The Literature of WAR

VOLUME **1** APPROACHES

The Literature of WAR

THOMAS RIGGS, *editor*

ST. JAMES PRESS
A part of Gale, Cengage Learning

GALE
CENGAGE Learning·

Detroit • New York • San Francisco • New Haven, Conn • Waterville, Maine • London

The Literature of War
Thomas Riggs, Editor
Marie Toft, Project Editor

For product information and technology assistance, contact us at
Gale Customer Support, 1-800-877-4253.
For permission to use material from this text or product,
submit all requests online at **www.cengage.com/permissions.**
Further permissions questions can be emailed to
permissionrequest@cengage.com

Artwork and photographs for *The Literature of War* covers were reproduced with the following kind permission.

Volume 1
For background photograph of American soldiers approaching Utah Beach on D-Day. June 6, 1944. © STF / AFP / Getty Images

For foreground painting *La Mitrailleuse* by C. Nevinson, 1915. © Tate, London 2012 / Art Resource, NY / © Estate of Christopher Richard Wynne Nevinson

Volume 2
For background photograph of U.S. helicopters landing near Bong Song in South Vietnam during Operation Eagle's Claw, February 16, 1966. © Bettman / CORBIS

For foreground woodcut of a Viet Cong soldier. © Christel Gerstenberg / Corbis

Volume 3
For background photograph of Hawker Hurricanes flying in formation during the Battle of Britain, WW II. © HIP / Art Resource, NY

For foreground painting *Death of Dresden* by Wilhelm Lachnit, 1945. Oil on canvas. © Galerie Neue Meister, Staatliche Kunstsammlungen, Dresden, Germany, Art Resource, NY; © The Estate of Wilhelm Lachnit.

Library of Congress Cataloging-in-Publication Data

The literature of war / Thomas Riggs, editor.
    p. cm.
    Includes bibliographical references and index.
    ISBN 978-1-55862-842-7 (set) -- ISBN 978-1-55862-843-4 (vol. 1) -- ISBN 978-1-55862-844-1 (vol. 2) -- ISBN 978-1-55862-846-5 (vol. 3)
    1. War and literature. 2. War in literature. I. Riggs, Thomas, 1963-
PN56.W3L55 2012
809'.93358--dc23

                 2012012026

Gale
27500 Drake Rd.
Farmington Hills, MI, 48331-3535

ISBN-13: 978-1-558-62842-7 (set)   ISBN-10: 1-55862-842-8 (set)
ISBN-13: 978-1-558-62843-4 (vol. 1)   ISBN-10: 1-55862-843-6 (vol. 1)
ISBN-13: 978-1-558-62844-1 (vol. 2)   ISBN-10: 1-55862-844-4 (vol. 2)
ISBN-13: 978-1-558-62846-5 (vol. 3)   ISBN-10: 1-55862-846-0 (vol. 3)

This title will also be available as an e-book.
ISBN-13: 978-1-558-62845-8 ISBN-10: 1-55862-845-2
Contact your Gale, a part of Cengage Learning, sales representative for ordering information.

Printed in the United States of America
1 2 3 4 5 6 7 16 15 14 13 12

 # ADVISORY BOARD

CHAIR

Kate McLoughlin

Lecturer in Modern Literature; Director of MA program in Modern and Contemporary Literature, University of London, England, Birkbeck. Author of *Authoring War: The Literary Representation of War from the Iliad to Iraq* (2011); and *Martha Gellhorn: The War Writer in the Field and in the Text* (2007). Editor of *The Cambridge Companion to War Writing* (2009). Co-general editor of the series Edinburgh Critical Studies in War and Culture. Cofounder of WAR-Net, a research network for scholars working on the representation of war.

ADVISERS

Khaled Al-Masri

Senior Preceptor of Arabic, Harvard University, Cambridge, Massachusetts. Author of the doctoral dissertation *Telling Stories of Pain: Women Writing Gender, Sexuality and Violence in the Novel of the Lebanese Civil War*. Contributor of English translations of Arabic poetry and short stories to various American and British literary magazines. Editor and cotranslator working on a Penguin anthology of Arabic short stories.

Aníbal González

Professor of Modern Latin American Literature, Yale University, New Haven, Connecticut. Author of books that include *Love and Politics in the Contemporary Spanish America Novel* (2010); and *Killer Books: Writing, Violence, and Ethics in Modern Spanish American Narrative* (2001). Founder and general editor of the series Bucknell Studies in Latin American Literature and Theory.

Edward Larkin

Associate Professor of English and Material Culture Studies; Director of Graduate Studies, University of Delaware, Newark. Author of *Thomas Paine and the Literature of Revolution* (2005) and editor of the Broadview Press edition of Paine's *Common Sense* (2004). Larkin's research focuses on loyalism and empire from the American Revolution through the 1820s.

Willy Maley

Professor of Renaissance Studies, University of Glasgow, Scotland. Author of books that include *Nation, State and Empire in English Renaissance Literature: Shakespeare to Milton* (2003). Coeditor of essay collections that include *Representing Ireland: Literature and the Origins of Conflict, 1534-1660* (1993); and *The Edinburgh Companion to Muriel Spark* (2010). Contributor to numerous publications and scholarly journals. Research interests include the representation of national and colonial identities in early modern texts, as well as deconstruction and postcolonialism.

Pamela Matz

Research Librarian, Widener Library, Harvard University, Cambridge, Massachusetts. Liaison to African and African-American Studies; Folklore and Mythology; Studies of Women, Gender, and Sexuality; and Study of Religion.

Victoria Stewart

Senior Lecturer in the School of English, University of Leicester, England. Author of *The Second World War in Contemporary British Fiction: Secret Histories* (2011); *Narratives of Memory: British Writing of the 1940s* (2006); and *Women's Autobiography: War and Trauma* (2003). Member of WAR-Net, a research network for scholars working on the representation of war. Associate member of the Stanley Burton Centre for Holocaust Studies.

John Whittier Treat

Professor of East Asian Languages and Literatures, Yale University, New Haven, Connecticut. Author of *Great Mirrors Shattered: Homosexuality, Orientalism and Japan* (1999); *Writing Ground Zero: Japanese Literature and the Atomic Bomb* (1995); and *Pools of Water, Pillars of Fire: The Literature of Ibuse Masuji* (1988). Editor of *Contemporary Japan and Popular Culture* (1995) and the *Journal of Japanese Studies*. Book projects, including a history of modern Japanese literature and a study of Korean writers under Japanese occupation.

Jing Tsu

Professor of Modern Chinese Literature and Culture, Yale University, New Haven, Connecticut. Fellow (2011–12) of the Center for Advanced Study in the Behavioral Sciences at Stanford University, California. Author of *Sound and Script in Chinese Diaspora* (2010); and *Failure, Nationalism, and Literature: The Making of Modern Chinese Identity, 1895-1937* (2005). Coeditor of *Global Chinese Literature: Critical Essays* (2010). Book project for study of Chinese migrant laborers and sinophone literature.

Editorial and Production Staff

ASSOCIATE PUBLISHER
Marc Cormier

PRODUCT MANAGER
Philip J. Virta

PROJECT EDITOR
Marie Toft

EDITORIAL SUPPORT
Reed Kalso, Rebecca Parks

EDITORIAL ASSISTANCE
Sara Constantakis, Matt Derda,
Shelly Dickey, Alan Hedblad, Linda Hubbard,
Jeff Hunter, Kathy Lopez, Carol Schwartz,
Lawrence Trudeau

ART DIRECTOR
Kristine Julien

COMPOSITION AND IMAGING
Evi Seoud, John Watkins

CUSTOM GRAPHICS
XNR Productions, Inc.

PROOFREADING
Wilbur Spotts

MANUFACTURING
Wendy Blurton

RIGHTS ACQUISITION AND MANAGEMENT
Margaret Chamberlain, Kimberly Potvin,
Robyn V. Young

TECHNICAL SUPPORT
Luann Brennan, Grant Eldridge, Andrea
Lopeman, Russel Whitaker

TABLE OF CONTENTS

Introduction

There is something counterintuitive about "the literature of war." How can war, a phenomenon of destruction, give rise to literature, an act of creation? What sort of fiction, poetry, or drama might thrive on mass death, injury, and loss, other than the voyeuristic, the exploitative, or the simply sadistic? Might war writing even perpetuate war, glorify violence, and obscure suffering?

War literature does all of these things. It also warns against pursuing armed conflict, exposes its atrocities, and argues for peace. It records the acts of war with as much accuracy as is possible, and it memorializes the dead. It is voyeuristic, exploitative, and sadistic; it is also tender, selfless, and comforting. It is gleeful and angry; inflammatory and cathartic; propagandist, passionate, and clinical. It is funny and sad.

The literature of war is a literature of paradoxes, the greatest of which is the fact that it comments continuously on its own failure. War writers often lament their incapacity to describe the realities of armed combat, the inexpressible nature of the subject matter, the inadequacy of language, and the inability of their audiences to understand. Here, for example, is a description by the American writer Tim O'Brien of the war he experienced in Vietnam:

> There is no clarity. Everything swirls. The old rules are no longer binding, the old truths no longer true. Right spills over into wrong. Order blends into chaos, love into hate, ugliness into beauty, law into anarchy, civility into savagery. The vapors suck you in. You can't tell where you are, or why you're there, and the only certainty is overwhelming ambiguity.[i]

Paradoxically, in stating what makes war impossible to represent, O'Brien represents it. The inversion of what he perceives as the normal order of things (though the definitions and sources of "truth," "right," "order," "law," and "civility" might be questioned) is matched physically in armed conflict.

O'Brien's list of inversions occurs in a story, presented in a series of textual shards, that details the blowing of a man's body to bits:

> The booby-trapped 105 round blew him into a tree. The parts were just hanging there, so Dave Jensen and I were ordered to shinny up and peel him off. I remember the white bone of an arm. I remember pieces of skin and something wet and yellow that must've been the intestines. The gore was horrible, and stays with me. But what wakes me up twenty years later is Dave Jensen singing "Lemon Tree" as we threw down the parts.[ii]

There are a number of reversals here. A GI, Curt Lemon (a name suggestive of lemming-like behavior, yellowness, cowardice, a life curtailed, things gone sour), has literally been blown from ground to treetops: the world turned upside-down. His innards have been externalized: the body turned inside-out. "Lemon Tree," in addition to invoking his name, refers to the Peter, Paul and Mary song of that title. With this allusion, O'Brien suggests that the GI's organs, which his comrades must symbolically harvest from the tree, have metamorphosed into fruit.

War's surreal inversions are not limited to the human body. When buildings collapse, rooms—enclosed and private spaces—are exposed to the air. George MacBeth's poem "The Land-Mine" (1967) describes this effect:

> It brought the garden to the house
> And let it in. I heard no parrot scream
> Or lion roar, but there were flowers
> And water flowing where the cellared mouse
> Was all before.[iii]

In this nightmarish invasion, objects have again lost their qualities: solid has turned to liquid, animal has turned to vegetable, and the house has taken on a surreal, jungle-like quality, evoked by the references to parrot and lion. On a larger scale, bombing makes, in the words of Robert Mezey, "bridges kneel down, the cities billow and plunge / like horses in their smoke."[iv]

Language and literary form are sensitive to the fragmenting effects that war has on individual lives, communities, the body, and the environment. Writing can itself shatter very finely. In Jerzy Ficowski's poem "Script of a Dead Cemetery" (1979), individual words break like the Jewish tombstones whose fragments are now "the predominant iconographic figure by which public memory of the Shoah is constructed" in present-day Poland[v]:

> Sandstone is good
> for honing scythes
> so all that is left
> is a rib of stone
> here a foot of stone
> a tibia
> there a shinbone
> a bone of sto
> a shank of st[vi]

Like the splinters of sandstone, the word fragments "sto" and "st" cannot stand alone: if they are to have meaning, it is only through being cemented, still jagged, with other shards.

In these examples from O'Brien, MacBeth, Mezey, and Ficowski, the peculiar paradox that is war literature is clearly visible. Destruction creates. Writing about war is akin to building—or rebuilding—a city. It is an act of creation, of binding together. In the extracts quoted above, destruction is captured and suspended in literary form (through such devices as rhyme, imagery, allusion, and juxtaposed opposites). The literature of war, then, is both dependent on, and the opposite of, armed conflict.

The examples considered so far display the experimental, self-reflexive nature of literature stretched to its limits in the task of representing the unrepresentable. The pioneering American war correspondent Martha Gellhorn argued:

> If you can't change it [war] you must at least record it, so that it cannot just be ignored or forgotten. It is some place on the record and it seemed to me personally that it was my job to get things on the record in the hopes that at some point or other, somebody couldn't absolutely lie about it.[vii]

The argument for realism in war literature is that the facts must be presented as accurately and objectively as possible, so that the record cannot later be distorted. Formal decoration and imaginative license have no place in this strict regard for truth. But the realist project falters as soon as it states its terms. "Fact," "accuracy," "objectivity," "truth," and "realism" itself are infinitely contestable concepts. And the realist approach has other problems. The more realistic the portrayal of war's atrocities, the greater the risk of sadistic enjoyment. It is impossible (and unwise) to ignore the fact that war literature delights in, and occasions delight in, violence. This is what David Bromwich terms "the non-moral theory of art."[viii] Bromwich draws attention to the pleasure that can be taken in the representation of suffering and destruction, which, he argues, is derived from a sympathetic engagement, a "state of being held to attention by helpless feelings about someone else, who at the moment is visibly suffering."[ix] Bromwich argues that war literature induces pleasure in the reader because it brings him or her "close to a scene of risk."[x] The reader, safely remote from the war zone, vicariously experiences danger and suffering and even imagines horrors greater than those represented. According to Bromwich, the experience may be positive, and even joyful—and the reader does not have to be a sadist to find it so.

In this understanding of war literature, the text becomes a place of rehearsal, and reading becomes a process of approaching and testing fears. The war writer thus serves as a knowledgeable guide to the "scene of risk." This is one reason why war, to a greater extent than other subjects (even subjects such as love, grief, and physical pain), requires personal experience on the part of those who seek to convey it. Eric J. Leed has suggested that battle is "learned" through "physical immersion": knowledge of war is, like sexual knowledge (or, more mundanely, the ability to ride a bicycle), "acquired in the body."[xi] To write about war—to guide the reader to and through "the scene of risk"—therefore becomes a right to be earned. As Jonathan Shay, a psychiatrist who has worked with Vietnam War veterans suffering from post-traumatic stress disorder, remarks, if a listener is willing to experience "some of the terror, grief, and rage that the victim did,"[xii] the combatant is more likely to feel understood and to trust the listener.

Confining the right to write about war to combatants, however, has the result that those traditionally denied access to the war zone (women are the most obvious example) are also denied access to the genre. Where women have historically gained firsthand experience of the war front, it has primarily been as caregivers rather than combatants. Consequently, women's war writing has often been limited to accounts of nurses or of those who assumed responsibility for maintaining the home front. Vera Brittain's World War I memoir *Testament of Youth* offers examples of both roles, moving between the home and war fronts. Combining retrospective autobiography and diary, Brittain reveals how direct contact with fighting rapidly diminished her idealism. The tendency to privilege firsthand accounts of combat, however, has not prevented civilian observers from writing about war. For instance, diarist Nella Last details the changes that World War II brought to domestic life in Britain, and Amrita Pritam's "Today I Invoke Waris Shah" reflects on the experience of becoming a refugee in the aftermath of the Partition of India. Such accounts demand recognition that the experience of war extends far beyond the field of battle.

In broadly defining the genre of war writing, *The Literature of War* considers texts treating the diverse impacts of war on those who experience it, whether as soldiers or civilians, and examines the ways in which war is transformed through writing. Because the experience of war transcends geographical boundaries, genres, and specific conflicts, this book is organized thematically, rather than chronologically or geographically.

The first volume highlights various approaches to war, from the theoretical to the experimental, discussing the works of writers as diverse as the ancient Chinese military strategist Sun Tzu, the Spanish conquistador Bernal Díaz del Castillo, and the twentieth-century African writer and political activist Ken Saro-Wiwa. Collectively, these and other texts in the volume demonstrate that there is no one approach to war—and that theoretical and artistic attempts to grapple with war (whether in theory or reality) have historically taken myriad forms, from popular songs to epic poems, speeches, and experimental fiction. The approaches to war considered in this volume have been employed as propaganda (both for and against war), offered rules for conducting war, and reflected on the impossibility of writing war experience.

The second volume considers texts centered on the experiences of those who encounter war, whether on the battlefield or the home front. Written by men and women of diverse backgrounds—from classical epic poets Homer and Virgil, to novelist and American Civil War hospital volunteer Louisa May Alcott, to Palestinian activist and writer Ghassan Kanafani, to First Gulf War veteran Anthony Swofford—these texts reveal the multiplicity of perspectives and experiences contained within any conflict. Combatants describe the fear and trauma of experiencing warfare firsthand, but they also occasionally celebrate its exhilarating and empowering effects. For some writers discussed in this volume, particularly women, war brings new opportunities and responsibilities as well as new dangers. The accounts of the men and women who have maintained the home front during a war reveal the state of anxious anticipation in which they await news of loved ones on the front, and, in many cases, their struggles with privation and change at home. For the displaced and alienated—the refugees, exiles, and prisoners of war—home is revealed to be a contested idea that can be a source of both strength and trauma.

The final volume explores a body of writing reflecting on the impacts of war on individuals, communities, cultures, and human values. The texts discussed in this volume, which range from memoirs and histories to epic poems, speeches, and works of fiction, are written by a diverse group of authors that includes ancient Greek playwright Aristophanes, Native American leader Black Hawk, British World War II fighter pilot Richard Hillary, and Nuruddin Farah, a Somali novelist whose family was displaced by political and military strife. Collectively these texts express the transformative power of war, which kills and wounds (both physically and psychologically), shifts geographical boundaries, and often challenges the meaning and worth of long-held values such as courage, loyalty, and sacrifice. War, these texts demonstrate, can also bring about liberation (both political and social), and it can engender new ways of conceptualizing and creating art when those impacted by war find old modes inadequate to the challenge of depicting war's realities.

The English novelist Henry Green, sensing that the Second World War was breaking up everything that he knew and relied on, nonetheless remarked, "these times are an absolute gift to the writer."[xiii] Created from destruction, the literature of war is writing stretched to its limits, demanding extraordinary resourcefulness from those who seek to produce it. Its readers also have significant responsibilities. Understanding how and why truths and lies about war are conveyed, perceiving the status of those who convey them, and appreciating the surrounding ethical issues are nothing less than necessary acts of global citizenship.

Kate McLoughlin,
Advisory Board Chair

---

[i] Tim O'Brien, *The Things They Carried* (London: Flamingo, 1991) 78.

[ii] O'Brien, 78-79.

[iii] George MacBeth, *Collected Poems, 1958-1982* (London: Hutchinson, 1989) 107.

[iv] Robert Mezey, "How Much Longer?" *Collected Poems, 1952-1999* (Fayetteville: U of Arkansas P, 2000) 80.

[v] James E. Young, *The Texture of Memory: Holocaust Memorials and Meaning* (New Haven: Yale UP, 1993) 185.

[vi] Jerzy Ficowski, *A Reading of Ashes*, trans. Keith Bosley and Krystyna Wandycz (London: Menard, 1981) 29.

[vii] Freedom Forum European Centre, "Freedom Forum Europe Pays Tribute to Martha Gellhorn" (London: Freedom Forum European Centre, 1996) 7.

[viii] David Bromwich, *Skeptical Music: Essays on Modern Poetry* (Chicago: U of Chicago P, 2001) 234.

[ix] Bromwich, 237.

[x] Bromwich, 234.

[xi] Eric J. Lead, *No Man's Land: Combat and Identity in World War I* (Cambridge: Cambridge UP, 1979) 74.

[xii] Jonathan Shay, *Achilles in Vietnam: Combat Trauma and the Undoing of Character* (New York: Schuster, 1995) 189.

[xiii] Quoted in Mark Rawlinson, *British Writing of the Second World War* (Oxford: Clarendon, 2000) 77.

EDITOR'S NOTE

The Literature of War, a three-volume reference guide, provides critical introductions to works in which military conflict is an important influence or setting. Most of the 300 entries discuss a single work of fiction, nonfiction, poetry, or drama. These texts, originally written in English, French, Spanish, Chinese, Arabic, and other languages, portray wars spanning from ancient times to the twenty-first century. Among the earliest works discussed in the guide is *The Trojan Women,* produced by Greek playwright Euripides in 1400-1200 BCE, which details violence inflicted by Greeks on the Trojan royal family. Later books include *Dien Cai Dau* (1988), a collection of poems concerned with the Vietnam War by American author Yusef Komunyakaa; *The Stone Virgins* (2002), by Zimbabwean writer Yvonne Vera, set in the 1980s during an era of civil distrust, paranoia, and violence in Zimbabwe; and *War Trash* (2004), a fictional memoir of a prisoner of war in Korea by Chinese writer Ha Jin.

The structure and content of *The Literature of War* was planned with the help of the project's advisory board, chaired by Kate McLoughlin, lecturer in modern literature at the University of London. Her introduction to this guide provides an overview of war literature.

ORGANIZATION

All 300 entries share a common structure, providing consistent coverage of the works and a simple way of comparing basic elements of one text with another. Each entry has six parts: overview, historical and literary context, themes and style, critical discussion, sources, and further reading. Entries also have sidebars discussing topics related to the works, authors, or conflicts. For example, the sidebar to the entry on *For Whom the Bell Tolls,* the classic novel by Ernest Hemingway, discusses the film adaptation starring Gary Cooper and Ingrid Bergman.

The Literature of War is divided into thematic sections, outlined in the table of contents. Volume 1, "Approaches," has six sections, each highlighting a way that literature represents war—through theories, histories, eye-witnessing, propaganda, satire, and experiments. "Propaganda," for instance, includes entries on works such as Julia Ward Howe's "Battle Hymn of the Republic" (1862), a patriotic poem serving the Northern cause during the Civil War, and Virginia Woolf's *Three Guineas* (1938), a feminist-pacifist treatise composed in response to the Spanish Civil War. The volume's preface, written by Walter W. Hölbling, professor of American Studies, Karl-Franzens-Universität, Graz, Austria, provides an overview and explanation of these approaches. Volume 2, "Experiences," includes five sections—combatants; women at war; prisoners, refugees, and exiles; the home front; and change—along with an explanatory preface by Victoria Stewart, senior lecturer at the School of English, University of Leicester, England. Volume 3, "Impacts," has ten sections: the body, the mind, gender and gender relations, families, communities, countries, death, values, aesthetics, and posterity; the volume's preface was written by Adam Piette, professor of English literature, University of Sheffield, England.

Among the criteria for selecting entry topics were the importance of the work in university curricula, the genre, the region and country of the author, the region and country of the conflict, and the time period. Entries can be looked up in the author and title indexes. There are also several resources in the back of the book, including a thematic outline for all three volumes; a chronology with geographic pointers; lists of entries by conflict and genre; a list of authors by nationality; as well as awards and media adaptations.

ACKNOWLEDGMENTS

Many people contributed time, effort, and ideas to *The Literature of War*. Early planning was overseen by Philip Virta, Marc Cormier, and Marie Toft at Gale, and Marie Toft served as the in-house manager of the project. This guide owes its existence to their involvement and interest.

We would like to express our appreciation to the advisers, who, in addition to creating the organization of *The Literature of War* and choosing the entry topics, identified other scholars to work on the project and answered many questions, both big and small. We would also like to thank the contributors for their accessible essays, often on difficult topics, as well as the reviewers, whose extensive knowledge of the works was essential in ensuring the quality of the text.

I am especially grateful to Erin Brown, the senior project editor, who was involved in every stage of the project, from working with advisers, training writers, and managing workflow to organizing the review process. Other members of the project's staff include Mariko Fujinaka, Anne Healey, Bob Anderson, Yvette Charboneau, Tony Craine, Mary Beth Curran, Stephen Davis, Lee Esbenshade, Laura Gabler, Harrabeth Haidusek, David Hayes, Joan Hibler, Janet Moredock, Wendy O'Donnell, Donna Polydoros, Robert Rauch, Mary Russell, and Treven Santicola.

THOMAS RIGGS

Contributors

ALISON BAILEY

Bailey holds a PhD in East Asian studies and is a university professor.

LISA BARCA

Barca holds a PhD in Romance languages and literatures and is a university professor.

ALLISON BLECKER

Blecker is a PhD candidate in Near Eastern languages and civilizations and a teaching fellow.

TODD BREIJAK

Breijak is a freelance writer.

ERIN BROWN

Brown holds an MFA in creative writing and has been a university instructor and a freelance writer.

JOSEPH CAMPANA

Campana holds an MA in English literature and has been a university professor.

TOM COLLIGAN

Colligan holds an MA in classics and is a freelance writer.

COURTNEY CONROY

Conroy holds an MA in literary studies.

MELISSA DOAK

Doak holds a PhD in history and is a freelance writer.

STEPHANIE D. FLORES-BRADSHAW

Flores-Bradshaw holds an MA in English literature and is a university instructor.

DANIEL FRIED

Fried holds a PhD in East Asian studies and is a university professor.

GEETHA GANGA

Ganga holds a PhD in English literature and is a university lecturer.

ELIZABETH GANSEN

Gansen holds a PhD in Spanish and has been a university instructor.

GRETA GARD

Gard is a PhD candidate in English literature and has been a university instructor and a freelance writer.

CYNTHIA GILES

Giles holds an MA in English literature and a PhD in interdisciplinary humanities. She has been a university instructor and a freelance writer.

NICHOLAS T. GOODBODY

Goodbody holds a PhD in Latin American literature and is a university professor.

QUAN MANH HA

Ha holds a PhD in American literature and is a university professor.

SETH HAGEN

Hagen holds an MA in literary studies and has taught high school English.

GREG HALABY

Halaby is a PhD candidate in Arabic and Islamic studies and a teaching fellow.

YEN-KUANG KUO

Kuo holds an MA in modern Chinese literature and is pursuing her PhD in modern Chinese history.

MARK LANE

Lane holds an MFA in creative writing and has been a university instructor and a freelance writer.

JESSICA TSUI YAN LI

Li holds a PhD in modern Chinese literature and is a university professor.

JENNY LUDWIG

Ludwig holds an MA in English literature and has been a university instructor and a freelance writer.

THEODORE MCDERMOTT

McDermott holds an MFA in creative writing and has been a university instructor and a freelance writer.

STEPHEN MEYER

Meyer holds an MFA in creative writing and has been a university instructor and a freelance writer.

JANET MOREDOCK

Moredock is an editor and has been a university instructor and a freelance writer.

JANET MULLANE

Mullane is a freelance writer and has been a high school English teacher.

MARC OLIVIER REID

*Reid holds a PhD in Spanish &
Portuguese and is a university
professor.*

JACOB SCHMITT

*Schmitt holds an MA in English
literature and has been a freelance
writer.*

GINA SHERRIFF

*Sherriff holds a PhD in Spanish and is a
university professor.*

CHRISTOPHER SIMONY

*Simony holds an MA in literary studies
and has been a high school AP English
teacher.*

SARA TAYLOR

*Taylor holds an MA in theatre history,
theory, and literature and is pursuing
her PhD in the same field.*

PAMELA TOLER

*Toler has a PhD in history and is a freelance
writer and former university instructor.*

JESSICA TOOKER

*Tooker is a PhD candidate in English
literature and a university instructor.*

RAUL VERDUZCO

*Verduzco holds a PhD in Spanish &
Portuguese and has been a university
professor.*

Academic Reviewers

ELIYANA R. ADLER

Research Associate, University of Maryland, College Park.

PATRICIA ALDEN

Professor of English and African Studies, St. Lawrence University, Canton, New York.

NATASHA ALDEN

Lecturer in Contemporary British Fiction, Aberystwyth University, Wales.

ROGER ALLEN

Professor of Arabic and Comparative Literature; Chair, Department of Near Eastern Languages and Civilizations, University of Pennsylvania, Philadelphia. Translator and editor.

DONALD ANDERSON

Professor of English and Writer in Residence, U.S. Air Force Academy, Colorado Springs. Editor, War, Literature and the Arts.

DEBRA D. ANDRIST

Professor of Spanish; Chair, Department of Foreign Languages, Sam Houston State University, Huntsville, Texas.

JOHN ANZALONE

Professor of French, Skidmore College, Saratoga Springs, New York.

HOLLY ARROW

Associate Professor of Psychology, Institute of Cognitive and Decision Sciences, University of Oregon, Eugene.

CHRISTIAN K. AWUYAH

Associate Professor of English, West Chester University, Pennsylvania.

MARK BAKER

Assistant Professor of History, Koç University, Istanbul, Turkey.

DOROTHEA BARRETT

Professor of Literature, Syracuse University in Florence and New York University at La Pietra, Florence, Italy.

ROBERT BARRETT

Associate Professor of English, Medieval Studies, and Theatre, University of Illinois at Urbana-Champaign.

SHANE JOSHUA BARTER

Assistant Professor of Comparative Politics, Soka University of America, Aliso Viejo, California.

RON BASHFORD

Assistant Professor of Theater and Dance, Amherst College, Massachusetts.

JOHN D. BAXENDALE

Visiting Fellow, Humanities Research Centre, Sheffield Hallam University, England.

DAVID BECK

Professor and Department Chair of Native American Studies, University of Montana, Missoula. Consultant and adviser for several U.S. programs for Native Americans.

PIERINA BECKMAN

Associate Professor of Spanish, University of North Texas, Denton.

STEPHEN BEHRENDT

University Professor and George Holmes Distinguished Professor of English, University of Nebraska, Lincoln.

WILLIAM BELDING

Lecturer, School of International Service, American University, Washington, DC.

AMY BELL

Associate Professor of History, Huron University College, London, Ontario.

PETER BEREK

Professor Emeritus of English, Mount Holyoke College, South Hadley, Massachusetts.

MICHAEL P. BREEN

Associate Professor of History and Humanities, Reed College, Portland, Oregon.

TIMOTHY BRENNAN

Professor of Cultural Studies and Comparative Literature and of English, University of Minnesota, Minneapolis and St. Paul.

PAUL BRIANS

Professor Emeritus of English, Washington State University, Pullman.

MARSHA BRYANT

Associate Professor of English, University of Florida, Gainesville.

JUAN E. CAMPO

Associate Professor of Religious Studies, University of California, Santa Barbara.

MICHAEL CHAPMAN

Professor Emeritus of English Studies;Research Fellow, University of KwaZulu-Natal, Durban, South Africa.

SARAH E. CHINN

Associate Professor of English, Hunter College, New York.

JULIE CODELL

Professor of Art History, Arizona State University, Tempe.

AMY COOK

Assistant Professor of Theatre History, Theory, and Literature, Indiana University, Bloomington.

JR. COOPER

Professor Emeritus of Slavic Languages and Literatures; Adjunct in Comparative Literature, Indiana University, Bloomington.

WILFRIDO CORRAL

Professor of Spanish, Sacramento State University, California.

ROBERT CRAIG

Adjunct Professor of History, University of South Florida Sarasota-Manatee, Florida.

ANNE CSETE

Associate Professor of Asian History, St. Lawrence University, Canton, New York.

VALENTINE CUNNINGHAM

Fellow and Tutor in English, Corpus Christi College, University of Oxford; Professor of English Language and Literature, University of Oxford, England.

JUAN PABLO DABOVE

Associate Professor of Spanish, University of Colorado, Boulder.

ROBERT DALY

Distinguished Teaching Professor of English, State University of New York at Buffalo.

JR. DEMARIA

Henry Noble MacCracken Professor of English Literature, Vassar College, Poughkeepsie, New York.

ELIZABETH EAMES

Associate Professor of Anthropology, Bates College, Lewiston, Maine.

CHARLES EASTMAN

Assistant Professor of English; Director of the Writing Program, Whittier College, California.

ANN-MARIE EINHAUS

Lecturer in Modern and Contemporary Literature, Northumbria University, Newcastle upon Tyne, England.

NADA ELIA

Faculty in Liberal Arts, Antioch University Seattle, Washington.

GEORGE ESENWEIN

Associate Professor of History, University of Florida, Gainesville.

DANINE FARQUHARSON

Associate Professor of English, Memorial University of Newfoundland, St. John's.

CÉSAR FERREIRA

Professor of Spanish, University of Wisconsin-Milwaukee.

DANIEL FRIED

Assistant Professor of East Asian Studies and of Comparative Literature, University of Alberta, Edmonton.

SUSAN STANFORD FRIEDMAN

Sally Mead Hands Bascom Professorship and Virginia Woolf Professor of English and Gender and Women's Studies, University of Wisconsin-Madison.

JAY GELLER

Associate Professor of Modern Jewish Culture, Vanderbilt Divinity School and Vanderbilt University, Nashville, Tennessee.

SHARI GOLDBERG

Assistant Professor of Literary Studies, University of Texas at Dallas.

SHARON L. GRAVETT

Professor of English; Assistant Vice President of Academic Affairs, Valdosta State University, Georgia.

WENDY GRISWOLD

Professor of Sociology and Bergen Evans Professor of Humanities, Northwestern University, Evanston, Illinois.

QUAN MANH HA

Assistant Professor of American Literature and Ethnic Studies, University of Montana, Missoula.

JANE HARRIS

Professor of Slavic Languages and Literatures, University of Pittsburgh, Pennsylvania.

BRADY HARRISON

Professor of English, University of Montana, Missoula.

GREGORY HEYWORTH

Associate Professor of English, University of Mississippi, Oxford.

WALTER HÖLBLING

Professor of American Studies, Karl-Franzens-Universität, Graz, Austria.

VANCE HOLLOWAY

Associate Professor of Spanish, University of Texas at Austin.

ANDREW J. HUEBNER

Associate Professor of History, University of Alabama, Tuscaloosa.

JESÚS E. JAMBRINA

Associate Professor of Spanish and History; Coordinator, Latin American Studies; Research Fellow, D. B., Reinhart Institute for Ethics in Leadership, Viterbo University, La Crosse, Wisconsin.

ANGELA M. JEANNET

Charles A. Dana Professor Emerita of French, Franklin and Marshall College, Lancaster, Pennsylvania.

KELLY JEONG

Assistant Professor of Comparative Literature and of Korean Studies, University of California, Riverside.

CHRISTOPHER JESPERSEN

Professor of History; Dean, School of Arts and Letters, North Georgia College and State University, Dahlonega.

JEFFREY W. JONES

Associate Professor of History, University of North Carolina at Greensboro.

JANE JORDAN

Senior Lecturer in English Literature, Kingston University, Kingston upon Thames, England.

LAURIE KAPLAN

Professor of English; Academic Director, England Center, George Washington University, Washington, DC.

DANIEL KATZ

Associate Professor of English and Comparative Literary Studies, University of Warwick, Coventry, England.

STEVEN G. KELLMAN

Professor of Comparative Literature, University of Texas at San Antonio.

TIM KENDALL

Professor of English Literature; Head, Department of English; Director, Centre for South West Writing, University of Exeter, England.

YOUNGJUN KIM

Doctoral candidate in History of International Politics, University of Kansas, Lawrence; Professor of International Politics, Korea National Defense University, Seoul.

RICHARD KING

Professor of Chinese Studies, University of Victoria, British Columbia.

WILLIAM M. KING

Professor of Afroamerican Studies, University of Colorado, Boulder.

HIROSHI KITAMURA

Associate Professor of History, College of William and Mary, Williamsburg, Virginia.

J. ROGER KURTZ

Professor of English; Chair, Department of English, State University of New York at Brockport.

TYPHAINE LESERVOT

Associate Professor of Letters and of Romance Languages and Literatures, Wesleyan University, Middletown, Connecticut.

SHIMON LEVY

Professor of Theatre, Tel Aviv University, Ramat Aviv, Israel.

MARIA HELENA LIMA

Professor of English, State University of New York at Geneseo.

LISA SUHAIR MAJAJ

Independent scholar; PhD in American Culture, University of Michigan, Ann Arbor.

MARÍA DEL PILAR MELGAREJO ACOSTA

Assistant Professor of Spanish, University of Wisconsin-Milwaukee.

EYDA MEREDIZ

Associate Professor of Latin American Colonial Literature and Culture; Director, Graduate Studies, Department of Spanish and Portuguese, University of Maryland, College Park.

SHIGERU MIYAGAWA

Professor of Linguistics and Kochi-Manjiro Professor of Japanese Language and Culture; Head, Foreign Languages and Literatures, Massachusetts Institute of Technology, Cambridge.

SHAKIR MUSTAFA

Visiting Associate Professor of Arabic, Northeastern University, Boston, Massachusetts.

ROBERT NABORN

Lecturer in Dutch Language and Literature; Director, Dutch Studies Program, University of Pennsylvania, Philadelphia.

C. M. NAIM

Professor Emeritus of South Asian Languages and Civilizations, University of Chicago, Illinois.

WILLIAM F. NAUFFTUS

Professor of English, Winthrop University, Rock Hill, South Carolina.

DRAGANA OBRADOVIC

Assistant Professor of Slavic Languages and Literatures, University of Toronto, Ontario.

JAMES PALMITESSA

Associate Professor of History, Western Michigan University, Kalamazoo.

LIA PARADIS

Assistant Professor of History, Slippery Rock University of Pennsylvania.

PASCALE PERRAUDIN

Associate Professor of French, St. Louis University, Missouri.

ADAM PIETTE

Professor of English Literature, University of Sheffield, England.

JAMES I. PORTER

Professor of Classics, University of California, Irvine.

PATRICK QUINN

Professor of English; Dean, Wilkinson College of Humanities and Social Sciences, Chapman University, Orange, California.

PETRA RAU

Senior Lecturer in English and European Literature, University of Portsmouth, England.

JOHN R. REED

Distinguished Professor of English, Wayne State University, Detroit, Michigan.

BEATRIZ REYES-FOSTER

Assistant Professor of Anthropology, University of Central Florida, Orlando.

J. THOMAS RIMER

Professor Emeritus of Japanese Literature, Theatre, and Art, University of Pittsburgh, Pennsylvania.

MOSS ROBERTS

Professor of Chinese, New York University.

JULIO RODRÍGUEZ-LUIS

Professor Emeritus of Spanish, University of Wisconsin-Milwaukee.

PHILLIP ROTHWELL

Professor of Portuguese, Rutgers University, New Brunswick, New Jersey.

JASON RUDY

Associate Professor of English, University of Maryland, College Park.

PETER RUTLAND

Professor of Government, Wesleyan University, Middletown, Connecticut.

ALEXANDER SAMSON

Lecturer in Golden Age Spanish Literature, University College London, England.

GRAHAM SAUNDERS

Reader in Theatre Studies, University of Reading, England.

ARIEL SCHETTINI

Professor of Literary Theory, New York University Buenos Aires, Argentina.

HANS PETER SCHMITZ

Associate Professor of Political Science, Syracuse University, New York.

SIMONE SCHWEBER

Goodman Professor of Education and Jewish Studies, University of Wisconsin-Madison.

PAUL SEAWARD

Director, History of Parliament, London, England.

MARTIN J. SHERWIN

University Professor of History, George Mason University, Fairfax, Virginia.

PETER SIMPSON

Associate Professor and Director of the Holloway Press, University of Auckland, New Zealand.

AMARDEEP SINGH

Associate Professor of English, Lehigh University, Bethlehem, Pennsylvania.

REBECCA STANTON

Assistant Professor of Russian, Barnard College, Columbia University, New York.

GIUSEPPE STELLARDI

Faculty Lecturer in Italian and Fellow, St. Hugh's College; Lecturer in Italian, New College and Oriel College, University of Oxford, England.

SARAH STOECKL

Doctoral candidate in English, University of Oregon, Eugene.

JAMES T. F. TANNER

Professor of English, University of North Texas, Denton.

DANIEL TRAISTER

English-Language Literature Bibliographer; Curator, Rare Book and Manuscript Library, Van Pelt-Dietrich Library, University of Pennsylvania, Philadelphia.

VERONIKA TUCKEROVA

Texas Chair of Czech Studies, University of Texas, Austin.

JERRY VARSAVA

Professor of English and Comparative Literature, University of Alberta, Edmonton.

MICHÈLE E. VIALET

Professor of French and Women's Studies, University of Cincinnati, Ohio.

RICHARD A. VOELTZ

Professor of History, Cameron University, Lawton, Oklahoma.

LANCE WILCOX

Professor of English, Elmhurst College, Illinois.

JOHN H. WILSON

Associate Professor of English, Lock Haven University, Pennsylvania. Editor, Evelyn Waugh Newsletter and Studies.

JAY WINTER

Charles J. Stille Professor of History, Yale University, New Haven, Connecticut.

ISABEL WOLLASTON

Senior Lecturer in Jewish and Holocaust Studies, University of Birmingham, England.

ELIZABETH WOOD

Professor of History, Massachusetts Institute of Technology, Cambridge.

GUO WU

Assistant Professor of History, Allegheny College, Meadville, Pennsylvania.

GREGORY D. YOUNG

Affiliate Faculty in Political Science and International Affairs, University of Colorado, Boulder.

JOANNE ZERDY

Lecturer in Theatre, Behrend College, Pennsylvania State University, Erie.

DARREN ZOOK

Lecturer in Political Science, University of California. Berkeley.

PREFACE TO VOLUME 1

War, the socially sanctioned use of collective violence against a perceived enemy, suspends many of the values that govern society during peacetime. Killing and destruction are authorized, and citizens are asked to die prematurely. The subject has simultaneously troubled and fascinated writers, who have approached it from diverse perspectives ranging from the theoretical and the historical to the aesthetic. While some writers have embraced realistic or journalistic approaches to war, others have experimented with form in order to acknowledge that war defies traditional modes of representation. Whatever the approach, war writing, perhaps more so than any other type of literature, tends to reveal and question the essential cultural concepts, expectations, and stereotypes that have traditionally been used to justify war. Many works of war literature strive to expose how cultural myth and propaganda drive war; others have actively participated in the glorification of war and the sacrifices it requires. The texts discussed in this volume illustrate how authors from different times and places have approached the challenge of addressing war through literature.

The works discussed in the first section of the volume illustrate theories about war. Systematic thinking on the subject dates back over thousands of years. Some works, such as Sun Tzu's ancient treatise *The Art of War* and Carl von Clausewitz's nineteenth-century analysis *On War*, offer comprehensive philosophical approaches. Others, including Machiavelli's *The Art of War*, Mao Zedong's *On Guerrilla Warfare*, and Ernesto "Che" Guevara's *Guerrilla War: A Method*, focus on military tactics and strategies. In a quite different vein, Henry David Thoreau's concept of nonviolent "war" based on ethical principles, outlined in his "Civil Disobedience," has been successfully applied in the twentieth century by Mahatma Gandhi and Martin Luther King Jr., as well as in the peaceful protests that accompanied the collapse of the USSR and the nonviolent revolutions in Tunisia and Egypt in 2011.

We continually try to explain events with the wisdom of hindsight by studying the past. Wars, with their destruction of lives, material surroundings, and ideals, are in dire need of explanations that make sense. The second section of this volume includes texts by such early historiographers as Herodotus, Thucydides, Caesar, and Tacitus; factual and fictional histories of the Crusades, the conquest of the Americas, and civil and colonial wars in Africa, Europe, India, Korea, Latin America, and the United States; oral histories of the Vietnam War; and historical novels and documentaries about subjects such as U.S. warfare against Native Americans.

Unlike historians, writers of eyewitness accounts do not always attempt to interpret; rather, they try to re-create events and their impacts. These endeavors can take manifold shapes that span all literary genres. With the exception of Bernal Díaz del Castillo's memoir *The Conquest of New Spain* and Alonso de Ercilla y Zúñiga's epic poem *The Araucaniad*, all the texts in this section date from the past two hundred years. Their number and variety demonstrate not only that the eyewitness account is the most frequently chosen form of writing about war but also that individual opportunities to record personal war experiences have multiplied during this time. The accounts included here come from five continents, deal with wars from the sixteenth century to the present, and cover the literary genres of diary, drama, memoir, novel, poetry, reporting, and short story.

From the beginning of human history, propaganda has been an essential part of warfare. The famous phrase of the ancient Greek dramatist Aeschylus—"The first casualty of war is truth!"—is still valid. Traditionally, propagandistic writing either elevates one's own side to heroic, victorious heights or degrades the enemy to subhuman status, and it often does both. Rhetorical strategies in this vein, from medieval epics like *The Song of Roland* to "The Battle Hymn of the Republic" to novels such as Ken Saro-Wiwa's *Sozaboy*, show little change over time. Most of the texts included in this section are not candidly propagandistic; yet taking sides in a war almost inevitably leads to subjective representations. War propaganda exists across all literary genres and has been written by a substantial number of well-known authors, among them Shakespeare, Thomas Paine, Henry Wadsworth Longfellow, Virginia Woolf, W. H. Auden, John Dos Passos, Algernon Charles Swinburne, Sean O'Casey, Martin Luther King Jr., and Alfred, Lord Tennyson.

Satire is often effective as a writer's tool when traditional ways of making sense fail; Kurt Vonnegut Jr. expresses this state of affairs succinctly in his novel *Slaughterhouse-Five*: "There is nothing intelligent to say about a massacre." He does not mean that we should be silent, though, and after his initial statement, he continues speaking in a dry, humorous manner that often makes readers chuckle involuntarily and then feel embarrassed about it. Less subtle but rather more grim is the oldest known European satire on war, Hans Jakob Christoffel von Grimmelshausen's seventeenth-century *Simplicius Simplicissimus*, in which the hero's experiences during the Thirty Years' War are presented in gruesome detail. Most of the more recent satires are less appalling. In Jaroslav Hašek's classic World War I novel *The Good Soldier Švejk*; Joan Littlewood's musical about the same conflict, *Oh! What a Lovely War*; Joseph Heller's World War II novel *Catch-22*; and Richard Hooker's Vietnam-era *M*A*S*H*, comedy and black humor help mask the horrible realities of war. In other works, such as Richard Aldington's *Death of a Hero*, Evelyn Waugh's *Sword of Honour*, Saadat Hasan Manto's *Black Margins*, Wole Soyinka's *Madmen and Specialists*, and Sony Labou Tansi's *Parentheses of Blood*, disillusionment and resignation are only thinly veiled by bitter humor.

By necessity we usually try to understand current wars in terms of preceding ones, and only if our concepts can no longer justify events do we look for new explanatory systems. In such situations authors invent fresh techniques for telling their stories, and to their contemporary audience these efforts often look very experimental. In the final section of this volume, a representative selection of writings surveys innovations in war literature. For instance, Filippo Marinetti's *Zang Tumb Tuuum* employs the techniques of Dadaist sound and optophonetic poetry; Alejo Carpentier's *The Kingdom of This World* draws on magical realism; Alvaro Cepeda Samudio's *La casa grande* hints at harsh facts through the interrupted, frightened thoughts of the narrator; Tim O'Brien's *The Things They Carried* uses objects to signify emotions; Henri Barbusse's *Under Fire* offers gritty realism in the guise of a journal; H. G. Wells's *The War of the Worlds* presents science fiction as frightening reality; and Thomas Pynchon's *Gravity's Rainbow* puzzles its readers with multiple points of view and a phantasmagoric protagonist who ultimately disappears as a result of identity diffusion.

The six sections of this volume explore various authorial approaches to the literature of war. The entries in the subsequent volumes, titled "Experiences" and "Impacts," present works that deal with the often very personal and emotional residue war leaves in the hearts and minds of survivors.

Walter W. Hölbling

THEORIES

THE ART OF WAR

Niccolò Machiavelli

OVERVIEW

In *Dell'arte della guerra* (*The Art of War*, 1521) Italian Renaissance philosopher Niccolò Machiavelli establishes a link between the political and military arts and argues that the development of civil society is impossible without a properly functioning militia.

The treatise opens with a letter to Florentine nobleman Lorenzo di Filippo Strozzi in which Machiavelli claims that "all the arts that have been introduced into society for the common benefit of mankind, and all the ordinances that have been established to make them live in fear of God and in obedience to human laws, would be vain and insignificant if they were not supported and defended by a military force." In the seven books that follow therein, Machiavelli takes a strictly rational approach to all aspects of waging war, including recruiting infantry, maneuvering and quartering troops, conducting a siege, and keeping soldiers fit during peacetime.

Throughout the text, the author laments the deplorable state into which military affairs have fallen in the Italian city-states and calls for a return to the ideals of ancient Roman society. In essence, Machiavelli prescribes a military remedy for all of Florence's social ills, claiming that its citizens can recover their lost virtue by imitating "the ancients in warlike exploits."

Machiavelli's lasting reputation with contemporary readers rests primarily on *The Prince* (1531) and, to a lesser extent, on the *Discourses with Livy* (1532), two political works on how effective leaders should conduct themselves with their subjects and with their rivals. While the influence of *The Art of War* has also been significant, it is considerably more difficult to calculate its relevance to readers outside its immediate audience. For more than a century the text was among the most important works on military science in the Western canon, largely owing to the argument Machiavelli makes on behalf of Roman virtue and the benefits of severe discipline and rigorous training. However, the rapid increase in the use of artillery and other advances in military technology over the course of the sixteenth century quickly dated Machiavelli's specific discussions of troop deployment and fighting tactics.

Nevertheless scholars have noted that Maurice of Nassau, Gustavus Adolphus, and Raimondo Montecuccoli, three leaders credited with making sweeping military reforms in the sixteenth century, studied *The Art of War* and that Frederick the Great of Prussia and Napoléon Bonaparte admired Machiavelli's work. Philosophers Michel de Montaigne and Voltaire also remarked favorably upon *The Art of War* in their writings.

Machiavelli's influence waned considerably shortly after the conclusion of the Napoleonic Wars in 1815 with the 1832 publication of Carl von Clausewitz's *On War*, the seminal work on Western military theory. Whereas the passages on the characteristics of successful generals in *On War* share some of Machiavelli's ideas about ancient virtue, Clausewitz otherwise eschews Machiavelli's rational approach to the minutiae of military life.

HISTORICAL AND LITERARY CONTEXT

Machiavelli wrote during the Renaissance, an era of cultural rebirth that began in Machiavelli's native Florence in the thirteenth century and spread throughout Europe over the next four hundred years. One of the prominent features of this period was the resurgence of classical learning, with an emphasis on ancient Greek and Roman texts. Sometime around 1515, Machiavelli joined the Orti Oricellari, a group of intellectuals founded by Bernardo Rucellai who modeled themselves on Plato's Academy and took their name from the gardens on Rucellai's estate, where they held discussions on art, literature, history, and philosophy, as well as on the lamentable state of contemporary war and politics on the Italian Peninsula.

Warfare had deteriorated in the Middle Ages, the period between the fall of the Roman Empire and the Renaissance, when there was no centralized state to codify military law and guarantee a hierarchy of command. During this time, armies were typically formed shortly before battle commenced and disbanded immediately afterward, which meant that troops were ill-disciplined and poorly trained.

In proposing solutions to these ills, Machiavelli relies heavily on the work of ancient thinkers, most notably Vegetius's *De re militari* from fourth-century CE Rome. In his introduction to the revised edition of the Ellis Farneworth translation of *The Art of War*, Neal Wood claims that Machiavelli lifted entire passages "almost word for word" from Vegetius on the

Key Facts

Conflict:
Siege of Pisa

Time Period:
16th Century

Genre:
Treatise

THE INFLUENCE OF VEGETIUS ON *THE ART OF WAR*

Flavius Vegetius Renatus, a minister of state in the declining years of the Roman Empire, wrote two books: a discourse on war and a guide to veterinary medicine. While the latter was quickly forgotten, *De re militari* was the most widely read military treatise of the Middle Ages. Commanders were known to take copies into the field and consult it during battle. The work was so frequently copied during this period that more than 320 copies of the manuscript have survived to modern times. The famous aphorism "If you want peace, prepare for war" comes from *De re militari*.

Medieval leaders found in Vegetius a reliable link to the glory of ancient Rome and a practical guide to waging war. Although little is known of the author's life, it is generally accepted that he had no military experience and that he does not say anything new about his subject. Instead, it is believed that in an attempt to return the degenerating Roman Empire to its former greatness, Vegetius catalogs the theories of leading Roman military thinkers such as Cato the Elder, Cornelius Celsus, Frontinus, and Paternus for his contemporaries in the military and for future readers. Of particular interest to medieval generals was book three of *De re militari*, which contains twenty-six chapters on strategy and tactics.

precepts of war, precautions to take during the march, and maintaining the health of soldiers. For his descriptions of Roman weapons and armor Machiavelli depends on Polybius, a Greek historian from the third century CE, whose seminal work *The Histories* covers the rise of the Roman Empire from 220 to 146 BCE.

Machiavelli came of age in a brutal period of Florence's history. When he was born in 1469, Italy consisted of a set of independent, fractious city-states that were frequently under attack by European forces seeking to unify the peninsula, often at the behest of the pope. In 1494, Charles VIII of France invaded the region hoping to conquer the Kingdom of Naples in the south. That same year, Florence managed to free itself from the rule of the Medici, a Florence-based banking family that sought to spread its political influence throughout the area. French campaigns in Italy continued sporadically for the next thirty years, and the Medici remained a constant threat to Florence.

Although he was never a soldier, Machiavelli had acquired considerable military experience by the time he began composing *The Art of War* in 1519. From 1498 to 1512 he served as secretary of the Florentine chancellery, a body established to oversee foreign affairs. His duties included meeting with military diplomats from across Europe and raising infantry for campaigns against rival Italian city-states.

The first and most strident argument Machiavelli makes in *The Art of War*—the need for Florence to dismiss its mercenary soldiers (or condottiere, as they were called) and raise a citizens' army modeled on the ancient Roman militia—comes from his experience in the wars against Pisa in 1504 and 1509. In the first encounter, Florence lost with an army of 3,500 mercenaries supplemented by two thousand conscripts from the rural provinces. In the second, Florence won with the ten thousand enlisted infantry that Machiavelli recruited according to the precepts of a civic ordinance he had drafted in 1507. Machiavelli's citizens' army

lost, however, to Spanish mercenary forces in 1512 at Prato, following which the Medici family was restored to power and Machiavelli was charged with treason and dismissed from his post.

THEMES AND STYLE

Machiavelli sets *The Art of War* in the Rucellai Gardens with Cosimo Rucellai, grandson to Bernardo, hosting a discussion in which he and three of his close friends, all of whom were part of Machiavelli's intellectual circle, question papal captain Fabrizio Colonna, a visiting mercenary, about military tactics. In all of his responses, Colonna rejects contemporary military practice and praises the habits of the ancient Greeks, Romans, and Carthaginians. For example, in book six, while discussing the soldier's diet with Battista della Palla, Colonna says, "How well these excellent rules are observed in our armies at present, I need not tell you; everyone knows that our soldiers, instead of imitating the regularity of sobriety of the ancients, are a parcel of intemperate, licentious and drunken fellows."

The entire work takes the shape of a series of Socratic dialogues, a genre familiar to Renaissance readers wherein an expert and a novice discuss a moral or philosophical issue. Playing the role of the expert, Colonna engages in an extended conversation with one interlocutor at a time, using their brief questions as prompts to articulate his views on basic military practice and on the issues confronting the Florentines.

In books one and two, Colonna discusses the recruiting and training of troops with Cosimo Rucellai. Luigi Alamanti poses questions on battle formations in book three. Books four and five cover tactics and the order of the march, respectively, with Zanobi Buondelmonti as Colonna's sounding board. In the final two books, Colonna discusses encampment and the defense and attack of towns and fortresses with Della Palla, the youngest and most eager of his interlocutors.

Colonna is a curious choice to voice the arguments Machiavelli develops throughout *The Art of War*. Though all historical records indicate that Colonna was a distinguished commander, he had served the French in their quest for Naples and had attacked Florence with a legion of Spanish mercenaries in the service of the Medici family. In many ways Colonna was the antithesis of Machiavelli's ideal soldier and was a more apt example of the corruption and opportunism in sixteenth-century Florence. When Cosimo asks him how he can speak to the virtues of the ancients if he himself has not practiced them in his career, Colonna replies that practicing such virtues requires unique circumstances and that "since

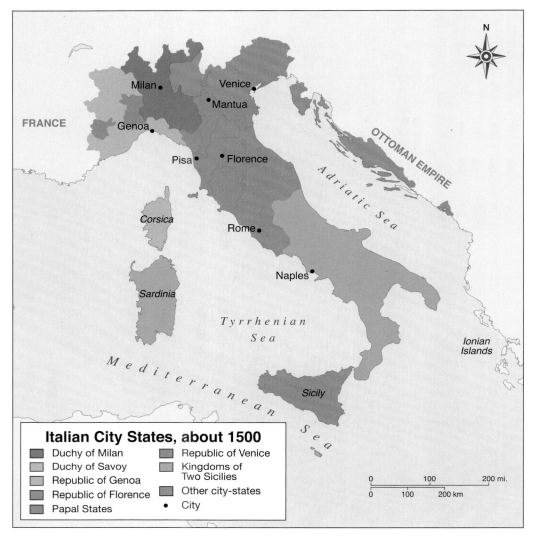

Italian City States, about 1500

- Duchy of Milan
- Duchy of Savoy
- Republic of Genoa
- Republic of Florence
- Papal States
- Republic of Venice
- Kingdoms of Two Sicilies
- Other city-states
- City

© MAP BY XNR PRODUCTIONS. CENGAGE LEARNING, GALE.

I have never had any such opportunity of showing what preparation I have made to revive among us the military discipline of the ancients, nobody can reasonably blame me for not doing so." It is a guarded response that Cosimo accepts but that also puts distance between Machiavelli and his primary speaker and precludes the reader's assumption that Colonna is merely voicing the author's unmediated opinions.

His past as a mercenary notwithstanding, Colonna sets virtue, which the translator keeps in the Italian (*virtù*), above all of the particular aspects of military strategy discussed throughout the text. Colonna opens his remarks by saying that he would have the ancients teach the Florentines "to honor and reward *virtù*; not to scorn poverty; to value good order and discipline in their armies; to oblige citizens to love one another, to decline faction, and to prefer the good of the public to any private interest."

Later, in his most sustained treatment of the subject, Colonna offers a social theory on the concept of *virtù*, arguing that republics nurture it but monarchies thwart it. "Men become excellent and show their *virtù* according to how they are employed and encouraged by their sovereigns." According to Colonna, republics are typically small and are surrounded by other republics. Thus their leaders require men of *virtù* to advance the military and commercial aims of the republic in a competitive regional environment. Monarchies, which tend to be large and to subsume neighboring states, view men of *virtù* as a threat to their political goals. "Where there are many states, there will be many great men; but where there are few states, there will not be many great men," Colonna says.

CRITICAL DISCUSSION

Military scholars have debated the relevance of *The Art War*, given that many of the strategies discussed in the text became obsolete shortly after it was published and that Machiavelli failed to acknowledge the impact that cavalry and gunpowder would have on battle in the near future.

In a thoroughly considered defense of Machiavelli, Ben Cassidy first outlines the scope of Machiavelli's errors and argues that of all the charges against him, those pertaining to his apparent dismissal of gunpowder are the most damaging to Machiavelli's reputation as a military thinker. To highlight this point Cassidy notes Sir Charles Oman's famous line that when forecasting military innovations Machiavelli "'backed the wrong horse' in almost every instance." Cassidy also quotes the more damning remarks from Azar Gat in *The Origins of Military Thought from the Enlightenment to Clausewitz*, where the Israeli military theorist claims, "Machiavelli could not accept firearms as a significant military and political innovation because this would have undermined not only his model for military organization and virtues—the Roman army—but also the foundations of his historical and theoretical outlook." Ultimately, Cassidy rejects these criticisms, declaring instead that *The Art of War* "is more than simply a pamphlet on military tactics" and that thinkers like Oman and Gat "condemn [Machiavelli] for not possessing the powers of prophecy."

Scholars have also examined the implications of placing Fabrizio Colonna at the center of the treatise. Marcia L. Colish claims that an eminent and respectable mercenary could speak to Machiavelli's views on ancient virtue with the most authority because such a figure had witnessed the degeneration of the art of war firsthand. Considering the protocols of the genre as well as the content of Machiavelli's argument on behalf of ancient virtue, Colish observes that within the framework of a Renaissance dialogue, "no personage of the day was more richly equipped to convey that message than Fabrizio Colonna."

Timothy J. Lukes disagrees with Colish and finds instead that Machiavelli's position on hired soldiers is more nuanced than it appears. According to Lukes, Colonna serves as evidence that Machiavelli "is willing to tolerate, or even cautiously ratify, a certain kind of paid warrior, one not necessarily assigned mercenary status." As Lukes points out, since Colonna is "not in it only for the money, he is not, in fact, a mercenary."

SOURCES

Cassidy, Ben. "Machiavelli and the Ideology of the Offensive: Gunpowder Weapons in 'The Art of War.'" *Journal of Military History* 67.2 (2003): 381+. JSTOR. Web. 24 Oct. 2011.

Colish, Marcia L. "Machiavelli's 'Art of War': A Reconsideration." *Renaissance Quarterly* 51.4 (1998): 1151+. JSTOR. Web. 24 Oct. 2011.

Lukes, Timothy J. "Martialing Machiavelli: Reassessing the Military Reflections." *Journal of Politics* 66.4 (2004): 1089+. JSTOR. Web. 24 Oct. 2011.

Machiavelli, Niccolò. *The Art of War*. Trans. Ellis Farneworth. Cambridge: Da Capo, 2001. Print.

Wood, Neal. Introduction. *The Art of War*. By Niccolò Machiavelli. Cambridge: Da Capo, 2001. Print.

FURTHER READING

Gat, Azar. *The Origins of Military Thought from the Enlightenment to Clausewitz*. New York: Oxford UP, 1991. Print.

Kubik, Timothy R. W. "Is Machiavelli's Canon Spiked? Practical Readings in Military History," *Journal of Military History* 61 (1997): 7+. Print.

Oman, Sir Charles. *A History of the Art of War in the Sixteenth Century*. Mechanicsburg: Stackpole, 1999. Print.

Paret, Peter, Gordon A. Craig, and Felix Gilbert, eds. *Makers of Modern Strategy from Machiavelli to the Nuclear Age*. Princeton: Princeton UP, 1986.

Ridolfi, Roberto. *The Life of Niccolò Machiavelli*. Trans. Cecil Grayson. Chicago: U of Chicago P, 1963. Print.

Taylor, F. L. *The Art of War in Italy, 1494-1529*. Cambridge: Cambridge UP, 1921. Print.

Vegetius Renatus, Flavius. *Vegetius: Epitome of Military Science*. Trans. N. P. Milner. Liverpool: Liverpool UP, 1997. Print.

Joseph Campana

THE ART OF WAR

Sun Tzu

❖ *Key Facts*

Conflict:
Warring States period

Time Period:
5th–3rd Centuries BCE

Genre:
Treatise

OVERVIEW

The Art of War is the oldest and most widely studied military treatise in human history. The ancient Chinese text is generally recognized as the work of Sun Tzu, a distinguished military general who is believed to have lived during the fourth century BCE. The work is organized into thirteen chapters, each addressing a different aspect of warfare, such as analyzing military strength, planning offensives, maneuvering troops, and the effective use of spies. At only about six thousand Chinese characters in length, *The Art of War* is a highly compressed, aphoristic text, both pragmatic and philosophical in its discourse on essential military principles.

In the opening lines of the text, Sun Tzu introduces what will become the overriding message of his doctrine, that military conflict is a matter of grave consequence, which must be approached with the utmost rationality, awareness, and diligent consideration. He says:

> War is a matter of vital importance to the State; the province of life or death; the road to survival or ruin. It is mandatory that it be studied thoroughly.

Indeed, what is striking about the body of Sun Tzu's military tract is the extent to which it is devoted to avoiding battle altogether. War is not something to be entered into rashly or for petty reasons, the author emphasizes, nor is the primary objective to bring physical destruction to the enemy. Rather, the height of military skill is to subjugate one's opponent strategically—by infiltrating his alliances, confounding his plans, and coercing him diplomatically—without ever resorting to armed combat.

Ultimately, as it draws on the principles of Taoist thought, *The Art of War* demonstrates that war, however much it may require physical regimentation and technical expertise, is at last a deeply human affair, in which moral strength, intellectual agility, and emotional restraint necessarily prevail.

Described by British military historian B. H. Liddell Hart as a work of "eternal freshness," it is believed to have been studied and employed by such diverse modern military leaders as the French emperor Napoleon Bonaparte, members of the Nazi High Command, Chinese Communist leader Mao Tse-tung, American general Douglas MacArthur, North Vietnamese general Vo Nguyen Giap, and American general Colin Powell.

HISTORICAL AND LITERARY CONTEXT

Questions surrounding the date and authorship of *The Art of War* have been the subject of vigorous critical debate for nearly as long as the text has existed in print. When did Sun Tzu live? Was he the sole author of *The Art of War*, or should the work be attributed to a disciple or school of disciples? Was Sun Tzu a real person or only a mythical figure?

Traditionalist scholars credit the historical figure Sun Wu, who was active in the late sixth century BCE during China's Spring and Autumn period (722–481 BCE), as the author of *The Art of War*. This assertion is based largely upon portrayals of Sun Wu in the *Shi chi*, by China's "Grand Historian" Sima Qian (c. 145-87 BCE), which is considered the first systematic history of China; and in *The Spring and Autumn Annals*, a classic Confucian text.

Modern scholars, however, have identified aspects of the technology, terminology, philosophical attitudes, and battle tactics in *The Art of War* as incompatible with the Spring and Autumn period. Based on this textual evidence, they argue that the text could not have been written until the subsequent Warring States period (453–221 BCE), a time of social and political upheaval during which the nature of warfare was radically changed.

In the feudal society of ancient China, war was largely a ritualized activity, governed by a chivalric code that called for various forms of decorum and courtesy. Battle was forbidden during planting and harvesting seasons, at times of year when it was deemed too hot or too cold to fight, and during periods of communal mourning. Military ranking was determined according to aristocratic hierarchy rather than skill or experience, and engagement was restricted to terrain that could accommodate chariots. Small armies were composed of untrained peasants, who tended to be poorly organized and equipped; they were commanded, often ineffectively, by powerful vassals or members of the ruler's inner circle. Battles amounted to little more than crude skirmishes, waged without clearly defined objectives and concluded without quantifiable results. Many campaigns ended in ruin simply because the soldiers ran out of food.

During the Spring and Autumn period, the Chinese feudal system descended into inexorable decline. Just as the hereditary aristocracy began to dissolve, large-scale commerce began to flourish. Increasingly, power was consolidated among a handful of large states, within which the great families vied with one another for dominion. Once internal control of the various states was established, those rulers directed their military ambitions outward, as each state sought to conquer and absorb the remaining smaller principalities and to gain economic and political advantage over rival states.

Thus began the Warring States period, an expanse of more than two centuries when six of the eight principal states of China remained at war with each other almost continuously. In response to this protracted crisis, traditional modes of warfare were abandoned. Rulers formed large standing armies of disciplined troops, which were led by professional generals and capable of mobilizing on short notice at any time of year. The introduction of the lethal crossbow and various forms of iron weaponry also contributed to the transformation of Chinese warfare, as soldiers began to play specialized roles in combat, and sophisticated troop formations and maneuvers were devised to maximize their expertise. Moreover, just as waging war became indispensible to the survival of the state, so, too, rulers abandoned old notions of moral code, seeking strategic advantage over their adversaries through a new brand of political diplomacy that was characterized by manipulation and deceit.

Because the unprecedented military and political innovations of the Warring States period are so clearly reflected in *The Art of War*, and because the text introduces the idea of war as an instrument for promoting the concerns of the state, modern scholars conclude that the work most likely emerged during this period and not before it. Further, while centuries of critical analysis have been unable to resolve definitively the identity of the text's author, most scholars agree that *The Art of War* is distinguished by such originality of thought and integrity of style that it must necessarily be the work of only one person, whose ideas were informed by extensive real practical experience in battle.

THEMES AND STYLE

Sun Tzu understood that protracted war was tremendously costly. Not only did it consume lives and capital, but it also undermined the morale of troops and citizens, compromising their loyalty to their ruler and, in turn, the unity and security of the state. As such, the author urged that when military engagement is unavoidable, the general must take every available measure to achieve victory quickly and with minimal casualties, suffering, and loss of capital on both sides. To this end, *The Art of War* dis-

cusses many practical matters, from the calculation of military strength and the difficulty posed by weather and physical terrain to the importance of using flags, torches, and drums to communicate with one's troops in the field.

Although it contains plenty of concrete detail, *The Art of War* is foremost a philosophical text, which holds that military success depends upon the cultivation of certain abstract qualities. Perhaps the most paramount of these is self-knowledge and knowledge of one's opponent:

> Know the enemy and know yourself; in a hundred battles you will never be in peril. When you are ignorant of the enemy but know yourself, your chances of winning or losing are equal. If ignorant both of your enemy and of yourself, you are certain in every battle to be in peril.

In the opening chapter, as Sun Tzu outlines the five fundamental factors that must be considered in measuring one's military strength relative to that of one's enemy, it becomes clear that to know oneself and one's enemy, one must consider not only physical conditions and circumstances but also psychological and moral factors, such as the discipline and training of troops, their degree of allegiance to their leader, and the extent to which that leader is wise, sincere, humane, courageous, and strict.

For Sun Tzu the character of the general is particularly critical to military success. The general must maintain a high level of rationality, resisting anger, arrogance, impatience, desire for fame, excessive benevolence, and other indulgences that render him vulnerable to poor decision making. The general must also guard his plans with utmost secrecy and remain unknowable, even to his own men.

According to Sun Tzu, success in battle depends on manipulating the enemy in order to attack when

In the hills of Burma in 2001, a guerrilla fighter from the rebel Shan State Army reads *The Art of War* by Sun Tzu, 2001. © JENNY MATTHEWS / ALAMY

THE ART OF WAR AND BUSINESS

Composed sometime between the years 722 and 481 BCE, Sun Tzu's *The Art of War* remains one of the most influential works on military tactics and strategy in the history of warfare. While designed for military purposes, the work has also proved influential in other spheres of human activity, notably business. In Japan, reading *The Art of War* is often mandatory for top managers and executives, whereas a number of Western firms have employed the work in training employees to strengthen their negotiating skills when brokering contracts. Indeed, the work's breadth of scope has provided a wealth of applications in the world of commerce, as corporations use the text to control interpersonal office dynamics, develop long-term business strategies, and anticipate the actions of competitors. The work's relevance in the sphere of business affairs earned widespread recognition following the release of Oliver Stone's *Wall Street*, a film exposing the excesses and corruption that governed the world of high finance during the 1980s. In one of the movie's most quoted scenes, ruthless executive Gordon Gekko advises his protégé: "Read Sun Tzu, *The Art of War*. Every battle is won before it is ever fought."

and where he least expects it. "All warfare is based on deception," the author famously states:

> Therefore, when capable, feign incapacity; when active, inactivity. When near, make it appear that you are far away; when far away, that you are near. Offer the enemy a bait to lure him; feign disorder and strike him.

The strategic importance of deceit is one of the most often noted themes of *The Art of War*. Although the text contains only two explicit references to deception, it repeatedly invokes the benefits of concealment, dissimulation, and trickery in the effort to take the enemy by surprise and exploit his weaknesses. Significantly, too, the successful employment of such tactics depends upon the quality of the general's imagination, creative responsiveness, and ability to adapt to ever-changing circumstances.

As many scholars have observed, the themes that circulate in Sun Tzu's text are strongly rooted in Taoism, a school of Chinese philosophical and spiritual thought that arose out of the Warring States period. Sun Tzu's ideas about leadership and strategic advantage reflect the Taoist emphasis on emotional composure and the need to refine one's faculties of perception and responsiveness in order to master life's challenges. Also notable is the foundational Taoist principle of inaction, or "non-doing," which is echoed in Sun Tzu's governing tenet that military combat should be avoided whenever possible and that the enlightened strategist can achieve victory without fighting.

Stylistically *The Art of War* also resembles the texts of the Taoist canon, including the *Tao Te Ching* (*The Way and Its Power*), in the simplicity and elegance of its aphorisms, the depth of its wisdom, and the overall unity of its recurring themes.

CRITICAL DISCUSSION

The most important of the Seven Military Classics of ancient China, *The Art of War* was considered necessary reading for military officers to earn promotion in Imperial China. According to traditional histories, it was instrumental to Qin Shi Huang (259–210 BCE) in his effort to end the Warring States period and become the first emperor of a unified China in 221 BCE. By the end of the first century CE, knowledge of the work had spread to Japan, where its teachings were embraced by some of the fiercest and most renowned warriors of the premodern era, including Oda Nobunaga (1534–82) and Toyotomi Hideyoshi (1536–98), who were instrumental in unifying the warring political factions of Japan.

Still, while *The Art of War* has been tremendously influential in Asia for more than two millennia, it remained unknown to Western readers until 1772, when it was translated into French by Jean Joseph Marie Amiot (1718–93), a French Jesuit missionary to Peking. The first significant English edition of the work was published in 1910 by the Victorian scholar and translator Lionel Giles (1875–1958). In the 1960s the text gained wider exposure among English readers with the publication of a new, critically acclaimed translation by American Marine commander and Chinese military scholar Samuel B. Griffith (1906–83).

In 1972 archaeologists uncovered a tomb dating to the Han dynasty (206 BCE–220 CE) that contained a nearly complete copy of *The Art of War* printed on bamboo slips. The Yin Chueh Shan text, as it became known, predated all previously known copies of the manuscript by more than a thousand years; its discovery helped to resolve certain longstanding questions about the date and composition of the original text.

Since the late twentieth century, Western scholars have devoted increased attention to the subtleties and implications of Sun Tzu's philosophy. Dennis and Ching Ping Bloodworth, Ronald Glasberg, and others have compared *The Art of War* to other such seminal tracts on war and power as *The Prince*, by Italian statesman Niccolò Machiavelli (1469–1527), and *On War*, by Prussian army officer Karl von Clausewitz (1780–1831). Another fruitful mode of critical inquiry has sought to understand *The Art of War* in terms of Taoist philosophy. Following Christopher C. Rand's work in this vein, Roger T. Ames and Thomas F. Cleary published new English translations of *The Art of War* concerned with elucidating Taoist elements of the text.

The Art of War has also been widely adapted to a business context. Numerous books have applied its precepts to the fields of management, corporate politics, and negotiating.

SOURCES

Cleary, Thomas F. Translator's Introduction. *The Art of War*. By Sun Tzu. Trans. Thomas F. Cleary. Boston: Shambhala, 1988. xi–lxv. Print.

Griffith, Samuel B. Introduction. *The Art of War*. By Sun Tzu. Trans. Samuel B. Griffith. London: Oxford UP, 1963. 1–56. Print.

Hart, B. H. Liddell. Foreword. *The Art of War*. By Sun Tzu. Trans. Samuel B. Griffith. London: Oxford UP, 1963. v–vii. Print.

Phillips, Thomas R. Introduction. *The Art of War*. By Sun Tzu. Trans. Lionel Giles. Harrisburg: Military Service Publishing, 1953. 9–39. Print.

Sawyer, Ralph D. Introduction. *The Art of War*. By Sun Tzu. Boulder: Westview, 1994. 79–162. Print.

FURTHER READING

Ames, Roger T. *Sun-tzu: The Art of Warfare: The First English Translation Incorporating the Recently Discovered Yin-ch'üeh-shan Texts*. New York: Ballantine, 1993. Print.

Bloodworth, Dennis, and Ching Ping. *The Chinese Machiavelli: three thousand Years of Chinese Statecraft*. New York: Farrar, 1976. Print.

Cleary, Thomas F. *The Essential Tao*. New York: HarperCollins, 1993. Print.

Glasberg, Ronald. "Toward a Cross-Cultural Language of Power: Sun Tzu's *The Art of War* and Machiavelli's *The Prince* as Exemplary Texts." *Comparative Civilizations Review* 27 (1992): 31–50. Print.

McNeilly, Mark R. *Sun Tzu and the Art of Modern Warfare*, New York: Oxford UP, 2001. Print.

Rand, Christopher C. "Chinese Military Thought and Philosophical Taoism." *Monumenta Serica: Journal of Oriental Studies* 34 (1979-80): 171–218. Print.

MEDIA ADAPTATIONS

Art of War: Sun Tzu's Legendary Victory Manual Comes to Life. Dir. David Padrusch. Perf. James Wong. A & E Television, 2009. Television special.

Art of War. Dir. Kuang Hui. 1981. Documentary film.

Erin Brown

"CIVIL DISOBEDIENCE"

Henry David Thoreau

✥ *Key Facts*

Conflict:
Mexican-American War

Time Period:
Mid-19th Century

Genre:
Essay

OVERVIEW

Originally published as "Resistance to Civil Government" in the periodical *Aesthetic Papers* in May 1849, Henry David Thoreau's "Civil Disobedience" is one of the most influential essays of all time. In it, Thoreau, an ardent abolitionist, condemns the U.S. government for perpetuating slavery and rejects the Mexican-American War (1846-48) as an unjust conflict. He reminds his fellow citizens that supporting the government makes them complicit in these immoral acts and states that conscience should dictate action in cases where conscience conflicts with law.

Thoreau originally delivered what would become the essay as a lecture on January 26, 1848, at the Concord Lyceum. It was given its present title when published in a collection of Thoreau's works, *A Yankee in Canada, with Anti-Slavery and Reform Papers*, in 1866. The essay has remained relevant for over a century. It is known to have influenced important political figures around the globe, including Mohandas Gandhi (1869-1948) and Martin Luther King Jr. (1929-68). King wrote in his *Autobiography* that "as a result of his [Thoreau's] writings and personal witness, we are the heirs of a legacy of creative protest."

HISTORICAL AND LITERARY CONTEXT

In "Civil Disobedience," Thoreau responds to what he perceived to be the injustice of the Mexican-American War. The war began in April 1846 after the United States annexed Texas, which Mexico claimed as a territory. The annexation was fueled by the popular doctrine of Manifest Destiny, which held that the United States was destined to stretch from coast to coast. Despite widespread opposition by abolitionists, who feared that another large Southern state would extend the political power of slaveholders, Texas officially became a state on December 29, 1845. In response to the annexation, Mexico broke off diplomatic ties to the United States. Fearing an attack, President James K. Polk ordered troops to the Mexican border. After U.S. attempts to purchase California and New Mexico were rebuffed, hostilities escalated. When Mexican forces allegedly killed American soldiers who were patrolling in contested territory, Polk pushed for war, which was officially declared on May 13, 1846. The conflict was unpopular due to its high cost in both money and human life, and many, including Abraham Lincoln, questioned its legitimacy.

After nearly two years of intense fighting, the war ended on February 2, 1848, with the Treaty of Guadalupe Hidalgo, which codified U.S. control of Texas. Under the terms of the treaty, the United States also acquired the territories that would become California, Nevada, Utah, and New Mexico, as well as parts of modern-day Colorado, Oklahoma, Kansas, and Wyoming, at a price significantly lower than had been offered prior to the war. Despite the fact that the acquisitions allowed the nation to fulfill its Manifest Destiny, public opinion remained sharply divided over the war even after it ended. Thoreau, who was active in the abolition movement, was an outspoken opponent. In July 1846 he was famously jailed after refusing to pay his taxes because he did not want to contribute financially to the war effort. Soon after, he gave the lecture that would become "Civil Disobedience," in which he reflects on his brief incarceration.

Thoreau's essay responds in part to a work by British philosopher William Paley (1743-1805) titled "Of the Duty of Civil Obedience" (1785), which argues that obedience to the state is dictated by Christian theology. In arguing against this view, Thoreau aligns himself with other figures who challenged injustice, including Jesus Christ, astronomer Nicolaus Copernicus (1473-1543), Protestant reformer Martin Luther (1483-1546), and George Washington (1732-99). The essay also draws on literary works ranging from Greek mythology to the plays of Shakespeare. It notably quotes from Charles Wolfe's influential 1817 poem "The Burial of Sir John Moore after Corunna," which details the hasty burial of a revered military leader after a battle in the Peninsular War (1808-14).

In the century and a half since it was first published, "Civil Disobedience" has been embraced by leaders seeking political change through peaceful resistance. Gandhi credited the essay as being an important influence on his strategy of nonviolent civil resistance to colonial rule in South Africa and India in the early twentieth century, and King embraced Thoreau's model of civil disobedience as a guide for the American Civil Rights Movement of the 1960s. Thoreau's protest against the war was the

theme of the 1970 two-act play *The Night Thoreau Spent in Jail*, written by Robert Edwin Lee and Jerome Lawrence, which dramatized Thoreau's brief imprisonment and celebrated conscientious objection and civil disobedience at a time when the American public was polarized by U.S. involvement in the Vietnam War (1965–75).

THEMES AND STYLE

The central theme of "Civil Disobedience" is that individuals' consciences are often in conflict with majority rule and government policy, and that in such cases those individuals owe a moral duty to themselves to obey the dictates of their consciences over those of the government. Thoreau offers the war with Mexico as a prime example of the misuse of government by a powerful few. "Witness the present Mexican war," he asserts, "the work of comparatively a few individuals using the standing government as their tool; for, in the outset, the people would not have consented to this measure." He suggests that the majority, who did not support the conflict, nevertheless bowed to the desires of the small number of powerful (pro-slavery) governmental figures who did. Both the war and the institution of slavery, he says, are so morally repugnant that they demand immediate action; since the government is unwilling to change course, people must work outside it.

A related theme in the essay is that citizens need to eschew blind allegiance to government. Thoreau spells out the conflict among individual morality, failed government, and alleged civil obligation in the following terms: "How does it become a man to behave toward this American government to-day? I answer, that he cannot without disgrace be associated with it. I cannot

for an instant recognize that political organization as *my* government which is the *slave's* government also." Thoreau emphasizes that this applies as much to the local government of Massachusetts—which he accuses of being unprepared or unwilling to intervene in either the Mexican-American War or slavery because its members are "more interested in commerce and agriculture than they are in humanity"—as it does to the federal government. Thoreau notes his surprise at how few others are willing to take a stand against the government, and he reminds his readers that it is theirs to shape. He urges "every man [to] make known what kind of government would command his respect," adding "that will be one step toward obtaining it."

Stylistically, "Civil Disobedience" is notable for Thoreau's frequent use of questioning as a rhetorical technique ("Must the citizen ever for a moment, or in the least degree, resign his conscience to the legislator?" "Unjust laws exist; shall we be content to obey them, or shall we endeavor to amend them, and obey them until we have succeeded, or shall we transgress them at once?"). At times entire paragraphs are composed of questions. This strategy, which reflects the text's origins in oratory, is employed to persuade readers, in part by asking them to consult their consciences for the answers.

CRITICAL DISCUSSION

Early critical reaction to Thoreau's essay was virtually nonexistent, in large part because the work was not widely read. Although the Mexican-American War had ended by the time "Civil Disobedience" was published, over time scholars began to recognize its broad applicability to a number of political and moral crises. The publication in 1890 of a widely circulated edition

Thoreau's disgust with the Mexican-American War informed his essay, "Civil Disobedience." James Walker (1819-1889), *Battle of Chapultepec*, (*Storming of Chapultepec*), 1858. Oil on canvas. © THE ART ARCHIVE

DRAMATIZING THE NIGHT THOREAU SPENT IN JAIL

More than a century after Thoreau's refusal to pay a tax that would support the Mexican-American War landed him in the Concord jail, Jerome Lawrence and Robert Edwin Lee memorialized the event in their play *The Night Thoreau Spent in Jail* (1970). The two-act drama draws on Thoreau's essay "Civil Disobedience." It depicts Thoreau's interactions with a fellow prisoner, the homeless Bailey, who has been wrongfully accused of arson. It also includes Thoreau's reflections on important moments in his life, including his unrequited love for Ellen Sewall, the traumatic time he spent teaching in a school that required him to flog his pupils, the death of his beloved brother John, and his friendship with fellow writer Ralph Waldo Emerson.

First produced when the United States was five years into its nearly decade-long involvement in the unpopular Vietnam War, the play struck an immediate chord with theatergoers, who recognized the intended parallel between Thoreau's act of civil obedience and the actions of contemporary antiwar protestors. Upward of eighty sold-out performances of the play were staged on college campuses in 1970 alone. It debuted on the professional stage at Washington, D.C.'s Arena Stage in November of that year, and it remains popular today.

of Thoreau's work that included the essay as well as an influential article about it by Russian novelist Leo Tolstoy is widely credited with bringing the piece to the attention of modern readers. Subsequently, the work was embraced by political figures such as Mohandas Gandhi, Martin Luther King Jr., and President John F. Kennedy. The popular and political interest in it led to increased scholarly attention as well. Today a wide body of academic commentary treating the essay has developed, and it continues to draw scholars from a number of disciplines, including sociology, history, and literature.

A central strand of academic discussion focuses on the political implications of "Civil Disobedience." For example, in an article in *Southern Quarterly*, Raymond Tatalovich argues that Thoreau's position descends into anarchy in its attack on majority rule. Pointing to the fact that Thoreau is "particularly critical of majority rule and political processes," especially in a moral sense, Tatalovich suggests that Thoreau's emphasis on individual morality is "incompatible with the requirements of contemporary society as we know it." Other scholars point out that while Ralph Waldo Emerson's "Self-Reliance" and Walt Whitman's poetry (in particular "Song of Myself") also espouse anarchic elements, Thoreau's "Civil Disobedience" focuses on a rigorous protection of individual and minority rights against the rule of a majority that in some democracies may represent as little as 50.1 percent of the voting public—a circumstance that makes necessary an avenue for resolving daily civil rights issues.

Critics have also debated whether the essay rejects democratic principles or represents an attempt to perfect them. For instance, while commentators often accept Thoreau as an advocate of democracy, Leigh Kathryn Jenco's article in the *Review of Politics* questions this conventional wisdom, arguing that

Thoreau's writings "reveal a much deeper concern that the theory and practice of democracy itself, not just democracy in its current manifestation, threaten the commitments that facilitate moral practice in our personal lives."

In an article in *Modern Age*, Carl L. Bankston III questions the prevailing approaches to Thoreau's political vision. He argues that Thoreau, in "Civil Disobedience," was outlining a theory not of political activism as we generally understand it but of a variety of "inactivism" that Thoreau, he says, posited as "a necessary condition of personal conscience." Bankston relates the choice of inactivism to the mid-twentieth century concept of the "inner-directed" social personality (as opposed to the "other-directed" type). Accordingly, in urging that an individual follow his own conscience rather than "buy in" to popular social trends, Thoreau was proposing a new perspective on civic engagement and moral decision making that has much to offer contemporary political discussion.

Another debate regarding the text arises from what commentators see as a contradiction between Thoreau's position in the essay and his later support of John Brown, the militant abolitionist who in 1859 unsuccessfully attempted to lead an armed slave uprising in Harpers Ferry in what is now West Virginia. While some suggest that Thoreau's support of Brown's active and armed resistance to the government marks a change in philosophy from that advocated in "Civil Disobedience," others argue that the two positions are completely compatible. For example, Jack Turner suggests in *Political Theory* that Thoreau advocates what Turner describes as "a politics of *performing conscience*" through which the individual conscience is made public, spurring others to feel and act likewise. Subsequently, he argues, "Thoreau values and encourages acts [like Brown's] that take a stand for moral right against immoral law and spark wonder in their audience at the power of individual agency, especially moral agency."

SOURCES

Bankston, Carl L., III. "Thoreau's Case for Political Engagement." *Modern Age* 52.1 (2010): 6–13. Print.

Jenco, Leigh Kathryn. "Thoreau's Critique of Democracy." *Review of Politics* 65.3 (2003): 355–81. Print.

King, Martin Luther, Jr. *The Autobiography of Martin Luther King, Jr.* New York: Warner, 1998. Print.

Lee, Robert Edwin, and Jerome Lawrence. *The Night Thoreau Spent in Jail.* New York: Hill, 1971. Print.

Tatalovich, Raymond. "Thoreau on Civil Disobedience: In Defense of Morality or Anarchy?" *Southern Quarterly* 11.2 (1973): 107–13. Print.

Thoreau, Henry David. "Civil Disobedience." Boston: Godine, 1969. Print.

Turner, Jack. "Performing Conscience: Thoreau, Political Action, and the Plea for John Brown." *Political Theory* 33.4 (2005): 448–71. Print.

FURTHER READING

Arendt, Hannah. *Crises of the Republic.* New York: Harcourt, 1972. Print.

Campbell, Randolph B. *Empire for Slavery: The Peculiar Institution in Texas, 1821-1865.* Baton Rouge: Louisiana State UP, 1989. Print.

Gross, Robert A. "Quiet War with the State: Henry David Thoreau and Civil Disobedience." *Yale Review* 93.4 (2005): 1–17. Print.

Lens, Sidney. *The Forging of the American Empire.* New York: Crowell, 1971. Print.

Paley, William. "Of the Duty of Civil Obedience." *The Principles of Moral and Political Philosophy.* Indianapolis: Liberty Fund, 2002. Print.

Powell, Brent. "Henry David Thoreau, Martin Luther King, Jr. and the American Tradition of Protest." *OAH Magazine of History* Winter 1995: 26–29. Print.

Richardson, Robert D. *Henry Thoreau: A Life of the Mind.* Berkeley: U of California P, 1986. Print.

Greta Gard

GUERRILLA WARFARE
A Method
Ernesto "Che" Guevara

❖ Key Facts

Conflict:
Cuban Revolution

Time Period:
Mid-20th Century

Genre:
Manual

OVERVIEW

Guerrilla Warfare: A Method is the English title of an article ("*Guerra de Guerrillas: Un Metodo*") written by Ernesto "Che" Guevara in 1963 for the Cuban journal *Cuba Socialista* and subsequently published as a pamphlet. Guevara, who played a strategic military role in the successful Cuban Revolution (1953–59) led by Fidel Castro, had presented a detailed account of his views on the theory and practice of unconventional war in a 1960 manual titled *Guerrilla Warfare*. Together the two works present Guevara's foco theory (*foquismo* in Spanish; also called focalism), an important departure from the dominant theory of guerrilla warfare articulated in the 1930s by Chinese revolutionary leader Mao Zedong. Whereas Maoist orthodoxy viewed guerrilla warfare as a tool to be used in support of a politically inspired revolution, Guevara came to believe that a guerrilla organization could itself create the conditions of revolution, without depending on a political vanguard. Although *Guerrilla Warfare* provides more practical detail concerning the conduct of irregular military operations, *Guerrilla Warfare: A Method* is important because it significantly modified Guevara's theoretical stance. In particular it argued that even superficially democratic regimes in Latin America were in fact oppressive oligarchies and were therefore appropriate targets for destabilization. Guevara suggested that guerrilla warfare could be used to provoke a violent response from such governments, thereby unmasking their true character.

Although Guevara's ideas were based largely on the success of the Cuban Revolution, he believed they could be applied effectively in other developing countries. His theories about fomenting revolution did not hold up well in application, however, and after several failed attempts to implement the foco strategy in Africa and Latin America, Guevara was killed by the Bolivian army in 1967. Nevertheless, Guevara's charismatic personality, impassioned idealism, and prolific writing have established him as an icon of the revolutionary spirit. Born into an upper-middle-class family in Argentina, Guevara was a well-educated medical doctor who combined an intellectual grasp of Marxism with a willingness to live the hard life of a guerrilla soldier. His selfless commitment to the cause of social justice attracted admiration, and "Che" (a nickname given him by Cuban revolutionaries) epitomized for many the idea of a leader who could not only overthrow corrupt governments by clever means but also inspire a new social order after the fighting ended. The continuing influence of *Guerrilla Warfare: A Method* comes primarily from this image of Guevara as the ideal revolutionary rather than from the ideas he put forth.

HISTORICAL AND LITERARY CONTEXT

Guerrilla warfare is a specific type of the irregular or unconventional military action used by weaker forces against stronger opponents. The goal of guerrilla warfare is to weaken and demoralize the enemy, using tactics such as ambush and assassination, as well as disrupting transportation, communications, and supply lines. This style of warfare uses a hit-and-run strategy rather than pitched battle, and guerrilla forces typically depend on greater mobility and on the support of local populations to offset their unequal position against better-trained, better-armed regular troops. Guerrilla forces are often indistinguishable from noncombatants, and their operations are designed to continue for long periods of time, gradually depleting enemy resources and exhausting an opponent's political will. It is very difficult to gain a conventional military victory against a determined guerrilla organization.

Irregular warfare is well suited to resistance against foreign invaders and has often been used in civil wars, independence movements, and insurgencies. Although there have been instances of irregular warfare throughout military history and in every part of the world, the word *guerrilla* (a diminutive of *guerra*, the Spanish word for "war") was first used in 1807 to describe the activities of partisan fighters who harassed Napoleon's army in the countryside of Spain. Guerrilla warfare was used in a variety of conflicts during the nineteenth century but continued to be regarded primarily in military terms, as an adjunct or an alternative to conventional warfare. Marx, however, recognized the political potential of insurgent warfare in 1849, and during the early twentieth century guerrilla warfare began to be viewed as a strategy that could be useful in a communist revolution. Although Russian revolutionaries Vladimir Ilich Lenin, Leon Trotsky, and Joseph Stalin all acknowledged the importance of irregular warfare, it was the Chinese revolutionary leader Mao Zedong who focused on guerrilla warfare as an indispensable aspect of the communist movement. As explained by Mostafa Rejai in *Political Ideologies: A Comparative Approach*, the idea of "guerrilla communism" came to be characterized by an almost exclusive association with underdeveloped countries; a focus on the countryside rather than the cities; a reliance on the rural peasantry rather than urban workers; and an expectation of protracted military conflict, with several distinct stages of development.

Maoist theory was aligned with the historic tendency to situate guerrilla operations in rural areas, where mountains, jungles, and other difficult terrains may offer better cover, while also providing additional challenge for conventional forces. Traditional Marxist/Leninist ideas had developed in the context of industrialized society, however, and were based on the assumption that political change would be driven by rising discontent of urban workers. Mao's emphasis on the politicization of rural peasants therefore represented a new approach to revolutionary strategy, more suited to conditions in the vast, largely preindustrial country of China. Cuba, by contrast, was a small country with an established middle class, a more modern economy, and a different set of political conditions, so its strategy for revolutionary success diverged in turn from the Maoist version. Guevara elaborated these Cuban modifications into a streamlined version of guerrilla warfare that was designed to drive rather than serve political revolution. Because China and Cuba were the only modern instances in which a guerrilla war was successfully carried out against a native government (rather than a foreign invader or colonial occupation), Mao Zedong's *On Guerrilla Warfare* and Guevara's *Guerrilla Warfare: A Method* were very influential among aspiring revolutionaries during the second half of the twentieth century.

THEMES AND STYLE

In *Guerrilla Warfare: A Method*, Guevara begins by restating the lessons of the Cuban Revolution, which he had outlined in the manual *Guerrilla Warfare*. These "three fundamental contributions to the laws of the revolutionary movement in the current situation in America" state that people's forces can win a war against a conventional army; that the insurrection itself can create conditions favorable to revolution; and that armed struggle should take place mainly in the countryside. Although Guevara claimed not to have read Mao's *On Guerrilla Warfare*, the first and third of the contributions he named were in keeping with Mao's views. The second, however, was significantly different. It suggested that the guerrilla band, or *foco*, could bring about revolution by its own actions

The author and revolutionary Che Guevara in a photo taken after he addressed the UN General Assembly in 1964. © CSU ARCHIVES / EVERETT COLLECTION

instead of by supporting a revolution instigated by others. As a corollary, this meant revolution need not require a "protracted" process of political preparation, as described by Lenin and Mao. By contrast with the communist revolution in China, which took more than twenty years in all, the revolution in Cuba was brief, lasting only from 1953 to 1959. Guevara gave much of the credit for this rapid success to the accomplishments of the *foco*, and this emphasis gave rise to the foco theory as a new approach to revolution. He also acknowledged, however, that while guerrilla warfare could be used successfully as a means to revolution against "corrupt Caribbean dictatorships," it could not be applied "where a government has come to power through some form of popular vote, fraudulent or not, and maintains at least an appearance of constitutional legality." In such cases, he concluded, "the guerrilla outbreak cannot be promoted, since the possibilities of peaceful struggle have not yet been exhausted."

In *Guerrilla Warfare: A Method*, Guevara reversed this position, contending that "we should not allow 'democracy' to be utilised apologetically to represent the dictatorship of the exploiting classes." He suggested instead that a superficially democratic regime should be forced to resort to violence, "thereby

A COMPLICATED LEGEND

Ernesto "Che" Guevara is among the most fascinating and controversial figures of the twentieth century. He was incontestably handsome and charismatic, a doctor who renounced a life of privilege to devote himself to the achievement of social justice. He was also an innovative thinker, a persuasive (even poetic) writer, and a tireless worker for the causes he believed in. His willingness to live a difficult, often dangerous life with little personal reward made him an icon of the revolutionary spirit.

It is generally acknowledged that he could be ruthless toward those he perceived as enemies and that he was often inflexible in his views. Critics contend that Guevara's ideological influence was severely detrimental to postrevolutionary Cuba, especially in terms of his early pro-Soviet stance and his forceful attempts to base the new Cuban economy on "moral" rather than financial incentives. As his role in Cuba began to decline, Guevara's attempts at exporting foco theory to other countries resulted in costly failures, and in the end, his death was as controversial as his life: was it a martyr's death or the predictable outcome of ill-conceived actions?

Debate continues over the "real" story of Guevara. For some he represents the epitome of principled commitment; for others he seems an empty figure whose fame was merely an accident of history. Some believe his ideas succeeded in Cuba only because of Castro's political skills; others think that Castro could never have succeeded without Guevara. He is seen as a saintly visionary by some, and by others as a violent fanatic.

To a large extent the legend of "Che" overshadows the ideas and actions of Ernesto Guevara, making it difficult to form an objective assessment of his achievements or influence. Long after his death, he continues to be a polarizing figure.

unmasking its true nature as the dictatorship of the reactionary social classes." Guevara argues that such an event "will deepen the struggle to such an extent that there will be no retreat from it." In this view "the performance of the people's forces depends on the task of forcing the dictatorship to a decision—to retreat or unleash the struggle." This rhetoric demonstrates that *Guerrilla Warfare: A Method* is more obviously Marxist in tone than his earlier work, and it suggests a shift of emphasis from revolution in Cuba to the achievement of world socialism.

CRITICAL DISCUSSION

According to Matt Childs, whose article in the *Journal of Latin American Studies* offers an extensive historical examination of foco theory, Guevara's changed views reflected the shifting politics in post-Revolution Cuba. He notes that "in 1960, when *Guerrilla Warfare* was published, the socialist nature of the Cuban Revolution had yet to be declared, [but by 1963] the Soviet Union had admitted Cuba to the socialist camp," and foco theory took a more clearly Marxist turn. It also occupied an important place in Cuba's foreign policy. Based on the idea that *focos* could drive revolution in other Latin American countries, the new Cuban regime attempted to establish or support revolutionary groups in Nicaragua, Guatemala, Venezuela, Argentina, Colombia, the Dominican Republic, and Peru. Their efforts failed in every case, driving Cuba further into international isolation and suggesting, as Childs points out, that "overthrowing an established government [is] clearly a more uncertain enterprise than Che's stylized interpretation of the Cuban revolutionary experience made it appear."

Soon after Guevara's death, Cuba began to pull back from its sponsorship of revolution in Latin America. In addition, Guevara's closest collaborator in the development of foco theory, the French writer Régis Debray, revised his own views on the matter after 1967, writing in the essay "Time and Politics" that "it is impossible to provoke or improvise crisis situations artificially; every country, every locality, has its own special historical time, its own pace, its speed of development." In addition to Debray and other revisionists, who recognized that Guevara had misinterpreted aspects of the Cuban Revolution, there were also outright detractors, who contended that Guevara's personal egotism and stubborn adherence to the foco theory had cost the lives of followers. Yet Guevara's treatises on guerrilla warfare remain among the best-known commentaries on modern revolutionary action.

As Gordon McCormick observes in *Queen's Quarterly*, on one level Guevara's message is dated, as he was "the product of a different era, fighting and dying in the name of a political program that has been thoroughly discredited with time." On a higher level, however, "Che Guevara continues to stand for a set of values that are more significant to the human condition than the particular features of his political philosophy." McCormick suggests that Guevara fulfills the enduring image of a hero—not only "an intellectual man of action" but also "a person of strong conviction and great physical and moral courage."

SOURCES

Childs, Matt D. "An Historical Critique of the Emergence and Evolution of Ernesto Che Guevara's Foco Theory." *Journal of Latin American Studies* 27:3 (1995): 593–624. Print.

Debray, Régis. "Time and Politics." *Prison Writings*. Trans. Rosemary Sheed. New York: Random, 1973: 130+. Print.

Guevara, Ernesto. *Che: Selected Works of Ernesto Guevara*. Ed. Rolando E. Bonachea and Nelson P. Valdes. Cambridge: MIT, 1969. Print.

McCormick, Gordon H. "Revolutionary Odyssey of Che Guevara." *Queen's Quarterly* 105.2 (1998): 168–85.

Rejai, M. *Political Ideologies: A Comparative Approach*. Armonk: Sharpe, 1991. Print.

FURTHER READING

Chaliand, Gérard. *Guerrilla Strategies: An Historical Anthology from the Long March to Afghanistan.* Berkeley: U of California P, 1982. Print.

Guevara, Ernesto. *Episodes of the Cuban Revolutionary War: 1956-58.* New York: Pathfinder, 1996. Print.

Guevara, Ernesto, and David Deutschmann. *Che Guevara Reader.* Havana: Centro de Estudios Che Guevara, 2003. Print.

Harris, Richard L. *Che Guevara: A Biography.* Santa Barbara: Greenwood, 2011. Print.

Hart, Joseph. *Che: The Life, Death, and Afterlife of a Revolutionary.* New York: Thunder's Mouth, 2003. Print.Bottom of Form

Robinson, Donald B. *The Dirty Wars: Guerrilla Actions and Other Forms of Unconventional Warfare.* New York: Delacorte, 1968. Print.

Weir, William. *Guerrilla Warfare: Irregular Warfare in the Twentieth Century.* Mechanicsburg: Stackpole, 2008. Print.

Cynthia Giles

ON GUERRILLA WARFARE

Mao Zedong

✧ **Key Facts**

Conflict:
Chinese Revolution of 1911

Time Period:
Early to mid-20th Century

Genre:
Treatise

OVERVIEW

On Guerrilla Warfare is the English title of a document written in 1937 by Chinese communist leader Mao Zedong (also transliterated as Mao Tse-tung). Although the document was originally developed as an argument for using unconventional military action to combat the Japanese invasion of China, it went on to become a standard treatise on guerrilla warfare as a tool of political revolution.

On Guerrilla Warfare summarized the lessons Mao had learned during a decade of conflict with the Nationalist Chinese government, and defined a specific methodology for achieving military success against a stronger opponent. Equally important, the document put forth a view of practical revolution that differed in an important respect from traditional Marxist theory. Mao outlined an approach to revolutionary action that depended on the peasantry rather than the urban working class and was therefore more suitable to an agrarian society such as China. This strategy proved to be important in revolutionary movements of the later twentieth century, most notably in Southeast Asia.

Mao wrote *On Guerrilla Warfare* at a point of intersection between the long internal campaign to create a communist government in China and a recurrence of the external threat posed by Japanese invaders. The work is divided into seven chapters, the first of which defines guerrilla warfare as "a powerful special weapon" that combines political and military aspects. In chapter two Mao examines the relationship between guerrilla operations and those of the regular army. Chapter three summarizes the history of guerrilla warfare, and the following chapter discusses the means by which guerrilla operations may defeat a superior force. Chapter five provides details regarding the principles of organization for guerrilla warfare, which include independence from hierarchical leadership, commitment to "the people's emancipation," and strategic acquisition of supplies. In the last two chapters, Mao explains the mutual interdependence of military action and political affairs and then concludes with specific observations on guerrilla strategy.

This combination of practical advice, political inspiration, and theoretical innovation made *On Guerrilla Warfare* a widely influential document.

In particular, Mao introduced ideas for converting deficits into advantages that became standard operational principles for guerrilla forces. These included the use of intelligence provided by sympathetic locals, the value of deception and surprise as an equalizing strategy against superior firepower, the importance of mobility, and the use of retreat as an offensive tactic.

Although Mao went on to become a prolific author, whose works included political analysis, propaganda, poetry, and autobiography, *On Guerrilla Warfare* was arguably his most important work in terms of its impact on world affairs.

HISTORICAL AND LITERARY CONTEXT

Mao Zedong was born in the Hunan Province of China in 1893. His formal education was minimal, but he studied on his own and read widely throughout his life. Rebelling against his harsh and demanding father, a grain merchant, Mao secured a modest position in the Peking University library, where he met radical intellectuals. The 1917 revolution in Russia, which ended with a Marxist government in power, had raised hopes for the triumph of an international communist movement, and by 1920 Mao was a professed Marxist. In 1921 he served as one of twelve delegates to a meeting that established the Chinese Communist Party (CCP).

At that time a Nationalist faction in China had succeeded in displacing the imperial Manchu dynasty, and the Nationalist leader Sun Yat-Sen seemed interested in a cooperative relationship with the Chinese communists. After Sun's death in 1925, however, the communists were regarded as a threat by his ultraconservative successor, Chiang Kai-shek, who in 1927 wiped out much of the CCP in an attack on the party's urban enclaves.

A few months later Mao, who was serving as a provincial party leader in Hunan, failed in his attempt to stage a peasant uprising. With a small number of armed followers, he retreated into the mountains. There he began to establish a base of support, implementing land reforms and creating a peasant government. In 1934, when Chiang Kai-shek initiated an all-out assault on the communists, Mao was forced into a retreat that became his most famous exploit. With about one hundred thousand men, he crossed six thousand miles of deserts, mountains, and rivers in a yearlong journey known as the Long March. Although most of his forces were lost during the trek, Mao learned valuable lessons, established a new stronghold, and soon took over leadership of the CCP.

When Japan invaded China in 1937, the CCP and the Nationalists set aside internal divisions to concentrate on defense of the country. Mao's tactical ideas, as set forth in *On Guerrilla Warfare*, were important to that defense, but his strategic understanding of revolution proved to be even more crucial once the Japanese surrendered in 1945. The communist forces were able to shift quickly from a defensive action against the Japanese to a "people's war" against Chiang Kai-shek and the Nationalist army. By 1949 the Nationalists had been forced to retreat from the mainland of China to the island of Taiwan, and Mao was declared leader of the Chinese People's Republic.

THEMES AND STYLE

Prior to Mao, unconventional warfare had a long but unsystematic history. The practice is recorded in ancient Hittite and Chinese writings, accounts from Jewish and Roman history, medieval chronicles, and analyses of almost all modern conflicts. According to Brian Loveman's overview in *The Oxford Companion to Politics of the World*, "There is no major part of the world in which some sort of guerrilla warfare has not been utilized by the weak against the strong, by resistance forces against foreign invaders, by technically or numerically inferior armies against better-equipped, larger, or more powerful forces." Similarly, Loveman continues, "no single theater of operations or mode of combat defines guerrilla warfare." Its hallmark, however, is the use of small mobile forces to harass and demoralize a regular army, often over a long period of time. By keeping their operations modest and their casualties low, guerrilla forces can outlast opponents whose requirements for money, men, and matériel are much greater.

The importance of scale as a characteristic of unconventional warfare is reflected in the word *guerrilla*, a diminutive form of *guerra*, the Spanish word for "war." In his chapter on the history of guerrilla warfare, Mao, recounting its use in the Russian Revolution and in earlier episodes from Chinese history, provides a context familiar to his audience.

In other parts of *On Guerrilla Warfare*, Mao offers a systematic view of guerrilla operations that addresses the need for repeatable results. Previously, unconventional warfare had been regarded as improvisational for the most part, depending for its effectiveness on elements of surprise and invention. Although Mao does not reject these qualities, he also does not rely on them. His approach creates a more stable form of guerrilla warfare, with a coherent set of underlying principles.

Legions of Chinese soldiers use the Great Wall as a military highway during the Second Sino-Japanese War in 1937, the year Mao Zedong wrote *On Guerrilla Warfare*. © AP IMAGES

One strategic component is emphasis on the political dimension of guerrilla warfare, which requires "indoctrination of both military and political leaders" and depends on three factors: "first, spiritual unification of officers and men within the army; second spiritual unification of the army and the people; and, last, destruction of the unity of the enemy." In explaining the relationship that should exist between the people and the troops, Mao employs one of the poetic analogies that make his writing so effective. After likening the people to water and the troops to fish that inhabit the water, he asks, "How may it be said that these two cannot exist together?" The answer articulates a key precept of Mao's philosophy: "It is only undisciplined troops who make the people their enemies and who, like the fish out of its native element cannot live."

Mao goes on to suggest scrupulous rules of behavior for guerrilla troops, both toward the people and within their units, stressing courtesy and self-

THE LITTLE RED BOOK

Mao was a prolific writer, and all of his books were popular in China. *Quotations from Chairman Mao Tse-Tung*, however, was in a class by itself. By many estimates it is the most widely distributed secular work in history, with as many as one billion copies printed.

The book began as a selection of inspirational quotes compiled in 1964 for use by communist party officials and military leaders, but the original idea expanded into something of a national obsession. Between 1965 and 1967, the book was finalized in an edition that included 427 quotations organized in thirty-three topic categories such as "Imperialism and All Reactionaries are Paper Tigers" and "Building Our Country through Diligence and Frugality." An extensive printing program was initiated to ensure that copies would be available to everyone in China. The most commonly manufactured version of the book was small enough to be portable and was bound in a durable bright-red cover, giving rise to the well-known nickname "Little Red Book" (LRB).

Owning and reading the LRB was effectively mandatory in China during the early years of the Cultural Revolution—a movement intended to purge all traces of capitalism and traditional culture in China, ensuring a pure form of socialism. The Cultural Revolution was closely tied to a cult of personality centered on Mao, in which the image and ideas of the Chinese leader dominated all forms of media. The same approach had previously been used by German fuehrer Adolf Hitler and Soviet premiere Joseph Stalin to create national enthusiasm for their totalitarian regimes.

The Cultural Revolution was initiated in 1966, but its damaging effects—which included widespread social dislocation, violent factional struggles, and the destruction of historical and religious sites and artifacts—were so great that Mao called for an official end to the movement in 1969. Some aspects continued for several years afterward, however, further impairing China's political stability.

discipline. In both style and content, *On Guerrilla Warfare* reflects the tradition of Chinese wisdom literature, particularly through echoes of Sun Tzu's classic military treatise *The Art of War* (sixth century BCE). This confluence of clear writing, practical advice, moral instruction, and original thought made *On Guerrilla Warfare* a widely popular manual, with an influence that extended far beyond China and long after Mao's death in 1976.

CRITICAL DISCUSSION

Historically, the flexible nature of guerrilla warfare made it a useful tool for almost every sort of cause or ideology. In the twentieth century, however, guerrilla warfare came to be viewed primarily as an instrument of communist revolution. Both Marx and Lenin, the primary architects of communist theory, had commented on the usefulness of unconventional warfare, but it was Mao Zedong who elaborated and intensified the connection. As Mostafa Rejai observes in *Political Ideologies: A Comparative Approach*, Mao, "the foremost theoretician-practitioner of guerrilla communism," was responsible for formulating "an explicit and self-conscious statement of the ideology and practice of guerrilla communism, [which he proclaimed] as a model for all developing countries."

Consequently, *On Guerrilla Warfare* is discussed more often in terms of its relationship to revolutionary communism than in terms of the advice and insight it offers regarding operational aspects of unconventional warfare. Although this emphasis is due in part to the later impact of Maoist ideology, both inside and outside of China, it also reflects Mao's approach to the practice and theory of guerrilla warfare. As Bernard Norling observed in his review of *On Guerrilla Warfare*, Mao regards war as "merely another instrument of policy" and he "stresses that neither war in general nor guerrilla war in particular is ever an end in itself." While his tactical prescriptions are not very different from those practiced by guerrilla leaders throughout history, Mao's focus on co-opting the peasantry by means of political education provides a dynamic new key to revolutionary success.

Mao's emphasis on winning the countryside was closely tied to his theory of "protracted struggle," which assumed that a long period of preparation—the organizational phase—would be required in order to build sufficient support among the masses. That would be followed by a defensive (guerrilla) phase, and the struggle would end with a final offensive phase, marked by a clash of regular armies. Thus guerrilla warfare could be crucial to the revolution, but in the end, conventional military action would be required to complete the process.

The most successful replication of Mao's strategy was carried out by the Vietnamese military leader Võ Nguyên Giáp in the First Indochina War (which resulted in the establishment of the Democratic Republic of Vietnam under HồChí Minh) and the subsequent Vietnam War. Giáp made some pragmatic adaptations, based on local conditions, but fundamentally adhered to the Maoist model.

In Cuba guerrilla leader Ernesto "Che" Guevarra made a sharper departure from the model. As Ian F. W. Beckett explains in *Modern Insurgencies and Counter-Insurgencies: Guerrillas and Their Opponents since 1750*, Mao's theory "stressed the importance of parallel but separate military and political organisations," whereas Guevara "argued that the guerrillas themselves could be a revolutionary fusion of political and military authority, with the guerrillas acting as a revolutionary 'vanguard' party in embryo." Guevara propounded this theory, known as *foquismo*, in *Guerrilla Warfare* (1960). Although the charismatic Guevara became a revolutionary icon, and his writings on guerrilla warfare compare with Mao's in terms of influence, his approach never proved effective in practice outside of Cuba.

SOURCES

Beckett, I. F. W. *Modern Insurgencies and Counter-Insurgencies: Guerrillas and Their Opponents since 1750.* London: Routledge, 2001. Print.

Griffith, Samuel B. *Mao Tse Tung: On Guerrilla Warfare.* New York: Praeger, 1961. Print.

Loveman, Brian. "Guerrilla Warfare." *The Oxford Companion to Politics of the World.* New York: Oxford UP, 1993. 372–73. Print.

Norling, Bernard. "Peace and the Waging of War." Rev. of *On Guerrilla Warfare*, by Mao Zedong. *Review of Politics* 25:2 (1963): 248–54. Print.

Rejai, Mostafa. *Political Ideologies: A Comparative Approach.* Armonk: Sharpe, 1991. Print.

FURTHER READING

Chaliand, Gérard. *Guerrilla Strategies: An Historical Anthology from the Long March to Afghanistan.* Berkeley: U of California P, 1982. Print.

Chou, Eric. *Mao Tse-tung: The Man and the Myth.* Briarcliff Manor: Stein, 1982. Print.

Robinson, Donald B. *The Dirty Wars: Guerrilla Actions and Other Forms of Unconventional Warfare.* New York: Delacorte, 1968. Print.

Weir, William. *Guerrilla Warfare: Irregular Warfare in the Twentieth Century.* Mechanicsburg: Stackpole, 2008. Print.

Womack, Brantly. *The Foundations of Mao Zedong's Political Thought, 1917-1935.* Honolulu: UP of Hawaii, 1982. Print.

Cynthia Giles

ON WAR

Carl von Clausewitz

❖ *Key Facts*

Conflict:
Napoleonic Wars

Time Period:
Early 19th Century

Genre:
Treatise

OVERVIEW

On War (*Vom Kriege*), Prussian general Carl von Clausewitz's unfinished treatise on military strategy and the nature of war, was published posthumously in 1832 by his wife, Marie von Clausewitz. Although it was originally dismissed as romantic and antirational, the book is now widely regarded as one of the most meticulously crafted, comprehensive, and controversial works on its subject.

Unlike the leading strategists of his day, Clausewitz does not enumerate a set of military principles or prescribe a list of techniques meant to increase the likelihood of success in combat. In the book he is less concerned than his contemporaries with an abstract theory of war and the minutiae of troop formations, munitions stores, casualty rates, and the geometry of the battlefield. Instead, Clausewitz introduces several new, less measurable considerations, such as the socioeconomic conditions and political policies that underwrite a given conflict, the genius of the commanding officer, the troops' morale, the role of chance, and the corresponding inevitability of things going wrong in combat. Clausewitz's book is not intended to endorse a particular method of waging war or indoctrinate the student in a given philosophy but rather to present a set of observations that nurture in him presence of mind and the capacity for good judgment in the heat of battle.

HISTORICAL AND LITERARY CONTEXT

The Napoleonic Wars (1803–15), and more specifically the French invasion of Russia in 1812, form the backdrop and inform most of the arguments in *On War*. Clausewitz also frequently cites the campaigns of Frederick the Great during the First Silesian War (1740–42) and the War of Austrian Succession (1740–48) to substantiate his claims.

Clausewitz uses Frederick's and Napoleon's campaigns to illustrate one of his central theses: that the nature of war changes radically with alterations in politics and society and with advances in technology, and therefore there is no surer way to court annihilation than to deploy yesterday's tactics in today's war. For example, because of the limited range of munitions at the time and the relatively small size of fighting forces, Frederick was able to conduct troop movements in full view of the enemy. In contrast, by Napoleon's time, circumstances had changed considerably. Rifles were more accurate and their range was expanded. Furthermore, they were easier to fire while lying prostrate, and one was thus more likely to encounter shelling from concealed troops. In addition, whereas Frederick drew his army mainly from groups of mercenaries and specifically trained soldiers, Napoleon, because of the changes in society following the French Revolution, was able to form an army from a much broader segment of the population. Thus, while Frederick took tens of thousands of soldiers to the battlefield, Napoleon routinely took more than 200,000.

Clausewitz served in the Russian army during the Battle of Borodino (September 7, 1812), which involved more than 250,000 troops, resulted in at least seventy thousand casualties, and was believed to be one of the bloodiest days in the history of warfare up to that point. He also witnessed several of the battles in the ensuing months as the Russians chased Napoleon's fast-depleting forces back across the Russian border. Although he would draw many of his most famous conclusions from what he saw during that time, Clausewitz was not considered the leading expert on the Napoleonic Wars, nor even a foremost military strategist in European circles in the aftermath of the wars. The most respected theorist of Clausewitz's time was Antoine-Henri Jomini, a Frenchman who served as general in the Russian Army during Napoleon's invasion. Unlike *On War*, Jomini's *The Art of War* (1838) is a didactic text that offers a rich explication of tactics and formations and prescribes a method for achieving success in battle. It, too, is still widely read.

THEMES AND STYLE

Clausewitz began recording observations that would later appear in *On War* in his mid-twenties while being held prisoner by Napoleon's army for two years, between 1806 and 1808. He then composed the majority of the work between 1816 and 1830, when he served as the director of the Prussian War Academy. Portions of the text were published separately as essays during his lifetime. At the time of his death in 1831, Clausewitz had finished an initial draft of six of the eight books he had planned for the final volume and had sketched notes for the two others. He had, however, revised only a small segment—chapter 1 of the first book—to his satisfaction.

Given the circumstances of its composition, *On War*'s style is varied and, in places, inconsistent. Book 1, "On the Nature of War," is succinct and aphoristic and contains many of Clausewitz's best-remembered lines. For example, it is here that Clausewitz, noting the connection between politics and combat, remarks that "war is nothing but the continuation of policy by other means." Elsewhere in Book 1 he writes, "War is thus an act of force that compels our enemy to do our will" and "War is such a dangerous business that the mistakes that come from kindness are the very worst." Other parts of the book, such as the accounts of maneuvers by Napoleon, Frederick the Great, and several more obscure commanders, can be sprawling and are remarkable both for the precision of the author's memory and for the depth of his analysis. Still other observations, such as Clausewitz's deliberations on boldness, daring, intellect, and genius, seem unfinished and at times contradictory.

Throughout his work, Clausewitz employs a dialectic approach to his analysis of war. When formulating a thought, he poses a thesis and an antithesis, and from these extremes he arrives at a conclusion that is a synthesis of the two propositions. For example, one such distinction Clausewitz makes is between absolute war and limited war. On the one hand, he notes that absolute war, which represents the ideal state of conflict, involves "the maximum use of force" to "render the enemy powerless." He writes, "War is an act of force; there is no logical limit to the application of that force. Each side compels its opponent to follow suit; a reciprocal action is started, which must lead, in theory,

to extremes." On the other hand, Clausewitz observes that war never reaches its extreme, because in reality the aims of war are always limited. For the author, war is never an end in itself but rather an instrument of policy, be it to defend a plot of land, acquire new territory, or meet any number of other objectives. This link between policy and war is the central thesis in Book 1. Moreover, there were two memoranda found among Clausewitz's notes indicating that his intention was to return more frequently to this point as he revised the remaining books of his manuscript.

Clausewitz based one of his most radical propositions on what he witnessed at the Battle of Borodino. Considering the relative strength of both armies after the Russian forces' retreat into the interior of the country, Clausewitz concluded that, of the two, defense was the stronger form of war than offense, an idea that contradicted the established wisdom of the day. In Book 6 of *On War* Clausewitz subjects the principle to an exhaustive dialectical analysis before confirming it. First establishing attack and defense as antithetical principles, Clausewitz argues that after the initial foray, the forces switch roles, putting the attacking army at a distinct disadvantage. While the attacking force must adopt a number of defensive positions, most notably securing the new terrain it has conquered and maintaining lines of communication with its base, the defending army, if it has respectably held forth, has the opportunity to launch a counteroffensive in close quarters against a battalion that has likely established a makeshift defensive position on unfamiliar territory.

CLAUSEWITZ'S POSSIBLE INFLUENCE ON JIHADI MILITARY THEORY

Since 2001 U.S. military theorists have debated whether Carl von Clausewitz's ideas are relevant to the nation's fight against Islamist paramilitary cells. Less attention has been paid, however, to the influence Clausewitz's thought may have on the formulation of jihadi military strategy in the Islamist fight against the United States. According to Norwegian defense researcher Thomas Hegghammer, in early 2002 Majallat al-Ansar and the Center for Islamic Studies and Research, two online sources of Islamist propaganda (both defunct since 2003), began to abandon religious rhetoric and instead run articles that made reference to Western academic research on warfare. They frequently quoted Clausewitz along with other Western military theorists. Other al-Qaeda-affiliated online publications quickly followed suit.

Hegghammer calls this series of texts "Jihadi strategic studies" and notes that by autumn 2002 the military analysis in the articles had become "remarkably sophisticated." "A particularly interesting development," Hegghammer observes, "is the widening of the notion of strategy to include much more than purely military factors" as Jihadi thinkers "put increasingly more emphasis on the political, economic, and psychological dimensions of the confrontation with the US." Of particular interest to Hegghammer is a prescient article from 2003 titled "Jihadi Iraq—Expectations and Dangers" in which the anonymous author argues that the most effective way to force the United States to withdraw from Iraq is to increase the economic strain on Washington by pressuring its allies to leave the coalition.

With all of his formulations, Clausewitz recognizes that the ever-present elements of chance and difficulty make any theory a gamble on the day of battle. In particular, he gives difficulty, which he calls friction, considerable attention. "Countless minor incidents—the kind you can never really foresee—combine to lower the general level of performance, so that one always falls short of the intended goal," he observes. For Clausewitz, it is friction, more than anything else, that distinguishes "real war from war on paper."

CRITICAL DISCUSSION

On War was largely ignored in the years immediately following its publication, with the initial run of fifteen hundred volumes selling few copies in the first two decades after its release, despite Clausewitz's widely acknowledged success in his military career. In his introduction to the 1984 edition, Michael Howard notes that fellow military strategists found the work "hard going." Howard speculates that Clausewitz's contemporaries may have disregarded his work because they were aware that it undermined the accepted dogma of Prussian military circles. Howard writes, "But even those who had not read him knew that his teachings embodied that freedom of thinking, that emphasis on the creative action of the individual and disdain for formalism," which, Howard contends, Prussian military conservatives had "tried to keep alive during the sterile and reactionary period of the 1840s."

Clausewitz began to acquire a larger readership nearly forty years after *On War*'s publication when, following his victories in the German wars of unification (1866 and 1870), Helmuth von Moltke, the chief of the Prussian General Staff, named *On War*, along with the Bible and the works of Homer, as the

Joseph Mallord William Turner (1775–1851), *The Field of Waterloo*, exhibited 1818. Oil on canvas.
© TATE, LONDON / ART RESOURCE, NY

books most responsible for his success. There is, however, considerable scholarly debate as to whether or not Moltke's praise of Clausewitz caused the shift or coincided with it. Howard argues that by the time of the wars of unification, Clausewitz's ideas were pervasive in Prussian military circles, though many in the new generation of strategists may not have been entirely aware of their origin. As Howard notes, "Many of the ideas we now think of as peculiarly Clausewitzian and to which Moltke was to so signally give effect in his campaigns … were commonplaces among young Prussian officers who had shared the Napoleonic experience. As with so many thinkers, many of the ideas which Clausewitz codified and transmitted to posterity may have been shared generally, if unconsciously, among his contemporaries." According to this view, Moltke attached Clausewitz's name to what had existed for decades in Prussian military circles as a set of unattributed assumptions that had been proven reliable by victory in a series of important military campaigns.

In 1873 *On War* was translated into English by British colonel J. J. Graham, which he did, many scholars believe, because of Moltke's praise of the book. According to Christopher Bassford, it was F. N. Maude's frequent mention of Moltke in his introduction to the 1908 edition of the English translation that firmly established the link between Moltke and Graham. Bassford halfheartedly accepts this link but also claims that Clausewitz had been well received in British military circles before the translation appeared. "There may be some truth to the view that it was Moltke's praise that drew British attention to Clausewitz, but this translation was also the logical outcome of a long-standing interest in Clausewitz in Britain," he writes. As further evidence that Moltke's influence was minimal, Bassford notes that sales of the Graham's first edition were miniscule.

For English military historian B. H. Liddell Hart, the work's place in the canon of military texts is attributable to nothing more than the license to naked aggression granted by Clausewitz's theory of absolute war. In *The Ghost of Napoleon*, Hart argues that Clausewitz "was the source of the doctrine of 'absolute war,' the fight-to-a-finish theory, which, beginning with the argument that 'war is only a continuation of state policy by other means,' ended by making policy

the slave of strategy." Hart recognizes that Clausewitz did not intend to endorse wanton violence, but he nevertheless blames the writer for allowing himself to be too easily misunderstood:

> Not one reader in a hundred was likely to follow the subtlety of his logic, or to preserve a true balance amid such philosophical jugglery. But everyone could catch such ringing phrases as—'We have only one means in war—the battle.' 'The combat is the single activity in war.' 'We may reduce every military activity in the province of strategy to the unit of single combats.' … For, by making battle appear the only 'real warlike activity,' his gospel deprived strategy of its laurels, reduced the art of war to the mechanics of mass slaughter, and incited generals to seek battle at the first opportunity, instead of creating an *advantageous* opportunity.

SOURCES

Bassford, Christopher. *Clausewitz in English: The Reception of Clausewitz in Britain and America, 1815-1845*. New York: Oxford UP, 1994. Print.

Clausewitz, Carl von. *On War*. Ed. and trans. Michael Howard and Peter Paret. Princeton: Princeton UP, 1989. Print.

Hart, B. H. Liddell. *The Ghost of Napoleon*. Westport: Greenwood, 1980. Print.

Howard, Michael. "The Influence of Clausewitz." *On War*. Ed. and trans. Michael Howard and Peter Paret. Princeton: Princeton UP, 1989. Print.

FURTHER READING

Fraser, David. *Frederick the Great*. New York: Penguin, 2002. Print.

Hart, B. H. Liddell. *Strategy*. New York: Plume, 1991. Print.

Jomini, Antoine-Henri. *The Art of War*. Trans. G. H. Mendell and W. P. Craighill. Westport: Greenwood, 1971. Print.

Lieven, Dominic. *Russia against Napoleon: The True Story of the Campaigns of War and Peace*. New York: Penguin, 2011. Print.

Montross, Lynn. *War through the Ages*. New York: Harper, 1960. Print.

Joseph Campana

STRATEGY
The Indirect Approach
B. H. Liddell Hart

❖ *Key Facts*

Conflict:
Various European wars

Time Period:
5th Century BCE–mid-20th Century

Genre:
Treatise

OVERVIEW

In *Strategy: The Indirect Approach* (1954), British military theorist B. H. Liddell Hart reviews the campaigns of fourteen European conflicts spanning 2,500 years to demonstrate the advantages of an indirect approach over a direct approach to waging war. Liddell Hart defines the direct approach as a simple matter of concentrating the better part of an entity's force against the enemy's strongest point of resistance. The indirect approach, on the contrary, is a complicated process whereby one side weakens the opposition by gaining physical and psychological advantages before the battle starts and then choosing an opportune time to strike swiftly at the enemy's most vulnerable points. Covering an exhaustive set of examples, Liddell Hart argues that the most famous commanders in Western history, including Alexander the Great, Julius Caesar, and Napoleon Bonaparte, won their greatest victories through intimidation, cunning, speed, and surprise—all of which are key aspects of the indirect approach. He notes that these same commanders failed when they practiced the direct approach. For Liddell Hart, their defeats show "how rarely the possession of superior force offsets the disadvantage of attacking in the most obvious way."

Liddell Hart first proffered the theory of the indirect approach in *The Decisive Wars of History* (1929) and expanded on it in 1941's *The Strategy of the Indirect Approach*, which was reprinted in 1942 as *The Way to Win Wars*. These texts contain a survey of Western military history beginning with the Athenian victory over the Persians at Thermopylae in 480 BCE and ending with World War I (1914–18). In 1954's *Strategy: The Indirect Approach*, Liddell Hart adds an analysis of World War II (1939–45) and a section on the fundamentals of strategy in which he distinguishes political policy from military strategy. Over the course of twenty-five years between the four publications, he came to regard the indirect approach as one of life's core principles. He writes in the preface to the 1954 volume, "When ... I first came to perceive the superiority of the indirect over the direct approach, I was looking merely for light upon strategy. With deepened reflection, however, I began to realize that the indirect approach had a much wider application—it was the law of life in all spheres: a truth of philosophy."

HISTORICAL AND LITERARY CONTEXT

Liddell Hart began his writing career after World War I. He had served from 1914 to 1916 in the British army before being relieved from combat duties because of injuries suffered in a gas attack. By the early 1930s—after publishing biographies of Roman General Scipio Africanus in 1926 and U.S. Civil War General William Tecumseh Sherman in 1929 as well as a widely acclaimed analysis of World War I (*The Real War 1914-1918*) in 1930—Liddell Hart had emerged as a leading military theorist in the West. He is credited with being among the first to understand that the new technologies of the twentieth century, especially tanks and aircraft, rendered manpower considerably less important than it had been in the past.

As early as 1925, in *Paris or the Future of War*, Liddell Hart wrote that air and tank raids would be the key offensive elements in upcoming wars and that speed and maneuverability would trump any strength provided by numbers of troops. He was one of the first proponents of detaching armored divisions from the main body of infantry and cutting deep into enemy lines with tanks. He also studied the best means of cutting enemy lines of communications. In *The British Ways in Warfare* (1932), he famously notes that cuts made close to the front had the most immediate effect on the enemy but that cuts made close to the source of communications had the greater effect. While his work in the interwar period was largely ignored in British military circles, it is known that German and Italian commanders studied his writings closely and deployed his tactics against the British in World War II. In 1944, while visiting Liddell Hart's estate, U.S. General George Patton, commander of the North African Campaign in World War II, told the author that he had learned a great deal about how to fight Nazi General Erwin Rommel in the desert by reading Liddell Hart's analysis of Sherman's march through Georgia during the U.S. Civil War.

Liddell Hart's work belongs to a tradition of military writing that dates to *The Art of War*, a composition ascribed to Chinese General Sun Tzu (544–496 BCE) but which is believed to have been completed in the third century BCE, more than two hundred years after Sun Tzu's death. Like Sun Tzu, Liddell Hart advocates for discretion and, whenever possible, minimizing bloodshed in war. There are numerous other texts in this tradition, including Italian Renaissance philosopher Niccolò Machiavelli's *Dell'arte della guerra* (1521; *The Art of War*, 1560) and French General Antoine-Henri Baron Jomini's *Precis de l'art de la guerre* (1838; *Summary of the Art of War*, 1868). But Liddell Hart regards Carl von Clausewitz's *Vom Kriege* (1832; *On War*, 1832) as the work that had the greatest impact on warfare in the twentieth century. He believes that Clausewitz was deeply misunderstood by policymakers and generals alike and that his book is responsible for a great deal of unnecessary bloodshed in World War I and World War II.

THEMES AND STYLE

In the opening pages of *Strategy: The Indirect Approach*, Liddell Hart expresses his theory on strategy in an aphorism that has since become famous: "In strategy, the longest way round is often the shortest way home." Over the course of the book, he makes numerous clear, simple comparisons to demonstrate what he means by the indirect approach and to show how useful it is. For example, he compares the indirect approach to a martial artist who waits for the opponent to overextend himself and then turns the opponent's strength into a weakness. Liddell Hart explains that the Greeks deployed this tactic at the Battle of Salamis in 480 BCE, when they drew a vastly superior Persian fleet into the narrow straits close to shore. Once the Persians had overcommitted, the size of their fleet became a detriment as they lost their maneuverability, and the Greeks launched their artillery at easy targets from the flanks. Elsewhere, Liddell Hart draws similes between using the indirect approach in war and soft-selling products and feigning indifference while courting a loved one.

These succinct explanations, however, belie the complexity of Liddell Hart's theory, which rests on the ideas that psychological aspects of war take precedence over the physical aspects and that smart leaders are more important than vast numbers of troops. Each of the examples Liddell Hart provides confirms what he calls "the immemorial lesson that the true aim in war is in the mind of the hostile rulers, not in their troops; that the balance between victory and defeat turns on mental impressions and only indirectly on physical blows." Victory at Salamis, for example, turned on a mental impression. According to Liddell Hart, Xerxes drew his fleet in too far because Themosticles, a Greek soldier that Xerxes believed to be a traitor, had convinced the Persian ruler that the Greeks were prepared to surrender. For Liddell Hart, a leader pursues the indirect approach by putting the enemy in a state of physical and psychological dislocation. The leader establishes physical dislocation by separating

THE BLITZKRIEG CONTROVERSY

A 1940 German attack on London, World War II. © NATIONAL GEOGRAPHIC SOCIETY / CORBIS

In the early years of World War II, German panzer divisions, which included tanks, aircraft, and infantry, overwhelmed the enemy with their force and speed, striking by surprise from many different angles with the most technologically advanced artillery that had been used in combat up to that point in history. After the war, analysts coined the term "blitzkrieg" to describe such assaults that hit the opposition like an avalanche or a torrent. In his postwar writings, Liddell Hart claimed that the Germans based this method of attack, in part, on his theories. *Panzer Leader* (1952), the English translation of Nazi General Heinz Guderian's memoirs, verifies Liddell Hart's assertion.

The evidence suggests, however, that Liddell Hart may have had a hand in manipulating the historical record to get his influence on the Germans documented in such convincing fashion. In *Alchemist of War: The Life of Basil Liddell Hart*, Alex Danchev reports that the original German edition of the memoir, *Erinnerungen eines Soldaten* (1950; Memories of a Soldier), makes no mention of Liddell Hart's influence on German strategy. According to Danchev, British military historian Kenneth Macksey found among Guderian's files a letter from Liddell Hart in which he asks Guderian to mention in the English edition that between the wars he, Liddell Hart, had written at length about the swift, multifaceted armored attack later deployed by the Germans. In the letter, Liddell Hart also requests that Guderian acknowledge that he was impressed by these observations. When questioned about the letter, Liddell Hart said that he had no record of such correspondence but that he was thankful to have been mentioned in the book.

the opposition's forces, cutting off their supplies, and eliminating the means of retreat. Physical dislocation, in turn, creates psychological dislocation by making the opposing commander feel trapped or paralyzed, which causes what Liddell Hart refers to as "a double D—demoralization and disorganization." Frightening troops is more effective than killing them because, as Liddell Hart notes, "a man killed is merely one man less, whereas a man unnerved is a highly infectious carrier of fear, capable of spreading an epidemic of panic."

Liddell Hart devotes the final section of the book to grand strategy, or the overriding political policy that he contends must always guide military strategy. In general, he claims that the goal of all grand strategy "is to obtain a better peace—even if only from your point of view." Throughout the passages on grand strategy, Liddell Hart condemns Prussian military strategist Clausewitz for stirring a lust for absolute war in future generations of military leaders in his seminal work *On War*. Liddell Hart claims that Clausewitz's "gospel deprived strategy of its laurels, and reduced the art of war to the mechanics of mass-slaughter." Although Liddell Hart concedes that the author likely did not intend his work to have this effect on readers, he also writes that "Clausewitz invited misinterpretation more than most."

CRITICAL DISCUSSION

Reviewers of *Strategy: The Indirect Approach* often recognize Liddell Hart as the foremost military theorist of the twentieth century and claim that his work is required reading for statesmen, generals, and lay students of military history alike. Ronald Lewin in his review in *International Affairs* calls the book "one of the seminal military studies of this century." Robert H. Larson concurs, arguing in his article "Liddell Hart: Apostle of Limited War" that "in formalizing the concept of the indirect approach, Liddell Hart produced what may well be his most important contribution to strategic thought." Although he finds Liddell Hart's text to be "a work of uneven quality," M. E. Howard nevertheless agrees with the relevance of Liddell Hart's ideas. At the end of his notice, he claims, "Our only hope of survival is that the conflicts of the future will either be 'cold' or limited; and in both the strategy of the indirect approach will play a paramount part."

Some scholars, however, such as Jay Luvaas and Alex Danchev, claim that Liddell Hart's theory governed the way he read military history. While defending Liddell Hart against one of his critics in "Liddell Hart and the Mearsheimer Critique: A 'Pupils' Retrospective," Luvaas, who spent a summer at Liddell Hart's estate, concedes that "once Liddell Hart had worked out his theory he used it ... as the basis for making judgments on past and present." According to Danchev, in his article "Liddell Hart and Indirect Approach," "Liddell Hart's hypothesis ruled his proofs. He did not sift evidence discriminately to see what would turn up; he ransacked it thievishly and bagged what he could find .... The same conclusions would have emerged from dinner at the Savoy and viewing *Gone with the Wind*."

Luvaas and Danchev also note that toward the middle of his career Liddell Hart despaired of the utility of combat and argued against it. Considering his work in the years prior to World War II, Luvaas argues that Liddell Hart "emerges, it must be admitted, almost as a pacifist, intrigued with the intellectual problems of the strategist but shrinking from that fatal step that could lead to war and a possible return to the conditions of 1914–18." Liddell Hart's commitment to avoiding bloodshed deepened with time. Luvaas cites a memorandum that Liddell Hart wrote in the early 1960s when Western powers were considering declaring war on the Soviet Union after Nikita Khrushchev authorized construction on the Berlin Wall. In that note Liddell Hart writes, "Would any sane man stake his life on a game of cards where the opponent held all the trumps, and the only possible alternative to losing every trick in turn would be to commit suicide? Yet the policy and contingency planning of the Western powers amount to nothing better than that! Khrushchev 'holds the trumps.'" Likewise, Danchev observes, "In Liddell Hart the pacifist streak was ineradicable. As time went on his unbelief yawned wider. By the mid-1930s he was convinced that, far from being a deliverance, war was an abhorrence (and total war a nonsense), victory a semblance, and battle an excrescence." Yet the author continued to be interested in military issues until the end of his life, and in the posthumously published *History of the Second World War* (1971), he expresses pride in the British Royal Air Force's role in the conflict.

SOURCES

Danchev, Alex. "Liddell Hart and the Indirect Approach." *The Journal of Military History* 63.2 (April 1999): 313+. JSTOR. Web. 26 Oct. 2011.

Howard, M. E. Rev. of Strategy by Liddell Hart. *International Affairs (Royal Institute of International Affairs 1944-)* 33.1 (1955): 96. JSTOR. Web. 26 Oct. 2011.

Larson, Robert H. "B. H. Liddell Hart: Apostle of Limited War." *Military Affairs* 44.2 (1980): 70+. JSTOR. Web. 26 Oct. 2011.

Lewin, Ronald. Rev. of Strategy by Liddell Hart. *International Affairs (Royal Institute of International Affairs 1944-)* 44.3 (1968): 527+. JSTOR. Web. 26 Oct. 2011.

Liddell Hart, B. H. *Strategy*. 2nd rev. ed. New York: Plume, 1991. Print.

Luvaas, Jay. "Liddell Hart and the Mearsheimer Critique: A 'Pupils' Retrospective." Rev. of *Liddell Hart and the Weight of History* by John J. Mearsheimer. *The International History Review* 11.3 (1989): 572+. JSTOR. Web. 26 Oct. 2011.

FURTHER READING

Bond, Brian. *Liddell Hart: A Study of His Military Thought*. Piscataway, NJ: Rutgers UP, 1977. Print.

Clausewitz, Carl von. *On War*. Trans. Michael Howard and Peter Paret. Princeton, NJ: Princeton UP, 1989. Print.

Danchev, Alex. *Alchemist of War: The Life of Basil Liddell Hart*. London: Weidenfeld & Nicholson, 1998. Print.

Guderian, Heinz. *Panzer Leader*. Trans. Constantine Fitzgibbon. Cambridge: Da Capo, 2001. Print.

Lawrence, T. E. *Seven Pillars of Wisdom: A Triumph: The Complete 1922 Text*. Radford, VA: Wilder, 2011. Print.

Liddell Hart, B. H. *The German Generals Talk*. New York: William Morrow, 1971. Print.

Naveh, Shimon. *In Pursuit of Military Excellence: The Evolution of Operational Theory*. London: Frank Cass, 1997. Print.

Joseph Campana

HISTORIES

An Account, Much Abbreviated, of the Destruction of the Indies

Fray Bartolomé de las Casas

OVERVIEW

Since its publication in 1552, *An Account, Much Abbreviated, of the Destruction of the Indies*, by Fray Bartolomé de las Casas (1484–1565), has provoked debates as well as misunderstandings regarding the early Spanish presence in the New World. Above all, the document should be viewed in the context of ongoing discussions in the sixteenth century about what qualified as a just war and whether or not the Indians of the Americas should be subdued by force before being introduced to the Christian faith. Las Casas published *Destruction of the Indies*, which offers brief descriptions of the atrocities committed by the Spanish against native peoples of the Americas, in the hope of influencing the Spanish Crown's policies towards its indigenous New World subjects. The work is divided into sections, each pertaining to a specific geographical area and organized chronologically according to the dates of each conquest. Although after its initial printing this document would not be published again in Spain until 1646, the polemical reception of *Destruction of the Indies* throughout Europe assured Las Casas's lasting fame.

Destruction of the Indies reflects Las Casas's life-long dedication to ending Spanish violence in the Americas, as well as his firsthand knowledge of its inhabitants. Indeed, from 1502, when he assumed management of his father's *encomienda* (a land grant from the Spanish government) in the Antilles, until his death in 1565, Las Casas resided at different periods in Cuba, Mexico, and Hispaniola (Haiti). His experiences in these places, which account for roughly thirty years of his life, not only indicate the personal nature of his political endeavors in the Spanish Court but also the fact that many of the episodes recounted in *Destruction of the Indies* are based on his own eyewitness testimony. The most important of these events was, without a doubt, the 1514 massacre of the Taíno Indians on the island of Cuba, which became the source of Las Casas's activism.

HISTORICAL AND LITERARY CONTEXT

Spain commenced its colonizing efforts in the Americas with the arrival of Christopher Columbus in the Bahamas in October 1492. On his second expedition, in 1493, Columbus claimed the island of Hispaniola (present-day Haiti and the Dominican Republic) for Spain. In the early years of the sixteenth century, Spanish expeditions seeking gold and slaves traveled throughout Central America and into North America. Subsequent conquests of the Aztec, Maya, and Inca peoples led to the establishment of the viceroyalties of New Spain and Peru by the mid-1500s. For Spain, the colonies were a source of immense wealth and their indigenous populations, in addition to providing slaves, represented a tremendous opportunity for the expansion of the Catholic Church. Although initial contacts between the Spanish newcomers and indigenous peoples were usually friendly, the native peoples began to resist Spanish efforts to control or exploit them, and the Spanish increasingly resorted to violence to achieve their aims.

Although *Destruction of the Indies* was neither the first nor the last of Las Casas's attempts to end Spanish violence in the Americas, it remains the most widely read and discussed of his publications. Las Casas presented a preliminary version of the document to the Council of Castile in 1542, during a meeting convoked by Carlos V to examine problems in the Indies. In consequence of Las Casas's court appearance, the New Laws were enacted on November 20, 1542. Generally speaking, the laws attempted to curtail the enslavement of the natives and to abolish the most harmful aspects of the *encomienda*, an economic system that placed parcels of land and their native inhabitants in the hands of Spanish settlers and that ultimately led to abuses of the native populations. Due to the violent backlash against them on the part of the *encomenderos*, the New Laws were revoked three years later. This setback was one of the reasons that Las Casas decided to publish *Destruction of the Indies* in 1552 in Seville.

The 1552 publication of *Destruction of the Indies* differs from the 1542 version in that the later document includes an argument and a prologue. In the argument, Las Casas recalls the circumstances underlying the initial redaction of the text and his continued responsibility to document the injustices being perpetrated in the Indies. The prologue, dedicated to Prince Philip of Spain, emphasizes the obligation of

THE SURVIVAL OF THE TAÍNO

In his *Account, Much Abbreviated, of the Destruction of the Indies*, Fray Bartolomé de Las Casas notes that the massacre of Taíno Indians by Spanish conquistadors in Cuba helped turn his sympathies toward the plight of the indigenous peoples of the New World. The Taíno were one of three ethnic groups living on the island, which had an estimated population of slightly more than one hundred thousand inhabitants when Christopher Columbus arrived in 1492. By the 1530s the indigenous population had diminished to just five thousand.

Las Casas landed in Cuba in 1511. He served as the chaplain for an expedition on the eastern side of the island led by the Spanish conquistador Pánfilo de Narváez. In his *History of the Indies* (probably drafted in 1552), a multivolume work that elaborated on many of the stories in *Destruction of the Indies*, Las Casas describes the brutal treatment of the Taíno people by Narváez's soldiers:

> One time, the Indians came out to greet us with food and gifts … they gave us fish in abundance, bread, food, to the limit of their larder. All of a sudden the devil got into the Christians. Right before my eyes, they put to the sword without provocation or cause more than three thousand souls who sat in front of us, men, women, and children. I saw there cruelty on a scale no living being has ever seen or expects to see.

As a result of such massacres, as well as of the unbearable hardships of the *encomienda* system, the introduction of infectious diseases, and widespread suicides among the indigenous people of Cuba, nearly 90 percent of the Taíno population was wiped out under Spanish rule. Until recent years, historians believed that the conquest of Cuba had rendered them extinct, but since 1997 the descendants of the Taíno have gathered annually in Baracoa, Cuba's oldest city. Their numbers are estimated to be in the thousands and growing.

kings, once they are informed about or become aware of a problem, to remedy it. In episode after episode of *Destruction of the Indies*, Las Casas presents the prince with a horrific vision of the conquest, in which the Indians are subjected to all manner of cruelties without first being taught the Christian faith. In addition, as Las Casas reports, they are called "rebels" if they do not profess their allegiance to Spain even though this allegiance implies their enslavement and eventual death.

The harsh criticism of the behavior of the conquistadores in *Destruction of the Indies* is related to general discussions about the nature of the Spanish conquest that reached their high point in the mid-sixteenth century. In 1519 Las Casas participated in a debate with Fray Juan Quevedo with respect to the rationality of the Indians. Quevedo argued that the Indians were natural slaves, a position he supported by citing the ancient Greek philosopher Aristotle's *Politics*. The text advocated for the natural superiority of certain human

beings over others. Similarly, in 1550 Las Casas participated in a well-known debate with Juan Ginés de Sepúlveda in Valladolid. The question discussed was: Is it lawful for the Spanish king to wage war against the Indians before preaching faith to them, with the condition that, once having been subdued, they learn the Christian faith? Sepúlveda sustained the affirmative, and like both Quevedo and Las Casas, he availed himself of Aristotle to support part of his argument that the Indians were not capable of self-government. Las Casas, on the other hand, argued that the Indians had a right to sovereignty regardless of whether or not they had accepted the Christian religion.

Las Casas's stance regarding the debate at Valladolid is related to his understanding of what constituted a just war. Specifically, he believed that the war being waged in the Americas against the Indians was not just because it did not fulfill any of the three criteria for such a war. These criteria include the need (1) to defend a Christian nation against an invasion; (2) to defend a Christian nation against those who seek to destroy Christianity and to spread their own religious beliefs; and (3) to avenge those who have wronged a Christian nation and who refuse to restitute wrongs committed. Las Casas's entrenched opinions about these issues are very clearly seen in *Destruction of the Indies*, in which he vigorously defends the Indians' right to defend their physical and spiritual well-being at the same time that he denounces the abuses of the Spanish.

THEMES AND STYLE

Much of the continued appeal of *Destruction of the Indies* can be attributed to its brevity. Instead of trying to overwhelm the reader with the sheer volume of the atrocities committed by the Spanish, Las Casas attempted to shock readers by depicting the inexplicable cruelty of the Spanish in a handful of carefully selected episodes. In addition, the violent incidents he describes are organized on an ascending scale: each new encounter between the Spanish and the Indians is worse than the last. Las Casas's concise and simple writing style also helps to retain the reader's attention.

Since *Destruction of the Indies* is essentially a work of propaganda, it is no surprise that Las Casas avails himself of all of the rhetorical tools necessary for the success of his project. Without doubt, Las Casas's repeated claim to be an eyewitness to many of these massacres had a tremendous impact on the work's credibility. He also uses irony and hyperbole to exaggerate the antagonistic relationship between the Indians and the Spanish. This dichotomy between the Spanish and the Indians is the thematic cornerstone of *Destruction of the Indies*. On the one hand, Las Casas describes the Indians as the "most humble, most patient, meekest and most pacific, slowest to take offense and most tranquil in demeanor, least querulous, most lacking in rancour or hatreds or desire for vengeance of all the peoples of the earth." On the other, the Spanish behave as "fierce wolves and tigers and lions who have gone many days without food or nourishment" who throw themselves among "gentle sheep." This metaphor, which evokes the image of Jesus leading his flock, creates an ironic contrast between the figure of Christ and the Spaniards' forsaken religious duties in the New World.

Las Casas emphasizes the fact that the behavior of the Spanish conquistadors inevitably led to a reluctance on the part of the Indians to recognize the sovereignty of the Spanish Crown. If the Indians did not accept the authority of the Spanish Crown, as Las Casas relates, the Indians were subdued by force—either enslaved or killed. In *Destruction of the Indies*, Las Casas counters the conquistadores' use of violence by arguing that the Indians have the natural, divine, and human right to defend themselves and their land against the attacks of the Spanish. As he writes, "And I know, too, as a sure and infallible truth, that the Indians always waged the most just and defensible war against the Christians, albeit the Christians never waged just war against the Indians, but rather were diabolical and infinitely unjust." The Indians, Las Casas maintains, are the natural possessors of their land and their dignity, both attributes that cannot be taken without permission or just cause. This is

not to say that Las Casas did not support the Spanish Crown's presence in the New World, especially for the purposes of evangelization; however, he argued that the spiritual needs of the Indians could only be met by peaceful means.

CRITICAL DISCUSSION

The publication of *Destruction of the Indies* in 1552 in Spain immediately initiated a series of translations throughout Europe: the first translation, in Flemish, was published in 1578, and was quickly followed by a French translation in 1579 and a Latin translation in 1598. The illustrations of Theodore de Bry in the latter did much to heighten the appeal of the horrors in the text. In the seventeenth century, numerous translations in English, German, Italian, Dutch, Latin, and French were published. These translations however, were read in a much different cultural and political context than Las Casas had originally intended: specifically, *Destruction of the Indies* was used as a weapon against Spain in the religious wars that were taking place between Protestant and Catholic nations. Many of the translations were politically motivated in other ways, as well. The first translations in Flemish and French, for example, included a warning for citizens of the Netherlands, at that point under Spanish rule, of the extent of Spanish cruelty. The feelings of ill will

This engraving by Theodor de Bry (1528–98) depicts one of the massacres Fray Bartolomé de las Casas recorded, in which Columbus and his soldiers used their greyhounds to slaughter about 100 Taíno Indians. © HARPER COLLINS PUBLISHERS / NEW YORK PUBLIC LIBRARY / THE ART ARCHIVE / THE PICTURE DESK, INC.

on the part of rival nation empires towards Spain that are reflected in this proliferation of translations led to the creation of the Black Legend, which promoted the view of Spain as a violent and morally corrupt country.

Las Casas became a central figure in the Latin American wars of independence in the late eighteenth and early nineteenth centuries. Intellectuals and leaders like Fray Servando Teresa de Mier and Simón Bolívar hailed Las Casas as one of the first Spanish intellectuals to recognize the sovereignty of the Indians in the New World. Mier, a Dominican Friar from Mexico, dubbed Las Casas the father of the Creoles in the Americas as well as the protector of the Indians.

Las Casas's writings continued to figure in scholarly discussions of ethics and human rights in the twentieth and twenty-first centuries. In "Bartolomé de Las Casas and the Spanish Empire in America: Four Centuries of Misunderstanding," Lewis Hanke provides an account of the historical ramifications of Las Casas's defense of the Indians' rights and their capacity for self-rule, as well as the impact of his writings on Spain's image through the centuries. Hanke also cites Las Casas's significant contributions to the early modern development of such fields as political theory, anthropology, and history. Similarly, Martin E. Marty recognizes the direct link between modern conceptions of individual rights and Las Casas's arguments on behalf of the Indians but warns that some aspects of his thought are likely to make today's readers uncomfortable. In his foreword to a 1992 translation of Las Casas's *In Defense of the Indians*, Marty provides a brief account of the zeitgeist of sixteenth-century Spain in order to show that Las Casas's arguments were both ahead of his time and yet still reflective of it, as in the case of "his defense of the natives on the grounds that they were not Catholic heretics, against whom war would be just" and his early support (later vehemently withdrawn) for the enslavement of Africans.

Recently, some scholars have focused on how Las Casas's ideas anticipated the egalitarian ideals of the French Enlightenment. In "Equal Rights and Individual Freedom: Enlightenment Intellectuals and the Lascasian Apology for Black Slavery," for example, Santa Arias describes how a hotly contested eighteenth-century debate concerning Las Casas's early recommendations for enslaving Africans led to his becoming an important source for French philosophers. The debate attracted a powerful advocate to Las Casas's cause: Henri Grégoire, a revolutionary leader and ardent critic of racism, wrote an essay staunchly defending Las Casas against the charge that he was responsible for initiating the African slave trade. Arias's analysis demonstrates that the endorsement of Grégoire and other Enlightenment leaders, including Mier, helped make Las Casas's sixteenth-century recommendations for reform a cornerstone of the Enlightenment's revolutionary idealism more than two centuries later.

SOURCES

Adorno, Rolena. *The Polemics of Possession in Spanish American Narrative*. New Haven: Yale UP, 2007.

Arias, Santa. "Equal Rights and Individual Freedom: Enlightenment Intellectuals and the Lascasian Apology for Black Slavery." *Romance Quarterly* 55.4 (2008): 279. Print.

Hanke, Lewis. "Bartolomé de Las Casas and the Spanish Empire in America: Four Centuries of Misunderstanding." *Proceedings of the American Philosophical Society* 97.1 (1953): 26–30. Print.

Las Casas, Bartolomé de. *An Account, Much Abbreviated, of the Destruction of the Indies*. Ed. Franklin W. Knight. Trans. Andrew Hurley. Indianapolis: Hackett, 2003. Print.

———. *Brevísima relación de la destrucción de las Indias*. Ed. André Saint-Lu. Cátedra: Madrid, 2005.

———. *Brevísima relación de la destrucción de las Indias*. Ed. José Miguel Martínez Torrejón. Alicante: Universidad de Alicante, 2006. Print.

Marty, Martin E. Foreword. *In Defense of the Indians*. By Fray Bartolomé de Las Casas. Ed. and trans. Stafford Poole. DeKalb: Northern Illinois UP, 1992. xiii-xvii. Print.

FURTHER READING

Arias, Santa, and Eyda M. Merediz. *Approaches to Teaching the Writings of Bartolomé de Las Casas*. New York: MLA, 2008. Print.

Benavente, Fray Toribio de. *Motolinía's History of the Indians of New Spain*. Trans. and ed. Elizabeth Andros Foster. Westport: Greenwood, 1973. Print.

Hanke, Lewis. *All Mankind Is One: A Study of the Disputation between Bartolomé de Las Casas and Juan Ginés de Sepúlveda on the Intellectual and Religious Capacity of the American Indians*. DeKalb: Northern Illinois UP, 1974. Print.

Las Casas, Bartolomé de. *The Only Way*. Ed. Helen Rand Parish. Trans. Francis Patrick Sullivan. New York: Paulist, 1992. Print.

MacNutt, Francis Augustus. *Bartholomew de Las Casas: His Life, Apostolate, and Writings*. Cleveland: Clark, 1909. Print.

Elizabeth Gansen

BACKLANDS

The Canudos Campaign

Euclides da Cunha

OVERVIEW

The 1893 War of Canudos is one of the most famous—or perhaps infamous—events in the early history of Brazil, occurring as the country adjusted to the recent overthrow of the monarchy headed by Dom Pedro II. Despite the fact that the war only affected a marginalized population settled in a remote northeastern corner of the country, it has since been recognized as a major turning point in Brazilian history, one that foreshadowed the young nation's turbulent transition from its colonial roots to modernity and republicanism. The great importance of this event became clear after the publication of *Os Sertões*, Brazilian intellectual and journalist Euclides da Cunha's 1902 account (sometimes called a novel) about the Canudos conflict. *Os Sertões* (*Rebellion in the Backlands*, 1944; *Backlands: The Canudos Campaign*, 2010), now a classic of Brazilian literature, depicts a nation going to war against its own people in the context of a charismatic religious overlay and the potential for a popular political struggle for power.

Backlands: The Canudos Campaign is the story of a unique, populist, racially mixed religious community of the sociopolitically disenfranchised that had essentially exiled itself to the remote town of Canudos in northeastern Brazil. The community lived at odds with the newly formed republican government, disagreeing with their separation of church and state, taxes, and other impositions. Amid growing concerns that the Canudos settlers—or backlanders, as they were called—were planning subversive, anti-republican activity, including a reversion to monarchy (their leader had predicted the return of a famous Portuguese king), the government intervened in the name of protecting national interests and the future of the republic. A violent encounter between the community and authorities and some rabble-rousing by traditional priests fed the government's fears. In order to neutralize the threat, the Brazilian military invaded and attacked the community. The backlanders answered with violent resistance, however, and the military was defeated in three successive campaigns.

Many of the settlers at Canudos were wounded or killed in the first three conflicts, and those who remained were weak from religious fasting. They became dispirited after their leader, Antônio Conselheiro, died of starvation while fasting. In a fourth campaign in 1897, the military retaliated for its previous defeats by wiping out the Canudos community, slaughtering men, women, and children and leveling the remaining edifices. The soldiers exhumed Conselheiro's body, beheaded it, and took the head back with them to the capital as a symbol of their victory.

Da Cunha witnessed parts of the war firsthand. His account draws on anthropology, psychology, and social Darwinism to explain the popular interest in the Canudos religious community and its relationship with the whole of Brazil. He also attempts to place the conflict within the larger context of an emerging Brazilian nation, with its conflicting institutions and interests. In the introduction to the English translation of the work, Ilan Stavans notes that da Cunha "portrays a struggle between Brazil's past and future, between Catholicism, a Portuguese import, and an unruly indigenous society." The author is equally critical of the Canudos community and the new republican government, illustrating the ways in which both parties acted irrationally.

HISTORICAL AND LITERARY CONTEXT

After its declaration of independence from Portugal in 1822, Brazil was a constitutional monarchy ruled by Dom Pedro I and then by his son, Dom Pedro II. In 1889, despite Dom Pedro II's popularity among the people, the monarchy was overthrown, and Brazil was declared a republic. This new republic was considered a constitutional democracy, although it had more in common with a military dictatorship: The right to vote was severely restricted, and a small group of landed elites maintained control of national politics. Political power was concentrated in the larger cities of Rio de Janeiro and São Paulo and the states of Minas Gerais and Rio Grande do Sul, with their large agricultural estates, while areas of north and northeastern Brazil had little say in national affairs. Brazilians became increasingly dissatisfied with the republican government, and the military feared pro-monarchy uprisings among the people.

It was in this atmosphere that Antônio Vicente Mendes Maciel began roaming the backlands of

❖ *Key Facts*

Conflict:
War of Canudos

Time Period:
Late 19th Century

Genre:
Novel

JOASEIRO: A POPULAR RELIGIOUS MOVEMENT THAT FARED BETTER THAN CANUDOS

Canudos was not the only popular religious movement to arise during the early days of the republic in Brazil. In 1889, only two years after the destruction of Canudos, another community was formed in Joaseiro, Ceará, also in the northeastern part of the country. Headed by a former Catholic priest, Father Cícero Romão Batista, this religious community persisted for nearly fifty years and grew to thirty-five thousand settlers. Father Cícero was thought to be a mystic, claimed to have religious visions, and was allegedly involved in a miracle in which the host he administered was transformed into blood thought to be the blood of Christ. News of this miracle captured the attention of the ecclesiastical authorities as well as devout Catholics from all over the country; while Father Cícero was suspended from his orders, the community at Joaseiro was flooded with pilgrims looking to witness the miracle.

Several scholars have compared and contrasted the communities of Canudos and Joaseiro, attempting to explain why the former was the target of such violence while the latter was allowed to continue for half a century. One of the main distinctions is that while Antônio Conselheiro opposed the government and church authorities, Father Cícero was much more politically savvy, working with local leaders in exchange for their support.

northeastern Brazil, preaching and attracting a religious following among the peasants. In 1893 he and his followers created their own "holy city" in Canudos in a remote area of the state of Bahía. Canudos quickly became a refuge from national politics for its settlers. Their leader christened himself Antônio Conselheiro ("counselor") and established his own social and religious codes, including communal production and distribution of goods, the abolition of civil marriages (which were replaced by religious unions, presided over by Conselheiro), and the prohibition of alcohol. As the community grew to nearly thirty thousand followers, the government became concerned that the backlanders might actually incite a monarchist rebellion.

The mayor of the neighboring town of Juazeiro appealed to the government for help after a number of disputes between Conselheiro's followers and area residents. The first expedition, consisting of one hundred soldiers, ended in disaster as the backlanders, assisted by *jagunços* (mercenary fighters), launched a surprise attack at daybreak, killing thirty people and defeating the military forces. The second conflict had a similar result: The military was repelled by more than 500 men armed with cattle prongs, pitchforks, and machetes.

The next two expeditions were more carefully planned. Colonel Antônio Moreira César, a military

hero who had crushed a rebellion in Rio Grande do Sul some years earlier, was brought in to lead the third expedition. He and his troops were overconfident, however, and made a number of tactical mistakes. They advanced too quickly and were ambushed by the backlanders. Rumors began to circulate that rather than being a small religious community, Canudos was a pro-imperialist army that threatened the security of the nation. Under pressure from the government, the minister of war personally oversaw the preparations for the fourth and final expedition. This time government forces attacked with heavy artillery and the help of auxiliary forces. The military encircled the settlement and made their assault, destroying most of the buildings and leaving only a few hundred survivors.

Backlands: The Canudos Campaign is not the only treatment of the Canudos War. Da Cunha's work inspired Nobel Prize-winning author Mario Vargas Llosa to write *The War of the End of the World* in 1981. While Vargas Llosa's novel is based on the events of the war, he delves into the realm of fiction by focusing on the characters in the Canudos camp, turning them into mythical, larger-than-life figures. He offers a distinct, more sympathetic view of Antônio Conselheiro than da Cunha does in *Backlands*, giving readers some idea of how this strange character came to lead a messianic cult. Vargas Llosa pays strange homage to the author of *Backlands* by placing him in his novel: Da Cunha is re-created in *The War of the End of the World* as "the nearsighted journalist," a nameless lackey who travels with the Brazilian soldiers as they destroy the Canudos community. The work is considered one of Vargas Llosa's best novels and presents readers with a different perspective on the Canudos War.

These events continue to resonate in Brazil; they inspired a 1978 documentary by Ipojuca Pontes titled *Canudos* and a 1997 movie directed by Sergio Rezende titled *Guerra de Canudos*, as well as a yearly commemorative mass. Ironically, the physical remains of the community are now under the waters of a major modern dam, just as the members of the community were overwhelmed by the rush to "modernity" at the time.

THEMES AND STYLE

Da Cunha was embedded with the São Paulo battalion to cover the Canudos War for the newspaper *O Estado de São Paulo*, and although he was present for less than a month of the four-year conflict, he reports on the entire war with the intensity of an eyewitness. But *Backlands* is not only a war report. Da Cunha wanted to give his readers context and help them understand the causes of the war as well as its possible consequences for a modern Brazil. His text is divided into three parts: "The Land," "Man," and "The Battle." This progression from landscape to psychology to historical event shows the author's belief in environmental determinism. He describes the backlands of the northeast as rustic and primitive; likewise, its inhabitants are pre-modern, in a state of nature but also less civilized than those who live in the larger Brazilian cities.

Da Cunha also considers Conselheiro's teachings primitive, describing the religious leader as "a second-century heretic in the modern age." Yet despite being "clownish and grotesque," Conselheiro entranced his followers and managed to maintain complete spiritual and physical control over them. They welcomed suffering and, when faced with the certain destruction of their lifestyle, were willing to sacrifice their lives in defense of the Canudos community. In *Backlands* da Cunha shows some sympathy for Conselheiro's followers, considering them victims of both a charismatic leader and a repressive government.

The description of the Canudos War in *Backlands* is richly detailed, with an analysis of nearly every move in each battle. Da Cunha supplies a great deal of factual information supported by direct quotations from historical documents and news reports of the war. Yet his opinion emerges from the factual narrative in the form of sharp commentary and dry witticisms. He notes, for example, that during the first expedition "the troops decided to leave on the twelfth to avoid a departure on the thirteenth, an unlucky day. And their mission was to fight fanaticism!" The author analyzes the war from the perspective of the Brazilian urban elite, comparing Canudos to the 1793 peasant revolt in Vendée, France. Like many Brazilian intellectuals of his time, da Cunha looked to Europe for cultural and historical references and believed that his readers would immediately recognize the connection between the Canudos War and an episode from the French Revolution.

In *Backlands* da Cunha is not only interested in the conflict itself but also in the psychological factors involved. In his discussion of the selection of Moreira César as the leader of the third assault on the community, he comments that "the fetishistic tendencies of the times called for idols in uniform. He was chosen as the latest one." Da Cunha strongly believes that the excessive faith in Moreira César was one of the weaknesses of the expedition and contributed to the military defeat. He describes the massacre of the Canudos community with the pathos and humanity of an overwhelmed eyewitness but finishes his book in the more detached tone of the scientist. In his last section, titled "Two Lines," the author laments the fact that "we do not have a Maudsley … to prevent nations from committing acts of madness and crimes against humanity." Henry Maudsley was a British psychiatrist who worked in asylums and mental hospitals during the late nineteenth century. This reference to Maudsley was da Cunha's final psychological evaluation of the Canudos War: As Stavans explains, the author promotes "a psychiatric system able to identify dangerous lunatics who … might organize a sinister revolt and, in doing so, threaten an emerging republic." Da Cunha

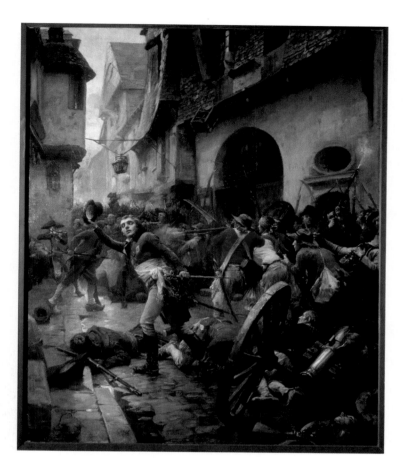

completes his war report by focusing on the role of science—and more specifically on the budding science of psychology—in maintaining peace within the Brazilian nation.

CRITICAL DISCUSSION

The Canudos War was covered extensively by the newspapers of the time; many Brazilians (and the republican government) feared the possibility that the conflict could become the catalyst for all-out civil war. Although by the time *Os Sertões* was published in 1902 the government was slightly more stable and the threat of civil war had diminished greatly, the book was well received for the wealth of information it contained. For many Brazilians the backlands of the northeast were remote and mysterious, and da Cunha's text was a geographical and sociological guide to the area and to the Canudos community.

Os Sertões was first translated into English in 1944, bringing da Cunha's work to a much larger audience. Anthropologist Claude Lévi-Strauss reviewed the translation, describing it as a work of art and claiming that da Cunha "authentically started a Brazilian national literature." To help guide the reader through the various folkloric terms and descriptions

Henri de la Rochejaquelein, au Combat de Cholet en 1793, painted in 1900 by Emile Boutigny, portrays the peasant revolt in support of the monarchy in Vendée, France, during the French Revolution. Backlands author Euclides da Cunha compares the people of Canudos, Brazil, to the royalist peasants of Vendée. © ROGER-VIOLLET / THE IMAGE WORKS. REPRODUCED BY PERMISSION.

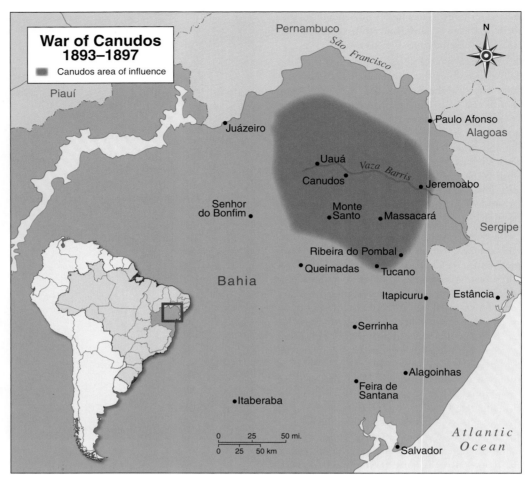

War of Canudos
1893–1897

Canudos area of influence

Pernambuco

São Francisco

Piauí

Juázeiro

Paulo Afonso
Alagoas

Uauá

Vaza Barris

Canudos

Jeremoabo

Senhor
do Bonfim

Monte
Santo

Massacará

Sergipe

Bahia

Ribeira do Pombal

Queimadas

Tucano

Itapicuru

Estância

Serrinha

Alagoinhas

Feira de
Santana

Itaberaba

0   25   50 mi.
0   25   50 km

*Atlantic
Ocean*

Salvador

N

© MAP BY XNR PRODUCTIONS. CENGAGE LEARNING, GALE.

of Brazilian flora and fauna in the book, the English translation was augmented with maps, drawings, and a glossary.

More modern scholarship has called into question da Cunha's depiction of the Canudos community and its leader. In *Vale of Tears*, Robert M. Levine argues that Conselheiro was not a religious fanatic or rogue prophet but rather a Christian lay preacher interested in social reform who was followed by a relatively innocuous group of believers rather than the religious extremists that da Cunha described in his book. Lori Madden makes a similar statement in her article "The Canudos War in History," also suggesting that Conselheiro "initiated his own brand of land reform." In *The Brazil Reader* Dain Borges shows how da Cunha's view of the government's role in the Canudos War was somewhat distorted as well. He explains that da Cunha's harsh criticism of the Brazilian government may have been in part a result of his own experiences in life, which made him "wary of both democracy and military government."

Yet despite da Cunha's subjective take on the events at Canudos, *Backlands: The Canudos Campaign* is a classic of Brazilian literature and fundamental to understanding the early days of the Brazilian republic. In addition, the book is a product of its era, in which writers and intellectuals were working to comprehend Brazil as an emerging nation, with all of its contradictions and violent conflicts. For da Cunha, as for many of his contemporaries, the tragic Canudos War was one more stop on the road to modernity.

SOURCES

Borges, Dain. "A Mirror of Progress." *The Brazil Reader: History, Culture, Politics.* Ed. Robert M. Levine and John J. Crocitti. Durham: Duke UP, 1999. 93–99. Print.

Da Cunha, Euclides. *Backlands: The Canudos Campaign.* Trans. Elizabeth Lowe. London: Penguin, 2010. Print.

Levine, Robert M. *Vale of Tears: Revisiting the Canudos Massacre in Northeastern Brazil, 1893–1897.* Stanford: Stanford UP, 1990. Print.

Lévi-Strauss, Claude. Rev. of *Rebellion in the Backlands*, by Euclides da Cunha. *American Anthropologist* 46.3 (1944): 394–96. Print.

Madden, Lori. "The Canudos War in History." *Luso-Brazilian Review* 30.2 (1993): 5–22. Print.

Stavans, Ilan. Introduction. *Backlands: The Canudos Campaign.* By Euclides Da Chunha. Trans. Elizabeth Lowe. London: Penguin, 2010. Print.

FURTHER READING

Campos Johnson, Adriana Michéle. *Sentencing Canudos: Subalternity in the Backlands of Brazil.* Pittsburgh: U of Pittsburgh P, 2010. Print.

Della Cava, Ralph. "Brazilian Messianism and National Institutions: A Reappraisal of Canudos and Joaseiro." *Hispanic American Historical Review* 48.3 (1970): 402–20. Print.

Freyre, Gilberto. *The Masters and the Slaves: A Study in the Development of Brazilian Civilization.* Trans. Samuel Putnam. New York: Knopf, 1959. Print.

González Echvarría, Roberto. "A Lost World Rediscovered: Sarmiento's *Facundo* and E. da Cunha's *Os Sertões.*" *Myth and Archive: A Theory of Latin American Narrative.* Cambridge: Cambridge UP, 1990. 93–141. Print.

Hobsbawm, Eric J. *Primitive Rebels: Studies in Archaic Forms of Social Movement in the Nineteenth and Twentieth Centuries.* New York: Norton, 1959. Print.

Vargas Llosa, Mario. *The War of the End of the World.* Trans. Helen R. Lane. New York: Farrar, 1984. Print.

Gina Sherriff

BLOODS

An Oral History of the Vietnam War by Black Veterans
Wallace Houston Terry II

÷ *Key Facts*

Conflict:
Vietnam War

Time Period:
Mid-20th Century

Genre:
History

OVERVIEW

In *Bloods: An Oral History of the Vietnam War by Black Soldiers* (1984), twenty African American service-men reflect on their roles in the Vietnam War and trace the conflict's lasting effects on their lives. Edited by journalist Wallace Terry, the book explores the unique experiences of black soldiers who were fight-ing an unpopular war in Vietnam at a time when the civil rights movement was at its height at home. The soldiers' stories span all but the final two years of the decade-long involvement of the United States in the war, all four branches of the U.S. military, and all ranks from private to colonel. Reginald Edwards, whose narrative opens the book, was among the first Americans to arrive in Vietnam in 1965. Colonel Fred V. Cherry, whose story closes the collection, remained in Vietnam as a prisoner of war until 1973. Many of the soldiers featured in the book came from socioeco-nomically disadvantaged households, and many were targets of racism before, during, and after their service. Many came home devastated by their wartime experi-ences only to encounter the disappointing injustices of continued racism. Their stories depict their varied reactions to postwar life. A number turned to religion for comfort, others embraced political activism, and some became involved in criminal activity.

Upon its publication, *Bloods* quickly became a best seller. Commentators praised its uncensored depictions of wartime atrocities and racism and the authenticity of its language. Well reviewed in the popular press, the book quickly became a staple in high school and college classrooms, where it generated some controversy over of its graphic detail. Today it remains central to discussions of race in the context of the Vietnam War and of oral history as a means of conveying the experience of war.

HISTORICAL AND LITERARY CONTEXT

Roughly 300,000 African Americans served in Vietnam, their numbers constituting approximately ten percent of the American forces. Early in the war African American soldiers accounted for a dispro-portionate number of war deaths, in part because a greater number of them were assigned to combat duty than soldiers of other races and also because disproportionately few were officers. As the war dragged on, however, commanders, aware of the sta-tistics, worked to bring the African American casualty rate to a number more consistent with averages for all service personnel.

While many African Americans were drafted into service, others, including some of the subjects of *Bloods*, joined the military because they lacked oppor-tunities at home. Many wanted to go to college but were unable to afford tuition. The lack of prospects for African American citizens was a prominent concern in the 1960s and 1970s. In the years immediately before the war, the civil rights movement had succeeded in bringing about important legislation, including the *Civil Rights Act of 1964*, which banned discrimina-tion based on race, sex, religion, or national origin; and the *Voting Rights Act of 1965*, which eliminated such impediments to voting as literacy tests and poll taxes. Despite these measures, African Americans still faced prejudice and economic inequality. As the war began to dominate the public imagination, many people feared that it was diverting much-needed attention and funding from civil rights crises, an argu-ment voiced by prominent figures, like Martin Luther King Jr. Before long, frustration with the war, anger over the 1968 assassination of King (which features in the stories of several men in *Bloods*), and the desire to combat unremitting discrimination fueled the rise of the Black Panther Party, founded in 1966 as a means of protecting African Americans from police brutality. Many of the men who tell their stories in *Bloods* became involved with the Black Panthers after returning home from the war.

The Vietnam conflict presented unique chal-lenges to all who served. Despite attempts to prepare the soldiers for the climate and terrain of Vietnam, some of which are depicted in *Bloods*, the realities of jungle warfare and intense heat overwhelmed many combatants. Moreover, soldiers had to contend with the Viet Cong, a communist guerrilla group that used surprise ambushes, traps, and land mines. In *Bloods* Harold "Light Bulb" Bryant describes the dangerous nature of the work in which he was engaged: "We probed for mines, blew up mines, disarmed and blew up booby traps." Many of the stories in the collection illustrate the difficulties of identifying Viet Cong among the villagers the troops encountered. Several men express feelings of guilt over their participation in the unintentional killing of civilians.

Bloods was not the first oral history of the Vietnam War. Al Santoli's 1981 book *Everything We Had: An Oral History of the Vietnam War by Thirty-three American Soldiers Who Fought It* helped establish the genre and demonstrated its potential for popular success. Santoli's work was quickly followed by Mark Baker's *Nam: The Vietnam War in the Words of the Men and Women Who Fought There* (1982). Also published in 1982, the oral history *Brothers: Black Soldiers in the Nam* described the Vietnam experiences of Stanley Goff and Robert Sanders.

THEMES AND STYLE

Bloods emerged from a series of interviews with the men whose stories it tells. That the accounts originated in oral language is an important aspect of the book's style. Although Terry edited the men's reflections, he worked to retain a sense of their actual speech. The men often use improper grammar, slang, and foul language. Typical of such language is Arthur E. "Gene" Woodley's description of his feeling that the U.S. government had betrayed his trust in sending him off to war: "They had us naïve, young, dumb-ass niggers believin' that this was for democracy and independence. It was fought for money."

In his introduction to the volume, Terry establishes one of the central themes of the book—the complex relationship between the Vietnam War and the American civil rights movement. Many of the men talk about the racism they experienced while serving. Haywood T. Kirkland tells of being forced to contend with "rednecks flying rebel flags from their jeeps." Others offer similar stories of disrespect and of discriminatory treatment, but they note that racism tended to dissipate during battle, when men relied on each other for survival. Bryant describes a self-proclaimed member of the Ku Klux Klan who, after his life was saved by an African American comrade, "said that action had changed his perception of what black people were about." Such moments of understanding could not counteract the persistent discrimination and lack of opportunities African American soldiers faced on returning home, however. Kirkland expresses the desire, experienced by many of the veterans interviewed for the book, to do something to better the lives of African Americans after the war: "I started talking with friends before leaving 'Nam about being a part of the struggle of black people. About contributing in the world since Vietnam was doing nothin' for black people." For Kirkland, this aspiration initially prompted him to commit a crime: he and his friends robbed a mail truck and used a share of the money to buy Christmas presents for the impoverished people of their community. Several other men joined the Black Panthers in an attempt

WALLACE TERRY AND VIETNAM

This May 5, 1968, photograph shows what journalists Wallace Terry and Zalin Grant found when they searched for four colleagues who had reportedly been ambushed by the Viet Cong. Although American forces said the mission was too dangerous, Terry and Grant brought back the bodies of John Cantwell, Ronald B. Laramy, Michael Birch, and Bruce S. Pigott. © AP IMAGES

Although *Bloods* tells the stories of other men's service in Vietnam, author Wallace Terry (1938–2003) had direct experience of the war as a journalist. After making history as the first African American newspaper editor-in-chief at an Ivy League University (Brown), Terry attended graduate school, taught at Howard University, and wrote briefly for the *Washington Post* before accepting a position at *Time* magazine. In 1967 his work at *Time* took him to Vietnam, where he spent two years as the magazine's deputy bureau chief in Saigon. In this capacity he covered some of the major events of the war, including the Tet Offensive, a series of North Vietnamese surprise attacks on South Vietnamese and American forces. He gained firsthand knowledge of the fighting by flying on combat missions and traveling with assault troops. Terry won praise in May 1968 when he and *New Republic* correspondent Zalin Grant carried out a dangerous but successful mission to recover the bodies of four fellow reporters killed by the Viet Cong. After returning from Vietnam, Terry was appointed Frederick Douglass Professor of Journalism at Howard University. In the decades following the war, he established himself as one of the foremost authorities on African American service in Vietnam.

to bring about change. Some, including Bryant and Cherry, became involved in nonprofit work to aid the African American community.

Another theme that emerges from stories in the book is that the war turned the men who fought it into "animals." According to Kirkland, the instinct was cultivated in training when soldiers were told not to refer to the enemy as Vietnamese but to "call everyone gooks, dinks" in order to dehumanize them. Many of the soldiers suggest that the war instead dehumanized the American soldiers themselves. Woodley,

Allen Payne in the 1995 film *The Walking Dead*, about African American soldiers in the Vietnam War. © SAVOY PICTURES / COURTESY EVERETT COLLECTION

describing his participation in brutal acts against Viet Cong prisoners, explains, "I was some gross animal." Others tell of how they shocked their loved ones with their flashbacks and violent outbursts. Edwards attests to the lasting influence of the war when he reflects, "I used to think that I wasn't affected by Vietnam, but I had been livin' with Vietnam ever since I left."

CRITICAL DISCUSSION

When *Bloods* first appeared in 1985, it was widely embraced by both readers and critics, drawing the attention of both black and white audiences and garnering glowing reviews in the mainstream media. Writing in *Time*, Paul Gray notes, "The twenty blacks who discuss their experiences while serving in the Viet Nam War are uniformly eloquent." A reviewer for *Ebony* calls the work "an incisive and explosive account of the experiences of Black soldiers" and states that the men who tell their stories are "symbols of the large number of low-income Blacks who shouldered a cruelly disproportionate share of the burden of an American tragedy." Commentators have often emphasized that, in addition to exposing the unique experiences of African American combatants, *Bloods* offers valuable insight into the experience of war more generally. Reviewing the book for *Military Affairs*, Alan M. Osur writes, "Wallace Terry has given us a book important for the study of Blacks in the military and military history in general. He presents accounts that shake our senses and sensitize us to the reality of war, and especially to the trauma and turmoil that was Vietnam."

One of the major critical disputes to emerge from discussions of the work involves the authenticity of its language and the accuracy of its stories. Reviewing the book for the *School Library Journal*, Jacqueline Brown

Woody praises its style: "These experiences are told candidly and explicitly in the language of men who have been frightened, threatened, tortured, shamed, maimed, betrayed, and ignored." Interest in linguistic style is evident in scholarly examinations of the work as well. Patrick Hagopian—who includes *Bloods* in "Oral Narratives," his study of the enduring popularity of Vietnam War stories—traces the book's origins and publication history; he argues that Terry's approach is unique in that he "allows the distinct grammar of Black English, when used, to survive the editing, rather than 'correcting' it." Hagopian also believes that Terry's editorial hand is sufficiently visible in the work to contradict the common claim that the men were all extremely eloquent. Some commentators have gone further, questioning Terry's methodology and the truth of the men's stories. In his book *"War Stories,"* Gary Kulik writes, "Terry offered no evidence of his methods—what were his questions? Are the transcripts verbatim?—and no evidence that he sought any form of corroboration." In particular, Kulik questions the veracity of the account given by Woodley, which, he suggests, "is not a believable story." He points to evidence that Woodley, and perhaps several of the other men whose stories are included in the volume, lied about their experiences. Such accusations have undoubtedly hampered the scholarly reception of the work.

SOURCES

Rev. of *Bloods: An Oral History of the Vietnam War*, ed. Wallace Terry. *Ebony* 1 Nov. 1984: 25. Print.

Gray, Paul. "Beleaguered Patriotism and Pride." Rev. of *Bloods: An Oral History of the Vietnam War by Black Soldiers*, ed. Wallace Terry. *Time.* Time Inc., 20 Aug. 1984. Web. 10 Aug. 2011.

Hagopian, Patrick. "Oral Narratives: Secondary Revision and the Memory of the Vietnam War." *History Workshop* 32 (1991): 134- 50. Print.

Kulik, Gary. *"War Stories": False Atrocity Tales, Swift Boaters, and Winter Soldiers—What Really Happened in Vietnam.* Washington, D.C: Potomac, 2009. Print.

Osur, Alan M. Rev. of *Bloods: An Oral History of the Vietnam War by Black Soldiers*, ed. Wallace Terry. *Military Affairs* 51.1 (1987): 45. Print.

Terry, Wallace, ed. *Bloods: An Oral History of the Vietnam War by Black Soldiers.* New York: Random, 1984. Print.

Woody, Jacqueline Brown. Rev. of *Bloods: An Oral History of the Vietnam War by Black Soldiers*, ed. Wallace Terry. *School Library Journal* 1 Aug. 1985: 89. Print.

FURTHER READING

Baker, Mark. *Nam: The Vietnam War in the Words of the Men and Women Who Fought There.* London: Sphere, 1982. Print.

Brinker, William J. "Oral History and the Vietnam War." *OAH Magazine of History* 11.3 (1997): 15–19. Print.

Budra, Paul, and Michael Zeitlin. *Soldier Talk: The Vietnam War in Oral Narrative.* Bloomington: Indiana UP, 2004. Print.

Goff, Stanley, and Robert Sanders, with Clark Smith. *Brothers: Black Soldiers in the Nam.* Navato: Presidio, 1982. Print.

Graham, Herman, III. *The Brothers' Vietnam War: Black Power, Manhood, and the Military Experience.* Gainesville: UP of Florida, 2003. Print.

Nielson, Jim. *Warring Fictions: American Literary Culture and the Vietnam War.* Jackson: UP of Mississippi, 1998. Print.

Olson, James Stuart, and Randy Roberts. *Where the Domino Fell: America and Vietnam, 1945 to 1995.* New York: St. Martin's, 1996. Print.

Santoli, Al. *Everything We Had: An Oral History of the Vietnam War by Thirty-three American Soldiers Who Fought It.* New York: Random, 1981. Print.

Terry, Wallace. *Missing Pages: Black Journalists of Modern America: An Oral History.* New York: Carroll, 2007. Print.

Westheider, James E. *Fighting on Two Fronts: African Americans and the Vietnam War.* New York: New York UP, 1997. Print.

Greta Gard

THE BROKEN SPEARS
The Aztec Account of the Conquest of Mexico
Miguel León-Portilla

✣ *Key Facts*

Conflict:
Conquest of Mexico

Time Period:
16th Century

Genre:
History

OVERVIEW

The Broken Spears: The Aztec Account of the Conquest of Mexico (1962) is an anthology intended to provide an alternative historical vision of the sixteenth-century encounters between the Spanish and the Native Americans living in the Aztec empire, located in present-day Mexico. Miguel León-Portilla, who compiled the documents included in the book, observed that, until the publication of *Visión de los vencidos: relaciones indígenas de la conquista* in 1959, very few accounts of the Spanish conquest from the Aztec point of view were available to the general public. He declared the main purpose of his compilation, which features Spanish translations from the original Nahuatl (the Aztecs' language), to be the widening of readers' knowledge about a chapter of history that has traditionally been known almost exclusively through chronicles and histories written by and about the victorious Spanish, including the *Letters of Relation* written by Hernán Cortés, who led the conquest of Mexico, and *The True History of the Conquest of New Spain*, by Cortés's lieutenant Bernal Díaz del Castillo. León-Portilla's anthology contains a full array of testimonies dating from 1527—several years after the Spanish conquest of Mexico (1519–22)—to the twentieth century. The more recent entries include accounts by Nahuatl-speaking Indians as well as others who wrote in favor of Indian rights, like the revolutionary leader Emiliano Zapata, who reappraised the value of the Nahuatl community for Mexico in two manifestos made public in 1918, during the Mexican Revolution.

HISTORICAL AND LITERARY CONTEXT

Despite the presence of more recent accounts in *The Broken Spears*, the majority of the documents are sixteenth-century accounts of the Spanish conquest of the Aztec Empire. Although Cortés's expedition to the Yucatán Peninsula was not the first Spanish visit to the region, it proved to be definitive. He and the 530 soldiers who accompanied him landed on Cozumel Island in February 1517. Here, Cortés began to convert the Indians to Christianity and also to form alliances against the Aztecs with the local tribes, many of whom were already resentful of the powerful hold that the Aztecs exerted over the region. During his travels in the Yucatán, Cortés met Doña Marina, an Aztec noblewoman who had been given to local Mayans as a gift. Doña Marina, commonly called La Malinche, proved to be a key figure in the conquest, as she and Jerónimo Aguilar, a Spaniard who had been stranded in the Yucatán on a previous voyage and who had lived among the Maya, worked as interpreters for Cortés. Both La Malinche and Aguilar took very active roles in translating messages and speeches for the Spaniards. In addition, La Malinche became Cortés's lover.

Although the Spanish conquest of Mexico was the impetus behind all of the accounts included in *The Broken Spears*, Miguel León-Portilla includes in his introduction an overview of the pre-Columbian history of the Aztec Empire and the characteristics of the empire's governance that would later be important in encounters with the Spanish. The Aztecs arrived in the Valley of Mexico sometime during the thirteenth century in successive migrations from the north. They settled on a very inhospitable island in the middle of a lake, but they quickly began to prosper and expand their lands through war and conquest. Their capital, Tenochtitlan, was founded in the fourteenth century, a period that marked the empire's height as a political and economic power whose borders extended to the Atlantic Ocean in the east and the Pacific Ocean in the west.

In his introduction, Léon-Portilla also points out several characteristics of Aztec culture that would have a crucial effect on the speed with which the Spaniards were able to take over the empire. First, Aztec prophecies had predicted the imminent arrival of the god Quetzalcoatl, who, according to their mythology, had exiled himself to the East and whose second coming was expected to provoke a deep change in the universe. Cortés's arrival in Mexico was understood by the Aztecs to be the fulfillment of this prophecy, and Cortés himself was initially identified as Quetzalcoatl due to his physical appearance and the unknown objects and animals that he brought with him, mainly firearms and horses. Second, the Aztecs had a highly codified system of warfare that treated armed encounters as a form of ritual. This made it difficult for the Aztecs to comprehend the sudden and violent changes that overtook their relationship with the Spanish.

The sixteenth-century Nahuatl accounts that form the foundation of Léon-Portilla's book were drawn from the records of Franciscan missionaries, who began arriving in Mexico from Spain in the 1520s. The Franciscans devised an alphabetic transliteration of Nahuatl, and they taught some Aztecs how to write using this alphabetic representation of their language. An ongoing debate surrounds the question of whether the Nahuatl histories of the conquest contained in the Franciscan codices could have been written by Aztec authors. Even if the writers were Aztecs, however, the very earliest any of the accounts could have been written was the late 1520s, a fact that calls into question their faithfulness to actual events surrounding the 1521 conquest.

During the early period of Spanish colonialism in the Americas, other indigenous authors also recorded the histories of their peoples, including their encounters with the Spanish. El Inca Garcilaso de la Vega (1539–1616), for example, whose parents were a Spanish conquistador and an Inca princess, wrote a history of the Inca Empire prior to the Spaniards' arrival (*Comentarios Reales de los Incas*, 1609; *First Part of the Royal Commentaries which Treats of the Origin of the Yncas*, 1864; *Royal Commentaries of the Inca*, 1961). His *Historia General del Peru* (1617; *General History of Peru*, 1966) describes, with sympathy for both sides, the history of Spanish-Inca relations in Peru through the end of the sixteenth century. Another Inca of noble family, Felipe Guaman Poma de Ayala (c. 1535-c. 1615), is known for his *El primer nueva corónica y buen gobierno* (1612–15; *The First New Chronicle and Good Government*, 1961), a vividly illustrated account of the injustices resulting from imperialism and a proposal for the reform of the colonial governmental addressed to the Spanish king Philip III.

THEMES AND STYLE

Many of the themes that recur throughout Léon-Portilla's anthology derive from the particular historical context of the Spanish conquest of the Aztecs. For example, in the texts' portrayal of the events leading up to the meeting of the Aztec ruler Motecuhzoma and Cortés, there is an emphasis on soothsayers' prediction of their encounter. Through the soothsayers' interpretation of the prophecy, Cortés is ascribed the characteristics of Quetzalcoatl. Faced with this interpretation, Motecuhzoma is described as uncertain about what he should do: many of his subjects are uneasy about the strangers in their lands, and as their emperor, Motecuhzoma must make important decisions about how the strangers will be received and how he will interact with their leader, Cortés. His uncertainties give way to erratic behavior as he requests, on the one hand, that the Spanish stop their march to Tenochtitlan while, on the other, he welcomes them with open arms. Several times Motecuhzoma is criticized for taking no action whatsoever and for responding passively to

A detail from the Aztec document known as the *Codex Borbonicus*, which was written by Aztec priests around the time of the Spanish conquest of Mexico. © PRIVATE COLLECTION/ JEAN-PIERRE COURAU/THE BRIDGEMAN ART LIBRARY INTERNATIONAL

the Spaniards' actions. Tensions between Motecuhzoma and those whom he once considered his allies heighten his doubts.

It should be noted that the long-standing view of Motecuhzoma as an indecisive leader has been qualified by recent studies. Scholars have suggested that the appearance of a comet may have influenced the Aztecs' interpretation of Cortés's arrival. They have also emphasized the fact that Motecuhzoma's identification of Cortés with Quetzalcoatl was short-lived and was not a factor in his dealings with Cortés by the time the Spanish reached Tenochtitlan in November 1519.

The Spaniards' violence towards the natives caused even more confusion and hostility among the native populations that made up the Aztec Empire. Accounts in *The Broken Spears* depict encounters in which the Spaniards massacre entire towns for no apparent reason, actions that heighten the ambiguity surrounding their presence in Mexico. In addition, the physical appearance of the strangers, with their beards and strange clothing, as well as the new objects and technologies they bring with them, provokes both curiosity and suspicion among the natives. The Spaniards' greed, another topic frequently touched on in these texts, elicits the natives' disdain.

Another important aspect of the texts included in Léon-Portilla's anthology is their descriptions of the exhaustive process of translation in the conversations between Cortés and Motecuhzoma. Evident in these descriptions is an awareness, not always seen in the

THE FIRST ANTHROPOLOGIST

In collecting the chronicles that comprise his landmark anthology *Broken Spears: The Aztec Account of the Conquest of Mexico*, anthropologist Miguel León-Portilla relied to a large extent on the documentary records of Franciscan missionaries, who played a central role in spreading Christianity throughout the newly conquered territory over the course of the sixteenth century. Among León-Portilla's most important sources was Bernardino de Sahagún, a priest and ethnographer who dedicated his life to chronicling the vast cultural and religious history of New Spain. His magnum opus, *La historia general de las cosas de Nueva España* (c. 1545–90; The general history of the things of New Spain), contains the earliest systematic study of Aztec society and culture. Better known as the *Florentine Codex*, after the city where the manuscript was eventually housed, Bernardino's massive work consists of approximately 2,400 pages and 2,000 illustrations and covers such subjects as history, religious rituals, and economics. Composed in both Spanish and Nahuatl, the *Florentine Codex* is particularly noteworthy for including Bernardino's extensive interviews with Aztec natives, which he conducted over a fifty-year span. Bernardino's innovative approach to gathering information, combined with his dedication to providing an exhaustive account of native customs, practices, and beliefs, has earned him a reputation among scholars as the world's first anthropologist.

accounts written by the Spanish conquistadors, of the potential difficulties of such chaotic linguistic situations, as not one but several people attempt to translate from one language to another.

The Spaniards marching to Tenochtitlan had an advantage in being fully aware that they were going to witness the meeting of two very different cultures. Despite the Aztecs' lack of foreknowledge, their accounts of the conquest contain a wealth of information that is lacking from Spanish accounts. First, they include images that offer a unique, visual perspective on the violence and destruction of the conquest. Second, the native accounts give a more complete version of the encounter between the Spaniards and the native populations in the sense that they describe the events leading up to the conquest, the conquest itself, and the physical and psychological devastation that followed the conquest. The title *The Broken Spears* was taken from the early-sixteenth-century Nahuatl poem "Epic Description of the Besieged City," which contains images that recur throughout Léon-Portilla's anthology. The first stanza of a poem describes the natives' reaction to their defeat:

> Broken spears lie in the road;
> We have torn our hair in grief.
> The houses are roofless now, and their walls
> Are red with blood.

The section of the poem recounting the effects of the conquest is particularly important in illustrating the deep scars that are the legacy of the Spanish conquest of Mexico.

Although the Nahuatl accounts in *The Broken Spears* have been generally accessible only since the book's publication in 1959, they have been widely embraced in Mexico as a contribution to national memory and, to a certain extent, to the formation of Mexican identity.

CRITICAL DISCUSSION

Prior to the publication of *Visión de los vencidos*, the existence of a Nahuatl literature or system of knowledge had gone unacknowledged for centuries. It was simply omitted from discussions of Mexico's cultural heritage; thus, the impact of Léon-Portilla's anthology was immediately felt. As described by Rolena Adorno in *Colonial Latin American Literature: A Very Short Introduction* (2011), León-Portilla "charted an entirely new course for colonial writings by publishing Spanish translations of the Nahuatl accounts of the conquest of Mexico." In "The Pre-Columbian Past as a Project; Miguel Léon-Portilla and Hispanism," Ignacio M. Sánchez-Prado credits León-Portilla more specifically with the "construct[ion] and institutionaliz[ation of] something we might call 'Pre-Columbian knowledge.'"

The main difficulty Léon-Portilla faced in assembling the Aztec reports of the conquest was the paucity of sources. He was forced to rely heavily on the sixteenth-century records of Fray Bernardino de Sahagún's *Florentine Codex* (originally called *Historia general de las cosas de la Nueva España*), in which the Franciscan friar (who was living in Mexico) documented the history and culture of the Aztecs, often including descriptions by the Aztecs themselves. León-Portilla's dependence on Sahagún and his alphabetic transliteration of the oral conventions of the Nahuatl language have led to the questions about the authenticity of the narratives in *The Broken Spears*. Some scholars have claimed that finding an authentic Nahuatl literature of any kind using León-Portilla's method is impossible. Sánchez-Prado, however, asserts that the importance of the anthology "rests

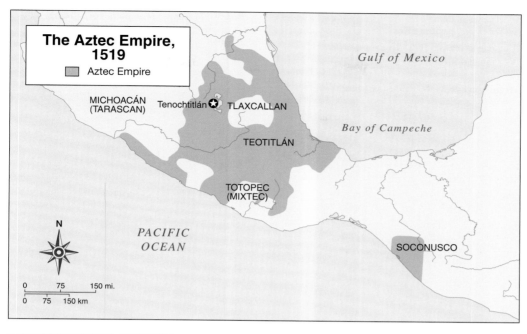

The Aztec Empire, 1519

© MAP BY XNR PRODUCTIONS. CENGAGE LEARNING, GALE.

not so much on [its] rigor in recovering the indigenous textualities, but on the very gesture of recovering those textualities and presenting them as voices silenced by the colonial process."

In his foreword to the expanded and updated edition of *The Broken Spears*, J. Jorge Klor de Alva also acknowledges that the origin of the Nahuatl narratives suggests that they may not be accurate. He nevertheless defends Léon-Portilla's method, making the case that the accounts included in the Franciscan codices could in fact have been written by Aztec eyewitnesses to the conquest. He also describes Sahagún's careful, systematic approach to his work of recording the Aztecs' history, citing the friar's personal testimony in Book 12 of the *Florentine Codex* that "this history … was written at a time when those who took part in the very Conquest were alive. … And those who gave this account [were] principal persons of good judgment, and it is believed they told all the truth."

As a work that recognized for the first time in hundreds of years "voices silenced by the colonial process," *The Broken Spears* became a touchstone of movements to recognize the rights of indigenous peoples, both in Mexico and in other parts of the world grappling with the legacies of colonialism. Sánchez-Prado observes that in Mexico, the "official discourse has claimed Léon-Portilla's work as part of the construction of Mexican nationality," and Klor de Alva notes the popularity of the anthology among Mexican readers, remarking that hundreds of thousands of copies of the book have been sold in the country, whereas the typical nonfiction work records sales of about three thousand copies. For some critics, however, the adoption of the anthology as a monument to Mexican national identity is problematic; these commentators are concerned that the work has been co-opted by the very Creole culture and political structures that sought to erase Mexico's indigenous history in the first place. Supporters of Léon-Portilla's effort to recover Nahuatl literary culture defend him against charges of elitism, however, citing his long-standing personal advocacy of indigenous rights.

SOURCES

Adorno, Rolena. *Colonial Latin American Literature: A Very Short Introduction.* Oxford: Oxford UP, 2011. Print.

Klor de Alva, J. Jorge. Foreword. *The Broken Spears: The Aztec Account of the Conquest of Mexico.* By Miguel León-Portilla. Expanded and updated ed. Boston: Beacon, 1992. Print.

León-Portilla, Miguel. *The Broken Spears: The Aztec Account of the Conquest of Mexico.* Boston: Beacon, 1992. Print.

Sánchez-Prado, Ignacio M. "The Pre-Columbian Past as a Project; Miguel Léon-Portilla and Hispanism." *Ideologies of Hispanism.* Ed. Mabel Moraña. Nashville: Vandberbilt UP, 2005. Print.

FURTHER READING

Cortés, Hernán. *Fernando Cortés, His Five Letters of Relation to the Emperor Charles V (1519–1526).* Trans. and ed. Francis Augustus MacNutt. 2 vols. Glorieta: Rio Grande, 1977. Print.

Díaz del Castillo, Bernal. *The True History of the Conquest of New Spain.* Nendeln: Kraus Reprint, 1967. Print.

Garcilaso de la Vega, El Inca. *Royal Commentaries of the Inca, and General History of Peru.* Trans. H. V. Livermore. 2 vols. Austin: U of Texas P, 1966. Print.

Guaman Poma de Ayala, Felipe. *The First New Chronicle and Good Government: On the History of the World and the Incas up to 1615.* Trans. Roland Hamilton. Austin: U of Texas P, 2009. Print.

Wright, R. *Stolen Continents: Conquest and Resistance in the Americas.* Toronto: Penguin, 2003. Print.

Elizabeth Gansen

THE CIVIL WAR
A Narrative

Shelby Foote

OVERVIEW

Shelby Foote's *Civil War* (3 vol.; 1958, 1963, 1974) remains one of the most comprehensive accounts of the American Civil War. Foote's narrative is noteworthy for the engaging, novelistic manner in which it chronicles this traumatic, and in many respects epic, chapter in American history. As noted by many critics, Foote aimed to convey to his readers the reality of the conflict—that is, "how it was." The massive, ambitious work—more than 1,500,000 words and almost three thousand pages long—illustrates the conflict with unprecedented dramatic scope and force. Foote took twenty years to complete this history, which features vivid portrayals of the hundreds of battles and skirmishes that defined America's most tragic war.

Foote's narrative revolves primarily around the opposing efforts of two determined political leaders: Jefferson Davis, president of the Confederacy, and Abraham Lincoln, newly elected president of the United States. Volume 1 opens with Jefferson Davis's farewell speech to the Senate in 1861 and moves on to Abraham Lincoln's first presidential orders. The volume gives an account of the secession and examines the early battles, starting with Fort Sumter and culminating with Perryville. It closes with the scene of Davis preparing for war, alongside Lincoln's emphatic message to Congress in 1862, in which he made a case for the urgency of abolishing slavery. Volume 2 traces the struggles of the Confederacy against the Union, ending with a portrait of the resolute William T. Sherman. Recounting the war's middle period, this volume traces the war's trajectory from the Battle of Fredericksburg to the Battle of Meridian. Focusing on the final year of the Civil War, volume 3 brings the conflict to its climax and ends with the dramatic final encounter between Confederate general Robert E. Lee and Union Army commander Ulysses S. Grant at Appomattox.

HISTORICAL AND LITERARY CONTEXT

Foote's *Civil War* is often described as combat history; that is, the text recounts the military aspects of the war, focusing on the actual fighting, tactics, battles, and men and leaders of the conflict as opposed to the social, economic, or political factors that influenced the war. More significantly, *Civil War* aims to reveal the humanistic elements of war, profiling figures from both the Union and Confederate armies. In keeping with his novelistic strategies, Foote profiles the leading figures of the conflict over time, revealing their characters within the broader framework of the narrative as it unfolds. In this way historical context becomes crucial to understanding the various motivations, pressures, and other factors guiding the actions of individuals. As Douglas Mitchell writes in "The Conflict Is Behind Me Now" the "narrative form rehumanizes history by recapturing the context of human action." Indeed, *Civil War* opens in a distinctly dramatic fashion, depicting Jefferson Davis at the moment he resigns from Congress to become president of the newly formed Confederacy. In a similar way, Foote brings the narrative to a close with a description of the Lee's momentous surrender to Grant. According to Mitchell, Foote treats the war itself as "a matter of art … of triumphs and failures of human imagination."

Foote had already published four novels and a collection of short stories before undertaking *Civil War*. His decision to represent the Civil War as a coherent, temporal narrative invites an analysis of its literary formations and rhetorical strategies. Most scholarly debate surrounding the work centers on the ostensible polarity of history and narrative. "History," as an academic discipline, traditionally suggests an attempt to order and interpret events that are regarded to be, for the most part, concrete and established as fact. "Narrative," on the other hand, suggests some degree of creative freedom on the part of the author. Hans H. Skei addresses this issue in his article "History as a Novel":

> Narrative history is a product of individual imagination: it often scrupulously relies on the available and accessible facts, but it is nonetheless an *artifice*. Which is to say that the gap between historical narrative and fictional narrative is reduced considerably. The historical narrative makes a claim upon truth, and the very form may indeed have been chosen as a vehicle for rendering the complexities of past events.

Even considering the muddled lines between truth and imagination in a narrative history, however,

⁜ Key Facts

Conflict:
American Civil War

Time Period:
Mid-19th Century

Genre:
Fletcher Pratt Award, 1964

MOVING PICTURES: KEN BURNS BRINGS THE CIVIL WAR TO LIFE

Largely influenced by the work of such Civil War scholars and authors as Shelby Foote, Ken Burns's 1990 film *The Civil War* is considered the definitive documentary of the conflict that shaped American history. The film is made up primarily of firsthand accounts taken from the writings of those who lived through the war and played a role in deciding its outcome. Famous actors and public figures including Sam Waterston (as Abraham Lincoln), Morgan Freeman (as Frederick Douglas), and Garrison Keillor (as Walt Whitman) read from diaries and letters that provide a personal, subjective perspective on the war. Many of the accompanying visuals are still photographs taken by Civil War photographers, among them Mathew Brady, and the soundtrack uses songs that were written and performed during the war period. A companion book titled *The Civil War: An Illustrated History* was also published in 1990, providing further detail about the images featured in the film.

The Civil War was first broadcast by the Public Broadcasting Service (PBS). At more than ten hours in length, it was broken into five separate episodes that aired on consecutive nights from September 23 to 27. The documentary was a massive hit, drawing the largest audiences in the history of PBS, and it won two prime-time Emmy awards, a Peabody award, and numerous other accolades. Foote's performance as one of the historians interviewed throughout the series was also very well received, and he enjoyed a spike in sales of his *Civil War: A Narrative* in the months after the film aired. Burns's film was digitally remastered and released on DVD in 2002, an indication of its enduring popularity.

few critics have questioned the credibility of the history presented in *Civil War*. Skei writes, "Facts remain facts, research remains research, evidence can still be controlled and evaluated." Throughout all three volumes of the work, Foote authenticates his narrative by continually drawing information from army dispatches, charge orders, soldiers' letters, newspaper reports, and generals' memoirs. In doing so, the author manages to create some of the most detailed portraits of significant places, events, and individuals in the entire corpus of Civil War literature.

THEMES AND STYLE

Foote's storytelling strategies are evident from the beginning to the ending lines of his history. The first line of *Civil War* reads, "It was a Monday in Washington, January 21; Jefferson Davis rose from his seat in the Senate." Rounding out the Confederate president's story, Foote ends *Civil War* with Davis's response to a reporter's question regarding the travesty and bloodshed of the war. In a simple but powerful statement, Foote writes of Davis (in volume 3), "'Tell them—' He paused as if to sort the words. 'Tell the world I only

loved America,' he said." The author's literary mastery likewise creates vivid visual imagery, as in his description of the Fredericksburg battle in volume 2:

> Staged as it was, with a curtain of fog that lifted, under the influence of a genial sun, upon a sort of natural amphitheater referred to by one of the two hundred thousand participants, a native of the site, as 'a champion tract inclosed by hills,' it quite fulfilled the volunteers' early-abandoned notion of combat as a picture-book affair. What was more, the setting had been historical long before the armies met there to add a bloody chapter to a past that had been peaceful up to now.

By alternating the point of view between east and west, commander and soldier, movement and countermovement, Foote creates a varied, panoramic portrait of each battle. Mitchell writes, "We see the broad sweep and large-scale movement of men and arms, but then the close-up gives us the concrete experience of which these consist." In depicting one Union assault on Orchard Knob, Foote opens a paragraph (in volume 2) presenting the viewpoint of a Union colonel as he watched the gallant movements of sixty regiments: "at times their movements were in shape like the flight of migratory birds, sometimes in line, sometimes in mass, mostly in V-shaped groups, with the points toward the enemy." Foote quickly contrasts the privileged perspective with the immediate experience of the battling soldier: "Up close, there was the gritty sense of participation, the rasp of heavy breathing, the drum and clatter of boots on rocky ground, and always the sickening thwack of bullets entering flesh and striking bone."

Foote takes particular interests in the soldiers' stories, seeking to capture the horror of their encounters: "No one assigned to one of the burial details ever forgot the horror of what he saw; for here, close-up and life-size, was an effective antidote to the long-range, miniature pageantry of Saturday's battle as it had been viewed from the opposing heights" (volume 2). Helen White and Redding S. Sugg Jr., in their article "Shelby Foote's *Iliad*," concur: "The narrator is balanced, generous, seeing many sides from many angles, and from a late position within a long tradition—one almost says Christian-humanist—with a Southern quality, involving piety real but rueful and pervasive irony." James Panabaker in *Shelby Foote and the Art of History* writes that Foote found it important to address the human condition: "Foote demonstrates a deeply humanistic perspective—ironic and sympathetic in equal measure."

Foote's characterizations are made more realistic through his liberal use of colloquialisms and humor (Mitchell). He retells one paradoxically humorous story: "One [soldier], about to remove a shoe from what he thought was a Federal corpse, was surprised to see the 'corpse' lift its head and look at him reproachfully. 'Beg pardon, sir,' the would-be scavenger said, carefully lowering the leg; 'I thought you had gone above" (volume 2). White and Sugg write,

> Although epic in magnitude, seriousness, and scope and tragic in impact, the book conveys much of the human quality of events through humor. Foote appreciates and features Confederate humor, shares it, and develops it by the special touches of the literary man. … In spite of destruction, carnage, and pain—unforgettably rendered, as in the account of Sharpsburg, where the wounded crept into hayricks for shelter only to be burned when fire swept the field—Foote blends humor into whole sections.

Similarly, Panabaker regards Foote's artistry as an aesthetic treatment of chaos: "Foote's writing conveys the paradoxical blend of loss and discovery offered by an artistic rendering of the past."

CRITICAL DISCUSSION

Civil War did not achieve critical acclaim until Foote's appearances on Ken Burns's 1990 television documentary series, *The Civil War*. Critics largely acclaim the book for its comprehensive treatment of the war and its balanced account of the Northern and Southern perspectives. Some critics and historians, however,

criticize Foote for overemphasizing the battle scenes while ignoring the sociopolitical aspects of the war. Thomas Landess writes in his article "Southern History and Manhood" that "any full-blown account of the Civil War must of necessity involve political considerations." According to Landess, Foote "seems to have adopted too simple a view of the political implications of the War and to have allowed that view to color his renditions of such a 'character' as Abraham Lincoln. … What is wrong with Foote's composite picture of Lincoln's career is his failure to understand the political motives that lay behind it, the president's concept of his own destiny." In his article "Foote's *The Civil War*: The Version for Posterity?" George Garrett defends Foote's seeming blunder:

> Because *The Civil War* is primarily, though not entirely, a combat history of the war, the other elements, political and social and economic, are realized dramatically and in that context. They, too, are shown and implied, or are to be inferred, in action and in character. It would be a serious misreading to conclude that any of these elements are missing, but it would be a critical mistake to look for their exploitation in conventionally analytic and expository terms.

Moreover, even Landess later concurs: "In his accounts of the battles themselves, probably the best

ever written on the subject, he gives ample evidence to undercut his questionable political assumptions."

Critics also widely note that Foote omits footnotes throughout his research. Various historians chide the author for his lack of documentation. In his review of *Civil War*, James Robertson points out that "it is difficult to criticize Foote's research because the literature of the Civil War is so immense. … He has carefully digested a mass of printed material and then rewritten the story to suit the tenets of his own presentation." Still, Robertson considers the absence of documentation a "serious flaw": "No one will challenge the authenticity of statements made by Foote, but it would have been extremely helpful to serious readers and working historians to know the sources for some of his facts." Foote foreknowingly responds to his critics in the biographical note of the first volume:

> Nothing is included here, either within or outside quotation marks, without the authority of documentary evidence which I consider sound. … I have left out footnotes, believing that they would detract from the book's narrative quality by intermittently shattering the illusion that the observer is not so much reading a book as sharing an experience. … In all respects, the book is as accurate as care and hard work could make it … for in writing a history, I would no more be false to a fact dug out of a valid document than I would be false to a "fact" dug out of my head in writing a novel.

Foote's disclaimer failed to appease certain academics, but by and large, his quality (and quantity) of writing in *Civil War* garners the respect and commendation of most critics. Mitchell writes, "Unlike meaning in the work of the professional historian, based on objective judgment of facts and sound generalizations from them, meaning here is rendered through artistic vision and sensed by the reader through the dynamic experience of the work's structure." Panabaker furthers the praise: "Foote is one of a rare breed of artists who combine the tools and sensibility of a writer of modernist fiction with the discipline of a historian." Overall, Foote attempted to illustrate—and, judging by the critical reception, succeeded in doing so—a vast but balanced account of the American Civil War, concentrating on the militaristic elements of the war and the individuals who participated in that conflict.

SOURCES

Foote, Shelby. *The Civil War: A Narrative.* 1958. Vol. 1: *Fort Sumter to Perryville.* New York: Random, 1986. Print.

———. *The Civil War: A Narrative.* 1963. Vol. 2: *Fredericksburg to Meridian.* New York: Random, 1986. Print.

———. *The Civil War: A Narrative.* 1974. Vol. 3: *Red River to Appomattox.* New York: Random, 1986. Print.

Garrett, George. "Foote's *The Civil War*: The Version for Posterity?" *Mississippi Quarterly* 28.1 (1975): 83–92. Print.

Landess, Thomas H. "Southern History and Manhood: Major Themes in the Works of Shelby Foote." *Mississippi Quarterly* 24.4 (1971): 321–47. Print.

Mitchell, Douglas. "'The Conflict Is Behind Me Now': Shelby Foote Writes the Civil War." *Southern Literary Journal* 36.1 (2003): 21–45. *Academic Search Complete.* EBSCO. Web. 9 Oct. 2011.

Panabaker, James. *Shelby Foote and the Art of History: Two Gates to the City.* Knoxville: U of Tennessee P, 2004. Print.

Robertson, James I., Jr. "*The Civil War: A Narrative.*" *Civil War History* 22.2 (1975): 172–75. Print.

Skei, Hans H. "History as a Novel: Shelby Foote's *The Civil War: A Narrative.*" *Notes on Mississippi Writers* 13.2 (1981). 45–63. Print.

White, Helen, and Redding S. Sugg Jr. "Shelby Foote's *Iliad.*" *Virginia Quarterly Review* 55:2 (1979): 234–50. Print.

FURTHER READING

Carter, William, ed. *Conversations with Shelby Foote.* Jackson: UP of Mississippi, 1989. Print.

Chapman, Stuart C. *Shelby Foote: A Writer's Life.* Jackson: UP of Mississippi, 2003. Print.

Foote, Shelby. Interview. *Parting the Curtains: Interviews with Southern Writers.* By Dannye Romine Powell. Winston-Salem: Blair, 1994. Print.

Kreyling, Michael. *Figures of the Hero in Southern Narrative.* Baton Rouge: Louisiana State UP, 1987. Print.

Phillips, Robert L., Jr. *Shelby Foote: Novelist and Historian.* Jackson: UP of Mississippi, 1992. Print.

White, Hayden. "The Historical Text as Literary Artifact." *The Critical Tradition: Classic Texts and Contemporary Trends.* Boston: Bedford, 2007. 1383–97. Print.

Stephanie Flores-Bradshaw

THE CRUSADES THROUGH ARAB EYES

Amin Maalouf

OVERVIEW

The journalist and novelist Amin Maalouf, an Arab Christian, immigrated to France in 1976 to avoid civil war in Lebanon. For the most part he has written historical fiction in which he takes what Hamid Bahri and Francesca Canadé Sautman describe in the article "Crossing History, Dis-Orienting the Orient" as "an unorthodox, nomadic and nonidentarian view of the cultural and political history of the Middle East from Ancient times to modernity."

The Crusades through Arab Eyes, published in French in 1983 and in an English translation in 1984, is Maalouf's single work of popular history. In many ways the work continues the themes of Maalouf's novels, in which he challenges the distortion of the Muslim Arab past in European historiography and refuses to accept what he calls the "lethal identities" developed within that tradition. According to Kathleen Davis and Nadia Altschul, in *Medievalisms in the Postcolonial World*, Maalouf "recognizes and deploys the explanatory power of a 'medieval' past, not by simply reversing its paradigms, but by setting it in motion, emphasizing its heterogeneity and withdrawing the grounds for 'lethal identities.'"

Based on chronicles written by medieval Arab historians, the work presents the history of the Crusades from the Muslim side in a format accessible to readers with no special knowledge of Islam, the Middle East, or the Arab world. The book is organized into six chronological parts: "Invasion," "Occupation," "Riposte," "Victory," "Reprieve," and "Expulsion." Unlike most accounts of the Crusades, Maalouf's narrative focuses on the actions, successes, and failures of Muslim leaders and armies, illustrated with quotations from Arab and Muslim historians and chroniclers of the period.

HISTORICAL AND LITERARY CONTEXT

The Crusades are a European historical concept. From the Muslim perspective the arrival of European knights in 1096 in what is now Palestine was known simply as the Frankish wars or, more accurately, the Frankish invasions.

In the mid-eleventh century the Islamic world was in political turmoil. Once united under the power of the Sunni caliph in Baghdad, the former caliphate was now divided into independent local states whose rulers fought over territory. Weakened by political strife and by sectarian divisions between Sunnis and Shiites, the Islamic heartland was not able to defend itself against a series of attacks by groups that Muslims saw as barbarians: the Berber tribes of North Africa, the Turks and later the Mongols from central Asia, and western Europeans, the last in a series of campaigns that became known as the Crusades.

The first wave of crusaders to respond to Pope Urban II's call in 1095 for an expedition to go to the aid of their Christian brothers in the Holy Land was made up of small groups of men and women led by people like Peter the Hermit. Often known as the People's Crusade, this group of amateur soldiers was poorly equipped and was untrained. The first Muslim leader to encounter soldiers of the People's Crusade was Kilij Arslan, a Seljuk Turk who controlled central Anatolia. Peter's small ragtag force was easily defeated outside the city of Nicaea in October 1096. Later, when Arslan heard that more Franks had landed, he was not expecting the battle-hardened group of knights and archers, led by experienced commanders, that had arrived. This second wave of crusaders defeated Arslan, seized his capital of Nicaea, and marched on to defeat the neighboring Islamic city-states. Over and over, Muslims rulers were defeated by their inability to recognize the threat posed by the European invaders and to unite against them.

By 1100 the crusaders controlled the area around Jerusalem, establishing four small principalities in the region, collectively called the Kingdom of Jerusalem These crusader states controlled the Holy Lands until 1187, when Islamic forces newly united under the Kurdish leader Saladin reconquered Jerusalem. Finally, in 1291 the city of Acre, the last crusader stronghold, fell to Muslim forces.

Most histories of the Crusades have been written from a Western perspective. The earliest accounts portray the Crusades as an expression of deep religious faith. Contemporary historians have looked at them in terms of military conquest as well as Christianity. Whether positive or negative, these accounts have all produced what Bahri and Sautman describe as "a history of a Western endeavor and of Western politics, in which those subject to attack and conquest were passive victims, ineffectual adversaries, or, perhaps,

❖ Key Facts

Conflict:
Crusades

Time Period:
11th–13th Centuries

Genre:
History

SALADIN

From the early nineteenth century Salah ad-Din Yusuf ibn Ayyub, known in the West as Saladin, has been a heroic figure in almost any account of the Crusades. He originally rose to power as a vassal of the Seljuk Turkish ruler Nur ad-Din, who wanted to unite the Muslim world under his control. In 1163 Nur ad-Din sent Saladin's uncle, Asad ad-Din Shirkuh, to conquer Fatimid Egypt. Accompanied by Saladin, Shirkuh captured Cairo. When he died two months later, Nur ad-Din appointed the twenty-nine-year-old Saladin as his vizier in Egypt.

Working first as Nur ad-Din's vassal and later ruling in his own right, Saladin reunited much of the Islamic heartland. He destroyed the Shiite power base in Egypt, faced down the extremist Shiite sect known as the Assassins, and seized control of Nur ad-Din's empire after the Seljuk ruler's death. Members of the Seljuk court and army swore allegiance to Nur ad-Din's eleven-year-old son and declared war on Saladin. It took Saladin twelve years of battle and diplomacy to unite Nur ad-Din's empire under one rule. In 1186, with Egypt and Syria united in a single kingdom, Saladin turned his attention to the Kingdom of Jerusalem, created by the Crusaders. In 1187 he reconquered Jerusalem and the greater part of the territories held by the Franks.

picturesque characters." As the Islamicist Carole Hillenbrand points out in *The Crusades*, this view is explained in part because the vast majority of Western medieval scholars do not read Arabic and thus depend on uneven and incomplete translations of the Arabic sources.

Only two works dealing with Muslim reactions to the Crusades were available to Western readers before the publication of *The Crusades though Arab Eyes*. Francesco Gabrieli's *Arab Historians of the Crusades* was published in Italian in 1957 and translated into English in 1963. Gabrieli's work consists of selected passages from Arab chronicles of the period and brief biographical sketches of their authors. The other work appeared in 1968 when the Israeli scholar Emanuel Sivan published *L'Islam et la Croisade: Idéologie et propagande dans la réaction Musulmane aux Croisades* (Islam and the Crusades: Ideology and Propaganda in the Muslim Reaction to the Crusades). Sivan's groundbreaking study has not been translated into English.

THEMES AND STYLE

Maalouf begins his book with a statement of intent: "The basic idea of this book is simple: to tell the story of the Crusades as they were seen, lived and recorded on 'the other side'—in other words, in the Arab camp." Telling a story is exactly what Maalouf does, producing a narrative that Mahmood Ibrahim sums up in a review of the book in *International Journal of Middle East Studies* as "an almost endless series of military encounters interspersed with intrigues, assassinations, alliances, counter alliances, battles lost and won, sieges raised and lifted … concentrating on the leaders and what they said and did and what they suffered and enjoyed." Maalouf describes his work as a "true-life novel" of the Crusades. He tells his story using devices more common to novelists than to historians, building dramatic tension and allowing his readers to share the emotions and inner thoughts of his characters. The result is what Bahri and Sautman call a "suspenseful and spry narrative."

Maalouf's narrative is not limited to what James Brundage, in a review for the *Journal of Near Eastern Studies*, dismisses as "a banquet of blood and gore, kings and battles." Interested in the pluralism and tolerance of the medieval Muslim world, Maalouf emphasizes the passages in the chronicles in which the Jewish population of the region allies itself with the Muslims against the Christian invaders. He also discusses the longstanding caravan trade between East and West, which continued unmolested throughout the era of the Crusades. He quotes a chronicler who reports that "the Christians … make the Muslims pay a tax, which is applied without abuses. The Christian merchants in turn pay duty on their merchandise when they pass through the territory of the Muslims. There is complete understanding between the two sides, and equity is respected. The men of war pursue their wars; but the people remain at peace."

Although Maalouf does not spend much time on historical analysis, he does not simply accept his sources without question, and he urges his readers to use their own judgment. For example, after presenting Ibn al-Qalansi's estimate of Frankish losses in a battle, Maalouf cautions the reader that "here or elsewhere, the figure should not be taken too literally. Like all his contemporaries, the chronicler of Damascus was no slave to precision, and it would have been impossible for him to verify these estimates in any event." In addition, in *The Crusades through Arab Eyes*, as in his novels, Maalouf reads the past through the lens of the present. In the epilogue he draws an explicit comparison between the Crusader states and modern Israel.

CRITICAL DISCUSSION

With the publication of the English translation, *The Crusades through Arab Eyes* generated strong responses from the academic community. Some, like M. L. J. Young, in his review in the *Bulletin of the British Society for Middle Eastern Studies*, praises the work as a landmark. Others have attacked Maalouf's scholarship and his celebration of Muslim victories. Brundage, for example, praises Maalouf's prose as attractive and pleasant but ultimately rejects the account as "journalistic in the worst sense of the term. His tale is superficial, anecdotal, and over simplified." Similarly, Ibrahim acknowledges that the book is useful to students but complains that Maalouf does not

This 1954 painting by Syrian artist Saed Tahssin depicts the Crusaders surrendering to the Sultan Saladin after the battle of Hattin in 1187. Early 20th century. © NATIONAL MUSEUM/DAMASCUS SYRIA / GIANNI DAGLI ORTI / THE ART ARCHIVE / THE PICTURE DESK, INC.

provide "any analysis of the ideology of the Crusades, of the contemporary conditions in the Middle East and of the Crusaders' final failure to establish a permanent presence in the area."

Despite scholarly complaints about Maalouf's lack of analysis and novelistic style, *The Crusades through Arab Eyes* is regularly included on recommended reading lists of introductory books on the Crusades. Hillenbrand sums up the consensus of critics that, while the book is neither comprehensive nor academic, it "came as a breath of fresh air into the field; it is lively and always popular with students."

SOURCES

Bahri, Hamid, and Francesca Canadé Sautman. "Crossing History, Dis-Orienting the Orient: Amin Maalouf's Uses of the 'Medieval.'" *Medievalisms in the Postcolonial World: The Idea of the "Middle Ages" outside Europe.* Ed. Kathleen Davis and Nadia Altschul. Baltimore: Johns Hopkins UP, 2009. Print.

Brundage, James A. Rev. of *The Crusades through Arab Eyes,* by Amin Maalouf. *Journal of Near Eastern Studies* 47:2 (April 1988): 149–50. *JSTOR.* Web. 24 Aug. 2011.

Davis, Kathleen, and Nadia Altschul. Introduction. *Medievalisms in the Postcolonial World: The Idea of the "Middle Ages" outside Europe.* Ed. Kathleen Davis and Nadia Altschul. Baltimore: Johns Hopkins UP, 2009. Print.

Hillenbrand, Carole. *The Crusades: Islamic Perspectives.* New York: Routledge. 2000. Print.

Ibrahim, Mahmood. Rev. of *The Crusades through Arab Eyes,* by Amin Maalouf. *International Journal of Middle East Studies* 20:4 (Nov. 1988): 559–60. *JSTOR.* Web. 24 Aug. 2011.

Maalouf, Amin. *The Crusades through Arab Eyes.* Trans. Jon Rothschild. London: Al Saqi, 1984. Print.

Young, M. L. J. Rev. of *The Crusades through Arab Eyes,* by Amin Maalouf. *Bulletin of the British Society for Middle Eastern Studies* 15:1–2 (1988): 102–3. *JSTOR.* Web. 27 Aug. 2011.

FURTHER READING

Al-Azm, Sadik J. "Western Historical Thinking from an Arab Perspective." *Western Historical Thinking: An Intercultural Debate.* Ed. Jören Rüsen. New York: Berghahn, 2002. Print.

Constable, Giles. "The Historiography of the Crusades." *The Crusades from the Perspective of Byzantium and the Muslim World.* Ed. Angeliki E. Laiou and Roy Parviz Mottahedeh. Washington: Dumbarton Oaks, 2001. 1–22. Print.

Daniel, Norman. *The Arabs and Medieval Europe.* London: Longman, 1975. Print.

Finucane, Ronald C. *Soldiers of the Faith: Crusaders and Moslems at War.* New York: St. Martin's, 1983. Print.

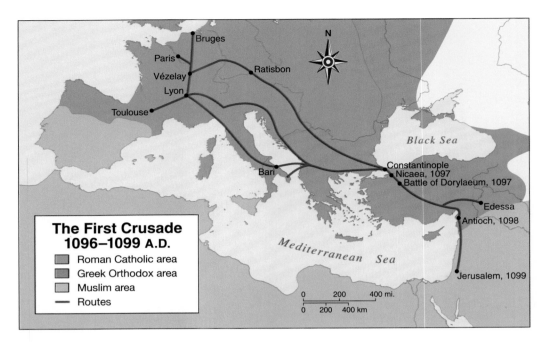

Gabrieli, Francesco, ed. *Arab Historians of the Crusades: Selected and Translated from the Arabic Sources*. Trans. E. J. Costello. London: Routledge, 1969. Print.

Holt, P. M. *The Age of the Crusades: The Near East from the Eleventh Century to 1517*. New York: Longman, 1986. Print.

Nicholson, Helen J. "Muslim Reactions to the Crusades." *Palgrave Advances in the Crusades*. Ed. Helen J. Nicholson. New York: Palgrave Macmillan, 2005. Print.

Nicolle, David. *Crusader Warfare*. New York: Continuum, 2007. Print.

Riley-Smith, Jonathan. *The Crusades: A History*. 2nd ed. New Haven: Yale UP, 2002. Print.

—, ed. *The Oxford Illustrated History of the Crusades*. Oxford: Oxford UP, 1995. Print.

Pamela Toler

Eighteen Fifty-Seven

Surendra Nath Sen

OVERVIEW

In 1955, in anticipation of the 100th anniversary of the Indian Mutiny, Maulana Abul Kalam Azad, then the India Minister of Education, invited historian Surendra Nath Sen to write "a new and objective history of the movement of 1857." Although the work would be published under the official sponsorship of the Indian government, Azad did not intend it to be an official government version of events. In his foreword to *Eighteen Fifty-seven*, Azad explains, "The only directive I issued was that he should write the book from the standpoint of a true historian. Beyond this general instruction, there was no attempt to interfere with his work or influence his conclusions."

In his preface to the resulting book, published in 1957, Sen states that he accepted the assignment because he believed that "though old controversies still persist, much of the bitterness has long since disappeared." Therefore, he believed, "a fresh review of the causes, character and consequences of the Sepoy war was well worth attempting." *Eighteen Fifty-seven* was Sen's last major work.

HISTORICAL AND LITERARY CONTEXT

By the mid-nineteenth century, the British East India Company had been the dominant power in the Indian subcontinent for one hundred years. Officially, the Mughal emperor still ruled in Delhi, and the East India Company, like the rulers of India's princely states, held its territory as a vassal of the emperor. The company maintained a private army, which was made up in large part of Indian soldiers known as sepoys. In 1857 the East India Company introduced a new weapon that caused concern among the sepoys: the Enfield rifle. The new rifle used greased cartridges made of paper wrapped around powder and a ball. Soldiers bit the cartridge open, poured the contents down the barrel of the gun, and rammed the cartridge after it. Word began to spread among the sepoys that the cartridges were greased with a combination of beef and pork fat, making them an abomination to both Hindus and Muslims. The wildest rumors claimed the British wanted to cause Hindu sepoys to lose their caste so it would be easier to convert them to Christianity. British officers were slow to respond to the rumors. By the time they assured their men that the cartridges were greased with beeswax and vegetable oils, the damage was done.

The sepoys were not the only group with reasons to be unhappy with the East India Company's rule. Beginning in the late 1820s, the company passed a series of reforms that were seen as attacks on traditional Hindu law, including allowing Christian converts to inherit property and the prohibition of child marriage and widow burning (*sati*). An aggressive policy of annexing Indian states created resentment among the Indian princes, who had traditionally supported the British. Land reform in Bengal imposed a new concept of private land ownership that displaced many landholders, creating yet another source of discontent with British rule.

On May 8, 1857, discontent turned to rebellion at the army garrison of Meerut in the state of Uttar Pradesh. Eighty-five sepoys refused to use the Enfield rifle. They were tried the next morning, stripped of their uniforms, and put in irons. On May 10, three of the regiments stationed at Meerut stormed the prison, freed the jailed sepoys, and killed the British officers and their families. The sepoys then marched toward Delhi, where the last Mughal emperor, Bahadur Shah II, ruled in name only.

The mutineers entered Delhi two days later and demanded an audience with the emperor. At first the Indian regiments stationed in Delhi continued to take orders from their British officers, but they soon joined the mutineers, who proclaimed revolution in the name of the unfortunate Bahadur Shah. Soon Indian rulers whose power had been threatened by British reforms rose up, adding their own private armies to those of the mutineers. What had begun as a mutiny expanded into a many-faceted resistance movement across northern India. Atrocities were committed on both sides. With only forty thousand European troops in India, the British were only able to keep the mutiny from spreading beyond northern India because a large majority of Indian sepoys in other parts of the subcontinent remained loyal to their officers. By 1858 the uprising was over, though bands of mutineers continued guerrilla actions well into the following year.

The Indian uprisings of 1857 are perhaps the most written-about events in Indian history. Histories of the mutiny began to appear as early as 1859. In the nineteenth century, most studies of the mutiny were written by British historians. These studies tended to

✧ *Key Facts*

Conflict:
Sepoy Mutiny/
The Great Rising

Time Period:
Mid-19th Century

Genre:
History

THE BRITISH ECONOMIC EMPIRE

At its height during the nineteenth century, the British East India Company controlled a vast colonial economic network, one that extended across the entire expanse of Asia. In order to retain its stranglehold on trade in the region, the company employed various forms of coercion and domination, including political bribery, propaganda, and violence. In addition to its concerns in the subcontinent, the East India Company established a powerful foothold in southeastern China as it strove to control the flow of precious metals and tea out of the country.

In his novel *An Insular Possession* (1986), Timothy Mo explores the sordid and nefarious aspects of British commercial practices in East Asia. Set in the years leading up to the first Opium War of 1839–42, Mo's narrative describes the unethical means by which the East India Company secured its interests in the region, notably its placations of the Chinese by supplying them with opium. Much of this opium was imported from the company's business holdings throughout India. This successful tactic was soon emulated by other firms in the area, including many American-owned companies. In Mo's novel, two disenchanted businessmen found a newspaper with the intent of using it to expose these execrable activities. Ultimately, it was the Chinese themselves who launched an attack against foreign economic interests, eventually expelling them from mainland China.

An illustration of the Indian Mutiny features William Stephen Raikes Hodson (right), commander of Hodson's Horse, a British cavalry unit. W R STOTT, *BATTLE OF ROHTAK*, ILLUSTRATION TO *STORIES OF THE INDIAN MUTINY* PAGE 84. MARY EVANS PICTURE LIBRARY. © MARY EVANS PICTURE LIBRARY / EVERETT COLLECTION.

focus on the military aspects of the uprisings, referring to them solely in terms of a "mutiny" or "Sepoy revolt." They described the atrocities committed by Indians against British civilians but seldom referred to the corresponding atrocities committed by the British against Indians in the conflict.

After India gained its independence in 1947, Indian scholars began to write revisionist histories that portrayed the mutiny as the first Indian war of independence. Many of these histories took the same Indian leaders that British historians had portrayed as villains and recast them as heroic freedom fighters. The most notable of these works is V. D. Savarkar's *The Indian War of Independence 1857*, described by G. P. Singh as the "Bible of the Indian Revolutionists."

THEMES AND STYLE

Sen began work on *Eighteen Fifty-seven* under handicaps that he describes in the book's preface: "The time allowed was by no means adequate, the source materials, though one-sided, were voluminous, the subject itself bristled with difficulties." The problem of source materials was a serious one. Sen's work as a historian is marked by his insistence on what Anil Chandra Banerjee describes as "the full exploration of source materials in the original, so that accurate and faithful interpretations of facts might follow." Most of the source materials used by previous historians were British. While Sen made full use of British official documents and memoirs dealing with the mutiny, he also worked with previously unstudied sources from the Indian viewpoint, including rare personal accounts and diaries.

"Preconceived theories and deep-rooted convictions" about the events of 1857 provided a problem that was less easy to address. Previous accounts of the mutiny had created national mythologies on both sides. Sen points out that, even a century later, "there are Englishmen who find it difficult to persuade themselves that the ruling race might have been guilty of some lapses and errors," and many Indians "are reluctant to admit that some of the rebel leaders might have been inspired by motives other than patriotic." His goal was to write a balanced account of events that avoided both sets of prejudice.

Assuming that most of his readers will be familiar with the main events of the mutiny, Sen is primarily concerned with understanding the causes and character of the revolt rather than creating a detailed narrative history. The first ten chapters of the book examine the underlying causes for discontent and then consider how those causes played out as the violence spread from the initial mutiny in Meerut through seven different regions of northern India. Sen sees no glory in the events he depicts: "It was an inhuman fight between people driven insane by hatred and fear. The non-combatants suffered as badly at the hands of infuriated soldiery as the men in arms: age and sex afforded scanty protection against primitive cruelty and even death brought no immunity from wanton insult." Unlike earlier historians of the mutiny, Sen draws no distinction between Hindu, Muslim, or Christian, stating that "all relapse into the primitive savagery from which religion and civilization has apparently reclaimed their remote ancestors."

In his final chapter, Sen addresses the questions of whether "the movement of 1857" was "a spontaneous outburst of sepoy discontent or a premeditated revolt engineered by clever politicians? Was it a mutiny limited to the army or did it command the support of the people at large?" He ultimately refuses either to idealize the mutiny as the "first Indian War of Independence" or to "dismiss it as a mere military rising." He argues that the uprising of 1857 cannot be described simply as a mutiny because it soon spread beyond the army to include the traditional leaders of northern India. However, he also refuses to claim that traditional Indian rulers were leading an independence movement. In Sen's view, the elite leaders who joined the uprising "wanted a counter-revolution" aimed at restoring their own power to the level they had enjoyed under Mughal rule. Nonetheless, he acknowledges that many members of the Indian nationalist movement in the early twentieth century were "inspired by the memory of the Mutiny."

CRITICAL DISCUSSION

Sen was a member of the first generation of professional Indian historians. He received an honorary doctorate from Oxford University in recognition of his outstanding contributions to the study of Indian history. Although his area of specialization was the Maratha dynasty, *Eighteen Fifty-seven* is generally considered one of the best one-volume histories of the mutiny.

Contemporaries praised the work for its balanced account of an event that was generally seen through the lenses of national prejudice. Jossleyn Hennessy describes this effect in glowing terms:

> The best proof that Dr. Sen has fulfilled his task is that while reading his pages the same feelings are experienced as when a well-known painting is seen again after it has been cleaned and restored. All the objects depicted are familiar but the colours, lights, and shades stand out revealing new detail and new perspectives where much has been dark and blurred.

Historian Daniel Thorner, believing that a decade of Indian independence was too brief a time to "permit thorough reworking of the available materials," is less enthusiastic, but he nonetheless describes Sen's book as "a convenient and useful account of the rising as a whole."

Later assessments of Sen's work have remained positive. Banerjee, writing in 1973, takes the position that "later research will supplement and correct his conclusions, but it is unlikely that they will ever be entirely superseded: they stand on the granite foundations of critical exploration of source-materials and uncompromisingly dispassionate interpretation of facts." Ainslie Embree, pointing out the difficulties of writing a government-sponsored book on a controversial subject, claims that "despite what must have been strong pressures to present the war of 1857 as a nationalist struggle, the book is remarkably judicious and free from rancour." Sen's final chapter is often printed in collections of essays related to the mutiny.

SOURCES

Azad, Maulana Abul Kalam. Foreword. *Eighteen Fifty-seven.* New Delhi: Government of India Publications Division, 1977. Print.

Banerjee, Anil Chandra. "Dr. Surendra Nath Sen" *Historians and Historiography in Modern India.* Ed. S. P. Sen. Calcutta: Institute of Historical Studies, 1973. Print.

Embree, Ainslie T., ed. *India in 1857: The Revolt Against Foreign Rule.* New Delhi: Chanakya, 1987. Print.

Hennessey, Jossleyn. Rev. of *Eighteen Fifty-seven,* by Surendra Nath Sen. *International Affairs* 34.2 (1958): 205. *JSTOR.* Web. 24 August 2011.

Sen, Surendra Nath. *Eighteen Fifty-seven.* New Delhi: Government of India Publications Division, 1977. Print.

Singh, G. P. *Indian Historians and Historiography in the Twentieth Century.* New Deli: Akansha, 2009.

Thorner, Daniel. Rev. of *Eighteen Fifty-seven,* by Surendra Nath Sen. *Victorian Studies* 1.4 (1958): 364–67. *JSTOR.* Web. 24 August 2011.

FURTHER READING

Edwardes, Michael. *Battles of the Indian Mutiny.* London: Batsford, 1963. Print.

Hewitt, James, ed. *Eyewitnesses to the Indian Mutiny.* Reading: Osprey, 1972. Print.

Hibbert, Christopher. *The Great Mutiny: India 1857.* New York: Penguin, 1980. Print.

Pati, Biswamoy. "Historians and Historiography, Situating 1857." *1857: Essays from Economic and Political Weekly.* Hyderabad: Orient Longman, 2008. Print.

Pati, Biswamoy, ed. *The 1857 Rebellion.* New Delhi: Oxford UP, 2007. Print.

Sen, Ronojoy. "Contesting 1857: Indian Historians and the Debate over the Uprising." *Revisiting 1857: Myth, History, Memory.* Ed. Sharmistha Gooptu and Boria Majumdar. New Delhi: Roli, 2007. Print.

Sen, Surendra Nath. "Writings on the Mutiny." *Historians of India, Pakistan and Ceylon.* Ed. C. H. Philips. London: Oxford UP, 1961. Print.

Thompson, Edward. *The Other Side of the Medal.* New York: Harcourt, 1926. Print.

Pamela Toler

FACUNDO
Civilization and Barbarism
Domingo Faustino Sarmiento

✣ Key Facts

Conflict:
Argentine Civil Wars

Time Period:
Mid-19th Century

Genre:
Novel

OVERVIEW

One of the foundational texts of modern Latin American literature, Domingo Faustino Sarmiento's *Civilización i barbarie o vida de Juan Facundo Quiroga* (1845; *Facundo: Civilization and Barbarism*, 1868) is believed to have inspired the genre of the Latin American dictator novel. Sarmiento wrote *Facundo* to denounce the dictatorship of Juan Manuel de Rosas in Argentina and to propose a European-style system of government. He believed that would bring "civilization" to the country and counter the "barbarism" of Rosas and other *caudillos*, leaders who controlled communities through violence. Sarmiento narrates the lives of Rosas, who was president of Argentina from 1829 to 1852, and Juan Facundo Quiroga, a military strongman and governor of the rural La Rioja. The novel portrays the ruthlessness of the caudillos during the civil wars of the mid-nineteenth century and their stranglehold on power in the country after the end of the wars.

Like the dictator novel of the twentieth century, *Facundo* examines the relationship between authority and brutality in Latin America and represents Sarmiento's attempt to understand the circumstances that led his country into dictatorship. It is difficult to assign *Facundo* to a single genre; as Roberto González Echevarría notes in *Myth and Archive*, "It is a sociological study of Argentine culture, a political pamphlet against the dictatorship of Juan Manuel Rosas, … a biography of the provincial *caudillo* Facundo Quiroga, Sarmiento's autobiography," and, most importantly, it is an analysis of the power of violence.

An author, educator, and politician, Sarmiento was a political exile in Chile when he wrote *Facundo*; as the director of the Santiago newspaper *El Progreso*, he published his work in his paper's literary supplement in 1845. Sarmiento drew many of the historical facts he manipulates in the novel from his own experience and knowledge. After returning to Argentina in the mid-1850s, he served as his country's ambassador to the United States from 1865 to 1868 and as president of Argentina from 1868 to 1874. During his presidential term, Saramiento implemented many of his progressive ideas, founding new schools and universities, installing telegraph lines throughout the country, and promoting industrial growth. Yet, it is the image he created of the powerful and charismatic caudillo for which he will be remembered. *Facundo* became an instant classic on the strength of its astute psychological sketches of Rosas and Quiroga and its establishment of the literary prototype of the caudillo, the wild, passionate military strongman who inspires both adoration and terror in his followers.

After gaining independence in 1816, Argentina was home to two political parties that were in fierce conflict, the *Unitarios* and the *Federalistas*. The *Unitarios* (members of the Unitarian party) supported a centralized government based in Buenos Aires, Argentina's largest city. The *Federalistas* opposed this idea and argued for a decentralized government, or a federation of provinces, each with its own power to make decisions about local or regional issues. The political tensions between the two parties came to a head in 1826 when the *Unitario* candidate, Bernardo Rivadavia, was elected president. Rivadavia favored the urban elite of Buenos Aires and persecuted the *gauchos* (Argentine cowboys) in the outer provinces, who were often forced into indentured servitude or prison.

The *Federalistas* challenged Rivadavia's power, and the presidency changed hands twice—first going to the *Federalista* Manuel Dorrego, and then to the *Unitario* Juan Lavalle—before Juan Manuel de Rosas took over the government by force in 1829. He led the country until 1852, setting up a dictatorial regime that forced all Argentines to support his *Federalista* government and cruelly persecuted those who did not. He established strict media censorship to silence opposition and formed the infamous *mazorca*, a personal armed force responsible for the violent enforcement of laws. Many *Unitarios*, including Sarmiento, fled to neighboring countries to avoid being tortured or murdered by the mazorca. Rosas was finally defeated in 1852 by another Argentine caudillo, Justo José de Urquiza, who fought against him with the help of Brazilian and Uruguayan soldiers.

Although he was not as central to national politics as Rosas, Quiroga was a well-known caudillo who wielded great power in the provinces in the nineteenth century. He was rumored to have killed a cougar near his home in La Rioja, a feat which earned him the nickname "Tiger of the Plains" in reference to his bravery and tendency towards violence. A charismatic and populist leader, he rose to become the commander of the provincial army, a post from which he fought the *Unitarios* until 1829. After the fighting was over, Quiroga transitioned from military service to diplomacy, promoting federalism throughout the provinces. In 1834, while traveling to mediate a dispute between two provincial governors, Quiroga was ambushed and assassinated. Although the governor of the province of Córdoba and two others were hanged for the crime, many believe that it was Rosas himself who orchestrated the assassination to rid himself of a political rival.

In his analysis of the rise to power of strongmen like Quiroga and Rosas, Sarmiento focuses on environmental, social, and psychological factors. This helped to establish the literary foundation for such novels as Miguel Ángel Asturias's *El Señor Presidente* (1946; English translation, 2007), Augusto Roa Bastos's *Yo el supremo* (1974; *I, the Supreme*, 1986), Gabriel García Márquez's *El otoño del patriarca* (1975; *Autumn of the Patriarch*, 1976), and Mario Vargas Llosa's *La fiesta del chivo* (2000; *The Feast of the Goat*, 2001). Presenting fictionalized versions of the dictatorships of Manuel Estrada Cabrera in Guatemala (Austurias), Dr. José Gaspar Rodríguez de Francia in Paraguay (Roa Basto), composites like García Márquez's, and Rafael Trujillo in the Dominican Republic (Vargas Llosa), these authors all borrow from Sarmiento's original reflections on the nature of power in a Latin American political context.

THEMES AND STYLE

In literature and visual art, much of the nineteenth century was dominated by the style known as *costumbrismo*, in which artists or writers depicted local customs, stereotypical characters, and the minute details of daily life. At a time of rapid industrial and urban growth in Europe and the Americas, *costumbrismo* offered a romantic view of provincial lifestyles that were becoming scarce within the bustle of the new metropolis. In Argentina, for example, the gauchos were immortalized in nineteenth-century literature for their unique lifestyle, traditions, and close relationship with the dry, infertile land of the Argentine *pampa* (prairie). Gauchos came to symbolize the heart of the Argentine character, though in reality they were economically disadvantaged, politically oppressed, and socially isolated. Sarmiento was clearly influenced by this nostalgic view while writing *Facundo*. He dedicated the first three chapters of the text to descriptions of the *pampa* and different types of gauchos, depicting them as both a colorful part of his country's past and an obstacle to its modernization.

The first chapter of *Facundo*, "Physical Aspect of the Argentine Republic, and the Ideas, Customs, and Characters It Engenders," also shows clear signs of geographical determinism, or the belief that physical surroundings determine culture and character. Sarmiento claims, for example, that the gaucho—inherently violent and ungovernable—is a product of the harsh, desert-like pampa where he lives and works. The caudillo, too, is a product of his environment, and his tyranny is born of necessity: "He needs a will of iron and a character so bold as to be rash, in order to control

The Battle of Monte Caseros, depicted in this lithograph, ended the dictatorship of Argentinian caudillo Juan Manuel de Rosas in 1852. © MUSEO HISTORICO NACIONAL CASA RIVERA, MONTEVIDEO, URUGUAY / INDEX / BRIDGEMAN ART LIBRARY INTERNATIONAL.

SARMIENTO'S AMERICAN EDUCATION

Civilización i barbarie o vida de Juan Facundo Quiroga was first translated into English in 1868 by Mary Mann, wife of the celebrated Massachusetts educator Horace Mann. Domingo Sarmiento, who met the Manns while traveling in 1847, shared their passion for public education and teacher training. (Sarmiento had taken a great interest in the United States and had studied the work of Benjamin Franklin and Abraham Lincoln.) With Mary Mann acting as interpreter, Sarmiento and Horace Mann discussed pedagogy, and Sarmiento returned to Latin America determined to implement many of Mann's ideas in the Argentine school system.

Sarmiento's relationship with Mary Mann continued after he left North America. He translated her biography of her husband into Spanish, and she translated *Facundo* for readers in the United States. As Kathleen Ross explains in her 2004 translation of the novel, Mary hoped that her own translation would help boost Sarmiento's political career: "Mann wished to further her friend's cause abroad by presenting Sarmiento as an admirer and emulator of U.S. political and cultural institutions." Following his election as president of Argentina in 1868, Sarmiento made American-style public education one of the cornerstones of his presidency.

A statue of Domingo Sarmiento stands in Boston in memory of his admiration for Massachusetts and its educational institutions and his friendship with Horace and Mary Mann.

the audacity and turbulent nature of the land buccaneers that he alone will govern and dominate, in the abandoned wilds of the desert." The caudillo is thus no more than a bad gaucho who has seized the reigns of power and held on through violence. In the insular world of the pampa, authority and justice are both local concerns, and the caudillo has absolute power to create and enforce the law as he sees fit. He does not hesitate to execute anyone who disobeys, and "[h]e who dies in these executions by the foreman leaves behind no rights to any kind of complaint, since the authority that has murdered him is considered to be legitimate." Sarmiento dedicates the first three chapters of the text to this kind of analysis, and only presents the history of armed struggle in Argentina in Chapter IV, "The Revolution of 1810."

In chapters IV through XIV, Sarmiento moves back and forth between the history of war in Argentina and his character study of Quiroga. Even in the historical chapters, he continues to focus on the character of the gauchos and the caudillos. He explains that during the armed struggle of the 1820s, many caudillos moved from the pampa into the army: "There were dozens of caudillos who in four years had

been elevated from bad gauchos to commanders, from commanders to generals, from generals to conquerors of towns, and finally to absolute sovereigns of the latter." In the army as in the pampa, their violent tendencies and domineering characters helped their rise to power. For Sarmiento, Quiroga and Rosas exemplified this move from caudillo to soldier to dictator. He explores their rise to power in depth. He begins with Quiroga, whom he both admires and disdains. Sarmiento seems in awe of Quiroga's political power, calling him "a great man, a man of genius in spite of himself and without knowing it, a Caesar, a Tamerlane, a Mohammed." Yet, he also describes Quiroga as the ultimate caudillo: "Ignorant, barbarous … brave to the point of rashness, endowed with Herculean strength, a gaucho on horseback before all else, dominating everything through violence and terror, he knew only the power of brute force."

Sarmiento covers the fighting between *Federalistas* and *Unitarios* in four chapters, focusing on Quiroga's movements and military tactics. He illustrates his character through his account of the Battle of La Tabada, early in the war: "Facundo attacked the city with his entire army, and during a day and night of attempted assaults, was forced back by one hundred young clerks, thirty artisan artillerymen, eighteen retired soldiers, six sick men in armor." The opposition surrenders when he threatens to burn the city to the ground; his army then shoots their leader, despite the fact that he is waving a white flag. For Sarmiento, this is but another example of the ruthlessness of the caudillo, who has no respect for the rules of warfare.

In *Facundo* Sarmiento argues that the assassination of Quiroga was "an official act, extensively discussed among various governments, planned in advance, and carried out with tenacity, like a state policy." Although the death of Quiroga may have helped Rosas politically, it also made the man a legend. In Sarmiento's view the assassination demonstrated Rosas's cold, calculating brutality, which would come to characterize his dictatorship. While Quiroga was wild and passionate and would resort to violence out of anger, Sarmiento saw a very different kind of violence in Rosas: "Rosas never goes into a fury; he calculates in the quiet and seclusion of his study, and from there, the orders go out to his hired assassins." For Sarmiento, Rosas was the more dangerous of the two caudillos, able to control the nation through the strategic use of terror.

For his vision of Argentina's future, Sarmiento looked north: he admired the educational system in the United States, and the country's assurance of basic rights for all citizens. He felt that a true democracy required its people to be educated, and, according to Dorothy Penn in "Sarmiento—'School-Master President' of Argentina," he is rumored to have said that "an ignorant people will always choose a Rosas." With regard to economics, he believed that Argentina needed to shift from agriculture to industry and trade in order to modernize.

CRITICAL DISCUSSION

From the time it was published in 1845, *Facundo* was highly regarded in Argentina as a political call to action for the burgeoning middle class. Elected president in 1868, Sarmiento is credited with putting an end to the caudillos' rule and focusing on education throughout the country. In *Facundo and the Construction of Argentine Culture*, Diana Sorensen Goodrich studies the novel's reception and suggests that it helped Sarmiento gain entrance into national politics. In addition, various critics have noted that one of the novel's most significant legacies is its characterization of the opposition between civilization and barbarism. Brian Gollnick writes in *The Cambridge Companion to the Latin American Novel* that Sarmiento's distinction between urban centers of progress and the wild, untamed space outside the city would reappear in the Latin American regional novel in the twentieth century.

In his essay "The Dictatorship of Rhetoric / The Rhetoric of Dictatorship," Roberto González Echevarría explores *Facundo*'s legacy to Latin American letters. Among the subsequent dictator novels, he notes that Alejo Carpentier's *El recurso del metodo* (1974; *Reasons of State*, 1976), García Márquez's *The Autumn of the Patriarch*, and Augusto Roa Bastos's *I, the Supreme*, all published in the mid-1970s, treat the topic with increasing complexity. Motivated by the rhetoric of *Facundo*, the later novels cast "the figure of the dictator … [as] part of a foundation myth that attempts to account for the modern history of Latin America."

A number of scholars have analyzed *Facundo* as a political and historical document, and some have focused in particular on the work's impact on the building of the modern Argentine nation. Paul H. Lewis's *Authoritarian Regimes in Latin America*, for example, traces the origin of the dictatorship in Latin America to the rule of the caudillos of the eighteenth and nineteenth centuries.

SOURCES

Gollnick, Brian. "The Regional Novel and Beyond." *The Cambridge Companion to the Latin American Novel.* Ed. Efraín Kristal. Cambridge: Cambridge UP, 2005. Print.

González Echevarría, Roberto. "The Dictatorship of Rhetoric / The Rhetoric of Dictatorship." *The Voice of the Masters: Writing and Authority in Modern Latin American Literature.* Austin: U of Texas P, 1985. Print.

———. "A Lost World Re-discovered: Sarmiento's *Facundo* and E. da Cunha's *Os sertões.*" *Myth and Archive: A Theory of Latin American Narrative.* Cambridge: Cambridge UP, 1990. Print.

Lewis, Paul H. *Authoritarian Regimes in Latin America: Dictators, Despots, and Tyrants.* Lanham: Rowman, 2006. Print.

Penn, Dorothy. "Sarmiento—'School-Master President' of Argentina." *Hispania* 29.3 (1946): 386–89. Print.

Sarmiento, Domingo Faustino. *Facundo: Civilization and Barbarism.* Trans. Kathleen Ross. Berkeley: U of California P, 2004. Print.

Sorensen Goodrich, Diana. *Facundo and the Construction of Argentine Culture.* Austin: U of Austin P, 1996. Print.

FURTHER READING

Criscenti, Joseph. *Sarmiento and His Argentina.* Boulder: Rienner, 1993. Print.

Halperín Donghi, Tulio, ed. *Sarmiento, Author of a Nation.* Berkeley: U of California P, 1994. Print.

Lynch, John. *Argentine Dictator: Juan Manuel de Rosas, 1829–1852.* Oxford: Oxford UP, 1981. Print.

Shumway, Nicolas. *The Invention of Argentina.* Berkeley: U of California P, 1991. Print.

Gina Sherriff

FORTY MILES A DAY ON BEANS AND HAY

The Enlisted Soldier Fighting the Indian Wars

Don Rickey Jr.

❖ *Key Facts*

Conflict:
Indian Wars

Time Period:
Late 19th Century

Genre:
History

OVERVIEW

Forty Miles a Day on Beans and Hay: The Enlisted Soldier Fighting the Indian Wars is a study of the men in the United States Regular Army (the country's standing army) who fought on the western frontier against Native Americans from 1861 to 1890. Published in 1963, the book is considered a Western history classic. Author Don Rickey Jr. interviewed surviving Indian Wars veterans in the 1950s and used the material to analyze the common soldier's experience, from enlistment and rudimentary training, to preparation for combat, to combat and its aftermath, to crime, punishment, and desertion. The uniqueness of the book—both its emphasis on the common soldier and its use of interviews as its main source material—inspired a new generation of historians. The book ran through sixteen printings between 1963 and Rickey's death in 2000.

In *Forty Miles a Day on Beans and Hay*, Rickey contends that the army regulars were neither the "romantic beau sabreur, knight-errant of the West" nor the "brutalized and degraded oppressor of noble red men" that historical and popular treatments of the Indian Wars had previously portrayed. He delves into each aspect of life as a member of the Regular Army fighting on the western frontier in order to provide a more balanced, human view of what the soldiers endured and accomplished. These men were ordered to keep Native Americans confined on reservations and to build the communications infrastructure required to open up the American West to white settlement. Rickey writes, "To the regulars was allotted the task of spearheading the great work, without receiving even crumbs of recognition or appreciation in the doing."

Rickey's own service in the military during World War II and the Korean War informed his view that no history of war is complete without an understanding of the experience of common soldiers. After receiving a doctorate in history from the University of Oklahoma, he worked for the National Park Service, beginning as a historian at the Little Bighorn Battlefield National Monument. This post most likely informed his choice to focus his studies on the Indian Wars. He maintained that the popular obsession with the "Wild West"—an obsession that reached a peak in the post-World War II period—"warped and romanticized" what took place in the 1800s on the western frontier.

HISTORICAL AND LITERARY CONTEXT

The post-Civil War West was the area west of the Mississippi stretching from the Great Plains to the Pacific Ocean. In the 1830s President Andrew Jackson pursued Indian removal policies that forced Native Americans in the Southeast and the old Northwest (present-day Ohio, Indiana, Michigan, Illinois, Wisconsin, and part of Minnesota) across the Mississippi River onto the Great Plains. Although Native Americans resisted this encroachment, sometimes violently, by the 1840s and '50s white settlers were pushing even further westward into the very lands that the government had promised to the Native Americans. Renewed hostilities resulted in another thirty years of Indian Wars, lasting from 1861 to 1890. It is this round of Indian Wars that Rickey examines in his book.

During the wars, the Sioux, Cheyenne, Arapaho, Nez Perce, Comanche, Kiowa, Ute, Apache, and Navajo nations fought encroachment on their lands and removal to Indian reservations managed by the inept and sometimes corrupt agents of the U.S. Bureau of Indian Affairs. Small and inadequate companies of army regulars were dispatched to protect the white settlers and force Native Americans onto the reservations. Both sides committed atrocities. In the 1864 Sand Creek Massacre, a force of 1,200 soldiers led by Colonel John Chivington killed 150 Cheyenne men, women, and children in a peaceful village. In 1866 Cheyenne and Sioux fighters ambushed and killed Captain William Fetterman and his eighty troops. Other impressive Sioux victories led to the Treaty of Fort Laramie in 1868, which guaranteed the Sioux control of the Black Hills in the Dakota Territory. Discovery of gold in the Black Hills led to a gold rush, however, and new conflicts between white miners and Native Americans flared up. When the U.S. government ordered the Lakota Sioux and Northern Cheyenne out of the Black Hills, some resisted under the leadership of Crazy Horse and Sitting Bull, uniting to push the whites out. In response, Lieutenant Colonel George Armstrong Custer led a force of 265 men against two thousand Sioux warriors at the Little Bighorn River in June 1876. All of Custer's troops died at the Battle of the Little Bighorn, a defeat that shocked the nation and resulted in increased military action.

Clearly, Native Americans were a formidable and much feared opponent of the army regulars; even small bands determined to avoid confinement on reservations could lead troops all over the prairie for months on end. An Apache band of thirty-three men and women led by Geronimo eluded a much larger pursuing force for five months in 1885 while the supplies, and the morale, of the U.S. troops dwindled. The eventual defeat of the last roaming bands resulted less from U.S. military power or prowess than from the destruction of the bison herds on the Great Plains by white hunters. To avoid starvation, Native Americans had to move to the reservations. The Indian Wars ended in 1890, after the U.S. army brutally repressed the Ghost Dance, a new Native American religious movement that prophesied that whites would be destroyed in an apocalypse. In December 1890 several thousand federal troops rounded up the Ghost Dancers and opened fire, massacring nearly 300 Sioux men, women, and children at Wounded Knee and ending Native American armed resistance in the West.

Forty Miles a Day on Beans and Hay has been called an early example of the "new" American military history. Rather than being concerned with analyzing battles, strategies, and military leaders, the new military history, as Peter Karsten describes it in the *American Quarterly*, involves "a fascination with the recruitment, training, and socialization of personnel, combat motivation, the effect of service and war on the individual soldier, the veteran, the internal dynamics of military institutions, inter- and intra-service tensions, civil-military relations, and the relationship between military systems and the greater society."

The use of this new method of research and documentation took off in the 1960s and '70s as social movements sought to establish equal rights, including equal political access and participation of groups formerly considered minorities. One of the tools of the new approach was the interview, or oral history, used to investigate perspectives that were unavailable through more conventional historical resources. Rickey's book was one of the first histories in modern times to incorporate oral testimony as a major source; other notable examples include Edward M. Coffman's *The War to End all Wars: The American Military Experience in World War I* (1968) and Stephen E. Ambrose's *Citizen Soldiers: The U.S. Army from the Normandy Beaches to the Bulge to the Surrender of Germany, June 7, 1944-May 7, 1945* (1997). In a separate article, "Talking About War: Reflections on Doing Oral History and Military History," Coffman documents that since World War II, university libraries and other institutions have amassed collections of thousands of oral histories of veterans of twentieth-century wars. Researchers increasingly use oral histories to illuminate the past experiences of common people, not only

BUFFALO SOLDIERS

Frederic Remington's *Cavalry Charge on the Southern Plains* (1907) depicts the Buffalo Soldiers. © GEOFFREY CLEMENTS/CORBIS.

At the conclusion of the Civil War, as the United States began to heal from four years of intense internecine conflict, Congress turned its attention to forming a peacetime army. Among the most celebrated fighting units to emerge during this time were the so-called buffalo soldiers, African American troops entrusted with defending territory in the Southwest and the Great Plains against hostile activity by Native Americans. Formed in 1866, the buffalo soldiers comprised two cavalry regiments and two infantry regiments and played a key role in the Indian wars over the remainder of the century. The buffalo soldiers served with distinction, earning nearly twenty Medals of Honor for their combat heroics. By the late 1890s, as hostilities with Native American tribes subsided, the buffalo soldiers continued to serve in other U.S. military operations, including the Spanish-American War. Although the regiments did not participate in World War I, they did fight Mexican and German forces at the third battle of Nogales in Arizona and joined the U.S. Cavalry in forcing the surrender of rebellious Yaqui tribes in the battle of Bear Valley in 1918, the final conflict of the Indian wars. By the Korean War, as the U.S. Army became integrated, the last of the buffalo soldier regiments was disbanded. The last surviving buffalo soldier, Mark Matthews, died in 2005 at the age of 111.

in the military but also in contemporary social movements and in many other areas of historical enquiry.

THEMES AND STYLE

Forty Miles a Day on Beans and Hay is wholly concerned with the enlisted soldiers' experience of the Indian Wars of the late nineteenth century. Examining the daily lives of U.S. Regular Army troops in the wars, Rickey contends, is crucial to gaining an understanding of the truth about that period in American history. He writes, "As members of the Regular Army, these men formed an important segment of our usually slighted national military continuum, upon and around which our massive armies have been created in times of crisis." Rickey believes this disregard extends to soldiers of all wars.

Rickey also seeks to dispel the mythology of the Wild West as a place full of heroes and villains, violence and valor, and above all, excitement and adventure. He contends, "Few aspects of the frontier past have been so routinely warped and romanticized as has that mixture of tragic folly, duplicity, savagery, heroism, waste, and costly establishment of order commonly referred to as the Indian Wars." The myths had been perpetuated in dime-store novels of the nineteenth and twentieth centuries and in the explosion of Westerns on the big screen in the early twentieth century, beginning with *The Great Train Robbery*, first shown in 1903. Rickey notes, "The men and events comprising the sweep of post-Civil War Western military history are customarily written and conceived of as storybook people and situations." *Forty Miles a Day on Beans and Hay* seeks to set the historical record straight.

Rickey's book examines all aspects of enlisted men's lives, from joining up and early training to routine duties at the Western posts and on Indian campaigns to how soldiers spent their free time. Far from having the glamorous adventures of the mythological Wild West, Rickey writes, the soldiers experienced "isolation, boredom, and monotony." Even facing Indian attacks or being ordered out on campaign could be welcome breaks from the tedium. The men's work often included logging, building structures, hauling drinking water, and sometimes acting as servants for officers and their families. Meanwhile, rations, clothing, and shelter were inadequate; severe frostbite and even deaths from exposure and freezing during winter campaigns were common. Rickey suggests that the "months of inactivity were depressing and psychologically deteriorating, and probably bred more serious trouble than any other single factor." Many soldiers turned to alcohol and prostitutes. Others deserted. Writes Rickey, "For some, the circumstances of enlisted soldiering became more than they were willing to endure."

Central to Rickey's project of writing a "real" history of the Indian Wars' rank and file was gathering information from the enlisted men themselves. Because many of these men were nearly illiterate, most of what had been written about them had come from officers or other sources. Therefore, Rickey undertook to interview more than 300 veterans still living in the 1950s. Because he was committed to telling the story of these men, *Forty Miles a Day on Beans and Hay* includes a multitude of lengthy quotes from Rickey's correspondence and interviews. "Wherever possible," he explains, "the old regulars have been allowed to speak for themselves." Rickey took great pains to authenticate what the men told him, however, anticipating potential criticism of his methods and ensuring that his work would be taken seriously.

An 1889 illustration depicting the Battle of Little Big Horn (1876). In his novel *Forty Miles a Day on Beans and Hay*, Don Rickey Jr. describes the experiences of enlisted soldiers during the Indian Wars, including this battle. © PRIVATE COLLECTION / THE BRIDGEMAN ART LIBRARY INTERNATIONAL.

The Army in
the Indian Wars,
1865–1890
■ Army Post
● Battle

WA

Blackfeet

MT Crow

ND

Sioux

MN

Nez Perce

ID

OR

Little Bighorn, 1876

Birch Coulee, 1862

Modoc

Sheepeater

Sioux

SD

Sioux

Bannock

Cheyenne

Shoshoni

WY

Paiute

Fort Laramie, 1848

Arapaho

NE

Pawnee

Fort Churchill, 1860

Fort Kearney, 1848

CA

NV

UT

Ute

CO

Southern Cheyenne

Fort Hays,
1865

Navaho

KS

Sand Creek, 1868

Arapaho

Kiowa

Adobe Walls, 1864

AZ

Apache

NM

OK

PACIFIC
OCEAN

Comanche

Apache Pass, 1862

TX

MEXICO

Gulf of
Mexico

0   125   250 mi.

0   125   250 km

© MAP BY XNR PRODUCTIONS. CENGAGE LEARNING, GALE.

CRITICAL DISCUSSION

Forty Miles a Day on Beans and Hay was one of the first histories of the western frontier in the post-Civil War era to shift the focus from the officers to the enlisted men. It quickly became a Western history classic, inspiring a generation of "new historians" working in both the Western history and military history fields. Reviewing the book in *Montana: The Magazine of Western History*, Dee Brown admits skepticism about the reliability of oral interviews as historical sources but praises Rickey for his painstaking use of military records, contemporary accounts, and printed sources to authenticate the information. In "Lost Soldiers: Re-Searching the Army in the American West," Sherry L. Smith calls Rickey's work "pioneering" but also criticizes him and other Western historians for omitting the experience of the Native Americans: "Given

today's sensibilities, the overwhelming focus on the army seems one-sided, myopic, ethnocentric." Brown would have liked more information on the women attached to the companies as wives of the enlisted men or as laundresses. Nevertheless, reviewers have acknowledged, in the words of Charles E. Rankin et al ("Two Gifted Historians: Aubrey L. Haines and Don G. Rickey, Jr."), that Rickey was "the only historian who dedicated himself to seeking out the last of the Indian Wars veterans, interviewing them, and accurately recording the story of their army service."

At Rickey's death in 2000, several historians wrote essays eulogizing him in *Montana: The Magazine of Western History*, a publication to which he had frequently contributed. All concur in calling *Forty Miles a Day on Beans and Hay* "path breaking," "unique," and "classic." Rankin emphasizes that Rickey had believed in "the obligation to represent the people of the past within the context and standards of their own times, rather than weighing their actions against the changing political philosophies of the present." Oral histories, while engendering misgivings among established historians at the book's initial publication in 1963, had become a respected resource by the time of Rickey's death—a trend in which the pioneering *Forty Miles a Day on Beans and Hay* had played no small part.

SOURCES

Brown, Dee. Review of *Forty Miles a Day on Beans and Hay: The Enlisted Soldier Fighting the Indian Wars*, by Don Rickey Jr. *Montana: The Magazine of Western History* 13.4 (1963): 87–88. Print.

Coffman, Edward M. "Talking About War: Reflections on Doing Oral History and Military History." *Journal of American History* 87.2 (2000): 582–92.

Karsten, Peter. "The 'New' American Military History: A Map of the Territory, Explored and Unexplored." *American Quarterly* 36.3 (1984): 389–418. Print.

Rankin, Charles E., et al. "Two Gifted Historians: Aubrey L. Haines and Don G. Rickey, Jr." *Montana: The Magazine of Western History* 50.4 (2000): 66–73. Print.

Rickey, Don, Jr. *Forty Miles a Day on Beans and Hay: The Enlisted Soldier Fighting the Indian Wars*. Norman: U of Oklahoma P, 1963. Print.

Smith, Sherry L. "Lost Soldiers: Re-Searching the Army in the American West." *Western Historical Quarterly* 29.2 (1998): 149–63. Print.

FURTHER READING

Adams, Kevin. *Class and Race in the Frontier Army: Military Life in the West, 1870–1890*. Norman: U of Oklahoma P, 2009. Print.

Ambrose, Stephen, E. *Citizen Soldiers: The U.S. Army from the Normandy Beaches to the Bulge to the Surrender of Germany, June 7, 1944-May 7, 1945*. New York: Simon, 1997. Print.

Coffman, Edward M. *The War to End all Wars: The American Military Experience in World War I*. New York: Oxford UP, 1968. Print.

Leckie, William H. *The Buffalo Soldiers: A Narrative of the Black Cavalry in the West*. Norman: U of Oklahoma P, 2003. Print.

Rickey, Don, Jr. "Fort Laramie in 1876: Chronicle of a Frontier Post at War." *Western Historical Quarterly* 21.2 (1990): 252–53. Print.

Van de Logt, Mark. *War Party in Blue: Pawnee Scouts in the U.S. Army*. Norman: U of Oklahoma P, 2010. Print.

Wooster, Robert. *The American Military Frontiers: The United States Army in the West, 1783–1900*. Albuquerque: U of New Mexico P, 2009. Print.

Melissa Doak

THE GALLIC WAR

Gaius Julius Caesar

OVERVIEW

The Gallic War is the English title most frequently used for *Commentarii de Bello Gallico* by Gaius Julius Caesar (100–44 BCE). The work is also referred to with the literal translation *Commentaries on the Gallic War* and sometimes as *On the Gallic War* or *About the Gallic War*. It comprises seven books written by Caesar himself and an eighth book written after Caesar's death by Aulus Hirtius, one of his officers. The text describes and discusses a series of military campaigns conducted by Caesar from 58 BCE to 51 BCE, now known collectively as the Gallic Wars because they took place largely in an area of Europe known at the time as Gaul. These campaigns produced a significant expansion in the territorial dominance of Rome and substantially increased Caesar's political power, so his personal account of the events is of great value to historians.

Scholars generally agree, however, that the commentaries are not merely a straightforward record but rather a series of carefully crafted presentations designed to enhance Caesar's reputation. The third-person narration and unadorned prose style provide the appearance of objectivity, yet a close reading of the text reveals that Caesar carefully selects and colors events to serve his own purposes. Therefore *The Gallic War* is of interest not only for the study of military strategy and ancient styles of battle but also for the understanding of early propaganda techniques and the psychology of power.

Caesar's clear, direct prose style is ideal for the practice of basic translation, and since the nineteenth century *The Gallic War* has been a standard text in Latin classes. Additionally, the text includes a good deal of information about the geography and ethnography of pre-Roman Europe and Britain, as well as insights into the Roman attitude toward other cultures. Caesar also wrote *Commentarii de Bello Civili* (*Commentaries on the Civil War*), a shorter set of accounts focusing on his political and military activities during the period 49–48 BCE, and the two works together are often referred to simply as "Caesar's commentaries."

HISTORICAL AND LITERARY CONTEXT

The opening sentence of *The Gallic War* is well known to anyone who has studied Latin, and familiar even to many who have not. It states that the whole of Gaul is divided into three parts; by "the whole of Gaul" Caesar meant the territory defined today by France, Luxembourg and Belgium, most of Switzerland, the western part of northern Italy, and the parts of the Netherlands and Germany that lay on the left bank (i.e., west) of the Rhine River.

The three parts to which Caesar refers were inhabited, respectively, by the Belgae, the Aquitani, and "those who in their own language are called Celts, and in ours, Gauls." These tribes, according to Caesar, differed from one another in language, customs, and laws, and the territory of the Gauls was separated from that of the Aquitani by the River Garonne, and from the Belgae by the rivers Marne and Seine. These made up the areas of Gaul not yet under Roman control, called by the Romans *Galla Comata*, or "Long-Haired Gaul." The Romans had occupied Cisalpine Gaul (most of northern Italy) and Transalpine Gaul (the French region of Provence today) in the second century BCE and had found the Gaulish tribes to be formidable opponents in battle. Although their fighting forces were undisciplined by Roman standards, the Gauls were nevertheless relatively prosperous and urbanized, with substantial armaments, manpower, and military competence.

During the first century BCE, some tribes in Gaul submitted to Roman rule or formed alliances with Rome, while others resisted Roman dominance. A migration of the Helvetii (an aggressive Germanic tribe) into parts of Gaul provided Caesar with an opportunity to launch campaigns that could be represented as aid to Rome's allies in the region but that were also recognized as preemptive strikes against Gaulish and Germanic tribes who might threaten Rome's interests. Caesar, who was at the time governor of the Roman provinces in Cisalpine and Transalpine Gaul, also had personal reasons for these military excursions. He had run up considerable debt in his earlier political and military activities and needed the spoils of war that might be attained through the Gallic campaigns. In addition, the ambitious strategy promised to build up his reputation and strengthen his political power.

Although the majority of his engagements were successful, Caesar encountered a number of substantial challenges, and his forays across the Rhine River into northern Germany and across the English Channel into Britain proved did not succeed. His most difficult adversary among the Gauls was Vercingetorix, a chieftain of the Arverni tribe who was able to unite a number of tribes in a coalition against the Romans.

❖ *Key Facts*

Conflict:
Gallic War

Time Period:
58–51 BCE

Genre:
History

CAESARS IN CINEMA

Few historical figures have been featured in more films than Julius Caesar. There is even a cinematic account of the Gallic War, released in 2001 under the title *Druids*. Klaus Maria Brandauer appears as Caesar and Christopher Lambert as the warrior Vercingetorix, who rallied the Gauls. Although the somewhat tedious film failed to please audiences, it is visually and historically interesting.

Shakespeare's tragedy *Julius Caesar* (c. 1599) focused on Roman politics and the complex relationship between Caesar and Brutus. A 1953 film version of the play starred Louis Calhern as Caesar and James Mason as Brutus. In a 1970 production John Gielgud took the role of Caesar, with Jason Robards as Brutus. Both films cast respected theatrical actors in the two principal parts and added Hollywood stars to play the role of Mark Antony—Marlon Brando in 1953 and Charlton Heston in 1970.

The other major play about Caesar was George Bernard Shaw's *Caesar and Cleopatra* (1898), a drama of ideas in which the title characters represent contrasting approaches to rulership. The play received a lavish Hollywood treatment in 1945, with Claude Rains as Caesar and the popular Vivien Leigh as Cleopatra. Leigh, of course, was widely known for her portrayal of Scarlett O'Hara in *Gone with the Wind*.

Elizabeth Taylor took the next star turn as Cleopatra in a 1963 extravaganza featuring Rex Harrison as Caesar and Richard Burton as Mark Antony. Although the film is famous largely for its huge scale (as well as the real-life romance of Taylor and Burton), it is worth watching from a historical perspective, especially in the original four-hour version available on DVD.

Caesar has been a fixture of television drama as well. The BBC Television Shakespeare series presented a faithful rendition of Julius Caesar in 1979, and an American television movie titled *Caesar* offered an accurate and interesting biographical account in 2002.

Caesar's hard-won victory over these forces at the Battle of Alesia ended the Gallic campaigns in 52 BCE. Thereafter, Caesar returned to Rome, where he utilized the fame he had achieved through his actions in Gaul as a platform for his claim to the consulship of Rome. This strategy was blocked by his political opponents, however, leading to a civil war. In 48 BCE Caesar defeated his rival Pompey and became the sole ruler of Rome.

THEMES AND STYLE

The Gallic War exemplifies a particular type of Roman literature, the *commentarius*, or commentary. Commentaries were typically compilations of notes and political reports that recorded events more or less as observed, without a great deal of analysis or expansion. They differed from *historia*, or histories, which were usually more unified literary works. The seven books of *The Gallic War* written by Caesar follow a regular pattern, divided by year and subdivided by summers (the active battle period) and winters (when troops returned to quarters). The individual books, however, vary widely in length, style, tone, emphasis, and perspective. Some scholars contend that Caesar wrote all of them during one period, the winter of 52–51 BCE, but contradictions among the books have led other scholars to conclude that they were composed annually, following each year's battle period.

Caesar ranges through a wide array of topics in *The Gallic War*, but the commentaries are not merely episodic. Among the thematic strands woven through the work is the concept of *virtus*. The Latin word

(which became "virtue" in English) probably derived from *vir*, the word for "man," and originally referred specifically to courage in battle and manliness in general. Over time, *virtus* expanded to signify worthiness in a broader sense, but it retained a connection with martial valor and the particular strength of mind needed for victory in any type of conflict.

In *Caesar in Gaul and Rome: War in Words*, Andrew M. Riggsby suggests that in *The Gallic War* Caesar develops a particular view of *virtus*, suggesting for example that Germans acquire their *virtus* through individual confrontations with nature and with enemies, while Romans acquire *virtus* in group experiences and especially through submitting to authority under challenging circumstances. Further, Riggsby asserts, "Caesar locates a tension within the nature of virtus: resisting outside forces (like the enemy) versus resisting internal ones (like the urge to rush into battle too soon)."

Caesar's distinctive view of *virtus* extends to his understanding and application of military theory. According to J. E. Lendon's analysis in "The Rhetoric of Combat," Caesar's battle narratives demonstrate a belief that not only tactics but also psychological factors are important in battle. This can be seen in the way Caesar divides battle descriptions into segments that focus variously on aspects of *impetus* (attack, tactical move), *animus* (spirit, morale), and *virtus*. This multilayered view of warfare differed from the Greek tradition of battle narration, which focused primarily on tactics. Lendon contends that Caesar intentionally developed this distinction in *The Gallic War*, "creating

QVANTA STRA
GE VIRVM SVBLI
MIS ALEXIA CESSIT
CÆSAREIS AQVI
LIS. PICTA TABEL
LA NOTAT

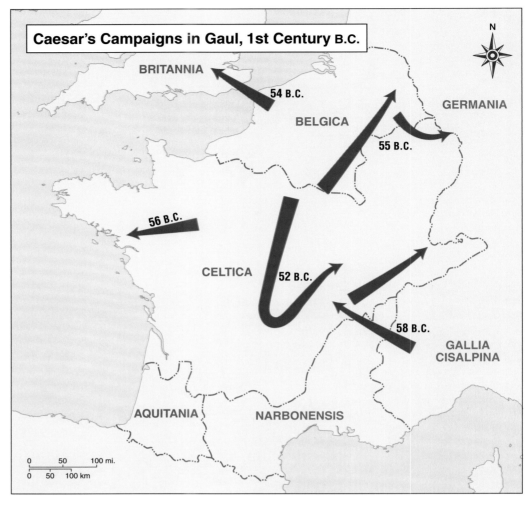

Caesar's Campaigns in Gaul, 1st Century B.C.

© MAP BY XNR PRODUCTIONS. CENGAGE LEARNING, GALE.

in his battle descriptions an artistic unity that blended Greek theory with aspects of traditional Roman military thinking and his own experience."

Caesar also uses subtle techniques of selection and implication to manipulate the reader's impressions of other groups and of Caesar's own expertise. In "Caesar's Construction of Northern Europe," for example, Hester Schadee argues that Caesar's presentation of ethnographic information is connected with his imperialist projects and military aims. In some cases, Caesar depicts himself as an explorer, inquiring about unknown peoples (such as the Helvetii and Nervii) and adding to Roman knowledge. In other cases (as with the German Suebi), he makes no inquiry, implying that certain "others" are not just unknown but in fact unknowable. In this way, Caesar presents a picture of Germania as "unknowable, incorruptible and therefore unconquerable." In writing about the British expeditions, Caesar takes a different approach, emphasizing the information he gains, as if to suggest

that by "controlling the island intellectually, Rome can control it militarily."

CRITICAL DISCUSSION

Historical evidence does not tell us whether Caesar's commentaries were written and published year by year or whether they were written yearly but published all at once. It is also possible that Caesar wrote them retrospectively, after the campaigns were ended. In any event, they were well known by 46 BCE, according to documents of the time. Even in the early days, however, some questioned the accuracy of Caesar's account. According to the biographic profile of Julius Caesar written by Suetonius in 21 CE, Asinius Pollio (who supported Caesar in the civil war) believed the commentaries "were put together somewhat carelessly and without strict regard for truth; since in many cases Caesar was too ready to believe the accounts which others gave of their actions, and gave a perverted account of his own, either designedly or perhaps from forgetfulness;

and [Pollio] thinks that [Caesar] intended to rewrite and revise them." Although critics since have differed in their interpretations of Caesar's intentions, most scholars today would agree that his seemingly transparent prose cannot be taken at face value.

This textual complexity can be viewed from multiple historical and literary perspectives. For example, in *The Eye of Command*, Kimberly Kagan contends that although self-promotion undoubtedly played a role in Caesar's presentation of events, his commentaries include not only successes but also failures that "reveal Caesar's effort to find the essential concatenation of events on the battlefield." Kagan argues that the commentaries can be viewed as an account of the command viewpoint, depicting Caesar's approach to understanding the dynamics of battle and recognizing the right events to focus on in pursuit of victory.

Taking another approach, Stephan Busch's article "Who Are 'We'? Toward Propagandistic Mechanism and Purpose of Caesar's *Bellum Gallicum*" analyzes the commentaries in terms of their intended effects on different audiences. Noting that "good propaganda is always multi-layered and typically offers more than one point of contact to the readers," Busch suggests that *The Gallic War* "offers a framework to which the readers can tie their personal experiences; outsiders are also invited to join and to read the story with sympathetic participation." To accomplish this aim, Caesar keeps his reports abstract for the most part but punctuates them from time to time with vivid details of battle and stories about individuals. By this means he offers something of interest to different audiences, "from the senatorial legate to the common legionnaire."

SOURCES

Busch, Stephan. "Who Are 'We'? Toward Propagandistic Mechanism and Purpose of Caesar's *Bellum Gallicum*." *The Manipulative Mode: Political Propaganda in Antiquity: A Collection of Case Studies*. Ed. Karl A. E. Enenkel and Ilja Leonard Pfeijffer. Boston: Brill, 2005. 164+. Print.

Hammond, Carolyn. *Caesar: The Gallic War*. Oxford: Oxford UP, 1996. Print.

Kagan, Kimberly E. *The Eye of Command*. Ann Arbor: U of Michigan P, 2006. Print.

Lendon, J. E. "The Rhetoric of Combat: Greek Military Theory and Roman Culture in Julius Caesar's Battle Descriptions." *Classical Antiquity* 18 (1999): 273–329. Print.

Riggsby, Andrew M. *Caesar in Gaul and Rome: War in Words*. Austin: U of Texas P, 2006. Print.

Schadee, Hester. "Caesar's Construction of Northern Europe: Inquiry, Contact and Corruption in *De Bello Gallico*." *Classical Quarterly* 58 (2008): 158–80. Print.

Suetonius. *Lives of the Twelve Caesars: And, Lives of Illustrious Men*. Trans. John C. Rolfe. London: Heinemann, 1964. Print.

FURTHER READING

Dillon, Sheila, and Katherine E. Welch. *Representations of War in Ancient Rome*. New York: Cambridge UP, 2006. Print.

Eden, P. T. "Caesar's Style: Inheritance versus Intelligence." *Glotta* 40 (1962): 74–117. Print.

Gelzer, Matthias. *Caesar: Politician and Statesman*. Trans. Peter Needham. Cambridge: Harvard UP, 1968. Print.

Gilliver, Kate. *Caesar's Gallic Wars, 58–50 BC*. Oxford: Osprey, 2002. Print.

Goldsworth, Adrian. *Caesar: Life of a Colossus*. New Haven: Yale UP, 2006. Print.

Krebs, Christopher B. "'Imaginary Geography' in Caesar's Bellum Gallicum." *Am. J. of Philology* 127.1 (2006): 111–36. Print.

Lendon, J. E. *Soldiers & Ghosts: A History of Battle in Classical Antiquity*. New Haven: Yale UP, 2005. Print.

McDonnell, Myles A. *Roman Manliness: "Virtus" and the Roman Republic*. Cambridge: Cambridge UP, 2006. Print.

Sidebottom, Harry. *Ancient Warfare: A Very Short Introduction*. Oxford: Oxford UP, 2004. Print.

Welch, Kathryn, and Anton Powell. *Julius Caesar as Artful Reporter: The War Commentaries as Political Instruments*. London: Duckworth, 1998. Print.

Cynthia Giles

HIROSHIMA

John Richard Hersey

✢ *Key Facts*

Conflict:
World War II

Time Period:
Mid-20th Century

Genre:
Essay

OVERVIEW

On August 31, 1946, the *New Yorker* magazine marked the one-year anniversary of the U.S. bombing of Hiroshima, Japan (which took place on August 6, 1945), with a special issue containing a single essay titled *Hiroshima*. The article was written by John Hersey, an American journalist who had won a Pulitzer Prize the year prior for his novel *A Bell for Adano* (1944). The essay's four sections trace the experiences of six bomb survivors from the moments before the blast through the challenging year that followed. Written in an understated style and eschewing moral commentary, the article allows the events and experiences it depicts to speak for themselves about the devastating effects of atomic warfare. Hersey, the son of American missionaries, had been born in China and had returned to Asia as a reporter at the close of the war. His knowledge of and respect for Asian cultures is reflected in his treatment of the people of Hiroshima. His six interviewees—the American-educated minister Reverend Tanimoto, the German Jesuit Father Kleinsorge, the Red Cross hospital physician Dr. Sasaki, the widowed Mrs. Nakamura, the private hospital owner Dr. Fujii, and the tin-factory worker Miss Sasaki—represented a diverse cross-section of Hiroshima's wartime residents.

Hiroshima experienced almost unparalleled success; issues of the *New Yorker* quickly sold out, and reprints of the essay appeared in numerous other publications before it was printed in book form three months later. The work is often credited with helping American readers to understand, many for the first time, that the victims of the atomic bomb were ordinary citizens to whom they could relate. Although it was occasionally criticized either for appearing too sympathetic to Japan or for not going far enough to condemn the bombing, it continues to be considered among the most important statements about the world's entry into the atomic age. An expanded version, which provided updated information about Hersey's six interviewees, was published in 1985, coinciding with the fortieth anniversary of the bombing.

HISTORICAL AND LITERARY CONTEXT

Hersey's essay chronicles the aftermath of the bombing of Hiroshima, which took place during World War II, on August 6, 1945. American president Harry S. Truman had made the difficult decision to use the atomic weapon in the hopes that it would bring an end to the war in Asia and thus prevent a lengthy and costly land battle. Hiroshima was chosen as a target because it was a large industrial city and was home to an army depot. Prior to the bombing, Hiroshima had been virtually ignored by American forces, and Hersey relays that "a rumor was going around that the Americans were saving something special for the city." Dropped by the B-52 bomber *Enola Gay*, the bomb, dubbed "Little Boy," was the first nuclear weapon ever used in war. It destroyed a nearly five-square-mile section of the city, which was then home to an estimated population of 200,000 to 300,000 people. More than 100,000 residents would die, either from the explosion itself or from the effects of radiation in its aftermath. The bombing of Hiroshima, coupled with the bombing of Nagasaki three days later, is generally credited with bringing about Japan's surrender on August 15, 1945, effectively ending World War II.

Hersey outlines the utter devastation of the city, describing scientists' calculations that the force and temperature of the blast were so great that it exerted "5.3 to 8.0 tons per square yard" and that "gray clay tiles of the type used in Hiroshima, whose melting point is 1,300° C., had dissolved." The essay's final section describes in some detail the lingering effects of radiation sickness, among them hair loss, high fever, anemia, infection, and wounds that were slow to heal, on those who survived the blast.

At the time of *Hiroshima*'s publication a year after the bombing, Americans were still debating the merits of the decision to use the bomb. As Michael J. Yavenditti points out in a 1974 article in the *Pacific Historical Review*, many Americans, convinced by widespread reports downplaying the power of atomic weapons and suggesting that much of the damage in Hiroshima resulted from the poor construction of its buildings, had become apathetic to the event and its victims. Hersey's great achievement, he suggests, was to force readers to reconsider their feelings about the bomb, in part by convincing them that "atomic bombing was qualitatively different from other kinds of bombings."

Prior to writing *Hiroshima*, Hersey had won praise for his war reporting and his novel writing, both of which informed the essay. His factual approach to the crisis reflects his journalistic training. In composing the essay, however, Hersey drew his primary inspiration not from other works of nonfiction but from Thornton Wilder's 1927 novel *The Bridge of San Luis Rey*, to which it has subsequently been compared. Like Wilder's novel, which tells the story of a group of characters whose lives intersect in the aftermath of a tragic bridge collapse, *Hiroshima* follows several parallel stories at once, tracing a diverse group of bomb survivors' experiences as they unfold over time. The work has also drawn comparisons to a range of other texts, including Robert Browning's historical verse novel *The Ring and the Book* (1868–69).

THEMES AND STYLE

Survival is a central theme of Hersey's essay. He alludes to the complex nature of survival in the essay's opening paragraph, in which he explains that "a hundred thousand people were killed by the atomic bomb, and these six were among the survivors. They still wonder why they lived when so many others died." This survivor's guilt is most notably embodied in Reverend Tanimoto, who, as he makes his way among Hiroshima's badly injured, feels the need to apologize for his relative fortune, telling them, "Excuse me for having no burden like yours." At the same time that they wonder why they escaped death, however, each of Hersey's subjects demonstrates strength and resiliency in the face of overwhelming devastation, going on with life because, in the words of Mrs. Nakamura, "It can't be helped." Such determination is epitomized by Dr. Sasaki, who, when the bomb first went off, "ducked down on one knee and said to himself, as only a Japanese would, 'Sasaki, *gambre*! Be brave.'" While in moments such as this one Hersey identifies what he sees to be distinctly Japanese reactions to adversity, the essay also emphasizes that one of the most remarkable things about the six survivors is how ordinary, and human, they ultimately are. Mrs. Nakamura worries about how she will provide for her children, Dr. Fujii mourns the loss of the hospital he had worked so hard to build, and Reverend Tanimoto is hurt by rumors that he is an American sympathizer and is not to be trusted.

Stylistically, the essay has drawn recognition for its unique narrative structure. It notably begins by describing in rapid succession the position of each of Hersey's six subjects just before the bomb exploded at 8:15 in the morning on August 6. It then circles back to the first of the six subjects, Reverend Tanimoto, detailing his experience at the time the bomb went off before moving on to do the same for each of the other five survivors. This pattern continues, as Hersey traces each person's experiences through each of the time periods that constitute the essay's four sections: the explosion ("A Noiseless Flash"), the ensuing fire that ravaged much of Hiroshima ("The Fire"), the confusion over the mysteriously destructive bomb ("Details Are Being Investigated"), and the lingering effects of radiation ("Panic Grass and Feverfew," named for the plants that began to grow rampantly in the city). At times the lives of the survivors intersect: Dr. Sasaki is one of the first to attempt to treat the badly broken

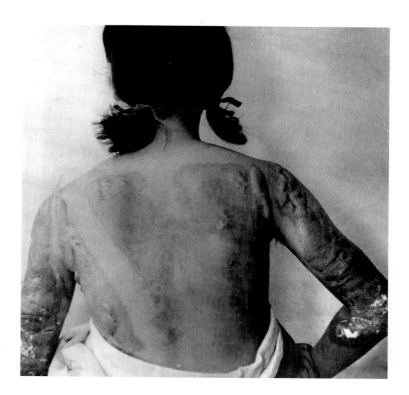

leg of the tin-factory worker who shares his last name; Reverend Tanimoto helps Mrs. Nakamura and her children reach safety; Father Kleinsorge advises Mrs. Nakamura about how best to support her family and visits Miss Sasaki during her recovery, eventually converting her to Catholicism.

The interconnected tales of the survivors are told in a straightforward, journalistic tone that shows the influence of Hemingway's works of the 1920s. The style of both writers owed much to their background as journalists, which had honed their ability to say much with few words. In writing his essay, Hersey aimed to give voice to the people of Hiroshima and to invite American readers to reflect on and draw their own conclusions about the use of atomic weapons. At times the work is deeply ironic, but it is never overtly judgmental or moralizing. Throughout, Hersey is careful to present his subject matter without editorializing, although he does include the subjects' own reflections on the event, including the reaction of Mrs. Nakamura and her family to rumors that the bomb had deposited poison in the city, rumors that "aroused them to more hatred and resentment of America than they had felt all through the war." Hersey's approach has drawn praise and criticism alike. While some commentators complained that Hersey was too restrained in his treatment of atomic destruction, Yavenditti suggests that the opposite is true: "The contrast between the apparently objective simplicity of his prose and the enormity of the phenomenon he described made *Hiroshima* all the more graphic and frightening for his readers."

A Hiroshima bombing victim photographed on September 1, 1945. Her skin is covered in burn scars that show significant keloiding. John Hersey's essay "Hiroshima" details the traumatic effects of the bombing on six of its victims. © LANDOV

REVEREND KIYOSHI TANIMOTO AND THE HIROSHIMA MAIDENS

Kiyoshi Tanimoto, the Methodist minister profiled in Hersey's book, won recognition for his postwar work with the *hiroshima otome*, or "Hiroshima Maidens," who had been horribly injured as a result of the 1945 atomic bombing. In 1955 Tanimoto worked with *Saturday Review* editor Norman Cousins to bring the women to the United States for corrective surgery. Although the Hiroshima Maidens Project was somewhat controversial in both Japan and the United States, Cousins and Tanimoto believed it would help promote understanding between the two nations. The women lived with volunteer host families while undergoing surgical procedures. Two of them appeared on the American television show *This Is Your Life*, bringing widespread attention to their plight for the first time. The Hiroshima Maidens were also introduced to Captain Robert Lewis, the copilot of the bomber *Enola Gay*. Lewis was moved to tears by the meeting.

The results of the Hiroshima Maidens Project were ultimately mixed. One woman died during surgery, but most enjoyed improved health as a result of the procedures. Years later, however, scholars have suggested that intense public scrutiny forced the women into a symbolic role (as embodiments of nuclear devastation) for which they were unprepared.

SOURCE: Foard, James H. "Vehicles of Memory: The *Enola Gay* and the Streetcars of Hiroshima." *Religion, Violence, Memory, and Place.* Ed. Oren Baruch Stier and J. Shawn Landres. Bloomington: Indiana UP, 2006. 117–31. Print.

CRITICAL DISCUSSION

Upon its publication in the *New Yorker* in the summer of 1946, *Hiroshima* was enthusiastically embraced by readers and critics alike, leading to its release in book form in November of that year. Reviewers embraced the work as an important statement about war and human resilience. Bruce Bliven of the *New Republic* declared that "Hersey's piece is certainly one of the great classics of war," going so far to suggest that "if it is eligible for a Pulitzer Prize and doesn't get it, the judges should go and take a Rorschach." Other commentators saw the essay as a dire warning about the destructive potential of future atomic warfare. Writing in the *Nation*, for example, Ruth Benedict predicted that the essay would "stir a new set of readers to an understanding that all other issues in the world today pale beside the necessity of outlawing war among the nations" (December 7, 1946).

Reviewers frequently drew attention to *Hiroshima*'s understated tone. Reviewing the work in *Queens Quarterly* in 1947, George Herbert Clarke noted that "in point of style, organization and sensitive perception, this is a memorable book. The style is clear and pure; and the organization uses balance and cross-reference with delicate skill." Where *Hiroshima* was criticized, it was generally for either appearing too sympathetic to Japan, whose forces had committed numerous atrocities during the war, or for failing to take a strong stance against atomic weaponry and what was seen to be the likely threat of its continued use.

The publication of an expanded version of the article in 1985 drew further praise for its updates on the fates of its subjects, as well as for its subtle warnings about contemporary nuclear escalation. Writing in the *Washington Post*, Chalmers M. Roberts asserted, for example, that "this little book brings the central problem of human existence today down from the often stupefying technical and theoretical to a reality no one can miss."

Although *Hiroshima* has been widely reviewed and reprinted in the decades since its original publication, it has not been subject to extensive scholarly commentary.

SOURCES

Benedict, Ruth. "The Past and the Future." Rev. of *Hiroshima*, by John Hersey. *Nation* 7 Dec. 1946: 656–58. Print.

Bliven, Bruce. Rev. of *Hiroshima*, by John Hersey. *New Republic* 9 Sept. 1946: 300–01. Print.

Clarke, George Herbert. Rev. of *Hiroshima*, by John Hersey. *Queen's Quarterly* 54.2 (1947): 251. Print.

Hersey, John. *Hiroshima.* New York: Knopf, 1985. Print.

Roberts, Chalmers M. "John Hersey Returns to Hiroshima." Rev. of *Hiroshima*, by John Hersey. *Washington Post* 11 Aug. 1985: 34. Print.

Yavenditti, Michael J. "John Hersey and the American Conscience: The Reception of 'Hiroshima.'" *Pacific Historical Review* 43.1 (1974): 24–49. Print.

FURTHER READING

Chase, Edward T. "Ross of the New Yorker Edits Hiroshima by John Hersey." *Yale Review* 88.3 (2000): 16–24. Print.

Guilfoil, Kelsey. "John Hersey: Fact and Fiction." *English Journal* 39.7 (1950): 355–60. Print.

Hersey, John. *A Bell for Adano.* New York: Knopf, 1944. Print.

Meredith, James H. *Understanding the Literature of World War II: A Student Casebook to Issues, Sources, and Historical Documents.* Westport: Greenwood, 1999. Print.

Sharp, Patrick B. "From Yellow Peril to Japanese Wasteland: John Hersey's 'Hiroshima.'" *Twentieth Century Literature* 46.4 (2000): 434–52. Print.

Takaki, Ronald. *Hiroshima: Why America Dropped the Atomic Bomb.* Boston: Little, 1995. Print.

MEDIA ADAPTATION

Valentine, John, adapt. *Hiroshima.* By John Hersey. Pacifica Radio Archives, 2004. Radio.

Greta Gard

THE HISTORIES

Herodotus

OVERVIEW

The Histories of the fifth-century-BCE Greek historian Herodotus of Halicarnassus presents the earliest-known attempt in Western literature to write a broad, accurate nonfiction record of the past. Preceded mainly by poets and mythographers, Herodotus sought to apply disciplined research to the craft of storytelling, taking as his subject the course of hostilities between the vast Persian Empire and the relatively loose affiliation of Greek city-states and what caused the animosity between them.

The Histories, organized at some point after the author's lifetime into nine chapters or books, starts with the first "of whom we know" that forcibly subjected the Greeks to foreign rule, King Croesus of Lydia (c. 560 BCE). After many lengthy digressions into the political and ethnographic backstories of most of the then-known world, *The Histories* turns to the momentous events surrounding the time of the writer's birth: the Ionian Revolt (492 BCE), in which the Greek cities along the coast of Asia Minor rebelled against Persian rule, and the subsequent, repeated Persian attempts to invade and conquer the Greek mainland between 490 and 479 BCE. This is the period that included the famous battles of Marathon, Thermopylae, Salamis, and Platea, all of which are known today primarily through Herodotus's accounts.

The importance of war as a subject worthy of exposition had clear antecedents in the Homeric epics and the heroic mythology that was pervasive in early, preliterate Greek culture. As the classical scholar Kenneth Waters has observed, the Greek escape from subjugation to the Persians dominated Greek political and cultural identity for generations, and Herodotus's public recitations of his historical writings about the Persian wars were consequently quite popular.

In researching and recounting in prose the triumph of the Greek cities over the immense invading Persian host (the size of which, among other things, Herodotus clearly exaggerates), Herodotus created a new type of literature—one that relied upon the historian's own critical evaluation of his research rather than on outside authority. This literary form aimed at turning away from mythmaking while retaining every bit of the defining national identity and pride that suffused the mythical epic poems that preceded his work.

HISTORICAL AND LITERARY CONTEXT

Herodotus was born in approximately 480 BCE in a Greek city on what is now the southeastern coast of Turkey. The place of his birth, Halicarnassus, was at that time ruled by a Persian tyrant named Lygdamis, who (according to later Roman historians) killed Herodotus's uncle Panyassis, a noted epic poet. After this Herodotus left for the island of Samos.

It is believed to be from this point that he completed his far-reaching travels around the Mediterranean that allowed him to describe in detail the distant lands of Egypt, Babylon, and Scythia in *The Histories*. Among the cities he visited was Athens, where he was paid large sums for his public appearances. In 443 BCE he traveled to the Athenian settlement at Thurii on the island of Sicily, where it is believed that he remained until his death around 425 BCE.

The date of Herodotus's writing in *The Histories* is difficult to know precisely. He produced no other known works. The scale of *The Histories* suggests that it was written over a long period, and allusions to the beginnings of the Peloponnesian War (431–404 BCE) seem to confirm that it was still a work in progress late in his life. His work was parodied in a comedy by Aristophanes in 425 BCE. And the fact that Thucydides, the great historian of the Peloponnesian War, felt compelled to begin his work precisely where Herodotus's writings left off indicates that Herodotus was very much a lasting part of the intellectual life of Athens during that city's most famous century.

When the Persian king Xerxes successfully invaded Athens in 480, his forces sacked the Acropolis and burned the Athenian temples, leaving the center of the city barren. It was not until the middle of the fifth century BCE—the period surrounding Herodotus's most likely travels to the city—that the Acropolis was beginning to be rebuilt. He had himself described in detail in book 8 of *The Histories* the Persian occupation of the Acropolis and the destruction of the temple of Athena Parthenos, the patron goddess of the city. The building of the Parthenon as it is known today took place in 447–438 BCE, and it is against this backdrop of rebuilding that Herodotus's patriotic and entertaining accounts of the Greeks turning away the great Persian army were so well received.

❖ *Key Facts*

Conflict:
Greco-Persian Wars

Time Period:
492–479 BCE

Genre:
History

THE BATTLE OF THERMOPYLAE AND THE LEGEND OF THE 300

Among the most vivid chapters in Herodotus's *Histories*, the recounting of the legendary Battle of Thermopylae has provided inspiration to artists and poets throughout history. One of the most original retellings of this fierce battle appeared in 1998, when author Frank Miller published his acclaimed graphic novel series titled *300*.

The narrative revolves around Leonidas, king of Sparta, as he rallies 300 of his best soldiers to defend the nation against a million invading Persian forces. Although overwhelmingly outnumbered, the Spartans manage to deter the enemy's progress at a range of high cliffs overlooking Thermopylae, or "Hot Gates." After two days, the Persian commander, Xerxes, offers Leonidas amnesty in exchange for his surrender; the Spartan leader refuses, however, even though he knows that defeat is inevitable. On the third day, the Spartans launch a fierce final attack on the Persians, even managing to wound Xerxes before they are finally slaughtered.

In spite of the defeat, the battle quickly assumes mythic proportions for the Spartans. Indeed, at the work's conclusion, the Spartan captain Dilios rallies his troops by recounting the story of Thermopylae before leading them to victory over the Persians at the Battle of Plataea. The graphic novel *300* eventually inspired the 2006 film adaptation of the same name, for which Miller served as technical director.

Often referred to as the father of history, Herodotus is widely credited for providing the very name still used today for research into the past. In the first line of *The Histories*, Herodotus states that he is presenting his *historiē*, or "inquiry," with the goal of preventing the deeds of men (both Greeks and foreigners) from being forgotten. Shortly after its creation, this relatively scientific approach to recounting the past was adopted by Herodotus's successor Thucydides, who completed his own *History of the Peloponnesian War* at the end of the fifth century BCE. Although their styles differed considerably, the accounts by these two historians of how the Greeks fought set the precedent for historical writing and narrative nonfiction for centuries to come.

THEMES AND STYLE

Herodotus composed *The Histories* in his native dialect of Ionian Greek and drew on the techniques of contemporary poets and dramatists. Employing artful word formations, such as *chiasmus*, *asyndeton*, and *hyperbaton*—which he used sparingly but effectively—the author follows the imperative of imposing literary craft on the presentation of his researches throughout. Writing in his influential study *Herodotus, Father of History*, John Linton Myres points out that extant fragments from the handful of contemporary storytellers, or logographers, whose interests seemed to encompass the same type of popular, anecdotal history that

Herodotus recorded, show surprisingly little stylistic resemblance, confirming that *The Histories* was, in its time, entirely novel in its style and approach.

Herodotus wrote in fairly colloquial language and often chose sensational effect over factual accuracy. His famous account of the Battle of Thermopylae, for example, in which a vastly outnumbered Greek force of a few thousand (led by the Spartan king Leonidas and his band of three hundred elite soldiers) held a high mountain pass against a Persian force of hundreds of thousands—so numerous that their arrows would block out the sun, Herodotus reports having heard—is often enlivened with such improbable, folkloric details.

His reliance upon speeches to illuminate the decisions of his characters follows epic and dramatic models and functions to explain not only the deeds of historic actors but also how their choices altered the subsequent course of human events. This practice stands in sharp contrast to the Homeric view of the past, in which divine intervention typically determines the outcome of human affairs.

Xerxes's conversations with his uncle Artabanus, for example, who stood alone among the Persians in counseling against the invasion of Greece, show the cause behind his decision to invade. Artabanus prudently counsels that the gods punish those who become too mighty and that the Persian expedition could easily be cut off from their homeland after crossing the Hellespont. Xerxes at first agrees but ultimately decides that the Greeks must be punished, he says, for burning the Persian city of Sardis during the Ionian Revolt. It is to be a mistake, as *The Histories* go on to show, but by presenting such deliberative speeches Herodotus heightens the instructive value of his work—in this case illustrating the dangers of hubris and of placing the satisfaction of retribution above all else. In this way Herodotus repeatedly uses the subject of war as an opportunity to examine the broader characteristics and frailties of human nature.

Similarly the conversation between Xerxes and the exiled Spartan king Demaratus, who becomes a valued adviser to the Persian king, drives home one of Herodotus's most prominent themes: the superiority of Greek freedom to Persian despotism. Xerxes argues that the Greek forces with whom he is preparing to engage might be better motivated if unified under a single leader whom they fear, whereupon Demaratus explains what makes the Greeks—the Spartans in particular—so formidable in battle:

> When the Spartans fight singly they are as brave as any man, but when they fight together they are supreme among all. For though they are free men, they are not free in all respects; law is the master whom they fear, far more than your subjects fear you. They do what the law commands and its command is always the same ... stand and win, or die.

Though Herodotus's fascination with the character and customs of the foreign invaders never wanes, the course of the conflict consistently reinforces the superiority of Greek virtue and how this concept of freedom under the law will forever compel the Greeks to victory.

CRITICAL DISCUSSION

From the time of Cicero, the estimation of the accuracy of Herodotus's *Histories* has swung back and forth, with the author being either praised as the father of history or pilloried as the "father of lies." Since the second half of the twentieth century, however, the former view prevailed, with scholars finding support for his research in the sparse Persian accounts and developing a renewed appreciation for his profound curiosity and skillful storytelling.

For an overtly patriotic history of war, there is an uncommon degree of ethnography in Herodotus's writing and what many have identified as a relatively modern-seeming appreciation for the cultures that the Greeks were exposed to during the Persian conflict. Writing in his influential 1988 study, *The Mirror of Herodotus*, François Hartog argues that Herodotus found a new way of examining Greek culture through contrast with alien societies.

The Scythians, for example (the previous victorious enemy of the Persians), were for his Greek audience an unimaginably exotic, nomadic (and, therefore, seemingly culture-less) society that achieved success against the massive Persian army through evasive tactics and, more important, decentralized authority. By casting this relative similarity with the political organization of the Greek city-states against a backdrop of profound cultural difference, Herodotus is better able to reveal the trait he considered central to retaining freedom from foreign dominion as being one rooted in the very core of human experience.

Herodotus often ascribes noble, even superior characteristics to foreign cultures, the Persians included. When Xerxes weeps after surveying his vast forces from a hilltop, because he realizes that in spite of their glory someday they will all be dead and gone, it is a touching, universally understood sentiment that animates the Persian king in a more sympathetic light than Herodotus ever casts on his Greek counterparts. Herodotus also devotes the very last lines of *The Histories* to a flashback in which the Persian king Cyrus wisely warns an adviser against the perils of imperialism. The Persians are portrayed here (as elsewhere in *The Histories*) as a culture in possession of great wisdom but one that suffers from hubris and the mistaken belief in the limitless power of its emperor, which makes its downfall inevitable.

Such warnings against expansionism must, in Herodotus's time, have seemed a direct criticism of the Delian League, the post-Persian Greek alliance that grew rapidly during the mid-fifth-century BCE

Ship dashed against ship, till the Persian dead strewed the deep 'like flowers'

into a de facto Athenian empire. For an analysis of this criticism as it recurs throughout *The Histories*, see J. Evans's essay "The Imperialist Impulse" in *Herodotus, Explorer of the Past*, in which Evans explains that Herodotus's audience would likely have felt that a continuum of vengeance extended directly from the end of *The Histories* into the contemporary struggles of their own time between the centers of power in Greece itself.

Among the preeminent modern studies of Herodotus are Henry Immerwahr's 1966 study *Form and Thought in Herodotus*, Charles Fornara's *Herodotus: An Interpretive Essay* (1971), and John Linton Myres's 1953 book *Herodotus, Father of History*. Among translations into English, several are excellent, though David Grene's is noteworthy for its fidelity to the original Greek text. *The Landmark Herodotus*, translated by Andrea Purvis and edited by Robert Strassler, first appeared in 2007. Its copious notes and maps illuminate the historical background of the expansive text.

The turning point in the Greco-Persian Wars, which are the subject of Herodotus's *The Histories*, was the Battle of Salamis (480 BCE), in which the Greek fleet of only 370 Vessels Triumphed Over The Persian Fleet Of More Than 1,000 Vessels. Illustration By Walter Crane. © MARY EVANS PICTURE LIBRARY/EDWIN WALLACE COLLECTION/ EVERETT COLLECTION.

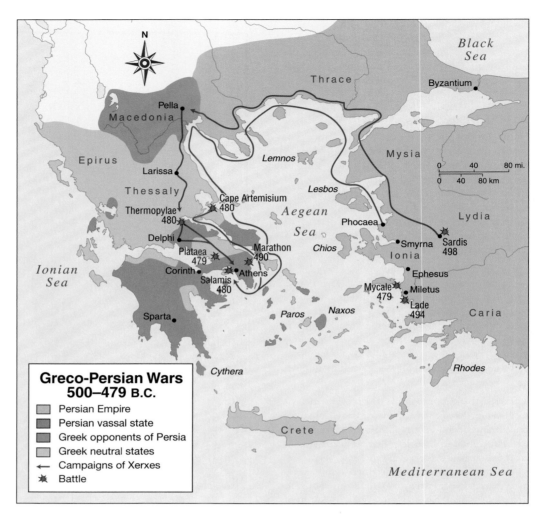

Greco-Persian Wars
500–479 B.C.
- Persian Empire
- Persian vassal state
- Greek opponents of Persia
- Greek neutral states
- ← Campaigns of Xerxes
- ✳ Battle

© MAP BY XNR PRODUCTIONS. CENGAGE LEARNING, GALE.

SOURCES

Evans, James A. S. *Herodotus, Explorer of the Past.* Princeton: Princeton UP, 1991. Print.

Hartog, François. *The Mirror of Herodotus.* Berkeley: U of California P, 1988. Print.

Myres, John Linton. *Herodotus, Father of History.* Oxford: Clarendon, 1953. Print.

Waters, Kenneth H. *Herodotus the Historian.* Norman: U of Oklahoma P, 1985. Print.

FURTHER READING

Brown, Irene. "Herodotus and the Strength of Freedom." *History Today* 31.2 (1981): 5–10. Web. Academic Search Premier. 22 July 2011.

Fornara, Charles. *Herodotus: An Interpretive Essay.* Oxford: Clarendon, 1971. Print.

Grant, Michael. *The Ancient Historians.* New York: Barnes, 1994. Web. *Google Book Search.* 13 Aug. 2011.

Green, Peter. *The Greco-Persian Wars.* Berkeley: U of California P, 1996. Print.

Herodotus. *The History.* Trans. David Grene. Chicago: U of Chicago P, 1988. Print.

Immerwahr, Henry R. *Form and Thought in Herodotus.* Cleveland: Case Western Reserve UP, 1966. Print.

Lateiner, Donald. *The Historical Method of Herodotus.* Toronto: U of Toronto P, 1989. Print.

Olmstead, A. T. *History of the Persian Empire.* Chicago: U of Chicago P, 1948. Print.

Romm, James. *Herodotus.* New Haven: Yale UP, 1998. Print.

Thomas, Rosalind. *Herodotus in Context: Ethnography, Science and the Art of Persuasion.* Cambridge: Cambridge UP, 2002. Print.

Thomas Colligan

HISTORIES

Tacitus

OVERVIEW

The *Histories* of the Roman historian Tacitus (in full, Publius [or Gaius] Cornelius Tacitus), written in 106–107 CE, were originally composed as fourteen books covering the rise and rule of the Flavian dynasty of Roman emperors, Vespasian, Titus, and Domitian, who held power from 69–96 CE. Today only the first four books and part of the fifth survive, restricting the *Histories* to the events of 69–70 CE and the particularly volatile period of Roman history in which several contenders vied for control of the empire. It addresses, most famously, the "year of the four emperors" (69 CE), in which Galba, Otho, and Vitellus each briefly held power over the principate, only to meet with violent ends. the senate declared Vespasian emperor in December of that year. This bloody transitional period of civil strife followed the suicide of the emperor Nero in 68. Nero's death marked the end of the first imperial family line of Rome—the Julio-Claudian dynasty—begun with the first emperor, Augustus, in 31 BCE.

The *Histories* today are generally overshadowed by Tacitus's greatest and final work, the *Annals*, which recounted, in similarly rigorous chronological fashion, the earlier history of the Julio-Claudian emperors. The threats of internal strife that make up the bulk of the *Histories* that survived marked a period of equal if not greater significance in Roman history. 69 CE was, as Tacitus describes it "a period rich in disasters, frightful in its wars, torn by civil strife … almost the last year of the Roman state." Covering conspiracies, assassinations, the burning of the Roman capitol—not by foreign invaders, but by Roman citizens—Tacitus's *Histories* stands as a potent document of the corrosive effects of supreme power being bestowed upon a single man. it is written in the swift, efficient style of the writer considered by many to have been the greatest of all Roman historians.

HISTORICAL AND LITERARY CONTEXT

Relatively little is known about the life of Tacitus. He is believed to have been born in northern Italy or southern France to a family of the elite equestrian order and to have begun his rise through the *cursus honorum*—the traditional sequence of public offices—as a quaestor (financial supervisor) during the reign of Titus. He was admitted to the senate shortly thereafter,

and following a hiatus in public service during which he is believed to have completed much of his writing (including the *Histories*), he was elevated to one of the empire's most prestigious governorships in Asia in 112–113. Following his return from the East, Tacitus published his final work, the *Annals*. Taken together, the *Histories* and the *Annals* originally formed a comprehensive record of Roman political history from the time of Augustus's death (14 CE) to the end of Domitian's reign in 96.

Tacitus published three minor works during his hiatus from public service: the *Germania*, an ethnographic description of the various German tribes; the *Agricola*, a biography of his father-in-law, Gnaeus Julius Agricola, the general and governor most responsible for expanding the empire in Great Britain; and the brief *Dialogus de oratibus*, a meditation on the art of rhetoric, of which Tacitus was an acknowledged master in his own time.

The tradition of annalistic history—the rigidly chronological recording of political affairs of the state—was longstanding in Roman historiography, beginning at least as early as the second century BCE with historians such as Cassius Hemina and Calpurnius Piso. In the Augustan era, Livy completed his monumental *History of Rome* in 142 books recounting the city's past from the year of its founding. Writing during the reign of Augustus, Livy brought rhetorical techniques and psychological interpretation to the annalistic tradition. Tacitus picked up these traits in writing his *Histories* and the *Annals*, though Tacitus's work remained considerably less ornate both in style and structure.

At the time of the events described in the beginning of the *Histories*, Tacitus was approximately thirteen years old. He thus relied heavily on the work of previous chroniclers (perhaps most notably that of Pliny the Elder) as well as firsthand accounts (most probably those of his father-in-law, Agricola), though the momentous events of that era surely would have been memorable even for an adolescent. In the first chapter of the *Histories*, Tacitus outlines the events to be covered. The period spanned three civil wars (Otho vs. Vitellius, Vitellius vs. Vespasian, and Domitian vs. Antonius Saturninus), each of which brought fighting to the streets of Rome. The northern frontiers of the empire in the Balkans and in Gaul were beginning

+ *Key Facts*

Conflict:
Flavian Dynasty

Time Period:
1st Century

Genre:
History

THE SILENCE OF WAR

In his *Histories*, a chronicle of Roman imperial rule during the first century CE, Tacitus argues that the empire must rely on the leadership of a strong emperor with the ability to centralize political power in order to survive. British playwright John Arden offers a radically different interpretation of the Roman Empire in his satirical novel *Silence Among the Weapons* (1982). Shortlisted for the Man Booker Prize, the novel follows the adventures of Ivory, a Roman theatrical agent whose career becomes derailed amidst political upheavals in Italy and Central Asia during the first century BCE. The novel depicts the violence and chaos that reigned throughout this period, while also providing a glimpse into the lives of the ordinary Roman citizens who were subject to forces beyond their control. Although set more than a century before the events recounted by Tacitus, Arden's novel addresses similar themes of imperial ambition during an era of great transition in early European history. At the same time, Arden's work stands as an allegory of political manipulation and intrigue in the twentieth century, in particular the various U.S. interventions in Latin America in the post-World War II era. The title derives from the Latin dictum *Inter arma silent leges*. Commonly attributed to Cicero, a first-century BCE Roman statesman and political philosopher, it translates roughly as "In times of war, the laws fall silent."

to fray. The Suebians (in modern day Germany), the Sarmatians (Iran), and the Dacian (Romania) all challenged Roman authority. Under the emperor Vespasian, Tacitus describes the beginning of a period about which he feels optimistic—including the final suppression of the Great Jewish Revolt, which was brought to a brutal conclusion in Jerusalem by Vespasian's son Titus in 70 CE. His optimism likely waned, however, in the now missing chapters of the *Histories* covering the broad persecutions that took place under the emperor Domitian. His "reign of terror," as Tacitus famously called it in the introduction to the *Histories*, saw at least twenty of Tacitus's colleagues in the senate executed, and as he writes in the second chapter of the first book, "The Mediterranean swarmed with exiles and its rocky islets ran with blood … rank, wealth, and office, whether surrendered or retained provided grounds for accusation, and the reward for virtue was inevitable death."

THEMES AND STYLE

With his *Annals*, Tacitus wrote of a relatively peaceful period in Rome under the Julio-Claudian emperors. The enemies Rome confronted were foreign, and conflict generally was kept far away from the peace of the city. With the *Histories*, however, Tacitus writes of a period in which Rome's enemies come from within. Galba, Otho, and Vitellius were all three leaders of frontier legions who marched upon the city to claim the throne, and such internal struggles provided the historian with a unique opportunity to examine both the nature and existence of the principate and what particular qualities were required of its ruler.

For the first time since the founding of the principate under Augustus, an emperor had to be named from outside the line of a dynastic succession. Tacitus appears to have been pessimistic about Rome's ability to find a good emperor. The civil wars demonstrate the corruption of the times, and throughout the *Histories*, Romans are forced to stand by in horror of the bloody drama unfolding in the streets before them. For the first time, these battles were not fought on some periphery of the empire (as at Actium) but at the very core of their social order.

Galba, Otho, and Vitellius each seem less fit for rule than the one before. Galba and Otho are doomed by their own hubris. Tacitus persistently describes Vitellus as a hopeless glutton. Moral decline had infected the ranks of the powerful, an affliction Tacitus attributes to the size and grandeur of the empire. "From time immemorial, man has had an instinctive love of power. With the growth of our empire this instinct has become a dominant and uncontrollable force," he writes.

Only Vespasian, he writes in the *Histories*, became better after he became emperor, and in Vespasian Tacitus begins to show optimism about the principate. Although Tacitus repeatedly praises the freedoms of the Republic and openly expresses a preference that power reside with the senate, he acknowledges that these are different times. As Herbert Benario observes in his comprehensive 1975 study, Tacitus consistently uses the word *principatus* with no apparent judgment, but he uses the word *dominatio*—"personal power without limit" (as a master's authority over his slaves or that of the paterfamilias over his wife and children)— to express the quality of governance opposite that of the traditional Roman value of *libertas*. Tacitus uses the term not only to describe Otho and Vitellius but also the Jewish "despots" of Jerusalem, for whom Tacitus displays deep contempt.

The credibility of Tacitus, a senator whose career had begun and prospered under the Flavian emperors, is questionable on certain matters. Anticipating the charge of bias he says in his introduction that he writes *neque amore et sine odio* ("without partiality and without hatred,"). Though he thoughtfully supports his claim of objectivity throughout the *Histories*, he fails to convince. The pro-Flavian bias is noteworthy through the extant portion of the *Histories*, but a foreshadowing to the later (now lost) books addressing the reign of Domitian suggest that the work might have presented a harsher view of the principate.

Tacitus's prose style is frequently observed to be similar to that of first century BCE Roman historian Sallust, who also wrote in a swift-moving, efficient style. It is this inclination toward brevity that often led Tacitus to pithy, epigrammatic statements. In the closing of his passage about the death of the emperor Galba, for instance, he effectively summarizes the man in a single sentence: "he seemed too great a man to be one, and by common consent possessed the makings of a ruler—had he never ruled."

CRITICAL DISCUSSION

Because of his demonstrated hostility towards Christians and Jews, Tacitus's work was not widely read in the Middle Ages. It regained appreciation in the Renaissance for its rich descriptions of imperial life. Tacitus has since been consistently acknowledged for having produced among the very highest quality Latin prose writing. In his essay "Of the Art of Discussion," sixteenth-century French philosopher Michel de Montaigne praises the *Histories* as "not a book to read[—] it is a book to study and learn; it is so full of maxims that you find of every sort, both right and wrong; it is a nursery of ethical and political reflections for the provision and adornment of those who hold a place in the management of the world." Another of his greatest admirers was the eighteenth-century English historian Edward Gibbon, who took Tacitus as his model and writes in one of his essays that his predecessor was alone in having risen to the level of a "philosophical historian." Gibbon continues, "Tacitus makes use of the dominion of eloquence of the heart, only to show you the connexion of the chain of events, and to instil into your mind the lessons of wisdom."

Ronald Syme, whose 1958 two-volume study *Tacitus* remains the definitive work on the subject, observes of the *Histories* that their organization and artful transitions display "perfect control." Syme points to eloquent speeches in the text that he calls "pure invention" and to events that are inaccurately condensed for the purpose of storytelling, but he roundly praises the historian for his ability to draw his characters in detail. On the subject of Tacitus's claims of impartiality, Syme writes, "History with Romans, never a subject of disinterested inquiry, could not be emancipated from political and moral preoccupations." And Syme comfortably overlooks inaccuracies in the *Histories* for the benefits to narrative. Tacitus's dramatic description of the burning of the temple of Jupiter on the Capitoline hill, for example, achieved its tremendous emotional force for Roman audiences by contrasting the sacrilegious fire of Vespasian's troops with the long pageant of visitors to this spot from a more perfect, more pious Roman past. Syme concludes: "To the power and splendour of Tacitus as a painter of historical scenes, no paraphrase or enumeration does justice."

Tacitus is not, however, without his harsh critics. The early twentieth-century Oxford historian R. G. Collingwood writes in his influential papers on historiography that Tacitus "coupled a contempt for peaceful administration with an admiration for conquest and military glory, an admiration blinded by his remarkable ignorance of the actualities of warfare." Collingwood defines Tacitus's approach as "psychological-didactic," relying on exaggeratedly good and exaggeratedly bad characters to draw moral lessons, without ever engaging in the work of trying to "re-enact in his own mind the experience of the people whose actions he is narrating."

The Oath of the Batavians. From the History of Tacitus, Claudius Civilis leads the conspiracy of the Batavians against Roman Emperor Vespasian. Painted for the Amsterdam City Hall. 1662. © ERICH LESSING / ART RESOURCE, NY

SOURCES

Benario, Herbert. *An Introduction to Tacitus*. Athens: U of Georgia P, 1975. Print.

Collingwood, Robin G. *The Idea of History*. Oxford: Oxford UP, 1993. Print.

Montaigne, Michel de. "Of the Art of Discussion." *The Complete Essays of Montaigne*. Trans. D. Frame. Stanford: Stanford UP, 1958. 3:8:719. Print.

Sheffield, J., ed. "Essay on the Study of Literature." *Miscellaneous Works of Edward Gibbon*. London: Blake, 1837. *Google Book Search*. Web. 6 Nov. 2011.

Syme, Ronald. *Tacitus*. London: Oxford UP, 1958. Print.

Tacitus, Cornelius. *Tacitus: The Histories*. Trans. K. Wellesley. New York: Viking, 1986. Print.

FURTHER READING

Classen, C. J. "Tacitus—Historian Between Republic and Principate," *Mnemosyne* 41 (1988): 93–116. Print.

Dudley, Donald. *The World of Tacitus*. London: Secker, 1968. Print.

Livy. *Ab urbe condita*. Trans. B. O. Foster. Cambridge: Harvard UP, 1919. Print.

Martin, Ronald. *Tacitus*. Berkeley: U of California P, 1981. Print.

Mellor, Ronald. *Tacitus*. New York: Routledge, 1993. Print.

Mendell, Clarence. *Tacitus: The Man and His Work*. New Haven: Yale UP, 1957. Print.

Sallust. *The war with Jugurtha*. Trans. J. C. Rolfe. Cambridge: Harvard UP, 1995. Print.

Tom Colligan

THE HISTORY OF THE PELOPONNESIAN WAR
Thucydides

OVERVIEW

The History of the Peloponnesian War is a work of non-fiction that chronicles the major events and figures of a war between the Greek city states of Athens and Sparta. The conflict, which stretched from 431 BCE to 404 BCE, was marked by long sieges. Atrocities were committed on both sides, creating devastation that was unparalleled in Greek history. The *History*, which is believed to have been organized into its present form by medieval editors, traces the war from its roots in Greece's distant past to 411 BCE, where the book breaks off in midsentence, never to be finished. The text was composed by Thucydides, an affluent Greek general who was exiled in 423 BCE after he was outmaneuvered by a Spartan commander in what was a devastating blow to the Greek cause. Thucydides drew on his personal experiences to compose the text. Although it was informed by both Athenian and Peloponnesian sources, the work has subsequently sparked much debate about the author's ability to present an unbiased account of the conflict.

Influenced by the logic and rhetoric of Sophist philosophy and the methodology of early Greek medical writings, Thucydides's *History* rejects mythologizing views of history in favor of fact and is notable for its early articulation of doctrines associated with political realism. Offering extended commentary on the frequent conflict between morality and power, the work has had a profound and global effect on philosophies of war, notably influencing prominent figures as diverse as Italian political theorist Niccolò Machiavelli (1469–1527) and American presidents Thomas Jefferson (1743–1826) and Woodrow Wilson (1856–1924).

HISTORICAL AND LITERARY CONTEXT

When decades-old tensions between Athens and Sparta ignited into warfare in 431 BCE, Thucydides sensed correctly that it would be a historically important conflict. By the time it drew to an end in 404 BCE, the lengthy war had radically changed Greece, bringing widespread destruction to urban areas and much of the countryside, impoverishing many citizens, and effectively ending Greece's golden age. The conflict transformed Athens from a position of superiority to one of subservience, from which it never fully recovered.

Modern knowledge of the Peloponnesian War has been deeply affected by Thucydides's account of it. Although in his day it was commonly believed that the war was caused by the refusal of the Athenian leader Pericles to lift trade restrictions against one of Sparta's allies, Thucydides questions this perspective, insisting that the origins of the war were far more complex, rooted in the history of the region and the imbalance of power between Athens and its neighbors.

The war is generally divided into three distinct phases, and it is largely due to Thucydides's influence that these phases are viewed as a single war rather than a series of related wars. At the heart of the conflict was the growing power of Athens and its allies (the Delian League), which was seen by Sparta and its allies in the Peloponnesian League as a threat that needed to be checked. The first major phase of the war began with Sparta's attacks on areas under Athenian control. After a brief lull during the Peace of Nicias in 421 BCE, fighting again broke out between the two factions in 415 BCE. The Athenians launched an expedition to Sicily to defend their allies there from the perceived aggression of the Peloponnesians. The conflict between Sparta and Athens reignited, fueled in part by the defection of the Athenian general Alcibiades. Alcibiades subsequently played on Sparta's fears about the spread of Athenian influence, intending to incite Sparta to enter the conflict. This phase of the war eventually ended with the destruction of the Athenian expeditionary forces, further reducing the power and reach of the Athenian empire. The defeat ushered in the third phase of the war, in which Sparta, now receiving support from Persia, undercut Athens's naval power and eventually claimed victory in 404 BCE.

Many scholars consider Thucydides's *History* the first attempt at rigorous historical scholarship. It builds, however, on a Greek literary tradition that stretches back to Homer (c. eighth century BCE), whose epic poems the *Iliad* and the *Odyssey* had chronicled the Trojan War and its aftermath. A more contemporary influence on the text was the work of Herodotus (c. 484–c. 425 BCE), who is generally considered the first Greek historian. Thucydides rejected both the form and the content of these earlier works, eschewing poetic language in favor of unadorned, factual prose. He also broke with tradition by marking time not in accordance with leaders' reigns, but by

✤ *Key Facts*

Conflict:
Peloponnesian War

Time Period:
5th Century BCE

Genre:
History

THE POWER OF ORATION IN WARTIME

One of the key passages in Thucydides's *History of the Peloponnesian War* comes in book 2, when the statesman Pericles delivers the annual funeral oration in honor of the Athenian war dead. Among the most influential military speeches in history, Pericles's address commemorates the Athenian soldiers who have fallen in the war against Sparta while also spurring the people to continue the battle. The oration formed part of an elaborate funeral ritual conducted in ancient Athens that included a procession and symbolic burial and culminated with a speech. While Thucydides attributes the speech to Pericles, he takes pains to note that the wording is an approximation. For this reason, while historians generally agree that Thucydides was likely present at the funeral ceremony where Pericles spoke, they remain divided on the exact content of the statesman's oration.

Stylistically, the speech is characterized by its linguistic complexity, employing a wide range of rhetorical techniques and figures of speech. The address is particularly noteworthy for its emphasis on the greatness of Athens itself, as Pericles relates the bravery of the city's fallen heroes to what they fought to preserve. One of the most stirring moments in the oration comes at the end, when Pericles issues his famous challenge to the surviving Athenians, calling on them to demonstrate the same bravery shown by their fallen compatriots. This aspect of the speech, in particular, has resonated with historians, who have found echoes of Pericles's stern reminder in Abraham Lincoln's Gettysburg Address.

years and seasons, which corresponded more clearly with military campaigns. The *History* is also notable for removing references to gods, which had dominated works by Thucydides's predecessors.

Scholars believe that in diverging from these older models, Thucydides was heavily influenced by both the Sophists, a group of philosophers known for their emphasis on logic and rhetoric, and the medical writings of contemporary Hippocratic philosophers. The *History* reflects the Sophist emphasis on antithesis, a rhetorical strategy in which opposing concepts are paired for effect. Like Hippocratic medical texts, it emphasizes careful observation as the foundation for argument. The Hippocratic influence is especially clear in Book 2, in which Thucydides discusses the plague that ravaged Athens during the first phase of the war.

THEMES AND STYLE

Although *The History of the Peloponnesian War* is focused primarily on the events of the twenty-seven-year conflict, it reflects on a far wider span of history. The text's first and longest book, also known as the Archaeology, examines the early history of Greece in the years leading up to the Peloponnesian War. This early history underscores the root causes of the conflict, emphasizing that the war was not caused by any one individual's actions but rather by the escalation of tensions over a long period.

Using techniques borrowed from the Sophists, Thucydides assails the common belief in Greece's former glory by suggesting that accounts of the Greek assault on Troy defy logic and reflect the exaggeration characteristic of poets (implicitly Homer). He also discredits historians (implicitly Herodotus) for favoring stories that are pleasing over ones that are true. In opposition to such models, he suggests, his work will offer an authentic account of a truly important war.

One of Thucydides's most important innovations in war literature was his exploration of the complex relationship between power and morality, which is a central theme in the *History*. The work has often been read as one of the earliest articulations of *realpolitik*, a political doctrine holding that the strong deserve to rule. Several key passages from the text have been offered in support of this view. The most notable of these occurs in the "Melian Dialogue" of Book 5, in which envoys from Athens enter into a debate with representatives of the Melians, a weaker people whom the Athenians expect to submit to their superior power. When the Melians refuse based on a belief that they have justice on their side, the Athenians dismiss the claim, emphasizing that power supersedes justice. When the Melians still refuse to yield, the Athenians slaughter all of the town's men and sell the women and children into slavery.

Many scholars have read this scene as evidence of the author's belief that moral concerns have no place in military decision making. Others, however, have suggested that Thucydides was simply articulating a common view without endorsing it and that he demonstrates a clear sympathy for the weak and the powerless in this and other passages. In a 1988 essay in the *American Political Science Review*, for example, Hayword R. Alker Jr. argues that Thucydides portrays neither side as truly in the right. Noting parallels between the use of dialogue in the *History* and contemporary tragedy, Alker suggests that "Thucydides's scientific study of power politics is essentially dramatic and ultimately tragic."

Further support for such a view can be found in the work's thematic emphasis on the physical and psychological damage caused by war. Early in the text, Thucydides outlines his belief that war breeds violence and brutality, a point he illustrates with scenes of unnecessary carnage. In Books 2 and 3, for example, he describes the effects of the Peloponnesian League's siege of Plataea, a city aligned with Athens. He describes how, upon their surrender, the Plataeans were systematically slaughtered by the victorious Peloponnesians. Even greater brutality is described in Book 7, in which Thracian forces invade the town of Mycalessus and mercilessly slaughter all of the children in the town's school.

Of particular stylistic note is Thucydides's use of oratory within his history. Although this technique was borrowed from Herodotus, Thucydides is credited with perfecting it. The work contains several speeches, attributed to prominent figures of the day. Although Thucydides may have witnessed some of the speeches he depicts, he makes it clear in the text that he had to re-create them from a sense of their content and purpose. The best known of these speeches is Pericles' funeral oration in Book 2. Given at the close of the first year of the conflict, the speech honors the Athenian dead and emphasizes the value of Athenian culture.

CRITICAL DISCUSSION

Little is known about the reception of *The History of the Peloponnesian War* among the author's contemporaries, although it appears to have carried some influence because other writers, most notably Xenophon (c. 431–350 BCE), attempted to complete it. Around 8 BCE, the work was evaluated by Greek historian Dionysius of Halicarnassus, who, though he faulted Thucydides stylistically, praised him as an innovator based on the fact that he "did not insert any of the mythical into his history, and he refused to divert his history to practice deception and magic upon the masses, as all the historians before him had done." The *History* was the subject of renewed scholarly interest in the fifteenth and sixteenth centuries, when the first Latin translations appeared in Europe and were embraced by influential thinkers as diverse as Machiavelli and British philosopher Thomas Hobbes (1588–1679).

In the nineteenth century Thucydides found an admirer in German philosopher Friedrich Nietzsche (1844–1900), who celebrated the Ancient writer's vision of power. The nineteenth century also saw an increase in speculation about the *History*'s composition, as scholars debated whether the work was composed all at once after the end of the war, or whether it was, as Thucydides suggested, written over many years and possibly subject to repeated revisions. Although this debate was never satisfactorily resolved, by the mid-twentieth century it no longer dominated scholarship. Another equally contentious debate has focused on whether Thucydides was as neutral in his depiction of the conflict as many early scholars of the work believed.

In recent years scholars have focused their attention on Thucydides's views regarding war and power. In a 1989 article in the *Review of Politics*, Michael Palmer draws parallels between the works of Thucydides and Machiavelli, arguing that there are significant distinctions between the two men's views. Discussing allegedly Machiavellian characters in the *History*, he suggests that "Thucydides wishes his most discerning readers to understand that neither these Athenian 'Machiavellians' and their 'nation,' nor any nation so conceived and so dedicated, can long endure." Other scholars have emphasized the

enduring relevance of Thucydides's work. Lawrence A. Tritle's 2006 essay "Thucydides and the Cold War," for example, explores the use of Thucydides's philosophy of war in the rhetoric surrounding the cold war. Tritle suggests that "political theorists and practitioners have regarded Thucydides as a paradigm for studying the ways of the world and the interactions of states."

Spartans asking Oracle at Delphi whether to make war against Athenians. Wood engraving 1910. © WORLD HISTORY ARCHIVE / ALAMY

SOURCES

Alker, Hayward R., Jr. "The Dialectical Logic of Thucydides' Melian Dialogue." *American Political Science Review* 82.3 (1988): 805–20. Print.

Dionysus of Halicarnassus. *On Thucydides*. Trans. W. Kendrick Pritchett. Berkeley: U of California P, 1975. Print.

Palmer, Michael. "Machiavellian virtù and Thucydidean aretē: Traditional Virtue and Political Wisdom in Thucydides." *Review of Politics* 51.3 (1989): 365–85. Print.

Tritle, Lawrence A. "Thucydides and the Cold War." *Classical Antiquity and the Politics of America: From George Washington to George W. Bush.* Ed. Michael Meckler. 127–40. Print.

FURTHER READING

Cornford, Francis M. *Thucydides Mythistoricus.* Philadelphia: U of Pennsylvania P, 1971. Print.

Dewald, Carolyn J. *Thucydides's War Narrative: A Structured Study.* Berkeley: U of California P, 2005. Print.

Forde, Steven. "Thucydides on Ripeness and Conflict Resolution." *International Studies Quarterly* 48.1 (2004): 177–95. Print.

Gromme, A. W. *A Historical Commentary on Thucydides.* 5 volumes. London: Clarendon, 1945–81. Print.

Hornblower, Simon. *Thucydides.* Baltimore: Johns Hopkins UP, 1987. Print.

Orwin, Clifford. "Piety, Justice, and the Necessities of War: Thucydides' Delian Debate." *American Political Science Review* 83.1 (1989): 233–39. Print.

Plutarch. *The Rise and Fall of Athens: Nine Greek Lives.* Trans. Ian Scott-Kilvert. Harmondsworth: Penguin, 1960. Print.

———. *On Sparta.* Trans. Richard J. A. Talbert. Harmondsworth: Penguin, 1960. Print.

Pouncey, Peter R. "Human Nature at War in Thucydides." *The Necessities of War: A Study of Thucydides's Pessimism.* 139–50. New York: Columbia UP, 1980. Print.

Romilly, Jacqueline de. *Thucydides and Athenian Imperialism.* Trans. P. Thody. Oxford: Blackwell, 1963. Print.

MEDIA ADAPTATION

The War That Never Ends. Dir. Jack Gold. Perf. Ben Kingsley, David Calder, Nathaniel Parker. British Broadcasting Corporation, 1991. Television movie.

Greta Gard

The History of the Rebellion and Civil Wars in England, Begun in the Year 1641

Edward Hyde

OVERVIEW

Edward Hyde, 1st Earl of Clarendon, was both a central player in the English Civil Wars and one of the period's earliest historians. The book now generally called *The History of the Rebellion and Civil Wars in England* is actually a combination of two quite different works created under very different circumstances and published in a form Clarendon never intended. He wrote what he titled *A True Historical Narration of the Rebellion and Civil Wars in England* between 1646 and 1648 while in exile in France. Using his personal knowledge of the political events of the 1620s and 1630s, he detailed the causes and incidents of the 1642–46 civil war between King Charles I and the British Parliament. He was able to fill the gaps in his account by obtaining information from others, most notably from his friend Lord Hopton and from King Charles I himself. In addition, Clarendon had access to many of the official documents he had written on behalf of the king and was able to incorporate them into the work. Twenty years later, when Clarendon began writing a personal memoir during a second exile, he was dependent on memory. The portions of the combined book that date from this period are more literary in style, less accurate in their details, and more direct in their historical judgments.

Clarendon's works remained unpublished until thirty years after his death, which occurred in 1674. Between 1702 and 1704 his sons combined Clarendon's *History* and his autobiographical writing into a single three-volume work and released it as part of a publishing battle between the Tory and Whig parties, respective political heirs to the Royalist (supporting King Charles I) and Parliamentarian sides in the civil war. Published in 1698, the *Memoirs of Edmund Ludlow* (c. 1617–92), was seen as a Whig historical manifesto. Clarendon's *History of the Rebellion and Civil Wars in England* was published as a Tory rebuttal.

Clarendon never meant his history to be simply a defense of Royalist views. First elected to the House of Commons in 1640, he was part of the reformist movement that tried to correct the misgovernment of Charles I. When the relationship between Parliament and the king broke down and turned into civil war, however, Clarendon joined the king, arguing that Parliament's increasingly desperate efforts to gain control of the country were the greater threat to the constitution.

The first two sections of the book are devoted to a detailed examination of the failures of both the Royalists and Parliament. The profits from the book's sales were dedicated to rebuilding the fortunes of the University of Oxford's printing house, which became known as the Clarendon Press.

HISTORICAL AND LITERARY CONTEXT

The English Civil War grew out of parliamentary opposition to the increasing power of the crown. When Charles I inherited the throne in 1625, he quickly found himself at odds with Parliament over his imposition of unconstitutional taxes and his leniency toward English Catholics. In 1628 Parliament passed *The Petition of Right* listing its grievances against the king. Charles responded by dissolving Parliament.

The king ruled without a Parliament for eleven years, relying instead on the advice of his French Catholic queen and the conservative Anglican bishop William Laud. In 1637, desiring uniformity among the churches of the realm, Laud convinced the king to impose a pre-Reformation version of the Anglican liturgy on Calvinist Scotland that included governance by bishops. The Church of Scotland resolved to reject the liturgy and depose the bishops, setting off a rebellion known as the Bishops' Wars of 1639 and 1640. Unable to pay for the wars, Charles reconvened Parliament in 1640 as a last resort, hoping to raise money quickly. After only a few weeks, however, he disbanded what is now called the Short Parliament, alarmed at the scale of the concessions the members demanded in return for funding the war against Scotland. Seven months later the beleaguered king was forced to convene what became known as the Long Parliament.

Hyde (not yet Earl of Clarendon) was elected to both the Short and the Long Parliaments. Although critical of the king's fiscal policies, he resisted Parliament's attempts to abolish the royal prerogatives. After the 1641 publication of a Parliamentary manifesto known as *The Grand Remonstrance*, Hyde tried unsuccessfully to reconcile the king and Parliament. By 1642 the differences between the two sides had escalated into civil war. The king attempted and failed to arrest the

Key Facts

Conflict:
English Civil Wars

Time Period:
Mid-17th Century

Genre:
History

THE GREAT TEW CIRCLE

Edward Hyde was deeply influenced by the group of poets, theologians, philosophers, and scholars that his friend Lucius Cary, the 2nd Viscount Falkland, brought together between 1633 and 1639 at his house at Great Tew. Both Oxford dons and members of the London literati came to use Falkland's impressive library and discuss their conclusions in congenial surroundings. Ben Jonson, Thomas Hobbes, George Sandys, and Isaak Walton were all members of the informal group at various times.

Writing a tribute to Falkland in his history, Hyde remembered his days at Great Tew as some of the happiest in his life.

He dubbed the group "the Great Tew Circle" and claimed that he learned more there than he had in his time at Oxford, stating that Falkland's guests came "to study in a purer air, finding all the books they could desire in his library and all the persons together whose company they could wish and not find in other society."

The group was interested in issues of theology and political philosophy as well as literature. Regular topics of discussion included the roles of reason and authority in religion, the nature of the Anglican church, and what the relationship between the church and the civil government of England should be.

leaders of Parliament, then fled London and raised his standard at Nottingham. During the first stage of the war, Hyde served as one of Charles I's chief advisers. After four years of fighting, Parliament gained the upper hand, and in 1646 Charles was forced to surrender. His son, Prince Charles, escaped to the continent and was followed by Hyde. After another two years of inconclusive negotiations over religious toleration and constitutional issues, including Parliament's control over taxation and limits on royal prerogatives, Parliament put the king on trial and executed him in early 1649.

In 1651 Scotland crowned Prince Charles as their king. From then Hyde established himself as the king-in-exile's most prominent aide. In 1660 Charles returned to England and was restored to the throne as King Charles II of England. Hyde was made Baron Hyde in 1660 and Earl of Clarendon in 1661. As Lord Chancellor under Charles II, Clarendon tried to find middle ground between former Royalists and Parliamentarians, making enemies among both. In 1667 he became the focus of a court conspiracy. Falsely accused of treason, he fled to France. Although Clarendon died in exile, he was the grandfather of two English queens. His daughter Anne married the Duke of York, later James II. Their daughters succeeded to the throne as Queen Mary and Queen Anne.

In his writing, Clarendon saw himself as working in the tradition of the Greek and Roman historians. Like many of his peers, he kept a "commonplace book" in which he recorded large extracts copied from various classical historians, among them Plutarch, Livy, Tacitus, and Thucydides. *The History of the Rebellion and Civil Wars in England* itself is full of classical allusions and quotations.

Clarendon's other avowed influence was Machiavelli, who declared that wise politicians could use history to understand the present and influence the future. According to Irene Coltman in *Private Men and Public Causes*, Clarendon noted in his commonplace books that if all histories were written by

men like Machiavelli and contained the true causes and remedies of political disease, rulers would need only to read history to become wise. He offered his own history as an analysis of what had gone wrong on the Royalist side—a book of advice about what policies should be adopted. It eventually became known as a more general "manual of advice" and guide to past mistakes for future rulers and their counselors.

During the time Clarendon wrote his works, the study of local history, using monuments, artifacts, and documents, was becoming a fashionable pastime for the educated classes. Influenced by this so-called antiquarian movement's approach to historical evidence, Clarendon supplemented his own memory and experience with those of others to the extent that he was able. Even though he was writing from exile and had limited access to public papers, he often quoted documentary evidence from both sides of the conflict in his narrative.

THEMES AND STYLE

In the opening pages of *The History of the Rebellion and Civil Wars in England*, Clarendon lays out his qualifications for writing the book:

> I may not be thought altogether an incompetent person for this communication, having been present as a member of Parliament in these councils before and till the breaking out of the Rebellion, and having since had the honour to be near two great kings in some trust.

Clarendon begins his history by assessing the errors of the past. In Book 1 he gives a narrative account of the government's errors prior to Charles I's summoning of the Long Parliament. He consistently places the responsibility on Charles's advisers rather than on the king himself. In Book 2 Clarendon provides a detailed description of a shift of power in Parliament from moderates to a more radical minority, and the subsequent transfer of power from the crown to the Parliament.

Although much of the later parts of the book deal with military action, Clarendon is more interested in the context and significance of events than in the specific details of battle. He is particularly concerned with understanding the character, motivations, and actions of individual men, believing that these shape history. He explains this in Book 7: "Celebrating the memory of eminent and extraordinary persons and transmitting their great virtues for the imitation of posterity [is] one of the principal ends and duties of history." In his introduction to the book, he is not as laudatory of all historical personages, declaring that he intends to focus on the individuals who created what he describes as this "mass of confusion."

The 130 character sketches in which he describes "the pride of this man, and the popularity of that; the levity of the one, and the morosity of another ... the spirit of craft and subtlety in some and the rude and unpolished integrity of others" are the most highly regarded sections of Clarendon's work. As George E. Miller observes in *Edward Hyde, Earl of Clarendon*, "The typical Clarendon character blends facts and judgments, balances strengths and weaknesses." Clarendon often brings his characters to life with one quick sentence. Thus the Earl of Arundel had a fine collection of rare medals but was "only able to buy them, never to understand them; and as to all parts of learning he was most illiterate." The Earl of Pembroke "paid much too dear for his wife's fortune by taking her person into the bargain."

The most vivid of his character sketches are his portraits of his best friend, Lucius Cary, the 2nd

Viscount Falkland, and "that brave bad man" Oliver Cromwell. Contrasted with what Royce MacGillivray describes in *Restoration Historians and the English Civil War* as "the pulsating life that suffuses Clarendon's satanic figure of Oliver Cromwell," his portrait of Charles I is tepid and unconvincing: "The worthiest gentleman, the best master, the best friend, the best husband, the best father and the best Christian, that the age in which he lived had produced."

CRITICAL RECEPTION

Clarendon wrote *The History of the Rebellion and Civil Wars in England* with an eye to posterity, intending that it should be published only when "the passion, rage, and fury of this time shall be forgotten."

According to Martine Watson Brownley in *Clarendon and the Rhetoric of Historical Form*, the work "immediately assumed a central place in English historiography after it appeared early in the eighteenth century. For the rest of the century, much English historical writing developed directly out of reactions to Clarendon, as historians from White Kennet to David Hume attacked, defended, annexed, or reworked the *History of the Rebellion*." It remained the subject of partisan commentary well into the nineteenth century.

Even those who disagreed with Clarendon's historical interpretations praised the literary qualities of the work, which went through at least twenty editions in the eighteenth and nineteenth centuries. His work continues to be included in anthologies of seventeenth-century writing.

Today *The History of the Rebellion and Civil Wars in England* is seen as the beginning of a tradition of

Charles I on the way to his execution, 1649. Illustration by Ernest Crofts (1847–1911). © TOWNELEY HALL ART GALLERY AND MUSEUM, BURNLEY, LANCASHIRE / THE BRIDGEMAN ART LIBRARY INTERNATIONAL

history writing that includes Edward Gibbon, Thomas Carlyle, and Thomas Babington Macaulay. It is generally considered the most important contemporary account of the English Civil War. In fact, historian Royce MacGillivray goes so far as to say that "Clarendon's *History* is so formidable an achievement that all historians writing about the war before its publication have an air of prematureness."

SOURCES

Brownley, Martine Watson. *Clarendon and the Rhetoric of Historical Form.* Philadelphia: U of Pennsylvania P, 1985. Print.

Clarendon, Edward Hyde, 1st Earl of Clarendon. *The History of the Rebellion: A New Selection.* Ed. Paul Seaward. Oxford: Oxford UP, 2009. Print.

Coltman, Irene. *Private Men and Public Causes: Philosophy and Politics in the English Civil War.* London: Faber, 1962. Print.

MacGillivray, Royce. *Restoration Historians and the English Civil War.* The Hague: Nijhoff, 1974. Print.

Miller, George E. *Edward Hyde, Earl of Clarendon.* Boston: Twayne, 1983. Print.

FURTHER READING

Fussner, Frank Smith. *The Historical Revolution: English Historical Writing and Thought, 1580–1640.* London: Routledge, 1962. Print.

Harris, R. W. *Clarendon and the English Revolution.* London: Chatto, 1983. Print.

Hicks, Philip. *Neo-Classical History and English Culture: From Clarendon to Hume.* New York: St. Martin's, 1996. Print.

Hughes, Ann. *The Causes of the English Civil War.* 2nd ed. New York: St. Martin's, 1998. Print.

Hutton, Ronald. "Clarendon's History of the Rebellion." *English Historical Review* 97.382 (1982): 70–88. Print.

Woolf, Daniel R. *The Idea of History in Early Stuart England Erudition, Ideology, and the "Light of Truth" from the Accession of James I to the Civil War.* Toronto: U of Toronto P, 1990. Print.

Woolrych, Austin. *Britain in Revolution, 1625–1660.* Oxford: Oxford UP, 2002. Print.

Wormald, B. H. G. *Clarendon—Politics, Historiography and Religion, 1640–1660.* Cambridge: Cambridge UP, 1951. Print.

Greta Gard

THE LAST OF THE MOHICANS
A Narrative of 1757
James Fenimore Cooper

OVERVIEW

James Fenimore Cooper's *The Last of the Mohicans: A Narrative of 1757*, first published in 1826, is perhaps the best known of Cooper's *Leatherstocking Tales*. In the five books of the series, Cooper traces the character of Natty Bumppo from 1740 to 1806. Bumppo, a white scout at home in the social world of Native Americans, is known by various names in different books: Deerslayer, Pathfinder, Leatherstocking, the trapper, and, in *The Last of the Mohicans*, Hawkeye. The novel takes place in 1757 during the third year of the French and Indian War, a struggle between the French, along with their Native American allies, and the British for control of the North American colonies. Cooper creates the fictional Mohican tribe and uses the figure of Hawkeye to bridge the divide between white and Native American cultures.

The Last of the Mohicans is set in the wilds of New York State in the Hudson Valley, site of several battles during the war. It traces the journey of Cora and Alice Munro from Fort Edward to Fort William Henry, where they will join their father, Colonel Munro, commander of the fort. Escorted by Major Duncan Heyward, the sisters accompany a column of reinforcements. The traveling party's Huron guide, Magua, is revealed to be a traitor allied with the French. Hawkeye and his Mohican companions, Chingachgook and his son Uncas, rescue Cora and Alice from the clutches of Magua and the Hurons twice before reuniting them with their father. Cora and Uncas fall in love. Soon after the party's arrival, Munro is forced to surrender the fort, and in the Hurons' brutal attack on the withdrawing troops, Cora and Alice are recaptured. Heyward, Hawkeye, Munro, Chingachgook, and Uncas pursue the kidnappers. Alice is rescued, but Cora and then Uncas are killed during the battle before Hawkeye finally brings down the evil Magua. Cora and Major Heyward are engaged to be married, and Chingachgook mourns his son, who was the last of the Mohicans.

Cooper's *Leatherstocking Tales* were hailed at their publications as distinctive, great American novels. In fact, *The Last of the Mohicans* became a classic, inspiring a long line of American Westerns—books that portray the struggles between Native Americans and settlers, cowboys, and bandits on the American

frontier, glorifying battles, all-out warfare, and the participants. Westerns sold as mass-market paperbacks. Like Cooper's novels, the majority of them were of dubious literary quality. Among these titles were Ann S. Stephens's *Malaeska, the Indian Wife of the White Hunter* (1860); Edward Willett's *Black Arrow, the Avenger, or Judge Lynch on the Border* (1871); and Frederick Whittaker's *Hawkeye the Hunter* (1908).

HISTORICAL AND LITERARY CONTEXT

During the colonial period the French explored the interior of North America, while English colonists settled along the East Coast. English and French fur traders on the frontier competed with one another for furs, and various Native American groups vied for the right to trade furs to the Europeans. After the Iroquois trapped all the beavers in their own lands, they declared war on neighboring Huron and Algonquin tribes, driving them westward. Because the Iroquois expansion threatened the French fur trade, the French provided weapons to the Huron and the Algonquin, while the English armed the Iroquois. As British fur traders began moving west in the 1750s, the French became alarmed; they began attacking settlements and trading posts and building forts. The French assault on Fort Necessity (under the command of then British lieutenant colonel George Washington) on July 3, 1754, officially began the French and Indian War.

The French and Indian War was part of the Seven Years' War (1756–63), a global struggle for empire between Britain and France. The Seven Years' War was the last of three wars fought between England and France between 1689 and 1763 and the only one that produced a decisive victory. The first two years of the French and Indian War saw successive British defeats, but the war took a turn toward the British in its third year, when a new secretary of state in Britain, William Pitt, committed the best British generals and funds to raise troops in the colonies. During the next two years, the British took control of six French forts and marched toward Quebec, the capital of New France. Quebec surrendered to the British in August 1759. Although the fighting was over in North America, Britain and France continued to battle in other parts of the world until the Treaty of Paris finally ended the Seven Years' War in 1763.

✤ *Key Facts*

Conflict:
French and Indian War

Time Period:
Mid-18th Century

Genre:
Novel

FILM VERSIONS OF *THE LAST OF THE MOHICANS*

The enduring popularity of Cooper's *Last of the Mohicans* is evidenced by the number of film adaptations of the novel that were produced throughout the twentieth century. In 1911, American filmmaker Theodore Marston completed a version featuring silent-film stars James Cruze and William Russell. Another silent version, directed by Clarence Brown and Maurice Tourneur, appeared in 1920 and was selected for preservation in the National Film Registry by the Library of Congress in 1995. The first adaptation to feature synchronized sound was directed by George B. Seitz and was released in 1936, with Clem Beauchamp receiving an Academy Award nomination for best assistant director. A number of television miniseries and short films were produced in the 1960s and 1970s, including a 1971 eight-episode production by the British Broadcasting Corporation (BBC), which was nominated for two Primetime Emmy Awards.

Despite the long history of film and television adaptations of the novel, perhaps the most successful film version was also the most recent. Released in 1992, *The Last of the Mohicans* was directed by Michael Mann and starred Daniel Day-Lewis as Hawkeye. The film was a commercial success, grossing more than $75 million at the box office, with esteemed film critic Leonard Maltin calling it a "rousing, kinetic update of the James Fenimore Cooper classic" that "never fails to entertain." The film won several awards, including an Oscar for best sound and a BAFTA for best cinematography and makeup. In a nod to the film's many predecessors, Phillip Dunne's screenplay for the 1936 version of *The Last of the Mohicans* is listed in the credits as an inspiration for Mann's production.

While Cooper chose the French and Indian War as his backdrop, he was, in fact, responding to cultural and political trends of the 1820s, his own era. His story comments on the white colonizers' and American government's genocidal policies, which were destroying Native American peoples and cultures all over North America. Since its establishment, the U.S. government had repeatedly made treaties with Native Americans that drove them westward. In 1828, soon after the publication of *The Last of the Mohicans*, Andrew Jackson was elected president and promoted forceful removal as a government policy; in 1830 Congress passed the *Indian Removal Act*, which officially required the U.S. government to relocate Native Americans to the West.

Cooper and other early American writers were greatly influenced by Romanticism, a literary and artistic movement that originated in Europe in the second half of the eighteenth century. Romantics rebelled against the rationalism of the Age of Enlightenment, instead stressing individual experience and emotion and drawing inspiration from nature. Cooper's descriptions of the beauty of the frontier wilderness, the simplicity of heroism, and the Native Americans as "noble savages" placed him firmly within the Romantic tradition. He created a distinctly new American Romantic novel with a vision of the Native American past that idealized conflict and emphasized the honor, glory, and courage of Hawkeye and the Mohicans in their struggles against the European invaders.

THEMES AND STYLE

The overriding theme of *The Last of the Mohicans* is the conflict between Native Americans and European Americans on the frontier. Cooper's violent war scenes—flashing tomahawks, silent pursuits through pristine forests and across silver lakes, rifles and scalping—exalt and sentimentalize the Indian Wars. Critics generally agree that Cooper felt sympathetic toward Native Americans. Scholars such as Wayne Franklin, author of *James Fenimore Cooper: The Early Years*, have argued that Cooper empathized with Native American because he was experiencing the slow dissolution of the Cooper family estate in the Hudson Valley. Other critics have suggested that the focus on the noble Mohicans represents, in a sense, escapism to a mythological and "free" American past.

Chad T. May suggests that neither of these approaches to Cooper is nuanced enough. In "The Romance of America: Trauma, National Identity, and the Leather-Stocking Tales," May maintains that Cooper wrote in the Romantic tradition in order to contain the "traumatic suffering and loss" caused by Native American removal policies—suffering and loss that he recognized but believed was inevitable—and therefore keep that trauma from casting doubt on narratives that emphasized American civilization's march of progress. Most critics agree that the novel portrays the white settlers' displacement of native peoples as inevitable, justified, and an example of American "progress." In fact, the nostalgic depiction of the old way of life of Native Americans helps conceal the imperialist violence done them.

Cooper exaggerated real events of the French and Indian War in order to make his fiction more dramatic and appealing to an American readership hungry for stories about the dangerous Western frontier. For example, the massacre of the English as they left the besieged Fort William Henry in *The Last of the Mohicans* was based on real events but was greatly embellished. Cooper's characterizations, however, are not as rigidly racial as those of other authors of the period. Some whites are inept, like Heyward, who accepts Magua as a guide for himself and the Munro sisters; others are valiant, like Hawkeye. Besides portraying Chingachgook and his son Uncas as stereotypical "noble savages"—men untouched by civilization and therefore honorable and pure—Cooper also includes a formulaic "bad Indian," Magua, who seeks revenge for hurts he has suffered at the hands of the whites. As he explains to Cora:

Magua was born a chief and a warrior among the red Hurons of the lakes; he saw the suns of twenty summers make the snows of twenty winters run off in the streams, before he saw a paleface; and he was happy! Then his Canada fathers came into the woods and taught him to drink the firewater, and he became a rascal. The Hurons drove him from the graves of his fathers as they would chase the hunted buffalo.

CRITICAL DISCUSSION

Cooper's *Leatherstocking Tales* were initially met with critical acclaim, and Cooper himself was hailed as the first genuine American novelist. Ralph Waldo Emerson is commonly quoted as calling the first book of the series, *The Pioneers*, "our first national novel." After the next two books, *The Last of the Mohicans* and *The Prairie*, were published, Van Wyck Brooks wrote in *The World of Washington Irving*, "Natty Bumppo was destined to remain the symbol of a moment of civilization, the dawn of the new American soul." All five of the novels were extremely popular, both in America and in Britain.

Later critics were less kind to Cooper. In his famous essay "Fenimore Cooper's Literary Offenses," Mark Twain mocked Cooper's work: "[Cooper] prized his broken twig above all the rest of his effects […] It is a restful chapter in any book of his when somebody doesn't step on a dry twig and alarm all the reds and whites for two hundred yards around." Critics generally agree that Cooper's style was mediocre at best. In a 2001 introduction to *The Last of the Mohicans*, Leslie A. Fiedler writes, "These five Leatherstocking Tales, though they stay in print and are read still by a substantial though diminishing audience, chiefly juvenile, are quite unlike what we ordinarily think of as Classics or 'Great Books.' They are, in fact, on most counts—on all counts, if judged by rigorous critical standards—bad books: ineptly structured, shamelessly periphrastic, euphemistic and verbose; at last, unforgivably boring."

In general, twentieth-century critics have looked less at the quality of Cooper's writing and more at the novels' value in portraying American culture of the 1830s. All five of the novels were republished by the Library of America in the 1980s, prompting Andrew Delbanco to write in the *New Republic*, "In some ways the Leatherstocking novels were escapist, enacting a retreat into the past. But […] they were also a part of Cooper's effort to come to terms with a world from which all hierarchies of value seemed to be disappearing." *The Leatherstocking Tales*, and especially *The Last of the Mohicans*, remain an essential part of the American canon. Fiedler appreciates both sides of the critical divide. He writes that the novels are "regressive, reactionary, downright wicked in terms of the enlightened moral consensus of the late twentieth century. […] That is to say, racist, sexist and anti-democratic, based on an ethnocentric, culturally imperialist and hierarchal view

The Huron and the Mohican in single combat while Hawkeye and Uncas watch unable to intervene. © EVERETT COLLECTION

of society which serves to perpetuate, indeed celebrates the subservience of red and black men to white ones, of females to males, and of the uncultivated poor to the lettered rich." But he also states, "The good-bad *Leatherstocking Tales* represent our homegrown, wicked-holy Old Testament, from which all other mythic novels in our Classic tradition derive."

SOURCES

"The Art of the Western, or, Judging a Book by its Cover." *Exhibition of Cover Art from Western Fiction.* Special Collections and Archives. Boise State University, 2000. Web. 26 June 2011.

Brooks, Van Wyck. *The World of Washington Irving.* Philadelphia: Blakiston, 1944. Print.

Cooper, James Fenimore. *The Last of the Mohicans.* New York: Random, 2001. Print.

Delbanco, Andrew. "The Leatherstocking Tales." *The New Republic* 9 (1986): 38. Web. 26 June 2011.

Fiedler, Leslie A. "James Fenimore Cooper: The Problem of the Good Bad Writer." Introduction. *The Last of the Mohicans.* By James Fenimore Cooper. New York: Random, 2001. Print.

Franklin, Wayne. *James Fenimore Cooper: The Early Years.* New Haven: Yale UP, 2007. Print.

May, Chad T. "The Romance of America: Trauma, National Identity, and the Leather-Stocking Tales." *Early American Studies* 9 (2011): 167–86. Print.

Twain, Mark. "Fenimore Cooper's Literary Offenses." 1895. *Whole Earth Review* 78 (1993): 106. Web. 26 June 2011.

Pollard, Finn. *The Literary Quest for an American National Character.* New York: Routledge, 2009. Print.

Sanborn, Geoffrey. *Whipscars and Tattoos: The Last of the Mohicans, Moby-Dick, and the Maori.* New York: Oxford UP, 2011. Print.

FURTHER READING

Barker, Martin, and Roger Sabin. *The Lasting of the Mohicans: History of an American Myth.* Jackson: UP of Mississippi, 1995. Print.

Cooper, James Fenimore. *The Leatherstocking Tales.* New York: Viking, 1985. Print.

Dyar, Jennifer. "Fatal Attraction: The White Obsession with Indianness." *Historian* 65.4 (2003): 817. Print.

MacDougall, Hugh C. *James Fenimore Cooper: His Country and His Art: Papers from the 1995 Cooper Seminar.* Oneonta: SUNY, 1995. Print.

McWilliams, John. *"The Last of the Mohicans": Civil Savagery and Savage Civility.* New York: Twayne, 1995. Print.

MEDIA ADAPTATIONS

Last of the Mohicans. Dir. Arthur Wellin. Perf. Emil Mamelok, Herta Heden, and Bela Lugosi. Luna Film, 1920. Film.

Last of the Mohicans. Dir. George B. Seitz. Perf. Randolph Scott, Phillip Reed, and Robert Barrat. United Artists, 1936. Film.

Last of the Mohicans. Dir. Michael Mann. Perf. Daniel Day-Lewis, Russell Means, and Eric Schweig. Twentieth Century-Fox, 1992. Film.

Melissa Doak

Mao's Generals Remember Korea

Xiaobing Li, Allan R. Millett, Bin Yu

OVERVIEW

Mao's Generals Remember Korea is a compilation of materials excerpted from the published memoirs of seven Chinese army generals, selected and introduced by noted scholars Xiaobing Li, Allan R. Millett, and Bin Yu. Published in 2001, the work provides insight into how Chinese military and political leaders approached their nation's engagement in the Korean conflict. The generals include the highest-ranking military leaders involved in the war, and their writings draw upon personal reminiscences, archival documents, and the work of Chinese historians and analysts. As the editors explain in the book's introduction, "Each of the generals offers special, personal insight into specific aspects of the war, including combat operations, logistics, political control, field command, and communications." Most of their memoirs were published in China during the 1980s but are not available in English translation.

For the most part, the generals closely follow official Chinese positions on the war, consistently condemning Western imperialism and glorifying the Chinese intervention. Further, as reviewer Chen Jian points out in the *Journal of Asian Studies*, "Memoirs often have a self-serving tendency," and the accounts collected in *Mao's Generals Remember Korea* focus on successes rather than mistakes. In a review for the *Air and Space Power Journal*, Colonel Anthony C. Cain notes that from the Chinese perspective, the Korean War was not "a blot on the national strategic consciousness during the Cold War," but rather "a nationalistic battle that precluded inevitable aggression from an imperialist foe."

In compiling the volume, Li, Millett, and Yu set out to illuminate topics such as the decision to intervene in Korea, Chinese strategy and combat methods, the role of political mobilization, relations with the Soviet Union, and China's approach to the truce negotiations. *Mao's Generals Remember Korea* is rounded out with an essay by Bin Yu on lessons China learned in the Korean conflict, as well as helpful maps and a substantial bibliography.

HISTORICAL AND LITERARY CONTEXT

The Korean conflict, which took place between June 1950 and July 1953, has often been characterized as the "forgotten war." Yet it was the first important engagement of the Cold War, and its effects have lasted for more than half a century. Casualty figures can only be approximated, but the dead are thought to have included about 35,000 Americans, more than 400,000 South Koreans, at least 150,000 Chinese, and an unknown number of North Koreans (more than 200,000). In addition, the Korean economy and landscape suffered significant damage.

Circumstances leading up to the Korean conflict began in the aftermath of World War II, when Korea was liberated from thirty-five years of Japanese rule. In 1910, as part of its imperialist expansion, Japan had annexed the Korean peninsula. The peninsula is about 85,000 square miles in area with 5,600 miles of coastline, and its southern tip is only about 125 miles away from Japan. Following Japan's defeat in World War II, the peninsula was divided into "spheres of influence" along the thirty-eighth parallel, a geographical line that crosses the peninsula roughly in the middle. The postwar agreement called for U.S. troops to occupy the South, which had a population of more than twenty million, and Soviet troops to occupy the more mountainous North, which had a population of about nine million.

In the South the United States promoted a pro-Western, anti-Communist political system, while in the North the Soviet Union encouraged development of a Communist system. All attempts to reunify the peninsula failed, and in 1948 two opposing hardline governments were established: in the South the Republic of Korea (ROK) was led by Syngman Rhee, and in the North Kim Il Sung headed the Democratic People's Republic of Korea (DPRK). Tensions between North and South led to continuing skirmishes across the thirty-eighth parallel. Pursuant to the original agreement, the Soviet Union and the United States withdrew their troops from the peninsula in 1948 and 1949 respectively.

China, the other nation that was about to become involved in the Korean War, lies at the northern boundary of the Korean Peninsula, just across the Yalu river. In October 1949 the Communist People's Republic of China (PRC) was established under Mao Zedong, concluding a long civil war in that country. A few months later Kim Il Sung approached both Mao and Joseph Stalin, premier of the Soviet Union, seeking support for a plan to unify the Korean peninsula

⁜ Key Facts

Conflict:
Korean War

Time Period:
Mid-20th Century

Genre:
History

MIG ALLEY

Even though the Korean War was fought on a peninsula, naval activity played a relatively minor role in the conflict. Most of the action at sea involved artillery support and the disruption of supply shipping. Like the land war, the war at sea was primarily conducted with the same tactics and equipment used in World War II.

In the air, however, the Korean War marked an important transition in military aviation. Whereas World War II had been fought primarily with propeller-driven, piston-engine planes, the Korean War featured a new generation of jet fighters—and gave birth to a new style of aerial combat.

At the beginning of the war, North Korea had only World War II-vintage fighters, which were quickly outmatched by U.S. forces flying first-generation straight-winged jets. When China entered the war, however, the situation changed dramatically. The Chinese had Soviet-made MiG-15 fighters—swept-wing aircraft that were faster and more heavily armed than their straight-wing counterparts. With its advanced design the MiG-15 immediately challenged U.S. air superiority in Korea.

The U.S. countered with three squadrons of swept-wing F-86 Sabres, and the Korean air war quickly became defined by jet-on-jet "dogfights." So many of these took place in northwestern North Korea that the area was nicknamed MiG Alley. Although the Soviet Union did not openly participate in the Korean conflict, it is known that Soviet pilots flew some of the Chinese MiGs.

The Korean War proved to be a testing range and training ground for a new generation of planes and pilots. It was the first air-power confrontation between the U.S. and the Soviet Union and marked the beginning of an arms race that would continue to escalate throughout most of the Cold War.

under Kim's leadership. Mao and Stalin gave Kim their approval, but Stalin refused to become directly involved. Mao was reportedly unaware that Kim intended to commence a military action almost immediately.

On 25 June 1950 a substantial North Korean force crossed the thirty-eighth parallel and quickly overwhelmed the South Korean defenders. To prevent North Korea from taking over the entire peninsula, the United Nations (UN)—led aggressively by the United States—entered the conflict and forced the North Korean troops far north of the thirty-eighth parallel, almost to the Yalu River. At this point China joined the war in support of North Korea and pushed the UN forces back across the thirty-eighth parallel into South Korea. Following these rapid developments, the war entered a stalemate phase that lasted from summer 1951 until an armistice was signed two years later. Although bombing and pitched battles continued, resulting in heavy casualties, neither side made significant territorial gains, and at war's end a border was reestablished near the thirty-eighth parallel. The armistice also created a demilitarized strip about two miles wide to serve as a buffer zone between the two Koreas.

China never formally entered the Korean War, and the Chinese People's Liberation Army (PLA) was not involved in the conflict. Instead, China provided more than two million combatants through a special Chinese People's Volunteers Force (CPVF). The Soviet Union also never officially entered the war or sent troops, but they supplied material aid to both the Chinese and the North Koreans and dispatched thousands of military advisers to North Korea before and during the war. For this reason the Korean War is widely viewed as the first significant conflict of the Cold War, which continued until the collapse of the Soviet Union in 1991. During this period South Korea evolved into an economically successful industrial nation, while North Korea became a heavily militarized and largely impoverished Communist state.

Mao's Generals Remember Korea provides a view of the war not otherwise available to the general reader. The perspectives of Western commanders were presented in commentaries by, among others, U.S. generals Matthew Ridgway, Douglas MacArthur, and Lawton Collins as early as the 1960s, but political conditions in China delayed the publication of military memoirs related to Korea until the '80s and later. Several books have examined the Korean War from the Soviet perspective, including Andrei Lankov's *From Stalin to Kim Il Sung: The Formation of North Korea 1945–1960* and Sergei Goncharov, John Lewis, and Xue Litai's *Uncertain Partners: Stalin, Mao, and the Korean War*. The latter utilizes primary source material, such as cables and internal documents, to illuminate relationships among the Communist powers. Studies of the role of Koreans in the conflict include Allan R. Millet's *War for Korea*, which uses South Korean sources, and Charles K. Armstrong's *The North Korean Revolution, 1945–1950*, which supplies viewpoints of civilians in North Korea before the war and of their fellow citizens taken captive during the war.

THEMES AND STYLE

The content of *Mao's Generals Remember Korea* falls into three general topic areas: the decision to intervene, the conduct of the war, and the strategy of the peace negotiations. The brief chapter "My Story of the Korean War" touches on all three areas. It is taken from the autobiography of Marshal Peng Dehuai, the top Chinese military leader in Korea. Peng summarizes the moral and political reasons for China's aid to Korea, describes each of the "five offensive campaigns" (sometimes referred to as the five "phases") that were carried out during the first six months of the war, and concludes by characterizing the armistice as a result of Chinese victories that "reflected the integrity of our revolutionary army's superior political and military qualities."

In the chapter "Beijing's Decision to Intervene," Marshal Nie Rongzhen depicts the intervention as reluctant but unavoidable in the face of American imperialism. In addition, he presents a Chinese view of American politics and their effect on the U.S. war effort. Nie never went to Korea himself but served as the acting chief of staff of the PLA and was a close aide to Mao Zedong, so it is not surprising that his account is especially enthusiastic in its praise of Mao's decisions.

Nie's reflections also provide commentary on operational aspects of the war, analyzing the challenges that confronted the Chinese army in Korea. Among these were the problems of delivering logistical support and obtaining sufficient supplies, topics that are discussed at greater length in chapters by General Hong Zuezhi ("The CPVF's Combat and Logistics") and Marshal Xu Xiangqian ("The Purchase of Arms from Moscow"). Although China and the Soviet Union had a common interest in supporting North Korea and opposing the United States, relations between the two Communist countries were at times problematic. Xu, who was chief of the People's Liberation Army (PLA) general staff, made an unpublicized trip to Moscow in 1951 to acquire Soviet weapons and obtain assistance in modernizing the Chinese military. Xu's delegation found, however, that the Soviet Union—still struggling to recover from the effects of World War II—could not easily provide help. Furthermore, some of the Soviet negotiators displayed "impatience" and "chauvinism" that seem to have previewed later political strains between the two Communist powers.

General Du Ping's chapter ("Political Mobilization and Control") describes in detail the role of policy makers in creating and maintaining a climate of support among the military and civilian populations in China, utilizing a variety of propaganda techniques. According to Chen Jian, "Du's story makes it clear that from the beginning of China's intervention in Korea, for Beijing this was more a political struggle—with the aim of enhancing revolutionary China's international prestige and security interests—than a narrowly defined military conflict."

In "Command Experience in Korea," General Yang Dezhi provides an account of the war from a

全力支持抗美援朝志顾军部队 51.8

This 1950s Chinese Communist propaganda poster rallies support for the North Korean Army during the Korean War by urging, "Support the Resistance to the USA with All Your Strength and Aid the Volunteer Army."
© (COLOR LITHO), CHINESE SCHOOL, (20TH CENTURY) / PRIVATE COLLECTION / © THE CHAMBERS GALLERY, LONDON / THE BRIDGEMAN ART LIBRARY

combatant commander's perspective, as well as vividly portraying some of the personalities and social conditions in the CPVF. Yang's commentary reveals the aggregate of political pressures, ideological concerns, and battlefield conditions that shaped his personal approach to operations on the ground.

In the final chapter of *Mao's Generals Remember Korea*, Major General Chai Chengwen discusses "The Korean Truce Negotiations." As Anthony Cain explains, "General Chai patiently outlines the 'reasonable' expectations of the Chinese negotiating team and then shows how inconsiderate and obstructionist behavior by the American-led UN negotiating team unnecessarily extended the truce talks to the detriment of world peace." Chai's account, according to Cain, allows readers to "see the same issues that appear in Western narratives, but from a different viewpoint."

CRITICAL DISCUSSION

Reviewers widely recognized *Mao's Generals Remember Korea* as very useful for nonspecialists seeking a broader understanding of the Korean War. Colonel Mike Davino observes in *Infantry Magazine* that the compilation "fills a void in the available English language literature about the Korean War from the Chinese perspective," supplying insights that remain relevant today because "the Chinese continue to draw upon lessons learned during the war." *Parameters* reviewer Nicholas Evan Sarantakes asserts that the work "belongs on the reading list and bookshelves of anyone with an interest in the military past or future of the peninsula." Cain praises "the multifaceted nature of the memoirs," which give the reader "a 360-degree operational view of Chinese efforts to counter UN and US actions in the Korean War."

Michael Sheng, however, sounds a note of caution in the *Journal of Military History*. While agreeing that the volume "makes a welcome addition to the ever-growing corpus of literature in the field, shedding new light on the strategic thinking, ideological inclination, military planning, and execution of the 'other side' in the conflict," he suggests that "Western readers may find it awkward and unproductive to go through all the CCP [Chinese Communist Party] jargon and condemnations of 'American imperialist aggressors' that fill these pages just to get a little bit of useful information of substance."

Chen Jian has a different concern, arguing,

> [The] long survey essay by Bin Yu, which is, by itself, a very good piece of scholarship, fails to fulfill a major task that the essay is supposed to take [on]; that is, in addition to providing a general survey of the Chinese experience during the Korean War, it should offer critical comments on the Chinese generals' recollections, while, at the same time, providing comparisons between them and what scholars have

learned in the past decade through access to newly declassified Chinese and, in many cases, Russian, documents.

Nevertheless, Chen acknowledges that the volume "remains a unique and very useful source. Anyone who is interested in the Chinese perspective of the Korean War should read it."

Newly declassified Chinese documents have informed recent studies of that country's perspectives on the Korean War, including those produced by Kathryn Weathersby of the Cold War International History Project of the Woodrow Wilson International Center for Scholars.

SOURCES

Cain, Anthony C. Rev. of *Mao's Generals Remember Korea*, edited by Xiaobing Li, Allan R. Millett, and Bin Yu. *Air and Space Power Journal* 17:2 (2002): 114. Print.

Davino, Mike. Rev. of *Mao's Generals Remember Korea*, edited by Xiaobing Li, Allan R. Millett, and Bin Yu. *Infantry Magazine* 1 Mar. 2004: n.pag. Print.

Jian, Chen. Rev. of *Mao's Generals Remember Korea*, edited by Xiaobing Li, Allan R. Millett, and Bin Yu. *Journal of Asian Studies* 61:2 (2002): 704–05. Print.

Li, Xiaobing, Allan R. Millett, and Bin Yu, eds. *Mao's Generals Remember Korea*. Lawrence: UP of Kansas, 2001. Print.

Sarantakes, Nicholas Evan. Rev. of *Mao's Generals Remember Korea*, edited by Xiaobing Li, Allan R. Millett, and Bin Yu. *Parameters* Autumn 2002: 154. Print.

Sheng, Michael M. Rev. of *Mao's Generals Remember Korea*, edited by Xiaobing Li, Allan R. Millett, and Bin Yu. *Journal of Military History* 66.2 (2002): 619–20. Print.

FURTHER READING

Armstrong, Charles K. *The North Korean Revolution, 1945–1950*. Ithaca: Cornell UP, 2003. Print.

Chen, Jian. *China's Road to the Korean War: The Making of the Sino-American Confrontation*. New York: Columbia UP, 1994. Print.

Goncharov, S. N., John W. Lewis, and Litai Xue. *Uncertain Partners: Stalin, Mao, and the Korean War*. Stanford: Stanford UP, 1993. Print.

Lankov, Andrei. *From Stalin to Kim Il Sung: The Formation of North Korea 1945–1960*. New Brunswick: Rutgers UP, 2002. Print.

Li, Xiaobing. *A History of the Modern Chinese Army*. Lexington: UP of Kentucky, 2007. Print.

MacArthur, Douglas. *Reminiscences*. New York: McGraw, 1964. Print.

Millett, Allan R. *The War for Korea, 1945–1950: A House Burning*. Lawrence: UP of Kansas, 2005. Print.

———. *The War for Korea, 1950–1951: They Came from the North*. Lawrence: UP of Kansas, 2010. Print.

O'Neill, Mark. "Soviet Involvement in the Korean War: A New View from the Soviet-Era Archives." *OAH Magazine of History* 14.3 (2000): 20–24. Print.

Ridgway, Matthew B. *The Korean War*. Garden City: Doubleday, 1967. Print.

Stueck, William W. *The Korean War in World History*. Lexington: UP of Kentucky, 2004. Print.

Weathersby, Kathryn. "New Evidence on North Korea." *Cold War International History Project Bulletin* 14–15 (2003): 5–138. Print.

Zhang, Shu G. *Mao's Military Romanticism: China and the Korean War, 1950–1953*. Lawrence: UP of Kansas, 1995. Print.

Cynthia Giles

ROYAL COMMENTARIES OF THE INCA AND GENERAL HISTORY OF PERU

El Inca Garcilaso de la Vega

✣ **Key Facts**

Conflict:
Spanish Conquest of
Peru

Time Period:
16th Century

Genre:
History

OVERVIEW

El Inca Garcilaso de la Vega's *Royal Commentaries of the Inca and General History of Peru* may be one of the most complex literary creations to come out of colonial Latin America. Published in 1609 and 1617, this two-volume history presents a retrospective view of Francisco Pizarro's bloody conquest of present-day Peru, as well as the more personal story of the author's family history. The son of an Incan princess and a Spanish conquistador, the author, also known as El Inca Garcilaso and El Inca, is proud of his mestizo (mixed) heritage, and he interweaves the personal and the historical in his text. As he explains in the introduction, his objective is twofold: to honor his family by immortalizing their contributions to the nation and to serve the Spanish crown by writing a complete and accurate history of the conquest of Peru. A true mestizo history, the *Royal Commentaries* honors both the Incan empire and the Spanish conquistadors who destroyed it.

The first volume of the text, the *Royal Commentaries of the Inca*, traces the history of the indigenous people of Peru through the rise of the Incan empire. The author draws a strong parallel between the actions the Inca took to expand their empire and the Spanish conquest of the Inca themselves. He stresses the fact that the Incan empire provided indigenous Peruvians with a strong sense of civic duty and an organized religion, which paved the way for their government by the Spanish crown and for their conversion to Christianity. The second volume, the *General History of Peru*, provides the details of the Spanish conquest, beginning with the arrival of Pizarro in 1525.

Royal Commentaries of the Inca and General History of Peru is as much a response to colonial historians as it is a history in its own right. El Inca Garcilaso comments on and corrects a wide range of sources on a number of subjects related to the conquest of Peru and the history of the Inca, often citing his own authority as an eyewitness. In contrast to historians who viewed the Inca as primitive and uncivilized, he stresses that they possessed a highly advanced military culture that had already conquered the whole of Peru before the arrival of the Spaniards. He also laments the fact that much of the communication between the conquistadors and the Incan nobility was conducted through ill-educated translators, either Spaniards who had picked up only some of the Quechua language or young Incan boys who had learned rudimentary Spanish.

HISTORICAL AND LITERARY CONTEXT

Because the Inca had no written language and thus passed their history down orally, there were few texts for El Inca Garcilaso de la Vega to consult while composing the first part of his work. His two major sources of information, other than the stories passed down through his family, were works written by two Jesuit priests who had worked in Peru: José de Acosta's *Historia natural y moral de las Indias* (Natural and Moral History of the Indies), which was published in Seville in 1590; and "Historia del Perú" (History of Peru), an unpublished work by the mestizo priest Blas Valera. The works were given to him by Jesuit missionaries in Spain.

Beginning in the thirteenth century, the Inca ruled over a large area of western South America. They developed a highly advanced civilization headed by the nobility, which consisted of the descendants of the man considered to be the first Inca, Manco Capac. From their center in Cuzco, in the Peruvian Andes, the Inca conquered large portions of present-day Argentina, Bolivia, Chile, Colombia, Ecuador, and Peru, either through peaceful consolidation or by military force. Ambassadors from the conquered regions were sent to Cuzco to learn the imperial language and the rules of administration. The Incan nobility taxed their subjects and maintained a large and potent army in order to expand the territories under their control and to quell rebellions.

In 1529 a war of succession broke out between two Incan princes, Huáscar Inca and Atahualpa Inca. As the brothers pitted their armies against one another, their conflict split the empire. Atahualpa emerged triumphant and took control of the empire just as Francisco Pizarro began his campaign in 1532 to conquer Peru. Pizarro, Hernando de Soto, and Friar Vicente de Valverde met with Atahualpa and requested that he and his people convert to Christianity and pledge allegiance to King Charles

I of Spain. After some confusion and disagreement, Pizarro's troops attacked and took Atahualpa prisoner, later putting him on trial for crimes against Catholicism and executing him. After Atahualpa's death the conquistadores had little trouble in taking over the entire Incan empire.

The legacy of the conquest of the Americas was shaped, by and large, by the chroniclers and historians of the time. The first historians to write about the Spanish conquest were also conquistadores. Gonzalo Fernández de Oviedo participated in the conquest of the Caribbean in the early sixteenth century, was appointed historiographer of the Indies in 1523, and published his *Historia general y natural de las Indias* (*General and Natural History of the Indies*) in 1535. Pedro Cieza de León helped conquer cities in Peru and Colombia and, as an official chronicler, published his *Historia del Perú* (*History of Peru*) in 1554. Francisco López de Gómara, Hernán Cortés's personal secretary, did not participate in the conquests but based his 1552 *Historia general de las Indias* (*General History of the Indies*) and *La conquista de Méjico* (*Conquest of Mexico*) on the accounts of the conquistadors after they had returned from battle.

El Inca Garcilaso served as his father's scribe during much of the conquest of Peru, which gave him access to many of the chronicles of conquest as well as the education needed to read and comment on them. In his *Royal Commentaries* he frequently refers to other historians, either to support his own point of view or to correct errors in their histories. He insists on the truth of his version of the story, citing both himself as an eyewitness and testimony from other reliable sources. To support his story of a disagreement between Francisco Pizarro and Atahualpa, for example, he cites "the *quipus* [Incan historical records in the form of a system of knotted cords] kept in the archives of Cajamarca province; and those of the conquistadors who were eyewitnesses of this scene, among them Alonso Valera, Blas Valera's own father." Among the many histories of the conquest, *Royal Commentaries of the Inca and General History of Peru* is unique because its author, as a mestizo, had ties to both the conquerors and the conquered.

THEMES AND STYLE

The *Royal Commentaries of the Inca and General History of Peru* is carefully written and highly detailed, mimicking the style of the historians of the time. El Inca Garcilaso de la Vega shows great admiration for the documentation of history, and he points out the advantages of written history to one of his Incan elders: "Inca, my uncle, you have no written records, how then can you remember these things of the past ... The Spanish and the nations that are their neighbors possess books; they know their entire history." His history of the Incan empire is organized chronologically by the reigns of its rulers and includes accounts of their conquests and style of government. He compares the

Inca to the ancient Romans in terms of their military prowess, the infrastructure of their communities, and their political administration. He also explains that, in addition to its highly advanced methods of construction, agriculture, and government, the Incan empire established organized religion among the indigenous people of Peru. He explains that the Incan nobility enforced "natural and reasonable laws" that were surprisingly similar to Christian moral codes: for example, "each one should do unto others as he would have others do unto him." He stresses that the Inca adhered to a strong moral code long before the arrival of the Spaniards and that such actions as sodomy, adultery, homicide, and theft were punishable offenses in the Incan empire.

When discussing the Spanish conquest of Peru, El Inca Garcilaso focuses on the problems of translation and of the improper education of interpreters in particular. He lays much of the blame for the violence of the conquest on Felipe, a young Incan boy trained by the Spaniards as an interpreter. During the first encounter between Francisco Pizarro and Atahualpa, Felipe's clumsy translations created tension, as Atahualpa was led to believe that "the Emperor desired him to give up his kingdoms willy-nilly; that he would be compelled to do so by fire, sword, and bloodshed; and that, like Pharaoh, he would be exterminated with all his army." Yet El Inca concludes on a positive note, defending the conquest of Peru as its salvation. He maintains that the bloodshed of the Spanish conquest was the will of God, "to allow the preachers of His gospel and of His Catholic faith to more easily bring their enlightenment to the gentiles of Peru."

A banknote from Peru commemorating El Inca Garcilaso de la Vega. © GEORGIOS KOLLIDAS / ALAMY

EL INCA GARCILASO'S MILITARY SERVICE IN SPAIN

El Inca Garcilaso de la Vega witnessed not one but two wars in his lifetime. Before writing the *Royal Commentaries of the Inca and General History of Peru*, he enlisted as a soldier in the Spanish army. He entered military service in 1570 and fought in the Alpujarra region of southeastern Spain, where he helped quell the Morisco Revolt, a rebellion against the Spanish monarchy that began in 1568.

The Moriscos, Spaniards of North African ancestry who had converted from Islam to Catholicism, were fighting against the harsh restrictions on their culture decreed by King Philip II. They were prohibited from reading or speaking Arabic, wearing traditional North African dress, or giving their children non-Catholic names. With the help of Algeria, many rebellious Moriscos waged guerrilla warfare against the Spaniards in the Alpujarras. The Spaniards, supported by Italian troops, defeated the Moriscos in 1571. In 1609 all remaining Moriscos were expelled from Spain and transported to North Africa. For his service to the crown, El Inca Garcilaso rose to the rank of captain. He remained in Spain until his death in 1616.

CRITICAL DISCUSSION

El Inca Garcilaso de la Vega died in 1616, a year before the second volume of *Royal Commentaries of the Inca and General History of Peru* was published in Spain. He had become a well-known writer and translator, and the posthumous publication of his historical text increased his literary fame. The *Royal Commentaries* was read widely throughout Europe and was translated into French in 1633 and into English in 1688. Much of the work's immediate interest, however, was related to its sense of exoticism; it provided Europeans with an insider's view of the once-mysterious Incan empire. As Alain Gheerbrant notes in his 1961 introduction to the text, "a reprinting of the *Royal Commentaries* was enhanced with engravings … representing the heroes of the Tahuantinsuyu [Incan empire] as some sort of Orientalized Romans, which was how the Parisians of that time imagined them to be." It was only in the nineteenth century, when more material was available for cross-references, that historians were able to read the *Royal Commentaries* with a critical eye. In the 1840s the American historian William Hickling Prescott, in *The History of the Conquest of Peru*, was one of the first to question the historical accuracy of the text; later historians noted that the text reflects its author's motives rather than an objective view of the conquest. In his history *The Conquest of the Incas*, John Hemming describes El Inca Garcilaso's narration of the death of Atahualpa as "an intensely dramatic story" rather than a historical document.

As war literature, however, El Inca Garcilaso's work offers an intriguing perspective on the conquest of Peru. Acting as a sort of cultural ambassador, the author translates the history of the Incan empire and many of the most controversial events of the conquest of Peru into a story that his readers can comprehend. Much of the literary criticism of the *Royal Commentaries* focuses on the way in which the author employs established techniques of war literature to make the conquest of the New World more accessible to his

European audience. In "The Incas and the Renaissance," for example, D. A. Brading describes the influence of Renaissance literature, especially the novels of chivalry and medieval Spanish epic poetry, on El Inca's work. Sabine MacCormack explains in her book *On the Wings of Time* that the author used Roman and classical literature as the framework for his description of the Incan empire. José Antonio Mazzotti, in his article "The Lightning Bolt Yields to the Rainbow," analyzes El Inca's use of European literary themes to make the conquest of Peru, or at least his version of it, familiar to his Spanish readers. And Roberto González Echevarría, in his essay "The Letter of the Law," highlights the author's deft application of the Spanish legal code in petitioning for recognition of his father's deeds as well as for economic compensation for himself.

SOURCES

Brading, D. A. "The Incas and the Renaissance: The Royal Commentaries of Inca Garcilaso de la Vega." *Journal of Latin American Studies* 18.1 (1986): 1–23. Print.

Garcilaso de la Vega, El Inca. *The Incas: The Royal Commentaries of the Inca Garcilaso de la Vega, 1539–1616*. Trans. Maria Jolas. New York: Orion, 1961. Print.

Gheerbrant, Alain. Introduction. *The Incas: The Royal Commentaries of the Inca Garcilaso de la Vega, 1539–1616*. New York: Orion, 1961. Print.

González Echevarría, Roberto. "The Letter of the Law: Garcilaso's *Comentarios*." *Myth and Archive: A Theory of Latin American Literature*. Cambridge: Cambridge UP, 1990. Print.

Hemming, John. *The Conquest of the Incas*. London: Papermac, 1993. Print.

MacCormack, Sabine. *On the Wings of Time: Rome, the Incas, Spain and Peru*. Princeton: Princeton UP, 2007. Print.

Mazzotti, José Antonio. "The Lightning Bolt Yields to the Rainbow: Indigenous History and Colonial Semiosis in the *Royal Commentaries* of El Inca Garcilaso de la Vega." *Modern Language Quarterly* 57.2 (1996): 197–211. Print.

© MAP BY XNR PRODUCTIONS. CENGAGE LEARNING, GALE.

Prescott, William Hickling. *The History of the Conquest of Peru: With a Preliminary View of the Civilization of the Incas.* 1847. Philadelphia: Lippincott, 1998. Print.

FURTHER READING

Adorno, Rolena. *The Polemics of Possession in Spanish American Narrative.* New Haven: Yale UP, 2007. Print.

Anadón, José, ed. *Garcilaso Inca de la Vega, an American Humanist: A Tribute to José Durand.* Notre Dame: U of Notre Dame P, 1998. Print.

MacCormack, Sabine. "Religion and Philosophy: Garcilaso de la Vega and Some Peruvian Readers, 1609–1639." *Religion in the Andes.* Princeton: Princeton UP, 1991. Print.

Varner, John Grier. *El Inca: The Life and Times of Garcilaso de la Vega.* Austin: U of Texas P, 1968. Print.

Zamora, Margarita. *Language, Authority and Indigenous History in the* Comentarios reales de los Incas. Cambridge: Cambridge UP, 1988. Print.

Gina Sherriff

THREE KINGDOMS

Luo Guanzhong

❖ *Key Facts*

Conflict:
Fall of the Han dynasty

Time Period:
2nd–3rd Centuries

Genre:
Novel

OVERVIEW

Three Kingdoms, a long, semivernacular historical novel produced during the Ming dynasty (1368–1644), is a major work of world literature and is of enduring significance in Asian culture. Often likened to the *Iliad* (Homer's chronicle of he Trojan War), *Three Kingdoms* is a powerful national epic of warring states whose rulers, warriors, military strategists, and government ministers played central roles in both its popular and elite audiences' imagination. Based on the historical events and protagonists of the final years and fall of the great Han dynasty (206 BCE-220 CE), the novel charts the civil war between three main contesting kingdoms—Shu-Han, Wei, and Wu—in their bid for the prize of empire. The primary focus of *Three Kingdoms* is on the buildup to and waging of war, and there are virtually no scenes without martial significance. Stressing the traditional desire for national unity pitted against inevitable dynastic rise and fall, the novel begins with the well-known lines, "The empire, long divided, must unite; long united, must divide"; these words are reversed in the final chapter, when the short-lived Western Jin dynasty temporarily takes the spoils.

Literary critics and historians debate the degree of historical accuracy in the novel. The eighteenth-century historian Zhang Xuecheng (1738–1801; quoted in Li Wai-yee's article "Full-Length Vernacular Fiction") famously commented that it is "seven parts historical … three parts fictional," while in the late-twentieth-century *Classic Chinese Novel*, C. T. Hsia writes, "Hardly a single character in the book is ahistorical. And there is no plot to speak of beyond the plot of history." Contemporary historian Rafe de Crespigny disagrees, finding more fiction than fact in much of the story. Whatever the verdict, the combination of gripping events, military combat and strategic debates, broad geographical and temporal sweep, strong characterization, and the exploration of themes of ambition, power, hubris, honor, loyalty, fate, futility, and failure ensure that the work rises above popular history to great literature.

HISTORICAL AND LITERARY CONTEXT

The fall of the Han dynasty, which had ruled a vast empire for four centuries, can be attributed to a variety of factors, including increasingly weak emperors, the rise of powerful local warlords, economic problems, the untoward influence of eunuchs and other powerful factions, and popular religious uprisings. *Three Kingdoms* traces the dynasty's collapse and the ensuing rise of three contesting kingdoms, all fighting to establish their own power base while attempting to reunite China as a single empire. Ultimately, none succeeded. After the defeat of more minor warlords by the year 207, Cao Cao of the Wei kingdom held control over the North China plain; the Sun clan of the Wu kingdom had established their base in the fertile southeast Yangzi River area; and the weakest contender, Liu Xuande (sometimes known as Liu Bei), was attempting to build support in the strategically vital central Jing province. Liu Xuande and his military adviser and chief minister Zhuge Liang (more commonly known as Kongming), shared the cause of restoring the Han dynasty. Although they did not succeed, many commentators have regarded the western Shu-Han kingdom Liu Xuande ruled after 208 as the sole legitimate heir to the Han dynasty. In the pivotal 208 Battle of Red Cliff, the Wu forces of Sun Quan, in nominal alliance with Liu Xuande, fought Cao Cao for control of the middle Yangzi region and southern China. Cao Cao's massive army was defeated by Sun Quan's general Zhou Yu. His use of fire ships (boats filled with combustibles and ignited near an enemy fleet) led to a disastrous retreat and the division of the country into three kingdoms. The consequent incessant campaigns, alliances, and defeats fill the remainder of the narrative, which ends in the brief reunification of China under the Western Jin (265–317 CE).

The novel's origins lie in historical accounts written very soon after the events described. Chen Shou (d. 297) recorded a history of the period using the standard biographical format (focusing on the careers of rulers, generals, and officials), an important structuring and stylistic device for classical Chinese literature. Pei Songzhi (372–451) compiled a mass of historical, semifictional, and outright fantastical materials that were appended to Chen Shou's history and that served as the basis for many later popular elaborations. Other important influences on the novel, particularly in terms of their emphasis on warfare, strategy, and characterization, include Sun Tzu's military treatise *Art of War* (c. eighth to fifth century BCE), the early historical narrative *The Zuo Tradition* (c. fourth century BCE), Sima Qian's *Records of the Historian* (c. second to first century BCE), and the debates of strategists found in *Intrigues of the Warring States* (c. first century BCE). Later historical accounts by Sima Guang (eleventh century) and Zhu Xi (twelfth century) moved away from the capsule biographical approach of earlier writers to a more continuous narrative style that profoundly influenced the creation of *Three Kingdoms*. These nonfiction works, as well as poetry about the events and personalities of the Three Kingdoms period and a long tradition of oral storytelling cycles, popular fiction, and dramas, played a central part in the development of the novel. They also contributed to the long-standing politically and ethnically charged debates over legitimate claims to imperial power. The oral and written tales focused mainly on the rivals Cao Cao (regent to the last Han emperor) and Liu Xuande (remote relation of the Liu imperial clan).

THEMES AND STYLE

While strongly embedded within a historical framework and heavily reliant on historical sources, several elements of *Three Kingdoms* point to its literary status as fiction. It has a cohesive structure; it carefully modulates pace and geographical shifts between north, southeast, and west and among the three powers; and it invokes overarching themes of hubristic vainglory and failed hopes. Its 120 chapters abound with vivid descriptions of people and events, glorious accounts of the exploits of warriors and military strategists, and lively, highly pointed dialogue. Its greatest strength may lie in the characterization of the central contenders for power and their followers. These figures play out their roles against a frenetic backdrop of shifting alliances, sieges, single combat, major battles, defeats, victories, diplomatic exchanges, and heated debates on military strategy. The most important characters are the Shu-Han leader Liu Xuande and his sworn brothers Zhang Fei and Lord Guan (Guan Yü), his adviser Kongming, one of his other "tiger" generals Zhao Zilong, and Cao Cao, the novel's fascinating Wei antihero and Liu Xuande's chief rival. All perform vital parts in the lead-up to and aftermath of the decisive battle of Red Cliff that lies at the heart of the novel and that determines the tripodal division of the empire predicted by arch strategist Kongming.

Rivalry and ambitions to power are thematized through Liu Xuande and Cao Cao. They are introduced to readers in the first chapter, and their stories are intimately linked, providing a parallel structure

A nineteenth-century illustration depicting Chu-Ko-Liang (Zhuge Liang), a Shu-Han dynasty statesman who is a major character in *Romance of the Three Kingdoms.* © ARCHIVES CHARMET / THE BRIDGEMAN ART LIBRARY INTERNATIONAL

Les pirates étrangers mis en déroute par l'éventail sacré. — Allusion à la légende d'après laquelle Chu-Ko-Liang, ministre de l'empereur Liu-Pei, ayant régné de 181 à 234 de l'ère chrétienne, mit en déroute une flotte ennemie, après avoir obtenu par ses prières un vent favorable. L'image représente le grand patriote monté sur une jonque de guerre et brandissant l'éventail qui souffle l'incendie sur le vaisseau des barbares occidentaux. L'incendie détruit le navire, ajoute le texte chinois, et les pirates meurent tous dans les flammes.

POPULAR CULTURE AND *THREE KINGDOMS*

In addition to the strongly historical origins of *Three Kingdoms*, the novel's events and characters are embedded in popular cultural forms, both pre-modern and contemporary. Storytellers and opera singers at markets and temple fairs (and more recently on television) have recounted the deeds of Liu Xuande, Lord Guan, Zhang Fei, Cao Cao, and others for at least a thousand years. New Year's folk-art posters and temple murals use images from stories in *Three Kingdoms*, and Lord Guan is still revered as the God of War in many areas. The novel was one of Chairman Mao's favorite books and served him as a source for military strategy. Comic book versions abound, as do games, including many versions with cross-gender representations of all the major characters as women warriors. There have been several television adaptations and films, the most recent of which is John Woo's *Red Cliff* (released in two parts in Asia in 2008–09 and as a single film in North America in 2009). Recent books and television series have promoted the novel as a self-help or business-strategy manual. The novel continues to be a best seller, not only in China but also in Japan and Korea. In the latter country it has become so important that it is acclaimed as an integral part of Korean national culture.

within the novel's events. Vitally important to Liu Xuande's rise to power is his meeting with Zhang Fei and Lord Guan, with whom he swears the Peach Garden oath of brotherhood to remain loyal to the death. This oath serves to bind the two extraordinary lieutenants to Liu Xuande's cause; however, it is also the catalyst for the failure of his imperial bid. Against Kongming's advice, Liu Xuande embarks on a strategically disastrous and bloody campaign of vengeance against the Wu kingdom after his sworn brothers are killed. Liu Xuande's distant connection to the imperial Han family, with whom he shares a surname, and his reputation as a compassionate leader lend a certain legitimacy to his claim to be the rightful heir to the Han throne. as does his reputation as a compassionate leader, but he plays an increasingly passive role, and his wrong-headed insistence on revenge disastrously undermines the Shu-Han imperial enterprise. Liu Xuande's ambitious will to power is severely undercut by his weaknesses (characterized by frequent weeping) and his stubborn loyalty to his sworn brothers.

Loyalty, honor, and heroic restraint combined with rashness and arrogance are symbolized in Liu Xuande's two sworn Shu-Han brothers, Zhang Fei and Lord Guan. Zhang is a crude, tough warrior whose berserker cry strikes fear into his opponents—including Cao Cao, who flees, hairpins flying, from the sound of Zhang's roar. He remains loyal to Liu Xuande throughout the novel, but he is reckless and cannot be trusted to understand the finer points of

strategy. His downfall and death are swift and brutal, as is the vengeance wreaked on his killers by his son and Liu Xuande. Lord Guan, on the other hand, is the epitome of a great warrior (he was made God of War more than five hundred years after his death), and his dashing heroic exploits are a central reason for the novel's popularity. Lord Guan is a hero from the moment of his first victorious single combat. All the fighting occurs offstage before he returns with his enemy's head to his game of chess, a cup of wine he left behind still warm. Lord Guan continues to play, unflinching while a doctor operates on his wounded arm. His highly developed sense of honor (*yi*) coexists with an Achilles' heel: his overweening pride. Ignoring Kongming's instructions to conciliate with the Wu forces so that they can mount a joint attack on Cao Cao, Lord Guan instead attacks and alienates Wu ruler Sun Quan; loses a vital base; and dies ingloriously. In contrast to both sworn brothers and Liu Xuande, the general Zhao Zilong brings courage and honorable service to the Shu-Han cause and loyalty to Kongming and the Liu clan. He remains the perfect knight, untainted by the fatal flaws of his peers. The exploration of pairs—Liu Xuande and Cao Cao, Zhang Fei and Lord Guan, Kongming and Zhao Zilong—and the comparisons and contrasts among them, creates a parallelism in the novel's characterizations.

The Wei leader Cao Cao, the novel's villain, or antihero, also exhibits ambition and hubris. He is an extraordinarily compelling figure who actively engages in battle, and his characteristic mode is laughter in the face of adversity. An increasingly powerful hegemon, his arrogance leads to disastrous mistakes that bring about his defeat at Red Cliff. The scenes before and after the battle receive far more attention than the actual fighting (a common trait of the novel), but these scenes are justifiably famous. Kongming and Cao Cao pit wits against each other and against the Wu general Zhou Yu, the historical victor. Cao Cao's Wei troops, inexperienced at naval warfare, are defeated by Kongming's complex interlocking plan, which depends on a variety of ruses involving spies and counterspies. "There is no end to deception in warfare," says Kongming. He "borrows" Cao Cao's arrows, tricks Cao Cao into chaining his ships together, and then destroys them utterly with fireships borne by a magically summoned wind. In a darkly powerful scene on the eve of battle, Cao Cao tempts fate by scorning his opponents, singing a song that tells of his past victories, and killing an adviser who points to a bad omen in the shape of a raven. Remorseful, he nonetheless cannot avoid laughing at several warnings of the danger of fire to his ships, and he continues to laugh as he flees in defeat with a reduced force, dodging the Shu-Han general Zhao Zilong and his lieutenant Zhang Fei. Cao Cao is then ambushed by Lord Guan, but Guan frees him in an honorable but misguided gesture that fundamentally affects the balance of power. Kongming accepts this act by his ruler's sworn brother as inevitable; he knows that Cao Cao is not yet fated to die.

Kongming is for many the real hero of *Three Kingdoms*. He possesses an almost uncanny strategic wisdom coupled with an untimely fate that dooms his endeavors to fail. Wooed by Liu Xuande to join his ranks at the age of twenty-seven, Kongming is the consummate military adviser and chief minister. He is unswervingly loyal to the cause of reviving the Han dynasty in the form of the Shu-Han kingdom. His strategic and rhetorical skills are virtually unmatched, and his far-sighted understanding of the grand, violent chess game of empire is strengthened by his supernatural abilities to bring the power of nature to bear during battle. He asserts that a military commander "is a mediocrity unless he is well-versed in the patterns of the heavens, recognizes the advantages of the terrain, knows the interaction of prognostic signs, understands the changes in weather, examines the maps of deployment, and is clear about the balance of forces." In *Knowing Words: Wisdom and Cunning in the Classical Tradition of China and Greece*, Lisa Raphals likens him to Odysseus and places him in a tradition of Chinese military strategists imbued with cunning wisdom (*zhi*). He is a warrior of words and brilliant ruses rather than force, but he is tireless in the field during countless campaigns. Kongming's ability to summon fire to defeat his enemies is a recurrent motif, as is his trick of appearing nonchalantly in small carts and on empty besieged city walls in the midst of battle to unsettle his opponents. Despite his apparent invincibility and unshakable confidence, he is defeated by the foolish actions of the rulers he serves so well and, more importantly, by the inevitability of history or fate: he insists, "My fate is linked to Heaven." After Kongming's death, the struggle for power continues among the three kingdoms, their generals and rulers diminished in stature in comparison to the earlier heroes, culminating in the general victory of the Western Jin dynasty, recounted at the end of the book.

CRITICAL DISCUSSION

The authorship of *Three Kingdoms* has long been a topic of scholarly debate. The earliest extant published edition of the novel, the *Sanguozhi tongsu yanyi*, dates from 1522 and has a 1494 preface. The Chinese writer Luo Guanzhong (c. 1330–1400) was, and continues to be, associated with its authorship, although the only proof is the long tradition attached to his name. Early vernacular fiction did not enjoy the same canonical status as other literary genres, so authorship was often anonymous. Some scholars who accept Luo's authorship posit that *Three Kingdoms* was a response to the turmoil at the end of the Mongol Yuan dynasty that led to the rise to power of Ming founder Zhu Yuanzhang (r. 1368–98). Many scholars, most prominently Andrew Plaks, argue that the novel was produced in

the mid-Ming dynasty, long after Luo's death, and that it is the earliest example of a new genre described as the "four masterworks," written by members of the sixteenth-century scholar-elites. In *The Four Masterworks of the Ming Novel*, Plaks suggests these works share a strong tendency toward ironic revision of the popular images of well-known characters. Whoever the author was, he clearly possessed a deep familiarity with the historical and popular sources concerning the Three Kingdoms period and more than a passing knowledge of military strategy and practice.

In the mid-seventeenth century, in the aftermath of the Qing conquest of China, the father and son team Mao Lun and Mao Zonggang revised and edited *Three Kingdoms*. They added voluminous commentary and a reading guide (*dufa*) to what would become the standard edition of the novel for the following three centuries. In addition to emphasizing the novel's structural unity and its themes of failure and futility, the Maos strongly advocate for the Shu-Han cause, particularly Kongming's role in it, while betraying ambivalent sympathy for Cao Cao. Both major English translations of the novel are based on the Maos' edition, and scholars such as Plaks and Moss Roberts (the most recent translator of *Three Kingdoms*) are indebted to the Maos' commentary in their own analyses of the structuring and themes of the novel, its reliance on pairs and parallelism in characterization and events, and its discussions of individual personalities. The 2008 volume *Three Kingdoms and Chinese Culture*, edited by Kimberly Besio and Constantine Tung with a foreword by Roberts, is the first full-length book of criticism in English to focus on the novel, filling a major gap in the field. This multidisciplinary study approaches *Three Kingdoms* and its central place in Chinese culture from several angles, with essays on values embodied through key terms, tragic consciousness, historical background to key figures and events, representations in drama and folk art, and the novel's contemporary life in new media throughout Asia. The variety and scope of the essays are a fitting testament to the rich and enduring significance of *Three Kingdoms* as a major cultural document.

SOURCES

Hsia, C. T. *The Classic Chinese Novel: A Critical Introduction*. Bloomington: Indiana UP, 1984. Print.

Li, Wai-yee. "Full-Length Vernacular Fiction." *The Columbia History of Chinese Literature*. Ed. Victor H. Mair. New York: Columbia UP, 2010. 621–58. Print.

Luo, Guanzhong (attributed). *Three Kingdoms: A Historical Novel*. Trans. Moss Roberts. Abr. ed. Beijing: Foreign Languages; Berkeley: U of California P, 1999. Print.

Plaks, Andrew. *The Four Masterworks of the Ming Novel: Ssu ta ch'i-shu*. Princeton: Princeton UP, 1987. Print.

Raphals, Lisa. *Knowing Words: Wisdom and Cunning in the Classical Tradition of China and Greece*. Ithaca: Cornell UP, 1992. Print.

FURTHER READING

Besio, Kimberly, and Constantine Tung, eds. *Three Kingdoms and Chinese Culture*. Albany: State U of New York P, 2008. Print.

De Crespigny, Rafe. "The Three Kingdoms and Western Jin: A History of China in the Third Century AD." *East Asian History* 1 (1991): 1–36; 2 (1991): 143–64. Print.

Lo, Andrew Hing-bun. "*San-kuo chih yen-i*." *The Indiana Companion to Traditional Chinese Literature*. Ed. William H. Nienhauser Jr. Bloomington: Indiana UP, 1986: 668–71. Print.

Alison Bailey

EYE-WITNESSING

THE ARAUCANAID

Alonso de Ercilla y Zúñiga

OVERVIEW

Widely considered the Chilean national epic, *The Arauca-naid* narrates one of the most violent and prolonged conflicts in the conquest of Latin America, the Arauco War. Alonso de Ercilla y Zúñiga uses the ancient form of epic poetry to tell the story of the Araucanian Indians' fierce defense of their land in south-central Chile against the invading Spanish forces. The Araucanians demonstrated impressive courage and resolve as they resisted conquest and colonization for more than 300 years. Ercilla, who arrived in Chile in 1557 as a volunteer soldier for the Spanish army, composed his poem from notes that he had taken during battle. Although he only witnessed a year and a half of the war between the Spaniards and the Araucanians, *The Araucanaid* offers an intensely vivid picture of the lengthy struggle for the control of Chile.

The Araucanaid is composed of three parts, published in 1569, 1578, and 1589. In the first part of the poem, Ercilla presents the fearless and indomitable Araucanians in their fight against the Inca Empire and, later, the Spanish conquistadors. In the second part, the poet lauds the Spaniards for their military prowess, reminding readers of their previous victories in other parts of the world. The final part of the poem covers a number of topics, dramatizing the romantic relationships between soldiers and their female companions, describing the greatness of King Phillip II and of Spain's growing empire in the New World, and censuring the actions of Spanish soldiers in the Arauco War.

After its publication in Spain at the end of the sixteenth century, *The Araucanaid* was widely read in Europe and Latin America. Spaniards appreciated the theme of the drama of conquest, and they embraced the poem as the natural extension of the medieval romances of chivalry. Its detailed descriptions of Chile and its people were also popular with Europeans yearning for a glimpse of the New World. The poem has become a classic of the Spanish language because of its nuanced view of the Spanish conquistadors, the Araucanians, and the Arauco War in general. Ercilla managed to glorify both the victors and the vanquished and to engage in subtle criticism while maintaining respect and awe for his subjects.

HISTORICAL AND LITERARY CONTEXT

The Araucanian (or Mapuche) people of south-central Chile were legendary for their fierceness and strength in battle. They resisted colonization by the Inca Empire for centuries, and at the arrival of the conquistadors the Araucanians fought against Spanish domination. (It is believed that the Spanish name *Araucana* comes from "auca," the Quechua word for "rebel.".) In 1535 Diego de Almagro's troops entered Chile from Peru; as they moved south of the Maule River, however, they were met with violent resistance by the Araucanians, forcing them into full retreat. Pedro de Valdivia attempted to conquer Araucanian lands in 1540, founding the city of Santiago a year later. The Araucanians attacked the city, all but destroying it. When the city of Concepción was established, the Araucanians attacked that settlement as well.

Recognizing the strength and resolve of the Araucanian Indians, the conquistadors sent for reinforcements and continued to press into Araucanian lands. They established the forts of Imperial, Valdivia, Tucapel, and Arauco, and in 1553 they opened a gold mine in Quilacoya, coercing many of the Araucanian Indians into the grueling work of gold mining. That same year the Araucanians congregated and officially declared war on the Spaniards. In their first official conflict, the Battle of Tucapel, they demolished the Spanish fort, forced the Spaniards to retreat, and captured and killed de Valdivia. In 1555 Francisco de Villagra attempted to reconstruct the fort at Concepción but was attacked by the Araucanians. The next year the Araucanians joined forces with another Mapuche tribe to the north, and together they attacked Santiago. Because of internecine conflicts, however, the Araucanians were betrayed by their allies, allowing the Spaniards to launch a surprise attack and kill Lautaro, the Araucanian military leader.

In 1557 the Spanish government sent more reinforcements under the leadership of García Hurtado de Mendoza to reconstruct the fort at Concepción. When the Araucanians assailed the fort again, the Spaniards defeated them and captured and executed their other great military leader, Caupolicán. The loss of two of their greatest warriors weakened the Araucanians significantly, and, while they persisted in attacking Spanish camps and fighting against the conquest, they could not prevent the inevitable loss of their lands. The seventeenth century brought various treaties between the Araucanians and the Spaniards, although these were rarely respected by either group,

✣ *Key Facts*

Conflict:
Arauco War

Time Period:
16th Century

Genre:
Epic poem

LEPANTO AND SPAIN

The 1571 Battle of Lepanto was one of the most significant military battles in the history of Christianity, essentially pitting the forces of Christianity and Islam against one another for control of the Mediterranean Sea. In October 1571 the Holy League, a coalition of Catholic sea powers that included Spain, Venice, Genoa, Savoy, the Knights of Malta, and the Papacy, engaged with the Ottoman Empire in a naval battle in the Gulf of Lepanto off the coast of modern-day Greece. The cause of the conflict was twofold: The Holy League feared the encroachment of the Muslim Ottoman Empire into Catholic-controlled Western Europe, and they wanted to maintain control of the Mediterranean Sea as a commercial channel into western Europe and the ever-expanding New World.

On October 7 the Holy League celebrated a decisive victory over the Ottoman forces. The Christians overwhelmed the Ottomans with greater numbers of sailors, soldiers, ships, guns, cannons, and ammunition. Although there were large numbers of casualties on both sides, the Ottoman forces suffered much greater losses and were forced to admit defeat in a major naval battle for the first time since the fifteenth century. The victory was highly significant and symbolic for Christians, since they believed that it was divine will, rather than superior firepower, that guaranteed their success.

and fighting continued on both sides. Despite uprisings against the Spaniards in 1723, 1759, 1766, and 1769, two groups were finally able to broker peace in 1803 with the Parliament of Negrete. By this time the Araucanian population had been cut in half by illness and starvation, and the surviving Araucanians were rounded up and moved to reservations in Southern Chile. Approximately 200,000 Araucanian Indians live peacefully today in reservations throughout the country.

Ercilla was one of the soldiers who arrived with Hurtado de Mendoza in 1557. He quickly became familiar with the major battles and figures in the conflict and chose to memorialize them. *The Araucanaid* employs a poetic form that began with the oral transmission of history. A long narrative poem, the epic generally glorifies heroic deeds of national or regional importance; examples include Homer's *Illiad* and *Odyssey* (composed near the end of the eighth century BCE), which narrate events during and after the legendary Trojan War, and Virgil's *Aeneid* (composed in the first century BCE), an account of the founding of the Roman state by the Trojan hero Aeneas. The first great work of Spanish literature is the epic *Poema de mío Cid* (recorded around the year 1200), which celebrates the deeds of El Cid, a hero of the *Reconquista*, or the reconquest of Spain from the Muslims of North Africa that occurred in the Middle Ages. The *Araucanaid* follows in this tradition of the epic poem as a literary representation of war.

THEMES AND STYLE

In describing the warriors of the Arauco War, Ercilla includes various references to soldiers of the classical world, especially of ancient Greece and Rome, and even to mythological characters. The poem comprises thirty-seven cantos (the epic is traditionally divided into cantos, from the Italian for "songs") within its three parts. In the second canto Ercilla compares one of the Araucanian soldiers with both Apollo and "ever emboldened Mars." In Canto III he mentions a cadre of classical warriors, including the Romans Horace and Publius Decius and the Spartan Leonidas, who, like the Araucanians, were willing to risk their lives in defense of their homelands. These references to ancient war heroes help to bridge the gap between the new, unknown world of Araucania and the more familiar world of classical literature. Many critics have noted that even the least-educated Spaniards of Ercilla's time had some knowledge of Greek and Roman mythology, medieval European ballads, and novels of chivalry. As Frank G. Dawson explains in "Ercilla and *La Araucana*: Spain and the New World," "The ballads and tales of chivalric derring-do impinged upon Ercilla's literary consciousness, as well as upon that of all Spain."

Ercilla also makes use of an ancient literary motif that was popular during the conquest of the Americas: the theme of the dream or premonition. In canto XIII the Araucanian warrior Lautaro tells his lover Guacolda:

> I was dreaming
> that a scowling Spaniard faced me
> with ferocity depicted
> in his mien. With hands of violence
> He squeezed out my heart.

In classical literature only the oracle had access to knowledge of the future. In medieval Spanish literature, however, the motif of the dream as a prediction of the future was common. Harriet Goldberg's "The Dream Report as Literary Device in Medieval Hispanic Literature" cites the theme in popular texts such as *The Poem of mío Cid* and the chivalric novel *Amadís de Gaula*. Chronicles of the conquest of Latin America made reference to dreams and premonitions of the arrival and domination of the Spanish; for example, the Aztec chief Moctezuma and others reportedly had visions and perceived various omens predicting the coming of Hernán Cortés and his men to conquer Mexico. Ercilla's reference to premonitory dreams corresponds with the epic style of his poem.

The Araucanaid stands out among much of the literature of the conquest of the Americas in that Ercilla takes a complex stand on the war between the Spaniards and the Araucanians, in which neither side, and no individual soldier, emerges as victor or villain. He begins by dedicating his poem to Philip II of Spain, but his first verses glorify the Araucanians, "a monarch-scorning people." He centers much of the poem on the multifaceted character of the war-like tribe and their dedication to the defense of their homeland. In canto XV, he describes the Araucanians' valiant fight to the death: "Their swords were twisting / Some who on the sod lay writhing, / lunged to do the utmost damage." As William Melczer notes in "Ercilla's Divided Vision: A Re-Evaluation of the Epic Hero in 'La Araucana,'" the Araucanians are most righteous in defeat: "The deeper the Araucanians sink into the military quagmire, the stronger they sense the historical significance of their resistance." This image of their moral superiority and Ercilla's focus on such leaders as Lautaro and Caupolicán allow the poet to humanize the Araucanians and dignify their acts of resistance against the inevitable force of Spanish conquest.

Ercilla also praises the Spaniards for their military might and imperial aspirations. Most notably, he deviates from time and place to witness two very significant battles in which Spain triumphed over its enemies. First, in cantos XVII and XVIII, the poem moves back and forth between the conflict in Chile and the 1557 Battle of St. Quentin during the Franco-Hapsburg War. In cantos XXIII and XXIV, Ercilla narrates the Battle of Lepanto, in which an army of Catholic allied states, including Spain, Malta, and many of the various kingdoms and republics that make up modern-day Italy, defeated the forces of the Ottoman Empire, thus preserving the dominance of Christianity over Islam in western Europe. The ideological parallel between the Battle of Lepanto and the fight against the Araucanians is clear, as both entail the expansion of the Catholic faith throughout the world.

CRITICAL DISCUSSION

The late-sixteenth-century publication of *The Araucanaid* was met with astounding success, both in Spain and in the Americas, and Ercilla was lauded as one of the first poets of the New World. Not long after publishing the first part of his poem in 1569, he was inducted into the Order of Santiago, an ancient and prestigious military and chivalric association in Spain. In his study of the book trade in colonial Latin America *Books of the Brave*, Irving Leonard demonstrates that throughout the colonial period, *The Araucanaid* was one of the most widely read accounts of the conquest of Latin America. Only a few decades after its publication, Ercilla's poem appears in another seminal work of Spanish literature, *Don Quijote*, in 1605. As Don Quijote's family and friends examine his bookshelf in order to weed out unworthy titles, *The Araucanaid* is one of three books that are saved from the fire. The local priest explains that Ercilla's poem is among "the best books written in heroic verse in the Castilian language, and … the richest gems of poetry that Spain has."

In later periods of Latin American history, *The Araucanaid* has been reinterpreted and co-opted for various ideological and political campaigns. The nineteenth-century Venezuelan poet and politician Andrés Bello's reading of the poem inspired his revolutionary

Mapuche Indians demonstrating in Santiago, Chile, in January 2000. *The Araucanaid* tells the story of the Mapuche's fierce defense of their land against Spanish invaders in the sixteenth century. © FRANS LEMMENS / ALAMY

campaign in support of the independence of Chile and Venezuela. Chilean poet and famed socialist Pablo Neruda described Ercilla as the "inventor and liberator" of Chile. Given the complex and multifaceted nature of *The Araucanaid*, it is certain to be the topic of further discussion and interpretation in centuries to come.

SOURCES

Cervantes Saavedra, Miguel. *Don Quijote*. Trans. Edith Grossman. New York: HarperCollins, 2003. Print.

Dawson, Frank G. "Ercilla and *La Araucana*: Spain and the New World." *Journal of Inter-American Studies* 4.4 (1962): 563–76. Print.

Ercilla y Zúñiga, Alonso. *The Araucanaid*. Trans. Charles Maxwell Lancaster and Paul Thomas Manchester. Nashville: Vanderbilt UP, 1945. Print.

Goldberg, Harriet. "The Dream Report as Literary Device in Medieval Hispanic Literature." *Hispania* 66:1 (1983): 21–31. Print.

Kallendorf, Craig. "Representing the Other: Ercilla's *La Araucana*, Virgil's *Aeneid*, and The New World Encounter." *Comparative Literature Studies* 40.4 (2003): 394–414. Print.

Leonard, Irving. *Books of the Brave*. New York: Gordian, 1964. Print.

Melczer, William. "Ercilla's Divided Vision: A Re-Evaluation of the Epic Hero in "La Araucana." *Hispania* 56 (1973): 216–21. Print.

Neruda, Pablo. "El Mensajero." *Don Alonso de Ercilla, Inventor de Chile*. Santiago: Editorial Pomaire, 1971. Print.

Nicolopulos, James. *The Poetics of Empire in the Indies: Prophecy and Imitation "La Araucana" and "Os Lusíadas"*. University Park: Pennsylvania State UP, 2000. Print.

FURTHER READING

Adorno, Rolena. "Literary Production and Suppression: Reading and Writing about Amerindians in Colonial Spanish America." *Dispositio* 11.28 (1985): 15–19. Print.

Aquila, August J. "Ercilla's Concept of the Ideal Soldier." *Hispania* 60.1 (1977): 68–75. Print.

Camões, Luís Vaz de. *The Lusiads*. Trans. Landeg White. London: Oxford World's Classics, 2008. Print.

Cevallos, Francisco Javier. "Don Alonso de Ercilla and the American Indian: History and Myth." *Revista de Estudios Hispánicos* 23 (1989): 5–17. Print.

Mignolo, Walter. *The Darker Side of the Renaissance: Literacy, Territoriality, and Colonization*. Ann Arbor: U of Michigan P, 1995. Print.

Rodríguez de Montalvo, Garci. *Amadis of Gaul*. Trans. Herbert Behm and Edwin Place. Lexington: UP of Kentucky, 2003. Print.

Gina Sherriff

THE BATTLE OF TOMOCHIC
Memoirs of a Second Lieutenant
Heriberto Frías

OVERVIEW

The Battle of Tomochic: Memoirs of a Second Lieutenant is a historical novel by Mexican author Heriberto Frías that was originally published anonymously in the newspaper *El demócrata* in serial form in March and April of 1893. The work is based on a military campaign in Chihuahua, Mexico, that led to a massacre in the village of Tomochic in 1892. Several new policies advanced by Porfirio Díaz's government were the source of the conflict that led to this military disaster. In particular, the dictator attempted to restrict the political and economic autonomy of individual Mexican towns while also making concessions to foreign governments regarding the extraction of the country's natural resources. Both political maneuvers were widely criticized, and they led to insurrections in the states of Chihuahua and Sonora in the last decade of the nineteenth century. Tomochic was directly affected by the exploitative new policies, and its citizens participated in the uprisings against the government.

The protagonist of *Tomochic*, Miguel Mercado, is a fictionalized version of the author, who witnessed the conflict as a second lieutenant in the Ninth Battalion of the Mexican army. Frías's military career had begun in 1887, only a few years before the Tomochic rebellion, and it ended shortly after the event, in part because of the publication of *Tomochic*. Frías was provoked to write his fictional account of the events in Tomochic after reading a newspaper article that, in his opinion, did not accurately reflect the extent of the ambiguity involved in the conflict. Frías sought to capture the confusion that characterized the fighting and the mistakes made by both sides that only added to the death and destruction. It was no surprise that his thinly veiled criticism of the role of the Mexican government in the Tomochic incident and of the dictator Porfirio Díaz, in particular, was objectionable to government officials. Although his friends ensured that no manuscript of the novel containing his name ever surfaced, Frías was jailed for a brief time while military representatives looked for this type of incriminating evidence. In addition to its importance in inaugurating Frías's career in journalism, *Tomochic* occupies a prominence place in Mexican literature: not only does it offer a unique perspective on the conflicts taking place in Mexico at the end of the nineteenth century but it is also considered an important literary precursor to the novels of the Mexican Revolution.

HISTORICAL AND LITERARY CONTEXT

Of the rebellions that took place in reaction to the changing policies of Porfirio Díaz's government, the one in Tomochic stood out for a number of reasons. First, the rebels and the soldiers were racially similar: whereas other rebel groups were composed mainly of members of Mexico's indigenous population, those who fought in defense of Tomochic were mainly *mestizos* (people of mixed-race heritage) and *criollos* (people of Spanish descent born in Mexico), just like the soldiers in the Mexican military. That is to say, neither soldiers such as Frías nor the general public could explain the military's violence on the basis of supposed racial differences.

Secondly, there was a religious element that, to a certain extent, had farther-reaching repercussions than Porfirio Díaz's economic policies. The inhabitants of Tomochic, like other villagers throughout Chihuahua, were followers of Teresa Urrea, or the Santa de Cabora, who was venerated for the miracles she performed. The citizens of Tomochic placed an image of Teresa Urrea on the altar of their church. When the priest arrived for his periodic visit to the town, he demanded that the villagers remove the image, which they refused to do. In consequence, the priest refused to fulfill his own religious obligations to the town and filed an official complaint with the civil authorities, denouncing the heretical behavior of Tomochic's residents. The government, in an attempt to make an example of the rebellious Tomochic, sent part of its armed forces to make the town's citizens comply with religious and civil law. The Tomochicans, led by Cruz Chávez, refused and raised barricades; the government, in turn, ordered its military to attack and kill the rebels. Most of Tomochic's men died in battle, while many of the women and children died in a fire that broke out in the church. By the time the fighting ended, approximately three hundred villagers had died.

The ambiguity and disorientation that figure prominently in Frías's retelling of these historic events are important thematic precursors to the works that would make up the literary current known as the

❖ *Key Facts*

Conflict:
Tomochic rebellion

Time Period:
Late 19th Century

Genre:
Novel

"THE BALLAD OF THE MEXICAN REVOLUTION"

The Battle of Tomochic: Memoirs of a Second Lieutenant, by Heriberto Frías, is one of the earliest literary accounts of the bloody Tomochic massacre of 1892, told from the perspective of an officer fighting with the Mexican army. The peasant ballad "El Corrido del Tomóchic," on the other hand, describes the struggle from the point of view of the Tomochic people. The ballad first appeared in print as an appendix to the autobiography of a Mexican soldier, Francisco Castro, who participated in the attack on Tomochic; however, the exact authorship and origins of the ballad remain unknown. "El Corrido del Tomóchic" describes the bold resistance of the Tomochic people in the face of the Mexican onslaught, highly praising their willingness to sacrifice their lives in defense of their right to retain their homes and property. As Castro notes in his memoirs, the bravery of the Tomochic people on that day eventually inspired him to join the revolt against Porfirio Díaz's corrupt reign almost two decades later; indeed, many scholars consider "El Corrido del Tomóchic" to be the original rallying cry of the Mexican Revolution. With its poetic expression of the desire for autonomy and freedom in the face of oppressive government forces, the ballad remains well known throughout Mexico and is still sung by the descendants of the Tomochic peasants who first resisted the Mexican army in 1892.

novel of the Mexican Revolution, which includes *The Underdogs* (1915), by Mariano Azuela. Although Azuela read *Tomochic* only after he had published his own novel, his praise of Fría's work in a later book, *One Hundred Years of the Mexican Novel*, suggests a shared ideological agenda between the two authors. Their similar thematic and aesthetic concerns would likewise be reflected in later novels of the Mexican Revolution.

THEMES AND STYLE

Many of the themes in *Tomochic* are embodied in the figure of Miguel Mercado, a soldier of the Ninth Battalion who becomes increasingly disillusioned by the failures of the military at the same time that he is falling in love with the niece of one of Tomochic's most outspoken citizens. Mercado's disillusionment is evident in the uncertainty he experiences when contrasting his abstract knowledge regarding war, which he has gleaned from the many books he has read, with the actual events unfolding in Tomochic. From the beginning, he is out of place among the soldiers: His previous intellectual pursuits have not prepared him for the realities of war. It soon becomes clear, however, that this is the least of his problems, for, once in Tomochic, he realizes that no one in his battalion has the experience or the knowledge of the local terrain necessary to effectively wage war against the town. Throughout the novel, Miguel laments the indistinctness of the situation in Tomochic, as well as the violence and disorganization that characterize the skirmishes between the Tomochicans and the military. From the very first battle, which is led by military officials blind to the challenges of the terrain and the strategies of their enemy, the soldiers often panic and disperse; as a result of their fear, many of them even fire into their own columns. Death, so exalted in the epic poems that Miguel reads, is reduced to a commonplace occurrence with no special significance.

In order to justify his own participation in the conflict, Miguel creates an alternative narrative in which he becomes a hero. In this way, his love affair with Julia, which is the secondary plot of the book, is intimately related to the war theme prevalent throughout the text. In this fictional world that Miguel creates, which very closely resembles a fairy tale, he rescues Julia from her physically and sexually abusive uncle. Frías writes, "In his imagination, Miguel combined past and future events, composing one long, luxurious poem of love, incense, and blood, in which the nuptials of the Virgin of Tomochic and the Hero Miguel shone resplendent and victorious." Despite the ambiguity that surrounds the military campaign, here Miguel imagines his relationship with Julia in archetypal terms. This permits him to distance himself from the gruesome and embarrassing reality of the military's involvement in Tomochic and to reinvent himself and his relationship with Tomochic's citizens through his salvation of Julia.

Of course, these imaginings are merely momentary daydreams that distract Miguel from his actual role in the fighting. As the conflict continues and the townspeople begin to suffer large numbers of casualties, Miguel's poetic discourses prove useless in staving off the horrible reality in which he finds himself. After the military's victory, the tragic parade of widows and orphans to the enemy camp leaves the soldiers speechless. The terrible reality of what they have done forces Miguel to abandon the comfort of his imagination to confront the truth of the situation. Witnessing this parade, Miguel thinks that he "couldn't remember reading anything so utterly painful or pathetic in any novel or play."

CRITICAL DISCUSSION

After the first printing of *Tomochic* in *El demócrata* in 1893, the work was published in book form in 1899 and again in 1906 and 1911. It was only in the 1899 Maucci edition, however, that authorship was definitely attributed to Frías. Despite the novel's initial popularity, scholarly interest in *Tomochic* has been minimal. As recently as 2008, Paul Vanderwood alleges in the *Hispanic American Historical Review* that while *Tomochic* is a "fine historical novel," it lacks the intellectual depth necessary to be considered a classic. Although Frías's book is viewed as an important precursor of the novel of the Mexican Revolution, examples of the latter are much more widely studied than the work that anticipated their creation.

What appreciation *Tomochic* received has traditionally been centered on its historical value rather than on any literary merits it might possess. In this respect, it is often discussed in the context of the formation of Mexico's national identity, as well as the political and economic struggles that occurred under Porfirio Díaz's regime. Read as a work of history, the novel has been criticized for its inclusion of the amorous relationship between Julia and Miguel, which is regarded as an unnecessary subplot.

In the mid- to late twentieth century, a few scholars began to emphasize the text's literary uniqueness. In a 1967 commentary in *Hispania*, James W. Brown makes a correct but rather obvious identification of Frías with naturalism, calling him a "Mexican Zola." Aníbal González's 1983 study *La cronica modernista hispanoamericana* considers *Tomochic* as a "naturalist novel with strong Modernist inflections." Antonio Saborit, probably the foremost scholar on the novel, builds on these early literary interpretations in *Los doblados de Tomochic* (1994), shedding light on the complex interactions between the novel and its contexts of production and reception. Saborit further explores the implications of the work's publication for Frías's subsequent literary and political career, as well as the novel's influence on Mexican culture and politics at the end of the nineteenth century.

Twenty-first-century analysis has taken a decidedly more theoretical approach to the novel. Joshua Lund's *The Impure Imagination*'s illustrates how the repression of the Tomochic uprising (a very controversial event in its time) and the scandal surrounding the publication of Frías's novel at once questioned and confirmed the official ideology of *mestizaje* (racial mixture) as the social formula intended to achieve national cohesion. In "Tomóchic de Heriberto Frías: Violencia campesina, melancolía y genealogía fraticida de las naciones," Juan Pablo Dabove examines how the novel is a failed attempt to depict the marginalized peasant consciousness and at the same time an enactment of what Benedict Anderson (in his earlier *Imagined Communities: Reflections on the Origin and Spread of Nationalism*) calls "the reassuring effect of fratricide": the creation, through a conflict narrative, of a virtual space, an imagined community called "Mexico."

Portrait of Mexican president Porfirio Díaz. Heriberto Frías's novel *Tomochic* is a fictional account of the 1892 massacre of the village of Tomochic, Mexico, ordered by the Díaz regime. © GIANNI DAGLI ORTI / THE ART ARCHIVE AT ART RESOURCE, NY

Dabove, Juan Pablo. "Tomóchic de Heriberto Frías: Violencia campesina, melancolía y genealogía fraticida de las naciones." *Revista de crítica latinoamericana* 30 (2004): 351–73. Print.

Frías. Heriberto. *The Battle of Tomochic: Memoirs of a Second Lieutenant.* Trans. Barbara Jamison. Intro. Antonio Saborit. New York: Oxford UP, 2006. Print.

González, Aníbal. *La crónica modernista hispanoamericana.* Madrid: Porrúa Turanzas, 1983. Print.

Lund, Joshua. "They Were Not a Barbarous Tribe." *The Impure Imagination: Toward a Critical Hybridity in Latin American Writing.* Minneapolis: U of Minneapolis P, 2006. 89–103. Print.

Saborit, Antonio. *Los doblados de Tomóchic.* México DF: Aguilar, 1994. Print.

Vanderwood, Paul. Rev. of *The Battle of Tomochic*, by Heriberto Frías. *Hispanic American Historical Review* 88.2 (2008), 331–32. Print.

FURTHER READING

Chávez, Daniel. "Tomochic: Nationalist Narrative, Homogenizing Late Nineteenth-Century Discourse and Society in Mexico." *Chasqui* 35.2 (2006): 72–88. Print.

González, Aníbal. *Journalism and the Development of the Spanish American Narrative.* New York: Cambridge UP, 1993. Print.

Vanderwood, Paul. *The Power of God against the Guns of Government: Religious Upheaval in Mexico at the Turn of the Nineteenth Century.* Stanford: Stanford UP, 1998. Print.

SOURCES

Anderson, Benedict. *Imagined Communities: Reflections on the Origin and Spread of Nationalism.* New York: Verso, 1991. Print.

Brown, James W. "Heriberto Frías, a Mexican Zola." *Hispania* 50.3 (1967): 467–71. Print.

———. Prólogo. *Tomóchic.* By Heriberto Frías. 13th ed. México DF: Porrúa, 2004. Print.

Elizabeth Gansen

THE BOER WAR DIARY OF SOL T. PLAATJE

An African at Mafeking

Solomon Tshekisho Plaatje

✛ *Key Facts*

Conflict:
Second Boer War

Time Period:
Late 19th–early
20th Century

Genre:
Diary

OVERVIEW

Published for the first time in 1973, South African writer and political leader Sol T. Plaatje's *Boer War Diary* provides a new perspective on the siege of Mafeking during the second Anglo-Boer War.

An accomplished linguist, fluent in both English and Dutch as well as several African and other European languages, Plaatje was employed as an interpreter for the Resident Magistrate's Court in Mafeking when the Second Anglo-Boer War began in October 1899. Working with British authorities during the siege, Plaatje also served in the new courts established following the imposition of martial law, and he wrote intelligence reports taken from African spies and dispatch runners.

Plaatje kept a detailed personal diary during the siege, from October 29, two weeks after the start of the siege, through the end of March, six weeks before British forces relieved the city. Written primarily in English, the diary provides specifics about the day-to-day events of the siege that do not appear in other historical sources, with a particular emphasis on the often-ignored role played by black African soldiers and civilians.

Anthropologist John Comaroff accidentally discovered the diary while doing fieldwork for his doctoral dissertation among the Barolong in the Mafeking district in 1969. As Comaroff describes it in the preface to the published diary, Plaatje's grandson, in response to a request for "any letters or old documents that the tribesmen might have accumulated," brought Comaroff a scrapbook that had belonged to his grandfather. The scrapbook itself was of little interest, but when Comaroff tapped the scrapbook on a table to shake off the dust the diary slid out of the back cover. Comaroff edited the diary with the help of its owner and a team of historians, linguists, and indigenous Barolong.

In 1990 Plaatje's diary was published in a second edition as *The Mafeking Diary: A Black Man's View of a White Man's War*. Comaroff, aided by Brian Willan, Solomon Molema, and Andrew Reed, produced a newly edited centenary edition of the diary in 1999 under the title *The Mafeking Diary of Sol T. Plaatje*.

HISTORICAL AND LITERARY CONTEXT

Founded in 1885 when the British annexed Bechuanaland, the Cape Colony town of Mafeking was located adjacent to the previously existing African town of Mafeking. Together, the two communities had a population of roughly fifteen hundred Europeans and five thousand black Africans, mostly members of the Barolong. The European town was the administrative capital of the Bechuanaland Protectorate, a market center for both the Transvaal and Cape Colony and a railway junction on the line to Rhodesia.

Located on the border between British and Boer territory, the town became a liability to the Cape Colony government when tension developed between the British and the two Boer republics over control of the newly discovered South African goldfields. When Mafeking's political leaders requested military protection against the possibility of border raids, the Cape government—fearing a military presence on the border would trigger an invasion—refused. Mafeking then turned to the new commander of the Protectorate Regiment, Colonel Robert Baden-Powell, best known today as the founder of the Boy Scouts. In September 1899, Baden-Powell ignored official instructions and relocated the regiment to Mafeking.

Soon after war broke out on October 11, 1899, the Boers crossed the border and surrounded the town. After a few initial skirmishes, the Boers limited their efforts to shelling the town from a safe distance. The siege lasted 217 days, from October 1899 to May 1900.

Although historians of the Boer War generally consider the siege of Mafeking to have been unimportant in strategic terms, it caught the imagination of the British public. The siege was seldom out of the headlines. The besieged town included journalists from four London papers, who paid African runners to carry their dispatches through the Boer lines. When news of the garrison's relief reached England, public celebrations were so exuberant that "maffick" became a verb meaning to celebrate uproariously. In the years after the war, Mafeking became part of the mythology of the British empire, due in large part to the continued efforts of Baden-Powell.

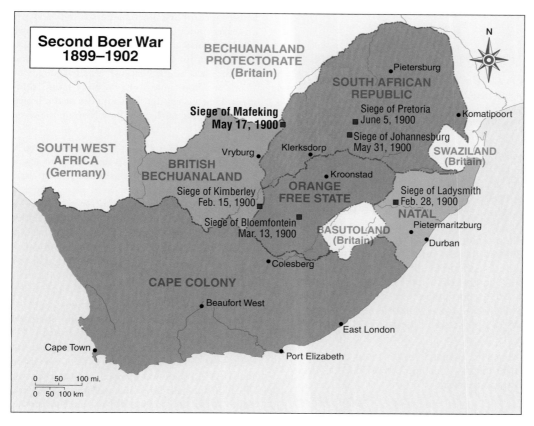

Second Boer War 1899–1902

BECHUANALAND PROTECTORATE (Britain)

SOUTH WEST AFRICA (Germany)

SOUTH AFRICAN REPUBLIC

Pietersburg

Siege of Mafeking May 17, 1900

Siege of Pretoria June 5, 1900

Komatipoort

BRITISH BECHUANALAND

Vryburg

Klerksdorp

Siege of Johannesburg May 31, 1900

SWAZILAND (Britain)

Kroonstad

ORANGE FREE STATE

Siege of Kimberley Feb. 15, 1900

Siege of Ladysmith Feb. 28, 1900

Siege of Bloemfontein Mar. 13, 1900

NATAL

BASUTOLAND (Britain)

Pietermaritzburg

Durban

Colesberg

CAPE COLONY

Beaufort West

East London

Cape Town

Port Elizabeth

0 50 100 mi.
0 50 100 km

© MAP BY XNR PRODUCTIONS. CENGAGE LEARNING, GALE.

Conscious that they were engaged in what one resident, quoted by Brian Willan, described as "making history for the British empire," many residents of the British town kept diaries. (Plaatje was given the task of typing up Resident Magistrate Charles G. H. Bell's daily entries.) A stream of these accounts of the siege, mostly written by war correspondents and army officers, were published soon after the war. These accounts uniformly treat the siege of Mafeking as an example of British heroism, minimizing the role played by black Africans in the defense.

In the years after the war, Plaatje became one of the leading African newspaper editors of his day and the first General Corresponding Secretary of the South African Native National Congress (later the African National Congress). He published several books, including a book-length policy analysis of the *Natives' Land Act of 1913*, collections of Sechuana proverbs and folktales, a translation of Shakespeare's *Comedy of Errors* into Tswana, and the historical novel *Muhdi* (1930), which was the first novel in English written by an African. Ironically, Plaatje's Mafeking diary, which he made no attempt to publish, is now his best-known work.

THEMES AND STYLE

Plaatje's diary overturns the traditional description of the Second Anglo-Boer War as a "white man's war." As historian P. L. Bonner points out, "Plaatje's observations were made from a very particular vantage point—that of a member of the African elite who was closely associated with the British authorities in the town." In fact Plaatje was uniquely placed to comment on the progress of the siege. Baden-Powell declared martial law shortly after the siege began, and Plaatje served as interpreter to two new courts in addition to continuing his work for the Resident Magistrate. He was the liaison between Bell and the Barolong population, organizing the "Native Runners and Spies" and writing reports on the information they brought back. He sold his secretarial services to various newspaper correspondents who were in Mafeking covering the war. Beginning in February 1900, he wrote weekly reports for Bell on what he described in the diary as "all the doings in connection with Native affairs."

Placed by education and profession between European and African worlds, Plaatje was in a better position than anyone else present during the siege of Mafeking to describe the activities of black Africans

MHUDI

Set in northwestern South Africa in the 1830s, Plaatje's novel, *Mhudi*, interprets the history of the period from an African (and specifically Barolong) point of view. The novel is often seen as an African corrective to Eurocentric histories that make the Boer Great Trek the central event of the period.

Plaatje's main characters, the Barolong couple Mhudi and Ra-Thaga, are displaced by the events known as the Mfecane: a period of widespread warfare and dispersal of ethnic groups throughout southern Africa that is often attributed to the expansion of the Zulu under Shaka and the Nbele under Mzilikazi. In their wanderings the couple becomes friends with a family of Voortrekkers, Boers who are part of the Great Trek into the interior of South Africa. The Voortrekkers have moved into what they believe to be empty lands. They soon find themselves at war when they encroach on territory controlled by the Matabele. An alliance between the Barolong and the Boers drives the Matabele away for a short period. The novel ends with the Matabele regrouping as a nation beyond South Africa's borders and the fate of the Boer settlers still in question.

In *Mhudi*, Plaatje combines elements from African oral history with Western narrative techniques, creating a style that has been adopted by many later African novelists.

to the town's defense. In his diary he recorded the contributions of messengers, spies, cattle rustlers, and "that gallant Britisher—the Barolong herdboy," as well as the role of the 750-member Black Watch, which Baden-Powell recruited to supplement the Protectorate Regiment, the police, and the 300-man civilian Town Guard.

Unlike any other contemporary account, Plaatje's details the experiences of the African population during the siege, including the extensive damages suffered by the black township, curfews, and increasing food shortages. His descriptions are expanded by barbed commentary. For instance, in discussing the details of rationing, he comments that conditions in the black township are made worse because arrangements are "in the hands of young officers who know as little about Natives and their mode of living as they know about the man on the moon and *his* mode of living."

Characters who play no role in British accounts of the siege come to life on his pages. Miss Ngono, whose lover was a member of the Black Watch and died of a head wound received while sniping at the Boer trenches, is "so broken-hearted that when I looked at her face I thought it was starvation telling on her constitution." The hapless Alfred Ngidi comes

before the court first "on a charge of being asleep while on sentry duty the previous night" and the following morning "on a charge of failing to hand over a bag of kaffircorn [or kafir corn, a grain that was a staple food for black South Africans]." Mathakgong, whose "name is a household word on every farm," supplemented the decreasing food supplies of the besieged town by raiding cattle from Boer farms in the western Transvaal.

Plaatje's style is often wry, self-deprecating, and humorous. Working in a private journal for his own pleasure, he consciously experiments with literary forms, language, and poetic word play, using words and phrases from Dutch, Sotho, Tswana, Xhosa, and Zulu to enrich his text. According to Patrick Furlong, the result is a style that makes Plaatje "more than a pale imitator of his British contemporaries ... overall, the style comes across as refreshing, vibrant, and always deeply humane."

CRITICAL DISCUSSION

Plaatje's writing received little financial or literary recognition during his lifetime. Biographer Brian Willan quotes an assessment of Plaatje's career by his friend Vere Stent, editor of the *Pretoria News*, who claimed that "if Mr. Plaatje was a French subject, they would fête him and make him a member of the *Academie*. In South Africa he is only a Native, and may not even ride a tram in the capital of the Union."

When Plaatje's diary was released in 1973, it was immediately hailed by Bonner and other historians as "a welcome addition to the literature of the Boer War, especially as it serves to underline still more emphatically the extent to which Africans became enmeshed in Anglo-Boer hostilities, and the often very important part they played in them." At the same time, critics recognized the insights the diary provides into the character of the young man who would become a prominent member of the Western-educated African elite and an early leader of the nationalist movement.

Plaatje's literary and political achievements have received renewed attention since the official end of apartheid in South Africa in May 1994. In the preface to the diary's 1999 centenary edition, John Comaroff goes so far as to say that "the metamorphosis of South Africa in the 1990s makes this an altogether new book ... It no longer appears as a literary curiosity from the African past, but as a crucial chapter in a history told *authoritatively* for the first time from a black perspective."

Historian Jane Starfield praises Plaatje's diary, not only for its "gifted, analytical, aesthetic and descriptive prose" but as "one of the Siege's most important records. Its rarity—being perhaps the only surviving diary of *any* war-time black South African—makes his observations and interpretations of British and Boer policy both rare and meaningful."

SOURCES

Bonner, P. L. "An African View of the Boer War." Rev. of *The Boer War Diary of Sol T. Plaatje*, by Sol T. Plaatje. *Journal of African History* 15.2 (1974): 341–43. Web. 14 June 2011.

Furlong, Patrick. Rev. of *The Mafeking Diary: A Black Man's View of a White Man's War*, by Sol T. Plaatje. *International Journal of African Historical Studies* 23.4 (1990): 733–35. Web. 21 June 2011.

Plaatje, Sol T. *The Boer War Diary of Sol T. Plaatje: An African at Mafeking.* Ed. John L. Comaroff. Johannesburg: Macmillan, 1973. Print.

Plaatje, Sol. T. *The Mafeking Dairy of Sol T. Plaatje.* Ed. John L. Comaroff and Brian Willan with Solomon Molema and Andrew Reed. Oxford: Currey, 1999. Print.

Starfield, Jane. "Re-Thinking Sol Plaatje's *Mafeking Diary*." *Journal of Southern African Studies* 27.4 (2011): 855–63. Web. 21 June 2011.

Willan, Brian. *Sol Plaatje: South African Nationalist, 1876–1932.* Berkeley: U of California P, 1984. Print.

FURTHER READING

Gardner, Brian. *Mafeking: A Victorian Legend.* London: Cassell, 1966. Print.

Lee, Emanoel C. G. *To the Bitter End: A Photographic History of the Boer War, 1899–1902.* New York: Viking, 1985. Print.

Marix Evans, Martin. *The Boer War: South Africa, 1899–1902.* Oxford: Osprey, 1999. Print.

Nasson, Bill. *Abram Esau's War: A Black South African War in the Cape, 1899–1902.* Cambridge: Cambridge UP, 1991. Print.

Pakenham, Thomas. *The Boer War.* New York: Random, 1979. Print.

Plaatje, Sol. *Selected Writings.* Ed. Brian Willan. Athens: Ohio UP, 1997. Print.

Saunders, Christopher. "African Attitudes to Britain and the Empire Before and After the South African War." *The South African War Reappraised.* Ed. Donal Lawry. Manchester: Manchester UP, 2000. Print.

Warwick, Peter. *Black People and the South African War, 1899–1902.* Cambridge: Cambridge UP, 1980. Print.

Willan, Brian. "The Siege of Mafeking." *The South African War: The Anglo-Boer War, 1899–1902.* Ed. Peter Warwick. Burnt Mill: Longman, 1980. Print.

Woeber, Catherine. "Plaatje Revisited." *English in Africa* 25.2 (1998): 111–21. Web. 21 June 2011.

Pamela Toler

A Barolong dispatch runner kneels to allow a British soldier to conceal a message in his clothing during the Second Anglo-Boer War, 1899–1902. © THE ART ARCHIVE / WAR MUSEUM OF THE BOER REPUBLICS, BLOEMFONTEIN / THE PICTURE DESK, INC.

CARTUCHO *AND* MY MOTHER'S HANDS

Nellie Campobello

✧ *Key Facts*

Conflict:
Mexican Revolution

Time Period:
Early 20th Century

Genre:
Novellas

OVERVIEW

Among the narratives of the Mexican Revolution, Nellie Campobello's *Cartucho* (1931) and *My Mother's Hands* (1937) stand out as manifestations of writing from the margins. Published originally as two separate but closely intertwined texts, *Cartucho* and *My Mother's Hands* portray everyday life in the northern state of Chihuahua during the harshest fighting of the Mexican Revolution (c. 1915–20). Instead of following the larger outlines of the war, *Cartucho* (literally, "cartridge") is based on Campobello's childhood memories of Hidalgo del Parral, an important mining town in Chihuahua and one of the centers of Pancho Villa's revolutionary movement. As Jorge Aguilar Mora writes in his introduction to the 2000 edition of *Cartucho* titled "El silencio de Nellie Campobello," the text expresses a "tension produced by the crossover of the personal with the historical" (trans. Raul Verduzco).

Cartucho consists of a series of vignettes, short narratives, or "still lives," as they are described by Tabea Alexa Linhard. The vignettes present episodes of the war as experienced by young Nellie, mostly from inside her house in Segunda del Rayo Street in Parral, where her mother works as a seamstress. Most depict loosely constructed scenes—fragmentary descriptions of the city under fire, portraits of anonymous and historical characters meeting their fate (usually death)—captured through the eyes of a young girl and stitched together with Campobello's adult literary skills. Instead of portraying picturesque regionalism or circumstantial events, *Cartucho*'s brief tales expose essential elements of the human spirit that drive the anonymous characters to embrace their fate as *revolucionarios*, along with grotesque or painful scenes of violence. Revenge, death, hatred, and cruel violence—interspersed with transient moments of innocent joy—are presented as part of Nellie's everyday life. Her protective, free-spirited mother, driven by affection for her own people, provides comfort, support, and, when possible, medical assistance to ease the pain, both physical or emotional, of the people in Parral—neighbors, soldiers, distressed women who have lost loved ones, and, of course, her children. *My Mother's Hands* is a eulogy for Campobello's mother (Rafaela Luna died in 1923 of natural causes), as well as an homage to her private struggle to help her people and

to set an example for her children. In that sense *My Mother's Hands* functions as a corollary to the autobiographical narrative underlying Campobello's work.

The first edition of *Cartucho* consisted of only thirty-three vignettes, the first of which, "Él" ("Him"), introduces Cartucho, the title character; for the second and definitive edition, which also includes *My Mother's Hands* (1940), Campobello omitted the prologue and one vignette (titled "Villa") and edited the rest of the previously published vignettes. She also added twenty-four new ones (for a total of fifty-six) as well as a dedication to her mother.

Campobello is considered the first woman to have written within the more general body of work treating the Mexican Revolution. Her important contribution to this current of literature gives us a unique perspective on the trauma of the revolutionary war in Mexico and its effects on the anonymous people who experienced it.

HISTORICAL AND LITERARY CONTEXT

The last ten years of Porfirio Díaz's presidency in Mexico were marked by the development of regional opposition movements. The rights granted to the middle class during his first period in office (1876–80) were gradually suppressed in the succeeding decades of his further terms in office (1884–1911). The *Pax Porfiriana*—intended to win over or neutralize the groups that traditionally led revolutionary uprisings—had become untenable.

Regional elites were relatively autonomous during the first twenty years of the Porfirian era, especially in the northern states of Sonora, Chihuahua, Durango, and Coahuila, where landowners created their own private militias, arming and training their peasants to defend their *haciendas*, thereby establishing ties of loyalty, consolidating local military power, and encouraging, perhaps unwittingly, a culture of violence in the region.

By 1910 a series of regional uprisings against Diaz's administration, unified under the Anti-Reelectionist Party, were led by Francisco I. Madero of Coahuila. Madero's movement was essentially political and lacked a firm national platform, especially in regards to agrarian and social programs; however, his was the only plausible alternative to Díaz's dictatorial regime. In order to unite factions within the revolt, Madero's

Plan de San Luis Potosí, which called for the people to revolt on November 20, 1910, included a clause promising to return lands unjustly confiscated by Díaz's administration to their legitimate owners.

Led by Pascual Orozco and Pancho Villa, the first important popular revolt broke out in the western mountains of Chihuahua. Local revolts throughout the country followed, and by April 1911 most of the countryside was controlled by the revolutionaries. On May 21 Madero and the federal government signed the Treaty of Ciudad Juarez, in which it was agreed that Diaz would resign, elections would be held in October, and the revolutionary army would be disbanded.

Soon after Madero's election in October 1911, it became clear that many of the stagnant institutions of the Porfirian era were to be maintained. This contributed to the fragmentation of the revolutionary movement into regional, guerrillalike uprisings, as before, though this time against the new president. Victoriano Huerta, commissioned by Madero to pacify the north, turned against him and led a coup d'état in February 1913. Madero and his vice-president, Pino Suárez, were murdered the night after Huerta took office.

Venustiano Carranza, governor of Coahuila, led a revolt against the "usurpation," forming an army intended to reinstate the constitutional order broken by Huerta. Several rebel units in Chihuahua who were operating under Villa joined Carranza, forming the Division of the North. Álvaro Obregón and Pablo Gonzalez commanded the Constitutionalists in the northwest and northeast, respectively. In the central state of Morelos, Emiliano Zapata led an independent guerrilla force attempting to restore land to the local population.

Villa decreed the confiscation of the largest *haciendas* in the state of Chihuahua, without compensation, to generate revenue and provide allotments for his troops. When Carranza opposed this plan, Villa resigned. In defiance of Carranza's orders, however, Villa's generals put him back in charge, and his troops defeated a federal force of twelve thousand in Zacatecas.

After Huerta was deposed, Carranza took over Mexico City with the support of Obregón's and González's divisions, leaving Villa—and his army of more than thirty thousand—out of the new arrangement, even as Villa strove to return lands to the peasants who had fought under him. Thus, the Division of the North, commanded by its *caudillo* (leader), Villa, began waging war against Carranza's troops. In this complex framework of treachery and empty promises, away from the country's political center, Nellie Campobello's characters wander like passers-by before the eyes of the young narrator, often fighting against the very forces to which they once belonged.

Campobello's work first appeared when the novel of the Mexican Revolution was on the rise and writing

VISUAL EXPRESSIONS OF THE REVOLUTION

As the author of the novellas *Cartucho* and *My Mother's Hands*, Nelly Campobello was one of the leading voices of the Mexican Revolution. Part of Mexico's cultural renaissance during the 1920s and 1930s, Campobello was associated with a number of leading writers and artists in the postrevolutionary period. Among Campobello's most renowned peers was the influential painter Diego Rivera (1886–1957). Known for his epic murals depicting the plight of the Mexican working class, Rivera developed his innovative style while living in Europe during the early twentieth century, when he was exposed to the formal experimentation of Paul Cézanne, Pablo Picasso, and other Cubist painters. Upon his return to Mexico in 1921, Rivera became involved with the revolutionary government's ambitious new cultural mission, through which it hoped to spread its radical artistic and political ideals to the general population. In the ensuing years, Rivera spearheaded the Mexican mural movement, an artistic project that aimed at depicting bold visions of an egalitarian future on the walls of public institutions throughout the country. Drawing from both European modernism and Aztec styles and motifs, Rivera painted some of the most daring frescoes of the period, executing major works for the National Palace in Mexico City and the National School of Agriculture. As the new government became increasingly repressive during the late 1920s, however, Rivera found himself expelled from the Mexican Communist Party and ultimately compelled to flee to the United States, where for the remaining decades of his life he continued to produce murals devoted to themes of economic and social justice.

about Pancho Villa was at its peak. According to Max Parra in *Writing Pancho Villa's Revolution: Rebels in the Literary Imagination of Mexico*, aside from *Cartucho*, three novels about and one biography of Villa were published in 1931. Nellie Campobello was the first woman to write about the revolution, and, though other works by women followed—including Carmen Baéz's short stories; Adriana García Roel's *Hombre de barro* (1943; Man of Clay), and Maria Luisa Ocampo's *Bajo el fuego* (1947; Under Fire)—she was the only woman whose works were included in Antonio Castro Leal's anthology *The Novel of the Mexican Revolution* (1961).

As recorded by Aguilar, Campobello believed that the negative critical reaction to *Cartucho* was not because of her being a woman but was rather an objection to "the authoritarianism of adults towards the young, the unscrupulous struggles for literary power, and the lasting repudiation of Villa 'the bandit' and his soldiers" (trans. Verduzco). Through an appraisal of Pancho Villa as a humane historical figure, Campobello attempted to redefine Villa's role in the official discourse; she reaffirmed a sense of communal identity unlike the unifying national identity imposed by the central power in the mainstream literature of the revolution. She writes from a feminine and domestic (as opposed to a male and public) perspective; her story is the narrative of a child, and it focuses on a regional conflict rather than the national war. In addition, she uses spare language and such literary devices as fragmentation, orality, irony, and the grotesque to portray the spirit of the community embodied in Villa.

THEMES AND STYLE

Two of the prevailing themes in *Cartucho* are anonymity and violence. According to Tabea Alexa Linhard in "A Perpetual Trace of Violence: Gendered Narratives of Revolution and War," violence is presented as a cyclical disease that exposes "a traumatic past, a haunted present, and an impossible future, inhabited by the specters of the revolution," while anonymity acknowledges the universal nature of the violence experienced by Campobello's characters.

Most of the characters are known by nicknames or pseudonyms. The main character in the first vignette in the collection, "Él," is called Cartucho, and to some extent, he represents the gallery of characters in the book. Like a gun cartridge in the war, he is only one among many thousands of others used by the war machine to inflict pain, and he is not expected to last for long. The vignette begins: "Cartucho didn't say his name" (trans. Verduzco). His appearance in the narrator's house is sudden, and so is his disappearance; when Nellie's mother asks about Cartucho, José Ruiz reflects, "Love made him a cartucho. And us …? Cartuchos—he said in a philosophical tone, while fixing his cartridge belt" (trans. Verduzco). The character retains his ambiguity—as did Pancho Villa (whose real name was Doroteo Arango) and Nellie Campobello herself—but his fate is implicit in his nickname. This vignette sets the tone for the rest of the book: It is laconic but forceful in its own silence. As Parra has noted, violence is a dominant theme in writings about Villa, since they call attention "to the brutalities of war and the emotions associated with it: fear, anger, hate, revenge, guilt, denial, and so on." What surprises most about Campobello's vignettes is the ease with which this violence is conveyed by the young narrator, who speaks of mutilated bodies, eyes, ears, guts, hands, and hearts.

These human elements, aside from grotesquely representing dismembered bodies, are also an important element in Campobello's writing style. Her laconic, meager idiom and fragmented syntax reproduce people's attempts to verbalize and "make sense of the disturbing experience of war" (trans. Verduzco). The deliberate insufficiency of language in representing such experience indicates a lack, even a traumatic mutilation, of the memory evoked. Campobello uses metonymy, a figure of speech in which the name of something is replaced by the name of one of its attributes or the name of an associated object, as a strategy for her characters to use in order to cope with a painful memory. Thus, a gun represents the war, a cartridge represents the combatants, and a scarf identifies the general who was strangled with it. On the other hand, metonymy has also been used as a mnemonic strategy in oral literature to ensure that the message is transmitted accurately to others; this strategy was used in most oral narratives that influenced Campobello's style, including the tales of the Tarahumara and Comanche peoples and the Mexican *corrido* (ballad). In *My Mother's Hands*, "hands" characterizes the mother figure as a provider who is both independent and protective.

CRITICAL DISCUSSION

When *Cartucho* was first published, it aroused the curiosity of the general public because of its humane approach to Pancho Villa, but only a few avant-garde writers—such as Germán List Azurbide, who wrote the prologue to the first edition—acknowledged its literary value. In 1935 literary scholar Berta Gamboa de Camino's essay "The Novel of the Mexican Revolution" placed *Cartucho* on the same footing as works by Mariano Azuela and Martin Luis Guzmán. During the following decades, however, criticism of Campobello's works was scarce. In *La novela de la revolución*, Antonio Magaña Esquivel quotes scholar F. Rand Morton's consideration of Campobello as a "halfway novelist." John S. Brushwood and José Rojas Garcidueñas do not even mention Campobello in *Breve historia de la novela mexicana* (1959). Antonio Castro Leal's inclusion of *Cartucho* and *My Mother's Hands* in the anthology *La novela de la revolución Mexicana*, however, helped her works regain the appreciation of academics.

After the publication of *Notes on the Military Life of Francisco Villa* in 1940, Nellie Campobello devoted herself to dance, and until recently, she was more widely known in Mexico as a dancer and choreographer than as a writer. Since her mysterious death in 1986 (apparently, she was kidnapped by one of her dance students and died in captivity), the study of her written works has been revived.

Several contemporary critics, including Margo Glantz, Kemy Oyarzún, Parra, and Aguilar Mora, praise Campobello's works as counter-hegemonic among the narratives of the Mexican Revolution. Aguilar Mora maintains that Campobello's writing paved the way for new literary and stylistic developments in the Latin-American narrative.

SOURCES

Aguilar Mora, Jorge. "El silencio de Nellie Campobello." Introduction. *Cartucho: Relatos de la lucha en el norte de Mexico*. Mexico: Era, 2000. 9–40. Print.

Campobello, Nellie. *Cartucho: Relatos de la lucha en el norte de México*. Mexico: Era, 2000. Print.

Glantz, Margo. "Vigencia de Nellie Campobello." *FULGOR* 3.1 (2006): 37–50. Print.

Linhard, Tabea Alexa. "A Perpetual Trace of Violence: Gendered Narratives of Revolution and War." *Discourse* 25.3 (2003): 30–47. Print.

Magaña Esquivel, Antonio. *La novela de la revolución.* 2nd ed. Mexico: Editorial Porrúa, 1974. Print.

Oyarzún, Kemy. "Mujer, memoria, historia: *Cartucho* de Nellie Campobello. *The Latin American Short Story.* Ed. Menton Seymour and Oyarzún. Riverside: U of California P, 1997. Print.

Parra, Max. *Writing Pancho Villa's Revolution: Rebels in the Literary Imagination of Mexico.* Austin: U of Texas P, 2006. Print.

Reyes Córdova, Bladimir. "Nellie Campobello: Una aproximación al discurso literario en *Cartucho.*" *La narrativa de la revolución mexicana. Primer período.* Ed. Renato Prada Oropeza. Puebla: U Iberoamericana Puebla, 2007. 203–31. Print.

FURTHER READING

Campobello, Nellie. *Cartucho; and, My Mother's Hands.* Trans. Doris Meyer and Irene Matthews. Austin: U of Texas P, 1988. Print.

Guzmán, Martín Luis. *Memoirs of Pancho Villa.* Austin: U of Texas P, 1965. Print.

Katz, Friedrich. *The Life and Times of Pancho Villa.* Stanford: Stanford UP, 1998. Print.

———. "Mexico: Restored Republic and Porfiriato, 1867–1910." *The Cambridge History of Latin America: c. 1870 to 1930.* Ed. Leslie Bethel. Cambridge: Cambridge UP, 1986. 3–78. Print.

Knight, Alan. *The Mexican Revolution.* Cambridge: Cambridge UP, 1986. Print.

McLynn, Frank. *Villa and Zapata: A History of the Mexican Revolution.* New York: Basic, 2002. Print.

Scheina, Robert L. *Villa: Soldier of the Mexican Revolution.* Washington: Brassey's, 2004. Print.

Tuck, Jim. *Pancho Villa and John Reed: Two Faces of Romantic Revolution.* Tucson: U of Arizona P, 1984. Print.

Womack, John, Jr. "The Mexican Revolution, 1910–1920." *The Cambridge History of Latin America: c. 1870 to 1930.* Ed. Leslie Bethel. Cambridge: Cambridge UP, 1986. 79–153. Print.

Raul Verduzco

DECENT INTERVAL

An Insider's Account of Saigon's Indecent End Told by the CIA's Chief Strategy Analyst in Vietnam

Frank Snepp

❖ *Key Facts*

Conflict:
Vietnam War

Time Period:
Mid-20th Century

Genre:
Autobiography

OVERVIEW

In *Decent Interval: An Insider's Account of Saigon's Indecent End Told by the CIA's Chief Strategy Analyst in Vietnam* (1977), Frank Snepp recounts his work as a CIA operative in Vietnam from October 1972 (the beginning of his second assignment there) to April 30, 1975 (the day on which U.S. personnel evacuated Saigon, the capital of South Vietnam). Throughout the book, Snepp argues that diplomatic arrogance, a myopic foreign policy, and duplicitous negotiations with both North and South Vietnam led to a hasty and embarrassing exit from Saigon and endangered the lives of the South Vietnamese, who were left at the mercy of the conquering North Vietnamese army.

Snepp begins *Decent Interval* with a lengthy review of the arduous discussions between Henry Kissinger (U.S. secretary of state and national security adviser) and Le Duc Tho (the North Vietnamese chief negotiator) that resulted in the 1973 Paris Peace Accords. For their work both men were awarded the Nobel Peace Prize, although Le Duc Tho refused to accept the award. The agreements ostensibly established a ceasefire and provided for the withdrawal of U.S. troops from the region. As Snepp points out, however, the resolution was deeply flawed because it never specified how South Vietnam would be governed and because it allowed for the continued presence of North Vietnamese troops there. Kissinger, Snepp contends, protected U.S. interests but left South Vietnam vulnerable. The book takes its title from a phrase coined by critics of the Paris agreements who claimed that by forging the treaty, Kissinger merely bought time and established a "decent interval" between an American departure and the final defeat of South Vietnam.

Although the Paris Peace Accords were supposed to have ended U.S. involvement in Vietnam, the fighting persisted, and North Vietnam continued to press its advantage against South Vietnam. Meanwhile, the U.S. commitment to the conflict diminished as public support for the war declined precipitously and the U.S. Congress grew reticent to fund the military effort. Snepp asserts that despite these obvious setbacks, the CIA was encouraged to ignore hard information and color its findings to represent the war as winnable.

Such reports would allow the Ford administration to secure more funds from Congress and stave off the defeat of South Vietnam. Because they were too busy covering up the truth, Snepp claims that the Americans never made adequate plans to leave the country. In the final third of *Decent Interval*, Snepp documents in exhaustive detail how all of this bungling led to the shameful, last-minute American departure from Saigon in April 1975.

To help recall his experiences, Snepp draws from a briefing notebook he used to log his official correspondence with colleagues and informants and a diary he began keeping in 1969, the start of his first assignment in Vietnam, "out of a vague impulse" to write a novel about what he had witnessed. He also bases his assertions on government documents and numerous interviews with former colleagues, many of whom were likewise disillusioned with CIA operations in Vietnam. To record the North Vietnamese point of view, Snepp relies heavily on *Our Great Spring Victory*, North Vietnamese commander Van Tien Dung's autobiography, which was first published in 1976, the year after North Vietnam assumed control of South Vietnam.

HISTORICAL AND LITERARY CONTEXT

The Vietnam War (1955–75) was fought between Communist-controlled North Vietnam, with the support of the People's Republic of China and the Soviet Union, against South Vietnam, which was supported by the United States. The U.S. government entered the conflict to contain the spread of communism and Soviet influence in Southeast Asia. For the North Vietnamese the war was a continuation of the First Indochina War with France (1946–54) and part of the effort to expel the colonial powers from the region. The North Vietnamese viewed South Vietnam as a puppet state controlled by the United States. U.S. involvement in the Vietnam War escalated in the mid-1960s during the presidency of Lyndon B. Johnson, peaking in 1969 when more than 500,000 U.S. troops were stationed there. Upon taking office that year, Richard M. Nixon pursued a twofold strategy: he escalated the air war by bombing Cambodia, hoping to hit

North Vietnamese sanctuaries and supply lines; and he pursued Vietnamization, whereby U.S. troops were gradually withdrawn and responsibility for conducting the war was turned over to South Vietnam. In January 1973, following Nixon's reelection in November the previous fall, Kissinger negotiated the Paris Peace Accords, which officially ended U.S. involvement in Vietnam. The fighting continued, however, until the fall of Saigon on April 30, 1975, when the last of the U.S. personnel stationed in South Vietnam withdrew from the country.

Books such as *Decent Interval* are often derogatorily called whistle-blowing exposés because their authors divulge inside information that some would say they are obligated to keep confidential. Several other books by former agents take the CIA to task in similar fashion. Victor Marchetti's *The Rope Dancer* (1971), one of the earliest of these books, documents the author's involvement in espionage against East Germany in the 1950s. John Stockwell's *In Search of Enemies* (1978) criticizes CIA actions during the U.S. intervention in the civil war in Angola (1975–76) and argues that the agency should be abolished. *Dirty Work* (1978), edited by former CIA agent Philip Agee and Louis Wolf, is a collection of essays that are critical of the CIA.

THEMES AND STYLE

Snepp's primary argument in *Decent Interval* is that the United States betrayed the South Vietnamese left behind in Saigon, endangering the lives of thousands of local contacts that supported the work of the CIA there. In the postscript to the book he writes, "The full impact of CIA losses and failures in Vietnam will probably never be known. There are too many unanswered questions. But based on what can be ascertained, it is not too much to say that in terms of squandered lives, blown secrets and the betrayal of agents, friends and collaborators, our handling of the evacuation was an institutional disgrace." Snepp estimates that less than one third of approximately ninety thousand South Vietnamese employed by the American embassy were evacuated from Saigon. He then adds that "to compound our errors and their costs we committed that unpardonable mistake of failing to ensure the destruction of the personnel files and intelligence dossiers we had helped the government assemble—and which identified so many of those left on the tarmac or outside the gates of the Embassy." To verify that the United States exposed these former employees to danger, Snepp notes that in June 1976 officials in Hanoi, the capital of North Vietnam, announced that "lackeys of imperialism" and those associated with South Vietnamese president Nguyen Van Thieu's puppet regime who refused "to repent their crimes" were to be tried in people's courts in the coming months.

According to Snepp, Kissinger and Graham Martin, the U.S. ambassador to South Vietnam, bear primary responsibility for the American failures in

the final years of the Vietnam War. With regard to the Paris Peace Accords, Snepp argues that Kissinger's "handiwork was faulty and too hastily done." He claims that Kissinger did not properly update Thieu while negotiating the agreement with Le Duc Tho and notes that Thieu was typically "flabbergasted and enraged" when the status of the discussions reached him secondhand. To appease Thieu, Kissinger and Nixon promised massive military support—just as they promised reconstruction assistance to North Vietnam; in both cases they did so without consulting Congress. Snepp claims that, when representing the agreement in the United States, "Kissinger, with his addiction to secrecy, never quite leveled with Congress or the American people about what was essential to preserving his imperfect peace." Snepp depicts Martin as a lackey sent to do Kissinger's bidding in the aftermath of the Paris Peace Accords. He writes that Martin "never appreciated the gravity of the military situation" and argues that "from the beginning, [he] approached his task as Kissinger wanted, as a kind of conjurer and Madison Avenue pitchman." When the situation deteriorated in 1974, he ignored the facts and "wanted no one around him who could effectively challenge or obstruct him." In the aftermath of the evacuation Snepp portrays Martin as a reflexively defensive man obsessed with salvaging his reputation and eager to persuade others that he managed affairs properly in South Vietnam.

On April 29, 1975, panic-stricken South Vietnamese civilians scale a wall at the U.S. Embassy in Saigon, trying to reach helicopters that are evacuating the last of the Americans. Saigon fell to the North Vietnamese communist troops the following day. © AP IMAGES / NEAL ULEVICH

UNITED STATES V. SNEPP, 1980

According to a secrecy agreement that he signed upon joining the CIA, Snepp was not permitted to publish any information obtained during the course of his employment without prior approval from the agency. Despite making assurances to CIA director Admiral Stansfield Turner that he would abide by the agreement, Snepp never submitted the manuscript of *Decent Interval* to the agency before publishing it in 1977. The CIA responded by initiating a civil suit against Snepp seeking to recover all profits from the sale of the book. In his defense, Snepp claimed that *Decent Interval* contained no classified information and that any censoring of the manuscript would have impinged his First Amendment rights. While the CIA conceded that the book contained no classified information, it claimed that the material in the book caused the agency "irreparable harm" by hampering its ability to gather intelligence in the future.

The court sided with the government, rejecting Snepp's plea for a jury trial and awarding the government all profits, past and future, from *Decent Interval*. The Fourth Circuit Court of Appeals upheld the constitutionality of the CIA's secrecy agreement but also held that the government was entitled to recoup only nominal damages from the publication of the book. The U.S. Supreme Court, however, overturned the findings of the Fourth Circuit Court of Appeals and upheld the initial decision. Snepp wrote about these trials in *Irreparable Harm: A Firsthand Account of How One Agent Took on the CIA in an Epic Battle over Free Speech* (1999).

As autobiography, *Decent Interval* differs from a confessional memoir in that Snepp does not focus on his own misdeeds but rather concentrates on the flaws and missteps of others. While acknowledging that he participated in espionage and procedures of questionable moral character, Snepp holds himself less accountable than he holds his superiors for the failure of those endeavors. He finds fault with the action taken by the CIA in Vietnam, but he does not dispute the CIA's right to be there and sponsor covert operations. In the postscript he writes, "As a former intelligence officer I must believe, perhaps naively, that the right decisions taken at appropriate moments on the basis of accurate information might have averted the outcome, or at least have modified it."

CRITICAL DISCUSSION

Reviews of *Decent Interval* have been mixed. In a *New York Times* review immediately following its publication, John Leonard finds *Decent Interval* "almost interminable" and claims that Snepp "is constantly straining for prose effects slightly beyond his powers of command; he piles on ironies he hasn't quite earned; he attitudinizes from an oddly empty center." Although Leonard concedes that Snepp offers a reliable account of the U.S. evacuation of Saigon, he chastises the author for his lack of insight, noting that "there isn't a gleam of political intelligence anywhere

in *Decent Interval*, a grain of historical sense, any feeling at all for the larger moral failure of which the fall of Saigon was merely a symptom." Seymour M. Hersh, who interviewed Snepp at length for a 1977 report for the *New York Times* about the CIA's reaction to *Decent Interval*, disagrees with Leonard's view of the book. Twenty-two years later, in a *Los Angeles Times* review of *Irreparable Harm* (1999), Snepp's memoir about his dealings with the U.S. Supreme Court, Hersh calls *Decent Interval* "a scathing critique of the CIA's bumbling, lying, and arrogance" and claims that the book is "brilliantly argued and elegantly written." He also praises Snepp for having the "courage and integrity to risk his career for the truth."

Many historians have treated *Decent Interval* as an important contribution to the study of the CIA's operations in Vietnam and of Kissinger's and Martin's mishandling of the evacuation of Saigon. In "Being Intelligent about Secret Intelligence Agencies," a survey of selected publications on U.S. secret intelligence agencies, Harry Howe Ransom argues that *Decent Interval* "gives rare insight into how well the CIA performed operationally overseas." Without evaluating Snepp's conclusions, Ransom nevertheless endorses his work, observing that "Snepp's purpose was to expose dramatically what he considered to be a poor operational performance. Whatever the merits of his judgments, we are supplied with a datum useful for an overall intelligence agency performance evaluation."

In "Kissinger, Ford, and Congress: The Very Bitter End in Vietnam" T. Christopher Jespersen draws extensively from *Decent Interval* to debunk the widely held perception that the United States was forced to evacuate Saigon in 1975 because Congress refused to appropriate the funds necessary to continue supporting the South Vietnamese. Instead, Jespersen argues that Kissinger, Nixon, and Gerald Ford recognized that the situation in Vietnam was rapidly deteriorating and deliberately tried to deflect responsibility for an embarrassing defeat to Congress. Echoing Snepp's observations from *Decent Interval*, Jespersen writes that Kissinger and other key members of the Ford and Nixon administrations "refused to acknowledge the rapidly deteriorating conditions in the months leading up to April 1975, delayed action repeatedly by pursuing unfeasible policies." Jespersen also agreed with Snepp's assessment of Graham Martin, writing that the ambassador was "steeped in denial" and that, in Martin's version of events, "everything revolved around what the United States had or had not done. The North Vietnamese had no agency or initiative of their own, and the same held true for the South Vietnamese." Most notably, Jespersen concurs with Snepp that the most troubling aspect of the U.S. withdrawal from Saigon "was the refusal of the Ford administration to provide adequate transportation for the thousands of South Vietnamese and Cambodians who had worked so closely with Americans and were very likely to be persecuted after the Communist victory."

SOURCES

Hersh, Seymour M. "Don't Ask; Don't Tell." Rev. of *Irreparable Harm*, by Frank Snepp. *Los Angeles Times*. Tribune Company, 11 July 1999. Web. 2 Dec. 2011.

Jespersen, T. Christopher. "Kissinger, Ford, and Congress: The Very Bitter End in Vietnam." *Pacific Historical Review* 71.3 (2002): 439+. *JSTOR*. Web. 2 Dec. 2011.

Leonard, John. "Saving Our White Skins." Rev. of *Decent Interval*, by Frank Snepp. *New York Times*. New York Times Company, 20 Dec. 1977. Web. 2 Dec. 2011.

Ransom, Harry Howe. "Being Intelligent about Secret Intelligence Agencies." *American Political Science Review* 74.1 (1980): 141+. *JSTOR*. Web. 2 Dec. 2011.

Snepp, Frank. *Decent Interval: An Insider's Account of Saigon's Indecent End Told by the CIA's Chief Strategy Analyst in Vietnam*. New York: Random House, 1977. Print.

FURTHER READING

Dung, Van Tien. *Our Great Spring Victory: An Account of the Liberation of South Vietnam*. Trans. John Spragens Jr. New York: Monthly Review, 1978. Print.

Ellsberg, Daniel. *Secrets: A Memoir of Vietnam and the Pentagon Papers*. New York: Penguin, 2003. Print.

Hoang, Van Thai. *How South Vietnam Was Liberated: Memoirs*. Hanoi: Gioi, 1992. Print.

Kissinger, Henry. *Ending the Vietnam War: A History of America's Involvement in and Extrication from the Vietnam War*. New York: Simon, 2003. Print.

Ninh, Bao. *The Sorrows of War: A Novel of North Vietnam*. Trans. Phan Thanh Hao. New York: Riverhead, 1996. Print.

Orentlicher, Diane F. "Snepp v. United States: The CIA Secrecy Agreement and the First Amendment." *Columbia Law Review* 81.3 (1981): 662+. *JSTOR*. Web. 2 Dec. 2011.

Snepp, Frank. *Irreparable Harm: A Firsthand Account of How One Agent Took on the CIA in an Epic Battle over Free Speech*. Lawrence: UP of Kansas, 1999. Print.

Stockwell, John. *In Search of Enemies: A CIA Story*. New York: Norton, 1984. Print.

Joseph Campana

DISPATCHES

Michael Herr

❖ *Key Facts*

Conflict:
Vietnam War

Time Period:
Mid-20th Century

Genre:
Memoir

OVERVIEW

Michael Herr's *Dispatches* (1977) provides a firsthand account of the author's experiences as a correspondent during the Vietnam War. The narrative chronicles Herr's forays into combat zones with U.S. military units, offering in-depth reporting on the critical battles of Hue and Khe Sanh following the Tet Offensive of 1968. Consisting largely of anecdotes, fragmentary descriptions of firefights and maneuvers, and quotations from American soldiers in the field, *Dispatches* creates an unorthodox, collage-like portrait of the fear, violence, and chaos that underlie the experience of armed conflict. At the same time, Herr's accounts provide a cohesive, ongoing philosophical meditation on the meaning of war in a postmodern, media-saturated world. Throughout the work, images of battle are seamlessly interwoven with references to rock-and-roll songs, counterculture slang, and other emblems of American culture, so that the distinction between reality and representation becomes hopelessly blurred. From Herr's perspective, the Vietnam War ultimately symbolizes the disintegration of traditional notions of American military power.

Dispatches is divided into six chapters. The first, "Breathing In," depicts the author attempting to establish his bearings soon after arriving in Vietnam. Herr's sense of dislocation becomes apparent on the book's opening page, in a description of an antiquated map hanging in his Saigon apartment. As Herr considers the artifact, he bluntly asserts that the territory on his wall no longer exists, that "for years now there had been no country here but the war." As he writes later in the chapter, there is ultimately no way to gain familiarity with Vietnam itself, only with the "saturating strangeness of the place."

The book's two long middle sections, "Hell Sucks" and "Khe Sanh," chronicle two of the bloodiest battles of the entire Vietnam conflict and contain the work's most detailed combat descriptions. These two chapters are followed by "Illumination Rounds," in which Herr describes the aftermath of the fighting through a series of portraits of American GIs. In "Colleagues" the author turns his attention to his fellow correspondents, in an effort to make sense of their role in the war. The chapter also levels a powerful critique at the mainstream media's coverage of the war, noting in particular its fundamental failure to "report meaningfully about death."

In the book's final section, "Breathing Out," Herr describes his surreal return to the United States, where he professes an inability to "tell the Vietnam veterans from the rock and roll veterans." The work concludes with a haunting incantation: "Vietnam Vietnam Vietnam, we've all been there."

Herr composed *Dispatches* over the course of a decade. Throughout this period, portions of his reporting were originally published in various periodicals. The earliest piece, "Hell Sucks," appeared in the August 1968 issue of *Esquire*, while Herr was still in Vietnam. A year later, the section "Illumination Rounds" was included in the seventh issue of the *New American Review* (August 1969). In 1977 Herr published two additional excerpts from the book. The first chapter appeared as "High on War" in the January 1977 issue of *Esquire*, and the last chapter was published in *Rolling Stone* on November 3, 1977, under the title "LZ Loon." That same year, Herr's Vietnam writings were published as *Dispatches* by Alfred A. Knopf.

HISTORICAL AND LITERARY CONTEXT

Michael Herr first arrived in Saigon in December 1967 as a correspondent for *Esquire*. In the book's early pages, he briefly describes the history of American involvement in the region, tracing its evolution from a relatively contained CIA operation to a "war bogged down in time, so much time so badly accounted for that it finally became entrenched as an institution."

Within months after his arrival, Herr found himself covering the Tet Offensive, a sweeping military campaign launched on January 31, 1968, by the North Vietnamese against U.S. forces and their South Vietnamese allies. The attack came as a surprise to the American military, owing both to its timing—the offensive was launched during the Vietnamese New Year, Têt, the country's most revered holiday—and to its ambitious scope. With the offensive, the North Vietnamese hoped to foment a widespread rebellion among the general population, with the aim of overthrowing the South Vietnamese government. Although the United States, by securing control over key territories while inflicting devastating casualties, ultimately achieved major tactical victories over the North Vietnamese forces, the Tet Offensive represented a strategic political victory for the North Vietnamese.

As Herr observes in *Dispatches*, the character of the war changed dramatically after Tet. In spite of its clear destructive power, America's conventional military suddenly seemed powerless in the face of such an unconventional conflict. In assessing the aftermath of the Tet attack, Herr describes the U.S. military as suffering a "huge collective nervous break-down" as the grim reality of the war began to sink in among American GIs. After Tet, Vietnam became a "dark room full of deadly objects," while the enemy forces suddenly seemed to be "everywhere all at once like a spider cancer." The pervasiveness of the North Vietnamese, along with their indomitable will, had become evident to those writing about the war: "Our worst dread of yellow peril became realized; we saw them now dying by the thousands all over the country, yet they didn't seem depleted, let alone exhausted." Within this context, Herr gives voice to the collective pessimism, claiming, "Instead of losing the war in little pieces over years we lost it fast in under a week."

Herr's innovative style of reporting in *Dispatches* marked a radical departure from traditional war narratives. Unlike realistic depictions of the Vietnam conflict, notably Philip Caputo's *A Rumor of War* (1977) and Larry Heinemann's *Close Quarters* (1977), *Dispatches* belonged to a postmodern vein of American writing known as New Journalism. Originally made famous by such writers as Truman Capote, Tom Wolfe, Hunter S. Thompson, and Norman Mailer during the 1960s and early 1970s, New Journalism was characterized by its unorthodox blending of diverse literary styles, creating a hybrid genre that drew freely from a range of motifs, narrative techniques, and authorial points of view. While conventional reporting was based on a fidelity to objectivity and fact, New Journalism stressed the inherently subjective position of the writer, insisting that any attempt to relate unbiased information was essentially impossible. At the same time, New Journalism writers typically blurred distinctions between high and low art, generating a pastiche of seemingly incongruent language, imagery, and ideas. With its free-ranging, wildly allusive style, its preoccupation with all aspects of contemporary society and culture, and its ability to develop a narrative perspective at once keenly focused on precise details and yet disconcertingly amorphous and decentered, Herr's book is a quintessential piece of New Journalism.

THEMES AND STYLE

Although a work of nonfiction, *Dispatches* displays certain distinctly novelistic qualities, particularly in its use of metaphoric language and in its inventive, elliptical narrative structure. Generally identified as postmodern in both style and sensibility, Herr's work incorporates a wide range of voices, storytelling methods, slang and military jargon, and literary and pop-culture allusions, employing a technique that Matthew C. Stewart (in *America Rediscovered*) identifies as *heteroglossia*. In

Vietnam, Summer, 1967, an anti-Vietnam War poster. © PETER NEWARK AMERICAN PICTURES / THE BRIDGEMAN ART LIBRARY INTERNATIONAL

constructing his story of the war, Herr draws freely from such literary antecedents as William Blake, Mark Twain, Charles Dickens, Wallace Stevens, and Graham Greene, among numerous others. While Herr occasionally notes the source of a particular literary allusion, at other times he allows certain words and phrases to flow, without attribution, within the relentless, pulsing energy of his own prose. In every sentence and paragraph, his writing is dazzling in its sustained verbal power and precision.

At the same time, the music and films of the 1960s are omnipresent in *Dispatches*, as Herr incorporates the prevailing cultural images and sounds of his generation into his accounts of battle. The text that emerges assumes a certain aspect of foreshortening, as if the impenetrable quality of the war has become merged with the disorienting proliferation of images. Indeed, Herr's prose style frequently takes on

DISPATCHES AND FILM REPRESENTATIONS OF THE VIETNAM WAR

Michael Herr's reporting from Vietnam represented a radical new type of war narrative, one marked by a high degree of subjectivity as well as a postmodern approach to the confusion and uncertainty that came to define the conflict. The author's unique sensibility exerted a profound influence on later chroniclers of the war, notably Francis Ford Coppola, director of the 1979 film *Apocalypse Now*.

Coppola's explorations into the technological terror associated with Vietnam, as well as into the absurd lack of clarity surrounding both America's objectives and its strategy, offer a stark visual echoing Herr's haunting literary account. At the same time, the film's numerous pop-culture references, its use of a psychedelic rock-and-roll soundtrack, and its fluid movement through a range of voices and perspectives find direct antecedents in *Dispatches*. Even the film's opening monologue, scripted by Herr, offers an uncanny refrain of the author's tentative, ambivalent point of view in the book.

Nearly a decade after *Apocalypse Now's* release, Herr wrote the screenplay for Stanley Kubrick's *Full Metal Jacket* (1987), another Vietnam War movie that employs postmodern techniques to convey the underlying sense of distortion and madness at the heart of the conflict.

a hallucinatory quality, as when he describes combat as both "dreaded and welcome," a moment that finds one's "senses working like strobes, free-falling all the way down to the essences and then flying out again in a rush of focus, like the first strong twinge of tripping after an infusion of psilocybin." This surge of linguistic energy is often accompanied by an almost preternatural power to recognize beauty in agents of destruction and death. At one point during his account of the Battle of Khe Sanh, Herr remarks how the sight of. 50 caliber tracers aimed at the helicopter in which he is flying can become momentarily "lovely," surprisingly "slow and graceful, arching up easily, a dream, so remote from anything that could harm you."

Still, as Michael Van Deusen notes in *Critique*, Herr's mission to incorporate these diverse texts into his narrative is in the end propelled by his "search for a language beyond the language of factual reporting as a way to bring other perspectives to bear on his experience." In spite of the qualities of ambiguity, confusion, and hypersubjectivity that characterize the work, Herr remains focused on locating some basic truth about the Vietnam experience. At times this truth seems impossible to attain, as when Herr quotes a hardened GI relating an inscrutable account of combat: "Patrol went up the mountain. One man came back. He died before he could tell us what happened." In other instances, the author locates this truth in a single

image from the field, as when he describes a marine "pissing into the locked-open mouth of a decomposing North Vietnamese solider."

Throughout the work, Herr continually strives to identify a larger, more elusive meaning in the war. Toward the end of the book, in "Colleagues," Herr attempts to encapsulate the essence of what he has witnessed in the image of "a dripping, laughing death-face," a horrific vision that lies concealed behind "every column of print you read about Vietnam," that remains as an "after-image" long after American TV viewers, safe in their homes back in the United States, have turned off the news. In this moment, Herr has tried to crack open what he describes at elsewhere in the narrative as the "secret history" of the war.

CRITICAL DISCUSSION

Dispatches was nearly universally hailed as a masterpiece of war writing at the time of its publication in 1977. Calling it "the best book to have been written about the Vietnam War," *New York Times* reviewer C. D. B. Bryan describes Herr's dispatches as "thoughtful, polished, tough, compassionate pieces." Bryan expresses particular admiration for the author's sympathy toward the soldiers in the field:

> To Michael Herr's everlasting credit, he never ceased to feel deeply for the men with whom he served; he never became callous, always worried for them, agonized over them, on occasion even took up arms to defend them.

John Leonard, also writing for the *New York Times*, hails the work as existing "beyond politics, beyond rhetoric, beyond 'pacification' and body counts" and also beyond the predictable lies surrounding the war. "It is as if Dante had gone to hell with a cassette recording of Jimi Hendrix and a pocket full of pills: our first rock-and-roll war." *National Review* contributor Joseph A. Rehyansky, on the other hand, takes issue with the author's "self-consciousness and cynical sentimentality," as well as the "endless pages of pointless, dreary intellectualizing" and "pompous introspection."

Over the years a number of scholars have focused on Herr's postmodern approach to narrative and language in *Dispatches*. David E. James, in *Representations*, examines Herr's use of popular culture as a linguistic and structural framework for his account of the Vietnam conflict, while Meghan Lau, in *Life Writing*, focuses her attention on Herr's deliberate fragmentation of the authorial self in the work. Conversely, some critics have suggested that the postmodern label is too strict a category for classifying the work's thematic and stylistic complexity. Writing in *War, Literature & the Arts* in 2009, Ty Hawkins examines the ways in which Herr's work "circumvents the dichotomous division of Vietnam War literature into realistic and postmodern camps." While Hawkins concedes that *Dispatches* represents a "canonical" work for those "critics inclined to celebrate the postmodern Vietnam War aesthetic," he ultimately identifies the book as "deeply essentialist" in its outlook, particularly in Herr's unflagging attempt to isolate a fundamental truth about the conflict.

SOURCES

Bryan, C. D. B. "The Different War." *New York Times* 20 Nov. 1977: BR2. Print.

Hawkins, Ty. "Violent Death as Essential Truth in *Dispatches*: Re-Reading Michael Herr's 'Secret History' of the Vietnam War." *War, Literature & the Arts* 21.1/2 (2009): 129–43. Print.

James, David E. "Rock and Roll in Representations of the Invasion of Vietnam." *Representations* 29 (1990): 78–98. Print.

Lau, Meghan. "Subverting Autobiography: War, Narrative, and Ethics in Michael Herr's *Dispatches*." *Life Writing* 6.2 (2009): 193–210. Print.

Leonard, John. Rev. of *Dispatches*, by Michael Herr. *New York Times* 28 Oct. 1977: C27. Print.

Rehyansky, Joseph A. "A Mortal S.I.W." *National Review* 17 Mar. 1978: 356. Print.

Stewart, Matthew C. "Style in *Dispatches*: Heteroglossia and Michael Herr's Break with Conventional Journalism." *America Rediscovered: Critical Essays on Literature and Film of the Vietnam War*. Ed. Owen W. Gilman Jr. and Lorrie Smith. New York: Garland, 1990: 189–204. Print.

Van Deusen, Michael. "The Unspeakable Language of Life and Death in Michael Herr's *Dispatches*." *Critique* 24.2 (1983): 82–87. Print.

FURTHER READING

Beidler, Philip D. "The Literature of Witness: Gloria Emerson, Frances Fitzgerald, Robert Stone, Michael Herr." *Re-Writing America: Vietnam Authors in Their Generation*. Athens: U of Georgia P, 1991: 206–87. Print.

Bonn, Maria S. "The Lust of the Eye: Michael Herr, Gloria Emerson and the Art of Observation." *Papers on Language and Literature* 29.1 (1993): 28–48. Print.

Carpenter, Lucas. "'It Don't Mean Nothin': Vietnam War Fiction and Postmodernism." *College Literature* 30.2 (2003): 30–50. Print.

Harrison, Brady, "'This Movie Is a Thing of Mine': Homeopathic Postmodernism in Michael Herr's *Dispatches*." *The Vietnam War and Postmodernity*. Ed. Michael Bibby. Boston: U of Massachusetts P, 1999: 89–108. Print.

Hellmann, John, "The New Journalism and Vietnam: Memory as Structure in Michael Herr's *Dispatches*." *South Atlantic Quarterly* 79 (1980): 141–51. Print.

Herr, Michael. *Dispatches*. New York: Vintage Books, 1991.

Thompson, Jon. "Ferocious Alphabets: Michael Herr's *Dispatches*." *Massachusetts Review* 43.4 (2002–03): 570–601. Print.

Stephen Meyer

THE EAGLE AND THE SERPENT

Martín Luis Guzmán

✢ Key Facts

Conflict:
Mexican Revolution

Time Period:
Early 20th Century

Genre:
Novel

OVERVIEW

The Eagle and the Serpent is the story of an idealistic university student who joins the Mexican Revolution (1910–20) and comes face-to-face with its brutal realities. Originally a series of chronicles published in Spanish, Mexican, and American newspapers, it was first released as a memoir in 1928 but was labeled as a novel in subsequent editions. In it a first-person narrator named Guzmán travels through Mexico and the United States and describes his encounters with the leaders of the revolution as well as its rank and file. Walking the line between eyewitness accuracy and literary embellishment, the book explores the role that one intellectual aspires to play in a chaotic civil war, the extent to which his ideas are able to influence the actions of others, and his eventual inability to reconcile his principles with the military and political realities of his country.

The novel opens with the narrator fleeing Mexico City to join the Constitutional Army in the north of the country. What follows is a string of loosely linked vignettes in which he comes into contact with various aspects of the war—everything except an actual battle. One night he attends a formal dinner with the first chief of the army; another night he is swept up in a drunken revelry of faceless soldiers. While he manages to save a high-society ball by swapping an old penny for a blown fuse, he utterly fails to improve conditions of a military hospital. When the narrator returns to Mexico City following the triumph of the Constitutional Army, he works first for the chief of police and then the minister of war. As the revolution begins to disintegrate into factionalism, he is thrown in prison by one band only to be freed by another. The novel ends with Guzmán fleeing the country as it descends further into civil war.

Guzmán's novel is best known for the author's portraits of the most prominent figures of the Mexican Revolution. Of these, his main subject is famed general of the Division of the North, Francisco "Pancho" Villa. When the narrator first meets him in a dingy house on the outskirts of a border town, he seems "more of a jaguar … than a man," a deadly force that must be controlled. Over the course of the novel, however, the general shows himself to be a rational, though often ruthless, leader—and even a master storyteller. Though the narrator decides in the end to abandon

Villa, it is the general who spares his life and allows him to go into exile.

Together with Mariano Azuela's *The Underdogs* (1915), *The Eagle and the Serpent* is the most important novel of the Mexican Revolution. While the former focuses on the movement's foot soldiers, the latter centers on its leaders. Some see this as elitism, and they critique the novel for not being ethically engaged. But this criticism begs the question of whether this aloofness is a strategy that Guzmán uses to show the limits of intellectualism and art when confronted with the horrors of war.

HISTORICAL AND LITERARY CONTEXT

The Mexican Revolution began in 1910, when a group of armies loosely allied under the leadership of Francisco I. Madero rebelled against the dictatorship of Porfirio Díaz (1896–1911). Madero was elected president in 1911, but he was deposed and assassinated in a plot orchestrated in part by General Victoriano Huerta and the American ambassador to Mexico. *The Eagle and the Serpent* begins in May 1913, during Huerta's short-lived presidency. During this time, armies in both the north and the south united in their push to unseat the usurper. The movement splintered into warring factions when Huerta's government finally fell, principally the Constitutional Army under Venustiano Carranza and the Conventionist Army under Pancho Villa. Guzmán's novel ends during this chaotic moment of multiple civil wars, in January 1915.

Though Carranza would defeat Villa and assume the presidency in 1917, he too would fall in 1920 to a military revolt, this time led by his former allies Álvaro Obregón, Plutarco Elías Calles, and Adolfo de la Huerta. This event marked the end of the military phase of the Mexican Revolution, but the country continued to experience armed conflict and political instability until the mid-1930s. In fact, Guzmán, exiled for his participation in De la Huerta's revolt against the government in 1923, would write *The Eagle and the Serpent* in Madrid. One year later, he would also publish a scathing roman à clef against Obregón and Calles titled *The Shadow of the Leader*.

The Eagle and the Serpent marks the beginning of a second wave of novels on the Mexican

Fresco in Chihuahua, Mexico depicting Pancho Villa, a legendary leader of the Mexican Revolution who is featured in *The Eagle and the Serpent.*
© HEMIS / ALAMY

Revolution, written a decade after the most violent phase of the movement had ended. Looking primarily to the first-wave *The Underdogs* as a model, these books abandoned the escapist fiction that had been in vogue since the reign of Porfirio Díaz and instead opted to confront Mexico's recent history and current reality (Rutherford). Much like Azuela's novel, *The Eagle and the Serpent* laments that the revolution merely replaced one corrupt government with another. Guzmán also follows Azuela in his effort to reproduce the colloquial, Mexican Spanish spoken by lower-class soldiers.

These realist tendencies, however, stand in contrast to another important influence on *The Eagle and the Serpent*, the social doctrine of *Arielismo*. Founded by Uruguayan thinker José Enrique Rodó (1872–1912), *Arielismo* maintained that "intellectual labor should not be reduced to utilitarian purposes, but … guided by the ethics of harmony and beauty" (Parra). While Rodó's direct influence over Guzmán as an author is highly debatable, this philosophy could account for the aesthetic distance that often separates the narrator from his surroundings and for his desire to find beauty in even the most bleak or horrifying moments of the revolution. For instance, when the narrator muses over how to best capture the nature of the Division of the North, he claims that only events with a "touch of poetic fancy" can bring out "their essence more clearly." Shockingly, Guzmán goes on to tell the story of a Division of the North officer who executes 300 prisoners of war, one by one with his revolver.

THEMES AND STYLE

The title, *The Eagle and the Serpent*, is a reference to the Mexican flag, which shows an eagle perched on a prickly pear cactus with a serpent in its claw. This coat of arms serves as an important interpretive tool for the novel. First it is indicative of Guzmán's preoccupation with understanding the essence of Mexico as a nation. Second it speaks to the way the author structures his narrative using a series of opposing pairs (Shaw). For instance, the "dense atmosphere of barbarism" that pervades the countryside stands in opposition to the refinement that "radiate[s] from the city." Likewise, the narrator's descriptions of the landscape and people that surround him often rely on a play of light and shadow, the former connoting tyranny and violence, and the latter symbolizing liberty and peace (Leal). Finally, the novel depicts the tension between the leaders of the revolution and the movement's poor and marginalized foot soldiers. For example, when the narrator is given a tour of the Presidential Palace by an officer in Emiliano Zapata's Liberation Army of the South, he notes that there is an "immediate incompatibility" between this rustic soldier and his opulent surroundings. Instead of a high-ranking official in a victorious army, he seems to be "a janitor showing a house for rent."

The tension between social classes in the novel is most apparent in the relationship that develops between Guzmán and Pancho Villa. The narrator describes their first meeting as an encounter between "two irreconcilable worlds" and the general as a "wild animal." For this reason, key moments in the book

TRANSLATION TROUBLES

The chapters that make up *The Eagle and the Serpent* are disjointed and autonomous enough that some critics have questioned whether the work can be categorized as a single, cohesive novel. For instance, the work begins not with the events of the Mexican Revolution per se but with a comedy of errors aboard a steamship. Traveling from Veracruz to New York City, the narrator finds himself caught up in the intrigues of an eccentric doctor who suspects an American passenger of spying on him. In order to evade capture, the doctor decides to seduce her, but his plan is as ineffective as it is illogical. The narrator ends up

rescuing him by telling the American woman that the doctor is secretly a serial killer.

More than critics, it has been publishing houses that have deemed this and similar episodes unnecessary. When Guzmán's work was released in English by Knopf in 1930, editors eliminated half of its chapters. The novel received similar treatment in French and German translations. In 1960 Guzmán wrote to Knopf about the possibility of a new, complete version of *The Eagle and the Serpent*. Knopf rejected Guzmán's many conditions, however, and it would not be until 1965 that Doubleday would publish the text in its entirety.

often involve the narrator controlling Villa's impulsive behavior with gentle reasoning, as when he convinces him to hand over his pistol or to spare the lives of 160 captured troops. These exchanges also embody another tension in Guzmán's work: the different roles that civilians and soldiers must play in revolutionary Mexico and, on a larger level, the dilemma of having to obey a military order even when that order should be questioned (Goodbody). But Guzmán's portrayal of Villa is more complex. While the narrator manages to take away Villa's pistol, Villa teaches the narrator how to properly shoot a revolver. And one of the most moving episodes of *The Eagle and the Serpent* is narrated by the general himself, revealing his intelligence, cunningness, and even his ability to tell a good story.

CRITICAL DISCUSSION

While some installments of *The Eagle and the Serpent* were censored in Mexican newspapers, the novel as a whole enjoyed a positive reception in both Mexico and Spain. As Mexican critics began to rediscover Mariano Azuela and focus on other novels on the Mexican Revolution, one writer held up *The Eagle and the Serpent* as far superior to *The Underdogs* as a work of art. A Spanish critic described Guzmán's work as a vivid film, full of visceral scenes captured with distance and objectivity, as if the narrator were more a camera than a person. Another aspect of the book that was and continues to be a subject of attention is Guzmán's decision to portray revolutionary leaders off the battlefield, allowing these more intimate moments to expose their true character. This is a strategy that he borrowed from first-century Greek biographer Plutarch, whose *Parallel Lives* makes an appearance in the novel. One evening Guzmán comes across a general reading the work and complaining that the Conventionist government is in such disarray because "among all these speechifiers, there's not a single Demosthenes."

More recently, these aspects of Guzmán's writing that had been praised have become a source of

criticism against the book. The distance that the narrator maintains from the chaotic world around him can be seen as a lack of compassion. As one critic puts it, "His indifference in the face of suffering can repel" (Rutherford). Also, the narrator's desire to find balance and beauty, his efforts to reveal men's essential character, speak to a certain elitism. The novel's characters are clearly organized into a social pyramid, with intellectuals at the top and the revolutionary masses at the bottom. Guzmán's *Arielismo*, then, seems a sort of social Darwinism, where the rank and file are "filthy and subhuman, … a setback for the cause of civilization" (Parra). These arguments, however, fail to consider the possibility that the author does this precisely in order to criticize the elitism and naïveté of his contemporaries during the early phase of the revolution. After all, for all the narrator's intellectual prowess, he is forced to abandon both his ideals and his country at the end of *The Eagle and the Serpent*. As he hurdles toward the border in a train, he exclaims with a mix of admiration for his country and anxiety about his escape, "Mexico is so big! Fourteen hundred kilometers to the border!"

SOURCES

Bruce-Novoa, Juan. "*El águila y la serpiente* en las versiones estadounidenses." *Plural: Revista Cultural De Excélsior* 17.193 (1987): 16–21. Print.

Goodbody, Nicholas. "Los tres Guzmán y el diálogo con Pancho Villa." *La Palabra y el Hombre* 129 (2004): 7–28. Print.

Guzmán, Martín Luis. *The Eagle and the Serpent*. Trans. Harriet de Onís. Glouster: Smith, 1969. Print.

———. *La sombra del caudillo [The Shadow of the Leader]*. México: Porrúa, 1997. Print.

Leal, Luis. "La caricia suprema: Contextos de luz y sombra en *El águila y la serpiente*." *Five Essays on Martín Luis Guzmán*. Ed. William W. Megenney. Riverside: Lat. Amer. Studies Prog. of the U of California, 1978. 72–82. Print.

Parra, Max. *Writing Pancho Villa's Revolution: Rebels in the Literary Imagination of Mexico*. Austin: U of Texas P, 2005. Print.

Rutherford, John. "The Novel of the Mexican Revolution." *The Cambridge History of Latin American Literature*. Eds. Roberto González Echevarría and Enrique Pupo-Walker. Cambridge: Cambridge UP, 1996. 213–25. Print.

Shaw, D. L. "*El águila y la serpiente*: *Arielismo* and Narrative Method." *Five Essays on Martín Luis Guzmán*. Ed. William W. Megenney. Riverside: Lat. Amer. Studies Prog. of the U of California, 1978. 1–18. Print.

FURTHER READING

Bruce-Novoa, Juan. "Martín Luis Guzmán's Necessary Overtures." *Discurso Literario: Revista de Temas Hispánicos* 4.1 (1986): 63–83. Print.

Curiel, Fernando. *La querella de Martín Luis Guzmán*. México: Coyoacán, 1993. Print.

Duffey, Patrick J. "Pancho Villa at the Movies: Cinematic Techniques in the Works of Guzmán and Muñoz." *Latin American Literature and Mass Media*. Eds. Edmundo Paz-Soldán and Debra A. Castillo. New York: Garland, 2001. 41–56. Print.

Gyurko, Lanin A. "Twentieth-Century Fiction." *Mexican Literature: A History*. Ed. David William Foster. Austin: U of Texas P, 1994. 243–303. Print.

Laraway, D. "Doctoring the Revolution: Medical Discourse and Interpretation in *Los de abajo* and *El águila y la serpiente*." *Hispanófila* 127 (1999): 53–66. Print.

Legrás, Horacio. "Martín Luis Guzmán: El viaje de la revolución." *MLN* 118.2 (2003): 427–54. Print.

Megenney, William W., ed. *Five Essays on Martín Luis Guzmán*. Riverside: Lat. Amer. Studies Prog. of the U of California, 1978. Print.

Pineda Franco, Adela. "Entre el exilio y el fuego revolucionario: La narrativa de Martín Luis Guzmán de 1925 a 1929." *Revista de Crítica Literaria Latinoamericana* 33.66 (2007): 29–51. Print.

Quintanilla, Susana. *A salto de mata: Martín Luis Guzmán en la revolución mexicana*. México: Tusquets, 2009. Print.

Williams, Gareth. "Sovereign (In)hospitality: Politics and the Staging of Equality in Revolutionary Mexico." *Discourse* 27.2 (2007): 95–123. Print.

Nicholas Goodbody

ECHOES OF VIOLENCE
Letters from a War Reporter

Carolin Emcke

❖ *Key Facts*

Conflict:
Kosovo War;
Second Intifada;
Iraq War;
War in Afghanistan

Time Period:
Late 20th Century;
Early 21st Century

Genre:
Letters

Award:
Political Book Award,
Friedrich Ebert
Foundation, 2005

OVERVIEW

The German war correspondent Carolin Emcke began writing the letters that make up *Echoes of Violence: Letters from a War Reporter* after returning from an assignment in Kosovo in 1999, during the aftermath of the withdrawal of Serbian troops from the contested region. Emcke had been shaken by her experience, and for two weeks after her return to Berlin she was unable to answer questions from friends and family about her time there. Finally she sent out a letter via e-mail to those closest to her, describing her activities and her reactions to the destruction she had witnessed in Kosovo. The practice became a ritual as Emcke traveled across the globe, covering wars in Lebanon, Nicaragua, Pakistan, Afghanistan, Colombia, and Iraq, as well as the terrorist attacks that took place in New York City on September 11, 2001.

The letters in *Echoes of Violence* are not merely descriptive. In them Emcke addresses philosophical issues raised by the work of war journalists, who are forbidden under any circumstance to take up arms or otherwise participate in the conflicts they cover and whose livelihoods depend on lethal violence and the misfortunes of others. Emcke discusses the guilt many war correspondents feel at only being able to write about the suffering of those who answer their questions. She also addresses the difficulties of representing the atrocities of war in words and of answering questions about her motives in choosing to work in war zones.

HISTORICAL AND LITERARY CONTEXT

The conflicts Emcke writes about in *Echoes of Violence* were ongoing in the late twentieth century or in the early twenty-first century. The period was characterized by numerous long-simmering and bitter regional conflicts whose victims were likely to be civilians rather than armed combatants. In Kosovo, Serbian forces attempted to drive out or destroy the ethnic Albanian population. In 2000 Israel withdrew the forces that had occupied southern Lebanon since the early 1980s in the short-lived hope of reducing Arab-Israeli tensions; the Second Intifada (also known as the al-Aqsa Intifada) against Israel began in September of that year. Even the so-called global war on terror, begun in the aftermath of the attacks in the United States in 2011,

eventually became concentrated in Iraq, Afghanistan, and Pakistan. Towns and villages were caught up in battles between Iraqi insurgents or, in Afghanistan and Pakistan, between Taliban militants and government and allied—mainly U.S.—forces. In cases like Nicaragua and Romania, the victims Emcke writes about did not have their lives and communities affected by armed conflict but instead by ruthless economic coercion and exploitation. Similarly, the armed depredations of the drug cartels brought life to a standstill in sections of Colombia. One of Emcke's letters describes people imprisoned in their meager homes while a battle raged between the local drug lord's minions and the army for control of a slum in Medellín, Colombia's second-largest city and the seat of the most powerful drug cartel.

Such conflicts are typically long running and unpredictable, capable of flaring into episodes of extreme violence. Writing in the *New York Review of Books*, Neal Ascherson compares the wars in Kosovo, Lebanon, Afghanistan, and Iraq to the Thirty Years' War (1618–48), when Central Europe "collapsed into a blackened gutted space traversed by sadistic mercenaries and warlord militias, into low-level war without rules or lines on the map." The complex histories and confusing arrays of opponents in such wars present difficult challenges for those reporting them as well as for those more directly involved. Emcke's letters chronicle her attempts to translate the darkened world of war into something that is "visible" to those who live outside it, to give "credible testimony to the wars and their victims."

THEMES AND STYLE

Emcke took the epigraph for the first chapter of *Echoes of Violence* from Michael Walzer's *Just and Unjust Wars*: "War kills. This is all it does." Although she returns repeatedly to the idea that war defies the attempt to represent it in language, Emcke's writing clearly expresses just how profoundly she was affected by the profligate killing in the war zones she visited. Her account ranges from mute shock—"At first there was only speechlessness"—to detailed and lucid explorations of her intellectual and emotional reactions. Her book is a meditation on war's destructiveness and on the journalist's responsibility to bear witness to human suffering during wartime.

Despite the book's somber emphasis on violence and destruction, Emcke's letters feature numerous accounts of resilience in the face of tremendous adversity. The stories of people's generosity despite their own deprivation, or of their helping members of the very group trying to destroy them, impress Emcke and the reader because they are tiny beacons that guide humanity out of the overwhelming chaos of war.

War correspondents often depend on local people in a combat zone for many things, from translation and transportation to basic necessities. Intimacy can develop quickly: "I am welcomed by strangers who open their hearts as few friends dare to do." But the intimacy cannot last, and the journalist has nothing to offer in return but the reports that he or she will write. For Emcke this form of giving does not entirely relieve her of a sense of guilt, because "nobody ever believed that I, as a journalist, could change his or her situation in the prisons, in the hospitals, in the refugee camps, at the front lines." In the end it is her commitment to the importance of bearing witness, of reminding the world that "the [victims of war] live in the same world as 'we,'" that spurs her to keep working despite conflicting emotions.

Near the beginning of her preface, as she is describing the difficulty of talking about her experiences of war, Emcke asks how one explains that "war and violence inscribe themselves on your soul and continue to live with you." She spends the remaining pages trying to do just this, drawing on her training in journalism and philosophy to give an account that is both clearly rendered and impassioned. Her style is laconic, but she chooses her stories and their details carefully so that the situations described seem to

unfold naturally before the reader, and suffering and anguish are laid bare. For example, in a single terse paragraph she recounts the desperate plight of a teenage girl in the hospital in Prizren, Kosovo. The girl, who must share a room with soldiers from all sides in the fighting, needs to be transferred to another hospital for treatment of a brain injury caused by a sniper's bullet. "She would probably die within the next five hours," writes Emcke, "because the hospital could not transfer her to Prishtina—the Serbian troops had stolen the only ambulance for their flight at the end of the war."

CRITICAL DISCUSSION

Echoes of Violence has enjoyed a positive critical reception. Emcke is widely respected as both a journalist and an academic, and reviewers have praised her letters for the insights they offer into the political realities of the countries she has visited, as well as for the intellectual and emotional scrupulousness of their author. As Kathy English observes in her review in *Biography*, Emcke's letters combine "gripping narrative with philosophic reflection on the meaning of war and the limitations of journalism to communicate the abyss of violence." Writing for *Bookforum*, Eliza Griswold praises the letters for being "unsentimental and immediate," noting that Emcke "handles battle with grace, both in the midst of the conflict and, later, on the page." Griswold is also impressed with Emcke's self-critical eye: "She never shies from owning her mistakes; this willing self-scrutiny is another of her strengths."

In his review in the *New York Review of Books*, Ascherson takes Emcke to task for underestimating the power of her pen, citing her declaration that it is the "burden" of the witness "to remain with a

Ethnic Albanian women weep for their husbands, who they believe were killed by Serbian militants after they were driven from their Kosovo homes in April 1999. © AP IMAGES / HEKTOR PUSTINA

THE PHILOSOPHY OF WAR

The search for underlying meaning in armed conflict is a question that has troubled philosophers, politicians, and writers for centuries. One of the most probing examinations of the subject is found in Michael Walzer's *Just and Unjust Wars* (1977). Originally inspired by his staunch opposition to the Vietnam War, Walzer's book provides a sweeping survey of war throughout history, from the Athenians' genocidal campaign against Melos during the Peloponnesian War to the infamous My Lai Massacre of 1968, during which hundreds of Vietnamese civilians were murdered by U.S. forces. In his exploration of the complex factors that lead to military confrontation, Walzer examines a wide range of moral issues, focusing on such themes as combat tactics, war crimes, and the prospect of achieving a just peace. Throughout the book, Walzer draws extensively from the firsthand writings and testimonies of participants as he seeks to comprehend the various moral and political justifications that have been given for waging war. His investigation points repeatedly toward a single question: In what cases can war be described as necessary? Widely hailed for its intellectual rigor, its thorough and detailed handling of specific events, and its moral passion, the book arguably finds its most compelling distillation in Walzer's dictum "War kills. This is all it does."

feeling of failure, of emptiness because even the most accurate account does not grasp the bleakness of war." Ascherson objects: "But here we are drifting into an acceptance that violent conflict is simply beyond representation … About writing, though, this is untrue. This is a matter of craft, a matter of devising the right technique. And it always has been." It is Emcke's underestimation of the power of language, rather than her writing itself, that Ascherson criticizes. Elsewhere in his review he praises her as being "courageous,"

"honest," and "wise" in her work as she "constantly contrast[s] the moral wreckage around her with the behavior of the few who try to keep their standards."

SOURCES

Ascherson, Neal. "Do They Crave War?" Rev. of *Echoes of Violence: Letters from a War Reporter*, by Carolin Emcke, and *Another Bloody Love Letter*, by Anthony Loyd. *New York Review of Books* 8 Nov. 2007. Print.

Emcke, Carolin. *Echoes of Violence: Letters from a War Reporter*. Princeton: Princeton UP, 2007. Print.

English, Kathy. Rev. of *Echoes of Violence: Letters from a War Reporter*, by Carolin Emcke. *Biography* Spring 2007. *Literature Resources from Gale*. Web. 25 May 2011.

Griswold, Eliza. "Post Traumatic: A War Correspondent's Letters View Conflict Up Close." *Bookforum* Apr.-May 2007. Web. 25 May 2011.

Walzer, Michael. *Just and Unjust Wars: A Moral Argument with Historical Illustrations*. New York: Basic, 1977. Print.

FURTHER READING

Beaumont, Peter. *The Secret Life of War: Journeys through Modern Conflict*. London: Harvill, 2009. Print.

Gellhorn, Martha. *Selected Letters of Martha Gellhorn*. Ed. Caroline Moorehead. New York: Holt, 2006. Print.

Hedges, Chris. *War Is a Force That Gives Us Meaning*. New York: PublicAffairs, 2002. Print.

Loyd, Anthony. *Another Bloody Love Letter*. London: Headline Review, 2007. Print.

McLoughlin, Kate. Rev. of *Echoes of Violence: Letters from a War Reporter*, by Carolin Emcke. *Times Literary Supplement* 1 June 2007: 31. Print.

Sontag, Susan. *Regarding the Pain of Others*. New York: Farrar, 2003. Print.

Janet Moredock

THE FACE OF WAR

Martha Gellhorn

OVERVIEW

The Face of War is a collection of the war correspondence of the U.S. writer Martha Gellhorn. Originally published in 1959, the collection was revised in 1967 and 1986. Beginning with the Spanish Civil War, the volume contains articles from the front in World War II, the Vietnam War, the Six Day War, and other major conflicts, including the Indonesian War of Independence and the late-century wars in Central America. Gellhorn prefaces the reports from each conflict with brief essays providing background and reflecting on her experiences covering the war.

A war reporter for sixty years, Martha Gellhorn covered many of the twentieth century's major armed conflicts from her favorite vantage point—on the ground. Widely acknowledged as one of the world's finest war correspondents, Gellhorn, who also published novels and short fiction, did not set out to be a journalist on the front lines. After graduating college she traveled to Europe, where she joined a group of young pacifists in France and tried to support her dream of a novelist's life by writing for *Vogue* magazine. Her travels brought her into close contact with the rise of Fascism in Europe, and by 1936 she "had stopped being a pacifist and become an anti-fascist." One year later she carried a letter of introduction from the editor of *Collier's* magazine to Spain, where she began to write about life in Madrid as civil war ravaged the city.

The enduring characteristics of Gellhorn's war reportage are clearly evident in her first dispatches from Spain: the focus on common soldiers and ordinary civilians, the incisively detailed descriptions of the impact of war on individual lives, and her unobtrusive but unmistakable way of letting the reader know exactly where her sympathies lay. In Spain she developed an unshakeable belief in the justice of the Republican (loyalist, antifascist) cause, and the moral dimension of her writing remained a strong and distinctive feature throughout her career.

Gellhorn was one of the first female war correspondents and a pioneer in other ways as well. Her close-up portraits of human courage, generosity, suffering, and cruelty in wartime significantly broadened war correspondents' fields of vision. Hers was never the view of any government; instead, her openly professed suspicion of governments set her apart.

Moreover, her fresh, ground-level perspective was later adopted by television journalists, whose medium also favors the specific and concrete over the distant and abstract. As well known for her audacity as for her personal charm, Gellhorn did not expect special treatment because she was a woman working in combat zones. She did not call herself a feminist, but she did as she pleased and thought every woman should simply do the same.

HISTORICAL AND LITERARY CONTEXT

Martha Gellhorn's talent for war reporting and her drive to be at the center of events coincided in dramatic fashion with the historical events of the twentieth century. In 1934 she traveled by train with fellow pacifists to meet young Nazis in Germany. When their newspapers were confiscated at the border by German police, Gellhorn and her friends were outraged, and their meeting with the Nazis, in "clean blond khaki-clad formation," only heightened Gellhorn's dismay. This journey marked the beginning of her transformation into a lifelong critic of Fascism and a passionate eyewitness to the unprecedented excesses of twentieth-century warfare.

Gellhorn's interest in the Spanish Civil War was sparked by references in German newspapers to the "Red Swine-dogs" of the Spanish republic. In 1936 the Spanish military attempted a coup after elections put power in the hands of the political left. The coup failed to bring the entire country under military control, and Spain became engulfed in a bloody struggle between the rebel Nationalists, including many right-wing elements, and the loyalist Republicans, consisting of left-wing and centrist elements. Nazi Germany, along with Italy's fascist government, supported the rebel Nationalists. They were also backed by the Roman Catholic Church, landowners, and other conservative groups within Spain, while the Republicans received aid from the Soviet Union, France, and Mexico, as well as thousands of European and U.S. volunteers who served in the International Brigades. Gellhorn, alarmed by the repressiveness she had witnessed firsthand in Germany, saw the Spanish Civil War in terms of a conflict between Fascism and freedom, and her view struck a sympathetic chord in the United States where—to her surprise—*Collier's* began publishing her accounts of the toll of war on noncombatants.

❖ *Key Facts*

Conflict:
Spanish Civil War

Time Period:
Mid-20th Century

Genre:
Journalism, Essays

DACHAU, MAY 1945: "NOWHERE WAS THERE ANYTHING LIKE THIS."

Reporting on the liberated concentration camp at Dachau, Germany, in May 1945, Martha Gellhorn recorded humankind's cruelty to humankind. The passion and skill with which she wrote is evident in the details she chose to describe the horror.

Witnessing a young man found under a pile of dead bodies in a train car, she writes, "What had been a man dragged himself into the doctor's office; he was a Pole and he was about six feet tall and he weighed less than a hundred pounds." Juxtaposed against this piteous figure is the German soldiers' casual murder of others dying inside the train who cried out as they succumbed to starvation and thirst: "From time to time, the guards fired into the cars to stop the noise." Gellhorn reveals that outside the crematorium "the clothing [of the prisoners] was handled with order, but the [naked] bodies were dumped like garbage, rotting in the sun, yellow and nothing but bones, bones grown huge because there was no flesh to cover them."

Despite the "hatred and sickness" Gellhorn felt toward the Germans, Caroline Moorehead records in her biography of the author that she did not consider the Allies heroes: "We are not entirely guiltless, we the Allies, because it took us twelve years to open the gates of Dachau. We were blind and unbelieving and slow, and that we can never be again ... If ever again we tolerate such cruelty we have no right to peace."

Without formal training as a reporter, Gellhorn at first "tagged along behind the war correspondents," among whom were two giants of twentieth-century literature, George Orwell and Ernest Hemingway. Orwell later published an account of his experiences in Spain and of the political situation there in *Homage to Catalonia* (1938). In addition to reporting for periodicals, Hemingway incorporated his experiences in Spain into his only full-length play, *The Fifth Column* (1938), and the acclaimed novel *For Whom the Bell Tolls* (1940). Having met in Key West in 1936 before traveling to Spain, Gellhorn and Hemingway cultivated their relationship while covering the war. They married in November of 1940, but Gellhorn left Hemingway in 1945.

Between 1939 and 1941, Gellhorn visited Finland and China, where she wrote about regional wars that became subsumed in the conflagration of World War II. Germany under Adolf Hitler was poised to avenge the humiliation it had suffered at the conclusion of World War I and to expand across Europe. Of the resulting global conflict, Gellhorn wrote, "The sense of the insanity and wickedness of this war grew in me until, for purposes of mental hygiene, I gave up trying to think or judge, and turned myself into a walking tape recorder with eyes."

In such articles as "Three Poles" and "A Little Dutch Town," Gellhorn used the stories of individuals

to convey the horrors and depredations of the German war machine, and several of her best-known articles focus on the Holocaust. In "Dachau," she records several conversations with doctors and former inmates at that concentration camp in May 1945, and she frequently comments on the calm with which her interviewees recounted the horrors they had witnessed. At the end of the article, Gellhorn tells of hearing the news of Germany's unconditional surrender, remarking that "the accursed cemetery prison ... seemed to me the most suitable place in Europe to hear the news of victory. For surely this war was made to abolish Dachau, and all the other places like Dachau, and everything that Dachau stood for, and to abolish it forever."

During the Cold War that ensued after World War II, the United States became involved in a number of conflicts with the declared aim of containing communism. The most controversial of these was the Vietnam War. In 1946 communists in Vietnam had taken up arms against French colonial forces, which finally withdrew in 1954. The country was divided between a communist-controlled North and the shaky government of the former emperor Bao Dai in the South. As it became increasingly involved in Vietnam, the U.S. government sought to cast the war as a struggle between the free world and the repressive forces of communism. On the ground, Gellhorn saw the conflict differently.

Gellhorn's reports from Vietnam in 1966 emphasized that the very people who were said by the U.S. government to be benefiting from the struggle against communism were, in fact, its greatest victims. American bombs, bullets, and napalm (a form of jellied gasoline) were "killing and wounding three or four times more [South Vietnamese] people than the [North Vietnamese and the] Vietcong do." Gellhorn made no effort to conceal her outrage at the conditions faced by civilians in South Vietnam, and as a result her reports from overflowing hospitals and orphanages there were not published by American newspapers. Eventually, the London-based *Guardian* printed six of her articles, after which the government of South Vietnam barred Gellhorn from returning.

THEMES AND STYLE

Throughout the reports and essays that make up *The Face of War*, Gellhorn writes of war in terms of crime and disease. With the nuclear arms race in high gear, she declares in her introduction to the first edition, "If we make or allow war, we deserve it; but we must limit our weapons and our locales, and keep our crime under control." Almost thirty years later, she opens her introduction to the 1986 edition with this observation: "After a lifetime of war-watching, I see war as an endemic human disease, and governments are the carriers." As the century progressed, Gellhorn became increasingly critical of the U.S. government, which she blamed for infecting its citizens with fears of external threats where no great danger existed (among the

Sandinistas in Nicaragua, for example) and for relying on propaganda and the "rehabilitation" of history in much the same way the communists themselves did.

In seeking what she called the face of war, Gellhorn rarely mentions prominent political or military figures in her reports. Instead, she focuses on ordinary individuals who are most vulnerable to the destruction and disruption of war. In the faces of bone-weary Free French soldiers in Italy, liberated inmates of concentration camps, and Vietnamese orphans disfigured by napalm attacks, she reads the cost of war.

Gellhorn's writing style contributed a great deal to the impact of her reporting from the ground. Deeply committed to her work, she argued that "the point of these articles is that they are true; they tell what I saw." This simple telling of what one sees involves innumerable skillful decisions about where and how to focus one's gaze. In making these decisions Gellhorn frequently relied on her experience as a fiction writer.

Scholars such as Maureen Mulligan have speculated that Gellhorn's lack of professional training as a war reporter "enabled her to create a style of journalism which was exceptionally flexible, original, and idiosyncratic." (She also benefited from the advice of her fellow correspondents, including Hemingway, though the question of the extent of his influence became a source of great irritation throughout her life.) Mulligan says that Gellhorn's unwavering first-person narrative voice "[forces] her readership to become involved on a personal level with those affected by war and its consequences." Nigel Nicolson, writing in the *New Statesman*, states that although "war reports like Miss Gellhorn's appear to write themselves," the path to such transparent prose is beset with potential pitfalls, from "indiscretion" to "overwriting" to "making your word-pictures unbelievably neat or heroic"; but Gellhorn, he adds, avoids these mistakes.

Gellhorn's direct, "tape-recorder" style also enabled her to place the moral problems of war squarely before the reader. Implicit in her careful, precise descriptions of terrible suffering is the question, Isn't there a better way? But rather than voice the question directly or propose a solution herself, she leaves the question open, placing her hope in the "memory and imagination" of ordinary people as the means of putting the faces of war behind us.

CRITICAL DISCUSSION

By the time *The Face of War* was published, Gellhorn's reputation as one of the best war journalists of the twentieth century was already well established. "Undoubtedly she was one of the best correspondents whom [World War II] produced," avers Nigel Nicolson, "and today her articles are as fresh as striped shirts back from the wash." The *Times Literary Supplement* also affirmed the superlative quality of Gellhorn's work, noting somewhat wryly that "only her belief that men must by now have learnt the lesson of

self-interest vitiates her thesis." In his 2002 study of the role of journalists in modern politics, Fred Inglis declares, "There cannot be a journalist's file of reports to match Martha Gellhorn's from November 1943 through to May 1945."

Students of Gellhorn's work have highlighted her unique contributions to journalism. Deborah Wilson asserts that Gellhorn's "legacy to journalism was to develop a different perspective for war correspondents." This difference, according to Wilson, is based in Gellhorn's preference for "first-person narrative and acute observations of people, their lives and situations."

Gellhorn was at her best when writing from the front, where, Wilson argues, she was driven by the drama of violence and her own anger. In a *Los Angeles Times* obituary, Bill Buford refers to the "Gellhorn rage—the irrepressible, passionate rage against injustice." As Wilson points out, however, Gellhorn never expected that her work would "directly influence the outcome of events she was reporting ... But she was driven to bear witness to what she considered man's inhumanity to man." Most critics and scholars agree that Gellhorn's work was not spoiled by the potency of her anger and the transparency of her political leanings. A 1993 review in the *Independent* characterizes Gellhorn's style as "unobtrusively gentle, always involved but never strident." Clancy Sigal, writing for the *Guardian*, finds that there is "a hard, shining, almost cruel honesty to Gellhorn's work" and that "she never was woolly or sentimental." In his obituary for *Salon*, Kevin Kerrane writes that although Gellhorn "sometimes made fun of 'objectivity' as a byword ... she always remained a stickler for accuracy."

In her essay "Dachau," Martha Gellhorn reports on the horrors of this concentration camp, where Allied forces found piles of corpses in 1945. Rico Lebrun (1900–1964), *Dachau*, 1958. Ink, wax, and charcoal on canvas. Gift of Constance Lebrun Crown, 1986-224. © THE JEWISH MUSEUM OF NEW YORK / ART RESOURCE, NY; © THE ESTATE OF RICO LEBRUN.

Not all of her readers appreciated Gellhorn's willingness to take a stand in her writing, however. Rick Lyman notes in his *New York Times* obituary that political conservatives sometimes "painted her as a left-leaning dilettante whose writing was often didactic and sentimental." Furthermore, her unqualified support for Israel in her writings about the Six Day War and later developments, combined with her harsh censure of Arabs, particularly the Palestinians, has caused some to question her assessment of violence in the Middle East.

SOURCES

Buford, Bill. "Martha Gellhorn Remembered." *Los Angeles Times*. Los Angeles Times, 22 Feb. 1998. Web. 17 May 2011.

Rev. of *The Face of War*, by Martha Gellhorn. *Independent* [London]. Independent Print, 27 Feb. 1993. Web. 16 May 2011.

Gellhorn, Martha. *The Face of War*. 1959. New York: Atlantic Monthly, 1988. Print.

Inglis, Fred. *People's Witness: The Journalist in Modern Politics*. New Haven: Yale UP, 2002. Print.

Kerrane, Kevin. "Martha's Quest." *Salon*. Salon Media Group, 12 Mar. 1998. Web. 17 May 2011.

Lyman, Rick. "Martha Gellhorn, Daring Writer, Dies at 89." *New York Times*. New York Times, 17 Feb. 1998. Web. 17 May 2011.

Mulligan, Maureen. "History Written in Flesh and Blood: Rebecca West, Martha Gellhorn, and María Martínez Sierra." *Nations, Traditions, and Cross-Cultural Identities: Women's Writing in English in a European Context*. Ed. Annamaria Lamarra and Eleonora Federice. Bern: Peter Lang, 2010. Print.

Nicolson, Nigel. "A Woman at the Wars." *New Statesman* 17 Oct. 1959: 517–518. Print.

Sigal, Clancy. Rev. of *The Face of War*, by Martha Gellhorn. *Guardian* [London]. Guardian News and Media, 3 Apr. 1986. Web. 16 May 2011.

"The War to End War." Rev. of *The Face of War*, by Martha Gellhorn. *Times Literary Supplement* 11 Sept. 1959: 515. Print.

Wilson, Deborah. "'An Unscathed Tourist of Wars': The Journalism of Martha Gellhorn." *The Journalistic Imagination: Literary Journalists from Defoe to Capote and Carter*. Ed. Richard Keeble and Sharon Wheeler. London: Routledge, 2007. 116–129. Print.

FURTHER READING

Dell'Orto, Giovanna. "'Memory and Imagination Are the Great Deterrents': Martha Gellhorn at War as Correspondent and Literary Author." *Journal of American Culture* 27.3 (2004). Web. *Literature Resource Center*. 16 May 2011.

Gellhorn, Martha. *The View from the Ground*. New York: Atlantic Monthly, 1988. Print.

Hemingway, Ernest. *For Whom the Bell Tolls*. New York: Scribner, 1940. Print.

Horwell, Veronica. "Martha Gellhorn: A Witness to Our World at War." *Brick* 59 (1998). Web. *Literature Resource Center*. 16 May 2011.

McLoughlin, Catherine Mary. *Martha Gellhorn: The War Writer in the Field and in the Text*. Manchester: Manchester UP, 2007. Print.

Moorehead, Caroline. *Gellhorn: A Twentieth-Century Life*. New York: Holt, 2003. Print.

Orwell, George. *Homage to Catalonia*. London: Secker and Warburg, 1938. Print.

Janet Moredock

"FIREMAN FLOWER"

William Sansom

OVERVIEW

"Fireman Flower," the centerpiece in a 1944 collection of short fiction by William Sansom (1912–76), follows the title character's thoughts as he fights the largest fire of his career. The story takes place in London during the Blitz (1940–41), when nightly German bombing raids set much of the city ablaze. As Flower hunts through a bombed warehouse in search of the all-important "kernel of the fire," he is faced by a series of disappointing dead ends and surreal experiences that call into question the stability of perception and the nature of truth itself. In this sense, both the fire and the war are presented as catalysts that lead the fireman to examine his life and philosophical outlook. The story is largely allegorical, with Fireman Flower's search through the mazelike warehouse corresponding to an Everyman's search for truth and meaning.

In composing the story, Sansom drew on his own experiences as a fireman during the Blitz. The success of the publication in Britain led to an American edition the next year, which caught the attention of noted fiction writer Eudora Welty (1909–2001). Welty particularly admired the work's surrealistic elements. Despite such endorsements, however, Sansom's writing has not experienced the enduring success that has met many other works of war fiction, perhaps because its focus is more philosophical than martial. The story does, however, continue to draw the attention of scholars interested in its reflections on the nature of human experience.

HISTORICAL AND LITERARY CONTEXT

"Fireman Flower" draws on Sansom's experience in the Auxiliary Fire Service (AFS) during World War II. The AFS was initiated in 1938 when rising militarism in Germany made it appear that another global war was inescapable. The AFS supplemented the work of local fire brigades, which were inadequately staffed to meet the demand that would accompany another war. Many AFS recruits received little training, and tensions were often high between AFS members and brigade members whose service predated the war. The animosity was strengthened because many AFS members were from the educated elite of British society (many, like Sansom, were writers or artists), and longtime brigade members often viewed them as either draft dodgers or opportunists seeking to usurp the working-class firefighters' positions.

Britain's firefighters became crucially important in September 1940, when the German Luftwaffe began running near-nightly bombing raids on England that would continue through May of the next year. Known collectively as the Blitz (from the German word *blitzkrieg*, or "lightning war"), these raids were intended to cause both physical devastation and psychological terror. The Blitz killed more than forty thousand people and destroyed upwards of a million homes in London alone. In addition to striking residential areas, the raids often focused on buildings considered to be strategic economic and military targets, such as warehouses and factories. The contents of these buildings made them especially prone to fire, and the bombings frequently resulted in blazes that were difficult to control. The most notable of these attacks on London occurred on December 29, 1940, when incendiary bombs ignited a massive firestorm. Sansom had joined the AFS as the Blitz was beginning in 1940, serving in the hard-hit area of Westminster. He was on duty during the December 29 raid.

Sansom's first published story, "The Wall" (1941), was based on his wartime service, and firefighting features prominently in several of his other stories. His fiction has often been compared to the work of British novelist Henry Green, another AFS veteran whose 1943 novel *Caught* traces the relationship between two firefighters. Thematically and stylistically, however, Sansom's work may be closer to the writings of Czech novelist Franz Kafka (1883–1924), who is known for his use of allegory and enigmatic narratives.

THEMES AND STYLE

"Fireman Flower" has often been interpreted as an allegory in which characters, objects, and events are used to symbolize broader ideas or concepts, often of a religious or philosophical nature. The story's title character has frequently been read as a symbol of humanity, his fellow firemen as reason and sense experience, and the twisting passages of the burning warehouse as life itself. Flower's quest for the center or "kernel" of the blaze is thus an extended metaphor for the human search for truth and balance in life. Sansom's depiction

Key Facts

Conflict:
World War II

Time Period:
Mid-20th Century

Genre:
Short story

PAINTING THE BLITZ

Leonard Henry Rosoman, *A House Collapsing on Two Firemen, Shoe Lane*, 1940. Oil. © THE ART ARCHIVE / IMPERIAL WAR MUSEUM

Sansom's work with the AFS was memorialized in the 1940 painting *House Collapsing on Two Firemen, Shoe Lane, London, 1940*. The piece is the work of Leonard Rosoman (1913-), a young artist who served with Sansom in the AFS. On the night depicted in the painting, Sansom, Rosoman, and another AFS colleague were sent to fight a warehouse fire in London's Shoe Lane. The firestorm was one of the greatest challenges that Sansom and his colleagues faced during their service. After battling the blaze for several hours, Sansom and the third man became trapped when a building next to the warehouse collapsed. Rosoman's painting depicts the two men confined between the warehouse and the toppled wall of the adjacent building as debris falls around them. Tones of orange and black convey the smoke, soot, and fire that surrounded them.

Sansom was able to escape serious injury in the collapse, but the third firefighter did not survive the incident. Rosoman painted the incident as a means of handling his grief. He later became an Official War Artist to the Admiralty in 1943. The painting is now part of Britain's Imperial War Museum Collections.

of his protagonist's intense, often fantastical mental experiences bears the marks of the surrealist movement of the interwar and post-World War II era. Surrealist writers attempted to depict the substance and processes of the subconscious, often through dreamlike imagery. In "Fireman Flower" Sansom suggests parallels between the content of the subconscious and the dark and chaotic experiences brought on by the war in general and the Blitz in particular.

In presenting Flower as an eyewitness to events of the war, Sansom's story explores the immediate, wartime experiences of the fireman and the larger, global experience of human existence. The story begins by framing Flower as both a unique individual and a nameless member of a larger body of firefighters. Observing himself among his colleagues, he asks "How should I be unique? ... As our uniforms depict us, so are we uniform." This passage establishes Flower as a representative fireman (and, allegorically, a representative human), but it proceeds to emphasize his uniqueness. Flower notes, for example, that on further inspection the uniforms reveal subtle differences. Also, though others accompany him to the fire, he will ultimately seek its "kernel" alone, and his experience of the fire will be unique, shaped by his own mental processes, memories, and subconscious desires. Flower's two subordinates, who pull him in different directions as he searches, represent two possible approaches to life—reliance on reason, and indulgence of the senses. Flower is briefly seduced by both outlooks, which divert him from his search for the seat of the blaze, lulling him into complacency and a false sense of security in the first instance, and deluding him into believing, in the second, that pleasurable sense experience is akin to spiritual enlightenment. He also faces a third distraction when he is momentarily pulled into pleasant memories of the past that tempt him away from his quest.

Flower's quest raises questions about attempts to bear accurate witness. After realizing for the second time that he has pursued the wrong path, he asks himself, "Am I too easily led? Or is the appearance of things at first so persuasive that it deceives each man?" Soon after, Flower is deceived by his reflection in a mirror, first mistaking it for another firefighter and then seeing it as "a ghost of himself." The nature of reality is also called into question when the intensity of the fire causes Flower to hallucinate (for example, when he sees his old friend Chalmers and objects from his childhood) as well as in surrealistic scenes in which it is unclear whether the described events are real, delusional, or a mixture of both (most notably when Flower finds himself in a room full of foamy, fragrant water from broken soap and perfume containers and briefly languishes in the pleasant sensory experience). In blurring the distinctions between reality and hallucination, and between past and present, the story also questions the priority of immediate experience. At one point Flower observes that "The past was more real than the present because the picture was clearly defined." This is especially true in the smoky warehouse, where objects fade in and out of the smoke, such that they "seemed to have been only a flutter of the imagination."

Each of Flower's encounters in the warehouse calls into question not only a philosophical outlook but also the reliability of any claim to know truth or certainty. After his brief seduction by reason, for example, he admonishes himself for pursuing enlightenment in the wrong way, as "freedom from doubt has nothing whatsoever to do with pure freedom. Freedom from doubt, the greatest deception of all!" He also links these discoveries to philosophical positions, noting that the "little offshoots of the fire are the most deceptive. They are like certain freak ideas and barren philosophies that in their novelty intrigue and seduce but never finally satisfy." At the end of the story, Flower believes he has located the roaring center of the fire, but the discovery leaves him unfulfilled. He flees to the roof of the building, where he embraces a life that will ostensibly value the balanced contributions of reason, sense, and memory.

CRITICAL DISCUSSION

Although it is not as well known as some works of war literature, "Fireman Flower" has, from the time of its original publication, garnered a steady stream of critical responses. A review of Sansom's collection in 1945 by Welty describes it as producing "an abundance of surrealist effects, wonderful and explicit and authentically 'sur-real'"; the review subsequently notes, hwoever, that "it would be incorrect and misleading to call the stories surrealist. It must be remembered that these effects come from an energy at work not for its own sake, in free-association or in any form of irresponsibility, but altogether purposeful and highly in control." Following Welty's lead, one thread of scholarly discussion has explored Sansom's use of surrealist techniques. Another arises from the story's alleged debt to Kafka. Critical comparisons between the two writers began almost as soon as Sansom's book was published, although some commentators suggested that Sansom was a mere, and exceptionally poor, mimic of the Czech writer. In an influential 1966 article in *Wisconsin Studies in Contemporary Literature*, Peter F. Neumeyer summarizes scholarly debate on the issue. His essay includes excerpts from a letter in which Sansom notes similarities between Kafka's writing and his own but rejects the idea that Kafka was a driving influence on his work. Neumeyer ultimately suggests that the two writers share a common perspective—"specifically the technique of meticulous and unornamented delineation of the object described."

Many critics have attempted to define Sansom's style. Discussing "Fireman Flower" in a 1988 article in *Studies in Short Fiction*, for example, William H. Peden suggests that the story "illustrates Sansom's almost uncanny blending of the real and the fantastic." Writing in *Short Stories and Short Fictions* in 1985, Clare Hanson explores the ends to which Sansom employed this hybrid technique, arguing

that Sansom's "war fictions contain hallucinatory and distorted images, but this is to make the point that war in its modern form is the ultimate distortion, a violation of almost all the normal impulses of life." Discussing "Fireman Flower" specifically, she emphasizes the protagonist's disorientation, noting that as the crisis unfolds, he "runs backwards, literally and metaphorically, to scenes from his former life." The distortion of time and reality has also been explored by Lara Feigel who, in an article in the 2011 book *Bombing, States and Peoples in Western Europe 1940–1945*, argues that Flower "experiences the bombing from the start in visually photographic terms," though he sees the photographs of the past more clearly than those of today, "rendering Flower himself ghostly in the present."

Other scholars, in attempting to assign "Fireman Flower" to a literary genre, have suggested it is best described as philosophical fiction. Paulette Michel-Michot argues in her book *William Sansom: A Critical Assessment* (1971), that the fireman is well-suited to Sansom's "philosophy of effort, of active and perpetual questioning and search." Ultimately, she says, the story reveals that "By nature man wants to find an absolute and final truth, but by nature life is dynamic, forever changing and transforming itself."

SOURCES

Feigel, Lara. "'The Photograph My Skull Might Take.' Bombs, Time and Photography in British and German Second World War Literature." *Bombing, States and Peoples in Western Europe, 1940–1945*. Ed. Claudia Baldoli, Andrew Knapp, and Richard Overy. London: Continuum, 2011. 121–135. Print.

Hanson, Clare. "The Free Story." *Short Stories and Short Fictions, 1880–1990*. New York: St. Martin's, 1985. Print.

Michel-Michot, Paulette. *William Sansom: A Critical Assessment*. Paris: Société d'Édition Les Belles Lettres, 1971. 132–139. Print.

Neumeyer, Peter F. "Franz Kafka and William Sansom." *Wisconsin Studies in Contemporary Literature* 7.1 (1966): 76–84. Print.

Peden, William H. "The Short Stories of William Sansom: A Retrospective Commentary." *Studies in Short Fiction* 25.4 (1988): 421–431. Print.

Sansom, William. "Fireman Flower." *Fireman Flower and Other Stories*. New York: Vanguard, 1945. 184–236. Print.

Welty, Eudora. Rev. of *Fireman Flower and Other Stories*, by William Sansom. *A Writers Eye: Collected Book Reviews*. Ed. Pearl Amelia McHaney. Jackson: UP of Mississippi. 66–67. Print.

FURTHER READING

Calder, Angus. *The Myth of the Blitz*. London: J. Cape, 1991. Print.

Demarne, Cyril. *The London Blitz: A Fireman's Tale*. London: Battle of Britain Prints International, 1991. Print.

Harris, Carol. *Blitz Diary: Life Under Fire in World War II.* Stroud: History Press, 2010. Print.

Piette, Adam. *Imagination at War: British Fiction and Poetry, 1939–1945.* London: Papermac, 1995. Print.

Sansom, William. *The Blitz: Westminster in War.* Oxford: Oxford UP, 1990. Print.

Wallington, Neil. *Fireman at War: The Work of London's Fire-fighters in the Second World War.* Newton Abbot: David & Charles, 1981. Print.

Welty, Eudora. Rev. of "Fireman Flower," by William Sansom. *Today* May 1945: 69–70. Print.

Greta Gard

HOMAGE TO CATALONIA

George Orwell

OVERVIEW

In *Homage to Catalonia*, George Orwell recounts the six months he spent fighting in the Spanish Civil War against the Fascist coalition later led by Generalissimo Francisco Franco. Orwell arrived in Barcelona, Spain, in December 1936 intending only to write a series of articles. Inspired by a kinship he immediately felt with the workers there, however, he hastily joined the Trotskyist militia Partido Obrera de Unificacion Marxista (POUM; Workers' Party of Marxist Unification) and took up arms with them along the Zaragoza front in northeastern Spain.

Orwell quickly became disenchanted with the progress of the fighting and was ultimately betrayed when the aims of the war shifted. From the outset, the POUM militia was badly trained and ill equipped and encountered almost no action. Bored and disillusioned, Orwell also did not understand the extent to which foreign intervention was dictating the course of the conflict. Joseph Stalin, leader of the Soviet Union, which was funding the Spanish defense, instituted a purge against the POUM and other groups within the coalition that he suspected were not loyal to the cause of defending the Second Spanish Republic. Forced to flee Spain shortly after he was injured in battle, Orwell concludes *Homage to Catalonia* by renouncing Stalin and accusing the Communist Party of betraying their ideals.

First published in England in 1938, *Homage to Catalonia* met with a great deal of hostility in leftist intellectual circles throughout Europe. The book was not published in the United States until 1952.

HISTORICAL AND LITERARY CONTEXT

The Spanish Civil War began on July 17, 1936, when a coalition of conservative generals revolted against the Second Spanish Republic, an elected government led by Manuel Azana. Collectively known as the Popular Front, the defenders of the Second Republic comprised a host of disparate factions, including anarchists, Marxists, socialists, and liberal democrats, each with varying degrees of loyalty to the government and united only in their hatred of the nationalist forces that had launched the coup. The rebels, or Nationalists, as they were called, consisted of a reactionary party called the Spanish Confederation of the Autonomous Right, a group of monarchists known as Carlists, and the Fascist Falange.

The conflict quickly acquired great significance as support for both coalitions came flooding into Spain from across Europe, turning the Spanish Civil War into a dress rehearsal for World War II. Despite having signed the Non-Intervention Agreement in August 1936, Nazi Germany and the Kingdom of Italy gave munitions and funds to Franco's forces and used the war to perfect tactics of air and tank attacks that they would deploy in the forthcoming war on the Continent. The USSR broke the agreement by supporting the Popular Front, and the International Brigades, consisting of leftist volunteers from all over Europe, also supplied soldiers and arms to defend the Second Republic.

In effect, the conflict grew into a proxy war (a war in which antagonistic powers who do not wish to fight each other directly take opposite sides in a smaller, local war) between Nazi Germany and Fascist Italy on the one side and Communist Russia, with hordes of foot soldiers from England and France, on the other. By the time the war ended and Franco had secured power on April 1, 1939, as many as five hundred thousand people had died. Meanwhile, World War II had begun seven months prior, on September 1, 1939, when Germany invaded Poland.

In addition to Orwell, many other writers, including Ernest Hemingway and Arthur Koestler, traveled to Spain to cover the war. In 1940 Hemingway published *For Whom the Bell Tolls*, considered by many scholars to be one of the best war novels of the twentieth century. Set in Spain in 1937, the book chronicles the experiences of Robert Jordan, an American volunteer for the International Brigade who must go behind enemy lines and blow up a bridge. The following year, Koestler produced *Darkness at Noon*, his masterpiece, in which, like Orwell, he renounces Joseph Stalin and the Communist Party. Although the book never explicitly mentions Stalin, Russia, or the Soviet Union, Koestler sets the novel in 1938 in a place that resembles Moscow during the Stalinist purges.

The atrocities committed by the Communist Party of Soviet Russia produced several dystopian political novels. As far back as 1921, Russian novelist Yevgeny Zamyatin published *We*, based on his experiences in the Russian revolutions of 1905 and 1917. Zamyatin set the novel in a nation called One State,

Conflict:
Spanish Civil War

Time Period:
Mid-20th Century

Genre:
Autobiography

THE SOVIET BETRAYAL
OF THE POUM

As the main source of arms to the Second Republic, the Soviet Union came to direct the military and domestic policy of the Spanish government during its fight against Generalissimo Francisco Franco and the Nationalists. At the top of Soviet leader Joseph Stalin's agenda was eliminating all potentially disloyal factions among the various communist organizations there. Stalin considered the POUM, the party with which George Orwell had enlisted, a threat because it openly endorsed the views of Leon Trotsky, a rival whom Stalin had exiled from the Soviet Union in 1929.

In his memoir *Yo fuí un ministro de Stalin (I Was a Minister of Stalin*, 1953), Jesús Hernández, a leading figure in the Partido Comunista de España (Spanish Communist Party, or PCE) during the 1930s, offers an account of the campaign Stalin initiated to slander the POUM and assassinate its leaders. A willing participant in these measures, Hernández verifies that Stalin's secret police force, the NKVD, tortured and murdered POUM cofounder Andreu Nin i Pérez. Following the murder, the NKVD produced false evidence portraying Nin i Pérez as a Fascist spy and leaked reports that he had fled the country to live in Italy.

Communists in Great Britain accepted the NKVD's account of Nin i Pérez's treachery and the entire frame-up of the POUM and rejected Orwell for censuring Stalin and disparaging the Communists in Spain in *Homage to Catalonia*. Contempt for Orwell among some British Communists and left-wing intellectuals has not diminished with time.

which was made entirely of glass so that its citizens could be easily monitored. Influenced by this work, Orwell, at the end of his career, abandoned realistic prose and produced two novels in this genre, *Animal Farm* (1945) and *1984* (1949), both of which satirize the evils of Stalinism.

THEMES AND STYLE

In *Homage to Catalonia*, Orwell's clarity of expression, concision, and knack for the curmudgeonly, understated turn of phrase result in a certain level of detachment that might shock some readers. For example, when Orwell reports on the first casualty in his unit, rather than lamenting the loss of a comrade, he chastens the group for its incompetence. "He had fired his rifle and had somehow managed to blow out the bolt; his scalp was torn to ribbons by the splinters of the burst cartridge case. It was our first casualty, and, characteristically, self-inflicted," he writes. Later when he encounters eleven- and twelve-year-old boys in the trenches, Orwell remarks, "Boys of this age ought never to be used in the front line, because they cannot stand the lack of sleep which is inseparable from trench warfare."

Opposite page:
Painting by Wyndham Lewis (1882–1957), depicting the surrender of Barcelona during the Spanish Civil War. *The Surrender of Barcelona,* 1934–1937. Oil on canvas. Tate Gallery, London, Great Britain. © TATE, LONDON / ART RESOURCE, NY / © ESTATE OF PERCY WYNDHAM LEWIS / BRIDGEMAN COPYRIGHT SERVICE

Not all of *Homage to Catalonia* is delivered in this cranky, deadpan tone. There are moments of boyish enthusiasm and unabashed idealism, such as when Orwell describes his initial impression of Barcelona. He explains that he joined the militia "because at the time and in that atmosphere it seemed the only conceivable thing to do … It was the first time I had ever been in a town where the working class was in the saddle." Orwell had explored his fascination with the lower classes in *Down and Out in Paris and London* (1933), the story of two years he spent living in poverty, working menial jobs, and traveling as a tramp; and in *Road to Wigan Pier* (1937), which includes a sociological study of working-class conditions in industrial northern England and an essay on his own middle-class background and socialist politics. Of the optimism he sensed in Barcelona, Orwell writes, "Above all there was a belief in the revolution and the future, a feeling of having suddenly emerged into an era of equality and freedom."

Orwell's central theme in *Homage to Catalonia* is the Soviet betrayal of the Marxist ideal of creating a classless, egalitarian society. On leave from the front, Orwell returns to Barcelona to discover that whereas earlier "every wall was scrawled with the hammer and sickle," now "fat prosperous men, elegant women, and sleek cars were everywhere." Acting on instructions from Stalin, Spain's Civil Guards open fire on POUM and anarchist strongholds in Barcelona and start spreading lies about them in military circles and in the press. After participating in the street fighting, Orwell returns to the front, where he is shot through the throat and nearly killed. His convalescence over, he returns to Barcelona to discover that he must flee the city as the Civil Guards are indiscriminately jailing anarchists and members of the POUM.

CRITICAL DISCUSSION

Upon the release of *Homage to Catalonia* in 1938, critical response was largely partisan, with Communist critics who supported the Soviet regime and Catholic critics dismissing Orwell's politics as naive and ill informed. For example, regarding the split in the Popular Front, a reviewer in the *Times Literary Supplement* argues, "This long-drawn-out party squabble is pathetic and has contributed sensibly to Franco's success. It is difficult to see how any revolutionary triumphs were possible so long as the chaotic military conditions which are described in this book were unchanged." Douglas Woodruff, writing for *Tablet*, an English Catholic weekly, claims that Orwell "had neither the occasion nor, apparently, the inclination to find out much about the ideas behind the Nationalist movement … It is curious that a man who tells us that for a year or two past the international prestige of Fascism had been haunting him like a nightmare, should not display more intellectual curiosity."

Supporters of Orwell's politics and admirers of his staunch individualism praised the book for its literary merit and the author for his clear-sightedness. Writing in *Time and Tide*, Geoffrey Gorer, a close friend of Orwell's, comments, "In a period of literary groups he has remained fiercely individualist, in a period of literary affectations he has developed a prose style so simple that its excellencies pass unperceived, in a period of lip service to collective ideas and ideals he has maintained passionately his own integrity and independence."

In 1952, when the book was first published in the United States, the critical consensus remained that Orwell's closing polemic was injudicious and ill informed but that his arguments were nevertheless an important contribution to the debate on communism and Soviet Russia. After observing that *Homage to Catalonia* "contains passages comparable to the best writing of our time," George Mayberry, writing in the *New Republic*, also remarks, "The weakness of the book, and this is a purely personal observation, is its politics ... To say that the liberals and socialists in accepting Communist aid from within and from without Spain was a betrayal is to ignore the rudiments of politics in a time of crisis."

In addition to the ongoing debate over Orwell's politics, literary scholars have analyzed the work for its rhetorical strategies and for what it reveals about the challenges of representing war from the perspective of the eyewitness. In "Facing Unpleasant Facts: George Orwell's Reports," George Watson claims that, for Orwell, in order to be believed the writer must participate in the events he writes about. Watson also argues that Orwell sought a greater degree of belief from his readers than did most other writers. "You are not reading Orwell as he would wish unless you believe him, and he demands that sort of credence not often given to twentieth century writers—as a truth-teller," Watson writes.

In order to establish such a high level of credibility, however, Watson notes that Orwell often had to "create events in order to turn himself into an author": he chose circumstances and took on roles in order to give himself the opportunity to write about his experiences. For Watson there is something less authentic about voluntarily subjecting oneself to hardship and deprivation than having these trials forced upon one. "To say that Orwell demands credence is not to say that he deserves it," Watson explains. "One initial difficulty here is the subtle but crucial difference between choosing an experience and accepting one."

SOURCES

Gorer, Geoffrey. Rev. of *Homage to Catalonia*, by George Orwell. *Time and Tide* 36 (30 Apr. 1938). Rpt. in *George Orwell: The Critical Heritage*. Ed. Jeffrey Meyers. New York: Routledge, 1997, 121–23. Web. 19 May 2011.

Mairet, Philip. Rev. of *Homage to Catalonia*, by George Orwell. *New English Weekly* 26 May 1938: 129–30. Rpt. in *George Orwell: The Critical Heritage*. Ed. Jeffrey Meyers. New York: Routledge, 1997, 127–29. Web. 19 May 2011.

Mayberry, George. Rev. of *Homage to Catalonia*, by George Orwell. *New Republic* 23 June 1952. Rpt. in *George Orwell: The Critical Heritage*. Ed. Jeffrey Meyers. New York: Routledge, 1997, 141–42. Web. 19 May 2011.

Orwell, George. *Homage to Catalonia*. Los Angeles: IndoEuropean, 2011. Print.

Watson, George. "Facing Unpleasant Facts: George Orwell's Reports." *Sewanee Review* 96.4 (1988). 644–57. Web. 21 May 2011.

Woodruff, Douglas. Rev. of *Homage to Catalonia*, by George Orwell. *Tablet* 40 (9 July 1938). Rpt. in *George Orwell: The Critical Heritage*. Ed. Jeffrey Meyers. New York: Routledge, 1997, 131–33. Web. 19 May 2011.

FURTHER READING

Borkenau, Franz. *The Spanish Cockpit: An Eyewitness Account of the Spanish Civil War*. London: Phoenix, 2000. Print.

Brenan, Gerald. *The Spanish Labyrinth: An Account of the Social and Political Background of the Spanish Civil War*. Cambridge: Cambridge UP, 1990. Print.

Crick, Bernard. *George Orwell: A Life*. Boston: Little, 1980. Print.

De Meneses, Filipe Ribeiro. *Franco and the Spanish Civil War*. New York: Routledge, 2001. Print.

Hemingway, Ernest. *For Whom the Bell Tolls*. New York: Scribner, 1996. Print.

Hitchens, Christopher. *Why Orwell Matters*. New York: Basic Books, 2003. Print.

Jerez-Farran, Carlos, and Samuel Amago, eds. *Unearthing Franco's Legacy: Mass Graves and the Recovery of Historical Memory in Spain*. South Bend: U of Notre Dame P, 2010. Print.

Koestler, Arthur. *Darkness at Noon*. Trans. Daphne Hardy. New York: Scribner, 2006. Print.

Thomas, Hugh. *The Spanish Civil War*. New York: Modern Library, 2001. Print.

Joseph Campana

MAN'S HOPE

André Malraux

OVERVIEW

French novelist and intellectual André Malraux's *L'espoir* (1937; *Man's Hope*, 1938), set in 1936 Madrid at the beginning of the Spanish Civil War, follows the story of a group of Republicans fighting against Francisco Franco's Nationalist Movement. The three parts of the novel—"Careless Rapture," "The Manzanares," and "Hope"—follow the rebels through the early months of the war, as they realize that the spirit of anarchy that rages at the heart of their efforts will not allow them to win the political victory they desire. Rather it is only when the soldiers and commanders are able to temper their passion for freedom with structured goals and fighting strategies that they are able to succeed in battle. Through a series of philosophical discussions staged between characters, the novel exposes the ideological and aesthetic conflict between his intellectual and activist sides, or between ideas and action, that concerned Malraux throughout his career. Though the titles of both the novel and its final section refer to hope, the book (which was published while the war was still raging) attempts to find it even in the anticipated defeat instead of foreseeing a positive outcome for the Republican side of the Spanish Civil War.

The original French version, *L'espoir*, was published in book form in December 1937, after having been excerpted in slightly different forms earlier that year. It had appeared in the bimonthly *La Nouvelle Revue Française*, the daily newspaper *Ce Soir*, and the literary and political weekly *Vendredi*.

HISTORICAL AND LITERARY CONTEXT

The Spanish Civil War (1936–39) was a military- and conservative-led revolt against the Republican government of Spain. Social unrest had been rising in Spain throughout the 1920s and '30s, mostly because of an extreme rise in poverty among the peasantry. In the fall of 1936, several military officers led the right-wing and fascist-aligned Nationalist faction in a coup attempt against the Popular Front, which had been elected on a platform of social reform and economic justice. The wider rebellion that followed plunged the nation into a civil war that captured the attention of the international community. During the conflict, which to many seemed to represent the defining struggle of the age, between socialism and Fascism, the Nationalists received aid from the fascist governments of Italian dictator Benito Mussolini and German dictator Adolf Hitler, while the Republicans received aid from the Soviet Union and, to a lesser extent, from Mexico, as well as from thousands of volunteers from western Europe and the United States. To the United Kingdom and France the war seemed representative of growing international instability in the wake of World War I. This led to a policy of nonintervention, endorsed publicly by many other nations.

The Spanish Civil War galvanized the international artistic community, capturing the imaginations of Spanish artists such as Pablo Picasso (in his painting *Guernica*) and Joan Miró (in his Black and Red series) as well as international novelists such as Malraux, Ernest Hemingway, John Dos Passos, Claude Simon, and George Orwell. In *Romanic Review*, Leslie Anne Boldt-Irons quotes novelist Upton Sinclair as commenting that the war attracted "probably the most literary brigade in the history of warfare," writers devoted to the communist/socialist desire to meld intellect and action. Malraux, Boldt-Irons continues, was one of the authors for whom "writing was an insufficient commitment to the fight against Fascism: the final test was action—to expose the body to danger and discomfort and to offer it, if necessary, in sacrifice."

In the decade preceding the Spanish Civil War, Malraux was engaged in numerous antifascist and liberal causes in his native France. In 1925 he founded the journal *L'Indochine*, which articulated the struggle of the Annanites against colonial landowners in Indochina. In 1934 he was a founding member of the International League against Anti-Semitism; in 1936 he assembled a fleet of planes, the Escuadrilla Espana, which flew missions against Franco's forces in the early years of the Spanish Civil War; and he was a member of the French Resistance during World War II. Veering toward the right later in life, Malraux worked as a cultural minister in the administration of Charles de Gaulle and spearheaded a revival of French cultural nationalism.

Man's Hope is most often contextualized with other novels about the Spanish Civil War, specifically Ernest Hemingway's *For Whom the Bell Tolls* (1940), in which an American, Robert Jordan, joins the International Brigades during the war. While Malraux's panoramic, philosophical novel differs formally from

Key Facts

Conflict:
Spanish Civil War

Time Period:
Mid-20th Century

Genre:
Novel

THE SPANISH CIVIL WAR AND THE FATE OF EUROPE

In many respects, *Man's Hope* represents the definitive ideological expression of Republican resistance during the Spanish Civil War. Gustav Regler's monumental novel *The Great Crusade* (1940), by contrast, focuses on the deep emotional and intellectual bonds forged between the individuals who fought in defense of the loyalist government. The novel is based on Regler's own experiences fighting with the Twelfth Brigade, a band of international volunteers who participated in a series of military victories between 1936 and 1937. Drawing heavily from real events, Regler's account of the war contains an objectivity and directness that is unusual for a work of fiction. At the same time, the work offers a profound meditation on the nature of such themes as loyalty, solidarity, and the struggle to achieve social justice in the face of violent political oppression. Even in the midst of this sense of camaraderie and optimism, however, Regler's narrative foreshadows the eventual unraveling of the Republican cause. As *The Great Crusade* unfolds, it becomes increasingly clear that the absence of a clear strategy, combined with a lack of vital material support from the Soviet Union and other foreign backers, will ultimately doom the efforts of the international brigades. One of the novel's most poignant sections describes the creeping sense of disillusionment among the young fighters as they learn of the bloody Stalinist purges occurring in the Soviet Union in 1937. This growing sense of uncertainty and dread, both toward the loyalist cause and the future of international communism, serves as a haunting portent of the tide of Fascist forces that will soon overwhelm all of Europe.

Hemingway's trademark realism, each novel is based on the author's personal experiences during the war and both express support for the rebel Republicans. Perhaps more significantly, Malraux addressed the conflict as an *engagé* ("engaged") writer, one who was ideologically aligned with his subject matter. Indeed, Malraux participated in the Spanish Civil War, serving as a gunner and squadron leader in the Republican air force. In this sense, *Man's Hope* has a great deal in common with works by other authors involved in the conflict, notably George Orwell's nonfiction *Homage to Catalonia* (1938) and Gustav Regler's novel *The Great Crusade* (1940). Indeed, Malraux's firsthand experience of the civil war lends his novel its underlying sense of authenticity.

THEMES AND STYLE

Malraux's epic novel, which promotes the Republican side of the Spanish Civil War, is clearly an example of what is known as *littérature engagé*, or literary works that intentionally and directly address the contemporary political situation. Formally, the work represents a hybrid of powerful fiction and nonfiction elements, interweaving conventional narrative techniques with direct, almost diary-like reports from the field. This strategy lends the work an immediacy and earnestness not often evident in traditional novel forms. Dennis Boak points out in *Revue André Malraux/Review*, however, that "one of the most remarkable features of *L'espoir* is that Malraux succeeded in writing a book for immediate consumption with a direct political message, yet which can be read half a century later … as a literary masterpiece—metamorphosing the transient into the timeless." Boak attributes the novel's longevity and its ability to transcend its "unashamed propaganda intentions" to Malraux's use of metaphoric schemes. Many critics point out that there are so many characters in *Man's Hope* that traditional novelistic features, such as characterization and interpersonal relationships, are largely lacking. Nonetheless, Boak says, Malraux's use of "shorthand" to describe his characters is part of the "systematic use of metaphoric imagery" that "assimilat[es] a whole world of culture and history to his story," developing the "'eternal' imagery [that] pull[s] against the political thesis of the novel."

Malraux's clear and unabashed support of the communist cause comes through consistently in *Man's Hope*. As such, the work did ultimately become a form of propaganda for the Popular Front, both in openly promoting the justice of its ideological goals and in endorsing the specific methods and techniques believed by members of the front to be essential to military success. In particular, as Malraux's continued emphasis on the need for discipline and pragmatism corresponded directly with the Popular Front's public image of itself, *Man's Hope* became a useful tool in recruiting volunteer efforts and resources in support of the communist struggle. At the same time, the novel's clear antifascist message serves to glorify the cosmopolitan character of the International Brigade, contrasting the belligerence and chauvinism of the Nationalist cause with the fundamental righteousness and solidarity of international communism. In this respect Malraux's work differs sharply from *Homage to Catalonia*, which depicted what Orwell perceived to be the corruption, deceit, and lack of clear organization that threatened to undermine the Popular Front's resistance efforts.

Man's Hope thematizes the conflict between what Malraux calls *être* (being) and *faire* (doing), between the idealistic beliefs that inform a political cause, on the one hand, and the disciplined action and potential compromises necessary to win a war, on the other. In the novel this contrast is enacted in the opposition between the anarchist and communist factions of the Republican forces. As the anthropologist-turned-intelligence-chief Garcia, often used to articulate the overarching themes of the novel, describes it, the communists' aim is to make something, while the anarchists want to be something. The values that the anarchists ascribe to—pacifism and justice—may be morally superior, but Garcia says, "We have to bring some order into these myths and transform our Apocalypse into an army, or die. There are no two ways about it." Although he himself agreed with the anarchists' beliefs, Malraux is aware of the necessity of violence and war to achieve those beliefs. The novel shows that the anarchist attitude that begins the war, when men who have been oppressed for decades are suddenly faced with a "carnival of freedom," is a "lyrical illusion." While, as the anarchist leader Negus declares, it is time "to live as life ought to be lived, here and now, or die," the Spanish Civil War was a peasant uprising fighting a mechanized army, and this fatalistic attitude would merely end in the defeat of the revolution. As Negus himself comes to realize, martial organization within the rebel ranks is necessary to win any kind of permanent political freedom. As Garcia puts it, the communists "have all the virtues of action, and those alone—but action is what is needed at this time."

CRITICAL DISCUSSION

Malraux's novel, released while the Spanish Civil War still raged, was lauded by intellectuals and activists on both sides of the political spectrum. Cecil Jenkins in *André Malraux* quotes Spanish anarchist Ramon Fernandez (1898–1936) as saying that "there is in this book a desire to win and yet a subtle dislike of winning which for me constitutes its principal beauty." Jenkins adds, however, that critics and readers saw from the beginning that the novel exceeded propaganda and was praised by conservatives such as the fascist writer Robert Brasillach (1909–48).

Some critics read *Man's Hope* retrospectively, in contrast to Malraux's later turn toward French cultural nationalism and his role as cultural minister in de Gaulle's conservative government. As Herman Lebovics explains in the *Wilson Quarterly*, it remains difficult to reconcile the rebel figure of Malraux and his early militant liberalism with his later attempt to define a specifically French culture as part of a larger movement of French nationalism.

Most critics, however, analyze *Man's Hope* in relation to the thematics of Malraux's earlier novels, particularly *La condition humaine* (1933; *Man's Fate*, 1934). His novels are, in general, read in terms of his interest in violence and death. Victor Brombert, in a 1969 lecture, says that "death and the human condition are for Malraux almost synonymous," and his novels illustrate this by showing how men behave in extreme situations such as in the midst of war. *Man's Hope*, Brombert continues, deploys apocalyptic imagery in the context of the Spanish Civil War to indicate the end of an era in which Europe was the political and cultural center. ... While, as one character says, "no painting stands up in the face of blood stains," Brombert asserts that "th[is] very negation implies a positive note" identifying the attempt to address the "mystery of suffering" as a precondition for "great art." Boldt-Irons says that Malraux's fascination with death in *Man's Hope* conflicts with political

activism and is detrimental to the direct political goals of the Spanish revolutionaries, a conflict that the novel exposes. Kerry H. Whiteside writes in *French Forum*, however, that in *Man's Hope* Malraux sees life and death as part of a larger metaphysics that defines the possibility of political action. Individuality, Whiteside argues, becomes a pragmatic question about leadership rather than a purely existential problem, allowing the author to develop a unique metaphysics in which "authority and artifice mediate fulfillment," a practical lesson that allows the book to transcend propaganda.

In *Comparative Literature Studies*, Ben Stoltzfus compares *Man's Hope* to Hemingway's *For Whom the Bell Tolls*, arguing that, despite the personal rivalry between the two authors, the books have a similar message. Although the novels differ formally, the works justify the people's challenge to the authoritative figures of the Church and the Spanish government by exposing the terrible conditions of poverty that affected most of the Spanish citizens in the prewar years.

A poster for the Republican army promoting unification during the Spanish Civil War, 1938. André Malraux's 1937 novel *Man's Hope* praises the Republican cause. © PETER NEWARK MILITARY PICTURES

SOURCES

Boak, Dennis. "*L'espoir*: From the Transient to the Timeless." *Revue André Malraux/Review* 19.1/2–20.1 (1987): 102–11. Print.

Boldt-Irons, Leslie Anne. "Military Discipline and Revolutionary Exaltation: The Dismantling of 'L'illusion lyrique' in Malraux's *L'espoir* and Bataille's *Le bleu du ciel.*" *Romanic Review* 91.4 (2000): 481–504. Print.

Brombert, Victor. "Malraux: Poet of Violence and Destiny." *Proceedings of the American Philosophical Society* 114.3 (1970): 187–90. Print.

Jenkins, Cecil. *André Malraux.* New York: Twayne, 1972. Print. Twayne's World Authors Ser. 207.

Lebovics, Herman. "Malraux's Mission." *Wilson Quarterly* 21.1 (1997): 78–87. Print.

Malraux, André. *Man's Hope.* Trans. Stuart Gilbert and Alastair McDonald. New York: Grove, 1938. Print.

Stoltzfus, Ben. "Hemingway, Malraux and Spain: *For Whom the Bell Tolls* and *L'espoir.*" *Comparative Literature Studies* 36.3 (1999): 179–94. Print.

Whiteside, Kerry H. "Malraux and the Problem of a Political Metaphysics." *French Forum* 18.2 (1993): 195–212. Print.

FURTHER READING

Bloom, Harold, ed. *André Malraux.* New York: Chelsea, 1988. Print. Modern Critical Views.

Boak, Denis. *Malraux: L'espoir.* London: Grant, 2003. Print. Critical Guides to French Texts 131.

Fisher, David James. "Malraux: Left Politics and Anti-Fascism in the 1930s." *Twentieth Century Literature* 24.3 (1978): 290–302. Print.

Golsan, Richard J. "Countering *L'espoir*: Two French Fascist Novels of the Spanish Civil War." *The Spanish Civil War in Literature.* Ed. Janet Perez and Wendell Aycock. Lubbock: Texas Tech UP, 1991: 43–53. Print.

Harris, Geoffrey T. *André Malraux: A Reassessment.* New York: Macmillan, 1996. Print.

Hemingway, Ernest. *For Whom the Bell Tolls.* New York: Scribner, 1940. Print.

Malraux, André. *Man's Fate.* New York: Vintage, 1990. Print.

Romeiser, John B. "His Master's Voice: Leadership Lessons in *L'espoir.*" *André Malraux: Across Boundaries.* Ed. Geoffrey Harris. Amsterdam: Rodopi, 2000: 117–39. Print.

MEDIA ADAPTATION

L'espoir. Dir. André Malraux and Boris Peskine. Perf. Andrés Mejuto, Nicolás Rodríguez, José Sempere. Lopert Pictures Corporation, 1945. Film.

Jenny Ludwig

MEMORY FOR FORGETFULNESS

Mahmoud Darwish

OVERVIEW

Through the synthesis of verse and prose poetry, excerpts from historical and literary texts, and fragments of memories and dreams, Mahmoud Darwish's semi-autobiographical *Memory for Forgetfulness* portrays a day under the Israeli siege of Beirut (June 6-August 12, 1982). While Darwish is concerned with the distinctly Palestinian experience of this event, his description of the details of everyday life shifts the focus of *Memory for Forgetfulness* to the broader human experience in a war zone. Darwish survived the siege and wrote *Memory for Forgetfulness* in 1985. The narrator of *Memory for Forgetfulness* justifies his, and Darwish's, silence during the war, insisting that "Beirut itself [was] the writing, rousing and creative." The Arabic literary magazine *Al-Karmel* published the text the following year as *The Time: Beirut/The Place: August*, and though the title has changed, its themes of memory, identity, language, and the role of literature and the author have endured.

Memory for Forgetfulness unfolds over a single day, beginning before daybreak as the narrator awakens and ending after sunset as he falls asleep. A dream of his former Israeli lover opens the narrative and introduces the complicated question of the relationship between Israel and the Palestinian people. Under the pretext of searching for a newspaper, the narrator leaves the shelter of his apartment seeking human contact, "running from a solitary to a collective death." As he wanders the streets of West Beirut, he encounters friends, acquaintances, and politicians, the general framework for numerous digressions and meditations on subjects ranging from coffee to Arab nationalism. The text also repeatedly revisits certain key episodes, creating a circular and fragmented narrative. Although *Memory for Forgetfulness* is limited in time and space, Darwish declares: "On borders, war is declared on borders," and the text, in both form and content, struggles against borders and limits of all types—political, historical, temporal, linguistic, and literary.

HISTORICAL AND LITERARY CONTEXT

Darwish was a child when his family fled its home in the Upper Galilee in 1948. The period before the end of the British Mandate for Palestine and the establishment of the State of Israel in 1948 was characterized by fighting between Jewish forces and the Arab majority population. These events created the first wave of refugees, which would be followed in 1948 by a mass exodus as the Jewish state sought to consolidate and expand its territory. Darwish's birthplace of Birweh fell victim to Israel's "campaign against potentially hostile Arab villages." Darwish relates that the villagers who had not fled successfully defended Birweh against Israeli soldiers. However, the village was then destroyed. Darwish discovered upon his return a year later that "it had been razed and replaced by two colonies, one for Yemeni Jews, the other for Europeans." The census of Palestinian Arabs had also already been completed, so Darwish was denied citizenship and an identity card. It is estimated that by 1949 more than 500,000 Arabs had become refugees, leaving only 160,000 of the original population within Israel.

In 1973 Darwish joined hundreds of thousands of Palestinian refugees in Beirut. The capital, and primarily West Beirut, had also become the headquarters of the Palestine Liberation Organization (PLO), an organization created in 1964 to centralize the Palestinian resistance movement. This made for an uneasy peace with many Lebanese since the PLO's staging of its often violent resistance from within Beirut was used as a justification by the Israelis for their extended siege of the capital. The Palestinians felt isolated as a people without a homeland, unwelcome in their adopted country, as Darwish describes: "'You're aliens here,' they say to them *there* [Israel]. / 'You're aliens here,' they say to them *here* [Lebanon]." The themes of identity, memory, and belonging stem from Darwish's own experiences as a Palestinian.

On June 6, 1982, Israel invaded Lebanon, implementing "Operation Peace for Galilee" in reaction to a series of PLO attacks against northern Israel as well as an earlier assassination attempt, erroneously attributed to the PLO, against the Israeli ambassador to the United Kingdom. Although one of Israel's goals was certainly the expulsion of the PLO from Lebanon, its plan was also to set up a friendly government with Christian Maronite Bashir Gemayel as president, leading to a warm welcome of the invasion by the Maronite population of East Beirut. One of the sources of Lebanon's long history of conflict is its confessional diversity—significant populations of a variety of Muslim and Christian sects, including the Maronite Church, a form of Eastern Catholicism, led to divisions along

Key Facts

Conflict:
Lebanese Civil War

Time Period:
Late 20th Century

Genre:
Prose poem

"WRITING TO FORGET"

The title of *Memory for Forgetfulness* has puzzled many readers over the years. Throughout the text Darwish plays with the opposing concepts: armies fight "anti-forgetfulness wars" to ensure that certain memories are preserved. At the same time, the narrator tells his Israeli lover, "if only one of us would forget the other so that forgetfulness itself might be stricken with memory." Here he seems to suggest that the only path to a lasting relationship involves the recovery of a more peaceful past, which can only be attained if the present animosity is forgotten.

One understanding of the title also lies in the experience of writing itself. Darwish wrote *Memory for Forgetfulness* in just three months while living in Paris. After sending it to his publisher, he claims to have never read it again. He explains that at that time in his life, his memories of the siege were creating a block that prevented him from writing poetry. The writing process was an act of liberation. *Memory for Forgetfulness* was a love song to Beirut, a mourning of the loss of Palestine and ultimately, an act of witnessing, a kind of anti-forgetfulness war that would simultaneously allow Darwish to forget while creating a record so others would always remember.

religious lines. When Gemayel eventually assumed the presidency, one of his collaborators called it "the longest *coup d'état* in the history of Lebanon."

When the Israeli siege began Beirut had already been weakened by prolonged civil war, a sectarian conflict that had divided the city since 1975: "the distance between one window and another facing it could be greater than that between us and Washington." Lebanon had also become a proxy for struggles between foreign powers: "if two intellectuals got into an argument in Paris, their dispute could turn into an armed encounter here." During the siege Israel cut off the water and electricity to West Beirut, prevented the delivery of supplies, and bombarded the capital, striking civilians and noncivilians alike. Darwish describes his encounters with the diverse weapons employed during the siege. His narrator faces the aftermath of a vacuum bomb during his walk and imagines the targeted building disappearing intact beneath the surface of the earth, so that "the residents … [kept] their previous shapes and the varied forms of their final, choking, gestures" underground while the birds "remained alive, perched in their cages on the roof."

It is estimated that eighteen thousand people were killed and thirty thousand wounded during the Israeli siege. *Memory for Forgetfulness* takes place on August 6, Hiroshima Day, inviting comparisons with World War II. The bombing only intensified during the final days of the siege. A cable from the U.S. ambassador to Lebanon described the violence on the following day, August 7, as "a blitz against West Beirut," suggesting its similarity to the German Blitz.

Both the Lebanese Civil War (1975–1990) and the post-1948 Palestinian experience have generated rich literatures, which frequently employ elements of the absurd, fractured prose, and nonlinear narrative to reflect the incomprehensibility of reality. Examples include Rashid al-Daif's *Passage to Dusk*, Elias Khoury's *Little Mountain* and *Gate of the Sun*, and Emile Habiby's *The Secret Life of Saeed: The Pessoptimist*. *Memory for Forgetfulness* straddles both traditions but is also unique because of its depiction of a specific historical moment during the Lebanese Civil War, the Israeli siege of Beirut, from a Palestinian perspective. Additionally, no other work so skillfully challenges generic conventions, combining storytelling and political commentary while maintaining the feel of poetry.

THEMES AND STYLE

One of the primary themes explored in *Memory for Forgetfulness* is the relationship between identity and place, a concern stemming from Darwish's location within the Palestinian diaspora. The narrator writes his double displacement. First, he has been exiled from his birthplace, Palestine, where without an identity card he must continually assert "I exist!" Second, he will soon be driven from Beirut. The city has become a kind of home for him, as it has for many Palestinian refugees: "Beirut has become my song and the song of everyone without a homeland." But he is not Lebanese, and with the siege of Beirut "the period of hospitality is over."

Without a true home Palestinians of this new generation build their identity on the idea of Palestine rather than memory of the physical place, "defending the scent of the distant homeland—that fragrance they've never smelled because they weren't born on her soil." However, any imagining of Palestine and Palestinian identity must now also include Israel and Israeli identity, a complicated reality embodied by the narrator's relationship with his Israeli lover. He tells her, "I don't love you. Or, I love you," indicating the complex history of hatred and kinship that bind these two peoples to a single physical place.

The layered narrative, through its incorporation of numerous voices and understandings of Palestine, reflects the fractures that prevent the writing of a single Palestinian identity. However, while the narrator can only directly give expression to his individual identity, the structure of the text encourages the emergence of a collective understanding as well, although it is a collectivity based on fragmentation exacerbated by Darwish's historical moment.

Another major theme treated in *Memory for Forgetfulness* is the role of literature and the author during war. The narrator discusses his inability to write during the siege, asserting that the sound of the guns "is louder than my voice." At the same time, however, the silence of Arab authors and poets leaves a void that other voices fill: "Is there anything more cruel than this absence: that you should not be the one to celebrate your victory or the one to lament your defeat?" Ultimately, Darwish advocates a marriage of "pure literature" and "political literature," arguing that "we want to heal the damage inflicted by the current trend to separate revolution from creativity and set the two in conflict."

Memory for Forgetfulness demonstrates this successful fusion of the creative and the political. Much of the text can be described as prose-poetry that elevates the details of everyday life as they are viewed through the lens of war. However, the numerous digressions, particularly those including material from other sources, lends a cobbled-together feeling reminiscent of earlier works of premodern Arabic literature. *Memory for Forgetfulness* is also an attempt to represent a reality that defies representation because of its incomprehensibility. Darwish claimed in an interview that "the role of the poet as witness, as objective witness, has declined, because the camera is more accurate than the writer. I believe the poet today must write the unseen." It is this history, based on dreams and emotions rather than names and numbers, that Darwish writes.

CRITICAL DISCUSSION

Although Darwish is best known for his poetry, *Memory for Forgetfulness* is an important work within both his own corpus and the field of Arabic literature more generally. In some ways, *Memory for Forgetfulness* serves as a necessary complement to Darwish's poetry. Ghassan Zaqtan highlights the unguarded expression found in the prose of *Memory for Forgetfulness* as one of the elements that grant it a special place within Darwish's body of work. He refers to the text as an "exercise" that reveals "what poetry does not allow to be exposed" because of the poet's careful attention to every word and phrase when composing poetry. Writing in the *Guardian* Radwa Ashour further calls *Memory for Forgetfulness* a "unique [contribution] to modern Arabic prose."

Critics have debated how to characterize *Memory for Forgetfulness*. In *Writing the Self: Autobiographical Writing in Modern Arabic Literature*, Yves Gonzalez-Quijano labels it as an autobiography, which he describes as "an attempt at introspection born out of the desire, in the face of death, to inscribe the most powerful moments of an existence in order to grasp its ultimate significance." Terry DeHay, in *Ethnic Life Writing and Histories: Genres, Performance, and Culture*, argues that the text should be considered a memoir since "memoirs privilege the relationship of memory to history." Challenging the classification of the text as a work of pure nonfiction, Gil Z. Hochberg asserts in her book *In Spite of Partition: Jews, Arabs, and the Limits of Separatist Imagination* that "the tension between the factual and the imagined is purposely sustained" throughout *Memory for Forgetfulness*.

West Beirut is shelled on June 1, 1982, during the Israeli siege, which Mahmoud Darwish depicts in *Memory for Forgetfulness*. © DAVID RUBINGER / CORBIS

Memory for Forgetfulness is most often studied within the framework of postcolonial studies, with scholars underlining its role in the creation of a Palestinian national identity in what some call a post-national world. DeHay is confident that *Memory for Forgetfulness* "is part of the process of regeneration of a national narrative, the production of an alternative narrative toward the re-imagining of national identity." Hochberg offers a more subversive reading, highlighting "Darwish's *deconstructive* and critical account of 'national memory.'" Focusing on the forbidden love affair between the narrator and his Israeli lover, Hochberg points to "the ambiguity and instability of identity that identity politics and the politics of national memory tend to erase and make forgotten," arguing that *Memory for Forgetfulness* in fact "asks us to view 'the national' itself with more suspicion, reminding us that for memory to appear as a national possession … the memory of the love that precedes 'the idea of the enemy' must disappear."

SOURCES

Ashour, Radwa. "Mapping a Nation: The Legacy of Darwish." *Guardian* [London] Guardian News and Media, 11 Aug. 2008. Web. 20 Oct. 2011.

Cleveland, William L. *A History of the Modern Middle East.* 3rd ed. Boulder: Westview, 2004. Print.

Darwish, Mahmoud. *Memory for Forgetfulness*. Trans. Ibrahim Muhawi. Introd. Ibrahim Muhawi. Berkeley: U of California P, 1995. Print.

———. Interview by Adam Shatz. "A Love Story between an Arab Poet and His Land." *Journal of Palestine Studies* 31.3 (2002): 67–78. JSTOR. Web. 20 Oct. 2011.

DeHay, Terry. "Remembered Community: Memory and Nationality in Mahmoud Darwish's *Memory for Forgetfulness*." *Ethnic Life Writing and Histories: Genres, Performance, and Culture.* Ed. Rocío G. Davis, Jaume Aurell, and Ana Beatriz Delgado. Berlin: Lit, 2007. 58–75. Print.

Gonzalez-Quijano, Yves. "The Territory of Autobiography: Mahmud Darwish's *Memory for Forgetfulness.*" *Writing the Self: Autobiographical Writing in Modern Arabic Literature.* Ed. Robin Ostle, Ed de Moor, and Stefan Wild. London: Saqi, 1998. 183–91. Print.

Hochberg, Gil Z. *In Spite of Partition: Jews, Arabs, and the Limits of Separatist Imagination.* Princeton: Princeton UP, 2007. Print.

Lamb, Franklin P., ed. *Israel's War in Lebanon: Eyewitness Chronicles of the Invasion and Occupation.* Boston: South End, 1984. Print.

Traboulsi, Fawwaz. *A History of Modern Lebanon.* Ann Arbor: Pluto, 2007. Print.

Zaqtan, Ghassan. "O Poet, What Did You Write During the War?" *Mahmoud Darwish: The True Difference.* Arabic. Amman: Dar al-Sharouq, 1999. 254–60. Print.

FURTHER READING

Darwish, Mahmoud. *State of Siege.* Trans. Munir Akash and Daniel Moore. Introd. Munir Akash. Syracuse: Syracuse UP, 2010. Print.

———. *Unfortunately, It Was Paradise.* Trans. and ed. Munir Akash and Carolyn Forché with Sinan Antoon and Amira El-Zein. Introd. Munir Akash and Carolyn Forché. Berkeley: U of California P, 2003. Print.

Hovsepian, Nubar, ed. *The War on Lebanon: A Reader.* Forward by Rashid Khalidi. Northampton: Olive Branch, 2008. Print.

Isaksen, Runo. *Literature and War: Conversations with Israeli and Palestinian Writers.* Northampton: Olive Branch, 2009. Print.

Mahmoud Darwich: As the Land is the Language. Dir. Simone Bitton. 1997. Film.

Nassar, Hala Khamis, and Najat Rahman, eds. *Mahmoud Darwish: Exile's Poet.* Northampton: Olive Branch, 2008. Print.

Notre musique. Dir. Jean-Luc Godard. Wellspring Media: 2005. Film.

Allison Blecker

NELLA LAST'S WAR
A Mother's Diary, 1939–45
Nella Last

OVERVIEW

First published in 1981, *Nella Last's War: A Mother's Diary, 1939–45* collects the World War II diaries of Nella Last, a British housewife who was forty-nine when the war broke out. Last wrote the diary, which begins with Britain's declaration of war against Germany, as part of the Mass Observation Project, a research venture established in 1937 and intended to gauge the lives and thoughts of ordinary citizens. The revival of Mass Observation allowed the 1981 publication of the diary. The work traces the everyday events of Last's life in Barrow-in-Furness, describing the frustrating experiences of rationing and blackouts, the anxieties caused by air raids at home and one of her two sons' service abroad, and her passionate work as a wartime volunteer. *Nella Last's War*, which represents just the first installment of the diary, concludes soon after the war's end.

Last, who confesses in the diary that "next to being a mother I'd have loved to write books," took great pains in filling her account with details about her everyday life, the fears brought on by the war, her aspirations, and also characters she meets in her daily round. The diary has subsequently caught the attention of readers and critics alike with its honest depiction of one family's wartime experiences. Last's frank discussions of her worries about her son's safety, her gripes about her in-laws, and her newfound sense of pride and strength as a woman have appealed to even those who didn't live during the war. In 2006 the diary was adapted as the television drama *Housewife, 49* (the name under which Last wrote for Mass Observation), which won the British Academy Television Awards for Best Single Drama and Best Actress (Victoria Wood) the following year. The success of *Housewife, 49* generated renewed interest in Last's diary, leading to two published sequels that collect Last's diary entries from the decades after the war: *Nella Last's Peace* (2008) and *Nella Last in the 1950s* (2010).

HISTORICAL AND LITERARY CONTEXT

Nella Last's War offers insight into the lives of ordinary British citizens during the Second World War. The entries cover almost the entire span of the war, excepting a period between December 30, 1944, and May 4, 1945; these entries were lost at some point

after Last submitted them. The book begins with Last's comments about Britain's declaration of war on Germany, which occurred on September 3, 1939, following the German invasion of Poland two days earlier. She reports that Britain's entry into the war is at once expected, frightening, and anticlimactic. In the final entry, dated August 14, 1945, Last records that the war ended as anticlimactically as it began: "I feel disappointed in my feelings. I feel no wild whoopee, just a quiet thankfulness and a feeling of 'flatness.'"

Last describes the evacuations of children that began soon after the declaration, as people living in urban areas, which were predicted to sustain heavy damage from bombing raids, sought safety for their families. She details her own firsthand experience of the German bombing raids that devastated British towns. Although the "Blitz," the series of German air raids over London from September 1940 to May 1941, is well known, German bombers did not limit themselves to London. Barrow, where Last lived, was home to a shipyard and was among frequent targets of the German raids. Last describes the lack of adequate bomb shelters and the sleepless nights interrupted by air raid warnings. On May 8, 1941, for example, she opens her entry with "another night of terror, and more damage and death."

Last's diary also details her volunteer work with the Women's Voluntary Service (WVS). Established in 1938 as part of the Air Raid Precaution Services, the WVS was designed to mobilize women to help support and protect the home front in the event of war. During the war members of the WVS were involved in myriad tasks, including fundraising for the war effort, coordinating the evacuation of children from densely populated areas, and making and collecting clothing and blankets and distributing them to those in need. WVS members also often orchestrated events to honor soldiers returning from war and provided food for firefighters and other emergency personnel during the Blitz. Last's diary entries describe the great lengths to which she went to gather old linens and scraps of cloth, out of which she produced clothing and dolls to be distributed to those in need or raffled off in support of the war effort.

Last's diary was originally published in 1981 as *Nella Last's War: A Mother's Diary, 1939–45*, but

✤ *Key Facts*

Conflict:
World War II

Time Period:
Mid-20th Century

Genre:
Diary

BRITAIN'S MASS OBSERVATION PROJECT

Nella Last's diary began as part of Britain's Mass Observation Project. The project came about in 1937 when Tom Harrisson, who was researching the daily lives of citizens in the city of Bolton, joined forces with Charles Madge and Humphrey Jennings, who were carrying out a similar project in London. The organization's research was envisioned as a way to track the experiences and feelings of average people across Britain. At first the group collected information primarily through open-ended surveys, but by 1939, the first year of World War II, it had recruited a group of roughly five-hundred individuals, known collectively as the National Panel of Diarists, to write regular diary entries about their lives. Researchers subsequently sorted passages from these entries according to topic, and data from the project thus provides a sense of what was on people's minds during the war. Popular war-related subjects include air raids and air-raid shelters, evacuations, gas masks, wartime propaganda, and the difficulties of dog ownership during wartime. Last's diary, which spans a period from 1939 to 1965, is among the most extensive records to have emerged from the project. Other responses are preserved in the organization's archive at the University of Sussex and are available through online subscriptions.

after the success of the BBC's television adaptation, *Housewife, 49*, it was re-released under the title *Nella Last's War: The Second World War Diaries of "Housewife, 49."* Last was not the first woman to have her wartime diary published, but hers is likely the best known today. Other notable contributions to the tradition of World War II diaries by women include Clara Emily Milburn's *Mrs. Milburn's Diary* (1979) and Vere Hodgson's *Few Eggs and No Oranges* (1976). Like Last, Milburn was a middle-aged mother, and her diary chronicles, among other things, the traumatic experience of having her son taken prisoner during the war. The diary of Hodgson, who was in her late thirties when the war broke out, shares with Last's diary an emphasis on the domestic struggles brought on by rationing as well as the outlet provided by wartime volunteering.

THEMES AND STYLE

Last's diary is presented largely as it was written for Mass Observation, although editor's notes are occasionally inserted between entries in order to provide context for some of the events described. For example, in between entries in which Last describes the bitter winter of 1940, the editor has added the explanatory note: "This winter was the coldest for forty-five years." Elsewhere, such notes give information about rationing, blackouts, and major events in the war. In a concluding section titled "Preparation of

the text," the editor explains that he at times standardized punctuation in order to make the text more accessible for the readers, while working to preserve as much as possible of Last's unique style and voice. Last's voice comes through particularly in moments of characteristic humor in the face of adversity. Explaining that one of her neighbors was praying for "God to strike Hitler dead," she notes, for example, that she "cannot help thinking if God wanted to do that he would not have waited till Mrs. Helm asked him to do so."

The diary weighs in on events of the war, emphasizing the atrocities committed against Jews. Early in the war, for example, Last reports watching a play titled *I Am a Jew* and feeling for the Jewish mother who must explain the hatred of Jews to her young son. She writes that the play haunted her, making her think "of all the helpless women in Germany who dare not want their babies." As the war ends in Europe, she reports seeing the graphic images from liberated concentration camps, emphasizing that the images of such inhumanity inspired a conviction that at times the international community must step in to help countries recover from tragic events. Occasionally, however, Last's frank observations about the war are unsettling, such as when, in January 1941, she writes, "I never thought I'd admire anything Hitler did, but today when I read in the 'Sunday Express' that he 'painlessly gassed' some thousands of lunatics, I did so."

One of the central themes to emerge from Last's diary is that the war affected the lives of women in unique and diverse ways. The most striking aspect of the war's impact on women, Last suggests, is the emotional burden of sending husbands and sons off to war. Last experiences this firsthand when her younger son, Cliff, enlists and is sent overseas. She also notes the effects of this maternal anxiety on other women around her. She records, for example, noticing that the fingernails of a fellow volunteer, whose son is also at war, are "bitten to the quick," an observation that causes her to feel "pity wrap me like a flame." When her town becomes the target of frequent air raids, Last describes her outrage at the lack of bomb shelters, attributing it in part to her empathy for mothers attempting to protect their young children. She also relates several local "scandals" involving young women who have become pregnant outside of wedlock and whose soldier lovers have been sent overseas before they can legitimate their relationships. Many of her entries, however, focus on the opportunities afforded women by the war. She frequently mentions her volunteer work with the WVS, which is a source of immense pride. The strength she derives from this work forces her to realize her dissatisfaction with her marriage. Toward the end of the war, for example, she records her frustration at being "treated [by her husband] with less consideration than the average man would dare to treat a servant."

CRITICAL DISCUSSION

Nella Last's War was well received by critics but did not achieve widespread popular success when it was first published in 1981. Reviewing the work in *Oral History*, Elizabeth Merson notes the feminist streak in Last's writing, suggesting that "there is no doubt that the war liberated Nella from her subservience to her husband, and indirectly her sons." But it is the work's broad and authentic portrait of lower middle-class life that Merson finds most intriguing, writing, "here is a mine of information about day-to-day life written in a candid, unguarded way, with occasional passages of great beauty." Similarly, in another early review in the *New Statesman*, Gillian Wilce asserts that Last's diary "should also be on the reading list of any who still believe the need for women's liberation to be an invention of contemporary young women who have nothing better to do."

Over time a small body of scholarly criticism has developed around Last's diary, often emphasizing its protofeminism. In a 1990 article in *Oral History*, for example, Dorothy Sherridan offers an overview of women's roles in the Second World War, citing Last's diary as an example of the popular cultural image of what she describes as the "Homefront woman," a figure who becomes "the embodiment of the national 'hearth'—what the rest of the country (ie men) are fighting for."

James Hinton includes Last among the nine individuals whose wartime experiences and Mass Observation participation he analyzes in his 2010 book *Nine Wartime Lives*. Hinton argues that Last offers a unique literary voice on the war, in part because "unshaped by formal education, her writing is vivid, funny, sad, intensely personal, and often moving." Hinton, like many other critics, also points to the emphasis on female empowerment in the diary, arguing that Last's "story has been seen as an example of the emancipating impact of war work (in her case voluntary work) on women's lives." Other scholars have pointed out, however, that while the war provided women such as Last with an opportunity to leave the home and participate in public service, the kinds of service in which many excelled were decidedly domestic in nature. Last, for example, wins praise for her ability to create dolls, clothing, and blankets from scraps of cloth, just as at home she sets herself apart through her skills as a shrewd household manager. Annamaria Lamarra argues in an article in *Memories and Representations of War* that Last's diary offers evidence that the war afforded new opportunities for women, in part by allowing them to play mother to the nation. "The pages of Nella Last's diary," she suggests, "provide glimpses of themes that we are still reflecting on today, for example, the interference of the obligations of equality with … traditional female duties."

SOURCES

Hinton, James. *Nine Wartime Lives: Mass-Observation and the Making of the Modern Self.* Oxford: Oxford UP, 2010. Print.

Lamarra, Annamaria. "War in Women's Experience and Writing." *Memories and Representations of War: The Case of World War I and World War II.* Ed. Elena Lamberti and Vita Fortunati. Amsterdam: Rodopi, 2009. 145–59. Print.

Nella Last was a proud member of the Women's Voluntary Service (WVS), which mobilized women to support the home front during the war. The WVS members depicted here pose with carts they will use to transport supplies to bombed areas after air raids. © AP IMAGES

Last, Nella. *Nella Last's War: A Mother's Diary, 1939–45.* Ed. Richard Broad and Suzie Fleming. Bristol: Falling Wall, 1981. Print.

Merson, Elizabeth. Rev. of *Nella Last's War: A Mother's Diary, 1939–45*, by Nella Last. *Oral History* 10.2 (1982): 76–77. Print.

Purcell, Jennifer. "The Domestic Soldier: British Housewives and the Nation in the Second World War." *History Compass* 4:1 (2006): 153–60. Print.

Sherridan, Dorothy. "Ambivalent Memories: Women and the 1939–45 War in Britain." *Oral History* 18.1 (1990): 32–40. Print.

Wilce, Gillian. Rev. of *Nella Last's War: A Mother's Diary, 1939–45*, by Nella Last. *New Statesman* 25 Sept. 1981: 30–31. Print.

FURTHER READING

Bell, Amy Helen. *London Was Ours: Diaries of the London Blitz.* London: Tauris, 2008. Print.

Fussell, Paul. *Wartime: Understanding and Behavior in the Second World War.* New York: Oxford UP, 1990. Print.

Hinton, James. "The 'Class' Complex: Mass-Observation and Cultural Distinction in Pre-War Britain." *Past & Present* 199 (2008): 207–36. Print.

Hodgson, Vere. *Few Eggs and No Oranges: A Diary Showing How Unimportant People in London and Birmingham Lived Through the War Years 1940–1945.* London: Dobson, 1976. Print.

Last, Nella. *Nella Last in the 1950s: Further Diaries of Housewife, 49.* Ed. Patricia E. Malcolmson and Robert W. Malcolmson. London: Profile, 2010. Print.

———. *Nella Last's Peace: The Post-War Diaries of Housewife, 49.* Ed. Patricia E. Malcolmson and Robert W. Malcolmson. London: Profile, 2008. Print.

Marwick, Arthur. "Print, Pictures, and Sound: The Second World War and the British Experience." *Daedalus* 111.4 (1982): 135–55. Print.

Milburn, Clara Emily. *Mrs. Milburn's Diaries: An Englishwoman's Day-to-Day Reflections, 1939–45.* London: Harrap, 1979. Print.

Schofield, Mary Anne. "Underground Lives: Women's Personal Narratives, 1939–45. *Literature and Exile.* Ed. David Bevan. Amsterdam: Rodopi, 1990. 121–47. Print.

MEDIA ADAPTATION

Housewife, 49. Dir. Gavin Millar. Perf. Victoria Wood, David Threlfall, Christopher Harper. ITV, 2006. Television movie.

Greta Gard

REQUIEM FOR BATTLESHIP YAMATO

Yoshida Mitsuru

OVERVIEW

Originally published in Japanese as *Senkan Yamato no Saigo* (1952) and translated into English by Richard H. Minear in 1985, *Requiem for Battleship Yamato* is a World War II memoir by Yoshida Mitsuru. In April 1945 Yoshida was a radar officer aboard the *Yamato* when it was sent on an ostensible suicide mission against American troops in the Pacific. Yoshida was one of only several hundred out of a crew of roughly three thousand to survive the mission. His memoir traces the mission from the receipt of orders outlining the attack through preparations, launch, and the tense period in which the crew, knowing they were unlikely to survive, prepared for battle. It concludes with the ship's destruction by American torpedoes and the rescue of the few survivors. Yoshida chronicles the crew members' attempts to remain calm in the face of impending death and their worries about the families they will leave behind to face an uncertain future.

Yoshida wrote his memoir almost immediately following the war, in part to come to terms with what he had endured. He completed a draft of the memoir in October 1945, but it was rejected for publication because the American authorities occupying postwar Japan deemed it militaristic and propagandistic. Yoshida subsequently revised the work, which was published in 1952 to critical acclaim. He further revised the memoir in 1978, creating the definitive version, which was used as the basis for Minear's translation. Although not as well known to English speakers as many other accounts of World War II, *Requiem for Battleship Yamato* remains one of the best-known Japanese books written about the war and has been the subject of a Japanese film adaptation in 1953.

HISTORICAL AND LITERARY CONTEXT

The battle that Yoshida's memoir describes took place on April 7, 1945, as the war in the Pacific was beginning to wind to a close. The U.S. Navy had been gaining dominance in the region, island-hopping closer and closer to the Japanese mainland. In June 1944 American forces took the Marianas, a chain of islands south of Japan that they then used as a base from which to carry out bombing raids over Japan. In March 1945, American forces

reclaimed the Philippines, which had been lost to Japan earlier in the war. Soon after, they had taken the island of Iwo Jima.

At the time of the *Yamato*'s ill-fated mission, American troops were on the verge of capturing Okinawa, an island roughly 340 miles off the Japanese mainland. In his memoir, Yoshida relates the Japanese military's awareness that "the loss of Okinawa will mean that the decisive battle, on the main islands [of Japan], is at hand." Because of the widespread awareness of the importance of Okinawa, the fighting there was particularly bloody, kamikaze suicide attacks were numerous (nearly fifteen hundred total between the beginning of April and the end of June), and many civilians on Okinawa committed suicide rather than surrender to American forces.

Yamato's mission, which Yoshida explains was named "Operation *Ten'ichigo*," noting that "*ten* [heaven] probably comes from the phrase 'a heaven-sent opportunity to reverse one's fortunes,'" was to get as close to Okinawa as possible and fight to the death. The plan was for it to draw American fire, leaving the U.S. Navy more vulnerable to kamikaze attacks. Yoshida makes it clear that the crew understood that they were not expected to survive the mission—"What awaited us was death and nothing else. Death, beyond a doubt." All aboard were aware that they only had enough fuel for the voyage to Okinawa and none to return home (although Minear points out in his introduction that unbeknownst to the crew, this was not actually the case).

Requiem for Battleship Yamato repeatedly emphasizes that the Japanese troops were outnumbered and outmaneuvered by their American counterparts. They also lacked the technology that allowed the U.S. Navy to succeed. The crew is aware, for example, that were they to reach Okinawa, their nine ships would face at least sixty American ones. Moreover, while Yoshida notes that although "at the time Yamato was designed, ten long years ago, one could boast of the impregnability of her defenses," the ship cannot expect to stand up to American technology. He suggests, of the Americans, that "theirs is a strength we cannot divine, a force we cannot fathom." When the American attack gets under way, the crew notes this strength with a mixture of horror and admiration. The chief of staff comments to Yoshida that "at the beginning of the war we flung a challenge to the world: how to attack

❖ *Key Facts*

Conflict:
World War II

Time Period:
Mid-20th Century

Genre:
Memoir

THE LAST KAMIKAZE

The sinking of the battleship *Yamato* on April 7, 1945, effectively signaled the end of Japanese naval power during World War II. The ship's destruction also carried profound symbolic significance for the Japanese. As the largest battleship in the world, the vessel had become an emblem of the nation's dominance in the Pacific and of the resolute spirit of the Japanese people. In the same way, the kamikaze, or suicide air attacks, that began flying in October 1944 came to symbolize the nation's absolute refusal to surrender to Allied forces. Often fighting in tandem with the maneuvers of Japanese warships, kamikaze pilots flew their planes directly into Allied naval vessels, with the aim of slowing the enemy attack. Because these planes were typically filled with explosives, bombs, and extra fuel, and because the pilots were capable of striking with great accuracy, they became far more effective weapons than conventional missiles. For a Japanese military facing defeat, the sacrifice of human life was ultimately justified by the kamikaze's destructive power. Edwin P. Hoyt captures the commitment of the Japanese military officer in his book *The Last Kamikaze: The Story of Admiral Matome Ugaki* (1993). The book tells the story of the decorated Japanese admiral, who, upon learning of Japan's surrender in August 1945, embarks on a final suicide mission against a U.S. naval vessel. With two other Japanese servicemen in his cockpit, the admiral ultimately crashes his plane into the sea, in a final, futile gesture of resistance.

capital ships with carrier planes. Now we get a brilliant answer thrust upon us." Later, Yoshida finds himself thinking that "they may be the enemy, but they are doing a splendid job."

Yoshida's memoir is considered one of the best works in an extensive tradition of Japanese war literature, little of which has been translated into English. Among the most influential pieces to reach English-speaking audiences are Ōoka Shōhei's *Nobi* (1951; translated as *Fires on the Plain*, 1957), about a soldier's experiences in the Philippines, and Ōe Kenzaburō's essay *Okinawa nōto* (1970; translated as *Okinawa Notes*), which condemns the Japanese military's role in encouraging civilian suicides at Okinawa. In addition to the memoir, Yoshida published several other writings about the war, including a biography of Vice Admiral Seiichi Itō, *Yamato*'s commander.

THEMES AND STYLE

Yoshida chose to write his memoir in *bungotai*, a literary form of Japanese in use prior to the war. Minear notes in his introduction that this choice has often led to the work's being described as a prose poem. The memoir is organized into entries as though it were a diary, despite the fact that it was composed in

its entirety after the events that it describes. Written in the literary present, it conveys a sense of immediacy: "4 April, early morning: a report that American planes attack. We take our stations. Forenoon, afternoon: just as on the day before, we float at full alert, watching and waiting." Occasionally, however, Yoshida references the outcome of events in advance. For example, when describing the officers' discussion of the battleship's fate, he notes, of the suggestion that "midway we will fall victim to airborne torpedoes," that "this prediction, subscribed to by a large number of the young officers, will prove to be precisely on the mark."

The central theme to emerge from Yoshida's memoir is the idea that death is not something that ought to be glorified. "No matter how splendid its raiment," he writes, "death is death." During the intense air assault on *Yamato*, he is shocked by the realities of death, in particular by seeing fellow crew members reduced to "hunks of flesh." The brutal carnage, with its horrific sights and smells, stands in stark contrast to the glorified vision of dying for one's country that had been promoted in Japanese culture before and during the war. The horror is heightened by Yoshida's familiarity with the men who have lost their lives. He knows from their stories that among them are fathers and expectant fathers, newlyweds, and sons, some of whom leave their families without any means of support. For Yoshida, the realization of his own life's value finally comes as he is struggling to survive in the water after the explosion of the *Yamato*. "For the first time," he explains, "for really the first time, the will to live fills me. It is not a desire, that I should *like* to live; it is an obligation, that I *must* live."

The philosophical divide between Yoshida's realizations and the propaganda of Japan's military leaders is evident in the memoir's concluding paragraphs. Within this text, Yoshida juxtaposes the Imperial Japanese Navy's official message about the event ("Thanks to this task force, our special attack planes had great success") and the truth of the mission's failure and the loss of thousands of men, whose individuality he emphasizes in the book's final lines: "Three thousand corpses, still entombed today. What were their thoughts as they died?" This critique of official rhetoric is visible elsewhere in the memoir as Yoshida reflects on the effects of the intensely militaristic propaganda on *Yamato*'s crew. As the battleship sinks, for example, he watches two navigation officers tie themselves to each other and to the ship's binnacle in order to assure that they will die because surviving would be shameful. Yoshida reveres Vice Admiral Seiichi Itō, the commander who went down with the ship, as a hero because he was able to see behind the rhetoric that was driving the war and glorifying death. Discussing the admiral's decision to call off the mission, Yoshida writes, "what extraordinary resolve! At the time, 'One hundred million deaths rather than surrender' was a popular slogan; nevertheless, acting on his own initiative, he called a halt to this special attack mission on which so much had been staked." In aborting the mission, Itō made the rescue of Yoshida and his fellow survivors possible. Had other military leaders been so brave, the memoir implicitly suggests, the massive loss of life could have been avoided.

CRITICAL DISCUSSION

When Yoshida's memoir was first published in Japan in 1952, it drew widespread praise, much of which came from men who had, like Yoshida, served in the war. Some commentators, however, have questioned whether Yoshida sacrificed too much of his initial version in order to get around American censors.

Prior to Minear's translation, a small excerpt of *Requiem for Battleship Yamato* was translated into English in 1952 by Masaru Chikuami as "The End of Yamato," gaining a larger audience when it was condensed for publication in *Reader's Digest* soon after. When Minear's full-length translation appeared in 1985, it was well-reviewed. Writing in the *Journal of Asian Studies*, for example, Richard H. Mitchell describes the book as "a minor classic viewed by critics as one of the highest achievements of post-1945 Japanese literature." Elsewhere, Sato Kyozo's *Pacific Affairs* review perceives the work as "truly a story of life and death."

Much praise was also lavished on Minear for the quality of his translation. Mitchell asserts that "Minear is to be commended for providing English speakers with another Japanese viewpoint on the Pacific War and war in general," while Sato lauds Minear for his "superb job of translating this book into English, and his informative, thoughtful introduction is excellent." Sato writes that "there are a few differences in nuance between the original and the English version" but goes on to note that "this does not reflect on Minear's abilities; the extremely formalized Japanese (*bungotai*) can only be approximated in English."

To date, the majority of scholarly commentary treating *Requiem for Battleship Yamato* has been written in Japanese and remains untranslated. The work has, however, attracted some critical commentary from English-speaking scholars, who recognize its value as an important contribution to the literature of the Second World War. In an article about World War II literature in the *Sewanee Review*, Samuel Hynes counts Yoshida's memoir among "the most modest personal accounts … [that] tell ordinary stories in plain language … stories that could be multiplied by tens of thousands to express the experiences of the mass of indistinguishable individuals who filled the vast canvases of the war." As a whole, Hynes suggests, such works "come as close, I think, as we will get to the story that will tell us how it was in World War II."

SOURCES

Hynes, Samuel. "War Stories: Myths of World War II." *Sewanee Review* 100.1 (1992): 98–105. Print.

Minear, Richard H. Translator's Introduction. *Requiem for Battleship Yamato*. By Yoshida Mitsuru. Trans. Richard H. Minear. Seattle: U of Washington P, 1985. xi-xxxvi. Print.

Mitchell, Richard H. Rev. of *Requiem for Battleship Yamato*, by Yoshida Mitsuru. *Journal of Asian Studies* 45.4 (1986): 868–69. Print.

Sato, Kyozo. Rev. of *Requiem for Battleship Yamato*, by Yoshida Mitsuru. *Pacific Affairs* 59.3 (1986): 508–09. Print.

Yoshida Mitsuru. *Requiem for Battleship Yamato*. Trans. Richard H. Minear. Seattle: U of Washington P, 1985. Print.

FURTHER READING

Astor, Gerald. *Operation Iceberg: The Invasion of Okinawa in World War II*. New York: D. I. Fine, 1995. Print.

Dull, Paul S. *A Battle History of the Imperial Japanese Navy (1941–1945)*. Annapolis: Naval Institute, 1978. Print.

Morris, Ivan. *The Nobility of Failure*. New York: Holt, 1975. Print.

Ooka Shohei. *Fires on the Plain*. Trans. Ivan Morris. Baltimore: Penguin, 1972. Print.

Achille Beltrame's engraving, *Japanese Kamikaze Pilot Diving into American Warship*, appeared in the Italian newspaper *La Domenica del Corriere* in November 1943. In *Requiem for Battleship Yamato* memoirist Yoshida Mitsuru details the strategy for Battleship Yamato—itself on a suicide mission—to distract U.S. forces enough to allow for primary damage from Kamikaze pilots. © GIANNI DAGLI ORTI / DOMENICA DEL CORRIERE / THE ART ARCHIVE / THE PICTURE DESK, INC

Inoguchi Rikihei and Nakajima Tadashi. *The Divine Wind: Japan's Kamikaze Force in World War II.* Trans. Roger Pineau. Annapolis: Naval Institute, 1958. Print.

Spurr, Russell. *A Glorious Way to Die: The Kamikaze Mission of the Battleship Yamato.* New York: Newmarket, 1981. Print.

Tsouras, Peter G., ed. *Rising Sun Victorious: An Alternate History of the Pacific War: It Could Have Happened … and Nearly Did.* Mechanicsburg: Stackpole, 2001. Print.

MEDIA ADAPTATION

Senkan Yamato. Dir. Yutaka Abe. Perf. Toru Abe, Minoru Arita, Hiroshi Ayukawa, Miyuki Chiaki, Susumu Fujita, and Gen Funabashi. Shintoho. 1953. Film.

Greta Gard

A RUMOR OF WAR

Philip Caputo

OVERVIEW

A Rumor of War (1977) chronicles Philip Caputo's service as a Marine Corps officer during the Vietnam War. The memoir is divided into three sections. The first, "The Splendid Little War," describes Caputo's decision to enlist, which was fueled by his boredom with suburbia and his infatuation with President John F. Kennedy's vision for a new United States. It details his subsequent Marine training, arrival in Vietnam, and initiation into the unique demands of guerrilla warfare and jungle combat. The second section, "The Officer in Charge of the Dead," describes Caputo's desk job accounting for casualties of war. The book's final section, "In Death's Grey Land," describes his return to combat duty, his involvement in the killing of several civilians, and his subsequent soul-searching about his role in the war. An epilogue chronicles his return to Vietnam several years later as a journalist, where he witnessed the fall of Saigon to North Vietnamese forces in April 1975.

In composing his memoir, Caputo drew on the letters he had written home and the diary he had flouted regulations to keep during the war. Published just two years after the war's end, the book gave voice to the experiences and lasting trauma of the thousands who served in Vietnam. Raising questions about the efficacy of the war, the moral culpability of the men who fought it, and the relationship between fiction and history, the book captured the attention of a U.S. public still reeling from the traumatic national experience of the war.

In the years following its publication, the book garnered significant attention from scholars as well as critics, who saw it as an important and honest examination of the war experience. In 1996 Caputo wrote a postscript to a new edition of his work that discusses his writing of the book and his reaction to its immense and unanticipated success. After *A Rumor of War*, he turned to fiction writing and has continued to explore American involvement in wars and civil wars in developing nations. Among these works are *Horn of Africa* (1980), *In the Forest of the Laughing Elephant* (1997; a novella in which he returns to the topic of the Vietnam War), and *Acts of Faith* (2005).

HISTORICAL AND LITERARY CONTEXT

A Rumor of War examines the U.S. political climate that led up to the Vietnam War as well as the war itself. The conflict began in November 1955, as the Communist forces of North Vietnam clashed with the government of South Vietnam. Concerned about the further spread of communism, the U.S. government had sent military advisers to aid the South Vietnamese government as early as 1950. After war broke out, the U.S. presence in Vietnam slowly escalated, with combat forces first arriving in 1965.

The combat conditions in Vietnam were brutally intense. The enemy Viet Cong (South Vietnamese rebel forces allied with the North) relied heavily on guerrilla warfare, and servicemen had to learn quickly how to avoid land mines, snipers, and booby traps. The war was marked by atrocities on both sides. The best-known atrocity committed by the U.S. forces was the My Lai massacre of March 16, 1968, in which as many as five hundred unarmed civilians were raped, tortured, and killed.

In his memoir Caputo explains that he joined the Marines "because [he] got swept up in the patriotic tide of the Kennedy era," in which public and military service were glorified. Caputo was subsequently among the first U.S. combatants to arrive in Vietnam, and although he left before the My Lai massacre, his memoir depicts several instances in which civilians were targeted by U.S. forces and suggests how exhaustion, trauma, and anger may have led ordinary men to commit atrocities. The book depicts the treacherous and anxiety-ridden conditions of daily life during the war—the intense heat and the difficult jungle terrain to which U.S. soldiers were unaccustomed. Contrary to training manuals asserting that "the jungle can be your friend," Caputo describes the "unremitting heat" and the "dim, evil-looking jungle," noting that "there was nothing friendly about the Vietnamese bush."

In writing his memoir—one of the first major pieces of Vietnam War writing—Caputo drew on the rich literary tradition of World War I. Many of his chapters take their epigraphs from the works of the World War I combatant poets Wilfred Owen and Siegfried Sassoon. The memoir is itself part of an extensive tradition of U.S. literature that reflects on the Vietnam War experience. It appeared within a few years of several other U.S. memoirs about the war, most notably Ron Kovic's 1976 *Born on the Fourth of July*, which chronicles the author's attempts

✤ *Key Facts*

Conflict:
Vietnam War

Time Period:
Mid-20th Century

Genre:
Memoir

Award:
Sidney Hillman
Foundation Award, 1977

KENNEDY AND VIETNAM

In *A Rumor of War*, Philip Caputo explains that he joined the Marine Corps in the years before the Vietnam War because he was inspired by President John F. Kennedy's call to public service. He then suggests repeatedly that Kennedy led him astray. Although Kennedy was assassinated in 1963, two years before U.S. involvement in the war officially began, many scholars have argued, like Caputo, that Kennedy greatly affected the course of the war.

Not only had Kennedy inspired many in Caputo's generation to serve their country, but he was also a firm proponent of the domino theory, which held that when a country fell to communism, its neighbors would soon follow. Although Kennedy opposed sending American troops into Vietnam, believing that the South Vietnamese must defeat the Communist North on their own, he greatly increased the number of American advisers and other personnel in South Vietnam. Under his predecessor, President Dwight D. Eisenhower, fewer than one thousand advisers were in Vietnam. By the time of Kennedy's assassination in 1963, the number had grown to sixteen thousand. In part because of this buildup, historians continue to debate whether the escalation of the war under Kennedy's successor, Lyndon B. Johnson, was designed by Kennedy and not carried out before his assassination.

to overcome the trauma of a war that left him a paraplegic, and Michael Herr's *Dispatches* (1977), a memoir about the author's work as a Vietnam war correspondent.

THEMES AND STYLE

Unlike Herr's *Dispatches*, which is characterized by a literary style that often verges on prose poetry, *A Rumor of War* is written in a straightforward, journalistic manner. Caputo introduces his memoir with a prologue that explains, "This book is not a work of the imagination. The events related are true, the characters real, though I have used fictitious names in some places." The plot unfolds in simple, detail-driven prose, as in this example from Part I, "The Splendid Little War": "The battalion did not see any action until April 22, when B Company was sent to reinforce a reconnaissance patrol that had fallen into an ambush a few miles west of Hill 327."

Caputo frequently comments on the complex relationship between war, history, and literature. In the introduction to the memoir, for example, he asserts that "this book does not pretend to be a history. It has nothing to do with politics, power, strategy, influence, national interests, or foreign policy." What it is, he asserts, is "a story about war, about the things men do in war and the things war does to them." In making this claim, Caputo divorces his memoir from history but nonetheless attests to its truth.

As his story unfolds, Caputo also works to distinguish between war as reality and war as literary representation. He repeatedly notes the disparity between the war literature with which he had gained familiarity as a college English major and the reality of his experiences in Vietnam. The romanticized version of war that led him to enlist did not come entirely from literature and film, however. Caputo emphasizes the impact of President Kennedy on his decision. At one point he describes the president as "that most articulate and elegant mythmaker," suggesting that "if he was the King of Camelot, then we were his knights and Vietnam our crusade." Unlike Arthur's men, however, Kennedy's "knights" are seen not only to fail but often to do more harm than good.

Rejecting the version of combat depicted in numerous books and films, *A Rumor of War* works to demythologize war, in part by emphasizing the brutality of war and its corrupting influence on those who fight it. One of Caputo's comrades, Gonzalez, is severely injured soon after their arrival in Vietnam when he steps on a mine. Later Caputo describes his reaction to news of a comrade's death: "Death. Death. *Death*. I had heard that word so many times, but I had never known its meaning." He also has to come to terms with the effects of the war on his men and himself. Early in his tour of duty, he is shocked to see an officer proudly displaying the ears of a Vietnamese man as a trophy, particularly because the man relishing the brutality "was a mirror image of [him]."

Later, however, when his job brings him into routine contact with the casualties of war, Caputo begins to seethe with animosity toward the enemy. His resultant desire to inflict harm on the Viet Cong eventually leads him to request that he be reassigned. "I volunteered for a line company," he explains. "I wanted a chance to kill somebody." In his subsequent role as platoon commander, he gives an order for a raid against suspected Viet Cong, telling his men, "If they give you any problems, kill 'em." Unfortunately the raid results in the death of the young boy who had provided the initial intelligence.

Caputo feels intense guilt because he knows that when he gave the order for the raid "there was murder in my heart." He also feels anger, particularly when he is court-martialed (although the charges are ultimately dismissed). He eventually finds some resolution by declaring "a truce between [himself] and the Viet Cong." He explains, "I signed a personal armistice, and all I asked for now was a chance to live for myself on my terms. I had no argument with the Viet Cong. It wasn't the VC who were threatening to rob me of my liberty, but the United States government, in whose service I had enlisted."

The third section closes with Caputo awaiting his departure from Vietnam. In the short epilogue that follows, he describes the fall of Saigon, underscoring that the death and lingering trauma of the war had been for naught.

CRITICAL DISCUSSION

Upon publication, *A Rumor of War* quickly became a best seller, touching audiences with its frank insider's depiction of the circumstances and moral dilemmas of the war. The memoir was also widely embraced by the literary community, with writers and critics alike proclaiming its success. The *Virginia Quarterly Review* describes Caputo's memoir as "unquestionably the very best work to appear on the Vietnam war and one of the finest pieces of American writing on war from the ground in this century." Writing in the *New York Review of Books*, novelist William Styron describes the work as "among the most eloquent I have read in modern literature" and observes that "Caputo writes so beautifully and honestly about both fear and courage, writes with such knowing certitude about death and men's confrontation with the abyss."

In the decades since its publication, Caputo's memoir has attracted a growing body of scholarly analysis. Writing in *Contemporary Literature* in 1981, Peter McInerney examines the memoir in the context of other literature of the Vietnam War. He suggests that the strength of Caputo's work lies in part in its realization of its own relationship to history. The text, he suggests, depicts "Caputo's—and America's—loss of the illusion that an epic vision of American history was still possible as we entered and prosecuted the American war in Vietnam."

Considering the memoir in the context of other combatants' takes on war in his book *The Soldiers' Tale*, Samuel Lynn Hynes suggests that Caputo's work is an important testament to the fact that "no man goes through a war without being changed by it." He also, however, examines the complexity of the memoir's depiction of men's reactions to war. Pointing to Caputo's assertion that "anyone who fought in Vietnam, if he is honest with himself, will have to admit he enjoyed the compelling attractiveness of combat," Hynes argues that "most men do feel war's high excitement and romance, and even its beauty (to which there are many testimonies), and not only *before* they experience war, but *after*."

Because the work foregrounds the experiences of male soldiers in the masculine arena of war, some scholars have explored the gender politics of Caputo's memoir. In his book *From Chivalry to Terrorism*, for example, Leo Braudy discusses Caputo's depiction in the context of prominent models of masculinity in the Vietnam War era, noting that "Caputo indicts equally the glory-hunting cowboy politics of Kennedy and the briefcase-general abstraction of [commanding U.S. Army general] William Westmoreland, who in a war with few pitched battles determined victory primarily by counting bodies—like the toting of scalps or the piles of heads collected in primitive warfare."

SOURCES

Braudy, Leo. *From Chivalry to Terrorism: War and the Changing Nature of Masculinity*. New York: Knopf, 2004. Print.

Caputo, Philip. *A Rumor of War*. New York: Holt, 1977. Print.

Hynes, Samuel Lynn. *The Soldiers' Tale: Bearing Witness to Modern War*. New York: Penguin, 1997. Print.

Philip Caputo gave voice to the haunting trauma veterans endure long after they leave the war zone. © EVERETT COLLECTION

McInerney, Peter. "'Straight' and 'Secret' History in Vietnam War Literature." *Contemporary Literature* 22.2 (1981): 187–204. Print.

Rev. of *A Rumor of War*, by Philip Caputo. *Virginia Quarterly Review* 54.1 (1978): 25. Print.

Styron, William. "A Farewell to Arms." Rev. of *A Rumor of War*, by Philip Caputo. *New York Review of Books* 23 June 1977: 3–6. Print.

FURTHER READING

Caputo, Philip. *Exiles: Three Short Novels*. New York: Knopf, 1997. Print.

———. "Goodnight Saigon." *War, Literature, and the Arts* 12.1 (2000): 19–27. Print.

Herr, Michael. *Dispatches*. New York: Knopf, 1977. Print.

Herzog, Tobey C. *Vietnam War Stories: Innocence Lost*. New York: Routledge, 1992. Print.

Heusser, Martin. "The War Spangled Banner: Vietnam and the Fabrication of National Identity." *Representing Realities: Essays on American Literature, Art and Culture*. Ed. Beverly Maeder. Tübingen: Narr, 2003. 143–57. Print.

Kovic, Ron. *Born on the Fourth of July*. New York: McGraw, 1976. Print.

O'Brien, Tim. *The Things They Carried*. Boston: Houghton, 1990. Print.

———. "*Rumor of War*. A Conversation with Philip Caputo at 58." *War, Literature & the Arts: An International Journal of the Humanities* 12.1 (2000): 4–17. Print.

Stone, Robert. *Dog Soldiers*. Boston: Houghton, 1974. Print.

MEDIA ADAPTATION

A Rumor of War. Dir Rob Holcomb. Perf. Brad Davis, Brian Dennehy, Keith Carradine, Michael O'Keefe, Stacy Keach, Lane Smith, and Christopher Mitchum. Charles Fries Productions, 1980. Film.

Greta Gard

RUSSELL'S DESPATCHES FROM THE CRIMEA, 1854–1856

William Howard Russell

OVERVIEW

William Russell, "special correspondent" for the London *Times*, is considered by many to be the original war correspondent. His career began during the Crimean War. As he later wrote in *The Great War with Russia*, "When the year of grace 1854 opened on me, I had no more idea of being what is now—absurdly, I think, called a 'War Correspondent' than I had of being Lord Chancellor." Already a well-known "color" writer for the *Times*, Russell accompanied a British expeditionary force to Malta on a trip to demonstrate support for Turkey in the face of Russian aggression. When the show of force unexpectedly developed into a full-scale war, Russell was in place, ready to report on the war firsthand.

On his return from the Crimea, Russell quickly compiled his dispatches from the field into a two-volume collection, *The War: From the Landing at Gallipoli to the Death of Lord Raglan* (1856). His reports were reissued in 1858 as *The British Expedition to the Crimea*, edited by Russell himself, and again in 1966 as *Russell's Despatches from the Crimea, 1854–1856*, edited by Nicolas Bentley.

Russell's reporting from the Crimea made him famous. His talents in demand, he proceeded to report on the last stage of the Sepoy Rebellion in1857, the first stages of the American Civil War in 1861 and 1862, the Battle of Königgrätz in 1866, the Franco-Prussian War and the subsequent revolution in Paris in 1870 and 1871, and the Zulu War of 1879.

HISTORICAL AND LITERARY CONTEXT

The Crimean War began in 1853 when Tsar Nicholas I of Russia demanded that the Ottomans recognize him as the protector of all Orthodox Christians living under Ottoman rule. The Turks refused, and Russia responded by occupying Moldavia and Wallachia (present-day Romania), two of Turkey's Balkan provinces. The Ottomans declared war in October, and in March 1854 Britain and France entered the conflict on the side of the Turks, fearing that continued Russian expansion into the Balkans would threaten the Mediterranean and the overland routes to India. Initially, British and French involvement was limited to the presence of naval squadrons at the entrance to the Dardanelles and in the Black Sea. When Russian forces did not withdraw, British commander Lord Raglan decided to drive them out of the Black Sea by taking the Russian naval base at Sevastopol in the Crimea. Russia evacuated Sevastopol only after a year long siege that devastated both sides.

Before the Crimean War, British newspapers often employed "correspondents" who literally wrote letters home about affairs in foreign capitals, but they had limited access to news from the battlefield. Newspapers printed official dispatches, such as the Duke of Wellington's famous account of Waterloo, reprinted reports from foreign newspapers, and hired junior military officers to write letters from the front. By the mid-nineteenth century, the introduction of the railway, the steamship, the telegraph, and daily papers aimed at the middle classes had heightened expectations about how quickly news could be reported from a war zone. In an essay in *Popular Imperialism and the Military*, Roger T. Stearn explains, "'The news' in its modern sense was a nineteenth-century creation, and the Victorian war correspondents were, with a few arguable exceptions, the first."

When the Ottomans declared war on Russia, the *Times* followed tradition and hired Lieutenant Charles Nasmyth of the East India Company's Bombay Artillery to write letters from Gallipoli, where the British fleet was stationed. According to Stanley Morison's *The History of "The Times,"* newspaper manager Morris Mowbray quickly became frustrated with the arrangement. He wrote to the paper's correspondent in Istanbul: "I wish you would impress upon Nasmyth with all your eloquence the absolute necessity of writing as often as he can and sending his letters without delay. The idea of a newspaper correspondent keeping the journal of a siege till after the affair is over has driven me wild." In February 1854 *Times* editor John Delane took the unusual step of sending staff reporter Russell to Malta with the British Army Guards. Russell expected to spend only a few weeks in Malta with the expeditionary force. But he traveled with the army to the Crimea and remained until the last British soldier went home in July 1856.

Russell is often described as the first journalist to make use of the telegraph. Although he was aware

❖ *Key Facts*

Conflict:
Crimean War

Time Period:
Mid-19th Century

Genre:
Journalism

of the advantages of the system, wire service between Balaclava (a town in the Crimea) and London was under tight military control. Russell was actually only able to send brief statements of critical news by telegraph from Istanbul; most of his dispatches went to London by steamer. In those days, before the opening of the Suez Canal in 1869, the trip from Istanbul to London took two to three weeks. Sometimes five or six of Russell's letters would appear in the paper on the same day.

THEMES AND STYLE

Russell was a correspondent in the most literal sense. His reports were written in the form of letters to the *Times*'s editor John Delane. In *Man of Wars: William Howard Russell of the "Times,"* biographer Alan Hankinson writes, "For his readers it was like getting long letters, hastily but honestly set down, from a soldier son who was fair-minded and fearless, who had an insatiable appetite for information of all kinds and a lively no-nonsense way of putting it down on paper." Russell's reporting was accurate, intelligent, critical, and unrelenting. When he arrived at Gallipoli, Russell found that Britain's generals were mismanaging the war, on the field and off. His first reports to the *Times*, later included in *Russell's Despatches from the Crimea*, painted a picture of official incompetence and suffering among the troops. Comparing the "inefficiency of our arrangements" with "the excellence of the French commissariat administration," Russell describes "the privations to which the men were exposed": they "suffered exceedingly from cold. Some of them, officers as well as privates, had no beds to lie upon. None of the soldiers had more than their single regulation blanket. … The worst thing was the continued want of comforts for the sick."

Well aware that realistic images from the front were unknown, Russell asks Delane, in a letter quoted in Morison's *The History of "The Times,"* "Am I to tell these things or hold my tongue?" Delane told him to proceed. For the next two years, Russell reported on the lack of wholesome food and clean water, the absence of the most basic sanitary arrangements, unsuitable uniforms and equipment, the preoccupation of officers with regulations left over from the Napoleonic Wars forty years earlier, and inadequate medical facilities. Russell balanced his criticism with praise of the "steady courage" of the British soldier. His descriptions of battle are vivid and coherent, focusing on the overall scene rather than an individual's experience.

Although he had no official standing with the army, Russell sailed with them from Malta to Gallipoli in March and accompanied them to the Crimea in September. When the British went into action on September 20, Russell tried to attach himself to the staffs of various divisional commanders with no success. He saw little of the actual battle. Instead, he used tactics that he had developed while reporting on the Irish elections of 1841: he asked every officer and soldier who was willing to talk to him to describe what happened. He soon discovered there was no consensus among his witnesses. Biographer J. B. Atkins records in *The Life of Sir William Howard Russell* that Russell

The Relief of the Light Brigade (1897), by Richard Caton Woodville, depicts the intense combat at the Battle of Balaclava on October 25, 1854, during the Crimean War. Oil on canvas. © RICHARD CATON WOODVILLE / NATIONAL ARMY MUSEUM LONDON / THE ART ARCHIVE / THE PICTURE DESK, INC.

WILLIAM HOWARD RUSSELL REPORTS FROM AMERICA

Journalist William Howard Russell established his reputation—and indeed the genre of war reporting—with his coverage of the Crimean War in 1854 to 1856. A few years later he covered the American Civil War. The London *Times* sent him to the United States in 1861 to report on "the rupture between the Southern States and the rest of the Union, consequent upon the election of Mr. Lincoln and the advent of the Republicans to power." Russell sailed on March 1, a month before the fall of Fort Sumter, which marked the start of the Civil War.

The trip was not a success.

The *Times* declared its support for the South and secession while Russell was still at sea. Russell considered himself an independent voice, but Americans saw him as the foreign minister for the *Times*. He was initially welcomed by Union and Confederacy alike, but he soon made himself unpopular with both sides. Confederate leaders were displeased with his assessment that the North's industrial power would ensure

its victory, with his vivid and negative depictions of slavery, and with the publication of their military secrets in the pages of the *Times*. Union officers were angered by his unflattering description of the Union retreat after the first Battle of Bull Run (July 21, 1861) and repeatedly denied him accreditation to join the Union army in the field.

His editor, John Delane, who had committed the *Times* to the Southern cause, was unhappy with the content of Russell's reports and with his unwillingness to move to the front without gaining authorization. After a year of frustration, Russell returned home in April 1862.

Russell combined his Civil War dispatches and excerpts from his diary into *My Diary North and South*, which was published in 1863.

SOURCE: Miller, Ilana D. *Reports from America: William Howard Russell and the Civil War*. Stroud: Sutton, 2001. Print.

---

was overwhelmed: "How was I to describe what I had not seen? Where to learn the facts for which they were waiting at home?" The following day, he wrote his first description of battle in a notebook taken from a Russian corpse.

Russell's style often seems florid by the standard of modern newspaper reporting, but his descriptions are realistic, detailed, and clear. Many of his original phrases are now clichés of war writing. The best known of these is his description of the British infantry at Balaclava as "that thin red streak topped with a line of steel," which is often misquoted as "the thin red line."

CRITICAL DISCUSSION

Historians of both the Crimean War and journalism often debate whether Russell was actually the first war correspondent. Scholars have made arguments in favor of Xenophon (c. 430–354 BCE); Julius Caesar (100–44 BCE); an anonymous writer for the *Swedish Intelligencer* in the seventeenth century; John Bell of the *London Oracle* in the eighteenth century; and Henry Crabb Robinson of the London *Times*, Charles Lewis Gruneison of the London *Morning Post*, and George Wilkins Kendall of the *New Orleans Picayune* in the first half of the nineteenth century.

Whatever the quibbles raised by scholars, Russell's contemporaries had no doubt that he was doing something new. His reports from the Crimea had an enormous impact on the politics of the time. His contemporaries credited his dispatches with initiating the fall of the Liberal-Conservative government in 1855, with improved supplies for the troops, with public

demand for military reforms, and with the acceptance and recognition of Florence Nightingale and her nurses for their work tending wounded soldiers near Istanbul. His description of the fatal charge of the British cavalry's Light Brigade—the result of a scandalous failure of leadership in a war marked by official incompetence—inspired Alfred Lord Tennyson's poem "The Charge of the Light Brigade." Edwin Godkin, a reporter in the Crimea for the London *Daily News*, wrote of Russell twenty years later; his words were reprinted in *The Life and Letters of Edwin Lawrence Godkin*: "If I were asked what I thought the most important result of the Crimean War, I should say the creation and development of the 'special correspondents' of newspapers. ... The real beginning of newspaper correspondence was the arrival of 'Billy' Russell with the English army in the Crimea. He was then a man of mature age, had had long newspaper experience, and possessed just the social qualities that were needed for the place. ... In his hands, correspondence from the field became a power before which generals began to quail."

Modern scholarship suggests that the British public gave Russell more credit than he deserved. Some of the problems that Russell blamed on Lord Raglan were the fault of the supply system back home. Descriptions of the conditions of medical facilities in the Crimea by Godkin of the *Daily News* and Thomas Chenery, the *Times*'s correspondent in Istanbul, also made a strong impression, inspiring Nightingale to recruit her private nursing corps. Nonetheless, Russell is generally hailed as the "father of war journalism." Russell described his role in less grandiose terms, naming himself "the miserable parent of a luckless tribe."

SOURCES

Atkins, J. B. *The Life of Sir William Howard Russell: The First Special Correspondent.* London: Murray. 1911. Print.

Godkin, Edwin. *The Life and Letters of Edwin Lawrence Godkin.* Ed. Rolio Ogden. New York: Macmillan, 1907. Print.

Hankinson, Alan. *Man of Wars: William Howard Russell of the "Times."* London. Heinemann, 1982. Print.

Morison, Stanley. *The Tradition Established, 1841–1884.* London: Times, 1939. Print. Vol. 2 of *The History of "The Times."* 4 vols. 1935–52.

Russell, William Howard. *The Great War with Russia.* London: Routledge, 1895. Print.

———. *Russell's Despatches from the Crimea, 1854–1856.* Ed. Nicolas Bentley. London: Deutsch. 1966. Print.

Stearns, Roger T. "War Correspondents and Colonial War, circa 1870–1900." *Popular Imperialism and the Military.* Ed. John M. MacKenzie. Manchester: Manchester UP, 1992. Print.

FURTHER READING

Knightley, Phillip. *The First Casualty: From the Crimea to Vietnam: The War Correspondent as Hero, Propagandist, and Myth Maker.* New York: Harcourt, 1975. Print.

Royle, Trevor. *Crimea: The Great Crimean War.* New York: St. Martin's, 2000. Print.

Russell, William Howard, et al. *The Crimean War: As Seen by Those Who Reported It.* Ed. Angela Michelli Fleming and John Maxwell Hamilton. Baton Rouge: Louisiana State UP, 2009. Print.

Sweeny, Michael S. *From the Front: The Story of War.* Washington: National Geographic Society, 2002. Print.

Sweetman, John. *The Crimean War.* Chicago: Osprey, 2001. Print.

Pamela Toler

A SMALL CORNER OF HELL
Dispatches from Chechnya
Anna Politkovskaya

OVERVIEW

A Small Corner of Hell: Dispatches from Chechnya (2003) is a collection of newspaper reports and columns written by Russian journalist Anna Politkovskaya about the Second Chechen War. The war began in 1999 when Chechnya, located in the northern Caucasus region, was clinging to its recently declared independence from Russia. In August Russia launched bombing raids on Chechnya with the stated intention of destroying a radical Islamist militant force based there. The raids forced tens of thousands of Chechens from their homes and were soon followed by a brutal land war. As she notes in the prologue to *A Small Corner of Hell*, Politkovskaya was sent into neighboring Ingushetia to cover the flight of Chechen refugees. The editor in chief of her Moscow newspaper, *Novaya gazeta*, had decided that because Politkovskaya was "just a civilian," not a war correspondent, she would have "that much deeper an understanding of other such civilians … caught in the war."

Beginning in the summer of 1999, Politkovskaya made monthly trips to Chechnya, where she wrote about the war from the perspective of ordinary Chechens displaced and traumatized by the fighting. Few reporters traveled to the region because of the extremely dangerous conditions, and Politkovskaya's voice soon came to dominate coverage of the war. Her descriptions about abuses and atrocities committed by both sides in the conflict earned her the antipathy of both militant leaders and Russian authorities, including Russian president Vladimir Putin. Since 1992 dozens of Russian journalists had been murdered, and Politkovskaya was well aware of the dangers she faced. On October 7, 2006, she was shot to death in the elevator of her apartment building in Moscow. No one has yet been convicted of the murder.

HISTORICAL AND LITERARY CONTEXT

Annexed by the Russian Empire in the nineteenth century after a bitter struggle, Chechnya had long resented Russian control. Taking advantage of the instability in the newly formed Russian Federation in the early 1990s, Chechnya declared itself an independent republic. In August 1994, Chechens opposed to independence took up arms in an effort to remove the government of Dzhokhar Dudayev. Russia became directly involved in the conflict in December 1994, when President Boris Yeltsin ordered troops into the region to restore "constitutional order." The ensuing war engulfed much of Chechnya, leveled the capital, caused the deaths of tens of thousands of civilians, and shocked the Russian public and the world with its unrestrained brutality. A cease-fire agreement was signed in August 1996, but the issue of Chechnya's independence was deferred until 2001.

When Russian forces again appeared in Chechnya in the summer of 1999, Russia's government declared that they were involved in antiterrorist operations against the militant Islamist International Peacekeeping Brigade. The Russian advance, however, soon exceeded its stated aims and became a full-scale attempt to reestablish control of Chechnya. In October 1999 the Chechen president called for a holy war to repel the invaders.

Russian attacks were often carried out on civilians in "safe areas" that the Russians claimed were sheltering Islamist militants; tens of thousands of civilians died, and many more were wounded or displaced. Undisciplined soldiers brutalized Chechen citizens, murdering, raping, and stealing with impunity. The soldiers were brutalized in turn by an army leadership that sent its rawest conscripts into hellish situations, where they were largely left to fend for themselves. Meanwhile, the militants brought misery to the highland villages in which they sheltered. As soon as they moved on, Russian troops would purge the villages, torturing and killing those they suspected of aiding the militants and burning all of the buildings. Despite widespread acknowledgment that the situation in Chechnya was devolving into chaos, Western powers eschewed direct involvement, unwilling to confront Russia over what it insisted was an internal affair.

Politkovskaya returned repeatedly to Chechnya to gather the stories of villagers whose families and homes had been destroyed by the war. Her presence was illegal, and many of the people she interviewed were later killed. She took great personal risks herself, enduring harassment and death threats from both sides, as well as kidnapping and poisoning. As noted by Tony Wood in the *London Review of Books*, most of the more than 500 reports Politkovskaya filed for

✣ *Key Facts*

Conflict:
Second Chechen War

Time Period:
Late 20th–early
21st Centuries

Genre:
Journalism

A man holds the body of one of the thirty civilians, mostly children and elderly people, who were killed when Russia bombed the village of Elistandji in Chechnya in October 1999. Russian journalist Anna Politkovskaya was especially vocal about the atrocity. © ANTOINE GYORI / SYGMA / CORBIS

Novaya gazeta between 1999 and her death were about the fighting in Chechnya.

In some ways, Politkovskaya's career recalls that of American writer Martha Gellhorn, who also found her voice as a journalist in covering war, though she was not a war reporter by training. Both Gellhorn and Politkovskaya largely ignored the actions of armies and political and military leaders. They focused instead on the experiences of ordinary people and sought with their writing to win justice and compassion for those who bear the brunt of war.

THEMES AND STYLE

In a terse, journalistic style that sometimes betrays weariness or impatience and is often shot through with scathing irony, Politkovskaya bears witness to a war notorious for its waste of human life:

> The end of this hopeless war is nowhere to be seen. The "purges" never stop; they resemble mass autos-da-fé. Torture is the norm. Executions without a trial are routine. Marauding is commonplace. The kidnapping of people by Federal soldiers in order to conduct slave trading (with the living) or corpse trading (with the dead) is the stuff of everyday Chechen life.

The sheer volume of Politkovskaya's reports on the Second Chechen War, combined with their consistent focus on the same themes and the experiences of individuals, enables them to be read as a chronicle or memoir. One senses how central the war became to her life in her assertion that she was

"thankful" for it because "it has purified [her] of everything that was superfluous, unnecessary." Her writings about it became the vehicle for her critique of Russia under Vladimir Putin, which depicted the country as backsliding, its weak democracy caving in to the corruption, secrecy, and indifference of the old Soviet system.

In the preface to *A Small Corner of Hell*, Politkovskaya describes Chechnya's citizens as the victims of "a clear, obvious, unbelievable world-wide betrayal of humanitarian values." The world, she surmises, had turned its back on the people of Chechnya. The Russian army, come to liberate them from ill treatment at the hands of Islamist terrorists, was instead subjecting them to methodical torture, humiliation, and murder. As Politkovskaya sees it, the aim of the Russians was genocide: the obliteration of the Chechens as a people. The Russian soldiers ravaged Chechen society from top to bottom, destroying families, villages, factories, infrastructure—in short, any possible support of normal communal life. In one passage, Politkovskaya describes a group of Chechen men who were tortured (burned with cigarettes, nails pulled out, beaten in the kidneys) and then thrown into a pit of freezing water. Afterward, they were told they had "nice asses" and raped by Russian officers. The Chechens who survived now saw vengeance for the incident as "the only purpose of the rest of their lives."

Politkovskaya's chronicle of the suffering of Chechen civilians also records what happens to people when they have lived for too long without food, shelter, or the common bonds of humanity. The word "beasts" occurs frequently in people's descriptions of how the war has affected them: "'We can't survive *this*. We're beasts, even to each other.'" While watching a group of starving Chechen refugees in a frenzy over food handouts in the city of Shali, Politkovskaya "recall[s] Putin's well-groomed assistant Sergei Yastrzhembsky announcing that a humanitarian disaster does not exist."

According to Tony Wood, Politkovskaya saw in Chechnya a reflection of what Russia was becoming. "For her, the war in Chechnya was not a distant event," he writes, "but a direct, distorting influence on the Russian state." In her view the war had completely corrupted and dishonored Russia. War crimes were not punished but rewarded with medals for bravery and service. Meanwhile, the parents of missing Russian foot soldiers applied in vain to authorities for information about their sons' fates.

CRITICAL DISCUSSION

Although *A Small Corner of Hell* has been well received by critics, journalists, and students of Chechnya's history, reviewers frequently observe that the book, along with Politkovskaya's other writings, is difficult reading. Pointing out that Politkovskaya's works "contain rape, torture, injustice, and betrayal in every chapter," Anne Appelbaum writes in the *Spectator* that *A Small Corner of Hell* "ask[s] a lot of the reader." Politkovskaya's violent death, combined with the widespread perception that she was murdered by someone who wanted her silenced, adds weight to her criticisms of Russian society and politics. As Appelbaum observes, "[A]fter her death, it is impossible to read her books and not feel the … sense of foreboding. Her life, and her murder, were so much like one of the stories she would have told herself."

The value of Politkovskaya's reportage is beyond dispute. She was one of few journalists to venture into Chechnya during the second war, and she went back many times over the years, even as her personal risk increased. According to Zachary T. Irwin in the *Library Journal*, this demonstrates her "consistent bravery and unswerving commitment to revealing as much truth as possible about a war whose breathtaking brutality is suspected but not well known." In her report for the *New Statesman* on Politkovskaya receiving the first Lettre Ulysses Award for literary reportage (for her book *Tchétchénie: le déshonneur russe* [2003]), Isabel Hilton praises the author for her "extraordinary courage and tenacity in documenting the atrocities of Chechnya and the corruption of Russian society that has been one effect of this extremely dirty war."

Exact information about the wars in Chechnya is extremely difficult to unearth. Politkovskaya's writings, however, offer concrete images of what Martha Gellhorn calls the "face of war." Illustrating

A CASUALTY OF HER PROFESSION

The cases of eighteen journalists murdered in Russia since 1992 remain unsolved. Although Russia became a democracy in 1991, its leaders, particularly Vladimir Putin, have shown little tolerance for a free press, and many Russians suspect that the state is implicated in Anna Politkovskaya's murder, as well as attacks on other journalists who have dared to criticize the government.

Given Putin's antagonism toward Politkovskaya and his aggressive assertion following her death that no one in the government could have committed a crime so clearly intended to "create a wave of anti-Russian feeling," there has been little optimism that the full truth about her murder will ever be known. In 2009 three men accused of participating in the shooting were acquitted on lack of evidence, but the Supreme Court ordered a retrial. In May 2011 police arrested Rustam Makhmudov, whom they charged with carrying out the shooting in Chechnya. In August, Dmitry Pavlyuchenkov, a retired Moscow police officer who had been a prosecution witness in the earlier trial, was charged with organizing the murder, along with Lom-Ali Gaitukayev, Makhmudov's uncle. Although the lawyer for Politkovskaya's children called the arrest of Pavlyuchenkov "an important stage in explaining the event," the identity of the person who ordered the journalist's murder remains unknown.

Politkovskaya's "meticulous attention to detail," Tony Wood quotes her description of a Chechen man in her book *Nothing But the Truth* (2010): "'He limps clumsily, his weight falling heavily first on one leg then on the other, a common sign here of someone beaten on the kidneys.'" Wood notes that Politkovskaya's eye for detail could equally be an "instrument of compassion," or "a weapon." Her reconstructions of events led to the indictment and conviction of a number of perpetrators of atrocities in Chechnya.

As powerful as Politkovskaya's writing is, some critics have expressed concern that her message may be undermined to some extent by disorganization and inconsistencies in her thinking about political aspects of the war. Wood finds that her analysis of politics in Chechnya is sometimes "surprisingly naive," faulting her for not holding President Boris Yeltsin sufficiently to account for his instigation of Russia's "ruinous" depredations in Chechnya. While praising Politkovskaya as "an indefatigable chronicler of the single nastiest side of modern Russia" (i.e., the abuses of the Second Chechen War), a reviewer for the *Economist* asserts that her book "risks leaving the foreign reader not just aghast, but stunned and somewhat confused. … [The book] skips harrowingly from year to year and place to place."

The critical importance of understanding Chechnya's troubled history with Russia and gaining a fuller picture of the two recent wars is the topic of review articles by Raffi Khatchadourian in the *Nation* and Michael Church in the *Financial Times*. Both cite contemporary accounts of the Russian Empire's annexation of Chechnya in the nineteenth century that "shockingly adumbrate," in Church's phrase, Politkovskaya's *A Small Corner of Hell*.

SOURCES

Appelbaum, Anne. "Extraordinary Champion of Ordinary People." Rev. of *A Small Corner of Hell: Dispatches from Chechnya* and *A Russian Diary*, by Anna Politkovskaya. *Spectator* 28 Apr. 2007: n. pag. *Literature Resource Center*. Web. 30 June 2011.

Church, Michael. "A Thistle in Russia's Side." *Financial Times* 28 Jan. 2005: n. pag. Web. 5 July 2011.

Gellhorn, Martha. *The Face of War*. Rev. ed. New York: Atlantic Monthly, 1988. Print.

Greenslade, Roy. "Ex-police Colonel Charged over Murder of Anna Politkovskaya." *Guardian* [Manchester, UK]. Guardian News and Media, 5 Sept. 2011. Web. 6 Oct. 2011.

Hilton, Isabel. "A Prize for the Underrated Genre of Literary Reportage." *New Statesman* 13 Oct. 2003: n. pag. Web. 5 July 2011.

Irwin, Zachary T. "Hell Up Close." Rev. of *Madness Visible: A Memoir of War*, by Janine di Giovanni; *Chechnya Diary: A War Correspondent's Story of Surviving the War in Chechnya*, by Thomas Goltz; and *A Small Corner of Hell: Dispatches from Chechnya*, by Anna Politkovskaya. *Library Journal* 15 Nov. 2003: 84. *Literature Resource Center*. Web. 30 June 2011.

Khatchadourian, Raffi. "The Curse of the Caucasus." *Nation* 17 Nov. 2003: 31–36. Web. 5 July 2011.

Politkovskaya, Anna. *Nothing But the Truth: Selected Dispatches*. Trans. Arch Tait. London: Harvill-Secker, 2010. Print.

———. *A Small Corner of Hell: Dispatches from Chechnya*. Trans. Alexander Burry and Tatiana Tulchinsky. Chicago: U of Chicago P, 2003. Print.

"New Arrest for Anna Politkovskaya's Murder—Step in the Right Direction." Amnesty International. Amnesty International, 24 Aug. 2011. Web. 6 Oct. 2011.

"No Justice for Anna Politkovskaya." *New York Times*. New York Times, 13 Sept. 2011. Web. 6 Oct. 2011.

"The Murder of Anna Politkovskaya: Retired Police Officer Arrested in Russia." *Spiegel International*. Spiegel Online, 24 Aug. 2011. Web. 6 Oct. 2011.

"Where Life Is No Party." Rev. of *A Small Corner of Hell: Dispatches from Chechnya*, by Anna Politkovskaya. *Economist* 2 Oct. 2003: n. pag. Print.

Wood, Tony. "'I Dream of Him Some Day Sitting in the Dock.'" *London Review of Books* 24 June 2010: 15–18. Print.

FURTHER READING

Baddeley, J. F. *The Russian Conquest of the Caucasus*. London: Longmans, 1908. Print.

Gall, Carlotta, and Thomas de Waal. *Chechnya: Calamity in the Caucasus*. New York: New York UP, 1998. Print.

Gould, Terry. *Marked for Death: Dying for the Story in the World's Most Dangerous Places*. Berkeley: Counterpoint, 2009. Print.

Politkovskaya, Anna. *A Dirty War: A Russian Reporter in Chechnya*. Trans. John Crowfoot. London: Harvill, 2001. Print.

———. *A Russian Diary: A Journalist's Final Account of Life, Corruption, and Death in Putin's Russia*. Trans. Arch Tait. New York: Random, 2007. Print.

Tishkov, Valery. *Chechnya: Life in a War-Torn Society*. Berkeley: U of California P, 2004. Print.

Janet Moredock

TALES OF SOLDIERS AND CIVILIANS

Ambrose Bierce

OVERVIEW

Ambrose Bierce's *Tales of Soldiers and Civilians* can be seen as an extended comparison of the relative horrors of war and peace. The book is divided into two parts: the ten war stories of *Soldiers* and the nine horror stories of *Civilians*. In both sections, Bierce combines sardonic wit, the use of a heightened emphasis on physical sensations, and ironic plot twists to create a world where his characters believe perilous situations to be safe and safe situations to be perilous. In Bierce's hands, both misperceptions prove deadly.

After being rejected by major publishers in New York, *Tales of Soldiers and Civilians* was published locally by San Francisco merchant E. L. G. Steele in 1891. The book was issued the same year in England under the title *In the Midst of Life*. In an effort to reach the literary audience on the East Coast, Steele sold the printing plates to two successive publishing houses, both of which went bankrupt. The collection finally reached a national audience in the United States in 1898, when it was republished, with three additional stories, as *In the Midst of Life*. Three of the stories in the original collection—"An Occurrence at Owl Creek Bridge," "Chickamauga," and "The Man and the Snake"—are widely considered to be Bierce's masterpieces.

HISTORICAL AND LITERARY CONTEXT

Eighteen-year-old Ambrose Gwinnett Bierce enlisted as a private in the Union army six days after the bombardment of Fort Sumter on April 12, 1861: the second man in Elkhart County, Indiana, to respond to President Lincoln's call for volunteers. Over the course of the war, Bierce was repeatedly promoted, reaching the rank of first lieutenant and holding a staff position of topographical engineer in the Army of the Ohio. He fought in some of the bloodiest battles of the Civil War, including Shiloh, Stones River, and Chickamauga. He was wounded in the head at the battle of Kennesaw Mountain. After he recovered, he returned to service in time to fight in the battles of Franklin and Nashville.

Bierce was deeply influenced by his wartime experiences, but he did not write about them for almost twenty years. After working as a tax collector in Alabama, an engineer with an army mapping expedition in the West, and the general agent of a gold-mining company, Bierce settled down as a journalist in San Francisco. Between 1875 and 1899, he was best known for his weekly column, "Prattle." He developed a reputation for employing biting invective and being for his willingness to attack almost any aspect of contemporary culture, from mad dogs to corrupt politicians.

Bierce's first written account of the Civil War was "What I Saw of Shiloh," published in the *San Francisco Wasp* in 1881 and again in the *San Francisco Examiner* in 1898. As the title suggests, the account is consciously limited to Bierce's own experience of the battle. He describes the piece as "a simple story of a battle, such a tale as may be told by a soldier who is no writer to a reader who is no soldier." He begins the article with a peaceful scene in camp among young men who still hold romantic ideas about war. He ends with his own ambivalent memories: "Is it not strange that the phantoms of a bloodstained period have so airy a grace and look with so tender eyes?—that I recall with difficulty the danger and death and horrors of the time, and without effort all that was gracious and picturesque?"

Bierce wrote the Civil War stories on which his literary reputation rests between 1888 and 1891. It was a period marked by nostalgia for the Civil War among veterans and civilians alike and by the rising mood of jingoism that would lead to the Spanish-American War of 1898. Bierce's Civil War stories were an antidote to the sentimentality typical of Civil War memoirs popular at the time. In his stories, Bierce abandons the "gracious and picturesque" in favor of "the danger and death and horrors of the time."

THEMES AND STYLE

Bierce's biographer, Roy Morris Jr., sums up the quality that differentiates Bierce from his contemporaries Bret Hart and Mark Twain as "the personal quality of his witness." Morris adds that when all the legends that have accumulated around Bierce are stripped away,

> what finally remains is 1st Lt. Ambrose Bierce, Ninth Indiana Infantry, the bloodied veteran of Shiloh, Chickamauga, Pickett's Mill, and a dozen other battlefields, who had experienced war on a scale—both large and small—that no other American writer had ever known in the half century preceding World War I. His true significance as an artist, in contrast to his undeniable quotability as a drawing room curmudgeon … remains grounded in his undeniable pride of

Key Facts

Conflict:
American Civil War

Time Period:
Mid-19th Century

Genre:
Short stories

AMBROSE BIERCE—MAPMAKER

The Battle of Kennesaw Mountain, June 27, 1864, during which Civil War soldier, front-line mapmaker, and author Ambrose Bierce was wounded in the head. 19th century. Color litho.
© PETER NEWARK AMERICAN PICTURES / THE BRIDGEMAN ART LIBRARY INTERNATIONAL

Ambrose Bierce spent two years of the Civil War serving as the topographer on the staff of Brigadier General William B. Hazen. When the war was over, he spent five months as the engineering attaché of Hazen's expedition to inspect military posts from Omaha to San Francisco.

Bierce paints a vivid picture of the life of a military topographer in the short story "George Thurston," which first appeared in the *San Francisco Wasp* on September 29, 1889, and was later included in *Tales of Soldiers and Civilians.* His topographer-narrator spends "all day in the saddle and half the night at [his] drawing board, plating [his] surveys." It was hazardous work. "The nearer to the enemy lines [he] could penetrate, the more valuable were [his] field notes and resulting maps." At times it seemed like the lives of men were worth nothing compared to necessity of "defining a road or sketching a bridge."

In a *San Francisco Examiner* article dated June 12, 1887, more than twenty years after the war was over, Bierce claimed that his training in topography still shaped how he looked at the world. "To this day I cannot look over a landscape without noting the advantages of the ground for attack or defense." Certainly his eye for landscape affected his Civil War stories. He often describes the topography of his tales with a precision rooted in reality that increases their horror.

place as the first American witness to modern war and the evil banality with which men die.

The ten war stories in *Tales of Soldiers and Civilians* borrow both settings and incidents from Bierce's real-life war experiences, but they do not simply report what happened. Instead, Bierce uses realistic details and references to actual battles to create a feeling of authenticity while emphasizing the horror of the situation. As editor Tom Quirk explains in his introduction

to the collection: "The macabre quality of Bierce's imagination often consisted in humanizing the unimaginable, not in adding contrived or ghastly detail to his fiction." This quality is perhaps most strongly felt in the story "Chickamauga," in which a child who can neither hear nor speak plays on the battlefield after the fighting has ended. Bierce builds tension using the contrast between what the child and the reader understand. Where the reader sees maimed and bleeding men, the child sees a "merry spectacle": the blood streaked on their faces, "something too, perhaps, in their grotesque attitudes and movements—reminded him of the painted clown whom he had seen last summer in the circus."

The tales are uniformly short, driven by plot structure, irony, and voice rather than character development. The twist endings that are a trademark of Bierce's stories are more than a narrative or stylistic trick. His characters are subject to ironic turns of fate. Some are forced to choose between conflicting duties—at horrible personal cost. For example, in "A Horseman in the Sky," a young Union sentry from Virginia shoots his father to protect his unit's position. Others are trapped by their own mistaken perceptions. In at least two of his stories, Bierce's protagonists literally die of terror even though they are not in real danger.

Bierce's story "An Occurrence at Owl Creek Bridge" breaks stylistic ground in experimenting with the conventions of literary realism. The story fools the reader by describing what appears to be external reality but is later revealed as the internal, subjective experience of the protagonist. In this way, Bierce demonstrates that mimicking reality with a chronological, sequential narrative has no correlation with "truth." Much later writers such as Kurt Vonnegut and Tim O'Brien, who described their experiences in World War II and the Vietnam War, respectively, used this technique to convey the indescribable horrors they witnessed.

CRITICAL DISCUSSION

Ambrose Bierce was a prolific writer. His collected works, published between 1909 and 1912, fill twelve four-hundred-page volumes. Today he is remembered primarily for the epigrammatic *Devil's Dictionary* (1911), the short stories in *Tales of Soldiers and Civilians,* and his dramatic disappearance into Mexico at the end of his life.

Bierce was the best-known journalist on the West Coast in the 1880s and 1890s, but he did not develop a national following for his acerbic columns until 1896, when newspaper magnate William Randolph Hearst sent him to Washington, D.C. to report on a sensational antitrust investigation that had California roots. When the expanded and revised collection of *Tales of Soldiers and Civilians* was published in 1898 under the title *In the Midst of Life,* Bierce's short stories reached a national audience for the first time.

Their reception was disappointing. A few critics recognized the power of his war stories. (One anonymous reviewer clearly read the "grimly powerful vignettes" within the context of the contemporary Spanish-American War, saying, "This little volume could not have been revived at a more opportune moment, and deserves the widest circulation as a peace tract of the first order.") Most, however, were simply baffled. It was easy to compare Bierce's ghost stories and supernatural tales of horror to those of Edgar Allan Poe and Nathaniel Hawthorne. His war stories were like nothing the American reader had seen and were at odds with the popular jingoism of the time. When Bierce disappeared in 1913, he was largely forgotten.

Bierce's writing was rediscovered in the 1920s. His combination of realistic detail and ironic horror resonated with a generation disillusioned by World War I. H. L. Mencken, a journalist at least as irascible as Bierce, claimed that Bierce "was the first writer ever to treat war realistically. He antedated even [French writer Émile] Zola. … What he got out of his services in the field was not a sentimental horror of it, but a cynical delight in it." Later in the century, in *Patriotic Gore*, critic Edmund Wilson's assessment of Bierce's writing is attenuated. Wilson attributes the author's austere, terse style to his army career: the "best qualities of Bierce's prose are military—concision, severe order, and unequivocal clearness. His diction is the result of training and seems rather artificial."

Today, critics disagree over where to place Bierce's stories in the larger framework of American literature in the nineteenth century. His war stories are too graphic to fit into the sentimental conventions of the typical Civil War novel. His penchant for the supernatural and the hallucinatory, the internal perception rather than the external narrative, place him outside the conventions of realism. His biting humor found its closest relative in the work of Mark Twain.

Differences of label aside, critics agree that Bierce is the pioneer of the American war story, recognized for the importance of his influence on later authors of war fiction, including Stephen Crane, Ernest Hemingway, John Dos Passos, and O'Brien.

SOURCES

Bierce, Ambrose. "What I Saw of Shiloh." *A Sole Survivor: Bits of Autobiography*. Ed. S. T. Joshi and David E. Schultz. Knoxville: U of Tennessee P, 1998. Print.

Bierce, Ambrose. *Tales of Soldiers and Civilians*. Ed. Donald T. Blume. Kent: Kent State UP, 2004. Print.

Rev. of *In The Midst of Life*, by Ambrose Bierce. *Nation* 66.225 (1898). Print.

Mencken, H. L. "Ambrose Bierce." *Prejudices: Sixth Series*. New York: Knopf, 1927. Rpt. in *Critical Essays on Ambrose Bierce*. Ed. Cathy N. Davidson. Boston: Hall, 1982. 61–64. Print.

Morris, Roy, Jr. *Ambrose Bierce: Alone in Bad Company*. New York: Crown, 1995. Print.

Quirk, Tom. Introduction. *Tales of Soldiers and Civilians*. By Ambrose Bierce. Ed. Tom Quirk. New York: Penguin, 2002.

Wilson, Edmund. *Patriotic Gore: Studies in the Literature of the American Civil War*. New York: Oxford UP, 1962. Print.

FURTHER READING

Blume, Donald T. *Ambrose Bierce's "Civilians and Soldiers" in Context: A Critical Study*. Kent: Kent State UP, 2004. Print.

Davidson, Cathy N. *The Experimental Fictions of Ambrose Bierce: Structuring the Ineffable*. Lincoln: U of Nebraska P, 1984. Print.

Davidson, Cathy N., ed. *Critical Essays on Ambrose Bierce*. Boston: Hall, 1982. Print.

Fatout, Paul. "Ambrose Bierce, Civil War Topographer." *American Literature* 26:3 (1954): 391–400. Print.

Gale, Robert L. *An Ambrose Bierce Companion*. Westport: Greenwood, 2001. Print.

Owens, David M. *The Devil's Topographer: Ambrose Bierce and the American War Story*. Knoxville: U of Tennessee P, 2006. Print.

Schaefer, Michael W. *Just What War Is: The Civil War Writings of De Forest and Bierce*. Knoxville: U of Tennessee P, 1997. Print.

Talley, Sharon. *Ambrose Bierce and the Dance of Death*. Knoxville: U of Tennessee P, 2009. Print.

MEDIA ADAPTATIONS

Ambrose Bierce: Civil War Stories. Dir. Don Maxwell and Brian James Egen. Perf. Campbell Scott, Vivian Schilling, and Nathan Darrow. Hannover House, 2006. Television.

An Occurrence at Owl Creek Bridge. Dir. Brian James Egen. Perf. Bradley Egen and Jody Chansuolme. Hannover House, 2005. Film.

Pamela Toler

Captain Hickenlooper's Battery in the Hornet's Nest at the Battle of Shiloh, April 1862, an illustration by T. C. Lindsay, depicts one of the battles in which Ambrose Bierce fought during the American Civil War. Color Litho. Private Collection. © PETER NEWARK MILITARY PICTURES / THE BRIDGEMAN ART LIBRARY INTERNATIONAL

TRUE HISTORY OF THE CONQUEST OF NEW SPAIN

Bernal Díaz del Castillo

✢ *Key Facts*

Conflict:
Conquest of Mexico

Time Period:
16th Century

Genre:
Memoir

OVERVIEW

An eyewitness account of Spain's ninety-three-day battle to conquer Mexico in 1521, Bernal Díaz del Castillo's *The Conquest of New Spain* (1908–16; *Historia verdadera de la conquista de la Nueva España*, 1632) often reads more like a novel of chivalry than a historical document. For his European readers, Díaz del Castillo's tale is full of dangerous battles pitting the valiant conquistadors against natives given to idolatry, cannibalism, and human sacrifice. Yet for all the exoticism and entertainment it provides, *The Conquest of New Spain* is a document crucial to the understanding of the political and financial aspects of the conquest. As Rolena Adorno notes in her essay "History, Law and the Eyewitness," Díaz del Castillo's text records a significant point in the conquest of the New World, "where the quest for royal reward met the writing of history."

Díaz del Castillo participated in the conquest of Mexico under Hernán Cortés and, like most of the Spaniards who battled in the New World, expected both glory and compensation for his service to the Crown. With *The Conquest of New Spain* he hoped to gain both at once. One of his major motives for writing the book was his belief that he and the other conquistadors had not been adequately compensated but had been passed over in favor of Cortés. To remedy this error, he portrays the conquest as conducted in an honorable and fair manner and emphasizes the loyalty with which the soldiers fought, in hopes of showing that they are truly deserving of financial reward. He sent a copy of his book to the Spanish government, but when he died in 1581, he had received nothing further from the Crown for his military service. Díaz del Castillo's original manuscript was rediscovered and published in Madrid in 1632.

Díaz del Castillo was not a historian, and he did not set out to write a work of history. In fact, as both an eyewitness and a participant in the conquest, he stresses that he can offer what historians cannot: a moment-by-moment account of the events as they took place and a deeper understanding of the context, feelings, and motives of those involved. He argues that those educated as historians, such as his contemporary Francisco López de Gómara, may write more eloquently but, never having been in the New World,

they introduce grave errors of fact and also fail to capture the atmosphere of battle or portray the heroism of the foot soldier.

HISTORICAL AND LITERARY CONTEXT

The conquest of Mexico was not originally designed to be a conquest at all: Diego Velázquez, governor of Cuba, named Cortés commander of a trade expedition to the mainland in 1518 but withdrew the commission a year later. Cortés ignored Velázquez's orders and set off in February 1519. When Cortés and his troops arrived, they allied themselves with the Tlaxcalans, enemies of the Aztec empire that had colonized much of Mexico. This alliance would prove vital in the Spanish defeat of the Aztecs.

In October 1519 Cortés's troops and their Tlaxcalan allies invaded the city of Cholula. Accounts of what happened there differ, but the general consensus is that the conquistadors seized the city's leaders and then set the city on fire, killing thousands of Aztec civilians. The Spaniards arrived in the Aztec capital, Tenochtitlan, in November 1519 and met Motecuhzoma, the leader of the Aztecs. Motecuhzoma originally welcomed the conquistadors, though there were rumors that he was secretly planning an attack to expel them from the city. Cortés decided to arrest Motecuhzoma and imprison him in the Spanish quarters to avoid such a possibility.

While Cortés was in Tenochtitlan, he heard that Velázquez had sent a party to arrest him for mutiny and treason. Obliged to resolve this dispute, he left the city in the hands of his commander, Pedro de Alvarado. When he returned, he found that Alvarado had ordered his troops to attack the Aztecs and that the residents of Tenochtitlan were rebelling violently against the Spaniards. Cortés asked Motecuhzoma to reason with his people, but when the Aztec leader came out onto the balcony of his palace, he was pelted with stones, and later died from his injuries. The Spaniards fled the city in July 1520 but returned in April 1521 and, after a four-month battle, conquered the Aztec capital.

The conquest of Mexico raised a number of controversial issues, beginning with the question of whether Cortés and his troops were authorized to be there at all. Cortés, however, was a master manipulator of his own image. While still in Mexico, he wrote letters to King Charles V of Spain in order to lend legitimacy to his illegal expedition. In addition, he later commissioned López de Gómara (who entered his service as a personal secretary and chaplain in 1540) to write a history of the conquest of Mexico on his behalf, which was published as *Historia general de las Indias* (*General History of the Indies*) in 1552. López de Gómara's work glorifies Cortés as a military hero and, according to Díaz del Castillo, unjustly omits the role of his loyal troops. In *The Conquest of New Spain*, Díaz del Castillo counters López de Gómara and other historians by highlighting the contributions of the captains and soldiers in the conquering army.

Another significant issue at stake for Díaz del Castillo was the *encomienda*, the king of Spain's policy that gave Spanish colonists in the Americas the right to the labor and monetary tributes of the indigenous people. This was the sole remuneration granted the conquistadors who remained in Mexico. The colonists were expected to care for their Indians and teach them the Spanish language and the Catholic faith. By providing free labor, the *encomienda* formed the economic foundation of the Spanish colonies. Because of declining indigenous populations and protests

regarding the mistreatment of the indentured servants, however, the *encomienda* began to wane in the second half of the sixteenth century. Dominican missionary Bartolomé de las Casas, who spent time in Cuba and Guatemala, petitioned the Spanish government to end the policy altogether, citing the exploitation and neglect of the local people at the hands of the colonists. The protest angered Díaz del Castillo, who, as Adorno explains in "Discourses on Colonialism: Bernal Díaz, Las Casas, and the Twentieth-Century Reader," "expected to live out his life being served and supported by the heathens whose souls through just war of conquest he had helped to save."

THEMES AND STYLE

In his chronicle Díaz del Castillo explains that he is no scholar. He writes without elegance or rhetoric, describing every event as plainly and directly as possible, just as he experienced it. Other historians and writers of the time, such as López de Gómara and Las Casas, did not participate in the conquest, a fact that Díaz del Castillo felt gave him an advantage. When describing the battle of Cholula, he makes a point of contradicting Las Casas, who argued that the Spaniards massacred innocent Cholulans: "He writes so persuasively that

Emanuel Gottlieb Leutze, *The Storming of the Teocalli by Cortez and His Troops*, 1848. Oil on canvas. The Ella Gallup Sumner and Mary Catlin Sumner Collection Fund, 1985.7. © WADSWORTH ATHENEUM MUSEUM OF ART/ART RESOURCE, NY

THE GREAT VOLCANO

Bernal Díaz del Castillo supplies a large amount of useful information about the geography of Mexico in *The Conquest of New Spain*, including an account of the volcano Popocatepetl, the second-highest point in Mexico. The volcano, which erupted in 1539, was very active when Díaz del Castillo witnessed it in 1519: "[T]he volcano began to throw out great tongues of flame, and half-burnt stones of no great weight, and a great deal of ash, and … the whole mountain range in which it stands was so shaken that [the soldiers] stopped still, not daring to go forward for quite an hour." He notes that the sight of the volcano amazed the conquistadors, because they had never seen anything like it in Spain.

Díaz del Castillo also documents the first Spanish ascent of the volcano by Diego de Ordaz, one of Hernán Cortés's captains. He claims that Ordaz began his climb accompanied by indigenous guides, but they were too scared to reach the top, and Ordaz and two Spanish soldiers climbed into the crater without them. Ordaz was so impressed by his experience that he had the image of a volcano added to his coat of arms, which is still held by his descendants in Puebla, Mexico.

he would convince anyone who had not witnessed the event … that these and the other cruelties of which he writes … took place as he says, whereas the reverse is true." Sensitive to criticism of the conquest of Mexico, Díaz del Castillo constantly reiterates his belief that he and his fellow troops fought honorably.

The Conquest of New Spain stresses that the Spaniards only fought to defend themselves from Indian attacks. The author notes that in one battle, Cortés had his royal notary "watch what happened so that [the notary] could bear witness if it should be necessary, in order that we should not be made responsible at some future time for the deaths and destruction that might occur." In contrast, he describes their allies, the Tlaxcalans, as violent and malicious and declares them responsible for much of the devastation in the battle of Cholula. According to Díaz del Castillo, the Tlaxcalans plundered and took prisoners out of spite until Cortés and his troops forced them to leave the Cholulans in peace.

Díaz del Castillo also believed that the conquest of Mexico was a spiritual war in which the Spaniards were saving souls from such practices as idolatry, human sacrifice, and cannibalism. He refers to the number of sacrifices that the Indians made before battle and explains that the conquistadors lived in constant fear. At one point he even states that the Cholulans "were planning to kill us and eat our flesh, and had already prepared the pots with salt and peppers and tomatoes." Many of the battles end with the conquistadors asking the Indians to destroy their idols and replace them with

crosses or statues of the Virgin Mary. In an almost formulaic fashion, Cortés speaks to the tribes about "our lord the Emperor, and of his purpose in sending us to the country, which was that we should right wrongs."

In the face of much controversy over the Spaniards' treatment of Motecuhzoma, Díaz del Castillo depicts their behavior toward him as rational. When Cortés finds out that Motecuhzoma ordered his captains to attack the Spanish troops, he explains to the Aztec leader that "since our King's ordinances prescribed that anyone causing others to be killed, whether they were guilty or innocent, should himself die, [Motecuhzoma] deserved punishment." Out of compassion, Cortés chooses not to punish Motecuhzoma, but he establishes his right and obligation to do so under Spanish law and Christian moral code. This is a significant point for Díaz del Castillo because he must remind his readers, especially those who have any say in his compensation for military service, that the conquistadors were in the right and that they provided a great service for the Spanish empire and the Catholic Church.

CRITICAL DISCUSSION

Díaz del Castillo did not present his *Conquest of New Spain* to the Spanish rulers until 1575; he sent it to protest the end of the *encomienda*, the only coimpensation that had been awarded the conquistadors for their service (and even this they shared with other Spanish settlers). When his manuscript was published in Madrid in 1632, it gained popularity as a riveting story of the conquest of Mexico. Subsequent translations have been edited to exclude Díaz del Castillo's strong opinions about the *encomienda*, the legitimacy of the conquest, and other controversial issues of his day in order to focus on the narrative itself.

Since the publication of the text, historians have criticized it and its author for various reasons. In his seventeenth century "Historia de la Conquista de México," Antonio de Solís considers it "sloppy, styleless, subjective [and] excessively personal," and in the nineteenth century William Hickling Prescott described the work in his book *History of the Conquest of Mexico* as primitive and artless. Regardless of its historical accuracy, *The Conquest of New Spain* endures as a highly dramatic account of conquest, and it offers modern readers precious insight into the mindset of a Spanish conquistador in the sixteenth century.

Until the middle of the twentieth century, histories like Díaz del Castillo's were the only sources of information about the conquest of Mexico. In 1959 Miguel León-Portilla published *The Broken Spears*, a series of indigenous accounts of the conquest taken from manuscripts originally written in the Aztec language. This new perspective caused many readers to recognize the one-sided nature of the history of the conquest and inspired a rereading of such chronicles as *The Conquest of New Spain*. Matthew Restall's

Seven Myths of the Spanish Conquest is a good example of the ways in which historians now deconstruct the rhetoric of the chronicles of conquest.

SOURCES

Adorno, Rolena. "Discourses on Colonialism: Bernal Díaz, Las Casas, and the Twentieth-Century Reader." *MLN* 103.2 (1988): 239–58. Print.

———. "History, Law and the Eyewitness: Protocols of Authority in Bernal Díaz del Castillo's *Historia verdadera de la conquista de la Nueva España*." *The Project of Prose in Early Modern Europe and the New World*. Ed. Elizabeth Fowler and Roland Greene. Cambridge: Cambridge UP, 1997. 154–75. Print.

Díaz del Castillo, Bernal. *The Conquest of New Spain*. Trans. J. M. Cohen. London: Penguin, 1963. Print.

León-Portilla, Miguel, ed. *The Broken Spears: The Aztec Account of the Conquest of Mexico*. Boston: Beacon, 1962. Print.

Prescott, William Hickling. *History of the Conquest of Mexico*. New York: Modern Library, 2001. Print.

Restall, Matthew. *Seven Myths of the Spanish Conquest*. Oxford: Oxford UP, 2003. Print.

Solís, Antonio de. "Historia de la Conquista de México." *Biblioteca Virtual Miguel de Cervantes*. Fundación Biblioteca Virtual Miguel de Cervantes, 1999. Web. 15 Aug. 2011.

FURTHER READING

Adorno, Rolena. "The Discursive Encounter of Spain and America: The Authority of Eyewitness Testimony in the Writing of History." *William and Mary Quarterly* 49.2 (1992): 210–28. Print.

Brooks, Francis J. "Motecuzoma Xocoyotl, Hernán Cortés, and Bernal Díaz del Castillo: The Construction of an Arrest." *Hispanic American Historical Review* 75.2 (1995): 149–83. Print.

Cortés, Hernán. *Hernán Cortés: Letters from Mexico*. Trans. Anthony Pagden. New Haven: Yale UP, 2001. Print.

Elliott, J. H. *Imperial Spain: 1469–1716*. London: Penguin, 1953. Print.

———. "The Mental World of Hernán Cortés." *Transactions of the Royal Historical Society* 17 (1967): 41–58. Print.

Gibson, Charles. *The Aztecs under Spanish Rule: A History of the Indians of the Valley of Mexico, 1519–1810*. Stanford: Stanford UP, 1964. Print.

Iglesia, Ramón. *Columbus, Cortés, and Other Essays*. Berkeley: U of California P, 1969. Print.

Simpson, Lesley Byrd. *The Encomienda in New Spain: The Beginning of Spanish Mexico*. Berkeley: U of California P, 1950. Print.

Gina Sherriff

WE WISH TO INFORM YOU THAT TOMORROW WE WILL BE KILLED WITH OUR FAMILIES

Stories from Rwanda

Philip Gourevitch

✧ *Key Facts*

Conflict:
Rwandan Genocide

Time Period:
Late 20th Century

Genre:
Journalism

Awards:
George Polk Award for
Foreign Reporting, 1998;
Los Angeles Times Book
Prize, 1998;
National Book Critics
Circle Award nomination
for nonfiction prize,
1998;
Guardian First Book
Award, 1999;
Helen Bernstein Award,
New York Public Library,
1999;
PEN/Martha Albrand
Award for First
Nonfiction, 1999;
National Magazine
Award finalist;
Cornelius Ryan Award,
Overseas Book Club

OVERVIEW

Philip Gourevitch's *We Wish to Inform You That Tomorrow We Will Be Killed with Our Families* (1998) is a journalistic narrative of the Rwandan genocide of 1994, in which Hutu hardliners killed an estimated 500,00 to 800,000 Tutsis and some 10,000 moderate Hutus. Gourevitch made numerous trips to Rwanda between 1995 and 1998, and interviewed survivors, alleged perpetrators, and key political figures. The book weaves together the stories of individual Rwandans and sketches the historical and political context that underlay the atrocities of 1994. Gourevitch also considers the country's prospects in the aftermath of the genocide and reflects on the ethical complications of memorializing and writing about such horrors.

We Wish to Inform You is by far the most widely read book on the Rwandan genocide to have appeared in the United States, and Gourevitch has been credited with measurably increasing public consciousness of the atrocity. The book's reception in the general press was overwhelmingly positive, and it established Gourevitch as one of the most serious and admired journalists in the English-speaking world. *We Wish to Inform You* has also been taken seriously by academic readers in a variety of fields. Some Africanists and other specialists, however, fault it for supplying a dualistic and simplified view of the plot that led to the killings.

HISTORICAL AND LITERARY CONTEXT

The Rwandan genocide took place in the context of conflict between the Hutu and Tutsi ethnic groups. Rwanda's Tutsi minority, who accounted for roughly 15 percent of the population, had ruled the country during the precolonial era, but ethnic identity became more highly politicized when German colonizers arrived in the late nineteenth century. After World War I Rwanda came under the control of Belgium, which concentrated political power in the hands of the Tutsis. Discussion of racial superiority increased, and the government introduced racial identification cards. As the movement for political independence in sub-Saharan Africa gathered force in the 1950s, Belgium had to acknowledge the Hutu majority and its political role in a post independence nation. In 1959 Hutus rebelled against the ruling Tutsi authority. With the help of the Belgian government, a successful revolution brought about Hutu leadership. Rwanda was granted its independence from Belgium in 1962 under a Hutu president, Grégoire Kayibanda.

Periodic outbreaks of violence between Hutus and Tutsis in Rwanda and neighboring Burundi occurred in the subsequent decades, and discrimination against Tutsis was enshrined in law. The Hutu president Juvénal Habyarimana, who took power in 1975, sought to limit ethnic strife through the establishment of one-party rule, but by the late 1980s economic decline and the end of the cold war had undermined his regime. Tutsi exiles in neighboring Uganda began to pose a threat to Habyarimana's power, and tensions once again grew between the two ethnic groups. In October 1990, when a rebel group calling itself the Rwandan Patriotic Front (RPF) crossed into the country from Uganda, widespread violence engulfed Rwanda. The international community tried to end the violence through a peace agreement. The Arusha Accords between the Rwandan government and the RPF were signed in August 1993, and United Nations peacekeeping forces (UNAMIR) were deployed in October of that year.

The peace agreement and the presence of peacekeeping forces failed to end the violence, primarily because hardliners on both sides rejected the agreement and because UNAMIR troops were not allowed to use force except in self-defense. Meanwhile, propagandists in the Hutu Power movement, which was rabidly anti-Tutsi, increasingly influenced public discourse and government policy. When Habyarimana was killed on April 6, 1994, most likely by Hutu extremists, Tutsis were blamed, and a highly organized campaign of genocide began. Ordinary civilians, operating in bands led and funded by government functionaries, used machetes to hack their neighbors, friends, and associates to death.

Gourevitch writes that he cannot wholly justify his reasons for deciding to report on the conflict. Upon learning of the unthinkable magnitude and nature of

The Rwandan Genocide left an estimated 800,000 men, women, and children murdered, c. 1994. © DAVID TURNLEY / CORBIS

the violence in Rwanda, he notes, "All at once, as it seemed, something we could have only imagined was upon us—and we could still only imagine it. This is what fascinates me most in existence: the peculiar necessity of imagining what is, in fact, real." Why it was necessary to make such events as the Rwandan genocide real to readers who would otherwise be able only to imagine it, Gourevitch cannot say. He admits to being unable to assure readers that there is any moral or lesson to be derived from his book. "The best reason I have come up with for looking closely into Rwanda's stories," he explains, "is that ignoring them makes me even more uncomfortable about existence and my place in it."

THEMES AND STYLE

Gourevitch acquaints readers with the Rwandan genocide and its aftermath by blending eyewitness testimony, historical and political context drawn from his own research, firsthand observation of postgenocide Rwanda, and personal meditations on the meaning of what he has discovered. His narrative is divided into two main sections: one focusing on the events of 1994, and the other one focusing on the aftermath of those events. The first section attempts to bring the reality of the genocide to life in all its horror, and the second addresses the question of how Rwanda might reconstitute itself as a nation with a population largely made up of killers and those they had attempted to kill.

The eyewitness testimony constitutes the book's core, so that a mosaic of personal experience emerges

against the historical and political background. Among the individual stories is that of Odette Nyiramilimo, a Tutsi doctor married to Jean-Baptiste Gasasira, who is of mixed Hutu and Tutsi descent but who has Hutu identity papers. Odette's story embodies many of the complexities and contradictions of racial policies and violence under the Hutu regimes in the years after independence. Her account of surviving the genocide vividly conveys the harrowing reality of being hunted by people who were once neighbors and associates. Odette and Jean-Baptiste ultimately survive by taking refuge in the Hotel Mille Collines. A Hutu friend named Paul Rusesabagina, an executive with the company that owned the hotel—and a former director of the hotel itself—shielded them and other Tutsis from Hutu militias. Paul's instinctual and sustained heroism, which forms another prominent thread in the book, complicates simplistic notions of the enmity all Hutus were said to have felt toward all Tutsis.

Indeed, throughout the book Gourevitch is concerned to demonstrate that the genocide was neither inevitable nor unpreventable. Taking aim at the common journalistic cliché that the violence in Rwanda was one among many outbreaks of ancestral ethnic hatred, he shows that before the 1950s there had been little explicit conflict between the Hutus and Tutsis and that the conflict that emerged in the decades after independence was rooted in racial theories introduced by the Belgians. Moreover the genocide was not a function of chaotic intertribal warfare but of a sustained government propaganda campaign and of a history of

RWANDA SINCE 1994

At the close of *We Wish to Inform You That Tomorrow We Will Be Killed with Our Families*, Phillip Gourevitch expresses an understandable skepticism about the prospects for harmony between the two main ethnic groups in Rwanda. Following the genocide of hundreds of thousands of Tutsis, "it was hard to imagine in 1994 how you could put this country back together," he says on *Prospero*, the *Economist*'s literary and cultural blog. "Even dealing with poverty seemed like a luxury then."

Since 1994, under the leadership of President Paul Kagame, Rwanda has done what was seemingly impossible; it has been stabilized politically and economically, and it has become one of the most peaceful countries in Africa. There has even been a measure of reconciliation between Hutus and Tutsis, brought about in part by the prosecution, in improvised courts, of some 800,000 Rwandans for murder and other crimes. The process has required great fortitude, especially on the part of Tutsis who must live peacefully with neighbors who killed people they loved.

In 2009, to begin research for a book about the country's recovery, Gourevitch returned to Rwanda for the first time after finishing work on *We Wish to Inform You*. In describing the stories of recovery and reconciliation he found, he says in *Prospero*, "There are raw Shakespearean dramas that lead to very big questions."

directly manipulating ethnic hatred for political gain. "In 1994," he writes, "Rwanda was regarded in much of the rest of the world as the exemplary instance of the chaos and anarchy associated with collapsed states. In fact, the genocide was the product of order, authoritarianism, decades of modern political theorizing and indoctrination, and one of the most meticulously administered states in history."

Gourevitch does not suggest that, once the genocide was underway, Hutus killed Tutsis unwillingly. He notes that "assertive resistance" to the government's demands to kill was rare. "Killing Tutsis was a political tradition in postcolonial Rwanda," he writes. "It brought people together." The killings were not conducted in fits of passion or madness, however. In keeping with the deliberate way in which the genocide was plotted by the government, the actual killings required substantial management, discipline, and hard work. Gourevitch emphasizes the work involved in killing a single human with a machete, and his chilling depictions of mass slaughter elucidate the diligence required to exterminate the majority of the Tutsi in a matter of three months.

Gourevitch also devotes significant space to a consideration of the roles of Western governments in the genocide. In particular, he damns the United Nations as ineffective. He argues that not only did the UN ignore the genocide but that it also, as a body—and with the active encouragement of the French and U.S. governments—prevented actions that could have stopped the killings. The commander of peacekeeping forces in

Rwanda, Lieutenant General Roméo Dallaire, made it clear that with "five thousand well-equipped soldiers and a free hand to fight Hutu Power, he could bring the genocide to a rapid halt." Instead of granting his request, the UN Security Council passed a resolution to cut the peacekeeping force by 90 percent, "ordering the retreat of all but 270 troops and leaving them with a mandate that allowed them to do little more than hunker down behind their sandbags and watch."

In addressing the aftermath of the genocide, Gourevitch examines the profound effects of the violence on neighboring African countries. He outlines the complex ways in which the Rwandan civil war triggered the war that broke out in the Democratic Republic of the Congo (formerly Zaire) in 1998, which led to another estimated three to four million violent deaths. Meanwhile, in considering Rwanda's future, Gourevitch is less than sanguine. He writes that "a UNICEF study later posited that five out of six children who had been in Rwanda during the slaughter had, at the very least, witnessed bloodshed, and you may assume that adults had not been better sheltered. Imagine what the totality of such devastation means for a society." Nevertheless, interviews with General Paul Kagame, who was leader of the RPF forces that overthrew the Hutu government, and who became president of the country in 2000, suggest reasons for hope. "People are not inherently bad," Kagame told Gourevitch. "But they can be made bad. And they can be taught to be good."

CRITICAL DISCUSSION

We Wish to Inform You That Tomorrow We Will Be Killed with Our Families was greeted with reviews that primarily ranged from positive to reverential. The Nigerian Nobel laureate Wole Soyinka, writing in the *New York Times Book Review*, praised the book for fighting the tendency toward allowing perpetrators of atrocities to fade into history. He applauded Gourevitch for casting a wide enough net to note the degree to which colonial rule and its aftermath, and the ineffectiveness of the United Nations, contributed to the carnage. Himself a veteran journalist who covered the Rwandan genocide, Jonathan Randal of the *Washington Post* was equally positive about Gourevitch's work. The book won numerous awards, including the Los Angeles Times Book Prize, the George K. Polk Award for Foreign Reporting, the Helen Bernstein Book Award, the Overseas Press Club's Cornelius Ryan Award for print journalism, the PEN/Martha Albrand Award for First Nonfiction, and the National Book Critics Circle Award as the best nonfiction book of 1998.

The book has received substantial attention from academics as well. Colette Braeckman, writing in *World Policy Journal*, maintains that Gourevitch "offers his readers not simply an introduction to postgenocide Rwanda but a lesson in humanity...We sense that each of us at a moment in our lives could also have been a torturer or a victim, a coward or a hero; that each of us, in short, could have been a Rwandan." Scott Straus, writing in the *African Studies Review*, calls the book a "deft, smart rendering of disaster" that "will gain a wide readership, from policy-makers to poets," but he argues that it fails to satisfy standards of scholarly rigor. Chief among its deficiencies, in Straus's view, is the fact that the "book disavows explanation, preferring narrative and description, and it ends without providing a clear understanding of how or why the genocide occurred." More pointedly, René Lemarchand argues in an article in *Transition* that "the absence of attention to the history and politics of the country creates a portrait of genocide that is insensitive to the complexity of its circumstances. In essence, Gourevitch's story reduces the butchery to a tale of bad guys and good guys, innocent victims and avatars of hate."

SOURCES

Braeckman, Colette. "Cowardice and Conscience." *World Policy Journal* 15.4 (1998/1999): 99–104. *JSTOR.* Web. July 14, 2011.

Gourevitch, Philip. *We Wish to Inform You That Tomorrow We Will Be Killed with Our Families: Stories from Rwanda.* New York: Farrar, 1998. Print.

Lemarchand, René. "Hate Crimes." *Transition* 81/82 (2000): 114–32. *JSTOR.* Web. July 14, 2011.

Straus, Scott. "Genocide in Rwanda." *African Studies Review* 43.2 (2000): 126–30. *JSTOR.* Web. July 14, 2011.

FURTHER READING

Hatzfeld, Jean. *Life Laid Bare: The Survivors in Rwanda Speak.* Trans. Linda Coverdale. New York: Other, 2006. Print.

———. *Machete Season: The Killers in Rwanda Speak.* Trans. Linda Coverdale. New York: Farrar, 2005. Print.

King, Elisabeth. "Educating for Conflict or Peace: Challenges and Dilemmas in Post-Conflict Rwanda." *International Journal* 60.4 (2005): 904–18. *JSTOR.* Web. July 14, 2011.

Mueller, John. "The Banality of 'Ethnic War.'" *International Security* 25.1 (2000): 42–70. *JSTOR.* Web. July 14, 2011.

Power, Samantha. *A Problem from Hell: America and the Age of Genocide.* New York: Basic, 2002. Print.

Prunier, Gérard. *The Rwanda Crisis: History of a Genocide.* London: Hurst, 1997. Print.

Straus, Scott. *The Order of Genocide: Race, Power, and War in Rwanda.* Ithaca: Cornell UP, 2006.

Windrich, Elaine. "Revisiting Genocide in Rwanda." *Third World Quarterly* 20.4 (1999): 855–60. *JSTOR.* Web. July 14, 2011.

Mark Lane

ZLATA'S DIARY
A Child's Life in Sarajevo
Zlata Filipovic

❖ *Key Facts*

Conflict:
Bosnian War

Time Period:
Late 20th Century

Genre:
Diary

OVERVIEW

Zlata's Diary, the diary of a young girl living through the Bosnian War between 1991 and 1993, records the way the ordinary life of a child is interrupted by civil war. The constant violence surrounding her and the loss of friends and family members force her to mature before her time. In a child's voice, Filipovic bears witness to the way that the cosmopolitan city disintegrated and the middle-class life she knew was disrupted by the nearly continuous shelling of Sarajevo.

In 1992 Filipovic passed pages from her diary to a teacher, and UNICEF, the United Nations Children's Fund, published a portion of it as part of a program to draw public attention and support to children in Sarajevo. The full diary reached international audiences when it was published as *Journal de Zlata* in 1993 in France, where it became a best seller. The diary was the center of a bidding war among American publishing houses and was an immediate best seller in Europe, the United States, and Canada. In the years following the publication of her diary, Filipovic, who had moved with her family to Paris in 1993, became a "spokeschild" for the children of Bosnia. Spurred by her experiences in the Bosnian War, Filipovic spent her adolescence and young adulthood as an advocate for the human rights of children.

HISTORICAL AND LITERARY CONTEXT

Beginning on September 2, 1991, and ending on October 17, 1993, Zlata's diary covers the early years of the Bosnian War. Zlata, nearly eleven at the start of her diary, is unaware of the buildup to the war. In the political void following the 1990 breakup of Yugoslavia, there was growing tension regarding the formation of nation-states in Bosnia, Croatia, Slovenia, Macedonia, and Herzegovina. Croatia and Slovenia declared their independence in 1991, while the government of Bosnia-Herzegovina held a referendum on independence in early 1992. The Bosnian parliament declared independence in April 1992, but ethnic wars broke out before the European Community could ratify their claim. Bosnian Serb paramilitaries, who supported the annexation of the Serbian-dominated area of Bosnia by the Republic of Serbia, laid siege to Sarajevo. The city remained blockaded, and under mortar fire and sniper attack, until the 1995 cease-fire. During the war, Bosnian Serb armies began a policy of genocide against Muslim and Croatian citizens. Nearly two hundred thousand people were killed during the conflict, and tens of thousands of Bosnian Muslim women and children were raped.

Zlata's Diary is invariably compared to the diary of Anne Frank, the young Jewish girl who kept a diary during the last years of her life, hiding in an attic space in Amsterdam. Frank died in the concentration camp in Bergen-Belsen, and her diary, discovered after World War II, is one of the best-known accounts of the Holocaust. While *Zlata's Diary* bears similarities to Frank's, and Filipovic was almost immediately marketed as the "Bosnian Anne Frank," numerous critics found this parallel to be disingenuous, arguing that genocides cannot be compared and that Filipovic's situation was neither as dire nor as hopeless as was Frank's. While Filipovic herself encouraged the comparison privately, naming her diary "Mimmy" as Frank named hers "Kitty," Filipovic becomes wary when such parallels are drawn by journalists, noting "some people compare me to Anne Frank. That frightens me, Mimmy. I don't want to suffer her fate."

THEMES AND STYLE

As demonstrated by Zlata's descriptions of her life before the war—she has a summer home, watches American television, takes piano and tennis lessons, and talks about Elle Macpherson—the outbreak of war in Bosnia was additionally shocking because Sarajevo was a wealthy, Westernized city often referred to as part of the "New Europe." Zlata narrates how her life, initially much like that of any middle-class, Western preteen girl, becomes focused around the scarcity of food and medical supplies, the lack of running water and electricity, and her weakening mother. She eloquently conveys her growing isolation as schools are closed and streets become too dangerous, expressing her sense of being "caged," "spending [her] days in the attic and in the cellar." She describes the "park in front of [her] house": "Empty, deserted, no children, no joy. I hear the sounds of shells and everything around me smells of war."

Michael Biggins points out that Filipovic's "perception of the tragedy" is more personal than political. The term "genocide" is never used in the book, and

Filipovic's sense of the political situation is loose and indistinct. She expresses a general horror of death and destruction rather than placing blame or choosing sides. She does not indicate her own ethnicity—it goes unmentioned in the text, but she is of mixed ancestry—and her life and friends before the war were not defined by such divisions. She describes her family celebrating Christmas, but she also mentions Muslim holidays. Still, Filipovic is aware of the importance of ethnicity in the war that rages outside her door. She notes that "politics has started meddling around. It has put an 'S' on Serbs, an 'M' on Muslims and a 'C' on Croats, it wants to separate them. And to do so, it has chosen the worst, blackest pencil of all—the pencil of war which spells only misery and death."

While Filipovic refers to the political talks of the "kids" (as the politicians were referred to), she does not make partisan arguments nor does she express any opinions about the future of the country. She does, however, articulate her horror at the destruction of the city and the deaths of loved ones and voice her concern about international apathy. She repeatedly describes the politicians as "stupid" and agonizes over their inability to resolve the situation: "Are they thinking about us when they negotiate, or are they just trying to outwit each other, and leave us to our fate?"

Filipovic's diary recounts her own growing fame and her response to it, poignantly noting how glad she is to speak English with a handful of young journalists. She views the interest in her as "exciting. Nice. Unusual for a wartime child." She says of a French journalist's departure that she "is going back to her peaceful country, her peaceful town, to her friends and her job. AND ME? I have a burned-down destroyed country, a demolished town, friends-refugees all over the world."

CRITICAL DISCUSSION

Zlata's Diary was an immediate best seller in America and in Europe, and it received positive reviews from most trade publications. *Publishers Weekly* describes it as a "vivid, sensitive diary [that] sounds an urgent and compelling appeal for peace," while Nancy Vasilakis, in the *Horn Book Magazine*, emphasizes Zlata's "artlessness, her very ordinariness that brings this account home."

The publication of *Zlata's Diary* in English opened up a controversy about the authenticity of the book, which was challenged most notably by David Rieff for the *New Republic*. Rieff, a journalist who covered the Bosnian conflict, points to disparities between the initial publication of the diary entries by UNICEF and the Viking edition. He notes that "again and again the girl moves from detailing her own experiences during the course of the day to more general accounts of political developments or new horrors of the war, and the two strains of narrative do not cohere. ... Zlata's references to various political events are nowhere to be found in the original edition of her diary." Michael Ignatieff, in the *New York Review of Books*, agrees, adding that the popularity of *Zlata's Diary* is "symbolic of the often inconsequential character of Western grasp of the Bosnian story. ... Zlata's diary is moving, in a sentimental sort of way, but it asks few awkward questions."

A young girl sits on the curb in Travnik, Bosnia, with her few possessions. She was forced from her home in Banja Luka. This 1993 photograph, like *Zlata's Diary*, reveals a child's experience of war. © ROGER HUTCHINGS / ALAMY

YUGOSLAV WAR ORPHANS

Zlata's Diary chronicles the terrifying ordeal endured by a young girl during the Bosnian War. Although Zlata Filipovic eventually escaped the conflict with her parents, thousands of other children living in the former Yugoslavia were not so fortunate. Within the first few months of the fighting, hundreds of children had been orphaned, with their parents either missing or confirmed dead. In 1992, with the number of orphans in the region swelling rapidly, a Sarajevo-based attorney named Dushko Tomic founded the Children's Embassy, an organization dedicated to offering shelter and protection to children who had lost their families. With help from the United Nations, the Children's Embassy quickly began to evacuate hundreds of children from the area, establishing transportation convoys through various private and state bus companies. As Tomic's organization struggled to lead the children to safety beyond the Yugoslavian borders, they found themselves battling epidemics, extreme hunger, and constant harassment by soldiers and police. At the same time, relief workers had to contend with the psychological agony suffered by the orphans, who had been severely traumatized by the experience of living for several months in the center of intense fighting. By July 1992, the Children's Embassy had rescued roughly thirty five thousand children. Over the next two decades, Tomic's organization continued to provide relief and other essential services to the children of Bosnia and Herzegovina.

Still, Patricia Chisholm, writing in the *Globe and Mail*, notes that even the harshest critics of the book itself have only praise for Filipovic, who, she says, "has succeeded in putting a human face on a war that often seems incomprehensible." Similarly, Michael Biggins in *Slavic Review* comments that "anything that forces attention to the unending tragedy of Bosnia carries the potential for some good." Even Biggins, however, concludes that the usefulness of *Zlata's Diary* "will be limited to whatever compassion it can engender … among people who might make a difference." Sidonie Smith points out in *Women's Studies Quarterly* that the familiarity of Zlata's pre-war life allows the book "[to be] marketed to a broad middle-class audience educated about, familiar with and prepared to respond to stories of childhood suffering." Smith continues to argue that the comparison between Filipovic and Anne Frank draws on their identity as "figure[s] of universalized innocence and heroic suffering," which "may not so much illuminate the incommensurate differences and the specifics of ethnic histories as have the effect of flattening history through an appeal to empathetic, depoliticized sentimentality."

Most academic criticism addressing *Zlata's Diary* is in the fields of children's literature and education, evaluating the way that children learn about political atrocity and genocide. Mary Johnson, writing in *Fourth Genre*, asserts that "the power of memoir is to open up worlds not your own" and commends *Zlata's Diary* for "hid[ing] nothing of [the author's] anguished fears for family and friends, her confusion and disappointment

at the disruption of normal activities [through which] she conveys the personal immediacy of war in a truly poignant way." Beth Benjamin and Linda Irwin-DeVitis, in the *English Journal*, recommend *Zlata's Diary* as a countermeasure to continued gender bias in school classrooms, saying that "if girls are to make a difference in the world … they need to see other female youngsters struggle to overcome life's obstacles in literature." Stephen L. Esquith, writing in *Polity*, used Filipovic's account as part of what he refers to as "democratic liberal education … [which] enables citizens to be mindful of democracy's deepest shortcomings [which are] xenophobia and empire, not gridlock." Esquith's strategy for teaching his students—he worked with both undergraduates and fifth graders—to use "power responsibly and tak[e] responsibility for violence when it is appropriate" deployed stories of children uprooted by violence such as *Zlata's Diary* to bring home the idea of collective responsibility for war crimes and crimes against humanity. Esquith found that *Zlata's Diary* was particularly effective at reaching the younger students he worked with.

SOURCES

Benjamin, Beth, and Linda Irwin-DeVitis. "Censoring Girls' Choices: Continued Gender Bias in English Language Arts Classrooms." *English Journal* 87.2 (1998): 64–71. Print.

Biggins, Michael. Rev. of *Zlata's Diary*, by Zlata Filipovic. *Slavic Review* 54.2 (1995): 544–45. Print.

Esquith, Stephen L. "An Experiment in Democratic Liberal Education." *Polity* 36.1 (2003): 73–90. Print.

Filipovic, Zlata. *Zlata's Diary: A Child's Life in Sarajevo.* New York: Viking, 1994. Print.

Ignatieff, Michael. "Homage to Bosnia." *New York Review of Books* 21 Apr. 1994. 1962–2011. NYREV, Inc. Web. 18 July 2011.

Johnson, Mary. Rev. of *Zlata's Diary*, by Zlata Filipovic. *Fourth Genre: Explorations in Nonfiction* 5.1 (2003): 2311–14. Print.

Rieff, David. "Youth and Consequences." Rev. of *Zlata's Diary*, by Zlata Filipovic. *New Republic* 28 Mar. 1994: 31–36. Print.

Smith, Sidonie. "'Zlata's Diary' and the Circulation of Stories of Suffering Ethnicity." *Women's Studies Quarterly* 34.1–2 (2006): 133–52. Print.

Vasilakis, Nancy. Rev. of *Zlata's Diary*, by Zlata Filipovic. *Horn Book Magazine* 70.5 (1994): 605. Print.

Rev. of *Zlata's Diary*, by Zlata Filipovic. *Publishers Weekly* 21 Feb. 1994: 245. Print.

FURTHER READING

Crowe, Chris. "Young Adult Literature: Peace-Keeping Forces: YA War Books." *English Journal* 89.5 (2000): 159–63. Print.

Filopovic, Zlata, and Melanie Challenger, eds. *Stolen Voices: Young People's War Diaries from World War I to Iraq.* New York: Penguin, 2006. Print.

Frank, Anne. *Anne Frank: A Diary of a Young Girl*. Trans. B. M. Mooyaart. New York: Bantam, 1993. Print.

Fry, Leanna. "'Never Again': International Children's Genocide Literature." *Bookbird: A Journal of International Children's Literature* 47.1 (2009): 6–9. Print.

Mead. Alice. *Girl of Kosovo*. New York: Yearling, 2003. Print.

Myers, Mitzi. "Storying War: A Capsule Overview." *Lion and the Unicorn* 24.3 (2000): 327–36. Print.

Prose, Francine. "A Little Girl's War." Rev. of *Zlata's Diary*, by Zlata Filipovic. *New York Times Book Review* 6 Mar. 1994: 7. Print.

Sills-Briegel, Toni, and Deanne Camp. "Using Literature to Explore Social Issues." *Clearing House* 74.5 (2001): 280–84. Print.

Wagner, Sarah E. *To Know Where He Lies: DNA Technology and the Search for Srebrenica's Missing*. Berkeley: U of California P, 2008. Print.

Woodward, Susan L. *Balkan Tragedy: Chaos and Dissolution after the Cold War*. Washington, DC: Brookings Institute, 1995. Print.

Jenny Ludwig

PROPAGANDA

THE AMERICAN CRISIS

Thomas Paine

OVERVIEW

Originally published in the *Pennsylvania Journal* on December 19, 1776, and printed several days later in pamphlet form, Thomas Paine's *The American Crisis* offered encouragement to American patriots during the early years of the American Revolution (1775–83). Paine initially published the work as *The Crisis* but later added "American" to the title to distinguish it from a British periodical of the period. Over the course of the war, Paine augmented the collection with additional installments, the last of which was published on April 17, 1783. Collectively, the works reflect on the major events of the war and are addressed to a wide range of readers, including both British and American citizens and prominent political figures.

Paine wrote *The American Crisis* at a time when George Washington's army was in retreat and morale was low. It so impressed Washington that he had it read to the troops in an attempt to recommit them to the cause, and it has subsequently been credited with helping to inspire their victory at the Battle of Trenton (December 26, 1776). Notable for their plain language, the papers of *The American Crisis* were signed "Common Sense," the name of Paine's immensely popular 1776 pamphlet outlining the cause of American independence. Although today it is less well known than *Common Sense*, *The American Crisis* was acknowledged as an important revolutionary influence by prominent contemporaries of Paine's, including Washington and Benjamin Franklin, and it remains popular with modern scholars, who view it as an important contribution to the literature of the American Revolution.

HISTORICAL AND LITERARY CONTEXT

As an author of war literature, Paine is unique in having played a shaping role in the conflict about which he wrote. Prior to writing *The American Crisis*, Paine had gained fame for using his journalistic talents to advocate for American independence. His 1776 pamphlet *Common Sense*, which critiques what Paine saw as an unjust relationship between Great Britain and the American colonies and argues against the view that the colonies were too weak to stand up to Britain in battle, is considered among the most successful pieces of war propaganda ever written.

Paine wrote the first and best-known essay of *The American Crisis* (known as *Crisis 1*) in the second year of the war, as Washington's Continental army was in retreat. The dire situation in which the American troops found themselves was in stark contrast to the optimism and exhilaration of their early victory in the war's opening Battles of Lexington and Concord (April 19, 1775). By the time Paine wrote *Crisis 1*, enthusiasm had given way to defeat, exhaustion, and despair. Forced out of their positions in New York and retreating across New Jersey, Washington's men suffered from low morale and high rates of desertion. Even Washington feared that an American defeat was near. Paine, who was traveling with Washington's army, saw the troops' demoralized state firsthand and hoped to increase morale through his writing.

Paine's essay has been credited with helping to turn the tide of the war. With the Battle of Trenton, on December 26, 1776, American forces began to rally. The battle occurred after American forces under Washington's leadership crossed the Delaware River despite hazardous weather. Because the Hessian mercenaries guarding Trenton did not expect the patriots to mount an attack in such weather, they were caught off guard and defeated with little loss of American life. The victory at Trenton helped to boost both morale and enlistment.

After achieving his desired goals with the first installment of *The American Crisis*, Paine went on to add further segments reflecting on military and political events as they unfolded. Several of the installments were addressed to prominent figures of the day, including Richard Viscount Howe, a British officer sent to negotiate with the colonists, and General William Howe (Richard's brother), who had repeatedly bested Washington early in the war. Others installments were addressed more generally, as were "To the People of England" or "To the Inhabitants of America."

Paine referred to thirteen installments, or "numbers," in the series, a number he is believed to have chosen to reflect the number of American colonies. His numbering system, however, was inconsistent throughout the series—there is no essay numbered either ten or twelve, for example—and there are two unnumbered texts, "Crisis Extraordinary" and "Supernumerary Crisis," which are generally considered part of the collection. Alfred Owen Aldridge notes in his

Key Facts

Conflict:
American Revolution

Time Period:
Late 18th Century

Genre:
Journalism

THOMAS PAINE, GEORGE WASHINGTON, AND THE FRENCH REVOLUTION

Although Thomas Paine is best known for his role in the American Revolution, he was an ardent supporter of the French Revolution (1789–99) as well, and he almost lost his life in the violence that consumed France.

Paine had fled to France in 1792 after his book *The Rights of Man* (1791), which defended the French Revolution, led to his being charged with seditious libel (then a capital offense) in Britain, where he was living. In France, despite his championing of the Revolution, he soon found himself on the wrong side of revolutionary leader Maximilien Robespierre, who was angered by Paine's advocacy of sparing the life of the overthrown King Louis XVI.

Arrested on December 28, 1793, and held as a foreign conspirator, Paine feared that he would be guillotined. His appeals to George Washington's envoy in Paris failed to secure any support, despite his zealous defense of Washington during the American Revolution. After miraculously escaping the guillotine, Paine was released from prison only after the Terror had ended with Robespierre's execution.

Paine never forgave Washington for what he felt was an act of supreme betrayal, and he subsequently attempted to attack the reputation of the man he had so passionately defended during the war.

book *Thomas Paine's American Ideology* that, because of such anomalies, "one cannot be absolutely sure of what pieces he [Paine] felt should be included in the complete text of *The Crisis*."

Some confusion also exists concerning the relationship between Paine's text and a roughly contemporaneous British series also titled *The Crisis*. Popular in London during 1775 and 1776, *The Crisis* attacked government policies, including those affecting the American colonies. Because of its proindependence stance, the British periodical was widely circulated in the colonies. An early British printing of Paine's *The American Crisis* erroneously included a letter that was not written by Paine but was in fact part of the British series *The Crisis*.

THEMES AND STYLE

Like Paine's earlier works of journalism, *The American Crisis* is notable for its straightforward address to the common man. While other writers of the day tended to embellish their texts with Latin and frequent allusions to literature and philosophy that would have been meaningful only to the educated classes, Paine speaks primarily of current events and contemporary figures, using accessible language and often outlining his arguments in concise, numbered steps.

Opening with the celebrated sentence "These are the times that try men's souls," *The American Crisis* dramatizes the challenges facing American patriots and emphasizes the importance of persevering in the face of crisis. Criticizing the "summer soldier and the sunshine patriot [who] will, in this crisis, shrink from the service of their country," Paine calls upon soldiers and civilians to stand firm in the face of British tyranny. In the third installment he lambastes those

Americans who are not actively supporting the war, asserting that he can imagine only a few reasons why colonists might fail to support the cause of independence ("fear and indolence") or why they might choose to oppose it ("*avarice, down-right villainy*, and *lust of personal power*").

To encourage the bravery of soldiers and civilians, Paine repeatedly emphasizes that the American cause is just and therefore destined ultimately to succeed, a position he maintains even in the face of military setbacks. In the fourth entry of the series, for example, he reflects on the recent American defeat at the Battle of Brandywine (September 11, 1777), assuring his readers that, though the British have won the battle, "what they have gained in ground, they paid so dearly for in numbers that their victories have in the end amounted to defeats." He makes a similar argument in the ninth installment about the ongoing siege of Charleston, arguing that if the city were to fall it would only serve to "rouse us from the slumber of twelve months past, and renew in us the spirit of former days." Such bravado is clear as well in the opening of the fifth essay, where he writes confidently that "it is pleasant to look back on dangers past," despite the fact that an American victory was not yet assured.

Penning the final installment of the series in 1883, Paine, referring to his initial pamphlet, asserts that "the times that tried men's souls are over—and the greatest and completest revolution the world ever knew, gloriously and happily completed." This final essay marks the culmination of Paine's insistence that the American cause was destined for success and emphasizes that these same qualities ensure America's future. "Never I say," he writes, "had a country so many openings to happiness as this. Her setting out in life, like the rising of a fair morning, was unclouded and promising. Her cause was good. Her principles just and liberal. Her temper serene and firm."

Paine also repeatedly emphasizes that, in opposition to the providentially blessed position of the Americans, the British side is marked by errors of policy and judgment that necessitate its downfall. Paine suggests, for example, that King George III of England has no grounds on which to seek divine assistance against the Americans, asserting that "a common murderer, a highwayman, or a house-breaker, has as good a pretence as he." In the second installment Paine proclaims that the British purpose "is to kill, conquer, plunder, pardon, and enslave," going on to assert that "a bad cause will ever be supported by bad means and bad men." It is, in part, his aversion to the British agenda that leads him in the seventh installment to reject a recent British proposal that would accede to the colonists' demands without granting them independence.

Surrender of Colonel Rall at the Battle of Trenton, 1776, a painting by Alonzo Chappel (1828–1887), celebrates the victory of George Washington's army at the Battle of Trenton. Washington read Thomas Paine's The American Crisis to his troops, and it was credited with inspiring his retreating, demoralized army to rally and win this important battle of the American Revolution. Chicago History Museum, Chicago, IL, U.S.A. © UNIVERSAL IMAGES GROUP/ART RESOURCE, NY

CRITICAL DISCUSSION

When it first appeared, *The American Crisis* was embraced by both troops and citizens who were in need of reassurance in the face of a military crisis. In the decades following the war, however, Paine fell out of favor, largely because of his outspoken criticism of religion, and by the time of his death in 1809, his reputation had declined significantly. In the late nineteenth century, biographer Moncure Daniel Conway worked to collect Paine's works and reclaim the author's reputation, and by the end of the twentieth century, his place in American history and literature was restored.

The American Crisis has been widely studied by scholars of history and rhetoric, but it has never attracted the degree of attention paid to *Common Sense*. Aldridge suggests that one reason for the relative dearth of criticism treating *The American Crisis* is that the work "concerns itself primarily with events and circumstances in the military and diplomatic struggle and devotes relatively little attention to ideology." Aldridge goes on to argue that, collectively, the essays that make up *The American Crisis* "have more in common with exhortatory sermons than with political essays" but that they continue the themes of *Common Sense*, most notably "the uniqueness of America and its favored status in the divine dispensation." Aldridge also suggests that *The American Crisis* is of particular interest because, in it, "Paine writes as a full-fledged American and addresses himself to particular problems and policies of his country and his countrymen."

Studies of *The American Crisis* have tended to focus primarily on its opening essay. In an article in the *Explicator*, for example, Edward J. Gallagher examines the role of time in the first installment, arguing that Paine carefully orchestrated the essay's paragraphs to move from present, to past, to future in such a way that readers would understand that their current problems had been faced and overcome by others and that they, too, should persevere and anticipate a better future. The effect, Gallagher suggests, is that the essay "wrap[s] people in the comfort of time, something that panic and confusion had robbed them of."

Scholars have also examined *The American Crisis* in relation to *Common Sense*. In an article in *Studies in the Humanities*, Edward H. Davidson argues that these two works offer insight into Paine's later writings on religion, noting that both explore the relationship between religion and politics. Davidson suggests, however, that in attempting to offer a religious grounding for American political and military actions, Paine ends up presenting himself as "a biblically-authorized spokesman for nearly everything that the American cause declared," despite building much of his argument against the king of England on similar grounds. Elsewhere, Martin Roth argues in an article in *Early American Literature* that both of these influential works are "strangely personal," offering images of "men who are lost in a space beyond the solace of friendship or love, beyond the support of any community," an image, Roth suggests, that can be traced in the works of later American authors such as Herman Melville, Mark Twain, and William Faulkner.

SOURCES

Aldridge, Alfred Owen. *Thomas Paine's American Ideology.* Cranbury: Associated UP, 1984. Print.

Davidson, Edward H. "Authority in Paine's *Common Sense* and *Crisis Papers*." *Studies in the Humanities* 18.2 (1991): 124–34. Print.

Gallagher, Edward J. "Thomas Paine's CRISIS 1 and the Comfort of Time." *Explicator* 68.2 (2010): 87–89. Print.

Paine, Thomas. "The American Crisis." *Writings of Thomas Paine*. Ed. Moncure Daniel Conway. Vol. 1. New York: AMS, 1967. 168–380. Print.

Roth, Martin. "Tom Paine and American Loneliness." *Early American Literature* 22.2 (1987): 175–82. Print.

FURTHER READING

Aldridge, A. Owen. "The *Crisis*." *Thomas Paine's American Ideology*. Newark: U of Delaware P, 1984. 240–53. Print.

Bailyn, Bernard. *The Ideological Origins of the American Revolution*. Cambridge: Harvard UP, 1967. Print.

Cowell, Pattie. "Knowledge and Power: Cultural Scripts in Early America." *American Literary History* 4.2 (1992): 337–44. Print.

Foner, Eric. *Tom Paine and Revolutionary America*. New York: Oxford UP, 2005. Print.

Keane, John. *Tom Paine: A Political Life*. London: Bloomsbury, 1995. Print.

Larkin, Edward. *Thomas Paine and the Literature of Revolution*. New York: Cambridge UP, 2005. Print.

Warner, Michael. *The Letters of the Republic: Publication and the Public Sphere in Eighteenth-Century America*. Cambridge: Harvard UP, 1990. Print.

Greta Gard

"Astraea Victrix," "The Transvaal," and "A Word for the Navy"

Algernon Charles Swinburne

OVERVIEW

Published separately in the London *Times* newspaper during the Second Boer War (1899–1902), Algernon Charles Swinburne's "The Transvaal," "A Word for the Navy," and "Astraea Victrix" are among the best-known poems treating the conflict. Considered collectively, the poems, which were later published in *A Channel Passage and Other Poems* (1904), glorify Great Britain's history, valorize its imperial aspirations, and justify the war as a defense of British values such as justice and freedom. Although a number of prominent British poets wrote patriotic verses in support of the war, Swinburne's are among the most vitriolic and jingoistic. His poems celebrate the military and cultural traditions of England's past and disparage as godless animals those perceived to challenge the nation's objectives.

The poems' rhetoric and staunch defense of colonialism have made them unpopular with modern readers and scholars. Although they are frequently referenced as examples of nationalistic and pro-imperial poetry, they are largely ignored as works of literature and are frequently excluded from discussions of Swinburne's body of work. Few scholars would deny, however, that Swinburne's Boer War poems are an important reflection of a once widely embraced view of Britain's superiority and entitlement to global power at the turn of the twentieth century.

HISTORICAL AND LITERARY CONTEXT

"The Transvaal," "A Word for the Navy," and "Astraea Victrix" react to an imperial war that Britain fought in what is now South Africa. The war, which was also commonly known as the Second South African War, began in 1899, during the height of British imperialism. The British Empire then included not only the countries of the early twentieth-century United Kingdom (England, Scotland, Wales, and Ireland) but also Australia, India, and parts of Africa. With territory around the globe, Britain was the major world power of the day. British colonial aspirations were driven not only by the desire for additional territory but also by the commonly held conviction that England was bringing progress to other parts of the world by extending its technology, knowledge, and values across the globe.

The Second Boer War broke out in October 1899 with Great Britain sending troops to the African continent to fight against the armies of two Dutch Boer Republics: the Orange Free State and the South African Republic, or Transvaal. The war grew out of simmering tensions between the governments of the Boer Republics and British settlers who had come to the region after the discovery of diamonds there in the 1860s. Over time the settlers came to resent their exclusion from the franchise and their high rate of taxation.

When these tensions erupted in violence, Britain entered the fray on the side of the settlers, demonstrating its imperial might by sending a large military force to the Transvaal. In addition, Australia, New Zealand, Canada, and South Africa itself all contributed troops in support of the British cause. The British were surprised, however, at the martial skill of the Boers, who used the limited weaponry available to them and their knowledge of the region's difficult terrain to strategic advantage. Britain eventually sent more than 450,000 men to the Transvaal, and both sides suffered heavy losses. Eventually, the Boers succumbed to Britain's stronger and larger military, and the Transvaal and the Orange Free State became official colonies of Great Britain.

Despite its victory and imperial expansion, Britain faced a backlash over its use of concentration camps, in which more than twenty thousand Boer civilians, many of them children, had died from malnutrition and disease during the war. These atrocities, however, did not become common knowledge until late in the war, when journalists brought the plight of concentration camp inmates to the attention of the British public.

At the outset of the war, many in Britain saw the conflict as a defense of British citizens and interests abroad. Swinburne was one of several well-known British poets who wrote in support of the war and of British imperialism more generally. Other notable pro-war authors of the period include Rudyard Kipling (1865–1936) and William Ernest Henley (1849–1902), whose nationalistic poem "Pro Rege Nostro" (1900) was subsequently used as propaganda during World War I. Swinburne wrote several other

✣ Key Facts

Conflict:
Second Boer War

Time Period:
Late 19th Century

Genre:
Poetry

BOER WAR CONCENTRATION CAMPS

Swinburne's depiction in his poems of the Boers as savage animals is evidence of the rhetoric that fueled wartime atrocities. Among the most egregious of the Second Boer War's acts of brutality was the imprisonment of Boer civilians in concentration camps.

Very little food was provided to inmates (who were predominantly women and children), and the meager rations were reduced for those whose family members were involved in combat. Malnutrition, coupled with the lack of proper sanitation in the camps, led to rampant illness. It is believed that roughly 28,000 Boers, the majority of them children, died as a result of conditions in the camps.

The atrocities of the concentration camps might not have been exposed had it not been for Emily Hobhouse, a delegate of the South African Women and Children's Distress Fund sent from England to tour the camps. Hobhouse's detailed reports of what she witnessed quickly spread in the British press, causing outrage.

Revelations of camp conditions resulted in the formation of the Fawcett Commission, which, upon verifying Hobhouse's account, demanded reform. Although the resulting ameliorations greatly reduced mortality rates, British public opinion had soured towards the war, and today the treatment of the Boers at that time is widely viewed in Britain as a point of national shame.

patriotic poems about the Second Boer War, most notably "On the Death of Colonel Benson," which mourns the death of a British officer famous for his heroism during the war.

Not all British civilians supported the conflict, however, and some were openly critical of both the war and the desire for empire that was seen as its driving force. Novelist and poet Thomas Hardy wrote a number of antiwar verses, the best known of which is "Drummer Hodge," a poem that criticizes Britain's willingness to sacrifice its working class as soldiers in order to achieve its imperial goals.

THEMES AND STYLE

Swinburne's Boer War poems vary in length and form. The shortest and best known of the three, "The Transvaal," is a Petrarchan sonnet, a fourteen-line poem with a traditional (though slightly variable) rhyme scheme. "A Word for the Navy," a much longer poem, is made up of twelve numbered octaves, while "Astraea Victrix," another longer poem, comprises twelve stanzas, each of which follows a rhyme scheme of *aabccbdd*. This somewhat unusual rhyme scheme would have been most clearly recognizable in the period as that of John Milton's ode "On the Morning of Christ's Nativity." Swinburne's use of traditional poetic forms helps to reinforce his poems' message that the Boer War carries on a proud tradition of British cultural as well as military superiority.

All three poems emphasize England's history as a unique and cultured nation, favored by God and marked by the love of freedom. The opening stanza of "Astraea Victrix" presents an example of Swinburne's glorification of England:

> England, elect of time,
> By freedom sealed sublime,
> And constant as the sun that saw thy dawn

> Outshine upon the sea
> His own in heaven, to be
> A light that night nor day should see
>   withdrawn,
> If song may speak not now thy praise,
> Fame writes it higher than song may soar or
>   faith may gaze.

Similarly, "A Word for the Navy" describes the country as "Bright England, whose glories adorn her." "The Transvaal" repeatedly stresses England's historical investment in freedom and justice, describing the nation as "a commonweal that brooked no wrong."

This latter quality in particular is repeatedly used in all three poems to justify the war. It is Britain's moral duty, the poems collectively suggest, to stand up to the Boers, who are alternately depicted as "heartless hounds of hatred" ("Astraea Victrix") and "dogs, agape with jaws afoam" ("The Transvaal"). In defending British settlers in Africa from the Boers, "Astraea Victrix" suggests, Britain is striking a blow against "murderous fraud that lurks / In hearts where hell's craft works." Britain's courageous decision to reclaim her role as an advocate of justice, the poem declares, "brings back power and pride" to the nation and its people.

Swinburne's poems draw extensively on the British military and literary traditions they revere. The most famous line of "The Transvaal," "Strike, England, and strike home!" is borrowed from baroque composer Henry Purcell's "Britons, Strike Home," a selection from the 1695 opera *Bonduca, or the British Heroine*. The opera, an adaptation of an early seventeenth-century play attributed to John Fletcher, tells the story of a first-century Celtic queen, Boudica, leading a revolt against the Romans. The invocation of Boudica furthers the poem's emphasis on Britain's longstanding status as a defender of liberty.

Indeed, all three poems suggest that Britain ought to embrace its history of militarism and exploration. In "Astraea Victrix" Swinburne describes England's entry into the war as stemming from the nation feeling "her future kindle from her fiery past." In "The Transvaal" he calls for a return to the time of Oliver Cromwell (1599–1658), who used his abilities as a political and military strategist to overthrow the British monarchy in favor of a briefly lived British republic. "A Word for the Navy" similarly celebrates the contributions of men such as famed naval commander Sir Francis Drake (1540–96), Admiral Robert Blake (1598–1657), who is widely credited with ushering in an era of British naval supremacy, and Royal Navy officer Horatio Nelson (1758–1805), who won fame during the Napoleonic Wars (1803–15).

By calling to mind major conflicts of England's history, these poems position the war in faraway South Africa as a battle for the very future of Britain and British culture.

CRITICAL DISCUSSION

At the time they were initially published, Swinburne's poems received mixed reviews from his contemporaries. While some were moved by their patriotic rhetoric, others were troubled by their bitter and violent tone. When "The Transvaal" first appeared in the *Times*, for example, it provoked an outpouring of letters from readers reacting against Swinburne's stance. Frederick Courteney Selous, an explorer who had traveled widely in Africa, complained in one such letter to the *Times* that the poem "seems to have been written with the sole object of embittering feelings in this country against the South African Dutch." Reviewing *A Channel Passage* in *Academy and Literature* in 1904, Francis Thompson praised Swinburne's "metrical faculty" but complained that "rhetoric and invective, reinless and redundant, quite usurp the place of poetry" in the patriotic war poems.

Thompson's view of the Boer War poems as propaganda rather than poetry continues today. Although modern scholars consider Swinburne an important poet of the late Victorian period, none of the poems he wrote about the conflict are considered among his most esteemed works, and they are frequently omitted even from book-length discussions of his poetry. Very little scholarly attention has been devoted to analyzing the poems as serious works of literature, or independent of other works of the period. Where they are cited, it is primarily as the most egregious examples of literary jingoism to emerge from the war.

In his book *Drummer Hodge*, for example, M. van Wyk Smith describes Swinburne's war poetry as "illustrative of the culture of violence which accompanied the imperialist ideologies of the time" and suggests that they are "symptomatic of a profound insecurity and lack of focus in the imperial dream itself." Similarly, Kathryn R. King and William W. Morgan, in their essay in *Victorian Poetry*, consider "The Transvaal" in particular to be an example of Boer War poetry that "both appealed to and inflamed the aggressive nationalism which nourished a lust for conquest." Describing the poem as "unusually nasty in tone," King and Morgan suggest that it is otherwise marked by typical conventions of war poetry: "the abuse of the enemy, the celebration of power and might with the suggestion that the manly English spirit fulfills itself through the conquest of lesser peoples; and the appeal to a more militaristic English past."

Scholars have frequently discussed the poems in the context of other poems from the era that supported imperialism and defended or encouraged war. For instance, van Wyk Smith has compared the poems to Sir Henry Newbolt's poems "Clifton Chapel" (1899) and "Vitaï Lampada" (1897), both of which took a similar, though less vitriolic, stance toward empire and were widely used as propaganda during World War I. King and Morgan use Swinburne's poems as a point of contrast to the anti-Boer War poems of Thomas Hardy, who was openly critical of Swinburne's "The Transvaal."

Charles J. de Lacy's painting *Troops Leaving Southampton for Second Boer War, 1899–1902,* celebrates the British navy, as does Algernon Swinburne's poem "A Word for the Navy." © CHARLES DELACY / EILEEN TWEEDY / THE ART ARCHIVE / THE PICTURE DESK, INC.

SOURCES

King, Kathryn K., and William W. Morgan. "Hardy and the Boer War: The Public Poet in Spite of Himself." *Victorian Poetry* 17.1/2 (1979): 66–83. Print.

Selous, Frederick Courteney. *The War in South Africa: Letters Contributed to the "Times" by Mr. F.C. Selous, the Well-Known Traveller and Sportsman.* London: National Press, 1899. Print.

Swinburne, Algernon Charles. "Astraea Victrix." *A Channel Passage and Other Poems.* London: Chatto, 1904. 160–65. Print.

———. "The Transvaal." *A Channel Passage and Other Poems.* London: Chatto, 1904. 156. Print.

———. "A Word to the Navy." *A Channel Passage and Other Poems.* London: Chatto, 1904. 95–101. Print.

Thompson, Francis. Rev. of *A Channel Passage and Other Poems*, by Algernon Charles Swinburne. *Academy and Literature* 17 Sept. 1904: 196. Print.

Van Wyk Smith, M. *Drummer Hodge: The Poetry of the Anglo-Boer War (1899–1902).* Oxford: Clarendon, 1978. Print.

FURTHER READING

Doyle, Arthur Conan. *The Great Boer War.* Alberton: Galago, 2005. Print.

Franey, Laura E. *Victorian Travel Writing and Imperial Violence: British Writing on Africa, 1855–1902.* Basingstoke: Palgrave, 2003. Print.

Fremont-Barnes, Gregory. *The Boer War 1899–1902.* Oxford: Osprey, 2003. Print.

Krebs Paula M. *Gender, Race, and the Writings of Empire: Public Discourse and the Boer War.* Cambridge: Cambridge UP, 1999. Print.

Maxwell, Catherine. *Swinburne.* Tavistock: Northcote, 2006. Print.

Robinson, Ronald Edward. *Africa and the Victorians: The Official Mind of Imperialism.* London: Macmillan, 1981. Print.

Swinburne, Algernon Charles. *Algernon Charles Swinburne: Major Poems and Selected Prose.* New Haven: Yale UP, 2004. Print.

Greta Gard

AUTHORS TAKE SIDES ON THE SPANISH WAR

W. H. Auden, Nancy Cunard, Stephen Spender, Et. al.

OVERVIEW

Authors Take Sides on the Spanish War (1937) is a political pamphlet, published in Great Britain, that contains the opinions of 148 well-known writers on the Spanish Civil War, which began in 1936. Organized by heiress and writer Nancy Cunard and poets W. H. Auden and Stephen Spender, among others, the publication provided a forum for writers to declare their allegiance to either the democratically elected government of the Second Spanish Republic or the right-wing rebel army led by General Francisco Franco, which was attempting a coup d'état. Cunard and her associates, supporters of the Republican cause, mailed a questionnaire to hundreds of British, Scottish, and Irish writers, asking, "Are you for, or against, the legal Government and the People of Republican Spain? Are you for, or against, Franco and Fascism? For it is impossible any longer to take no side." The editors culled the responses and published 148 of them. The overwhelming majority of the respondents pledged support for the Spanish government and decried the evils of Fascism. Sixteen writers, including poets T.S. Eliot and Ezra Pound, took a stand the editors classified as neutral, and five writers, Evelyn Waugh the most prominent among them, supported Franco. A publisher's note preceding the text indicates that all neutral and pro-Franco opinions were included in the publication but that pro-government responses were so numerous that several had to be omitted.

At the time of its publication, the pamphlet was influential in the wider public debate about the threat of Fascism and the possible consequences of the Spanish Civil War for the rest of Europe. The document remains of interest to historians of the literary and intellectual culture of 1930s Great Britain.

HISTORICAL AND LITERARY CONTEXT

The Spanish Civil War began in 1936 as a military coup led by General Francisco Franco to overthrow the elected government of the Second Spanish Republic. The rebel forces—or Nationalists, as they called themselves—represented several right-wing groups, including conservative Catholics, monarchists, and Fascists seeking to create a single-party, totalitarian state. These forces received military aid from the German government under Adolf Hitler and from Benito

Mussolini's government in Italy. The defenders of the Second Spanish Republic, known collectively as the Popular Front, consisted of anarchists, Marxists, and liberal democrats. The Spanish government was supported by the Soviet Union, which was then led by Joseph Stalin, and by volunteer units from across Europe and the United States known as the International Brigades. Historians estimate that approximately thirty five thousand volunteers from fifty-three countries traveled to Spain to defend the government and stop the spread of Fascism. While Great Britain, France, and the United States officially took neutral positions, most of the volunteers in the International Brigades came from these three countries.

Initially the coup met with effective resistance from the Republican forces, especially in the country's major population centers. General Franco waged a violent war of attrition, however, and frequently engaged in high-profile attacks on civilians, most notably the bombing of Guernica on April 26, 1937, which killed between 200 and 300 non-combatants. The *Authors Take Sides on the Spanish War* pamphlet was circulated two months after this event. While such attacks provoked outrage in intellectual circles and aroused international sympathy for the Republican forces, Britain and France began encouraging their most prominent volunteers to withdraw from the fighting because many promising younger volunteers had been killed by Franco's forces. As the war continued, the Soviet military equipment proved expensive and unreliable, and the various factions backing the Second Republic succumbed to infighting when Stalin began purging volunteers he suspected of being disloyal to the Soviet Union. Republican morale also suffered considerably in 1938 when Great Britain and France permitted Hitler to annex the northern, western, and southwestern regions of Czechoslovakia. Franco won decisive victories in Catalonia and Tarragona in January 1939, and on February 27 Great Britain and France recognized him as the leader of Spain. Although the fighting continued, hundreds of thousands of Republicans fled Spain, and the last of the defending forces surrendered to Franco on April 1, 1939.

Throughout the war leftist writers, artists, and intellectuals from Great Britain strongly supported

✣ *Key Facts*

Conflict:
Spanish Civil War

Time Period:
Mid-20th Century

Genre:
Pamphlet

NANCY CUNARD AND THE SPANISH CIVIL WAR

Nancy Cunard, the driving force behind the assembly and publication of *Authors Take Sides*, openly supported the Spanish Republican forces against Franco's Nationalists. Although Cunard was an heiress, poet, fashion plate, and an intimate of many of the best-known modernist writers and artists in interwar London and Paris, her position on the Spanish Civil War was not the product of ivory-tower detachment. As Lois G. Gordon writes in *Nancy Cunard: Heiress, Muse, Political Idealist*, as soon as the war broke out in Spain, Cunard traveled to the front lines as a journalist:

> She reported for a number of newspapers, determined to cover the war firsthand, initially in Barcelona and its neighboring fronts, and then in Madrid and the war zones surrounding it. She left the cities and made her way to the battlegrounds by riding with local truck drivers as far as they would take her. Then she walked long distances, often in heavy rain, snow, or under enemy fire, to reach the fronts. While covering the war, she also engaged in humanitarian activities that similarly exposed her to grave danger. She gave aid to war-ravaged and starving soldiers and civilians by moving them to safety and distributing food and supplies.

Cunard initially wrote and acted in the belief that intervention by the governments of France, Great Britain, and the United States might yet prevent the world war that was then looming, and then as the Republican cause was lost, she remained in Spain after most other journalists had left. During 1939 she uncovered historically significant evidence of the French government's complicity with the Francoist government, including France's help in maintaining concentration camps to which Spanish Republicans were being sent.

the Republicans in Spain. In such circles, intervening against Franco was seen as crucial to stopping the spread of Fascism across Europe, and the Republican cause united factions on the British left that were otherwise opposed to one another. Among the writers affiliated with the Communist-oriented *Left Review* journal, which backed the publication of *Authors Take Sides on the Spanish War*, Fascism was generally considered an outgrowth of capitalism, and the civil war was seen as a way for Spanish peasants and workers to continue the Communist revolution. Intellectuals of the center left, many of whom responded to the prompts of Cunard and her associates, agreed on the necessity of fighting Fascism but remained wary of Communist objectives and of the Soviet Union's involvement in the Spanish Civil War. Thus, *Authors Take Sides on the Spanish War* was in part an attempt to demonstrate that, in spite of their many political differences, the country's writers and intellectuals overwhelmingly agreed on the need to intervene on behalf of the Republicans.

Among intellectuals, the enthusiasm for armed intervention in Spain was influenced by lingering memories of World War I. Leftist opposition to the Great War had been primarily pacifist in orientation, but these arguments had ultimately failed to influence government policy. The experience of pacifism's failure, together with an apprehension that the regimes in Germany, Italy, and Spain were intent on total domination of Europe and could not be resisted by any peaceful means, had by 1937 led many socialists and others on the left to adopt the belief that war against fascism was both justifiable

and necessary. Many well-known writers and intellectuals, most famously George Orwell and Ernest Hemingway, volunteered on behalf of the Spanish Republicans, and a number of others contributed eyewitness accounts of the fighting to prominent periodicals.

THEMES AND STYLE

Authors Take Sides on the Spanish War is a short pamphlet of approximately ten thousand words that is divided into four sections. The first section, "THE QUESTION," presents the questionnaire that was mailed to British writers. It begins by arguing that, given the advances of fascism, "the Ivory Tower, the paradoxical, the ironic detachment, will no longer do" and that writers must take sides. The following three parts of the pamphlet are separated into pro-government, neutral, and pro-Franco responses. In the second part, titled "For the Government," many respondents state their opposition to fascism and argue that this ideology threatens to undermine civilization as a whole. For example, Marcus Garvey calls fascism "the cult of organized murder" and says that Hitler and Mussolini "are playing hell with civilization." Oswell Blakeston writes, "Fascism is what men used to call 'original sin,' It is the essential core of evil in all of us. If we can rid the world of Fascism, we may know what men used to call heaven. If we do not, we will get our Hell as others have already found theirs." The philosopher C. E. M. Joad pointedly declares that "the success of Fascism is the collapse of civilization and the relapse into barbarism." Others, such as W. H. Auden, note the threat a Franco victory presents to the rest of Europe. "I support the Valencia government in

Spain because its defeat by the forces of International Fascism would be a major disaster for Europe." Likewise, Gerald Bullett writes that a Franco victory will "mark the end of freedom and civilization in Europe."

Some respondents link fascism to capitalism and note that Britain, France, and the United States participate in the same cruel system that was in place in Germany and Italy. For example, Leonard Barnes claims that "Fascism in Italy and Germany is largely the outcome of policies pursued by capitalist interests and Governments in Britain, France, and America. Moreover, British rule in India and Africa is a form of Fascism just as barbarous as the German or Italian." Liam O'Flaherty also makes a connection between Fascism and British colonial policy. He writes, "I am for the legal government and the people of republican Spain against Franco and Fascism. As an Irishman, I realize that the toiling masses of Spain are waging the same struggle which we have waged for centuries in Ireland against landlordism and foreign imperialism." Still other writers, perhaps suggesting that the reasons for siding against Franco were too obvious to require explanation, offer direct expressions of support without supplying their rationale. These include Samuel Beckett, whose complete response is, "¡UPTHEREPUBLIC!" and the novelist Rose Macaulay, who writes, "AGAINST FRANCO." The inverted exclamation point that opens Beckett's response imitates the Spanish style of punctuation and thus emphasizes his support for the legal government.

The third section of the pamphlet records the responses of those writers whose opinions, contrary to the compilers' claims that the Spanish Civil War required one to take sides, fall under the heading "NEUTRAL?" Of the seventeen responses in this section, perhaps the most noteworthy are those of modernist poets T. S. Eliot and Ezra Pound. Eliot, a political conservative, writes, "While I am naturally sympathetic, I still feel convinced that it is best that at least a few men of letters should remain isolated, and take no part in these collective activities." On the other hand, Pound, who while living in Italy became a supporter of Benito Mussolini and who later circulated anti-Semitic and anti-American radio broadcasts on behalf of the Axis powers during World War II, responds, "Questionnaire an escape mechanism for young fools who are too cowardly to think; too lazy to investigate the nature of money, its mode of issue, the control of such issue by the Banque de France and the stank of England. You are all had. Spain is an emotional luxury to a gang of sap-headed dilettantes."

The final section of *Authors Take Sides on the Spanish War* presents the contributions of five writers who were willing to voice their support for the Franco regime. The most prominent figure among these respondents is the satirical novelist Evelyn Waugh, a social conservative and Catholic convert. He declares, "I am no more impressed by the 'legality' of the [Republican] Government than are English

Communists by the legality of the Crown, Lords and Commons. I believe it was a bad Government, rapidly deteriorating. If I were a Spaniard I should be fighting for General Franco ... I am not a fascist nor shall I become one unless it were the only alternative to Marxism." Prior to the start of the Spanish Civil War, Waugh had completed a biography of Jesuit martyr Edmund Campion and written a series of essays commending Mussolini for his conquest of Abyssinia (now Ethiopia).

CRITICAL RECEPTION

Authors Take Sides on the Spanish War was effective as a public relations tool, a demonstration that writers and other left-wing intellectuals overwhelmingly supported the Republican government in Spain. Although that government eventually fell to Franco in 1939, the Republican cause nevertheless retained an aura of nobility, which was due in no small part to the central role that the Spanish Civil War played in the intellectual life of writers and artists who contributed to the pamphlet. According to Eric Hobsbawm, in a 2007 retrospective on the International Brigades published in the *Guardian*, "Writers supported Spain not only with money, speech and signatures, but they wrote about it, as Hemingway, Malraux, Bernanos and virtually all the notable contemporary young British poets—Auden, Spender, Day-Lewis, MacNeice—did. Spain was the experience that was central to their lives between 1936 and 1939, even if they later kept it out of sight." The pamphlet's success in documenting writers' political views made it a template for later attempts to mobilize writers and intellectuals in political debate. Among copycat projects in the years since its publication are *Authors Take Sides on Vietnam* (1967), edited by Cecil Woolf and John Bagguley, and *Authors Take Sides: Iraq and the Gulf War* (2004), edited by Woolf and Jean Moorcroft Wilson.

In academia the pamphlet primarily remains of interest to historians and literary scholars of the period. Angela Jackson, in *British Women and the Spanish Civil War* (2002), details Cunard's role in bringing *Authors Take Sides on the Spanish War* to fruition and provides valuable contextual information. Tom Buchanan discusses the project's broader relationship to British intellectual life in *Britain and the Spanish Civil War* (1997), as does James K. Hopkins in *Into the Heart of the Fire* (1998). Hopkins specifically addresses the involvement of Orwell, whose response was omitted from the pamphlet. Valentine Cunningham's *Spanish Front: Writers on the Civil War* (1986) records the responses to the Spanish Civil War of additional writers, including Graham Greene, John Dos Passos, Leon Trotsky, and Orwell. Like Hopkins, Cunningham finds Orwell's views particularly important, given the writer's experiences fighting in the Spanish Civil War with a Communist militia called the Workers' Party of Marxist Unification (Partido Obrero de Unificación Marxista, POUM). Orwell

was forced to flee Spain when Stalin designated the party hostile to his ideals and began executing its members. When he returned to Britain in 1937, Orwell alienated many leftist British intellectuals with his critical view of communism.

SOURCES

Authors Take Sides on the Spanish War. London: Left Review, 1937. Print.

Buchanan, Tom. *Britain and the Spanish Civil War*. Cambridge: Cambridge UP, 1997. Print.

Cunningham, Valentine. *Spanish Front: Writers on the Civil War*. New York: Oxford UP, 1986. Print.

Hobsbawm, Eric. "War of Ideas." *Guardian*. Guardian News and Media, 16 Feb. 2007. Web. 19 Dec. 2011.

Hopkins, James K. *Into the Heart of the Fire: The British in the Spanish Civil War*. Stanford: Stanford UP, 1998. Print.

Jackson, Angela. *British Women and the Spanish Civil War*. London: Routledge, 2002. Print.

FURTHER READING

Buchanan, Tom. *The Impact of the Spanish Civil War on Britain: War, Loss and Memory*. Eastbourne: Sussex Academic, 2007. Print.

Gordon, Lois G. *Nancy Cunard: Heiress, Muse, Political Idealist*. New York: Columbia UP, 2007. Print.

Monteath, Peter. *The Spanish Civil War in Literature, Film, and Art: An International Bibliography*. Westport: Greenwood, 1994. Print.

Woolf, Cecil, and John Bagguley, eds. *Authors Take Sides on Vietnam*. New York: Simon, 1967. Print.

Woolf, Cecil, and Jean Moorcroft Wilson, eds. *Authors Take Sides: Iraq and the Gulf War*. Melbourne: Melbourne UP, 2004. Print.

Mark Lane

"BATTLE HYMN OF THE REPUBLIC"

Julia Ward Howe

OVERVIEW

Written in November 1861 during the first year of the American Civil War (1861–65), Julia Ward Howe's "The Battle Hymn of the Republic" is one of the best-known pieces of writing to emerge from the conflict and one of the most celebrated war songs of all time. The hymn was published in the *Atlantic Monthly* in February 1862, with the magazine's editor, James T. Fields, providing its title. It was soon widely reprinted and embraced by Union soldiers.

Before Howe wrote her famous lyrics, the tune and chorus ("Glory, glory, hallelujah!") were associated with several songs, most notably the marching song "John Brown's Body," which, though popular, was considered by many to have unsettling lyrics. Howe reported that she was inspired to write new lyrics for the song during a trip to Washington, D.C. in 1861. In her autobiographical *Reminiscences* (1899), she attributes the impetus to Unitarian minister James Freeman Clarke, who heard her singing "John Brown's Body" and suggested she write more appealing lyrics. She relates that she awoke early in the morning with the words of the hymn in her head and quickly wrote them down. Over time, the story of the hymn's composition has been elevated to near-mythic status and has been the subject of much commentary.

Drawing on biblical and martial imagery, the hymn likens the war to a holy crusade and valorizes service and death for the cause of abolition. More so than many other songs of the Civil War, "The Battle Hymn of the Republic" endured well beyond the conflict. It was popular during subsequent military struggles that include the Spanish-American War (1898), World War I (1914–18), and World War II (1939–45) and was prominent in memorial services for those whose lives were lost in the September 11, 2001, terrorist attacks on the United States.

HISTORICAL AND LITERARY CONTEXT

"The Battle Hymn of the Republic" is remembered as an important cultural artifact of the Civil War, in which music played an important role in military pomp and tradition. Army bands on both sides of the conflict were used to inspire enlistment and to lift the morale of the soldiers. In the North in particular, these bands often included as many as twenty-four members and an assortment of brass, woodwind, and percussion instruments. In addition to marching songs, troops often sang popular ballads as a way to reminisce about their homes and families. Some of these songs were favorites among both the Confederate and Union armies and often could be heard coming from both camps in the evening, after the day's battles were over.

Howe's hymn was written in the fall of 1861, a time when Union losses were high and morale was low. When the war had begun in April of that year, the North was full of confidence, and many believed that the war would result in a swift Union victory. After a decisive and bloody defeat at the First Battle of Bull Run (July 21, 1861), however, optimism was beginning to evaporate, and the nation was faced with the reality that the war would likely be lengthy and the loss of life significant. With morale in decline, Howe's hymn, with its insistence on the divine blessing of the Union cause, quickly became a favorite. It gained so much fame that it was sung in the U.S. House of Representatives in 1863, where it is said to have deeply moved President Abraham Lincoln.

The music of "The Battle Hymn of the Republic" predated Howe's lyrics, initially having been written in 1858 by Thomas Brigham Bishop (1835–1905), a songwriter known for his work with minstrel shows. At the time Howe wrote her lyrics, the tune was best known as "John Brown's Body." Brown, a militant abolitionist who had been executed after leading a failed raid on a federal arsenal at Harper's Ferry in what is now West Virginia, was a rallying point for the Union cause. Howe's husband had contributed financially to Brown's cause, and she had met the abolitionist personally shortly before the failed raid. She held a great deal of admiration for him.

Although "John Brown's Body" was often sung by Union soldiers early in the war, many were displeased with its lyrics, which were thought to be somewhat uncouth ("John Brown's body lies a-mouldering in the grave"). "John Brown's Body" provided not only the tune and the chorus for Howe's hymn but also much of the theme. Most versions of the John Brown lyrics include the idea of "marching on," most explicitly in the assertion that Brown's "soul's marching on." This idea was incorporated by Howe, who replaced Brown with Christ.

In addition to remaining a favorite patriotic song, Howe's hymn has had a lasting impact on American

✥ *Key Facts*

Conflict:
American Civil War

Time Period:
Mid-19th Century

Genre:
Song

CLOUDSPLITTER: THE HUMANIZING OF A LEGEND

Inspired in part by "The Battle Hymn of the Republic," the song that became the rallying cry of the Union army, Russell Banks's novel *Cloudsplitter* (1997) offers a fictional portrayal of radical abolitionist John Brown, told from the perspective of Brown's son Owen. In the course of the narrative, *Cloudsplitter* delves into Brown's violent activities in the years preceding the Civil War, from his efforts to combat proslavery forces in Kansas to his death (which some see as martyrdom) during the raid at Harper's Ferry.

The novel deviates from actual history at numerous points, notably in its portrait of Owen. Although the real Owen Brown survived the raid merely by chance, Banks frames it as a form of personal failure, in which the narrator's inability to act ultimately seals his fate. In portraying Owen's inability to join the raid at Harper's Ferry as an instance of failure—one that spares him certain death while also forcing him to carry his guilt for the remainder of his life—Banks adds an element of human frailty to the now-mythic aspects of Brown's historic raid. In the end, however, Owen is redeemed as his memories of the tragic events become the authoritative source for Brown's true historical legacy.

literature and culture. Most notably, John Steinbeck's 1939 novel *The Grapes of Wrath* and John Updike's 1996 book *In the Beauty of the Lilies* take their titles from lines in the hymn. The poem's famous opening line, "Mine eyes have seen the glory of the coming of the Lord," also provided the closing line of Martin Luther King Jr.'s final public sermon, "I've Been to the Mountaintop," which was delivered on the eve of his assassination in 1968.

THEMES AND STYLE

"The Battle Hymn of the Republic" is made up of six verses plus a chorus that changes slightly between verses. The sixth verse, which was not included when the hymn was first published in the *Atlantic Monthly* in 1862, is not as well known as the other five verses and is often not included when the song is performed. Each verse comprises a quatrain, or four lines, with the final line repeating as the final line of the chorus that follows the verse. This line changes slightly from one verse to the next: "His truth is marching on," "His day is marching on," "Since God is marching on," "Our God is marching on," and "While God is marching on." The sixth verse closes with the same line as the fourth.

The central theme of "The Battle Hymn of the Republic" is that the cause of the Union army is just and mandated by God, who has "sounded forth the trumpet that shall never call retreat." The poem thus presents the army as the vessel through which God marches on, just as the soldiers and abolitionists in

"John Brown's Body" were the means through which the martyred Brown's soul would march on.

The second verse of Howe's hymn explicitly connects God to the Civil War soldiers in asserting, "I have seen Him in the watch-fires of a hundred circling camps, / They have builded him an altar in the evening dews and damps; / I can read His righteous sentence by the dim and flaring lamps: / His day is marching on." While Howe repeatedly emphasizes the divine mission of the Union, the Confederate army and its supporters are repeatedly represented as anti-Christian. They are "contemners" of the Lord, whom the Union army is encouraged to kill in God's name, and are associated with the devil through the image of the serpent, which was associated with both.

The hymn draws repeatedly on imagery from the Bible. Scholars have often noted that the Lord in the first four verses is most clearly associated with the vengeful God of the Old Testament, marked by "His terrible swift sword" and his role in "sifting out the heart of men before His judgment-seat." In contrast, the final two verses reflect the redemptive love of Christ, who has "a glory in His bosom that transfigures you and me," providing "Wisdom to the mighty" and "Succour to the brave."

The hymn repeatedly celebrates devotion to the cause at any cost. This is especially evident in lines encouraging enlistment ("Oh, be swift, my soul, to answer Him! Be jubilant, my feet!") and even death ("As He died to make men holy, let us die to make men free"). That the author of the hymn was a woman, who would not fight or die for her country, to some degree complicates this message. Howe later explained that she had desperately wanted to help the war effort in any way she could but had felt that her options were limited by her sex.

The role of women in war is reflected in a line from the third verse: "Let the Hero, born of woman, crush the serpent with his heel." Although an allusion to biblical doctrine, the line also suggests that women are meant to produce heroes for battle—both literally as mothers and figuratively as proponents of the cause—a role for which women often have been criticized historically.

CRITICAL DISCUSSION

Howe's hymn had an immediate impact on the North. Praised by prominent literary figures, including poets Ralph Waldo Emerson and Henry Wadsworth Longfellow, it was widely reprinted in newspapers of the day and spread quickly among the troops. In the decades immediately following the hymn's composition, much critical and popular discussion focused on its history and the life of its author.

Scholars who were aware of the story of the hymn's creation admired its sophistication and at times speculated how it could have been composed so quickly. Attempts to resolve this mystery endured well into the twentieth century. In a 1951 article in the *New England Quarterly*, for example, Edward D. Snyder describes the writing of the hymn as "Mrs. Howe's apparently unprepared stroke of genius" and attributes the rapid composition to Howe's thorough knowledge of the Bible and the strength of her commitment to abolition and the Union cause. He offers a close reading of the poem, with possible biblical inspirations for Howe's terminology and imagery.

Despite a relative dearth of critical attention to the hymn, a small number of scholars continue to examine its themes and influences. Although biblical readings of the poem have dominated criticism, scholars in the late twentieth century began to examine the hymn through other critical lenses.

In an article in the 1996 book *Worldmaking*, for example, Jeffrey J. Polizzotto argues that the hymn's lyrics have a feminist subtext, through which Howe reflects on her unhappy marriage and her growing commitment to the cause of women's rights. He suggests that in the hymn Howe figures herself as a replacement for Brown, a woman who will fight against patriarchy for oppressed women. Furthermore, he notes that she links the cause of abolitionism to the cause of women's rights, suggesting that "[c]onnections between the two crusades appear in the martial metaphors employed to describe women on the march" elsewhere in Howe's body of work. As Polizzotto's work suggests, there has also been some scholarly interest in the relationship between Howe, her hymn, and John Brown.

SOURCES

Howe, Julia Ward. "The Battle Hymn of the Republic." *The Columbia Anthology of American Poetry*. Ed. Jay Parini. New York: Columbia UP, 1995. 225. Print.

Polizzotto, Jeffrey J. "Julia Ward Howe, 'John Brown's Body,' and the Coming of the Lord." *Worldmaking*. Ed. William Pencak. New York: Lang, 1996. 185–91. Print.

Ravitch, Diane. *The American Reader: Words that Moved a Nation*. New York: Harper, 2000. Print.

Snyder, Edward D. "The Biblical Background of the 'Battle Hymn of the Republic.'" *New England Quarterly* 24.2 (1951): 231–38. Print.

Julia Ward Howe's *Battle Hymn of the Republic* roused Northern soldiers to charge into battle with the sort of fervor captured in this film still from the Civil War drama *Cold Mountain*, (2003). © MIRAMAX / COURTESY EVERETT COLLECTION

FURTHER READING

Clifford, Deborah Pickman. *Mine Eyes Have Seen the Glory: A Biography of Julia Ward Howe*. Boston: Little, 1979. Print.

Cornelius, Steven H. *Music of the Civil War Era*. Westport: Greenwood, 2004. Print.

Garofalo, Robert Joseph. *A Pictorial History of Civil War Era Musical Instruments & Military Bands*. Charleston: Pictorial Histories, 1985. Print.

Hattaway, Herman, and Archer Jones. *How the North Won: A Military History of the Civil War*. Chicago: U of Illinois P, 1991. Print.

Howe, Julia Ward. *Reminiscences, 1819–1899*. Boston: Houghton, 1899. Print.

McPherson, James M. *Battle Cry of Freedom: The Civil War Era*. New York: Oxford UP, 1988. Print.

Richards, Laura Elizabeth. *Julia Ward Howe, 1819–1910*. Boston: Houghton, 1925. Print.

Silber, Irwin. *Soldier Songs and Home-Front Ballads of the Civil War*. New York: Oak Archives, 1964. Print.

Woods, Ralph Louis. *Famous Poems and the Little-Known Stories behind Them*. New York: Hawthorne, 1961. Print.

Greta Gard

"BEYOND VIETNAM"

A Time to Break the Silence
Martin Luther King Jr.

✤ *Key Facts*

Conflict:
Vietnam War

Time Period:
Mid-20th Century

Genre:
Speech

OVERVIEW

Delivered on April 4, 1967, at the Riverside Church in New York City, Martin Luther King Jr.'s speech "Beyond Vietnam: A Time to Break the Silence" outlines his moral opposition to the Vietnam War. The speech was controversial among King's opponents, who pointed to it as further evidence of what they saw as his political extremism. It was also, however, unpopular with many supporters of his civil rights work, who feared that his opposition to the war would have a negative impact on the movement. Anticipating the latter charge, King explains in the speech that his commitment to equal rights and his commitment to global peace and justice originate from the same moral impulse and that those who argue otherwise "do not know the world in which they live." Noted theologian and activist Vincent G. Harding, a close associate of King, wrote the first draft of the speech.

King delivered the speech, which reflects on the unique obligations of the Christian community with respect to war, before the group Clergy and Layman Concerned about Vietnam. He repeatedly emphasizes the disproportionate costs of war to the poor and disadvantaged, both at home and in Vietnam. Linking the oppression of the Vietnamese people, in which he believes the U.S. government is complicit, to the oppression of racial minorities in the United States and a U.S. policy of colonial oppression abroad, King calls upon his listeners to stand up against the war and to decry oppression wherever it exists around the globe. At stake, he suggests, is nothing less than the moral health of the nation. The speech, which is the best known of several that King gave against the war, is regarded as an important piece of political history. The continued relevance of King's words is evidenced by references to the speech in contemporary debates over U.S. involvement in wars in Iraq and Afghanistan.

HISTORICAL AND LITERARY CONTEXT

"Beyond Vietnam" denounces the U.S. military intervention in Vietnam. U.S. involvement in the region began in 1941, when the military assisted the Viet Minh (a coalition fighting for independence from French colonial rule) in their efforts to contain Japanese expansion in Southeast Asia. By 1950 the Cold War was underway, and U.S. leaders—who were convinced that communism would quickly spread around the globe in what President Dwight D. Eisenhower described as the "Domino Effect"—began sending military advisers to Vietnam in an effort to support French rule. The French, however, abandoned their territorial ambitions in the country after their disastrous defeat at Dien Bein Phu in 1954. Determined to prop up South Vietnam against the Communist government of North Vietnam, the United States remained. The war officially began in November 1955, with the first U.S. combat troops deploying in 1965. By the time of the Communist victory in 1975, nearly sixty thousand U.S. troops had died, and as many as several hundred thousand Vietnamese civilians had been killed in U.S. bombings.

King's speech points to the moral and social ills he believed both drove and were exacerbated by the Vietnam War. "Beyond Vietnam" addresses in particular the socioeconomic makeup of the U.S. forces serving in Vietnam, which constituted a "cruel manipulation of the poor." While about 10 percent of the U.S. soldiers who served in Vietnam were of African American descent, the vast majority (roughly three-quarters) of U.S. troops were drawn from the working and lower-middle classes. As America's working poor went off to Vietnam to fight, U.S. commitment to the war drew both attention and funds away from the social programs that benefited the impoverished at home. Many of these reforms had been instituted as part of Lyndon Johnson's Great Society programs, which included the War on Poverty, an initiative introduced in 1964 to target growing indigence in the United States. King describes his belief that prior to U.S. involvement in Vietnam "there was a real promise of hope for the poor—both black and white—through the poverty program" but notes that in the wake of the war, "I watched the program broken and eviscerated as if it were some idle political plaything of society gone mad on war." Indeed, even before the end of the Vietnam War, the War on Poverty was beset by criticism from conservatives and liberals alike, and interest in the initiative waned.

King's speech was also motivated by another controversial Great Society program called Project one hundred thousand (also known as McNamara's one hundred thousand because it was implemented by secretary of defense Robert McNamara), which attempted to increase military recruiting numbers by drastically lowering the mental and physical standards traditionally required of U.S. soldiers. As part of this initiative, recruiters aggressively targeted impoverished areas of the country, particularly urban ghettos and the rural South. Promoted as a means of providing valuable training opportunities for poor young men, the project merely filled the country's military ranks with ill-prepared troops, many of whom quickly accounted for a disproportionate number of U.S. casualties in the conflict. Not surprisingly, the program had recruited heavily in African American communities.

In crafting the speech, King drew on both contemporary antiwar rhetoric and U.S. literature. The title of the speech was taken from a statement of the Clergy and Layman Concerned about Vietnam's executive committee, which King explains touched him with its sentiment that "a time comes when silence is betrayal." King also quotes from the work of two U.S. poets. Early in the speech, he includes several lines from the poem "Let America Be America Again" by Langston Hughes (1902–67), which emphasizes the need for a new America in which the descendants of slaves might truly be free: "America never was America to me, / And yet I swear this oath—/ America will be!" King closes the speech with an excerpt from the poem "The Present Crisis" by James Russell Lowell (1819–91). An ardent abolitionist, Lowell used his popularity as a poet to advocate for an end to slavery. In stanzas that King quotes, Lowell calls upon his listeners to make the choice of good over evil: "Once to every man and nation / Comes the moment to decide, / In the strife of truth and falsehood, / For the good or evil side." Drawing a connection between the conscientious objection to slavery and the conscientious objection to the Vietnam War allows King indirectly to solidify the connection between his opposition to the war and his advocacy of civil rights at home. King further emphasized this connection in "Why I Oppose the War in Vietnam," a speech he gave a few weeks later, on April 30, 1967.

THEMES AND STYLE

Throughout "Beyond Vietnam," King emphasizes that, despite what many of his critics have suggested, his opposition to the war is an extension of his civil rights work. He notes the ironies, for example, that "we are taking the black young men who had been crippled by our society and sending them eight thousand miles away to guarantee liberties in Southeast Asia which they had not found in southwest Georgia and East Harlem" and that African Americans and white soldiers "kill and die together for a nation that has been unable to seat them together in the same schools." King stresses, however, that the burden of the war disregards race in falling disproportionately on the nation's poor. For King, this fact underscores a broader issue: that the government prioritizes

Dr. Benjamin Spock and Martin Luther King, Jr. lead nearly 5,000 marchers through Chicago to protest U.S. policy on Vietnam. © EVERETT COLLECTION INC / ALAMY

its global ambitions at the expense of serving the domestic needs of the American people.

Civil rights violations, poverty, and violence are all symptoms, King suggests, of a larger problem—the spiritual and moral decline of the United States that is being fueled by a combination of "deadly Western arrogance" and loss of its once revolutionary spirit. War in particular, he notes, is tainting the nation to the degree that "if America's soul becomes totally poisoned, part of the autopsy must read Vietnam." He suggests that the United States has become "the greatest purveyor of violence in the world today," and thus he argues that it is a moral duty to stand up against the war "for the sake of those boys [fighting the war], for the sake of the government, for the sake of hundreds of thousands trembling under our violence." The moral duty to speak out against the war is, he emphasizes, an inherently Christian one. Questioning why his fellow Americans cannot see the connection between the teachings of Christ and opposition to the war, King asks, "Could it be that they do not know that the good news was meant for all men—for Communist and capitalist, for their children and ours, for black and for white, for revolutionary and conservative?" Moreover, he suggests that the U.S. government is behaving against Christian principles both in Vietnam, where it has destroyed the South Vietnamese people it claims to defend, and at home:

> This business of burning human beings with napalm, of filling our nation's homes with orphans and widows … of sending men home from dark and bloody battlefields physically handicapped and psychologically deranged, cannot be reconciled with wisdom, justice and love.

Stylistically, King often uses rhetorical questions to emphasize his points: "Shall we say the odds are too great? Shall we tell them [our brothers] the struggle is

THE STORY BEHIND THE SPEECH

When King gave his "Beyond Vietnam" speech on April 4, 1967, U.S. combat troops had already been involved in the Vietnam War for two years. King, a committed pacifist and Nobel Peace Laureate, had wanted to give an antiwar speech as soon as U.S. involvement began, but he had been advised against it by those in his inner circle. Fellow civil rights activists feared that the speech would be viewed as an indictment of Lyndon Johnson, whose presidency had seen more civil rights reforms than that of any other U.S. president. By 1967, however, King believed he could no longer remain silent. His decision to give what he knew would be an unpopular speech was motivated in part by his visceral reaction to photographs of children who had been severely burned by napalm. Realizing they could not change his mind, King's advisers suggested that the speech be given in front of a largely religious gathering at Riverside Church in order to soften the controversy. Despite this attempt, however, the speech generated an immense backlash. The speech was condemned by 168 newspapers the following day and effectively ended the previously positive relationship between King and President Johnson, who immediately retracted an invitation to King to visit the White House.

too hard?" He also works to convey a sense of urgency, particularly through the repetition of the words *must* ("We must speak"; "Somehow this madness must cease"; "We must be prepared to match actions with words"; "we must enter the struggle"; "We must find new ways to speak for peace in Vietnam") and *demand* ("The world now demands a maturity of America that we may not be able to achieve. It demands that we admit that we have been wrong from the beginning of our adventure in Vietnam"; "These are days which demand wise restraint and calm reasonableness"). Such rhetoric underscores King's message that opposition to the war is a pressing duty on which his listeners are morally bound to act.

CRITICAL DISCUSSION

King was a major public figure at the time he gave the speech, and his words were widely reported and drew extensive journalistic commentary. The *New York Times*, for instance, called into question King's linking of opposition to the war in Vietnam with his advocacy of civil rights at home, arguing, "This is a fusing of two public problems that are distinct and separate. By drawing them together, Dr. King has done a disservice to both." The author goes on to suggest that King "makes too facile a connection between the speeding up of the war in Vietnam and the slowing down of the war against poverty."

In the decades since King first delivered his speech, scholars have worked to analyze it in the context of his other statements about equality and justice. In an article in *Peace & Change*, for example, Thomas J. Noer traces King's reaction against the Vietnam War in his 1967 speech to his growing frustrations with U.S. foreign policy throughout the 1950s and 1960s. Noer suggests that the speech "was the culmination of a decade of dissent, targeting many of the nation's cold war assumptions and actions." Noer does, however, note what he sees to be several flaws in King's speech, among them that King's "critique of U.S. foreign policy was based on impressions and anecdotes rather than research and systematic study" and that "he tended to romanticize more than analyze, and he often simplified complex issues. He rather naively accepted an economic analysis for the root of American diplomacy, especially regarding Vietnam." Despite such criticisms, however, "Beyond Vietnam" has generally been viewed as an important and successful speech.

More than four decades after it was delivered, King's speech has remained relevant and interesting to scholars not only of the U.S. civil rights movement and the Vietnam War but of contemporary U.S. politics. Writing in the *New York Amsterdam News* in 2010, noted journalist Herb Boyd recalls King's speech in the context of deliberations over the amount of money being spent on wars in Iraq and Afghanistan, noting parallels between the Vietnam era and the contemporary political and social climate in which "millions are still without decent housing, on the verge of starvation and with little hope of relief from a federal government straining to finance a seemingly unwinnable war."

SOURCES

Boyd, Herb. "Dr. King Was Right." *New York Amsterdam News* 8 July 2010: 4. Print.

"Dr. King's Error." *New York Times* 7 Apr. 1967: 36. Print.

King, Martin Luther, Jr. "Beyond Vietnam: A Time to Break the Silence." *A Testament of Hope: The Essential Writings of Martin Luther King, Jr.* San Francisco: Harper, 1986: 231–44. Print.

Noer, Thomas J. "Martin Luther King Jr. and the Cold War." *Peace & Change* 22.2 (1997): 111–31. Print.

FURTHER READING

Budra, Paul, and Michael Zeitlin. *Soldier Talk: The Vietnam War in Oral Narrative.* Bloomington: Indiana UP, 2004. Print.

Fairclough, Adam. "Martin Luther King and the War in Vietnam." *Phylon* 45 (1984): 19–39. Print.

Hall, Jacquelyn Dowd. "The Long Civil Rights Movement and the Political Uses of the Past." *Journal of American History* 91.4 (2005): 1233–63. Print.

Ingram, Glen. "NAACP Support of the Vietnam War: 1963–1969." *Western Journal of Black Studies* 30.1 (2006): 54–61. Print.

King, Coretta Scott. "The Legacy of Martin Luther King, Jr.: The Church in Action." *Theology Today* 65.1 (2008): 7–16. Print.

King, Martin Luther, Jr. *The Autobiography of Martin Luther King, Jr.* Ed. Clayborne Carson. New York: Warner, 1998. Print.

King, William M. "The Reemerging Revolutionary Consciousness of the Reverend Martin Luther King, Jr., 1965–68." *Journal of Negro History* 71.1–4 (1986): 1–22. Print.

Lischer, Richard. *The Preacher King: Martin Luther King, Jr. and the Word That Moved America.* New York: Oxford UP, 1995. Print.

Greta Gard

"THE CHARGE OF THE LIGHT BRIGADE," AND "MAUD: A MONODY"

Alfred Lord Tennyson

✣ *Key Facts*

Conflict:
Crimean War

Time Period:
Mid-19th Century

Genre:
Poetry

OVERVIEW

Alfred, Lord Tennyson's "Maud: A Monody" and "The Charge of the Light Brigade" are the only major English-language poems about the Crimean War. "The Charge of the Light Brigade" commemorates a failed British cavalry charge during the Battle of Balaclava. While the poem is forthright about the failure of the charge, it concentrates on the heroic state of mind of the soldiers and their valiant efforts to defend Britain. The poem was extremely popular, especially among British soldiers, and it remains one of Tennyson's best-known poems.

"Maud: A Monody," a long, three-part poem composed of dramatic monologues, addresses the Crimean War in the final section, in which the narrator proclaims his belief that war will renew the moral and ethical heart of the nation. In contrast to the more popular "Charge of the Light Brigade," the political stance of "Maud" with regard to the conflict is difficult to establish. The narrator's decision to join the army comes at the end of the poem, after the repeated personal losses he has suffered have driven him mad. His decision makes sense in the context of his own need for redemption but is not necessarily a strong endorsement of the war itself.

"The Charge of the Light Brigade" was first published in the *London Examiner* on December 9, 1854. Both poems were included in the 1855 collection *Maud, and Other Poems.*

HISTORICAL AND LITERARY CONTEXT

The Crimean War (1852–56) began when Russia invaded territory held by the Ottoman Empire. Concerned that the defeat of the Ottomans would allow Russian influence to extend into Western Europe, Britain and France entered the war in 1854. It was mainly fought over the control of strategic ports on the Crimean peninsula in southern Ukraine, which juts into the Black Sea.

The charge of the Light Brigade, the incident on which Tennyson based his poem, occurred on October 25, 1854, during the Battle of Balaclava, an unsuccessful attempt by the British to wrest control of the supply port of Balaclava from Russian forces. Because of a communications error, 637 men of the Light Brigade were ordered into a valley, where the Russian cavalry was waiting, rather than to the heights surrounding the valley. The charge turned into a massacre in which nearly forty percent of the British troops died, and it is generally understood to have been one of the major tactical blunders of the Crimean War.

Writing in the *Yale Journal of Criticism*, Natalie M. Houston describes the Crimean War as the "first truly modern British war," pointing to the use of new military and communications technology. Despite "the chivalric models of warfare embodied in its dandy officers," she writes, "orders were communicated by telegraph, St. Petersburg was protected by the first naval minefield, and plans for the use of poison gas were considered." The Crimean War was also the first war to be covered by war correspondents; the Irish writer William Howard Russell (1820–1907) reported on the fighting for the *Times* (London). Journals printed engravings made from the war sketches of William Simpson (1823–99) and photographs of the battlefields by Roger Fenton (1819–69). Houston notes that the British public responded strongly to press accounts of the war, demanding that shipments of supplies be made to the troops, and that the fall of Lord Aberdeen's government in 1855 was a direct consequence of press coverage that exposed the mismanagement of the war.

Maud, and Other Poems was the first volume Tennyson published after "In Memoriam A. H. H." (1850), the immensely popular elegy on the death of his friend, the poet Arthur Hallam (1811–33). It was also his first publication after being appointed poet laureate in 1850, an honor he received mainly on the merits of "In Memoriam" and popular epics on medieval subjects like "The Lady of Shalott" (1832) and "Morte d'Arthur" (1842). After he became poet laureate, however, Tennyson began publishing public poetry alongside his more personal lyric and epic poems. Examples of the former include "Ode on the Death of the Duke of Wellington" (1852) and "The Charge of the Light Brigade." As Houston points out, the large number of patriotic works in support of the Crimean War produced by other British writers and artists are now largely forgotten.

THE ARGUMENT FOR FOREIGN INTERVENTION

Among military historians the Crimean War remains a controversial subject, with many experts regarding it as an unnecessary campaign for Britain and its allies. In England the most prominent proponent for intervention in the region was Lord Palmerston, the British home secretary. Although he no longer wielded as much influence over British policy as he had when he had been the country's foreign secretary, Palmerston remained a significant voice in matters of foreign affairs. In 1853, after Russian troops under Nicholas II began to threaten the eastern borders of the Ottoman Empire, Palmerston argued that the British navy should send ships to the Dardanelles. In spite of opposition from several members of Parliament, Palmerston's position eventually won approval. The maneuvers were intended primarily as a deterrent to the Russian advance, representing both a demonstration of British naval power and of solidarity with the Ottoman forces. The Russians interpreted the actions as hostile, however, and used the British naval presence as a pretense for invading the Ottoman provinces of Moldavia and Wallachia. As tensions between the two sides escalated, the prime minister, Lord Aberdeen, argued for peace, while Palmerston remained steadfast in his demand for military engagement. Aberdeen reluctantly agreed, and in March 1854 he declared war on Russia. Following a series of disastrous campaigns—including the infamous charge of the Light Brigade—the war became increasingly unpopular in England, and Aberdeen was eventually forced to resign as prime minister. A short time later he was succeeded by Palmerston.

THEMES AND STYLE

"The Charge of the Light Brigade" was written in 1854 in response to a report in the *Times* about the Battle of Balaclava. Tennyson said that he wrote the poem in a matter of minutes, inspired by a phrase in the article, "some hideous blunder," which he rendered in the poem as "someone had blunder'd." The poem reframes the massacre as an example of the heroism of British soldiers, its dactylic rhythm evoking the pounding of hooves as the cavalry charges into battle. The short lines, strict rhyme schemes, and multiple repetitions of lines and phrases accentuate the rapid movement of the poem, recalling the thrill of the charge and focusing on the soldiers as men of action—"Theirs not to make reply, / Theirs not to reason why, / Theirs but to do or die." The last stanza demands that they be remembered for their bravery and heroism rather than for the mistake that led to their deaths:

> When can their glory fade?
> O the wild charge they made!
> All the world wonder'd.
> Honour the charge they made!
> Honour the Light Brigade,
> Noble six hundred!

"Maud" provides a far more complicated vision of the conflict. Primarily a series of psychological portraits of a man as he slowly descends into madness, the poem addresses the war only in the last short section, when the narrator decides to volunteer for the war as a way of expiating his personal demons. Because the argument in favor of the war is made by a man whose sanity is in question, his reasons cannot be taken as a straightforward endorsement. Indeed, since the publication of the poem, critics have debated whether the claims made by the narrator express Tennyson's own views. Christopher Ricks, who served as an editor of the poet's works, notes that Tennyson addressed this argument somewhat evasively in a letter, dated December 6, 1855, to the poet and clergyman Archer Gurney (1820–87). Saying that he did not see how his own views could be deduced from the poem since "all along the man was intended to have a hereditary strain of insanity" and that he, Tennyson, would not have expressed his own views with "so little moderation," he avoided revealing his position.

"Maud" is composed of three sections containing a series of dramatic monologues, the genre of Victorian poetry associated most closely with Robert Browning's "My Last Duchess." A dramatic monologue is narrated in the first person by a single speaker. Narrators of dramatic monologues are often mentally disturbed in some way; thus, the reader is faced with the challenge of both understanding the narrator's psychology and determining the truth of his or her account.

The first two sections of "Maud," which make up most of the poem, describe the narrator's unhappy life, from his difficult youth to his mental decline after a disastrous love affair, before his final decision to go to war. While the nearly 1,200 lines of parts 1 and 2 of "Maud" contain a variety of rhyme schemes and verse forms, they are characterized throughout by the same melancholy and psychological agony, returning repeatedly to images of death and destruction and finding reflections of pain and morbidity in the landscape.

In the beginning of the third section, the narrator, having lost his mind, finds his salvation in the Crimean War. As he describes it, "My life has crept so long on a broken wing / through cells of madness ... when I thought that a war would arise in defense of the right." He sees the coming war as a fight against the Mammonism (greed and materialism) that he railed against in the earlier parts of the poem and for the values of the British nation. Unconcerned with his own fate, he portrays the army as a way to escape his intense isolation and to ensure that the death he foresees will benefit the nation: "I have felt with my native land, I am one with my kind, / I embrace the purpose of God, and the doom assigned."

CRITICAL DISCUSSION

"The Charge of the Light Brigade" is one of the best-known poems in English literature. It immediately captured the attention and imagination of the British nation and was a particular favorite among cavalry officers. Tennyson had one thousand copies printed for distribution to soldiers in August 1855. The poem's memorable rhythms and repetitions made it a popular choice for inclusion in English school anthologies and readers, and it was often chosen as a selection to be memorized and recited. The work was popular enough that Tennyson wrote a follow-up poem about a victory in the Crimean War. This poem, titled "The Charge of the Heavy Brigade," was first published in *Tiresias and Other Poems* (1885), but it was far less successful. Overall, "The Charge of the Light Brigade" is considered to be one of Tennyson's less critically important poems, even though it remains one of his most popular. In summarizing the general critical view, Thomas Rommel, in an article titled "Lines Suggested by the War in the Crimea," identifies the poem as a "typical piece of Crimean War poetry" in that it describes the battle from the vantage point of an observer, "rarely focussing on the agony of the individual."

"Maud" is not one of Tennyson's better-known works, and on publication it was panned in the press. In his analysis of the reception of "Maud," Edgar Shannon, in an article published in *PMLA*, observes that, while some reviewers "insisted that the hero's pronouncements were purely dramatic," most critics understood the poem to express Tennyson's own support of the war. Thus, reviews often turned into arguments about the justifiability of the Crimean War and of wars in general and whether poets should address such matters at all. Shannon himself suggests that the vehement critiques of Tennyson's attempt to be "a social critic and reformer" scared him away from writing about contemporary matters and led to his return to medieval subjects in *The Idylls of the King* (1856–85).

In one of the few essays on Tennyson's war poetry, an article in the *Journal of the History of Ideas*, Michael C. C. Adams gives an overview of the critical accounts of "Maud" from the 1950s through the 1970s. Adams suggests that the poem was severely criticized because readers found what they interpreted as Tennyson's pro-war stance to be at odds with the antiwar views of the day. Adams argues that "Maud" and "The Charge of the Light Brigade," when read in the context of what he calls a "cross-cultural approach," are illuminating examples of the pre-twentieth-century vision of war as

a "rejuvenating force for prosperous and commercial-industrial nations." The revival of Victorian studies since the 1980s, moreover, has produced several important critical reevaluations of "Maud." Jerome McGann, in his account of Tennyson and the aesthetics of melancholy in "Tennyson and the Artists of the Beautiful," declares the poem important precisely because it is not straightforward. He argues that Tennyson alternately rebelled against and conformed to the cultural and political beliefs of the Victorian age and that "Maud" embodies this conflict, expressing conventional support for the war and, at the same time, casting doubt on the validity of that support by having it voiced by a madman. Mauricio D. Aguilera, on the other hand, writes in *Atlantis* that the pro-war message in the final section of the poem is part of "a coherent, well-articulated political proposal." Applying the political philosophy of Tennyson's contemporary Thomas Carlyle (1795–1881), Aguilera argues that "Maud" advocates a social system based on the hierarchical structure of the army, which would counteract the materialism of modern society. In an article in *Victorian Poetry*, Stefanie Markovits analyzes Tennyson's difficult role as poet laureate during a war that was "marked by dissonance," seeing his efforts to address the conflict in "The Charge of the Light Brigade" and "Maud" as examples of "a complex negotiation of the terrain of patriotic martial poetry."

SOURCES

Adams, Michael C. C. "Tennyson's Crimean War Poetry: A Cross-Cultural Approach." *Journal of the History of Ideas* 40.3 (1979): 405–22. Print.

Aguilera, Mauricio D. "Maud's Wars: The Political Message." *Atlantis: Revista de la Asociación Española de Estudios Anglo-Norteamericanos.* 21.1–2 (1999): 7–27. Print.

Houston, Natalie M. "Reading the Victorian Souvenir: Sonnets and Photographs of the Crimean War." *Yale Journal of Criticism* 14.2 (2001): 353–83. Print.

Markovits, Stefanie. "Giving Voice to the Crimean War: Tennyson's 'Charge' and Maud's Battle-song." *Victorian Poetry* 47.3 (2009): 481–505. Print.

McGann, Jerome. "Tennyson and the Artists of the Beautiful." *The Scholar's Art: Literary Studies in a Managed World.* Chicago: U of Chicago P, 2006. 88–103. Print.

Rommel, Thomas. "'Lines Suggested by the War in the Crimea': Florence Nightingale and the Role of the Individual Soldier." *War and the Cultural Construction of Identities in Britain.* Ed. Ralf Schneider and Barbara Korte. Amsterdam: Rodopi, 2002. 109–24. Print.

Shannon, Edgar F., Jr. "The Critical Reception of Tennyson's 'Maud.'" *PMLA* 68.3 (1953): 397–417. Print

Tennyson, Alfred. "Maud: A Monody." *Tennyson: A Selected Edition.* Ed. Christopher Ricks. Berkeley: U of California P, 1989: 511–82. Print.

———. "The Charge of the Light Brigade." *Victorian Poetry: An Annotated Anthology.* Ed. Francis O'Gorman. Oxford: Blackwell, 2004. 165–67. Print.

FURTHER READING

Bevis, Matthew. "Fighting Talk: Victorian War Poetry." *The Oxford Handbook of British and Irish War Poetry.* Ed. Tim Kendall. Oxford: Oxford UP, 2007. 7–33. Print.

Browning, Robert. "My Last Duchess." *Men and Women, and Other Poems.* Ed. J. W. Harper. London: Dent, 1975. 207–8. Print.

Campbell, Matthew J. B. *Rhythm and Will in Victorian Poetry.* Cambridge: Cambridge UP, 1999. Print.

Lovelace, Timothy, J. *The Artistry and Tradition of Tennyson's Battle Poetry.* London: Routledge, 2003. Print.

Markovits, Stefanie. *The Crimean War in the British Imagination.* Cambridge: Cambridge UP, 2009. Print.

Mazzeno, Laurence. *Alfred Tennyson: The Critical Legacy.* Rochester: Camden, 2004. Print.

O'Neill, James Norman. "Anthem for a Doomed Youth: An Interdisciplinary Study of Tennyson's 'Maud' and the Crimean War." *Tennyson Research Bulletin* 5.4 (1990). 166–81. Print.

Tennyson, Alfred. *Tennyson: A Selected Edition.* Ed. Christopher Ricks. Berkeley: U of California P, 1989. Print.

MEDIA ADAPTATIONS

The Charge of the Light Brigade. Dir. J. Seatle Dawley. Perf. Ben F. Wilson, Richard Neill, James Gordon, and Charles Sutton. General Film Company, 1912. Film.

The Charge of the Light Brigade. Dir. Michael Curtiz. Perf. Errol Flynn and Olivia de Havilland. Warner Bros. Pictures, 1936. Film.

The Charge of the Light Brigade. Dir. Tony Richardson. Perf. Trevor Howard, Vanessa Redgrave, and John Gielgud. United Artists, 1968. Film.

Jennifer Ludwig

EIGHTEEN HUNDRED AND ELEVEN

Anna Laetitia Barbauld

✥ *Key Facts*

Conflict:
Napoleonic Wars

Time Period:
Early 19th Century

Genre:
Poetry

OVERVIEW

Anna Laetitia Barbauld's 1812 poem *Eighteen Hundred and Eleven* is a critique of Great Britain's participation in the Napoleonic Wars (1803–15). Barbauld argues that the homeland suffered financially and culturally for its involvement in the conflicts. The poem looks at into Britain's history of scientific and cultural innovation and into a future when the nation will no longer dominate the globe. Despite its emphasis on British achievements, *Eighteen Hundred and Eleven* was deemed unpatriotic by many of Barbauld's contemporaries. The reaction against the poem stemmed from its prophecy that the nation would soon be eclipsed by the colonies and the Old World overshadowed by the New. This sentiment that was particularly unwelcome as Britain was embroiled in war. Barbauld was in her late sixties when she wrote the poem, and its negative reception effectively ended her poetic career. Although she continued to write, she published little additional poetry during her lifetime.

Despite the fierce condemnation of Barbauld's contemporaries that her poem was unpatriotic and unwomanly in its rhetoric, the work has been widely embraced by twentieth- and twenty-first-century scholars. Offering insight into the politics, culture, and gender roles at the beginning of the nineteenth century in Britain, *Eighteen Hundred and Eleven* has generated a rich body of academic commentary.

HISTORICAL AND LITERARY CONTEXT

Although England's involvement in the Napoleonic Wars was the immediate inspiration for *Eighteen Hundred and Eleven*, Barbauld had been disapproving of British foreign policy even before its outbreak. Nearly two decades earlier, her essay *Sins of the Government, Sins of the Nation* (1793) had criticized the country's tendency toward war and its emphasis on imperial power. Coming on the heels of Britain's involvement in the French Revolutionary Wars (1792–1802), the Napoleonic Wars were unpopular with many in Britain. The conflict ignited over the attempts of post-revolutionary France, under the leadership of Napoléon Bonaparte, to expand its empire beyond Europe. Although France and Great Britain had signed the Peace of Amiens in 1802, war broke out between the two nations again in May 1803, as Britain sought to defend its colonial

and commercial interests in the West Indies and to support its allies in Europe. In 1808 Britain came to the aid of Spain, sending troops to the Iberian Peninsula in what would eventually be known as the Peninsular War (1808–13). The unified forces of Great Britain and the Spanish guerrillas were eventually able to repel Napoléon's armies. By the time of Napoléon's final defeat in 1815, however, the British government had spent an immense sum to finance its involvement in the Napoleonic Wars and more than 300,000 British troops had been killed in battle or were missing in action. Barbauld's poem draws attention to the high cost of the war in both money and lives and notes that it came at a time when Britain was already suffering from financial hardship at home.

Barbauld's poem was published in 1812, the year in which Britain was drawn into the War of 1812 (1812–15), its second major war with the United States. This war resulted in part from British trade restrictions imposed in response to the Napoleonic Wars, and from the British Royal Navy's repeated impressment of American sailors. Although the poem appeared several months before the outbreak of the war, Barbauld's emphasis on the waning of British fortune and the increasing power of its colonies did not sit well with British audiences.

Eighteen Hundred and Eleven is part of a large body of literature depicting or reacting to the Napoleonic Wars. The best known of these works are novels such as William Makepeace Thackeray's *Vanity Fair* (1847–48) and Leo Tolstoy's *War and Peace* (1869). The war also occasioned an outpouring of poetry that ranged from critiques (such as Samuel Taylor Coleridge's 1798 "Fears in Solitude") to support for action against Napoléon to calls for Napoléon's destruction (such as Robert Southey's "Ode Written during the Negotiations with Napoleon Bonaparte, January 1814"). Although Barbauld was not the only poet to oppose the war, her poem was among the most unusual and most controversial reactions to the conflict. In her book *Mothers of the Nation*, Anne Mellor reads the poem as a "feminist rewriting of a neoclassical progress poem." That tradition in poetry includes works such as Thomas Gray's "The Progress of Poesy" (1757), which traces the spread of poetry from the ancient world to England. Barbauld's poem offers a similar trajectory of human thought and culture but emphasizes that the continued march of progress eventually renders all great nations things of the past.

THEMES AND STYLE

Eighteen Hundred and Eleven is often classified as a Juvenalian satire, a mode that takes its name from the Roman satirist Juvenal. Such satire is characterized by its harsh critique of public figures or policies—in Barbauld's case Britain's entry into the Napoleonic Wars. The poem is written in heroic couplets, or rhyming pairs of lines in iambic pentameter. Barbauld's use of heroic couplets, which are commonly associated with epic poetry, emphasizes the scope and gravity of the circumstances she portrays.

A central theme of the poem is that Britain has been rash in entering a war against Napoléon. Barbauld asserts that the nation has become complacent, believing itself to be untouchable. Does Britain, she asks, truly believe it possible "To sport in wars, while danger keeps aloof, / Thy grassy turf unbruised by hostile hoof?" She also suggests that Britain suffers from involvement in the war whether or not combat reaches its shores. It threatens the foundations of Britain's economy. "Thy Midas dream is o'er," she writes, and "The golden tide of Commerce leaves thy shore." Later she laments, "Commerce, like beauty, knows no second spring." She also depicts the devastating effects of the war on families at home: "oft o'er the daily page some soft-one bends / To learn the fate of husband, brothers, friends."

In addition to emphasizing the immense costs of war, the poem argues that the enterprise is superfluous in any case, in part because no empire can sustain itself perpetually. Barbauld's prophecy of the inevitable decline of Britain is joined with the poem's conception of progress, which envisions the figure of "the Genius" moving through Babylon, Egypt, and Carthage, bringing about agriculture, animal husbandry, and the flowering of art. This genius, however, is unpredictable, as it inevitably "forsakes the favoured shore, / And hates, capricious, what he loved before." It is thus, she suggests, only natural that Britain, despite having produced the numerous scientific and literary geniuses mentioned in the poem, will eventually see its glory and power usurped: "fairest flowers expand but to decay; / The worm is in thy core, thy glories pass away." Moreover, she suggests, war, which stifles both nature and human liberty, will necessarily hasten this demise. As the British Empire declines, she predicts, "to other climes the Genius soars, / He turns from Europe's desolated shores." These "other climes" are implicitly Britain's colonies and former colonies, including, presumably, the United States; Barbauld's words also allude to emerging South American republics such as Argentina, Venezuela, and Colombia, which, under the leadership of José Francisco de San Martín and Simón Bolívar, were beginning to win independence from Spain at the time Barbauld was writing.

Battle of the Busaco, Peninsular War, Portugal, 1810. Portuguese and British troops commanded by the Duke of Wellington pushed back the French. Ann Ronan Picture Library. © HERITAGE IMAGES / CORBIS

This vision of Britain's legacy is not wholly pessimistic, however, as Barbauld notes, "If westward streams the light that leaves thy shores, / Still from thy lamp the streaming radiance pours." Britain has, she argues, influenced the direction of the nations that will inherit its place in the world, a point Barbauld makes more explicit several lines later when she asserts, "Thy stores of knowledge the new states shall know, / And think thy thoughts, and with thy fancy glow." While this vision is unappealing to a postcolonial sensibility, for Barbauld it was a reflection of patriotism and optimism in the face of unavoidable change.

CRITICAL DISCUSSION

When it was first published, *Eighteen Hundred and Eleven* received mixed reviews from Barbauld's contemporaries. Many reviewers were either bewildered or incensed by the poem. Writing in the *Quarterly Review*, John Wilson Croker famously poked fun at both Barbauld's writing and her sex, satirically noting, "We had hoped … that the empire might have been saved without the intervention of a lady-author." He goes on to offer a close reading of several passages

THE FRENCH REVOLUTIONARY AND NAPOLEONIC WARS

Eighteen Hundred and Eleven is a reaction against Great Britain's continued involvement in wars with France. Even before the Napoleonic Wars, Britain had become embroiled in the French Revolutionary Wars, which began in 1792 with France's declaration of war against Austria. Prussia soon entered an alliance with Austria against France. Worried about the growing recklessness of France's revolutionary government after the execution of the deposed French king, Louis XVI, in January 1793, Spain and Portugal joined the alliance. On February 1, France declared war on Great Britain. Eventually the Ottoman Empire, Portugal, Russia, Sweden, and the Papal States were also arrayed against France.

The war between France and Great Britain lasted until 1802, when it was formally ended by the Treaty of Amiens. Because tensions remained high between the two countries, there is debate about when the Revolutionary Wars ended and the Napoleonic Wars began, but the latter are conventionally considered to have commenced on May 18, 1803. Some historians have suggested, however, that the Napoleonic Wars should actually be dated to November 9, 1799, when Napoleon came to power. This scholarly disagreement underscores the continual and exhausting state of war that Barbauld's poem rejects.

from her poem but admits that he cannot "satisfactorily comprehend the meaning of all the verses which this fatidical [prophetic] spinster has drawn from her poetical distaff." Other reviewers were more positive in their assessment of Barbauld's poetic talents and her commitment to the nation. The *Monthly Review*, for example, suggested that, despite the dire prophecies the poem contained, "like a true patriot, Mrs. B. glows with strong affection for her native land, and knows how to appreciate the value of the many blessings which distinguish it."

Many scholars have been drawn to Barbauld's depiction of the Napoleonic Wars and their effects on Britain at home and abroad. Writing in the *European Romantic Review*, for example, Evan Gottlieb considers Barbauld's statements about the war alongside those of her younger female poetic contemporary Felicia Hemans. Ultimately, he argues, Barbauld's poem outlines the war as a series "of endless, restless calamity, rather than individual, historically specific events," a strategy which he maintains "allows her to compose situations that exemplify the eternal costs of war without becoming overly caught up in the details of individual historical events." He suggests that the poem was disturbing to many of Barbauld's contemporaries not "because it prophesies that Britain will be defeated by France ... but because it predicts that Britain and its imperial holdings are doomed to destruction regardless of the outcome of the Napoleonic Wars."

As Gottlieb's work makes clear, the role of empire in the poem has been an important topic of critical discussion. Scholars remain divided in regard to the poem's ultimate message about empire. Discussing the work in *Wordsworth Circle*, Francesco Crocco suggests that, despite its somewhat radical opposition to the war, the poem "in fact reifies colonial ideology." Ultimately, he suggests, "Barbauld is critical of empire, but uncritical of cultural imperialism," insofar as the poem suggests that "British imperialism is an innocuous instrument that spreads civilization" and that "while empire must fail, British civilization must live on in its colonies."

Scholars have also worked to unravel the gender politics of both Barbauld's poem and early critical responses to it. Likening Barbauld to the mythic Greek prophet Cassandra, Mellor suggests that "she relentlessly foretells the doom of her country, here defined as the end of the liberal public culture to which English women as well as men have contributed." Much attention has also been focused on Croker's attack on Barbauld for inappropriately entering what he saw to be the masculine realm of politics.

SOURCES

Barbauld, Anna Laetitia. *Eighteen Hundred and Eleven: A Poem*. London: Johnson, 1812. Print.

Crocco, Francesco. "The Colonial Subtext of Anna Letitia Barbauld's *Eighteen Hundred and Eleven*." *Wordsworth Circle* 41.2 (2010): 91–94. Print.

Croker, John Wilson. Rev. of *Eighteen Hundred and Eleven*, by Anna Laetitia Barbauld. *Quarterly Review* 7.14 (1812): 309–13. Print.

Rev. of *Eighteen Hundred and Eleven*, by Anna Laetitia Barbauld. *Monthly Review* Apr. 1812: 428–32. Print.

Gottlieb, Evan. "Fighting Words: Representing the Napoleonic Wars in the Poetry of Hemans and Barbauld." *European Romantic Review* 20.3 (2009): 327–43. Print.

Mellor, Anne K. *Mothers of the Nation: Women's Political Writing in England, 1780–1830*. Bloomington: Indiana UP, 2000. Print.

FURTHER READING

Bainbridge, Simon. *British Poetry and the Revolutionary and Napoleonic Wars: Visions of Conflict*. Oxford: Oxford UP, 2003. Print.

Barbauld, Anna Letitia. *The Poems of Anna Letitia Barbauld*. Ed. William McCarthy and Elizabeth Kraft. Athens: U of Georgia P, 1994. Print.

———. "The Uses of History." *The Works of Anna Letitia Barbauld*. Vol. 2. New York: Carvill, 1826. 283–310. Print.

Behrendt, Stephen C. "'A Few Harmless Numbers': British Women Poets and the Climate of War, 1793–1815." *Romantic Wars: Studies in Culture and Conflict, 1789–1822*. Ed. Philip Shaw. Aldershot: Ashgate, 2000. 13–36. Print.

Chandler, James. *England in 1819: The Politics of Literary Culture and the Case of Romantic Historicism*. Chicago: U of Chicago P, 1998. Print.

Esdaile, Charles. *Fighting Napoleon: Guerrillas, Bandits, and Adventurers in Spain, 1808–1814*. New Haven: Yale UP, 2004. Print.

Fremont-Barnes, Gregory. *Armies of the Napoleonic Wars*. Barnsley: Pen, 2011. Print.

Golland, Rachel A. "Otherness in Anna Letitia Barbauld's *Eighteen Hundred and Eleven*: Prophesizing Terror in 19th Century England." *Exit 9: The Rutgers Journal of Comparative Literature* 9 (2008): 35–48. Print.

Hadley, Karen. "'The Wealth of Nations,' or 'The Happiness of Nations'?: Barbauld's Malthusian Critique in *Eighteen Hundred and Eleven*." *CLA Journal* 45.1 (2001): 87–96. Print.

Kaul, Suvir. *Poems of Nation, Anthems of Empire: English Verse in the Long Eighteenth Century*. Charlottesville: U of Virginia P, 2000. Print.

Keach, William. "A Regency Prophecy and the End of Anna Barbauld's Career." *Studies in Romanticism* 33.4 (1994): 569–77. Print.

Levine, William. "The Eighteenth-Century Jeremiad and Progress-Piece Traditions in Anna Barbauld's *Eighteen Hundred and Eleven*." *Women's Writing* 12.2 (2005): 177–86. Print.

McCarthy, William. *Anna Letitia Barbauld: Voice of the Enlightenment*. Baltimore: Johns Hopkins UP, 2008. Print.

Rohrbach, Emily. "Anna Barbauld's History of the Future: A Deviant Way to Poetic Agency." *European Romantic Review* 17.2 (2006): 179–87. Print.

Greta Gard

HENRY V
William Shakespeare

✣ *Key Facts*

Conflict:
Hundred Years' War

Time Period:
14th–15th Centuries

Genre:
Play

OVERVIEW

Henry V is the title generally used for *The Life of King Henry the Fifth*, a history play by William Shakespeare. The drama is thought to have been performed first in 1599, and a smaller-format "quarto" version was published in 1600. The best-known written version of the play appeared in a larger-format "folio" version in 1623. Since there are significant differences between the two versions, scholars often distinguish between the quarto text and the folio text in discussing the play. *Henry V* is the final work in a tetralogy (a set of four related plays) that depicts the succession to the English throne from Richard II, whose rule began in 1377, through Henry V, who reigned from 1413 until his death in 1422. The tetralogy is sometimes referred to as the *Henriad*, because the first three plays (*Richard II*, *Henry IV, Part 1*, and *Henry IV, Part 2*) form a background for the culminating action presented in *Henry V*.

In the two plays that focus on his father (Henry IV), the young Henry (usually called Prince Hal, sometimes Harry) is portrayed as irresponsible and undisciplined. He avoids the royal courts in favor of taverns, fraternizes with questionable characters, and causes trouble of various kinds. Yet he also demonstrates prowess in war, and Shakespeare's audiences—most of whom had already seen the previous plays—would have looked forward to seeing Prince Hal transform into the heroic protagonist of *Henry V*. Audiences of the time were also very familiar with the exploits of the real Henry V, whose against-the-odds victory over French forces at Agincourt, France, in 1415 had made him a legendary figure in English history. The events of *Henry V* take place a little before and just after the Battle of Agincourt. In addition to focusing on the battle itself, the play sets up the political context that surrounded Henry's decision to invade France and depicts a little of the developing relationship between Henry and the French princess whom he ultimately marries. *Henry V* contains some of Shakespeare's most familiar phrases, including the exhortation "once more unto the breach, dear friends" and the poignant description of fellow soldiers as a "band of brothers."

Like most of Shakespeare's serious plays, *Henry V* includes comic interludes and farcical characters, which in this case are carried over from earlier plays in the tetralogy. These serve not only to amuse the audience but also to emphasize by contrast the dramatic scenes that reveal varied and, to some extent, conflicting aspects of Henry's personality. Scholars and viewers alike have debated Shakespeare's ambiguous portrayal of the king as well as the political and moral issues raised by Henry's resumption of a long-running armed conflict after years of peace.

HISTORICAL AND LITERARY CONTEXT

Shakespeare's "history plays" are so-called not only because they portray real characters and events from England's past but also because an awareness of their historical context is necessary in order to completely understand the dramas. This presents a challenge for modern readers, who are not usually acquainted with the complex issues that form the background for *Henry V*. Shakespeare's original audiences, however, could be counted upon both to recognize the historical references in the play and to make associations between the play and the politics of their own time.

Although the events depicted in the tetralogy took place about two hundred years before the plays were written, it is necessary to go back much further in English history to make sense of the main action in *Henry V*. Following the Norman Conquest in 1066, the French duke of Normandy became king of England, and for many years thereafter the ruling house of England also controlled a large and rich area of France. Most of their holdings in France were lost during the thirteenth century, but the French and English aristocracies were by then closely intertwined. When Charles IV, the last king in the hereditary ruling line of France, died without a male heir in 1328, a crisis of succession occurred. The English king Edward III was Charles IV's closest male relative, so by English interpretation of the laws of succession, Edward should have inherited the French throne. The French claimed, however, that, due to a legal doctrine called Salic Law, he could not succeed because he descended from a female rather than a male line. (Edward's mother was Charles IV's sister.) This dispute led to a long conflict known as the Hundred Years' War, which was fought intermittently from 1337 to 1453. *Henry V* begins more than halfway through this war-torn period, during a period of relative peace that had begun in 1389. Henry's decision to end the peace and renew combat with France

Ron Embleton (1930–88),
*Into Battle: Agincourt—
The Impossible Victory*,
Original artwork from
Look and Learn, no. 63
(30 March 1963).
© LOOK AND LEARN / THE
BRIDGEMAN ART LIBRARY
INTERNATIONAL

is the moral crux of the play, while his unexpected victory is a heroic climax in England's long-running attempt to gain sovereignty over France. As Shakespeare's audience would have known, Henry married the French king's daughter, and after Henry's death in 1422, their infant son, Henry VI, was crowned king of both France and England.

The conflict did not end, however. During the next half century, England not only lost its war with France but also became embroiled in a devastating civil conflict called the Wars of the Roses (1455–85). Shakespeare had dramatized the events of this period in the "first tetralogy," written around 1591 and

comprising *Henry VI, Parts 1–3* and *Richard III*. These popular plays were among the playwright's earliest works and helped to establish his reputation in the Elizabethan theater.

THEMES AND STYLE

Although both the Wars of the Roses and the Hundred Years' War were long concluded by the time Shakespeare wrote *Henry V*, the current events of his day were still very much connected to those watershed events. The Wars of the Roses concluded with the defeat of Richard III by Henry Tudor and the establishment of a new line of English rulers. Henry Tudor became

FROISSART AND THE HUNDRED YEARS' WAR

Many aspects of medieval European history remain unclear or unknown due to the lack of reliable written accounts. Although many historical narratives were written during the time, most merely recorded events—and stories of events—without a particular care for accuracy or organization. The "chronicle" was a popular type of documentation that arranged events in order of time, with little analysis or interpretation.

Despite their shortcomings, medieval chronicles are a key source of information concerning political events and social conditions associated with the Hundred Years' War. Among the most important is Jean Froissart's *Chroniques de France, d'Engleterre et des païs voisins*, which covers the period from 1322 until 1400 and recounts the circumstances leading up to the conflict as well as the first fifty years of the war.

There is little personal information about the chronicle's author, but he seems to have risen from humble origins to become historian in the court of Philippa of Hainault, a French noblewoman who married King Edward III of England.

Froissart traveled widely and recorded all sorts of information, much of which has proven vital to later interpretations of the fourteenth century. His chronicles also contain a good deal of incorrect or insignificant information, however, and tend to favor the political interests of his patrons while ignoring the common people.

More than one hundred manuscript copies of Froissart's *Chroniques* have been preserved, most illuminated with miniature illustrations. The most famous of these, commissioned sometime in the 1470s by Flemish nobleman Louis of Gruuthuse, contains 112 miniatures by the most skilled artisans of the time. Printed copies of the *Chroniques* became widely available in the sixteenth century, but since the complete work totals nearly three million words, published versions were typically abridged. An abbreviated English version was available in 1525, and the first complete English translation, prepared by Thomas Johnes, appeared in twelve volumes from 1803 to 1810.

Henry VII (reigned 1485–1509) and was followed on the throne by his son Henry VIII (reigned 1509–47), whose quest for a male heir became the partial cause of England's Protestant Reformation. Henry VIII's sickly son Edward VI ruled for just six years, and the young king was succeeded by his half sister Mary. She, however, failed in her attempts to restore Catholicism to England, and the crown passed to her half sister Elizabeth in 1558. Elizabeth I (who was born in 1533 and would die in 1603) never married, and by the time Shakespeare was writing *Henry V*, the problem of who would succeed the aging queen had become a pressing public concern. At the same time, Elizabeth was credited in part for England's defeat of the powerful Spanish Armada, an event that was widely regarded as England's most important military victory since Agincourt. These and other political circumstances of the late Elizabethan era clearly influenced the thematic emphasis of *Henry V*, which focuses to a large extent on issues related to kingship and war.

The connection between those themes centers on Henry's motive in resuming the war. Throughout the play there are implications that the motives for war are cynical, not only on Henry's part but also on the part of the church and other vested interests. One effect of the Hundred Years' War—which is considered a transformational event in the history of Western civilization—was the rise of nationalism in both England and France. Those in power recognized that it was important to capture this emerging sentiment and ensure that it strengthened rather than threatened

their personal security. In addition, the newly crowned King Henry V needed to counter his reputation as a wastrel and win recognition as a strong leader who could regain England's dominion in France. Yet Shakespeare also shows another side of Henry's deliberation, through comments (both in soliloquy and in dialogue) that reveal his consciousness of the war's human costs. Throughout the play there are reminders of war's horrific violence, even though most of the martial action takes place offstage. When Henry goes in disguise among the common soldiers, he is confronted by the complexities that arise from his decisions. For a time the English victory seems to vindicate Henry's rationalization of the war, but the play ends with a sobering reminder from the Chorus that everything won will be lost again, by Henry's own son.

CRITICAL DISCUSSION

Henry's stirring address to the troops on St. Crispin's Day, meant to rouse them for the forthcoming Battle of Agincourt, is so powerful that it has been taken by many critics as the heart of the play and the measure of Shakespeare's intention to glorify the king and his war. This view, which is reflected in Laurence Olivier's popular 1944 film adaptation of the play, largely prevailed in critical discussion throughout the nineteenth century and into the first half of the mid-twentieth century. Proponents ignored or explained away elements in the play that undercut and even oppose the patriotic rhetoric. Yet at the same time a negative characterization of Henry was developing, expressed

A page from a fifteenth-century illuminated manuscript of Froissart's *Chronicle*, depicting the death of Jean III (1286–1341) and the battles that followed. © GIRAUDON / THE BRIDGEMAN ART LIBRARY INTERNATIONAL

as early as 1818 by William Hazlitt, whose *Characters in Shakespeare's Plays* describes the king as an "amiable monster." Detractors focus on Henry's ruthlessness (for example, ordering the executions of the French prisoners of war) and the shifting justifications by which he avoids personal responsibility for the war. By the latter part of the twentieth century, the balance of critical opinion had tilted toward a negative reading of Henry's character, but there were still two clearly developed schools of interpretation. As Karl P. Wentersdorf summarizes in his 1976 essay "The Conspiracy of Silence in *Henry V*":

> For some [critics] the play presents the story of an ideal monarch and glorifies his achievements; for them, the tone approaches that of an epic lauding the military virtues. For others, the protagonist is a Machiavellian militarist who professes Christianity but whose deeds reveal both hypocrisy and ruthlessness; for them, the tone is predominantly one of mordant satire.

The question of whether Henry's war was a "just" cause by moral, legal, and theological standards has been debated since the time of its undertaking, and literary critics have been divided on whether Shakespeare intended *Henry V* as a justification of the war or as a condemnation. Along these lines, a number of later scholars have explored the relationship of religion and war in the play, often viewing these factors in the context of political and philosophical influences at work in Shakespeare's own time. Notable examples include Steven Marx's "Holy War in *Henry V*" (1995), Janet Spencer's "Princes, Pirates, and Pigs: Criminalizing Wars of Conquest in *Henry V*" (1996), and Jonathan Baldo's "Wars of Memory in *Henry V*" (1996). John Mebane's 2007 essay "'Impious War': Religion and the Ideology of Warfare in *Henry V*" examines the play from a perspective that Shakespeare's histories "dramatize the discrepancy between the pacifism grounded upon key elements of the New Testament, on the one hand, and the devotion of the aristocratic warrior classes to an ideology of warfare, on the other." This warrior ideology, he contends, was compounded of chivalric codes, the Judeo-Christian "just war" doctrine, and the heroic tradition of pagan myth. Thus Mebane, like a number of other contemporary commentators, expands discussion of the play to encompass the more complex analytical approaches that characterize postmodern criticism.

SOURCES

Baldo, Jonathan. "Wars of Memory in *Henry V*." *Shakespeare Quarterly* 47.1 (1996): 132–59. Print.

Marx, Steven. "Shakespeare's Pacifism." *Renaissance Quarterly* 45.1 (1992): 49–95. Print.

Mebane, John S. "'Impious War': Religion and the Ideology of Warfare in *Henry V*." *Studies in Philology* 104.2 (2007): 250–66. Print.

Spencer, Janet M. "Princes, Pirates, and Pigs: Criminalizing Wars of Conquest in *Henry V*." *Shakespeare Quarterly* 47.2 (1996): 160–77. Print.

Wentersdorf, Karl P. "The Conspiracy of Silence in *Henry V*." *Shakespeare Quarterly* 27.3 (1976): 264–87. Print.

FURTHER READING

Bloom, Harold. *William Shakespeare's "Henry V."* New York: Chelsea House, 1988. Print.

De Somogyi, Nick. *Shakespeare's Theatre of War*. Aldershot: Ashgate, 1998. Print.

Jorgensen, Paul A. *Shakespeare's Military World*. Berkeley: U of California P, 1956. Print.

McAlindon, Tom. "War and Peace in *Henry V*." *Shakespeare Minus "Theory"*: 45–76. Aldershot: Ashgate, 2004. Print.

Meron, Theodor. *Henry's Wars and Shakespeare's Laws: Perspectives on the Law of War in the Later Middle Ages*. Oxford: Clarendon, 1993. Print.

Rabkin, Norman. "Rabbits, Ducks, and *Henry V*." *Shakespeare Quarterly* 28.3 (1977): 279–96. Print.

Shakespeare, William. *Henry V*. Bloom, Harold, Ed. and Intro. New York: Chelsea House, 1988. Print.

Shaughnessy, Robert. "The Last Post: *Henry V*, War Culture and the Postmodern Shakespeare." *Theatre Survey* 39.1 (1998): 41–61. Print.

Smith, Gordon Ross. "Shakespeare's *Henry V*: Another Part of the Critical Forest." *Journal of the History of Ideas* 37.1 (1976): 3–26. Print.

Taunton, Nina. *1590s Drama and Militarism: Portrayals of War in Marlowe, Chapman, and Shakespeare's* Henry V. Aldershot: Ashgate, 2001. Print.

MEDIA ADAPTATIONS

Henry V. Dir. Laurence Olivier. Perf. Laurence Olivier, Robert Helpmann, Felix Aylmer. United Artists, 1944. Film.

Henry V. Dir. Peter Watts. Perf. John Clements, John Garside. British Broadcasting Corporation, 1953. Television movie.

Henry V. Dir. Kenneth Branagh. Perf. Kenneth Branagh, Simon Shepherd, James Larkin. Samuel Goldwyn Company, 1989. Film.

Cynthia Giles

Observe the Sons of Ulster Marching Towards the Somme

Frank McGuinness

OVERVIEW

First produced at Dublin's Peacock Theatre in February 1985, Frank McGuinness's *Observe the Sons of Ulster Marching Towards the Somme* is the story of Kenneth Pyper, an Irish World War I veteran looking back on his wartime experiences from a distance of many years. Shifting backward in time, subsequent scenes depict the zeal with which Pyper's fellow soldiers, fueled by the mythic bravery of men from their home province, embraced service in the name of Ulster; the fear that overcame them after experiencing combat; and the preparation for the Battle of the Somme.

Pyper's homosexuality and upper-class social status initially make him an outsider among his comrades, but by the time of the battle, which he alone survives, he has developed strong bonds with the other men, particularly the blacksmith David Craig. As the soldiers prepare to enter battle, Pyper's love for Craig and his connections with the other soldiers lead him to embrace their collective love of Ulster in order to rally them for the fight.

The play was initially staged during the Troubles, a term that refers to the internal political, military, and paramilitary conflict that began in Northern Ireland in 1968 and ended with the Good Friday Agreement in 1998. The clashes pitted unionists, who fought to remain part of the political entity of Great Britain, against republicans (or nationalists), who demanded independence from Britain. While the play does not directly address the Troubles, the action takes place during the years when the Republic of Ireland was fighting for independence from Britain, a period that is often seen as the root of the ethnic, religious, and political issues at the heart of the Troubles. The play is, therefore, often read as a reflection on questions of British nationality, Northern Irish identity, and the history of violence that surrounds the two.

Observe the Sons of Ulster Marching Towards the Somme garnered widespread critical acclaim and was embraced by audiences on both sides of the Irish political divide. In the decades since its publication, it has been the subject of a growing body of scholarly commentary that has examined its statements about Irish and British politics and mythology; the relationships among history, memory, and the present; and the intersections of gender, sexuality, and war. The work lends itself well to a number of political and social interpretations, and recent productions have rendered it in the context of the scourge of AIDS and of the Iraq War.

HISTORICAL AND LITERARY CONTEXT

Observe the Sons of Ulster Marching Towards the Somme draws on the events of July 1, 1916, the opening day of the Battle of the Somme, an Allied attempt to overrun German lines along the Somme River in France that lasted into November of that year. More than sixty thousand British soldiers lost their lives on the first day of the battle. Some six thousand of the dead were from Ulster, a predominantly Protestant Irish province. In the play Pyper notes "the amount of volunteers from [his] beloved province. They can't keep up with [them]." That McGuinness's characters are Ulster Protestants is significant not only because the region lost so many young men in the battle but also because it has a rich political and military history.

The play is set in 1915 and 1916, which were critical years in the history of Irish independence. Ireland, a British colony since the sixteenth century, had begun to agitate for home rule in the late 1880s. The struggle for independence incited an internal conflict between those who wanted to remain part of the United Kingdom and those who wanted to form a separate Irish state. This conflict led to a violent civil war that lasted from 1916 to 1922. The war officially ended in 1921 with the Anglo-Irish Treaty, which split Ireland into the Irish Free State (now the Republic of Ireland) and Northern Ireland; the latter, comprising six of the nine counties of Ulster, remained part of Great Britain.

After the partition, Northern Ireland has seen fluctuating periods of peace and internal turmoil. The Protestant unionist government that took control in Northern Ireland initiated decades of discrimination against the minority (mostly republican) Catholic population. This discrimination led to the development of pro-Catholic rights groups, and when a civil rights march in 1968 turned violent, civil war broke out again, this time within Northern Ireland. In the decades preceding the production of McGuinness's play, the struggles between British troops and guerrilla and paramilitary forces led to the deaths of more than

Key Facts

Conflict:
World War I

Time Period:
Early 20th Century

Genre:
Play

Award:
London Evening Standard Award for Most Promising Playwright

three thousand people. It was intended that audiences in the mid-1980s should see the play as a statement about the contemporary crisis in Northern Ireland.

The Battle of the Somme was significant for Ulster not only because of the extensive loss of life but because it was fought on the same day as a much earlier historically important event, the Battle of the Boyne, which occurred in Ireland on July 1, 1690. That fight pitted the forces of King James II (a Catholic) against those of King William (a Protestant). William had deposed James in the Glorious Revolution two years earlier, but James continued to have an extensive following in Ireland. Supported by the Protestants of Ulster, William was ultimately victorious and subsequently became a hero to the people of the region.

Toward the end of *Observe the Sons of Ulster Marching Towards the Somme*, Pyper and his comrades reenact the Battle of the Boyne. Their efforts go awry, however, when Pyper, playing the role of William's horse, trips and falls, upending his rider and seemingly giving victory to King James. The play also references the Easter Rising of April 1916, in which members of the Irish Volunteers, under the leadership of Pearse, seized locations in Dublin and proclaimed an independent Irish Republic. The men discuss news of the Rising, lampooning Pearse and remarking that "[t]he Irish couldn't spell republic, let alone proclaim it."

In an essay in the *Yearbook of English Studies*, Declan Kiberd suggests that the work's title "is a deliberate echo of an old Ulster saga, *Oidhe Chloinne Uisnigh*, or

The Fate of the Sons of Usna," in which a corrupt aristocracy takes advantage of a group of warrior brothers. This interpretation underscores the importance of history in both the play and the cultural imagination of Ulster. Kiberd's reading is supported by the soldiers' frequent mention of serving the king, as when one of the men proclaims that "[w]e will fight [the war] as we have fought in other centuries to answer our king's call."

THEMES AND STYLE

Observe the Sons of Ulster Marching Towards the Somme is composed of four parts. In "Part 1: Remembrance," an aged Pyper addresses the ghosts of the comrades with whom he fought during World War I. "Part 2: Initiation" opens with Pyper first encountering his comrades in the barracks and introduces the conflicts in philosophy, particularly over war and patriotism, that will dominate their early relationship. In "Part 3: Pairing," the men enjoy a brief respite from the fighting during leave. With their zeal for war shattered, their relationships with each other become central to their ability to continue the fight. In "Part 4: Bonding," the men prepare for the Battle of the Somme, realizing that they are unlikely to survive it. The play closes with the older Pyper addressing his younger self.

McGuinness focuses on the mythic patriotism of Ulster's men, both past and present. In the second act the soldiers are excited to follow in the footsteps of generations of Ulster men who have died for the causes of freedom and Protestantism. By the end, however, they are afraid of death, which seems inevitable.

The Royal Irish Rifles, members of the Ulster Division, on the first day of the Battle of the Somme, which is the focal point of Frank McGuinness's play *Observe the Sons of Ulster Marching Towards the Somme*. © WORLD HISTORY ARCHIVE / ALAMY

As they prepare for battle at the end of the play, Craig tells Pyper, "This is the last battle. We're going out to die," a sentiment his comrades share. Although Pyper's detached stance on life has previously made him critical of the men's unswerving loyalty to Ulster, he attempts to rally them by appealing to their love of home. When they smell the Somme River, he encourages them to imagine "We're not in France. We're home. We're on our own territory. We're fighting for home. This river is ours. This land's ours. We've come home." As the men gather for battle, he leads them in a prayer that ends with the words "I love my home. I love my Ulster. Ulster. Ulster. Ulster. Ulster. Ulster. Ulster. Ulster. Ulster." But this scene of bonding and optimism is framed by the words of the older Pyper, who, addressing the ghosts of his fallen comrades, says, "We claimed we would die for each other in battle. To fulfil that claim we marched into the battle that killed us all. That is not loyalty. That is not love. That is hate. Deepest hate. Hate for one's self." *Observe the Sons of Ulster Marching Towards the Somme* ultimately suggests that the Ulster for which the men gave their lives was both imagined and illusory, leading them willingly and pointlessly to their deaths, both in World War I and during the Troubles.

The men's patriotic attachment to Ulster is connected to another of the play's central themes: the military's demand for conformity to norms of masculinity and heterosexuality. Attempting to live up to the mythic status of Ulster men, the soldiers often engage in misogynistic rhetoric. One of them, complaining about having to make his bed, explains that "you don't join the army to do woman's work." Another chastises his comrades for behavior that is "more fit coming from crying women." Distinguishing the unionists from the nationalists by virtue of their masculinity, one of the men suggests that the nationalists are a "disgrace to their sex, the whole bastarding lot of them."

The men's emphasis on masculinity is threatened, however, by the presence of Pyper, an artist and stereotypically effeminate homosexual. In addition to challenging sexual norms, Pyper defies the men's romanticized view of Ulster and militarism, explaining that he joined the army because he wanted to die and thus belittling their visions of heroism. Ultimately, however, it is Pyper's love for his fellow soldier Craig that gives him the will to survive the war and drives the pro-Ulster rallying speech he hopes will similarly inspire his comrades.

CRITICAL DISCUSSION

Premiering during the continuing violence and destruction of the fighting between Irish nationalists and unionists, *Observe the Sons of Ulster Marching Towards the Somme* drew intense scrutiny from audiences, reviewers, and literary scholars. Interest in it was amplified by the fact that McGuinness is a Catholic from the Republic of Ireland, and the play's central characters are Northern Irish Protestants.

Issues of political and religious representation occupy most early critical reactions to the play. The

THE SHAM FIGHT: SCARVA'S ANNUAL PAGEANT

The reenactment of the Battle of the Boyne (1690) in which the characters of *Observe the Sons of Ulster Marching Towards the Somme* participate builds on a Northern Irish tradition associated with the village of Scarva in County Down, where King William and his army are said to have camped before the battle.

Although Scarva is home to a population of only three hundred people, it attracts tens of thousands of enthusiasts each July to its famous Sham Fight. The event, which is held annually on July 13, celebrates the battle and the Ulster pride with which it has become synonymous. The celebration includes a parade featuring the Royal Black Institution, a prominent Protestant society dating to 1797, as well as a keynote address, and, most notably, the Sham Fight itself, a reenactment of the famous battle. Participants in the Sham Fight wear elaborate period costumes, ride horses, and carry guns and swords similar to those the original combatants would have used in 1690.

The tradition of Battle of the Boyne reenactments began as early as the late eighteenth century. They remained popular throughout Northern Ireland in the nineteenth century, eventually coalescing into the annual event at Scarva, which was well established by the outbreak of World War I. The popularity of the Sham Fight has helped to preserve the Battle of the Boyne in modern memory. Subsequently, the Northern Irish understanding of the battle and its significance have been shaped by the patriotism and pageantry of contemporary reenactments.

mythic status of Ulster and its men is at the center of this discussion, with critics often debating whether the work celebrates or lampoons the devotion of the men of Ulster to unionism, war, and sacrifice. Writing in *Éire-Ireland*, Tom Herron argues that the play's use of the flashback conveys its message about the endlessness and pointlessness of war: "There is no 'final scene,' there is no knowledge securely gained, only an endlessly repeated movement toward what was already 'known' in the beginning, the repetition of which begins the process anew."

Writing in the *Irish University Review* about the work's use of history and memory, Emilie Pine suggests that its message is ultimately apolitical, noting that "certain forms of memory are divisive and destructive, and need to be dismantled. In their place, [McGuinness] crafts a new ritual, artfully transferring meaning from the public and the political to the private and the personal."

Questions about the role of gender and sexuality are also central to critical discussions of the play. Scholars have frequently explored McGuinness's depiction of both Pyper's homosexuality and the homosocial bonds between the soldiers more generally. In an article in the *Canadian Journal of Irish Studies*, Helen Lojek reads Pyper as an extreme outsider, ostracized by

Austin Osman Spare (1888-?), a soldier bandages a wounded companion on the battlefield. © SNARK / ART RESOURCE, NY

SOURCES

Herron, Tom. "Dead Men Talking: Frank McGuinness's *Observe the Sons of Ulster Marching Towards the Somme.*" *Éire-Ireland: A Journal of Irish Studies* 39.1–2 (2004): 136–62. Print.

Kiberd, Declan. "Frank McGuinness and the Sons of Ulster." *Yearbook of English Studies* 35 (2005): 279–97. Print.

Lojek, Helen. "Myth and Bonding in Frank McGuinness's *Observe the Sons of Ulster Marching Towards the Somme.*" *Canadian Journal of Irish Studies* 14.1 (1988): 45–53. Print.

———. "*Observe the Sons of Ulster*: Historical Stages." *Echoes Down the Corridor: Irish Theatre—Past, Present, and Future.* Ed. Patrick Lonergran and Riana O'Dwyer. Dublin: Carysfort, 2007. 81–94. Print.

McGuinness, Frank. *Observe the Sons of Ulster Marching Towards the Somme.* London: Faber, 1986. Print.

Pine, Emilie. "The Tyranny of Memory: Remembering the Great War in Frank McGuinness's *Observe the Sons of Ulster Marching Towards the Somme.*" *Irish University Review: A Journal of Irish Studies* 40.1 (2010): 59–68. Print.

FURTHER READING

Bardon, Jonathan. *A History of Ulster.* Belfast: Blackstaff, 1992. Print.

Beiner, Guy. "Between Trauma and Triumphalism: The Easter Rising, the Somme, and the Crux of Deep Memory in Modern Ireland." *Journal of British Studies* 46.2 (2007): 366–89. Print.

Cadden, Michael. "Homosexualizing the Troubles: A Short Query into Two Derry Airs by Frank McGuinness." *Princeton University Library Chronicle* 68.1–2 (2006): 560–71. Print.

Cregan, David. "Irish Theatrical Celebrity and the Critical Subjugation of Difference in the Work of Frank McGuinness." *Modern Drama* 47.4 (2004): 671–85. Print.

Gilbert, Martin. *The Somme: Heroism and Horror in the First World War.* New York: Holt, 2006. Print.

Grene, Nicholas. *The Politics of Irish Drama: Plays in Context from Boucicault to Friel.* Cambridge: Cambridge UP, 1999. Print.

Lernout, Geert, ed. *The Crows Behind the Plough: History and Violence in Anglo-Irish Poetry and Drama.* Amsterdam: Rodopi, 1991. Print.

Lojek, Helen. *Contexts for Frank McGuinness's Drama.* Washington, D.C.: Catholic U of America P, 2004. Print.

McKittrick, David, and David McVea. *Making Sense of the Troubles: The Story of the Conflict in Northern Ireland.* Chicago: New Amsterdam, 2002. Print.

Nally, Kenneth. *"Celebrating Confusion": The Theatre of Frank McGuinness.* Newcastle upon Tyne: Cambridge Scholars, 2009. Print.

sexual preference, social class, philosophy of life, and profession. She suggests that Pyper reflects the truth that for minority groups, "the dominant historical perspective created by white male heterosexuals is too narrow," and that, in focusing on the personal relationships between the men, the play argues that "the emotional truths of daily existence deserve as much attention as the public events stemming from the ballotbox and the battlefield."

Scholars also trace the numerous historical and political interpretations of the play reflected by different directors. In an article in *Echoes Down the Corridor*, Lojek offers an overview of the many ways in which it has been staged, including in its Dublin premiere, which "emphasized World War I and the play's religious dimension"; in subsequent Northern Irish productions that tended to accentuate "the play's use of the Battle of the Somme, generally regarded as a key event in the history of Ulster Protestantism"; in 1990s stagings that underscored the play's homosexual subtext; and in a 2003 American production that many commentators interpreted in the context of war in Iraq.

Greta Gard

"PAUL REVERE'S RIDE"
Henry Wadsworth Longfellow

OVERVIEW

Henry Wadsworth Longfellow's poem "Paul Revere's Ride" is generally credited with creating the legend of the Revolutionary War hero and his historic ride to warn Lexington and Concord of an impending British attack. First published in the *Atlantic Monthly* in 1860, the poem appeared at a time when the United States stood on the brink of civil war and served as an important piece of propaganda for the Northern cause. In mythologizing Revere as a courageous patriot, Longfellow aimed to rouse sympathy for the abolition movement and patriotism for the protection of the union that Revere's ride had helped to found.

In composing the poem, which was inspired by a visit to the Old North Church in April 1860, Longfellow researched the history of Revere and his ride but chose to reinterpret the event, collapsing the work of several men into the single heroic quest attributed to Revere in the poem. This strategy allowed him to emphasize the themes of courage and perseverance in the face of difficult times that was essential to his message. The poem transformed Paul Revere from a New England hero to a national legend, and has greatly impacted the popular understanding of Revere's role in the Revolutionary War. Although scholarly treatments of the poem as a work of literature have been notably rare, it remains among the best-known poems of its era, and has been widely anthologized in collections of American poetry. Longfellow later retitled the poem "The Landlord's Tale" for inclusion as the opening poem in his 1863 collection *Tales of a Wayside Inn.*

HISTORICAL AND LITERARY CONTEXT

"Paul Revere's Ride" is loosely based on a series of events that unfolded on April 18, 1775, the eve of the American Revolution. A group of American rebels in Boston had discovered that British forces quartered in the city were planning to advance on the Massachusetts towns of Lexington and Concord, where they planned to arrest John Hancock and Samuel Adams and seize the stockpile of weapons the rebels had amassed. The rebels were unsure, however, whether the British were planning to travel by land or across the Charles River. Although the poem depicts Revere instructing a fellow patriot to observe the British and hang a signal light or lights in the tower

of the Old North Church ("One if by land, and two if by sea"), in actuality, it was Revere himself who gained intelligence of the British plan. He delivered the news to Robert Newman, the unnamed patriot in Longfellow's poem and arranged for the signal. Thus, when Newman signaled that the British were coming by sea, he was alerting not Revere, but rebels on the other side of the river, who might relay the message on to Lexington if Revere was intercepted. While Revere set off on his ride, a second rider, William Dawes, also left Boston for Lexington, following an alternate route. Both made it to Lexington, but Revere, Dawes, and a third man, Samuel Prescott, were intercepted by British troops before they reached Concord. Revere was detained in Lexington; the other two riders escaped, but only Prescott made it to Concord. The next day, April 19, 1775, the Battle of Lexington and Concord broke out, marking the beginning of the American Revolution. The conflict would not end until 1783.

Longfellow's poem also draws on the political climate of the period in which it was composed. The poem was written in the spring of 1860, as tensions between the North and South over slavery and states' rights were reaching a boiling point. Longfellow, an outspoken opponent of slavery, had previously published a volume of abolitionist verses entitled *Poems on Slavery* (1842). A proud New Englander, he hoped that the heroic figure of Paul Revere would instill in his fellow Northerners the resolve they would need to endure the impending crisis. Ironically, the poem was published in December of 1860, the same month in which South Carolina, citing the right of its citizens to hold slaves and the North's failure to uphold the Fugitive Slave Act of 1850, became the first state to secede from the Union. The Civil War officially began a year after the poem's composition, on April 12, 1861. The war would stretch until June 22, 1865. As Longfellow predicted, it was a trying time, which saw the deaths of more than six hundred thousand soldiers and devastated the South.

Longfellow's poem was not the first to address Revere's ride (Eb Stiles had composed a poem on the topic in 1795), but it was certainly the most influential. Discussing the reception and influence of Longfellow's poem in his 1994 study of Revere's ride, David Hackett Fischer suggests that "the insistent beat

Key Facts

Conflict:
American Revolution

Time Period:
Mid-18th Century

Genre:
Poem

PAUL REVERE'S RIDE.

does so in part by exaggerating the role the silversmith played in the events of April 18, 1775. In the poem Revere is at once the innovator of the lantern signal, the recipient of the signal's message, and the messenger who single-handedly warns both Lexington and Concord of the impending British attack. Moreover, the ride itself is depicted as the action on which the fate of the rebels and America would ultimately depend, with the speaker asserting that "the fate of a nation was riding that night." The poet later invokes the courage of the rebels who the next day would organize to fight against British, suggesting that everyone knows the story of "How the British Regulars fired and fled,—/ How the farmers gave them ball for ball." In referring to the rebels as "farmers," Longfellow emphasizes their relative vulnerability compared to the "British Regulars" or "redcoats," who are clearly a trained and well-equipped army. The poem implicitly calls upon its audience to be as brave and patriotic as Revere and the "farmers" who repelled the British from Lexington and Concord and to honor the union that their collective and courageous effort made possible.

The relationship between the past, present, and future is also thematically central to "Paul Revere's Ride." The poem begins in the present, with the speaker invoking the past; in its opening stanza the speaker, referencing the date of the famous ride, asserts, "Hardly a man is now alive / Who remembers that famous day and year." After establishing the importance of the subject matter, the poem shifts in the second stanza, to the past, describing the circumstances of Revere's ride. The poem closes by uniting the three: "For borne on the night-wind of the Past, / Through all our history, to the last, / In the hour of darkness and peril and need, / The people will waken and listen to hear / The hurrying hoof-beats of that steed, / And the midnight message of Paul Revere." Suggesting that Revere's message has significance for the people of the future reinforces the importance of both the ride and Revere. More importantly, however, suggesting that Revere's message is relevant to the present would, for the poet's contemporaries, immediately have invoked the specter of civil war, which, by the time Longfellow was writing, was beginning to appear inevitable. The past as it is fictionalized by Longfellow is thus deployed in the present as a valuable form of propaganda that might directly shape the course of the future.

CRITICAL DISCUSSION

"Paul Revere's Ride" was embraced by Longfellow's contemporaries, among whom the poet was a minor celebrity. Over time it established a reputation as one of the best-known and frequently recited of American poems. Despite its immense popular appeal, however, the poem was largely dismissed by literary scholars as time wore on. There are several reasons for this trend. The first is that the poem's straightforward tale,

of Longfellow's meter reverberated through the North like a drum roll. It instantly captured the imagination of the reading public. This was a call to arms for a new American generation, in another moment of peril." The work also significantly shaped the legend of Paul Revere. In fact, many scholars suggest that Revere would have remained largely unknown to history if it had not been for Longfellow's work, and references to the poem can be found in nearly all works discussing Revere's ride.

THEMES AND STYLE

"Paul Revere's Ride" is a narrative poem, a form in which verse is used as a means of telling a cohesive story. As the poem's opening entreaty, "Listen my children and you shall hear," suggests, the poem was written with oral delivery in mind. Commentators have frequently noted that the poem's rhythm re-creates the urgent pounding of the hooves of Revere's horse. While the narrative form has fallen out of favor, few would deny the appropriateness of such a form for the task in which Longfellow employed it, particularly as the work, in presenting a speaker who tells Revere's story many years after the fact, takes storytelling as an explicit subject.

Heroism and courage are the central themes of the story that Longfellow tells, and to this end he goes to great lengths to mythologize Revere's heroism. He

THE MIDNIGHT RIDE OF WILLIAM DAWES

While Longfellow's poem ensured the lasting fame of Paul Revere, in crediting the silversmith as the sole rider, he also virtually guaranteed that the contributions of William Dawes to that ride would be forgotten. In a humorous attempt to set the record straight, Helen F. Moore wrote a satirical poem titled "The Midnight Ride of William Dawes," which was published in the *Century Magazine* in 1896. In the poem's opening lines, a long-suffering Dawes laments, "Never of me was a hero made; / Poets have never sung my praise." Making reference to the famous opening line of Longfellow's

poem, he argues, "'Tis all very well for the children to hear / Of the midnight ride of Paul Revere; / But why should my name be quite forgot, / Who rode as boldly and well, God wot [knows]?" The poem suggests that the choice of Revere was arbitrary, motivated by the ease with which "Revere" rhymes with key words such as *hear*, *fear*, and *near*. Dawes explains, "As I rode, with never a break or a pause; / But what was the use, when my name was Dawes!" and asserts, "Had he been Dawes and I Revere, / No one had heard of him, I fear."

historical lesson, and opening line ("Listen my children, and you shall hear") associated it with a children's rather than an adult literary tradition. A second reason was that the poem's form had fallen out of vogue. Lyric poetry gained ascendency over narrative verse, which was often seen as less sophisticated or literary. Richard Ruland speaks to this second point in a 1966 *English Journal* article in which, noting the conflict between the literalism of poems such as "Paul Revere's Ride" and the modern demand for poetry heavy on symbolism, he suggests that "no amount of re-assessment can rescue Longfellow from his own theory of poetry, and unless our own conception should change, Longfellow can never be thought 'great.'"

Despite its somewhat denigrated status among literary critics, however, Longfellow's poem has has been the subject of a substantial body of criticism in the century and a half since its publication. Much of this work, however, has focused on the text's publication history and historical accuracy rather than its literary qualities. In a 1951 article in the *New England Quarterly*, for example, James C. Austin explores the

influence of J. T. Fields, the editor and part-owner of the *Atlantic Monthly*, on Longfellow's work, arguing that he made "an important improvement" to "Paul Revere's Ride" by reordering and revising the poem's final lines to emphasize the lasting importance of Revere's message. Edward L. Tucker's article in *Studies in the American Renaissance* offers insight into the poem and the other verses in *Tales of a Wayside Inn*, by reading them alongside Longfellow's journals from the same period.

Writers have frequently worked to identify the numerous historical liberties that Longfellow took in composing the poem. Over time, commentators have come to view these manipulations as strategic or rhetorical, rather than as evidence of sloppy historiography or misinformation. Although scholars of other works of war literature have often debated whether fictionalized accounts of war might ultimately present a more truthful account of the war experience than do the facts alone, there has not yet been a sustained attempt to consider Longfellow's poem in the context of such discussions.

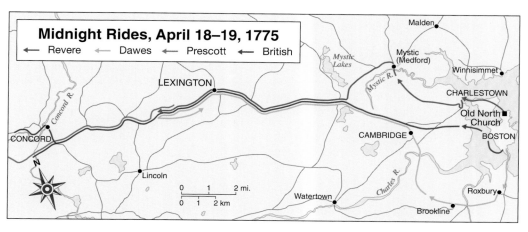

© MAP BY XNR PRODUCTIONS. CENGAGE LEARNING, GALE.

SOURCES

Austin, James C. "J. T. Fields and the Revision of Longfellow's Poems: Unpublished Correspondence." *New England Quarterly* 24.2 (1951): 239–50. Print.

Fischer, David Hackett. *Paul Revere's Ride.* New York: Oxford UP, 1994. Print.

Longfellow, Henry Wadsworth. "Paul Revere's Ride." *The Oxford Book of American Poetry.* Oxford: Oxford UP, 2006. 47–50. Print.

Ruland, Richard. "Longfellow and the Modern Reader." *English Journal* 55.6 (1966): 661–68. Print.

FURTHER READING

Calhoun, Charles C. *Longfellow: A Rediscovered Life.* Boston: Beacon, 2004. Print.

Langguth, A. J. *Patriots: The Men Who Started the American Revolution.* New York: Simon, 1988. Print.

Middlekauff, Robert. *The Glorious Cause: The American Revolution, 1763–1789.* New York: Oxford UP, 2005. Print.

Miller, Joel. *The Revolutionary Paul Revere.* Nashville: Nelson, 2010. Print.

Tourtellot, Arthur. *Lexington and Concord.* New York: Norton, 2000. Print.

Triber, Jayne E. *A True Republican: The Life of Paul Revere.* Amherst: U of Massachusetts P, 1998. Print.

Tucker, Edward L. "References in Longfellow's 'Journals' (1856–1882) to His Important Literary Works." *Studies in the American Renaissance* (1994): 289–345. Print.

Young, Alfred Fabian. *The Shoemaker and the Tea Party: Memory and the American Revolution.* Boston: Beacon, 1999. Print.

Greta Gard

THE SILVER TASSIE
A Tragi-Comedy in Four Acts
Seán O'Casey

OVERVIEW

Seán O'Casey's *The Silver Tassie* is one of the best-known plays depicting the lives of soldiers and their families during World War I. It is also one of the most experimental. O'Casey finished the play in 1928, but William Butler Yeats rejected it for production at Ireland's Abbey Theatre because its inflammatory subject matter didn't fit in with the increasingly conservative goals of the theater. O'Casey flouted convention by publishing it in print before it was staged. More than a year later, the play debuted in 1929 to mixed reviews at London's Apollo Theater.

The Silver Tassie examines the disparity between the common representation of the war as glorious sport or religious crusade and the reality of its damaging effects on young soldiers. Its protagonist, Harry Heegan, is a working-class Irish football hero whose athletic abilities have won him prestige in his community and the love of the popular Jessie Taite. As the play opens, Harry, home on leave from his service in France, leads his team to an unprecedented third consecutive championship. Remembering the song a fellow soldier sang in the trenches, Harry and his buddies dub the championship cup "the silver tassie." By the end of the war, however, Harry has been paralyzed, and Jessie has abandoned him for his friend and war comrade, the seemingly shallow and insincere Barney. Harry's suffering is compounded by the fact that Barney, who rescued him after he was paralyzed in battle, is celebrated as a war hero, gaining the community admiration that once belonged to Harry. As the play concludes, Harry, in a fit of anger and despair brought on by seeing Jessie and Barney together at the Football Club where he was once admired, flings the silver tassie to the floor.

Written in an innovative style that blends aspects of tragedy with comedy, naturalism with expressionism, and speech with singing and chanting, the play has polarized readers and audiences for decades. Although it is not widely staged, it continues to attract attention for both its innovative style and its blatant critique of the war and the propaganda that led a generation of men to their deaths.

HISTORICAL AND LITERARY CONTEXT

The Silver Tassie is set during World War I. The war, among the first to be fought with powerfully destructive modern weaponry, ultimately brought about the deaths of more than nine million men worldwide. In the United Kingdom the constant demand for more soldiers led to an extensive propaganda campaign. By the end of the war, such propaganda had encouraged the enlistment of more than 5,000,000 British soldiers, more than 800,000 of whom were killed in the conflict.

In depicting his protagonist's reversal of fortune, O'Casey critiques a tradition of war propaganda that compared military conflict to athletic contests or religious crusades. One of the most notable examples of the former tradition is Sir Henry Newbolt's 1897 poem "Vitaï Lampada," which explicitly likens war to a cricket match, calling upon soldiers to "Play up! Play up! And play the game!" Although it predated the conflict, Newbolt's poem was widely circulated in support of World War I recruitment. Elsewhere, the formation of Pals Battalions, which encouraged men to enlist in a group so they could fight alongside their colleagues, friends, and teammates, had helped to perpetuate the myth that war was a sport or an adventure that friends could experience together. O'Casey's play not only rejects the association of war with sport but also depicts its damaging effects on "pals" such as Harry and Barney, whose friendship is destroyed by the war. The play also critiques the use of propaganda that promoted World War I as a just and distinctly Christian cause, tied to Britain's role as an imperial power and bearer of the responsibility to spread enlightenment and Christianity around the globe.

In critiquing war and war propaganda, *The Silver Tassie* was part of a tradition of British anti-World War I drama that can be traced to 1917 when John Drinkwater's *X=O: A Night of the Trojan War* and Bernard Shaw's *O'Flaherty V.C.: A Recruiting Pamphlet* were first staged. O'Casey's play is more clearly associated, however, with a second wave of anti-World War I drama that was initiated in 1928 by R. C. Sherriff's popular and brutally realistic *Journey's End*. While Sherriff's play was set entirely in and immediately outside the trenches, *The Silver Tassie* largely avoids

❖ *Key Facts*

Conflict:
World War I

Time Period:
Early 20th Century

Genre:
Play

O'CASEY'S MOST FAMOUS AND ENDURING DRAMAS: *THE DUBLIN TRILOGY*

Before depicting the plight of Irish soldiers in Flanders in his World War I drama *The Silver Tassie*, playwright Seán O'Casey chronicled the Irish war for independence in his acclaimed work *The Dublin Trilogy*. In the trilogy's first installment, *The Shadow of a Gunman* (1923), O'Casey explores a working-class neighborhood in the Irish capital as the increasingly violent political situation wreaks havoc in the lives of the poor. A year later saw the premiere of the trilogy's second play, *Juno and the Paycock* (1924). In this work, O'Casey recreates Ireland's struggle for independence from the perspective of the Boyles, a typical working-class family torn apart by the alcoholism, moral corruption, and the pride of its men. The final installment of the trilogy, *The Plough and the Stars* (1926), offers a scathing critique of the fanatical and delusional side of Irish patriotism through its portrayal of several participants in the bloody Easter Rebellion of 1916. At the heart of all three plays lies the playwright's preoccupation with the divide between gender roles during the Irish Civil War. O'Casey reveals the extent to which traditional male tendencies toward egotism and violence ultimately destroy community and family. O'Casey's trilogy represents one of the first significant literary works to emerge from the Easter Rebellion.

depictions of battle. Instead, in settings that include the Heegan home, a destroyed monastery, a hospital, and a sports club, the work emphasizes the impact of the war away from the front lines. Thematically, the poem has much in common with combatant-poet Wilfred Owen's "Disabled," which dramatizes the experiences of a young football hero who returns from the war confined to a wheelchair.

THEMES AND STYLE

From the time it was written, *The Silver Tassie* has incited controversy over both its style and its thematic content. Although O'Casey was already an established playwright at the time it was written, the play, which the author labeled as a "tragi-comedy," diverged in important ways from his earlier works. It blends elements of tragedy with elements of comedy and includes experimental features such as singing and chanting. These experimental features are often associated with expressionism, an avant-garde artistic movement focused on conveying emotion and often emphasizing suffering and struggle. The style of the play varies, sometimes wildly, between acts. The opening act, which depicts the domestic life of the Heegan family, is largely in keeping with the traditions of naturalism, an aesthetic movement aimed at cultivating the appearance of reality. The second act, which takes place in a ruined monastery on the western front in France, displays techniques of expressionism, which often experiments with characters who are little more than types, exaggerated or dreamlike sets, and elements such as chanting and shadow that offer a distorted view of "reality." Prominent in the second act of *The Silver Tassie*, singing and chanting also substitute for dialogue in the concluding acts, which are otherwise more in keeping with the first act's naturalistic style.

What some commentators rejected as a lack of stylistic unity in the play, has been embraced by other scholars as an attempt on the part of O'Casey to realistically represent the fragmentation and chaos of modern warfare, an argument supported by the fact that act 2, the only scene set on the front, is also the most experimental. In this way the play's controversial stylistic elements are clearly tied to its antiwar message. In contrasting home and the front, the play also works against the depiction, common in wartime propaganda, of war as a patriotic and glorified form of sport. This dubious connection is emphasized in the second act, when a soldier receives a ball in a package from home, along with a note encouraging him to "play your way to the enemies' trenches when you go over the top." At the end of the play, Harry, paralyzed and demoralized, returns to the Avondale Football Club and notes a posted roll of honor that lists the names of men from the club who were killed in the war. Rather than extending their football glory, the war is shown to have ended the lives of its soldiers, literally in the case of the men on the list, and figuratively in the cases of Harry and his friend Teddy, who had been blinded in battle.

The play's critique of wartime propaganda is also reflected in its use of religious elements, which are especially central to the second act. The scene juxtaposes images of religion with images of war. Most notably a war-damaged crucifix, which is visually central to the scene, bears a plaque reading "PRINCEPS PACIS" (Prince of Peace). The contradiction between the Christian message of peace and the widespread death and destruction of a war that was often justified on religious grounds is further emphasized by the presence of a large howitzer artillery gun, bodies protruding from ruble, and the deathly character of Croucher, a skeletal soldier covered in blood. Religion and war are explicitly entangled in a repeated refrain in which soldiers, addressing their corporal, assert, "We believe in God and we believe in thee." The implication of

The Welsh at Mametz Wood, a painting by Christopher Williams (1873–1934), depicts the horrors of World War I, which Seán O'Casey portrays in his play The Silver Tassie. © NATIONAL MUSEUM WALES / THE BRIDGEMAN ART LIBRARY INTERNATIONAL

O'Casey's use of this refrain is that both religious and military figures are involved in leading a whole generation of young men to their deaths.

CRITICAL DISCUSSION

When it finally debuted on the stage in 1929, *The Silver Tassie* won the approval of many in the Irish literary community, including O'Casey's fellow playwright George Bernard Shaw. Audiences remained divided, however, about some of the play's more experimental aspects, most notably the staging of its second act. A division between those praising the play thematically and those criticizing it stylistically has endured in critical treatments as well. The drama is often considered to be a stylistically curious piece of war literature or a quasi-expressionist drama. Heinz Kosok's 1985 article in *Arbeitien aus Anglistik und Amerikanistik* situates the play in the context of other World War I dramas of the period, including W. Somerset Maugham's *For Services Rendered* (1932) and R. C. Sherriff's *Journey's End* (1928). Ronald G. Rollins, on the other hand, explores the role of expressionism in the play in a 1962 article in the *Bucknell Review*. He argues that the play's more experimental features reflect the fact that "these soldiers feel menaced by the inhuman, dissonant and mechanized elements in modern life; their halting speech and erratic actions point up their disillusionment, loneliness, and mystification in a disjointed world seemingly devoid of spiritual stability."

In a 1979 article in the *Canadian Journal of Irish Studies*, Carol Kleiman qualifies critical attempts to classify *The Silver Tassie* as a work of expressionism. She suggests that the play can be considered stylistically expressionistic insofar as its second act in particular is highly stylized, marked by distortion, exaggeration, and action that borders on pantomime. However, Kleiman rejects the notion that the play adopts wholesale the tradition of expressionism associated with continental playwrights such as Ernst Toller, whose *Masses and Man* (1922) provided O'Casey's introduction to the movement. Kleiman argues that instead, O'Casey developed a form of expressionism uniquely suited to his own objectives, rejecting elements of Toller's work (such as flat characters) that were ill-suited to his purposes.

Interest in the play's religious imagery and commentary has also led to a significant body of scholarship, with some commentators reading the play as antireligious and others suggesting that it merely takes aim at religious hypocrisy associated with war. Typical of the latter view is Jacqueline Doyle's 1978 article in *Modern Drama*, which offers an extended reading of O'Casey's use of religious imagery and ritual in the play, ultimately asserting that "the despairing yet hopeful conclusion of the play is not that God does not exist, but that man, through sacrilege, through self-sacrifice, through war, has driven God away."

Scholars in the early twenty-first century have attempted to address the play's central "problem"—namely, the perceived lack of unity between its acts. In a 2001 article in the *Canadian Journal of Irish Studies*, for example, Bernice Schrank offers an overview of the play's publication and performance history in order to argue that, despite the controversy surrounding it, act 2 is a logical part of the play as a whole. Despite such scholarship, commentators continue to debate the question of the play's unity or lack thereof.

SOURCES

Doyle, Jacqueline. "Liturgical Imagery in Sean O'Casey's *The Silver Tassie.*" *Modern Drama* 21.1 (1978): 29–38. Print.

Kleiman, Carol. "O'Casey's 'Debt' to Toller: Expressionism in *The Silver Tassie* and *Red Roses for Me.*" *Canadian Journal of Irish Studies* 5.1 (1979): 69–86. Print.

Kosok, Heinz. "*The Silver Tassie* and British Plays of the First World War." *Arbeitien aus Anglistik und Amerikanistik* 10:1/2 (1985): 91–96. Print.

Newbolt, Henry. "Vitaï Lampada." *Admirals All and Other Verses.* London: E. Mathews, 1897. Print.

O'Casey, Sean. *The Silver Tassie. The Complete Plays of Sean O'Casey.* Vol. 2. London: Macmillan, 1949. 3–111. Print.

Rollins, Ronald G. "O'Casey, O'Neill and Expressionism in *The Silver Tassie.*" *Bucknell Review* 10.4 (1962): 364–69. Print.

Schrank, Bernice. "Reception, Close Reading and Re-Production: The Case of Sean O'Casey's *The Silver Tassie.*" *Canadian Journal of Irish Studies* 26.2/27.1 (2000–01): 34–48. Print.

FURTHER READING

Brown, Terence. "Who Dares to Speak?: Ireland and the Great War." *English Studies in Transition: Papers from the Inaugural ESSE Conference.* Ed. Robert Clark and Piero Boitani. London: Routledge, 1993. 226–37. Print.

Gary, Brett. *Nervous Liberals: Propaganda Anxieties from World War I to the Cold War.* New York: Columbia UP, 1999. Print.

Horne, John. *A Companion to World War I.* Chichester: Wiley, 2010. Print.

Kingbury, Celia Malone. *For Home and Country: World War I Propaganda on the Home Front.* Lincoln: U of Nebraska P, 2010. Print.

Krause, David. *Sean O'Casey and His World.* London: Thames, 1976. Print.

Lasswell, Harold D. *Propaganda Technique in World War I.* Cambridge: MIT P, 1971. Print.

O'Connor, Garry. *Sean O'Casey: A Life.* New York: Atheneum, 1988. Print.

Templeton, Joan. "Sean O'Casey and Expressionism." *Modern Drama* 14 (1971): 47–62. Print.

Greta Gard

THE SONG OF ROLAND

OVERVIEW

The *Song of Roland* is the English title of the medieval epic poem *Chanson de Roland*, considered the first great work of French literature. Its authorship is unknown, and scholars disagree about whether it was the work of one poet or the result of oral composition over time. It was probably set down in the form now known around the time of the First Crusade (1095–99), when Christian forces began a series of attempts to drive Muslims from the Holy Land. There is no original manuscript of the poem, but a copy often referred to as the Oxford manuscript—also known as Digby 23, its designation in the collection of Oxford's Bodleian Library—is thought to be complete and has been the basis of most scholarship related to the work. The Oxford copy, which was made sometime in the middle of the twelfth century, contains about four thousand lines written in Anglo-Norman, a variant of Old Norman that developed after 1066. The *Song of Roland* is among the earliest examples of the *chanson de geste* (song of heroic deeds), a form of epic poetry that enjoyed great popularity in France during the twelfth and thirteenth centuries. Because of its compelling portrait of the heroic Roland and its skillful dramatization of events, the poem remains among the best-known works in Western literature.

The *Song of Roland* is set during the period when Charlemagne (c. 742–814) established his rule over most of Europe. However, the poem reflects the cultural conditions and political issues that were dominant when it was written rather than those that would have been current in the time of Charlemagne. It is regarded by many modern scholars not only as an epic tale designed to entertain but also as an endorsement of the Crusades and as a subtle study of the political forces that were moving France toward a more powerful form of monarchy in the twelfth century.

HISTORICAL AND LITERARY CONTEXT

The *Song of Roland* is connected to a historical event in 778, when Charlemagne's forces were attacked by a local ethnic group at Roncevalles Pass near the border between France and Spain. The poem is not a historical account, however, but rather an epic imagining of what might have taken place, and some aspects of the event were substantially changed. For example, the poem describes an attack on Charlemagne's party by

Saracens (Muslims), but the real attackers were almost certainly Basques, a non-Muslim people native to the western Pyrenees. The scope and importance of the battle may be exaggerated as well. There are only a few historical references to the incident at Roncevalles, and depending on how they are interpreted, the encounter may have been a major defeat for Charlemagne or only a minor setback. At that time he was king of the Franks, a people who were expanding their influence in Europe; he had not yet amassed the great power that would lead to his coronation as Holy Roman Emperor in 800. During his fourteen-year reign as emperor, Charlemagne established the geographic and political foundations of Western Europe and fostered a golden age of art and culture referred to as the Carolingian Renaissance.

By the time the *Song of Roland* was composed, almost three centuries after his death, Charlemagne was a figure of legend. A body of stories had developed that dramatized his great deeds, and in many of these he was accompanied by a fictional group of knights called the Twelve Peers. Among these knights (also known as the "paladins"), Roland was reputed to be the greatest. The character of Roland is believed to have derived from the mention of "Hruodland, Warden of the Breton Marches" in a biography of Charlemagne that was probably written between 817 and 833. Hroudland was listed as one of the Roncevalles casualties, but nothing else is known of the historical man.

In the poem Roland is depicted as an iconic hero who gives his life for king and honor. He commands the rear guard that protects Charlemagne's company, and when his men are attacked by an overwhelming Saracen force, Roland insists that it would be dishonorable to call for help. Despite the pleas of his friend Oliver, Roland waits until the entire rear guard has been killed before blowing his great horn to warn the king. He blows so forcefully that his temples burst, and he then arranges himself at the front of his slain men so that he may be found defiantly facing the enemy, even in death.

Roland dies midway through the poem, and although critical attention has largely focused on his character, the remaining episodes of the epic are at least as important when viewing the *Song of Roland* as literature of war. After defeating the forces that attacked Roland's men, Charlemagne is challenged

WAR AND THE EPIC

In modern times the word "epic" is often used informally to describe almost anything that is very large, goes on for a long time, or has extreme characteristics. In literary terms, however, an epic is usually a long poem that features a strong, courageous hero and deals with matters of historical importance, such as the founding of a city, the establishment of a dynasty, or the defeat of a great enemy. Epics typically use lofty language, and many include characters from myth or religion. From ancient times through the Middle Ages most epics developed through a process of oral composition, employing formulaic components that make the story easier to remember and retell.

The earliest known epic is the Mesopotamian *Gilgamesh*, which dates at least to 1000 BCE, and over the next millennium a great classical epic tradition produced the Indian *Mahbhrata* and the Greek *Iliad*, concluding with the Roman Virgil's *Aeneid* in the first century BCE. A new flowering of the genre began a few hundred years later with medieval works such as the *Song of Roland*, Russia's *Tale of Igor's Campaign*, Japan's *Tale of the Heike*, and Spain's *Poem of the Cid*.

Despite the many differences among the world's best-known epics, all have one element in common: war. As Masaki Mori explains in *Epic Grandeur: Toward a Comparative Poetics of the Epic* (1997), "The description of war and combat is so common to epics that it naturally appears to be an integral component of the genre." Yet war itself is seldom the true subject of an epic. For the most part warfare serves as a background for the hero's great deeds and creates a narrative landscape where questions of life and death, good and evil, right and wrong inevitably arise. War also provides the epic with a political, nationalistic, or ideological dimension that expands the importance of events and ties the story to communal concerns.

Opposite page:
Charlemagne: The Spanish March, circa 14th century. © GIANNI DAGLI ORTI / CORBIS

by another Saracen leader, Baligant, and the two meet in single combat. Charlemagne overcomes his opponent, though not without divine aid. He then must deal with political problems that arise from the discovery that Ganelon, a member of Charlemagne's own entourage, had arranged the attack on Roland's force. Ganelon defends his actions as personal revenge rather than treachery, a position that is supported by all of the peers except one man. The exception, Thierry, argues that Ganelon had committed treason because Roland should have been immune from personal attack while in the service of the king. The dispute is resolved by single combat between Thierry and Pinabel, Ganelon's champion. In another instance of divine intervention, Thierry defeats the much stronger Pinabel, and Ganelon is executed. A weary Charlemagne, who is two hundred years old in the poem, weeps when he receives divine instruction to continue the battle against the enemies of Christianity.

Charlemagne's commission from God highlights the relationship between the *Song of Roland* and the early-medieval politics of religious war. In the period during which the poem was probably written down, several factors were coalescing to initiate a series of Crusades (church-sanctioned military campaigns) that would last for the next two centuries. These factors included a rise in religious enthusiasm among the people, a power struggle taking place between the church establishment and various European monarchies, and divisions among various factions in the church. Tales of loyalty and sacrifice, such as the story of Roland, served to kindle enthusiasm for the Crusades, just as the poem's depiction of Roland's ascension into heaven echoed promises of redemption for those who volunteered in the Crusades.

The Oxford manuscript may be the earliest and most complete text available, but other versions of the narrative exist. Six additional texts, dating from the twelfth through the early fifteenth century, are included in *The Song of Roland: The French Corpus*, edited by Joseph Duggan. These versions vary substantially, and episodes are sometimes deleted, added, or recast, possibly reflecting shifts in cultural and political emphasis across different periods. Yet despite these transformations, the fundamental components of the poem are maintained, and its characters and themes can be clearly discerned. These components also persist as important elements in the European literary tradition. Roland and Charlemagne may be found in the *Paradiso* of Dante's *Divine Comedy* (1302), for example, and their story appears in German, Dutch, and Norse translations or adaptations during the Middle Ages. In the early sixteenth century the story was fantastically transformed in Ludovico Ariosto's romantic epic *Orlando Furioso*, counted among the masterworks of Italian literature, and it is later referred to in works by such diverse authors as Shakespeare, Robert Browning, and Graham Greene. Themes and characters from the *Song of Roland* continue to evoke the tension between heroic combat and mindless violence, between Roland's dramatic last battle and Charlemagne's poignant realization that the war never ends.

THEMES AND STYLE

The *Song of Roland* is the best-known example of the medieval literary works that focus on the "Matter of France," one of the three indispensable subjects of storytelling identified by the twelfth-century French poet Jean Bodel. Together with the "Matter of Britain" (stories about King Arthur and his knights) and the "Matter of Rome" (stories based on classical events and characters), the Matter of France provided a thematic organization for the emergence of a vernacular literature in both France and Britain over several centuries. In addressing these matters, literary works depicted idealized social systems governing relations among members of the aristocratic warrior class. By the later Middle Ages these representations formed the basis of the chivalric romance. This differed from the earlier

epic form by casting heroic deeds in the context of romantic love, spiritual quest, and fantastic adventure.

Works focusing on the Matter of France are also referred to as the "Carolingian Cycle" because many of them either feature Charlemagne as a character or focus on people and events from the time of Charlemagne. These stories incorporate secular political themes that reflect a transition from regional rule by powerful nobles to a greater concentration of power in the hands of the French king. A shifting view of the monarch's role is suggested by the ambiguous presentation of Charlemagne in the *Song of Roland*. Although he is portrayed at times as an almost superhuman hero, he can also seem surprisingly powerless, especially in relation to the peers. When they side with Ganelon, for example, Charlemagne does not overrule them but rather allows a resolution to emerge through the actions of others. In the end it is Thierry's improbable victory over Pinabel that serves to elevate the king over the peers.

A similar ambiguity surrounds Roland. In some respects he seems the epitome of a valiant Christian hero and in others an incarnation of classical protagonists such as Achilles and Oedipus, who were brought to their doom by pride and arrogance. From a modern perspective Roland's refusal to summon help seems prideful, especially when his noble friend Oliver pleads with him to act and blames him for the death of his men. Yet it is difficult to know how contemporary audiences would have regarded Roland's actions. Scholars differ strongly on this point, some contending that Roland is guilty of *démesure* (excessiveness or uncontrolled passion), others arguing that his actions follow the operative standards of feudal obligation and knightly honor.

The *Song of Roland*, as known from the Oxford manuscript, is composed of stanzas called *laisses*. Each line in the stanza has ten syllables, and the last stressed syllable has the same vowel sound as every other ending syllable of the stanza. Thus, the poetic effect depends on assonance rather than on rhyme. Repetition and parallelism create continuity on the narrative level, and the same scene is sometimes repeated several times with different details or from other viewpoints. There is little introspection or character development in the poem, which focuses on action and which treats the actors more as types than as individuals.

CRITICAL DISCUSSION

Despite its popularity and literary influence, serious scholarship on the *Song of Roland* was limited until the Oxford manuscript was published in 1837. Well into the twentieth century, most discussions of the work were dominated by controversies over authorship, dating, and translation. Scholars characterized as "traditionalists" regarded the poem as a product of tales that began soon after the battle at Roncevalles

and that eventually developed into songs performed by *jongleurs* (minstrels). From this perspective the Oxford manuscript merely captures a version of the story that was current at a particular time. Those known as "individualist" scholars, on the other hand, regard the *Song of Roland* as drawn from legendary tales but intentionally produced as a work of literature by one author. Similarly, rival views developed about the poem's central theme, with some critics contending that it is primarily a Christian story of Roland's redemption and martyrdom and others that it is essentially an account of heroic honor and valor. Further interpretive approaches shifted the thematic focus of the poem from Roland to Charlemagne or proposed a complexity that could accommodate multiple, even conflicting, themes.

It was not until most of the fundamental debates were either resolved or exhausted that critics began to place the work in a larger context and that textual analysis, or metacriticism, and the exploration of other topics opened new avenues for discussion. Peter Haidu's *The Subject of Violence* analyzes political themes in the poem's portrayal of violence, while Andrew Cowell's *The Medieval Warrior Aristocracy* explores the dynamics of reciprocity in the conflict between Roland and Ganelon. In "'Pagans are wrong and Christians are right': Alterity, Gender, and Nation in the *Chanson de Roland*," Sharon Kinoshita considers the poem's presentation of the Saracens as "a fierce and intractable Other" and discusses the meager attention accorded to women. Andrew Taylor's *Textual Situations* argues for a more interdisciplinary approach to the poem.

SOURCES

Cowell, Andrew. *The Medieval Warrior Aristocracy: Gifts, Violence, Performance, and the Sacred*. Woodbridge: Brewer, 2007. Print.

Duggan, Joseph J., and Karen Akiyama, eds. *La Chanson de Roland = The Song of Roland: the French Corpus*. Turnhout: Brepols, 2005. Print.

Haidu, Peter. *The Subject of Violence: The Song of Roland and the Birth of the State*. Bloomington: Indiana UP, 1993. Print.

Kinoshita, Sharon. "'Pagans are wrong and Christians are right': Alterity, Gender, and Nation in the Chanson de Roland." *Journal of Medieval and Early Modern Studies* 31.1 (2001): 79–111. Print.

Song of Roland. Translated and with introduction by W. S. Merwin. New York, Vintage Books, 1970. Print.

Taylor, Andrew. *Textual Situations: Three Medieval Manuscripts and Their Readers*. Philadelphia: U of Pennsylvania P, 2002. Print.

FURTHER READING

Ashe, Laura. "'A Prayer and a Warcry': The Creation of a Secular Religion in the *Song of Roland*." *Cambridge Quarterly* 28.4 (1999): 349–67. Print.

Cook, Robert Francis. *The Sense of the Song of Roland.* Ithaca: Cornell UP, 1987. Print.

Duggan, Joseph J. *The Song of Roland: Formulaic Style and Poetic Craft.* Berkeley: U of California P, 1973. Print.

Eisner, Robert A. "In Search of the Real Theme of the *Song of Roland.*" *Romance Notes* 14.1 (1972): 179–83. Print.

Kay, Sarah. "Ethics and Heroics in the *Song of Roland.*" *Neophilologus* 62.4 (1978): 480–91. Print.

Kinoshita, Sharon. *Medieval Boundaries: Rethinking Difference in Old French Literature.* Philadelphia: U of Pennsylvania P, 2006. Print.

Nichols, Stephen G. *Romanesque Signs: Early Medieval Narrative and Iconography.* New Haven: Yale UP, 1983. Print.

Pensom, Roger. *Literary Technique in the Chanson De Roland.* Geneva: Librairie Droz, 1982. Print.

Pratt, Karen. *Roland and Charlemagne in Europe: Essays on the Reception and Transformation of a Legend.* London: King's College London Centre for Late Antique and Medieval Studies, 1996. Print.

Vance, Eugene. *Reading the Song of Roland.* Englewood Cliffs: Prentice, 1970. Print.

MEDIA ADAPTATION

The Song of Roland. Dir. Frank Cassenti. Perf. Klaus Kinski. 1978. Film.

Cynthia Giles

Sonnets I–V

"I: Peace", "II: Safety", "III: The Dead", "IV: The Dead", and "V: The Soldier"

Rupert Brooke

+ *Key Facts*

Conflict:
World War I

Time Period:
Early 20th Century

Genre:
Poetry

OVERVIEW

Rupert Brooke's sonnets of 1914 ("I: Peace"; "II: Safety"; "III: The Dead"; "IV: The Dead"; "V: The Soldier") are among the best-known poems of World War I and the most famous to emerge from the early years of the war. Initially published in the journal *New Numbers* in December 1914, they attracted little attention until after Brooke's death, when they became immensely popular. In 1915, these sonnets were republished in *1914 and Other Poems* and then, in the same year, as *1914: Five Sonnets.*

After his death in 1915, Brooke became a legendary figure, a symbol of the ideal soldier his poems describe. He was known for his good looks, courage, and loyalty, and he became emblematic of the so-called Lost Generation, the idealistic young men who served and were slaughtered in the war. In her biographical note to Brooke's *Collected Poems,* Margaret Lavington records that, when he enlisted at the beginning of the war, Brooke said, "Well, if Armageddon's on, I suppose one should be there." His brief service in Belgium awakened a near-religious fervor to defend England that is central to his five sonnets.

The sonnets articulate a vision of the war as a noble cause, one that brings clarity and mission to lives that previously had none. Brooke diagnoses pre-war society as lacking in moral purpose and as psychologically ill. The war, by his account, marks the return of classic values such as nobility, honor, love, and holiness. For Brooke the worst things a soldier can suffer are pain and death, but they also mark a life well led and are a sacrifice for England that is ultimately redemptive.

HISTORICAL AND LITERARY CONTEXT

World War I, often known as the Great War, was the first global military conflict of the twentieth century. It pitted the empires of Germany, Austria-Hungary, and Turkey (the Central Powers) against the United Kingdom, France, and the Russian Empire (the Allies). The war, which began in 1914, was triggered by the assassination of Archduke Franz Ferdinand in June by a Serb nationalist. Attempts at reconciliation failed, and the war began on July 28 with the Austro-Hungarian invasion of Serbia, followed by the German invasion of Belgium, France, and Luxemburg and a Russian attack on Germany. The war caused a major power shift in Europe, bringing an end to two of the great European empires of the nineteenth century—the Austro-Hungarian Empire and the Ottoman Empire—and resulting in a massive reconfiguration of the European continent.

By the time the war began, the Industrial Revolution and developments in technology had drastically altered the kind of conflict that was possible. Each side used railways to mobilize large numbers of troops and to deploy them to the war front. Britain initially believed that the duration of the war would be several weeks, that the troops would be "home by Christmas." Brooke's poetry expresses this early enthusiasm, a faith in the British Empire, and a certainty that the honor and spirit of British troops will necessarily translate into a swift victory.

World War I inspired an enormous outpouring of unique poetry written by soldiers, often referred to as "trench poetry." The poetry was published in newspapers, journals, and anthologies during the war, circulated in broadsides, and included in letters and memoirs. The poets most often associated with the trench poetry movement include later writers such as Wilfred Owen (1883–1918) and Herbert Reed (1893–1968), whose verse depicts trench warfare as violent, miserable, and hopeless. Brooke is usually seen as their predecessor, a poet who still upheld beliefs the trench poets ultimately revealed to be myths. Some have suggested that Brooke, had he lived, might himself have reconsidered his vision of war. In its entry on him, the *Dictionary of Literary Biography* notes that in 1914 Brooke wrote from the trenches, "The eye grows clearer and the heart. But it's a bloody thing, half the youth of Europe, blown through pain into nothingness, in the incessant mechanical slaughter of these modern battles." Brooke died of blood poisoning early in the war, however, and the war sonnets stand as his greatest legacy.

THEMES AND STYLE

Brooke, who was educated at Cambridge, had become a well-known poet before the war. He was the most popular of the Georgian poets, a late-Edwardian group known for writing pastoral elegies in strict poetic forms. Brooke's sonnets are particularly Georgian in their use of pastoral themes. The soldiers in his poems are not portrayed in combat but are represented in a memorialized form that draws on consoling elegiac figures and symbols. His poem "Safety," for example, describes the emotional state of the soldier whose spirit finds "safety with all things undying, / The winds, and morning, tears of men and mirth, / The deep night, and birds singing, and clouds flying, / And sleep, and freedom, and the autumnal earth."

Thomas C. Ware, writing in *South Atlantic Review*, describes Brooke's use of Arcadian imagery as representative of the cultural background shared by the men who fought in the trenches, evoking "the ancient but lingering theme of the presence of death in Arcadia, as well as its corollary, the poignant yearning for comforts and reassurance in the horrifying wasteland of modern warfare." Pastoral elements are common images in depictions of home and the past in trench poetry, but Brooke also uses them to project a future utopia that is attainable only through a valiant death in combat.

Brooke's poems are overtly patriotic, deploying the structure of the sonnet to portray the strength and beauty of the soldiers fighting for England. One of Brooke's major themes is the glory of the soldier, particularly the glory of being a soldier fighting for England. The poems reflect the mythology surrounding the classic ideal that World War I would effectively destroy—a strong, valiant hero fighting for right and justice in the world.

Brooke's formal and technical perfection is displayed in the careful craftsmanship of his sonnets. Traditionally associated with love poetry—for instance, that of Petrarch and Shakespeare, Edmund Spenser and Christina Rosetti—the sonnet had been revived for use in elegies in the early 1800s, when poets began to write sonnets of mourning and sorrow in which the elegance and symmetry of the form stands for the beauty of the dead. The sonnet had also been associated with political occasional verse, which expresses adulation and attempts to provide a form of immortality for a worthy public figure. Brooke's sonnets play on both of these traditions, depicting the soldier as both a man to be mourned and remembered and as the equal of the military heroes of the past. The poet scorns those who did not voluntarily enlist at the start of the war, describing them as part of society's ills: "The sick hearts that honour could not move, / And half-men, and their dirty songs and dreary." The experience of enlisting, on the other hand, is like "waken[ing] … from sleeping," a spiritual awakening that is prolonged and intensified by death in battle. "The Soldier," for example, describes the fallen soldier's body as being purified and deified in death. Wherever the soldier's

CHARLES HAMILTON SORLEY'S WORLD WAR I SONNETS

The vision of death in war provided by the poetry of Charles Hamilton Sorley (1895–1915), whose posthumous *Marlborough and Other Poems* was as successful as Brooke's *Five Sonnets*, stands in nearly direct contrast to that of Brooke. The Scottish-born Sorley was educated at Marlborough College, Siefried Sassoon's alma mater, and had a scholarship to study at University College, Oxford. First, however, he spent several months in Germany, and he was studying at the University of Jena in 1914 when World War I broke out. When he returned to England, he volunteered for military service, joining the Suffolk regiment. Arriving on the western front as a lieutenant in May 1915, he soon became a captain, leading troops in the trenches in France. He was killed in action at the Battle of Loos on October 13, 1915.

Like Brooke, Sorley wrote a number of sonnets meditating on death in battle. Whereas Brooke's sonnets glorify such deaths, Sorley says in the second of "Two Sonnets" that death has "no triumph: no defeat: / Only an empty pail, a slate rubbed clean." Responding to Brooke, he remarks that "Ghosts do not say / 'Come, what was your record when you drew breath?'" Sorley's best-known sonnet, "When you see millions of the mouthless dead," written just before his death, rejects the very idea of remembrance, saying that "their blind eyes see not your tears flow. / Nor honour."

body lies, he will be a "heart, all evil shed away, / A pulse in the eternal mind."

Brooke's poems reflect a belief in the righteousness and strength of the British Empire, and in this respect they are strongly colonial. Brooke presents the fight for right and justice as a fight to spread Britishness throughout the world. In "The Soldier," an elegy in which a soldier anticipates his own death, the man directs his audience to celebrate rather than mourn his death, instructing them to understand it as a literal conquest of land. "If I should die," the poem begins, "think only this of me: / That there's some corner of a foreign field that is for ever England." The dead soldier's body is absorbed into the earth as a literal conquest of foreign lands: "There shall be / In that rich earth a richer dust concealed … A body of England's breathing English air."

England, unlike France and Belgium, was not invaded but entered the war in support of its allies. Brooke's work reinforces the idealized view of Britain's participation as an attempt to spread peace. The soldiers in Brooke's sonnets not only fight but also sacrifice themselves to bring "unbroken glory, a gathered radiance, / A width, a shining peace, under the night."

GREAT BRITAIN DECLARES WAR ON GERMANY.

The Daily Mirror

LATEST CERTIFIED CIRCULATION MORE THAN 1,000,000 COPIES PER DAY

No. 3,364.   Registered at the G.P.O. as a Newspaper.   WEDNESDAY, AUGUST 5, 1914.   One Halfpenny.

DECLARATION OF WAR BY GREAT BRITAIN AFTER UNSATIS-
FACTORY REPLY TO YESTERDAY'S ULTIMATUM.

The cover of the *Daily Mirror* on August 5, 1914, which was the start of World War I. © THE ART ARCHIVE / ROYAL AUTOMOBILE CLUB LONDON / NB DESIGN

a conventionality that is unlike his earlier work and that his patriotism is in conflict with his well-known distaste for imperialist poets such as Rudyard Kipling (1865–1936) and W. E. Henley (1849–1903). Some critics argue that Brooke's glorification of death is a symptom of his emotional confusion, a result either of questioning his sexuality, his unhealthy relationship with his mother, or the resurgence of his childhood religious indoctrination.

Most scholarship, however, continues to see the significance of Brooke's sonnets as an expression of the spirit of Britain before the war and as an example of the poetic forms the trench poets would so strongly rewrite to express their disillusionment. Margot Norris notes in the journal *College Literature* that Brooke is useful when teaching Isaac Rosenberg because the contrast helps students recognize the difference between Brooke's "romantic and patriotic image of the soldier's grave" and Rosenberg's ironic and literal accounts of death in the trenches.

Some critics have begun to reassess the popular poetry of the war, much of which took its cue both formally and thematically from Brooke. Nils Clausson points out in the *Journal of Modern Literature* that the development of the trench lyric is remarkable because Britain had no real tradition of poetry written by soldiers. He sees Brooke, despite his uncritical vision of the war, as a critical link between the abstraction of Georgian pastoral poetry and the hard edges of the trench poem, providing a model for revising poetic forms to allow them to address the topic of war realistically.

CRITICAL DISCUSSION

In *The Great War and Modern Memory*, Paul Fussell defines the literature of World War I as reflective of the disillusionment and tragic irony characteristic of the era as a whole. Trench literature, in Fussell's view, although less literary and less aesthetically important than high-modernist novels and poetry, is nonetheless a genre that belongs to the wartime era of black humor and hopelessness. Brooke's sonnets do not, in this sense, count as trench poetry, but rather belong to an innocent prewar era. In critical history Brooke's sonnets, which were written before he saw any actual fighting, are rarely taken seriously. Although they are among the most popular poems of the age, they also exemplify what, in retrospect, seems like childish naïveté in light of the age to come. Even among the early war poets, Brooke's optimism was seen as overwrought, and contemporary poets such as Charles Sorley (1885–1915), Isaac Rosenberg (1890–1918), and Edward Thomas (1878–1917) criticized the naïveté of his belief in the glory of war.

A number of critics have reevaluated Brooke's sonnets, often demonstrating that the poems show

SOURCES

Brooke, Rupert. *The Collected Poems of Rupert Brooke.* New York: Lane, 1915. Print.

Clausson, Nils. "'Perpetuating the Language': Romantic Tradition, the Genre Function and the Origins of the Trench Lyric." *Journal of Modern Literature* 30.1 (2006): 104–28. Print.

Fussell, Paul. *The Great War and Modern Memory.* Oxford: Oxford UP, 1975. Print.

Lavington, Margaret. Biographical Note. *The Collected Poems of Rupert Brooke.* By Rupert Brooke. New York: Lane, 1915. Print.

Norris, Margot. "Teaching World War I Poetry— Comparatively." *College Literature* 32.3 (2005): 136–53. Print.

"Rupert Brooke." *British Poets, 1880–1914.* Ed. Donald E. Stanford. *Dictionary of Literary Biography.* Vol. 19. Detroit: Gale, 1993. 55–61. *Dictionary of Literary Biography Complete Online.* Web. 13 June 2011.

Ware, Thomas C. "'Shepherd in a Soldier's Coat': The Presence of Arcadia on the Western Front." *South Atlantic Review* 68.1 (2003): 64–84. Print.

FURTHER READING

Bloom, Harold, ed. *Poets of World War I: Rupert Brooke and Siegfried Sassoon.* Broomall: Chelsea, 2003. Print.

Ebbatson, Roger. *An Imaginary England: Nation, Landscape and Literature, 1840–1920.* Burlington: Ashgate, 2005. Print.

Kendall, Tim. *The Oxford Handbook of British and Irish War Poetry.* Oxford: Oxford UP, 2007. Print.

Silkin, Jon. *Out of Battle: The Poetry of the Great War.* London: Macmillan, 1998. Print.

Stallworthy, Jon. *Great Poets of World War I: Poetry from the Great War.* New York: Carroll, 2002. Print.

Jennifer Ludwig

SOZABOY
A Novel in Rotten English
Ken Saro-Wiwa

✣ *Key Facts*

Conflict:
Nigerian Civil War/
Biafran War

Time Period:
Late 20th Century

Genre:
Novel

OVERVIEW

Sozaboy: A Novel in Rotten English is a 1985 book by Nigerian author and political activist Ken Saro-Wiwa. The book tells the story of Mene, a Nigerian youth coming of age during the Nigerian Civil War (1967–70). At the outset of the war, Mene is an apprentice driver learning to negotiate the corruption and bribery that rule his country's politics. Attempting to prove his manhood and impress Agnes, the young woman he eventually marries, Mene enlists as a *soza* (soldier) in the conflict. He soon finds, however, that the war is pointless; there seems to be little difference between the two sides, and death and destruction are everywhere. After his closest friend is killed in the war, and he realizes that his remaining companion, the allegiance-shifting soldier and opportunist Manmuswak, is not to be trusted, Mene runs away from the army. After a brief detention in a prison hospital, he escapes and returns to his home to find his village deserted. He sets off looking for his wife and mother and witnesses firsthand the destruction of the country and the deplorable conditions in refugee camps, where people are dying from disease and malnutrition as the corrupt elite continue to live in relative comfort. After narrowly escaping execution as a traitor only because of a shortage of bullets, Mene finds his way back to his village once again. Its surviving inhabitants are suffering from a cholera epidemic and he learns that his wife and mother were killed by a bomb. He is rejected by the remaining villagers because they believe he has returned as a ghost to "worry" the living. As the novel ends, Mene faces an uncertain future, armed only with the conviction that "if anyone say anything about war or even fight, [he] will just run and run and run and run and run."

Saro-Wiwa, who had supported the federal government in the conflict, drew on his experiences as a civilian administrator during the civil war. Written in what the author describes as "rotten English," a mixture of Nigerian Standard English (the country's official language) and pidgin English, the book re-creates the language of Nigeria's poor and dispossessed. When the book was published in 1985, the country was struggling with the political fallout of the revolution and the environmental ravages brought on by extensive oil exploration and extraction. These crises resonate

behind Saro-Wiwa's portrait of the war. Ten years after the book's publication, Saro-Wiwa's crusade against governmental and corporate corruption led to his execution. The international outrage that accompanied his death has fueled interest in the novel and its depiction of a simple man's attempt to survive in a society dominated by corruption, greed, and war.

HISTORICAL AND LITERARY CONTEXT

Sozaboy takes place during the Nigerian Civil War. The war grew out of tensions that had been simmering between the nation's diverse ethnic groups (including the predominately southeastern Igbo, the northern Hausa-Fulani, and the southwestern Yoruba), who had been forced together under British rule. These tensions rose to the surface when the nation gained independence in 1960 and governmental corruption escalated. A January 1966 coup led by a group of generals killed the prime minister and attempted to establish a new government. It was followed in July by a countercoup in which forces from northern Nigeria rose up against the generals and established Yakubu Gowon as the nation's head of state. Civil war ignited when several provinces in southeastern Nigeria, whose people had been persecuted following the failed January coup and feared genocide, seceded from the country and declared their independence as the Republic of Biafra. The subsequent conflict, which began on July 6, 1967, pitted Nigeria's federal government, under the leadership of Gowon, against the breakaway republic. By 1968 the war had largely reached a stalemate, and a federal blockade created a humanitarian crisis in Biafra as citizens ran out of food and supplies. With the aid of the British government, federal forces ultimately forced Biafra's surrender in 1970. The war was exceedingly costly, with as many as three million people dying from disease, hunger, or combat.

Sozaboy depicts the initial excitement that followed the coup ("Everybody was saying that everything will be good … because of the new government."), the slow realization that nothing had really changed, and the country's descent into war and disillusionment. The novel is part of an influential tradition of novel-writing that emerged from the Nigerian Civil War. Beginning with Sebastian Mezu's novel *Behind the Rising Sun* (1971) this tradition, which grew in the coming decade to include works such as Nkem Nwagboso's *The Road to Damnation* (1982), and Buchi Emecheta's *Destination Biafra* (1982), is often credited with helping to influence the development of contemporary Nigerian literature.

Sozaboy also reflects the postwar political climate of the author's country. By the time he wrote the novel, Saro-Wiwa's support for the federal government had been tempered by his work as an advocate for his people, the ethnic-minority Ogoni. After the war Saro-Wiwa had gradually attained a position of literary and social prominence in Nigeria. He ran a publishing house, wrote a popular television series, worked as a newspaper columnist, and served as president of the Association of Nigerian Authors in the early 1990s. He also began campaigning for Ogoni sovereignty and was soon actively engaged in a struggle against the federal government and the international oil companies. He used his relative fame to draw attention to the ways in which corporations were violating human rights and wreaking environmental havoc on Ogoni lands. Discussing *Sozaboy* in an essay in the book *Ogoni's Agonies*, Frank Schulze-Engler argues that this context is critical to understanding the novel, stating that "any attempt at assessing the political significance of Ken Saro-Wiwa's writings will necessarily have to begin with his involvement in the eco-political struggle of the Ogoni against the environmental devastation perpetrated by Shell and other oil multinationals and the political oppression engineered by Nigeria's military rulers."

THEMES AND STYLE

As its subtitle suggests, *Sozaboy* is written in a hybrid language that is, as Saro-Wiwa explains in the Author's Note that opens the collection, "a mixture of Nigerian pidgin English, broken English, and occasional flashes of good, even idiomatic English." Saro-Wiwa writes that the novel was "the result of [his] fascination with the adaptability of the English Language and of [his] closely observing the speech and writings of a certain segment of Nigerian society." Because of this "rotten English," which can be difficult to parse, the novel includes a glossary with more than a hundred words and phrases organized by the chapter in which they appear.

Language is itself an important theme in the novel. Mene relates that as a child he had enjoyed school and harbored dreams of entering a prestigious career such as medicine or law: "I wanted to be big man like lawyer or doctor riding car and talking big big English." Even as a young man, he associates English with power, and his nonstandard speech reveals the financial impediments that hampered his dreams. Moreover, the forces of oppression in Nigeria are frequently referred to as "grammar" or "big grammar," denoting their command of English, a result of the privileged class status and access to education that Mene lacks. Mene, explaining his country's descent into crisis, says

"as grammar plenty, na so trouble plenty. And as trouble plenty, na so plenty people were dying."

Another central theme of the novel is that war is a pointless and destructive exercise. As Mene himself proclaims near the book's conclusion, "War is a very bad and stupid game." Noting how many died on both sides of the war, and attempting to process acts of kindness on the part of his alleged enemies (such as the sharing of a cigarette), he ultimately concludes that "all this suffering is total useless. And to fight war is even more useless." Although the novel rejects war as a viable solution to Nigeria's political and social problems, it presents with sympathy the plight of young men like Mene, who, lacking education and opportunity, are tempted by the pageantry of the military and its empty promise of a better life. Discussing his early encounter with a group of soldiers, for example, Mene explains, "When I see how they are all marching, prouding and singing, I am very happy. But when I see all their uniform shining and very very nice to see, I cannot tell how I am feeling. Immediately, I know that this soza is a wonderful thing. With gun and uniform and singing." This vision, coupled with Agnes's desire that he become a "soza" eventually drives him to enlist. Saro-Wiwa emphasizes the dangerous and empty promises of military life when he figures Mene's disillusionment in similar terms: "that uniform that they are giving us to wear is just to deceive us."

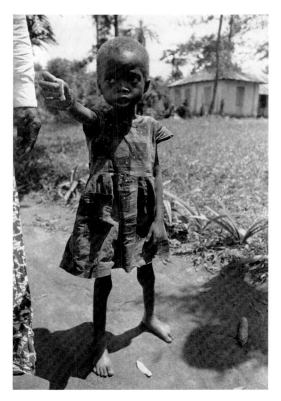

A victim of starvation, this little girl died just hours after her photograph was taken in Biafra, Nigeria on August 5, 1968. In *Sozaboy*, protagonist Mene witnesses the humanitarian crisis caused by the Nigerian Civil War, during which thousands of refugees died of starvation each day. © AP IMAGES / KURT STRUMPF

KEN SARO-WIWA'S POLITICAL ACTIVISM

While gaining fame as a novelist, Saro-Wiwa also made a name for himself as a member of the Movement for the Survival of the Ogoni People (MOSOP). The group called for an Ogoni Bill of Rights that would ensure increased tribal autonomy, protect tribal lands from destruction by oil companies, and guarantee the Ogoni a portion of oil profits. Saro-Wiwa's activism brought him into conflict with both foreign oil companies and the Nigerian government, a military junta led by General Sani Abacha. The struggle for autonomy was also resisted by some conservative Ogoni chiefs, and in 1994 four of these chiefs were murdered. Saro-Wiwa was arrested, tried, and sentenced to death for inciting the murders despite having been nowhere near the crime scene. The trial drew condemnation from the international community. Key witnesses later admitted that they had been bribed to testify against Saro-Wiwa and his fellow activists. On November 10, 1995, Saro-Wiwa and eight other men were hanged, despite international outrage. The executions led to a three-year suspension of Nigeria from the Commonwealth of Nations. In 2009, without admitting any guilt, Shell Oil agreed to a multimillion dollar settlement in a case brought by Saro-Wiwa's son accusing the company of extensive human rights violations.

CRITICAL DISCUSSION

Sozaboy was well received when it was first published in 1985. International attention to the work increased exponentially, however, following Saro-Wiwa's execution in 1995. Reviewing the novel in the *Nation* in 1996, Charles R. Larson described it as "one of the most devastating anti-war novels of the century." In Nigeria, however, Saro-Wiwa's conviction was used as a justification for banning his books from classrooms where *Sozaboy* had previously been popular following the author's work as a minister of education.

In the decades since its publication, much scholarly attention has been focused on *Sozaboy* both as an important piece of modern Nigerian literature and as a reflection of Saro-Wiwa's political activism. In an article in the book *Ogoni's Agonies*, Harry Garuba argues that, contrary to trends in literary criticism that have tended to downplay "concrete, historical struggles," Saro-Wiwa's work insists on being read in its cultural context. Garuba notes that Saro-Wiwa "believed that his ability to take literature into the streets or, put differently, to take the streets into literature was his ultimate triumph against those who sought to silence him." Garuba suggests that scholars of the novel have, following language-centered critical trends, too frequently put the novel's "rotten English" at the center of their readings. He argues that the work ought to be read as "as an allegorization of the minority experience in a postcolonial state." Wendy Griswold also interprets the novel allegorically. In her book *Bearing Witness*, she argues that Mene's experiences reflect Saro-Wiwa's own disillusionment with the direction of his country. Griswold situates *Sozaboy* within the context of both the Nigerian Civil War and society after the war and suggests that the novel is part of a larger trend in Nigerian literature that examines the isolation and despair of the country's intellectuals.

Scholars of the novel have also explored some of its less central themes, including the gender politics of oppression. In an article in the collection *Ken Saro-Wiwa: Writer and Political Activist*, for example, Maureen N. Eke suggests that Saro-Wiwa offers a pointed critique of how women suffer under systematic poverty and oppression, revealing that "women are objectified, and their lives are subsumed under the category of merchandise for barter, to be exchanged for the lives or freedom of the men."

SOURCES

Eke, Maureen N. "The Novel: *Sozaboy: A Novel in Rotten English.*" *Ken Saro-Wiwa: Writer and Political Activist.* Ed. Craig W. McLuckie and Aubrey McPhail. Boulder: Rienner, 2000. 87–106. Print.

Garuba, Harry. "Ken Saro-Wiwa's *Sozaboy* and the Logic of Minority Discourse." *Ogoni's Agonies: Ken Saro-Wiwa and the Crisis in Nigeria.* Ed. Abdul-Rasheed Na'allah. Trenton: Africa, 1998. 229–39. Print.

Griswold, Wendy. *Bearing Witness: Readers, Writers, and the Novel in Nigeria.* Princeton: Princeton UP, 2000. Print.

Larson, Charles R. "In Postcolonial Limbo." Rev. of *Sozaboy,* by Ken Saro-Wiwa. *Nation* 27 May 1996: 31–32. Print.

Mezu, S. Okechukwu, ed. *Ken Saro Wiwa: The Life and Times.* Randallstown: Black, 1996. Print.

Saro-Wiwa, Ken. *Sozaboy: A Novel in Rotten English.* London: Saros, 1985. Print.

Schulze-Engler, Frank. "Civil Critiques: Satire and the Politics of Democratic Transition in Ken Saro-Wiwa's Novels." *Ogoni's Agonies: Ken Saro-Wiwa and the Crisis in Nigeria.* Ed. Abdul-Rasheed Na'allah. Trenton: Africa, 1998. 285–306. Print.

FURTHER READING

Adagbonyin, Asomwan. "The Language of Ken Saro-Wiwa's *Sozaboy.*" In *Critical Essays on Ken Saro-Wiwa's "Sozaboy: A Novel in Rotten English."* Ed. Charles Nnolim. London: Saros, 1992: 30–38. Print.

Chabal, Patrick, ed. *Political Domination in Africa: Reflections on the Limits of Power.* Cambridge: Cambridge UP, 1986. Print.

Chukwuma, Helen. "Characterization and Meaning in *Sozaboy.*" *Critical Essays on Ken Saro-Wiwa's "Sozaboy: A Novel in Rotten English."* Ed. Charles Nnolim. London: Saros, 1992. Print.

Gikandi, Simon. *Reading the African Novel.* Portsmouth: Heinemann, 1987. Print.

Mair, Christian, "The New Englishes and Stylistic Innovation: Ken Saro-Wiwa's *Sozaboy: A Novel in Rotten English*." *Us/Them: Translation, Transcription and Identity in Post-Colonial Literary Cultures*. Ed. Gordon Collier. Amsterdam: Rodopi, 1992: 277–87. Print.

Meek, Sandra. "The Military and the (Re)making of African Postcolonial Identity in Ken Saro-Wiwa's *Sozaboy* and Manuel Rui's *Yes, Comrade*!" *Journal of Third World Studies* 16.2 (1999): 141–61. Print.

Ngugi wa Thiongó. *Decolonising the Mind: The Politics of Language in African Literature*. Portsmouth: Heinemann, 1987. Print.

Nnolim, Charles. "Saro-Wiwa's World and His Craft in *Sozaboy*." *Ken Saro Wiwa: The Life and Times*. Ed. S. Okechukwu Mezu. Randallstown: Black, 1996. 122–33. Print.

Saro-Wiwa, Ken. *A Month and A Day: A Detention Diary*. London: Penguin, 1995. Print.

Zabus, Chantal. "Mending the Schizo-Text: Pidgin in the Nigerian Novel." *Kunapipi* 14.1 (1992): 119–27. Print.

Greta Gard

"SPAIN"

W. H. Auden

❖ *Key Facts*

Conflict:
Spanish Civil War

Time Period:
Mid-20th Century

Genre:
Poetry

OVERVIEW

W. H. Auden's 1937 poem "Spain," written after his experiences driving an ambulance during the Spanish civil war, was first published in a pamphlet with the same name. A revised version was published in the collection *Another Time* (1940). Auden later disavowed "Spain" entirely, cutting it from collected editions of his poems.

Auden was one of a number of British writers, including the essayist George Orwell and the poet Stephen Spender, engaged by the Spanish civil war. Spain was torn between the left-leaning Republican government and the conservative-military Nationalist forces, including powerful fascist elements, that sought its overthrow. Auden's poem identifies the war as a symbol for "the struggle" of the present day, a pivotal point between the historical progression of the past and the potential of the future. While Auden's early poetry is generally socially committed and left-wing, his historical sensibility tends to be more overarching and abstract than that of his contemporaries, deploying Marxist and Freudian ideas as a lens through which to view the past. Similarly, while Spender's poems about the war were actively political and supported the Republican cause, "Spain" uses the war to examine the choice between fascism and liberalism that was the central political, ethical, and aesthetic question confronting the United Kingdom in the 1930s.

"Spain" was written in the last years of what is known as Auden's "English" phase and is one of his last overtly political poems. In 1939 he moved to the United States, converted to Christianity, and generally disavowed the attention to politics that characterizes his early work. The well-known elegy "In Memory of W. B. Yeats," written only a year later, remarks that "poetry makes nothing happen," and "Spain" is equally pessimistic about the possibility that art, including poetry, can directly instigate political action. It holds that poetry can, however, encourage readers to live more ethical lives. Rather than making a polemical point, as Spender's Spanish civil war poetry does, "Spain" encourages readers to act according to their own moral guidelines. Still, because the Spanish civil war was known as a "people's war" and the struggle against the military involved an uprising among the citizenry, the poem implicitly supports the Republican

government as a form that would allow people to make moral choices and to live ethically.

HISTORICAL AND LITERARY CONTEXT

The Spanish civil war (1936–39) was a military- and conservative-led revolt against the Republican government of Spain. Social unrest had been rising in Spain throughout the 1920s and 1930s, due mostly to an extreme increase in poverty among the peasantry. In 1936 the Popular Front, composed of moderate liberals as well as socialists and communists, were elected on a platform of social reform and economic justice. Soon afterward, General Francisco Franco led the right-wing and fascist-aligned Nationalist faction in an attempted coup, followed by a wider rebellion that plunged the nation into civil war. As the conflict became increasingly bloody and destructive, the Nationalists received aid from the fascist governments of the Italian dictator Benito Mussolini and the German leader Adolf Hitler, while the Republicans received aid from the Soviet Union, France, and Mexico as well as from thousands of volunteers from western Europe and the United States. Many felt that the polarization of political and social values in the war represented the defining struggle of the age: a clash not just between the opposing ideologies of socialism and fascism but also between civilization and barbarism, good and evil. The war was also seen as part of an international conflict between fascist and democratic styles of government. In addition, for the United Kingdom and France the war seemed representative of growing international instability in the wake of World War I.

In the 1930s the major poets of early modernism—notably T. S. Eliot and W. B. Yeats—were becoming more conservative, but a coterie of poets that included Auden, Spender, and Cecil Day-Lewis appealed to the left-leaning intelligentsia. This generation of poets, raised in the shadow of World War I, felt that their own political credibility was diminished by their lack of experience. Thus, the Spanish civil war beckoned to them as a source of artistic material and as a political cause, even as it captured the imagination of Spanish artists such as Pablo Picasso (in his painting *Guernica*) and Joan Miró (in his Black and Red series) as well as international novelists such as Ernest Hemingway, John Dos Passos, Claude Simon, and George Orwell.

But the conflict attracted poets most of all. It was "the poets' war," according to Stephen Spender, "because to many people the struggle of the Republicans has seemed a struggle for the conditions without which the writing and reading of poetry are almost impossible in modern society."

THEMES AND STYLE

Like most of Auden's poetry, "Spain" can be a difficult poem to read. Its narrator speaks from the present of "to-day," and both the narrator and the ventriloquized voice of Spain itself define the present as a turning point in human history. The 1937 version of the poem is written in 26 stanzas that can be roughly divided into three sections that contrast the past, the present, and the future. The poem begins with the phrase "Yesterday all the past," and the first six stanzas lay out much of human history, focusing on developments in trade and technology, such as "yesterday the invention / Of cartwheels and clocks, the taming of / Horses"; religion and spirituality: "the abolition of fairies and giants / ... / The trial of heretics among the columns of stone"; and history: "the classic lecture / On the history of mankind." Auden's sense of the past is cultural and not specifically political, as he is interested in the history of ideas.

Stanzas 3, 4, and 5 draw a contrast between the past—which is full of changes, ideas, and facts—and the future. Each of these three stanzas begins with the word "yesterday" and ends with the phrase "but to-day the struggle," defining the present as a pivotal point between past civilizations and any number of possible futures. Auden divides humanity into three categories: the poet, who appeals to nature and "vision" to "send me the luck of the sailor"; the investigator, who "inquires"; and the poor, who ask a greater power for the knowledge of "history" and "time." In Auden's poem nations "combine each cry, invoking the life / That shapes the individual belly" and demand that some greater power intervene.

That greater power—time, history, or the divine—responds, "O no, I am not the mover ... I am your choice, your decision. Yes, I am Spain," drawing a parallel between the political and moral conflict of the Spanish civil war and the question of human agency. Auden is less concerned with determining a course of action than with urging people to take any course of action and to live according to a moral code.

The poem holds that the future of human civilization is at stake but that it is in the hands of people strong enough to stand up for their beliefs. Action in the present translates into control of the future and "the rediscovery of romantic love, / The photographing of ravens; all the fun under / Liberty's masterful shadow." Such a future requires sacrifice from the present, however: "the deliberate increase in the chances of death ... the expending of powers / On the flat ephemeral pamphlet and the boring meeting."

When the poem was first published as a chapbook in 1937, it was well received. George Orwell, who was wounded in the war, considered it to be one of only a few moral works about the Spanish civil war. The next version of the poem, titled "Spain 1937," appeared in the volume *Another Time* with a number of changes. Most notably, Auden changed a controversial line that Orwell had objected to—"the conscious acceptance of guilt in the necessary murder"—to read "the fact of murder," weakening the suggestion that the poem condones violence.

Auden later rejected a number of his political poems, including "Spain," out of a concern that literature could be used as a tool of propaganda. According to Edward Mendelson, Auden's literary executor, Auden became increasingly anxious about the potential of poetic language to be "deceptive" or "flattering." Writing in "Revision and Power", Mendelson surmises that Auden dropped or revised poems not because he "disagreed with their politics" but because "he distrusted their power to convince readers that he and they were on the right side in the great struggles of the age." In "Squares and Oblongs," an essay on revisionism, the poet remarks that the "Orpheus [the singer of Greek legend whose music was so powerful that it affected even the natural world] who moved stones is the archetype not of the poet, but of [Paul Joseph] Goebbels," the Nazi propaganda minister.

CRITICAL DISCUSSION

Because of Auden's prominence as a poet and an important antifascist voice, "Spain" received much immediate attention. While the communist-affiliated left tended to criticize the poem for its refusal to make a strong polemic point, less partisan critics appreciated its ability to capture the complexity of the moral choices of the time. An anonymous review in *New Verse*, for example, commends the poem for avoiding partisanship.

Backdrop for Teatro Del Guinol (Puppet Show), painted in 1923 by Generation of '27 Spanish poet and playwright Federico García Lorca, who was executed in the Spanish Civil War. © J. BEDMAR / IBERFOTO / THE IMAGE WORKS

Critics often refer to "Spain" as one of the most important poems about the Spanish civil war as well as one of Auden's most impressive political poems. In his study of the political poetry of the 1930s, *The Auden Generation*, Samuel Hynes calls it "the best of the English war-poems from Spain" but also says, "it is also the least partisan, the least passionate, the least concerned with actual war, and the least Spanish … its subject is moral decision, not political action." Bernard Bergonzi, in *Wartime and Aftermath*, agrees with Hynes, referring to the Auden of the 1930s as "the political politician diagnosing the sickness of England." In *W. H. Auden*, Peter C. Grosvenor traces the complicated political debate about the poem, illustrating that the question of Auden's political sensibilities and the polemical aims of his verse remain in question.

The textual history of the poem—its revision between 1937 and 1940 and its eventual rejection from Auden's collected volumes—is often read in the context of the shift from his politically engaged English period to his later period of religious reflection. In this context Auden's career is exemplary of his generation's disillusionment after the loss of the Spanish civil war and of the general turn in British and U.S. poetry of the mid-twentieth century from politics to more individual concerns. Some critics, however, see the poem as exemplary of Auden's large-scale historical imagination, his tendency to see the present in allegorical rather than literal terms and his interest in general moral questions rather than historical specifics.

SOURCES

Auden, W. H. "Spain." *Selected Poems*. Ed. Edward Mendelson. New York: Vintage, 1989. 51. Print.

———. "Spain 1937." *The English Auden: Poems, Essays and Dramatic Writings 1927–1939*. Ed. Edward Mendelson. London: Faber, 1977. Print.

Bergonzi, Bernard. *Wartime and Aftermath: English Literature and Its Background, 1939–1960*. Oxford: Oxford UP, 1993. Print.

Grosvenor, Peter C. "Auden, 'Spain' and the Crisis of Literary Popular Frontism." *W. H. Auden: A Legacy*. West Cornwall: Locust Hill, 2002. Web. 12 May 2011.

Hynes, Samuel. *The Auden Generation: Literature and Politics in England in the 1930s*. Princeton: Princeton UP, 1976. Print.

Mendelson, Edward. "Revision and Power: The Example of W. H. Auden." *Yale French Studies* 89 (1996): 103–12. Web. 15 May 2011.

FURTHER READING

Deane, Patrick. *History in Our Hands: A Critical Anthology of Writings on Literature, Culture, and Politics from the 1930s*. London: Leicester UP, 1998. Print.

Grass, Sean C. "W. H. Auden, from Spain to 'Oxford.'" *South Atlantic Review* 66.1 (2001): 84–101. Web. 10 May 2011.

Kendall, Tim. "W. H. Auden's Journeys to War." *Modern English War Poetry*. Oxford: Oxford UP, 2006. Print.

Miller, John. *Voices against Tyranny: Writing of the Spanish Civil War*. New York: Scribner, 1986. Print.

Spender, Stephen. *New Collected Poems of Stephen Spender*. London: Faber, 2004. Print.

———. *Poems for Spain*. London: Hogarth, 1939. Print.

———. *The Thirties and After: Poetry, Politics, People*. New York: Random, 1978. Print.

Jennifer Ludwig

THREE GUINEAS

Virginia Woolf

OVERVIEW

Virginia Woolf's book-length essay *Three Guineas* is a feminist-pacifist polemic that has divided general readers, critics, and scholars since its publication in 1938. Written in response to the horrors of the Spanish Civil War and the rise of fascism in Germany and Italy, the book is framed as a letter to an imaginary male correspondent who has posed the question of how to oppose war effectively. It draws provocative connections between gender relations, economic power, and violence, suggesting that patriarchal societal structures in 1930s England represented "in embryo the creature, Dictator as we call him when he is Italian or German, who believes that he has the right, whether given by God, Nature, sex or race is immaterial, to dictate to other human beings how they shall live; what they shall do." Woolf supports her wide-ranging and discursive argument with historical and biographical materials from the women's movements of the nineteenth and early twentieth centuries and with keen analysis of current events and cultural figures of her own time.

Woolf's place as a modernist novelist of the first rank has been secure since the mid-twentieth century. However, her politically direct nonfiction works, including *Three Guineas* and its landmark predecessor *A Room of One's Own* (1929), were frequently dismissed as marginal texts within her larger body of work. This held true until the 1970s, when feminist scholars began urging a reconsideration of her contribution to social thought. Woolf became an important figure for these so-called second-wave feminists, and *Three Guineas*, like *A Room of One's Own*, became a central text in the burgeoning field of feminist literary studies.

The work's Marxist- and feminist-oriented approach to pacifism remains politically radical in the twenty-first century, upsetting dominant interpretations of the World War II struggle against fascism while continuing to serve as both provocation and inspiration to those who would seek to redefine gender relations in the service of social justice.

HISTORICAL AND LITERARY CONTEXT

Woolf, along with most of her friends in the Bloomsbury Group—a loose organization of intellectuals and artists, including the essayist Lytton Strachey, the novelist E. M. Forster, the economist John Maynard Keynes, Woolf's female lover Vita Sackville-West, and Woolf's husband, Leonard—objected strongly to the United Kingdom's involvement in World War I and to government policies that failed to establish grounds for sustainable peace in that conflict's aftermath. In the decades between World War I and World War II, Woolf increasingly perceived links between gender relations and capitalist power. She famously addressed these links as they affected women's writing in her 1929 book-length essay *A Room of One's Own*, which urges women to demand privacy and financial independence as a route toward fulfillment of their literary gifts. Soon after that book's publication, Woolf began collecting historical materials and newspaper clippings in preparation for a sequel, which she initially conceived as a fact-based essayistic novel about female sexuality and gender relations.

In 1935 Woolf and her husband, though he was Jewish, traveled through Fascist Germany and Italy, inadvertently witnessing a Nazi parade. That same year she was appalled at the defeat of the pacifist position within the United Kingdom's ruling Labour Party, which instead adopted a commitment to meet Italian aggression in Abyssinia with force, if necessary. In the wake of these developments, Woolf energetically worked on the projected novel-essay, and she became increasingly preoccupied with the notion that male domination of women was intricately linked with the pervasiveness of warfare.

Woolf's continuing research reflected this preoccupation, and it was further marked by the outbreak of the Spanish Civil War, which began in 1936 and involved the previously rare phenomenon of attacks on civilians. The conflict ended with the ascent to power of the military general Francisco Franco, a conservative dictator supported by the German and Italian regimes. Meanwhile Woolf's concept of her text changed. She eventually separated the fictional and the fact-based strands of the planned novel-essay into separate books. The first was published in 1937 as the novel *The Years*; the second became the essay *Three Guineas*, published in 1938 as the world prepared for war.

THEMES AND STYLE

Three Guineas is presented as a letter composed in response to a male barrister (attorney) who has supposedly written the author to inquire, "How in

✥ *Key Facts*

Conflict:
Spanish Civil War

Time Period:
Mid-20th Century

Genre:
Essay

FEMALE WARRIORS

In *Three Guineas* Virginia Woolf argues that war is inextricably bound up with patriarchal norms and societal structures. Some readers might conclude that Woolf believed women to be natural pacifists. She clearly demonstrates, however, that she does not hold such an essentialist view of gender.

For example, in *Three Guineas* she quotes from a newspaper interview of a female soldier in the Spanish Civil War. The thirty-six-year-old woman explains that her two daughters had joined the conflict and that she herself became a militiawoman to avenge the death of the younger daughter, recently killed in battle. The woman states that she has killed at least five men and stolen the horse of a sixth, who may or may not have died as a result of their encounter.

Woolf's argument does not rest on neat divisions between male and female capacities for violence. Rather, she focuses on the connections between societal structures, power, and violence. War is an outgrowth not of masculine nature but of the social and political configurations that men have established for their own benefit—and at others' expense—over time. Woolf contends that if war is to be avoided, society must be remade. Her belief that this is possible testifies to a more fluid conception of gender than that which underlies more clichéd arguments about gender and war.

your opinion are we to prevent war?" and to solicit funds for the pacifist cause. The epistolary form allows for a relatively informal and intimate tone. It also allows the author to embrace digression and structural looseness, all of which might initially seem at odds with the high seriousness of war as a subject. This casual style is offset, however, by the weight of obviously prodigious historical and cultural research, and it is in keeping with the nature of the argument as a whole. Because Woolf was theorizing about connections between gender relations and politics that had not yet been studied in any depth, she had to read between the lines of official history and journalism, recontextualizing her materials through juxtaposition and irony.

The correspondent to whom the text is addressed is, like the author, a member of "the educated class," but neither their common privileged social milieu nor their shared horror at photographs of the civilian men, women, and children killed during the Spanish Civil War can overcome a fundamental difference that profoundly affects their individual attitudes toward war. That difference is gender.

Thus, at the outset of *Three Guineas*, Woolf establishes her chief preoccupation. Her speaker maintains that the propensity of human societies toward war is inextricably bound up with patriarchal social and economic structures. Male social domination resembles and enables political fascism, she argues, so that

a patriarchal society invariably tends toward displays of power and aggression that lead to war. Women who do not have financial independence, meanwhile, have no choice but to support the warmongering political positions of their husbands, even though, as the speaker argues, wars are fought for reasons that are largely alien to them: "[Y]ou are fighting to gratify a sex instinct which I cannot share," Woolf's speaker writes to her male correspondent, "to procure benefits which I have not shared and probably will not share; but not to gratify my instincts, or to protect either myself or my country."

The book's title, like its form, works to convey the theme of society's inherently warlike underpinnings. By the time Woolf was writing, a British guinea had become an obsolete gold coin, but members of the upper class wrote checks in denominations of guineas (rather than British pounds and shillings) for the purchase of goods that signified their social status. As the Woolf scholar Jane Marcus notes in her annotated edition of the text, the guinea coin had been named after the African region Guinea and was initially minted with gold mined on the continent by British colonial forces using slave labor.

Thus Woolf's title indicates that the origins of her social class's wealth and lifestyle were made possible by imperial violence and inhumanity. Furthermore, the precise *three* guineas of the title refer to two one-guinea donations that the speaker proposes to make to charitable organizations for the support of women's education and professional development, as well as a final one-guinea donation to her correspondent. Each guinea, along with the discursive explanation behind the author's reasons for donating it, corresponds to one of the three chapters in the book.

Woolf's work clearly supports female education and professional advancement as a possible means of changing society for the better. *Three Guineas* also details the many ways in which these goals are thwarted by British society. A simple donation of money, as she sees it, will therefore do little to advance the social good. Without considering and addressing the complex interrelation of gender and politics, nothing will change. The thoroughness of her critique of existing social relations strongly suggests that the true equality upon which pacifism must be premised would require a radical dismantling of cultural norms and institutions.

CRITICAL DISCUSSION

Initial reactions to *Three Guineas* ranged primarily from mixed to hostile. Many among the Bloomsbury Group, including both Woolf's husband, Leonard, and her lover, Sackville-West, had serious reservations about the book's strident feminism and political audacity. And leading cultural figures, such as the novelist Graham Greene and the prominent female literary critic Q. D. Leavis, disparaged the book in no uncertain terms. Many of those who attacked the work, as Naomi Black notes in *Virginia Woolf as Feminist*, were obviously uncomfortable with the argument's underlying feminist outlook and "caricatured her as the ailing maiden queen of the snobbish Bloomsbury Group." Since Woolf was already an established and critically acclaimed author of highbrow novels, most reviewers dutifully applauded the artfulness of her writing while implying that her talent lay elsewhere than in the development of logical arguments. This trend was reinforced by Woolf's nephew Quentin Bell, her first biographer, whose two-volume *Virginia Woolf: A Biography* (1972) disparages *Three Guineas* as the insignificant foray into politics of an inherently apolitical writer.

Readers sympathetic to Woolf's feminist stance, on the other hand, immediately greeted the book with admiration and enthusiasm. In a study of the letters that Woolf received and wrote regarding the book, published in *Virginia Woolf: A Feminist Slant*, Brenda R. Silver demonstrates this trend.

With the rise of the second-wave feminists in the 1970s, the sympathetic audience for *Three Guineas* grew markedly, and that decade saw a concerted scholarly reconsideration of Woolf's reputation as a political and social thinker. In addition to Silver, such scholars and writers as Tillie Olsen, Naomi Black, Anna Snaith, and Jane Marcus led this effort. *A Room of One's Own* and *Three Guineas* became, as Marcus

writes in her introduction to the annotated edition of the text, "the 'Bible' of a new feminist movement for social change that succeeded the struggle of Woolf's generation."

In the mainstream press, debate continued as to the merits of *Three Guineas* and Woolf's political thought. The most prominent recent biography of Woolf, Hermione Lee's *Virginia Woolf* (1996), argues that *Three Guineas* has been misunderstood and generally undervalued. Recent detractors, meanwhile, have hewed closely to the line first established by the most virulently antifeminist of Woolf's 1930s detractors. These include Alison Light, who offers a negative review of a new edition of the book in the *London Review of Books*, and the conservative writer Theodore Dalrymple, whose essay "The Rage of Virginia Woolf" paints her as a contemptible Bloomsbury elitist who spawned generations of similarly contemptible liberal elitists.

Three Guineas is secure, however, in its status as a provocative classic of feminist thought. In its radical coupling of patriarchal structures and violence, it remains fertile ground for theorization about more recent political developments, such as the U.S. wars in Afghanistan and Iraq that followed the events of September 11, 2001. Marian Eide's "'The Stigma of Nation': Feminist Just War, Privilege, and Responsibility" (2008) is an example of a recent application of Woolf's ideas to new historical contexts.

Five distraught mothers who have just identified their children's bodies after a 1937 bombing in Lerida, Spain. In *Three Guineas*, written in response to the Spanish Civil War, Virginia Woolf addresses war from the perspective of women. © BETTMANN / CORBIS

SOURCES

Bell, Quentin. *Virginia Woolf: A Biography.* 2 vols. London: Hogarth, 1972. Print.

Black, Naomi. *Virginia Woolf as Feminist.* Ithaca: Cornell UP, 2004. Print.

Dalrymple, Theodore. "The Rage of Virginia Woolf." *City Journal* (2002). Web.

Eide, Marian. "'The Stigma of Nation': Feminist Just War, Privilege, and Responsibility." *Hypatia* 23.2 (2008): 48–60. *Project MUSE.* Web. 26 May 2011.

Lee, Hermione. *Virginia Woolf.* London: Chatto and Windus, 1996. Print.

Light, Alison. "Harnessed to a Shark." Rev. of *Three Guineas*, by Virginia Woolf. *London Review of Books* 21 Mar. 2002: 29–31. Print.

Silver, Brenda R. "*Three Guineas* Before and After: Further Answers to Correspondents."

Virginia Woolf: A Feminist Slant. Ed. Jane Marcus. Lincoln: U of Nebraska P, 1983. 254–76. Print.

Woolf, Virginia. *Three Guineas.* Annotations and introd. by Jane Marcus. Orlando: Harcourt, 2006. Print.

FURTHER READING

Barret, Michèle. *Virginia Woolf: Women and Writing.* London: Women's P, 1979. Print.

Carlston, Erin G. *Thinking Fascism: Sapphic Modernism and Fascist Modernity.* Stanford: Stanford UP, 1998. Print.

Hussey, Mark, ed. *Virginia Woolf and War: Fiction, Reality and Myth.* Syracuse: Syracuse UP, 1991. Print.

Levenback, Karen L. *Virginia Woolf and the Great War.* Syracuse: Syracuse UP, 1999. Print.

Majumdar, Robin, and Allen McLaurin, eds. *Virginia Woolf: The Critical Heritage.* London: Routledge, 1975. Print.

Marcus, Jane. *Art & Anger: Reading Like a Woman.* Columbus: Ohio State UP, 1988. Print.

Olsen, Tillie. *Silences.* New York: Delacorte, 1978. Print.

Pawlowski, Merry, ed. *Virginia Woolf and Fascism: Resisting the Dictators' Seduction.* New York: Palgrave, 2001. Print.

Mark Lane

THREE SOLDIERS

John Roderigo Dos Passos

OVERVIEW

Three Soldiers (1921) is the second of three fictional accounts of the First World War written by John Dos Passos, an American who served as a volunteer medic during the conflict. As its title suggests, the novel chronicles the war experiences of three very different soldiers: middle-class San Francisco native Dan Fuseli, rural Indiana farmer "Chris" Chrisfield, and affluent Virginia musician and scholar John Andrews. Despite their regional and socioeconomic differences, all three men are subjected to what Dos Passos depicts as the homogenizing "machine" of the military, and all three are ultimately disillusioned by the war and their roles in it. By the end of the novel, all three have been punished in some way for their resistance to the enforced uniformity of the military machine.

Published just two years after the end of the war, *Three Soldiers* was one of the earliest fictional treatments of the conflict. In condemning the war as a merciless and unreflective machine that destroyed the lives and individual identities of its soldiers, Dos Passos's novel was also one of the first pieces of war literature to question the validity of the war it describes. In so doing, it helped to establish a tradition of antiwar literature that persists today. While less famous than many other fictional responses to World War I, *Three Soldiers* remains relevant to scholars who value its unique depiction of multiple soldiers' perspectives, its emphasis on the mechanistic aspects of military life, and its unique reflections on the factors motivating desertion.

HISTORICAL AND LITERARY CONTEXT

Most of *Three Soldiers* takes place in France, which was the site of much of the most violent and deadly fighting of World War I. Although the novel makes reference to the 1916 Battle of Verdun, which claimed the lives of more than three hundred thousand men, making it one of the war's bloodiest battles, most of its action takes place away from the front. Unlike many other novels of the First World War, *Three Soldiers* does not concentrate on the details of combat but rather on the daily lives of soldiers being prepared for war and waiting to be sent into battle. Dos Passos details the propaganda films that the men watch as part of their training, the mindless chores they are forced to carry out as part of their service, and the prevalence of

desertion. Soldiers, often disillusioned by the realities of war and motivated by fear and/or frustration with the compulsory regimentation of military life, walked away from their posts. In total, thousands of Allied soldiers went AWOL, or absent without leave, during the war. This problem became increasingly prevalent as the war dragged on. In the novel Andrews at first goes AWOL on a whim in order to visit Paris with a fellow soldier, but, after he is subsequently imprisoned, beaten, and placed on a labor battalion as punishment, he escapes and goes into hiding with no intention of returning to service.

In detailing Andrews's plight during World War I, Dos Passos draws on a historical event that was important in the lead up to the American Civil War (1861–65). Andrews, a Harvard-educated musician, is the most intellectual of the novel's three protagonists; he repeatedly reflects on the militant abolitionist John Brown's 1859 raid on the federal armory at Harpers Ferry in what is now West Virginia. Andrews sees Brown, who was captured and ultimately executed for his role in the raid, as a kindred spirit who acted according to the dictates of his conscience rather than the law in attempting to end slavery. After the war, an AWOL Andrews begins work on a symphony entitled "The Soul and Body of John Brown" but, reflecting on his life, Andrews berates himself for the fact that "he had not lived up to the name of John Brown." The novel ends with the pages of the unfinished symphony blowing off his desk as he is arrested for desertionr.

Like Andrews, Dos Passos had benefitted from a Harvard education, and he, too, struggled with the moral implications of the war. Published in 1921, *Three Soldiers* was among the earliest works in a tradition of World War I writing that reached its peak in the late 1920s. Only one other major novel, Henri Barbusse's *Le Feu* (1916; *Under Fire*, 1917) preceded it. In its negative reaction against the war and its sympathetic treatment of desertion, *Three Soldiers* represented a new kind of writing that would resurface in later works of World War I fiction, including Erich Maria Remarque's *All Quiet on the Western Front* (1929) and Ernest Hemingway's *A Farewell to Arms* (1929). Although Dos Passos's novel is not among the most discussed of these works, it is generally credited with helping to pave the way for better-known texts about the First World War and later conflicts.

❖ *Key Facts*

Conflict:
World War I

Time Period:
Early 20th Century

Genre:
Novel

JOHN DOS PASSOS AND ERNEST HEMINGWAY

John Dos Passos and fellow writer Ernest Hemingway were friends who met when they served as volunteer ambulance drivers during World War I. Both would later turn their wartime experiences into novels. It was the two men's involvement in the later Spanish Civil War (1936–39), however, that ultimately ended their friendship and created an intense literary rivalry between them.

When the Spanish Civil War broke out, both men were, like numerous other intellectuals of the day, drawn to the cause of Spain's communists, who were fighting against a fascist takeover of the country. After Dos Passos's longtime friend José Robles Pazos was murdered by communists who claimed Robles was a fascist spy, however, Dos Passos began to retract his support for the Spanish communists. This created a rift with Hemingway, who was still deeply and idealistically committed to the communists. Although Hemingway would eventually become disillusioned with the cause, the two men never mended their friendship. Their disagreement over the war was so intense that Hemingway took aim at Dos Passos's work in his 1942 book *Men at War*. Hemingway suggested that *Three Soldiers* was derivative of the work of French war novelist Henri Barbusse and that it lacked realistic dialogue.

SOURCE: Koch, Stephen. *The Breaking Point: Hemingway, Dos Passos, and the Murder of José Robles.* New York: Counterpoint, 2005. Print.
MEYERS, JEFFREY. *HEMINGWAY: A Biography.* New York: Harper, 1985. Print.

THEMES AND STYLE

The central theme of *Three Soldiers* is that war is a dehumanizing experience that destroys individuality and breaks the human spirit. In order to emphasize the war's effects on its soldiers, Dos Passos begins by highlighting the cultural and socioeconomic differences between his characters. Nineteen-year-old Dan Fuseli, the descendant of Italian immigrants, is from a middle-class family in San Francisco. He sees the war as a means to gain experience and distinction. Twenty-year-old Chrisfield is from a farming family in rural Indiana. Having had little education, he has a natural resentment of authority. Twenty-two-year-old John Andrews, on the other hand, is from an affluent family in Virginia. He thinks about music as he works in boot camp. Ultimately, however, all three men begin to lose their individuality to the war, a homogenization that Dos Passos underscores by using mechanical metaphors to name the sections of the novel, each corresponding with a different moment or process in the men's indoctrination, disillusionment, and destruction: "Making the Mold," "The Metal Cools," "Machines," "Rust," "The World Outside," and "Under the Wheels." Early in the novel,

the comparison of soldiers to machine parts is made explicit by a soldier named Eisenstein, who notes that "in the tyranny of the army a man becomes a brute, a piece of machinery." Although Fuselli initially rejects such thinking, the effects of the daily routine of war and its attendant lack of physical and mental freedom eventually wear on him. Once full of zeal for military prestige, he ends up little more than a laughing stock among his fellow soldiers, suffering from venereal disease and assigned to a labor battalion after the war. The other two protagonists suffer even more disagreeable fates. Chrisfield is punished early on for insubordination. Later, after killing an officer with a hand grenade, he escapes punishment only because no one discovers what he has done. By the end of the novel, he, like Andrews, is living as a deserter in Paris. In depicting the constant fear under which both Chrisfield and Andrews live, Dos Passos casts the American military police, rather than the Germans, as the enemy, further underscoring the culpability of the larger military machine in the men's destruction.

Stylistically, the novel is notable for its gritty realism, which shocked many of its earliest readers. Dos Passos describes in great detail the daily rituals enforced upon the men by their officers. Although the protagonists see little combat, their discussions with fellow soldiers reveal the more graphic horrors of war: "fellers with their arms swelled up to twice the size like blisters" from mustard gas and a shell victim "with his chest split in half an' his head hangin' by a thread like." Dos Passos's realism is also reflected in the dialogue through which he captures the distinct speech patterns of characters drawn from different regions and social strata. Most notably, Chrisfield's language reflects his rural Indiana upbringing and includes words such as "feller" (fellow) and "mahn's" (mines). To increase the verisimilitude of the text, Dos Passos also uses common slang of the day and frequently includes fragments of the songs the soldiers sing to pass time or to remind themselves of home.

CRITICAL DISCUSSION

Upon its publication in 1921, *Three Soldiers* had a polarizing effect on readers and reviewers. While some recognized its innovative approach to war writing, some deemed it unpatriotic. Others, among them former soldiers, called into question the validity of Dos Passos's depiction of military service and the soldiers' emotional lives. Over time, however, the controversy concerning the novel began to fade, and its popularity has slowly been eroded by a combination of negative critical responses and scholarly preference for other texts. Although contemporary scholars have tended to produce less commentary on Dos Passos's novel than on other roughly contemporaneous treatments of World War I, it continues to attract critical attention.

Because Dos Passos wrote several works treating his wartime experiences, and because his attitude

toward war and representation evolved over time, scholars have frequently discussed *Three Soldiers* in the context of his other war writing. Typical of this vein of scholarship is Lois Hughson's 1980 essay in *Studies in the Novel*, which outlines the author's developing outlook from *One Man's Initiation: 1917* (1920) through *Three Soldiers* and the first two novels of the *U.S.A.* trilogy (1930–36). She traces a shift from detached observation in the first work to a more complex statement and narrative in *Three Soldiers*, which, she suggests, "initiates innovative divisions of consciousness, [and] communicates genuine suffering." She considers *Three Soldiers* a transitional rather than a mature work, however, and finds the author's use of Andrews as a mouthpiece for the complex intellectual ideas he wishes to convey awkward and distracting. Hughson argues that Dos Passos achieves a more sophisticated outlook in *U.S.A.* by removing the intellectual burden from his characters, such that "no one in the novel is capable of the perspectives that beget moral and social judgments, yet those judgments are made by the novel and communicated to the reader."

Another common critical approach to the novel has been to trace its relationship to other works of war literature. Commentators have frequently explored the impact on the novel of earlier American thinkers and writers, including Thomas Jefferson (1743–1826), Ralph Waldo Emerson (1803–82), Henry David Thoreau (1817–62), and Walt Whitman (1819–92). Owen W. Gilman Jr. suggests in a 1980 article in

Modern Fiction Studies that the influence of Thoreau in particular can be traced in what he views as one of the most unique aspects of Dos Passos's novel—John Andrews's moral struggles and his ultimate decision to desert his post. Reading the novel in the context of Thoreau's political essays, Gilman suggests, reveals Andrews as "Dos Passos' early personal tribute to Henry David Thoreau"; the critic explains, "When John Andrews thinks about his action, his thoughts reverberate with the feelings and ideas that Thoreau had put into his defense of the individual's responsibility to check the state." Scholars have also examined Dos Passos's influence on later works of war fiction. In *American War Literature: 1914-Vietnam*, for example, Jeffrey Walsh traces the influence of the novel in later works such as Norman Mailer's *The Naked and the Dead* (1948), James Jones's *From Here to Eternity* (1951), and the Vietnam War fiction of Tim O'Brien (1946-). Claudia Matherly Stolz discusses parallels between *Three Soldiers* and O'Brien's *The Things They Carried* (1990) in a 2004 article in *West Virginia University Philological Papers*.

SOURCES

Dos Passos, John. *Three Soldiers*. New York: Doran, 1921. Print Gilman, Owen W., Jr. "John Dos Passos: *Three Soldiers* and Thoreau." *Modern Fiction Studies* 26.3 (1980): 470–81. Print.

Hughson, Lois. "Don Passos's World War: Narrative Technique and History." *Studies in the Novel* 12.1 (1980): 46–61. Print.

In Wyndham P. Lewis's painting *A Battery Shelled* (1919), the British gunners in the background are depicted as faceless and mechanical, blending into the angular landscape. The metaphor of soldiers as machines is also employed in John Dos Passos's 1921 novel *Three Soldiers*. Oil. Imperial War Museum. © THE ART ARCHIVE / IMPERIAL WAR MUSEUM / THE PICTURE DESK, INC.

Red Cross volunteers load wounded soldiers into an ambulance in Verdun, France, during World War I. John Dos Passos's experience as a volunteer ambulance driver in France during the Battle of Verdun informed the writing of his novel *Three Soldiers*.
© BETTMANN / CORBIS

Stolz, Claudia Matherly. "Dos Passos's *Three Soldiers*: A Case Study." *West Virginia University Philological Papers* 51 (2004): 77–84. Print.

Walsh, Jeffrey. *American War Literature: 1914-Vietnam*. New York: St. Martin's, 1982. Print.

FURTHER READING

Carr, Virginia Spencer. *Dos Passos: A Life*. Garden City: Doubleday, 1984. Print.

Clark, Michael. *Dos Passos' Early Fiction: 1912–1938*. Cranbury: Associated UP, 1987. Print.

Cooperman, Stanley. "John Dos Passos' *Three Soldiers*: Aesthetics and the Doom of Individualism." *The First World War in Fiction: A Collection of Critical Essays*. Ed. Holger Klein. London: Macmillan, 1976. 23–31. Print.

Dos Passos, John. *The Fourteenth Chronicle: Letters and Diaries of John Dos Passos*. Boston: Gambit, 1973. Print.

Ellis, John. *Eye-Deep in Hell: Trench Warfare in World War I*. New York: Pantheon, 1976. Print.

Ludington, Townsend. *John Dos Passos: A Twentieth Century Odyssey*. New York: Dutton, 1980. Print.

Rosen, Robert R. *John Dos Passos and the Writer*. Lincoln: U of Nebraska P. 1981. Print.

Sassoon, Siegfried. *Memoirs of an Infantry Officer*. London: Faber, 1931. Print.

Simon, Zoltán. "World War I and the Technological Sublime in the Early Novels of John Dos Passos." *Hungarian Journal of English and American Studies* 8.2 (2002): 25–43. Print.

Weeks, Robert P. "The Novel as Poem: Whitman's Legacy to Dos Passos." *Modern Fiction Studies* 26 (1980). 431–46. Print.

Greta Gard

"Vitaï Lampada" and "Clifton Chapel"

Sir Henry Newbolt

OVERVIEW

"Vitaï Lampada" and "Clifton Chapel" are two of the best-known poems of British poet and novelist Sir Henry Newbolt. Originally published in *Admirals All* (1897) and *The Island Race* (1899), respectively, the poems share an emphasis on tradition and nationalism that compares war to athletic competition. They were considered technically innovative for their time, a quality contemporary scholars attribute to Newbolt's facility with Greek and Latin poetic traditions. Written when the British Empire was at its height, they struck an immediate chord with readers because of their emphasis on British cultural and imperial prowess and their glorification of serving, and even dying, for one's country. A decade and a half later, as Britain faced the challenges of World War I, Newbolt's poems were used as pro-war propaganda.

Not all of Newbolt's poetry promoted the glory of war, and prior to World War I some of his other verses were better known than "Vitaï Lampada" and "Clifton Chapel." The war, however, enshrined these poems in the country's collective memory, despite the growing popularity of the modernist tradition that arose from and reacted against the war. The modernists, in essence, viewed Newbolt's work as stylistically and thematically antiquated at best and morally irresponsible at worst. Today it receives little attention outside the academy, where it remains of some interest to scholars of British imperialism and the First World War.

HISTORICAL AND LITERARY CONTEXT

Written in the late 1890s, when the United Kingdom's reach was virtually unparalleled, Newbolt's poems reflect the historical and literary traditions of British imperialism. In addition to Ireland, Scotland, England, and Wales, the empire covered Canada, Australia, India, and parts of the West Indies and Africa. In addition, British commercial and naval power extended even farther. Newbolt's poems reflect the belief, widely accepted among his contemporaries, that Britain was spreading progress and knowledge around the globe.

Although today it is remembered for its use as propaganda during World War I, "Vitaï Lampada" references another conflict, the January 17, 1885, Battle of Abu Klea. Fought north of the Sudanese city of Khartoum, the battle pitted British forces against the army of the Mahdi of Sudan. British forces came

under attack as they attempted to reach Khartoum, where British general Charles Gordon was under siege. The battle resulted in the deaths of more than seventy British soldiers, many of them high-ranking officers. Although the British eventually claimed victory, they were too late to rescue Gordon, who was killed two days before British forces reached Khartoum.

In Britain the battle became famous as a near disaster in which troops were ill-equipped with guns that jammed and in which the popular Colonel Fred Burnaby was killed. Newbolt seized upon Abu Klea as an exemplar of victory achieved through perseverance and bravery. "Vitaï Lampada" claims that despite the fact that "The gatling's jammed and the colonel dead, / and the regiment blind with dust and smoke," the army is able to forge ahead by remembering the glory of past athletic triumphs.

When World War I began in 1914, Newbolt's poems were folded into a vigorous recruiting effort that was seen as necessary given the massive death tolls brought on by advanced weapons and the perils of trench warfare. With his metaphor of war as an athletic contest, Newbolt's work was particularly useful in the formation of "Pals battalions," in which men were encouraged to enlist to fight alongside men they knew.

The propaganda worked. Although more than eight hundred thousand British imperial soldiers were killed in the war, by 1918 more than five million men had joined the military. Commenting on the real-world effects of Newbolt's rhetoric, Colin Veitch in the *Journal of Contemporary History* offers the example of a British officer who kicked footballs toward the German trenches before leading an attack in which he and many of his men were killed.

As works emphasizing the prestige of the British imperial project, Newbolt's poems have often been compared to the better-known writings of British novelist Rudyard Kipling—whose name has become synonymous with British imperialism in the late nineteenth and early twentieth centuries. Newbolt was an unapologetic imperialist, and although he cautioned in less famous poems against going to war for the wrong reasons, his veneration of fighting and dying for one's country has become his literary legacy.

Such romanticized visions of martial pageantry and glory were soon challenged by poets reacting to the horrors of World War I. Ezra Pound (1885–1972),

✣ *Key Facts*

Conflict:
World War I

Time Period:
Early 20th Century

Genre:
Poetry

WORLD WAR I PALS BATTALIONS

Henry John Newbolt's poems reflect a popular association of war with the glory and camaraderie of sport, an association that was used to recruit soldiers during World War I. Such propaganda also helped to drive the creation of Pals battalions, some of which were derived from sporting leagues.

Begun in 1914, Pals battalions were not officially orchestrated by the British war office but were initiated by civilian leaders, who generally shouldered the financial burdens associated with starting them. Pals battalions encouraged men to serve with others who lived in the same city and/or shared their profession or recreational interests. The idea behind such battalions was that men would be more likely to enlist when guaranteed a sense of instant camaraderie with their fellow soldiers.

Appealing to local as well as national pride, Pals battalions soon accounted for a significant percentage of British recruits. Pals battalions were particularly popular in metropolitan areas such as Liverpool, Manchester, and Birmingham, which quickly raised multiple battalions each. Although popular with many who enlisted, Pals battalions were later criticized for perpetuating class segregation—with middle-class and working-class recruits generally forming separate battalions—and for creating conditions in which large segments of a community were wiped out in a single battle.

T. S. Eliot (1888–1965), and others of this generation rejected both the content and form of the imperial poetic tradition as incompatible with the postwar world.

THEMES AND STYLE

When *Admirals All* and *The Island Race* were published in the late 1890s, they were embraced for their fervent nationalism and for Newbolt's innovative adaptations of the classical meters he borrowed from Latin and Greek. Since "Vitaï Lampada" and "Clifton Chapel" are now remembered chiefly as examples of World War I propaganda, modern critics tend to see the most stylistically notable aspect of "Vitaï Lampada" as its use of an extended metaphor in which war is likened to sport.

The poem's opening stanza invokes a game of cricket at Newbolt's alma mater, Clifton College: "There's a breathless hush in the Close to-night—/ Ten to make and the match to win." On the field, each man gives his all because he is moved by the words of his captain: "Play up! Play up! And play the game!," a refrain that concludes each of the poem's three stanzas. In the second stanza the cry to "Play up" is voiced not in the Close but in the Sudan, where "The sand of the desert is sodden with blood." Here the troops are able to win the bloody battle of Abu Klea because "the voice of a schoolboy rallies the ranks" by evoking the spirit of youthful sporting competitions: "Play up! Play up! And play the game!"

Although the metaphor is less overt in "Clifton Chapel," it too likens military conflict to athletics, with the speaker entreating his son "To love the game beyond the prize." The conflation of military and sporting contests implies that war is not only glorious and heroic but also innocent and part of a tradition of British grandeur. In this way, the poem joins with the larger theme of Newbolt's writings, namely, that British traditions, whether academic, athletic, religious, or cultural, represent the pinnacle of human achievement and are worth fighting and even dying for.

"Vitaï Lampada" and "Clifton Chapel" also draw on the British "public" (in U.S. terms, "private") school tradition, in which the privileged elite are educated outside of the government-run education system. Both poems specifically reference the poet's alma mater, to which he was famously devoted. Both also make use of Latin, a language associated with a traditional British education. "Vitaï Lampada," for example, means "the torch of life," an allusion to *De rerum natura* (On the Nature of the Universe), by the Roman poet Lucretius.

In Newbolt's poems, public school nostalgia works to invoke pride in British culture more generally. In "Vitaï Lampada," the troops succeed abroad because they are able to draw on the shared traditions of their homeland. In "Clifton Chapel," the emphasis on British culture is more overt as a father addresses his son in the chapel of the noted public school, handing down knowledge and tradition from his generation to the next. He encourages the young man "To count the life of battle good, / And dear the land that gave you birth." Pride in school and country are further associated in the poem with faith in God, "Who built the world of strife, / Who gave His children Pain for friend, / And Death for surest hope of life." The poem closes with the father quoting from a plaque in the chapel, which, written in Latin, glorifies one "Who died in a foreign land, before his time, but as a soldier and for his country."

In connecting valued traditions of culture, education, and sport with war, Newbolt's poems encouraged military service as a chance for young men to escalate and consecrate the teamwork and pride that they had exhibited in school or on the sports field. The widespread appropriation of these verses during World War I indicate that they may, indeed, have held sway over the hearts and minds of the empire's once innocent youth.

CRITICAL DISCUSSION

When Newbolt's *Admirals All* was published in 1898, it was an immediate popular success. The work sold out quickly, and the publisher had to issue numerous editions to meet the demand. Some of Newbolt's literary contemporaries, however, doubted the artistic merits of his depictions of war.

A reviewer in the *Athenaeum*, for example, praises Newbolt's facility with poetic meter but questions the manner in which he discusses martial themes. Suggesting that Newbolt's failure to remain intellectually remote is a major problem, the reviewer asserts, "if a poem about war is to be really a poem, war, certainly, must be treated in the grand manner and with sufficient intellectual remoteness." The reviewer singles out "Vitaï Lampada" for its failures in this respect and states more generally that "if [Newbolt] wishes to indulge himself in a cheap popularity he has only to continue to mistake rhetoric for poetry." Similar concerns are evinced in a review of *The Island Race* in the *Academy*, which notes the collection's power as patriotic propaganda but questions its lasting literary value, saying, "It is good rhetoric; good wholesome doggerel for the camp fire and the quarter-deck; only rarely, in hints and touches, anything more."

Critical attention was again focused on Newbolt's poetry during World War I, when it was used to encourage young men to enlist and defend the empire. Writing in the *Fortnightly Review* in 1916, Herbert Warren notes a connection between poetry and heroism and says that in the context of the brutal destruction of the war, "poetry again will prompt a thousand heroic actions." He points to "Clifton Chapel" and "Vitaï Lampada" in particular as examples of contemporary verse with the heroism-inspiring qualities of famous poems of the past.

Today Newbolt is not nearly as well known as his contemporaries. Scholars interested in the literature of British imperialism are more inclined toward authors such as Kipling, while those studying nineteenth- and early-twentieth-century war poetry more broadly tend to favor Alfred, Lord Tennyson (1809–92), Walt Whitman (1819–92), and Wilfred Owen (1893–1918). In the 1990s several books were devoted to Newbolt's life and work, but there has been no sustained attempt to revalue his reputation as a poet.

Recent scholarship has primarily explored the power of Newbolt's rhetoric as a propaganda tool and his conflation of war and sport. Writing in the *Journal of Contemporary History*, for example, Colin Veitch describes "Vitaï Lampada" as "the ultimate poetic expression of the ideological transfer held to take place between public school playing-field and the battlefield." Conversely, Tony Collins suggests that the battlefield imagery has been used as pro-sport propaganda. In an article in the *Historical Journal*, Collins builds on the foundation laid by Veitch and others to argue that the English Rugby Football Union capitalized on the presumed relationship between sport, patriotism, and battle in order to promote itself during World War I. He cites "Vitaï Lampada" as a prominent example of the rhetoric of sport and war that the rugby association manipulated to its advantage.

Sir Henry Newbolt's poems were used to recruit "pals battalions," in which men enlisted and fought alongside their friends. In this undated World War I photograph, British Army soldiers march to the French front amid smiles and good cheer. © AP IMAGES

SOURCES

Rev. of *Admirals All*, by Henry Newbolt. *Athenaeum* 22 Jan. 1898. 111–12. Print.

Collins, Tony. "English Rugby Union and the First World War." *Historical Journal* 45.4 (2002): 797–817. Print.

"Lyra Heroica." Rev. of *The Island Race*, by Henry Newbolt. *Academy* 3 Dec. 1898: 371. Print.

Newbolt, Henry. "Clifton Chapel." *The Island Race*. New York: Lane, 1999. Print.

———. "Vitaï Lampada." *Admirals All and Other Verses*. London: E. Mathews, 1897. Print.

Veitch, Colin. "'Play Up! Play Up! And Win the War!' Football, the Nation and the First World War 1914–1915." *Journal of Contemporary History* 20.3 (1985): 363–78. Print.

Warren, Herbert. "The Appeal of Poetry at the Present Hour." *Fortnightly Review* July 1916: 110–23. Print.

FURTHER READING

Chitty, Susan. *Playing the Game: A Biography of Sir Henry Newbolt*. London: Quartet, 1997. Print.

Jackson, Vanessa Furse. *The Poetry of Henry Newbolt: Patriotism Is Not Enough*. Greensboro: ELT, 1994. Print.

Johnson, Robert. *British Imperialism*. New York: Palgrave Macmillan, 2003. Print.

Lasswell, Harold D. *Propaganda Technique in World War I*. Cambridge: MIT P, 1971. Print.

Newbolt, Henry John. *My World as in My Time: Memoirs of Sir Henry Newbolt, 1862–1932*. London: Faber, 1932. Print.

———. *Taken From the Enemy*. London: Chatto, 1892. Print.

Greta Gard

"WE'LL MEET AGAIN"

Hugh Charles

✦ *Key Facts*

Conflict:
World War II

Time Period:
Mid-20th Century

Genre:
Song

OVERVIEW

"We'll Meet Again" (1939) is a song written by Hugh "Hughie" Charles (with music by Ross Parker) and first recorded by the "Forces' Sweetheart" Vera Lynn near the outset of World War II. The song captured the mood in Britain as soldiers and their families prepared for war. After its success in Great Britain, "We'll Meet Again" was recorded in the United States by artists including Guy Lombardo (1941), Kay Kyser (1941), and Benny Goodman (1942). Slow and sentimental, it depicts a man's reassuring words to his sweetheart as he prepares to depart for war. By encouraging optimism about the duration and danger of World War II, the song attempted to boost morale among soldiers both before and during their service. Wartime critics felt it lacked the manly patriotic militarism some considered more appropriate for a war song. Subsequently, Charles has been criticized for presenting a sentimental vision of a military conflict in which hundreds of thousands of British soldiers died.

Despite criticism of its romanticization of the war, "We'll Meet Again" has had a lasting impact on popular culture in both Great Britain and the United States. During World War II the song was immensely popular, first in England and later in America. It fell out of favor after the war, as musical styles and tastes changed. During the 1960s, however, it attracted renewed attention when it was included in the soundtrack of *Dr. Strangelove or: How I Learned to Stop Worrying and Love the Bomb*, a 1964 antiwar film directed by Stanley Kubrick. "We'll Meet Again" notably plays as the film concludes with the mushroom cloud of an atomic explosion.

HISTORICAL AND LITERARY CONTEXT

When "We'll Meet Again" was first released in 1939, Great Britain was preparing for war. Alarmed by the rising militarism of Nazi Germany, Britain had already begun to build up its military, encouraging voluntary enlistment by allowing men to choose where and how they would serve. Just prior to Adolf Hitler's September 1, 1939, invasion of Poland, the British government passed legislation that required men ages twenty to twenty-one to enter military training. When Britain declared war on September 3, this conscription expanded to all men ages twenty to twenty-three. In the ensuing months much of the

British Expeditionary Force (BEF) and Royal Air Force (RAF) were mobilized to aid in the defense of France from Nazi invasion. With the fall of France in May 1940, England realized that its military, which was considerably smaller than that of its enemies, was woefully inadequate for the war ahead. Further recruitment measures were put in place, and by the end of the war, service was required of all able-bodied men ages eighteen to forty-one. Enlistment swelled from just more than one million men at the end of 1939 to a peak of slightly less than three million in 1945. In total, more than 3.5 million British men served in the war, and nearly four hundred thousand of them were killed.

With memories of the massive death toll of World War I still fresh in the minds of British citizens, anxiety was high upon the declaration of war and mass mobilization. Such unease was compounded by dire predictions of a war that would bring widespread destruction and civilian deaths in England. Men heading off to fight faced fear not only for their own safety abroad but also for their loved ones at home. Thus, while conscription obviated the need for propaganda aimed at boosting enlistment, efforts were made to reassure men about their service.

Music played an important role in raising both public and military morale about the war—the first major conflict during which most homes had access to a radio. On the warfront, music served to remind soldiers of home and to steel their resolve for the Allied cause. Armies also often broadcast music and political propaganda that would be picked up by enemy troops in the vicinity. Consequently, troops on both sides of the conflict were familiar with a wide range of war tunes. On the home front, music helped women pass the time as they worked in factories and helped boost the spirits of those who had loved ones overseas.

In their book *Music of the World War II Era*, William H. and Nancy K. Young describe the emergence, early in the war, of "a number of songs that celebrated courage, and looked to a more peaceful future." Charles's "We'll Meet Again" was part of this wave of war music. Prior to its release, Charles had penned "There'll Always Be an England," a wildly popular patriotic song celebrating England and its enduring traditions that was released in the summer of 1939. "We'll Meet Again," on the other hand, never mentions Britain or the war, instead expressing its patriotism by assuring men and their families that they will return from service unscathed. In depicting a soldier's departure for war, "We'll Meet Again" has much in common with one of the best-known songs of World War II, "Lili Marlene." Written in German after World War I, an English version of the song quickly became popular as well. "Lili Marlene" describes a soldier who leaves behind his beloved. He imagines her standing beneath the lantern where she often waited for him before the war, worries about another taking his place, and longs to be back home with her.

THEMES AND STYLE

On the surface, the central theme of "We'll Meet Again" is the need for optimism in the face of the adversity of war. The song's tone, like that of other war tunes of the period, is sweet and sentimental, reflecting upcoming hardship and deferring happiness to an unknown future date. This is reflected in its chorus: "We'll meet again, don't know where, don't know when, / but I know we'll meet again some sunny day!" The speaker encourages his sweetheart to "keep smiling through, just like you always do," secure in the knowledge that they will be reunited at some point in the future. Underscoring the optimistic message that the war will soon be over, he asks her to "say hello" to the people he knows and to "tell them I won't be long!" While the song does not deny that danger, or "darks clouds," loom, it tempers this threatening aspect of war with the promise of a happy ending. The speaker reminds his lover to keep up her spirits because "after the rain comes the rainbow, / You'll see the rain go, never fear" and to say "goodbye to sorrow." He also, importantly, promises to be true, pledging "I'll not forget you sweetheart."

Although Charles's lyrics display hopefulness, there is a distinct undercurrent that betrays the rosy picture presented by the song. For example, when the speaker refers to his friends and family—that "they'll be happy to know that as you saw me go, / I was singing this song"—he indirectly suggests that he is putting up a false front for their benefit. Similarly, the repetition of "we'll meet again," which opens many versions of the song and serves as its refrain, can be interpreted as an act of self-denial as well as national delusion that makes going off to war more palatable. Moreover, the indeterminacy regarding the future meeting, particularly with regard to where it will occur ("don't know where, don't know when"), has led some listeners to conclude that the song presumes the man's death in the war. Kate McLoughlin suggests in an article in the book *From Self*

In this 1940 photograph, which embodies the hope conveyed by the song "We'll Meet Again," a young woman leans over the barrier at a train station to kiss a British soldier returning from the front lines of World War II. © HULTON-DEUTSCH COLLECTION / CORBIS

THE "FORCES' SWEETHEART": VERA LYNN

"We'll Meet Again" owed much of its success to its recording by the "Forces' Sweetheart," Vera Lynn. Lynn, who was born Vera Welch in 1917, acquired her nickname in 1939, when she topped a newspaper poll of British servicemen's favorite entertainers. Although she had achieved some early success as a child performer, her wartime performances guaranteed her lasting fame.

In addition to recording songs such as "The White Cliffs of Dover" and "We'll Meet Again," Lynn hosted a popular wartime radio show, *Sincerely Yours*. The show, which allowed people at home to send messages to their loved ones overseas, further endeared her to the troops and their families. Lynn also traveled abroad, to countries such as Egypt, Burma, and India, to perform for Allied troops. She would dress up in formal attire despite the heat and insects in order to create a fantasy of wartime elegance for the soldiers.

After the war Lynn continued her career as a performer and immersed herself in charity work. In 1975 she was honored with the title Dame Commander of the Order of the British Empire. In Great Britain she remains one of the most honored and iconic figures of the World War II era.

to Shelf that the lyric "'I know we'll meet again some sunny day' might refer to a summer reunion, but it could with equal ease connote a bright afterlife."

CRITICAL DISCUSSION

When "We'll Meet Again" was recorded and released in Great Britain in 1939, it was immensely popular with listeners. Over the next few years, the song was rerecorded several times for release in the United States, but it did not achieve widespread popularity there until after America's entry into the war at the end of 1941. Despite, or perhaps because of, its intense popular appeal, Charles's song has not attracted the same degree of scholarly attention that has met other works of war literature. During the World War II era and the decades that immediately followed, popular music was not considered a legitimate topic of scholarly criticism (which was primarily limited to "high culture"). Thus, while the poetry and novels of the war received instant critical attention in the aftermath of the conflict, influential songs such as "We'll Meet Again" were overlooked. With the rise in the 1970s of cultural studies, an academic discipline aimed in part at collapsing the high culture/low culture distinction by applying critical lenses to popular works, such music became more attractive to scholars.

Some commentators have focused on the history and reception of "We'll Meet Again." In his book *The Songs That Fought the War*, John Bush Jones provides

cultural context for the song's popular reception, asserting that the war "made" music both by creating an audience and psychological demand for it and "in a larger sense by inspiring or occasioning the writing, publishing, and recording of thousands of songs by thousands of composers and lyricists, both professional career song writers and amateurs." Writing about the delayed reaction to Charles's song in the United States, Jones explains that it was initially released in the United States before the American people were ready for its message: "The song is a typical one of a soldier's parting words to his sweetheart as he is about to leave for war, in many ways a precursor of the numerous songs of parting by American songsmiths yet to come. When it was first released in the United States, we weren't even at war." Elsewhere, McLoughlin examines the song in the historical and cultural contexts of its performance by the popular Lynn.

Other scholars have contrasted the song's appeal with that of Charles's equally well-known "There'll Always Be an England." In an essay in the book *'Millions Like Us'?* John Baxendale counts both songs among a "handful of wartime songs still remembered 50 years after the event." He also suggests that "while the longevity of *We'll Meet Again* owes a great deal to that of dame Vera Lynn, *There'll Always Be an England* has lived on in a different cultural category: it is a national song."

The use of "We'll Meet Again" in Kubrick's *Dr. Strangelove* has attracted nearly as much scholarly commentary as the song itself. Discussing the song in that context, Alice Bach suggests in her book *Religion, Politics, Media in the Broadband Era* that Charles's "sugary lyrics underscore the death-dealing, ironic vision of Kubrick." Indeed, the film itself can be seen as critical commentary on the song, which uses sentimental optimism to conceal the massive destruction and loss of life wrought by the war.

SOURCES

Bach, Alice. *Religion, Politics, Media in the Broadband Era*. Sheffield: Sheffield Phoenix, 2004. Print.

Baxendale, John. "'You and I—All of Us Ordinary People': Renegotiating 'Britishness' in Wartime." *'Millions Like Us'?: British Culture in the Second World War*. Ed. Nick Hayes and Jeff Hill. Liverpool: Liverpool UP, 1999. 295–322. Print.

Jones, John Bush. *The Songs That Fought the War: Popular Music and the Home Front, 1939–1945*. Lebanon: Brandeis UP, 2006. Print.

McLoughlin, Kate, "Vera Lynn and the 'We'll Meet Again Hypothesis.'" *From Self to Shelf: The Artist under Construction*. Ed. Sally Bayley and Will May. Newcastle: Cambridge Scholars 2007. 112–20. Print.

Parker, Ross, and Hughie Charles. "We'll Meet Again." London: Irwin Dash Music, 1939. Print.

Young, William H., and Nancy K. Young. *Music of the World War II Era*. Westport: Greenwood, 2008. Print.

FURTHER READING

Beidler, Philip D. *The Good War's Greatest Hits: World War II and American Remembering.* Athens: U of Georgia, 1998. Print.

Bloomfield, Gary L. *Duty, Honor, Applause: America's Entertainers in World War II.* Guilford: Lyon's Press, 2004. Print.

Brewer, Susan A. *To Win the Peace: British Propaganda in the United States during World War II.* Ithaca: Cornell UP, 1997. Print.

Cull, Nicholas John. *Selling War: The British Propaganda Campaign against American "Neutrality" in World War II.* New York: Oxford UP, 1995. Print.

Horten, Gerd. *Radio Goes to War: The Cultural Politics of Propaganda during World War II.* Berkeley: U of California P, 2002. Print.

Lee, William F. *American Big Bands.* Milwaukee: Hal Leonard, 2005. Print.

MEDIA ADAPTATION

We'll Meet Again. Dir. Philip Brandon. Perf. Vera Lynn, Geraldo, and Patricia Roc. Columbia Pictures, 1943. Film.

Greta Gard

SATIRE

BLACK MARGINS
Stories

Saadat Hasan Manto

OVERVIEW

Black Margins: Stories (2003), by the Pakistani writer Saadat Hasan Manto, is a powerful collection of short fiction that deals with the Indian Partition of 1947 and with its aftermath. The stories were selected by M. Asaduddin from the fifteen short story collections Manto had written between 1948 and his early death in 1955.

Partition had a devastating effect on Manto's artistic life. He spent much of his adult life in Bombay, where he had a successful career as a screenwriter in India's nascent film industry. His wife and children emigrated to Lahore before Partition, but Manto refused to leave. In 1948 Manto and a friend, the popular Hindu film star Ashok Kumar, left Filmistan Studios for Bombay Talkies. Shortly after Manto's arrival, Bombay Talkies began to receive threats that the studio would be burned down if it did not fire all of its Muslim employees. Anonymous accusations that Manto was responsible for Muslim writers "infiltrating" the studio ultimately drove him to follow his wife and children to Lahore.

Once in Lahore, Manto suffered a major breakdown. For three months he was unable to adjust to his surroundings and unable to write. Aamir Mufti quotes Manto's later description of this period of confusion: "Despite great effort, I couldn't separate India from Pakistan. Repeatedly I was troubled by the same question: will the literature of Pakistan be a literature apart? If so, what will it be like? All that was written in undivided India, who is now its owner? Will that, too, be partitioned?"

HISTORICAL AND LITERARY CONTEXT

From the beginning of the twentieth century, Indian nationalists called first for a larger role in the government of British India and later for independence. At first, Hindu and Muslim nationalists worked together. By the 1930s, however, Muslim nationalists, under the leadership of Mohammed Ali Jinnah and the Muslim League, began to call for the creation of a separate Muslim state.

In 1947 the British government, overwhelmed by postwar problems at home and throughout the empire, announced that it would accede to Indian nationalists' demands for independence. Lord Louis Mountbatten was named viceroy of Indian with the mandate of resolving the differences between Hindus and Muslims and transmitting power into "responsible Indian hands." Within a month of his arrival, Mountbatten decided the only solution was to create two separate states. The original timeline called for the transfer of authority to occur no later than June 1948. Having reached the decision to partition India, however, the British government moved with speed. On July 15, 1947, it announced that the creation of two new South Asian states would occur one month later.

At midnight on August 15, 1947, the new states of India and Pakistan came into being. Independence was accompanied by fifteen months of violence. As communal violence increased, between ten million and twelve million Hindus, Muslims, and Sikhs migrated between India and Pakistan. Hundreds of thousands died in the process, and more died in the refugee camps that appeared on both sides of the border.

The event that came to be called partition occurred at midnight on August 15, 1947. Considerable effort went into the process of determining exactly where the border would lie between the new states of India and Pakistan. However, almost no thought was given to ensuring that the transfer of power would be peaceful. Faced with the prospect of being caught on the "wrong" side of the new border, between ten and twelve million Hindus, Muslims, and Sikhs migrated between India and Pakistan during a period of fifteen months. Hundreds of thousands died in the communal violence that accompanied the migrations. More died in the refugee camps that sprang up on both sides of the border.

THEMES AND STYLE

Manto's stories employ a combination of dark humor, surprise endings, and cinematic descriptions of violence. There are no heroes in the stories, although there are clear villains. "Toba Tek Singh" is generally considered Manto's masterpiece. In it he pushes the territorial logic of Partition to an illogical extreme. The governments of India and Pakistan decide that, since population and assets have been transferred between the two countries, it is only logical that the inmates

✣ *Key Facts*

Conflict:
Partition of India

Time Period:
Mid-20th Century

Genre:
Short stories

SIYAH HASHYE SKETCHES

In 1948 Manto published *Siyah Hashye* (Black Margins), a collection of thirty-two fragmentary sketches about the violence of Partition, ranging in length from two lines to five pages. A few focus on the ironic use of a single word. Short as they are, many depend on an ironic turn of the story or on dark humor. Each sketch is stripped down to its essential action, with neither character development nor the humanizing details that characterize Manto's short stories. According to Alok Bhalla, the cumulative effect of the sketches is "a nightmare landscape of random violence; a scandalous world where victims and predators interchange places needlessly and unpredictably." Like longer works of Partition fiction, the anecdotes in *Siyah Hashye* deal with looting, murder, rape, and attempts to escape violence. Unlike most works dealing with Partition, neither the perpetrators of violence nor its victims are identified by religion or region.

The reading public greeted the work with hostility. Manto was accused of sensationalizing the tragedies of Partition. The author defended himself in the introduction to his next collection of stories, *Yazid*, saying that in *Siyah Hashye* he had "dived into that ocean of blood shed by man of his fellow man, and selected some pearls, recording the tireless ferocity with which man had shed the last drop of the blood of his brother, recording the tears shed involuntarily by some who could not make out why they could not say good-bye to their inherent humanity."

In this September 25, 1947, photograph, Indian Muslim refugees wait in line for water for five hours at Purana Qila Fort on the outskirts of New Delhi, where they have taken refuge from the violence of the Partition. © BETTMANN / CORBIS

of lunatic asylums be exchanged as well. On the day of the transfer, one inmate refuses to move. Bishan Singh, a Sikh peasant popularly known as Toba Tek Singh because of his property holdings in that town,

says that he does not want to live in either India or Pakistan. He wants to live in Toba Tek Singh, the town where his family has always lived, which is now part of the Pakistani Punjab. When the guards try to push Singh into India, he resists. Ultimately, because he is a harmless old man, the guards allow him to stand straddling the border until the exchange is completed. The next morning Singh screams once, falls down, and dies: "There, behind barbed wire, on one side, lay India and behind more barbed wire, on the other side, lay Pakistan. In between, on a bit of earth which had no name, lay Toba Tek Singh." Manto continues his absurdist exploration of the logic of Partition in "The Dog of Tetwal." A dog is caught between communal camps on opposite sides of the border and killed when the camps' residents are unable to decide whether the dog is Indian or Pakistani.

In other stories in *Black Margins*, Manto focuses on violence against women within the context of the violence of Partition as a whole. In "Cold Meat" a Muslim man is rendered impotent by his memory of raping a Sikh girl whom he later realizes was dead. In "Open It" a Hindu man's efforts to find his daughter when they are separated in a refugee camp lead to her being repeatedly raped by a gang of Hindu youths. In both stories Manto is less concerned with the rape of the woman than with the effect of the rape on the men who survive and what he sees as the rape of the culture as a whole.

Manto writes in a simple style, defined by what the Indian writer and translator Alok Bhalla describes as "the grating roughness of his diction, the sardonic irony of his images and the harsh rhythms of his prose." Many of his stories are told through a third-party narrator called Manto, whose life is similar to but nonetheless distinct from that of Manto the writer. According to Bhalla, "The style of his best stories is devoid of all metaphoric excess and sentimental inflections, is always precise, bare-boned and conversational … Their descriptions, ironic and cold-eyed, seem to be authentic versions of life at a particular historical moment because they have the feel of the real and the pitilessness of stone." The writer and journalist Aatish Taseer sums up their effect by saying, "The stories are not forgiving, nor do they falsify the hard realities of India."

CRITICAL DISCUSSION

Manto was a controversial figure during his lifetime, both acclaimed for his work as an Urdu stylist and criticized for the content of his stories. He was widely condemned for his explicit use of sexual themes and was tried on several occasions by the governments of both British India and Pakistan for violating laws against obscenity. The progressive writers of the PWA rejected his work as reactionary at the same time that the Pakistani government blacklisted him as a communist.

Today Manto's reputation is based primarily on his short stories about Partition and its aftermath.

Critics regularly compare his stories to those of Guy de Maupassant and Anton Chekhov, citing his well-constructed plots, his realism, and his use of the unexpected ending. His best-known story, "Toba Tek Singh," appears in a number of anthologies, typically those that concentrate on Urdu or Pakistani short stories and those dealing with Partition. According to Bhalla, "The best of his partition stories surprise one by bringing together in darkly illuminating moments of existential understanding, terrible violence and the beauty of the human yearning for sex, children, home and community." Manto's short stories remain relatively unknown outside India and Pakistan, however.

Manto wrote his own assessment of his career in his proposed epitaph, which is published in almost every account of his career: "Here lies Saadat Hasan Manto. With him lie buried all the arts and mysteries of short story writing. Under tons of earth he lies, wondering if he is a greater story-teller than God."

SOURCES

Bhalla, Alok. "The Politics of Translation: Manto's Partition Stories in English." *The Place of Translation in a Literary Habitat and Other Lectures.* Mysore: Central Institute of Indian Languages, 2003. Print.

Manto, Saadat Hasan. *Black Margins: Stories.* Selected by M Asaddudin. Ed. Muhammad Umar Memon. New Delhi: Katha. 2003. Print.

Mufti, Aamir R. "Saadat Hasan Manto: A Greater Story-Teller than God." *Enlightenment in the Colony: The Jewish Question and the Crisis of Postcolonial Culture.* Princeton: Princeton UP, 2007. Print.

Taseer, Aatish. "Travellers of the Last Night." Introduction. *Manto: Selected Stories.* Ed. and trans. Aatish Taseer. Uttar Pradesh: Random, 2008. Print.

FURTHER READING

Arora, Neena, and R.K. Dhawan, eds. *Partition and Indian Literature: Voices of the Wounded Psyche.* 2 vols. New Delhi: Prestige, 2010. Print.

Asaduddin, M. "Manto in English: An Assessment of Khalid Hasan's Translations." *Life and Works of Saadat Hasan Manto.* Ed. Alok Bhalla. Shimla: Indian Institute of Advanced Study, 1997. Print.

Butalia, Urvashi, ed. *The Other Side of Silence: Voices from the Partition of India.* New Delhi: Viking, 1998. Print.

Flemming, Leslie A. *Another Lonely Voice: The Urdu Short Stories of Saadat Hasan Manto.* Berkeley: U of California, 1979. Print.

Street market in Bombay, India, the home of Muslim writer Saadat Hasan Manto, until his forced exile to Pakistan following Partition. © STEPHANIE COLASANTI / THE ART ARCHIVE / THE PICTURE DESK, INC.

Gopal, Priyamvada. "Dangerous Bodies: Masculinity, Morality and Social Transformation in Manto." *Literary Radicalism in India: Gender, Nation and the Transition to Independence.* New York: Routledge, 2005. Print.

Hasan, Mushirul, ed. *India's Partition: Process, Strategy and Mobilization.* New York: Oxford UP, 1993. Print.

———. *Inventing Boundaries: Gender, Politics and the Partition of India.* New York: Oxford UP, 2000. Print.

Khan, Yasmin. *The Great Partition: The Making of India and Pakistan.* New Haven: Yale UP, 2007. Print.

Manto, Saadat Hasan. *Partition: Sketches and Stories.* Trans. Khalid Hasan. New York: Viking, 1991. Print.

Wadhawan, Jagdish Chander. *Manto Naama: The Life of Saadat Hasan Manto.* Trans. Jai Ratan. New Delhi: Roli, 1998. Print.

MEDIA ADAPTATION

Toba Tek Singh. Dir. Afia Nathaniel, 2005. Film.

Pamela Toler

CATCH-22

Joseph Heller

OVERVIEW

Catch-22 (1961), a darkly comic novel by Joseph Heller, is widely considered to be America's most influential modern war novel. Its protagonist, Army Air Corps captain John Yossarian, is among the best-known characters in twentieth-century fiction, and the term *catch-22* came to be used to describe what the *American Heritage Dictionary* defines as "a situation in which a desired outcome or solution is impossible to attain because of a set of inherently illogical rules or conditions." In Heller's novel the term *catch-22* symbolizes the inherent absurdity created by a military bureaucracy in wartime. In particular, it establishes a circular-logic situation in which personnel can only be removed from the dangers of flight duty if they are insane, but an unwillingness to get killed is considered to be proof of sanity. Using multiple points of view, the episodic, non-chronological narrative of *Catch-22* depicts Yossarian's ongoing attempts to avoid being killed as well as his interactions with a large and colorful cast of characters.

Heller himself served as a bombardier in World War II, after which he finished graduate school, taught for a time, and wrote short fiction. The basic idea for *Catch-22* came to him in 1953, and he worked on the novel intermittently for the next eight years. When it was published in 1961, some reviewers were enthusiastic, while others were put off by its edgy mixture of biting satire and grotesque realism. Until the publication of *Catch-22*, novels about World War II had typically been realistic in their portrayal of the conflict's violence and hardship but had not overtly questioned the moral legitimacy of the war. *Catch-22* marked a sharp departure from that approach, and the novel's iconoclasm proved to be a good fit for the disillusionment and antiwar sentiment of the 1960s. Although it was not an immediate hit, *Catch-22* quickly gained a following in Britain, and by 1963 the paperback edition was a best seller in the United States. Commenting on Heller's death in 1999, novelist E. L. Doctorow observed: "When *Catch-22* came out, people were saying 'Well, World War II wasn't like this.' But when we got tangled up in Vietnam, it became a sort of text for the consciousness of that time. They say fiction can't change anything, but it can certainly organize a generation's consciousness" (quoted in the *New York Times*, December 14, 1999).

Catch-22 is not just noteworthy for its social impact, however; it has also come to be recognized as a virtuoso literary performance, even by those who may disagree with its message.

HISTORICAL AND LITERARY CONTEXT

World War II was an epic conflict, engaging most of the world's nations. Fighting took place on numerous fronts—by land, sea, and air—from September 1939 until September 1945. Heller was among the millions of U.S. fighting forces deployed in combat, and in certain respects *Catch-22* echoes his personal experiences as a bombardier stationed in Italy. He had enlisted in 1942 as an enthusiastic nineteen-year-old and remained in service though the later years of the war, when patriotic urgency began to wane both at home and in the ranks. Although Heller survived sixty combat missions and was awarded the Air Medal, ending the war as a first lieutenant, he often recounted a traumatic realization of his own mortality that occurred during his thirty-seventh mission, a recognition that is dramatized in *Catch-22* as Yossarian's reaction to the death of Snowden. After the incident Heller was in constant terror that each mission would be his last.

Two important links between Heller's experience and Yossarian's are the geographic setting and the type of service they perform. By 1943 much of Italy had already signed an armistice with the Allies, and Fascist dictator Benito Mussolini was effectively out of power, but the northern part of the country was still under German control. This division created the strange situation depicted in the novel, as U.S. soldiers bombed parts of Italy and visited other parts on tourist excursions. Those who served primarily in Italy thus had a somewhat different view of the war than had those who fought in eastern Europe and liberated the German concentration camps. In addition, bomber crews, typically at a great distance from their human targets, had a different experience of combat than soldiers on the ground. These factors may have contributed to the fact that Heller's experience of the war was generally positive until the day he became suddenly and intensely aware that he was himself a target. The same factors also created perfect conditions for the kind of surrealistic experience depicted in *Catch-22*.

Robert Merrill observes in his 1987 biography of Heller, "The fact that *Catch-22* appeared sixteen years after the end of World War II suggests that its author was not primarily interested in recapturing the intensity of his own experiences." Nor was Heller narrowly concerned with a specific war. He incorporated anachronistic references to combat helicopters, McCarthy-style loyalty oaths, and other details more often associated with the Korean War period (1950–53) than with World War II. In this way he ensures that *Catch-22* is not limited to a specific conflict but rather addresses facets of human nature brought to the surface by war and its aftermath in general.

THEMES AND STYLE

Although *Catch-22* is often described as an antiwar novel, the dominant subject of the work is not war but mortality. For Yossarian, the problem with war is that it might lead to his death. Thus the novel provides no political or moral reflections on war as a human activity or on World War II as a particular instance of war (just or otherwise). In this sense, *Catch-22* is not antiwar. Nor is it antimilitary, for all its satirizing of bureaucratic illogic. In Yossarian's view, the problem with the military is simply that it is intent on keeping him in mortal danger. In one of the novel's funniest and most telling scenes, Yossarian explains the basic reality of his situation to the doggedly optimistic Clevinger:

> "They're trying to kill me," Yossarian told him calmly.
>
> "No one's trying to kill you," Clevinger cried.
>
> "Then why are they shooting at me?" Yossarian asked.
>
> "They're shooting at everyone," Clevinger answered. "They're trying to kill *everyone*."
>
> "And what difference does that make?"

Yossarian has no interest in understanding the war, refuting the war, or changing people's opinions of the war. He only wants to be safe, and his persistent attempts to subvert the rules are always linked to the avoidance of personal danger. This drive for survival forces him to oppose the military establishment, and his antiestablishment tactics take on a kind of heroic inventiveness that highlights the absurdity and chaos of the war. Noted critic Alfred Kazin (in *Bright Book of Life*, 1973) summarizes a general view that "the theme of *Catch-22* is the total craziness of war, the craziness of all those who submit to it, and the struggle of one man, Yossarian, who knows the difference between his sanity and the insanity of the system." Kazin also observes, however, that the novel "is really about the Next War, and thus about a war which will be without limits and without meaning, a war that will end when no one is alive to fight it."

Although *Catch-22* may appear on first view to be a disordered romp through various time frames

Captain John Yossarian (played here by Alan Arkin in the 1970 film adaptation of Joseph Heller's *Catch-22*) sits naked in a tree to watch Snowden's funeral. © PARAMOUNT / FILMWAYS / THE KOBAL COLLECTION

and viewpoints, according to some critics, it is actually Heller's tight command of style that makes the novel so effective. J. P. Stern notes in his essay "War and the Comic Muse" that the novel's "mode of composition and organization […] is anything but naive." Stern continues: "It has a complex time scale, a structure of leitmotifs and carefully wrought repetitions and parallels, its verbal texture varies and is carefully modified according to its narrative situations—and all these devices give it the highly sophisticated form of a post-Joycean novel." As the narrative ground of the novel continually shifts (changing voices, cycling through slightly altered versions of the same events), the reader is drawn off-balance and propelled into the very absurdity the story describes.

CRITICAL DISCUSSION

The immediate critical reaction to *Catch-22* ranged from one extreme to another. Writing in the *Nation* (November 4, 1961), respected novelist Nelson Algren calls it not only "the best American novel to come out of World War II," but also "the best American novel to come out of anywhere in years." On the other hand, Richard G. Stern observes in the *New York Times Book Review* that Heller's novel "gasps for want of craft and

THE CATCH

The phrase "catch-22" has become so familiar in popular culture that it might be a shock to learn the title of Heller's novel was originally intended to be *Catch-18*. In 1961, the year the novel was published, Leon Uris's *Mila 18* was on the best-seller lists, and Heller's publisher was concerned that two similar titles might be confusing. Popular lore has it that Catch-11, Catch-17, and Catch-14 were all considered as replacements, but Catch-22 was finally considered the most appealing. The number was apparently not considered meaningful by Heller, even though commentators have occasionally linked it to themes and techniques of the work.

In 1970 the movie version of *Catch-22* also collided with another work, Robert Altman's irreverent *M*A*S*H*. A film adaption of *Catch-22* was scripted by Buck Henry and directed by Mike Nichols—the same duo that had produced an immensely popular satire, *The Graduate*, just a few years earlier. The strong cast of *Catch-22* included Alan Arkin as Yossarian and Bob Newhart as Major Major, as well as stars Anthony Perkins, Paula Prentiss, Jon Voight, and Orson Welles.

The film, however, was not especially successful with audiences or critics. Although Heller reportedly approved the script, it was so different from the novel that fans of the original work were disappointed. At the same time, Nichols and Henry may have been *too* literal in the translation from novel to screen, disappointing critics with a production that lacked cinematic energy.

In other words, a classic "catch-22" situation.

Over time unflattering comparisons to the novel, *The Graduate*, and *M*A*S*H* subsided, and the Nichols and Henry version of *Catch-22* was viewed more favorably and on its own terms. The film found a fresh audience when the DVD version came out in 2001.

sensibility," calling it "repetitive and monotonous" and "an emotional hodge-podge." Stern objects more to the execution of the novel than to its theme, but other critics rejected Heller's work on substance. As John W. Aldridge points out in his reflections on twenty-five years of *Catch-22* criticism (*New York Times*, 1986), most critics of the time were "conditioned by the important novels of World War I and reconditioned by the World War II novels of Norman Mailer, Irwin Shaw, John Horne Burns, James Jones and others to expect that the authentic technique for treating war experience is harshly documentary realism." Many literary critics were not prepared for the zanily comic portrayal Heller offered, nor were they comfortable with the novel's sudden turn in the final chapters from biting humor to phantasmagoric horror. Yet readers sensed early on, according to Aldridge, "that beneath the comic surfaces Mr. Heller was saying something outrageous, unforgivably outrageous, not just about the idiocy of war but about our whole way of life and the system of false values on which it is based. The horror he exposed was not confined to the battlefield or

the bombing mission but permeated the entire labyrinthine structure of establishment power."

As literary scholarship became more sophisticated and diverse in its approaches during the latter half of the twentieth century, the artistic achievement of *Catch-22* was recognized more widely. Cultural arguments continued, however. As the novel's fortieth anniversary drew near, neoconservative commentator Norman Podhoretz reflected on its impact. In Podhoretz's view, Heller's portrayal of war was a resurrection of discredited pacifist ideas "that war is simply a means by which cynical people commit legalized murder in pursuit of power and profits; that patriotism is a fraud; and that nothing is worth dying for." Although an early supporter of the work, Podhoretz had come to question whether "the literary achievement was worth the harm—the moral, spiritual, and intellectual harm—*Catch-22* has managed to do [to American culture]" (*Commentary*, February 2000).

Heller was also criticized by some Jewish commentators for ignoring the Holocaust and the evils of Hitler's Germany. Other scholars, however, note the influence of Heller's own Jewish background in the language and storytelling styles of *Catch-22*. Sanford Pinsker's essay "Reassessing *Catch-22*" comments on these differing views, conceding that some critics have "overdone the case for *Catch-22*'s covertly 'Jewish' sensibility," but admitting that he sees "lots of Yiddish flavoring just beneath the novel's gallows humor." Pinsker goes on to defend Heller by saying that "the bitterly satiric book [Heller] set out to write left no space for ruminations about the systematic destruction of European Jewry." At the same time, however, Pinsker concludes that despite the relevance of some of its social commentary, in considering *Catch-22* we must confront "the conspicuous absence of any acknowledgement that the real enemy was not Milo Minderbinder or ex-PFC Wintergreen or even General Dreedle, but Hitler. A World War II novel that leaves this crucial fact out begs for moral reassessment."

SOURCES

Aldridge, John W. "The Loony Horror of It All: *Catch-22* Turns 25." *New York Times* 26 Oct. 1986: 3. Print.

Algren, Nelson. "The Catch." Rev. of *Catch-22*, by Joseph Heller. *Nation* 4 Nov. 1961: 357–58. Print.

Kazin, Alfred. *Bright Book of Life: American Novelists and Storytellers from Hemingway to Mailer*. Boston: Little, Brown, 1973. Print.

Merrill, Robert. *Joseph Heller*. Boston: Twayne, 1987. Print.

Pinsker, Sanford. "The State of Letters: Reassessing *Catch-22*." *Sewanee Review* 108.4 (2000): 602. Print.

Podhoretz, Norman. "Looking Back at *Catch-22*." *Commentary* 109.2 (2000): 32. Print.

Severo, Richard, and Herbert Mitgang. "Joseph Heller, Darkly Surreal Novelist, Dies at 76." *New York Times* 14 Dec. 1999: A1+ ProQuest. Web. 15 May 2011.

Stern, J. P. "War and the Comic Muse: *The Good Soldier Schweik* and *Catch-22*." *Comparative Literature* 20.3 (1968): 193–216. Print.

Stern, Richard G. "Bombers Away." Rev. of *Catch-22*, by Joseph Heller. *New York Times Book Review* 22 Oct. 1961: n. pag. Print.

FURTHER READING

Aichinger, Peter. *The American Soldier in Fiction, 1880–1963: A History of Attitudes Toward Warfare and the Military Establishment*. Ames: Iowa State UP, 1975. Print.

Bloom, Harold. *Joseph Heller's "Catch-22."* Philadelphia: Chelsea House, 2001. Print.

Brosman, Catharine Savage. "The Functions of War Literature." 9.1 (1992): 85–98. Print.

Bryfonski, Dedria. *War in Joseph Heller's "Catch-22."* Detroit: Greenhaven, 2009. Print.

Craig, David M. "From Avignon to *Catch-22*." *War, Literature, and the Arts* 6.2 (1994): 27–54. Rpt. in *Twentieth-Century Literary Criticism*. Ed. Linda Pavlovski. Vol. 151. Detroit: Gale, 2004. *Literature Resources from Gale*. Web. 10 May 2011.

Heller, Joseph. *Catch-22*. New York: Simon, 1961. Print.

———. "*Catch-22* Revisited." *Holiday* Apr. 1967: 44+. Print.

———. *Closing Time: A Novel*. New York: Simon, 1994. Print.

Heller, Joseph, Matthew J. Bruccoli, and Park Bucker. *Catch as Catch Can: The Collected Stories and Other Writings*. New York: Simon, 2003. Print.

Walsh, Jeffrey. "Towards Vietnam: Portraying Modern War." *American War Literature, 1914 to Vietnam*. New York: St. Martin's, 1982. 185–207. Rpt. in *Contemporary Literary Criticism*. Ed. Roger Matuz and Cathy Falk. Vol. 63. Detroit: Gale, 1991. *Literature Resources from Gale*. Web. 10 May 2011.

MEDIA ADAPTATIONS

Catch-22. Dir. Mike Nichols. Perf. Alan Arkin, Martin Balsam, Richard Benjamin, Art Garfunkel, Jack Gilford, Buck Henry, and Bob Newhart. Paramount Pictures, 1970. Film.

Catch-22. Dir. Richard Quine. Perf. Richard Dreyfuss, Dana Elcar, Stewart Moss, and Andy Jarrell. American Broadcasting Company (ABC), 1973. Television.

Cynthia Giles

DEATH OF A HERO
Richard Aldington

❖ *Key Facts*

Conflict:
World War I

Time Period:
Early 20th Century

Genre:
Novel

OVERVIEW

Richard Aldington's novel *Death of a Hero* (1929) follows the life of George Winterbourne, the "hero" of the title. The novel describes George's typical Edwardian middle-class upbringing and his rebellion against the socially and sexually restricted society of his parents.

George moves to London, where he is the perfect embodiment of the hopefulness of his generation, becoming a painter, marrying, taking a mistress, and adopting the values of free love, pacifism, and political interest that surround him as Europe drifts toward World War I. As the war begins, George enlists in the army and is sent to fight in France. When he returns home on leave, he finds that his experiences as a soldier have isolated him: The horrors he saw are incomprehensible to his wife and friends, who are expecting tales of heroism.

Back at the front, his fellow officers have become so cynical that hope for the future has no place anymore, and he cannot relate to them, either. Having lost faith in the war and mankind, he stands up during a machine-gun barrage and is killed. His death is emblematic of the death of a generation, representing not only the senseless loss of life but also the loss of ideals once held dear. Aldington is not sparing in his portrayal of the hypocrisy of the era and the irony of glorious expectations completely gutted by reality.

Like his protagonist, Aldington traveled in bohemian circles in prewar London. Influenced by the ideals of classical Greece, Aldington strongly identified with an avant-garde group of poets known as the Imagists. He and his future wife, poet, novelist, and memoirist H.D. (Hilda Doolittle; 1886–1961), were introduced into the core of the group by Ezra Pound (1885–1972). Breaking with Romantic and Victorian literary tradition, the Imagists defined their aesthetic according to a new emphasis on spare language and clear, precise visual imagery as a vehicle for poetic statement. Ten of Aldington's poems appeared in Ezra Pound's first anthology of Imagist verse, *Des Imagistes* (1914).

Aldington enlisted in the army in 1916 and fought in France. Though he survived, he experienced the worst of trench warfare and returned home shell-shocked and sick from gas exposure. He also found that his wife had borne a child with the artist Cecil Gray (1895–1951) while Aldington was on the battlefield. He retreated to the Berkshire countryside, where he wrote the first draft of *Death of a Hero*, the novel that would occupy him for the next ten years.

That Aldington turned to writing prose is itself an indication of how much the war had affected him. His prewar writings were almost entirely poetic; at the time, he scorned prose for its inability to register strong emotions. By 1924, however, when he was composing his novel, Aldington had come to eschew the aesthetic values of Imagism—the "extreme compression and essential significance of every word"—and to favor instead "intense production and [a] widening audience" (quoted in Caroline Zilboorg, "Richard Aldington in Transition"). In *Death of a Hero*, aesthetic form gives way to the expression of a generation's disillusionment and the attempt to reconcile Aldington's own survivor's guilt. His wife's betrayal also influenced the novel, negatively affecting his depiction of his female characters.

A letter Aldington wrote to his friend Halcott Glover (1877–1949), the English dramatist and novelist, was added as a prelude to the novel. The letter recounts Aldington's struggle to write the novel, describing the narrative as "a threnody, a memorial in its ineffective way to a generation which hoped much, strove honestly, and suffered deeply." In a preface to the story, the narrator, an unnamed veteran who served with Winterbourne, similarly explains that he has written the novel as an attempt to expiate his war guilt, and that Winterbourne is a symbol of the guilt that everyone should feel about the war dead.

HISTORICAL AND LITERARY CONTEXT

World War I, also known as the "Great War," was the first global military conflict of the twentieth century. When the war began in the summer of 1914, Britain was confident in the superiority of its troops, their honor and spirit, and the empire's organizational power and use of industrial technology. The British military believed that it would swiftly overrun the German army and that the troops would be "home by Christmas." After the first weeks, however, the war settled into a violent stalemate, with soldiers held up in trenches and dugouts for weeks on end. The war consisted of short violent battles with bayonets and rifles and long periods of waiting on either side of the area known as "no-man's-land," the battlefield that separated the opposing sides.

Life in the trenches gave rise to a new form of writing called trench literature, which depicts the filth, boredom, fear, and violent death experienced by the troops, as well as the deleterious effects of poisonous gas and the constant noise of guns. In *Rites of Spring*, the historian Modris Ekstein remarks that, in the years after World War I, art took on the role previously fulfilled by history of explaining the events of the age. The war, he says, "was a matter of individual experience rather than collective interpretation." While historians were unable to produce accounts that "correspond[ed] to the horrendous reality, to the actual experience of the war," the psychological novel proved to be the perfect form for examining the collapse of the ideals of glory, honor, and duty that heretofore had been mainstays of the war novel.

Writing in *Twentieth Century Literature*, J. H. Willis Jr. explains that Aldington's novel is one of many war novels published in the 1920s that fell victim to censorship laws. In 1929 alone, versions of Ernest Hemingway's *A Farewell to Arms*, Erich Maria Remarque's *All Quiet on the Western Front*, and Frederick Manning's *Her Privates We* appeared only in expurgated form. Willis writes that while the poets and memoirists whose work came out soon after the war often used "euphemism and metaphor" to describe their experiences or used language that was crude but not profane, the novelists of the twenties wanted to be "faithful to the bitter, life-changing experience of modern warfare in a realistic depiction of both action and dialogue." They were "determined to depict accurately and unblushingly the sexual behavior of men at war and the four-letter language they used with regularity."

THEMES AND STYLE

Aldington's novel is a passionate and indignant book. The narrator, a fellow soldier of Winterbourne, communicates Aldington's disgust at the loss of his generation:

"The death of a hero! What mockery, what bloody cant. What sickening putrid cant! George's death is a symbol for me of the whole sickening bloody waste of it, the damnable stupid waste and torture of it."

Aldington attacks the possibility of "atoning" for "the lost millions and millions of years of life … for those lakes and seas of blood" and assaults the hypocrisy of the system that sent a generation off to die and yet honors the sacrifice with only token gestures. While the "Army did its bit," Aldington says, it could not "individually mourn a million heroes"; the "Two Minutes' Silence" held once a year is "doing nothing"; and "headstones and wreaths and memorials and speeches and the Cenotaph" are not individual enough. The novel is intended to both transmit the experience of the war and link that experience to George's inability to rejoin the society that he left behind or connect with his fellow officers.

Aldington's approach in *Death of a Hero* is strongly satirical, harshly criticizing Edwardian society. From the first pages of the novel, the narrator uses savage irony to comment on the "hypocrisy and prosperity and cheapness" of English society in the 1890s, portraying the English middle class as obsessed with keeping up appearances and making it clear that though George's parents appear to maintain a "loving and united home," they do not love him, and they disown him as soon as he declares his intention to become a writer. Moreover, the novel sees neither prewar life in London nor the wartime period as marking a real change from the sexual repression and duplicity of Edwardian society; rather, the war is depicted as the culmination of that society. George's death, which the novel hints is a suicide, stands for the failure of British society to support its individual members, particularly the young men.

Scholars have noted that many of the novel's characters are based on figures from Aldington's own life: his parents are the model for Winterbourne's parents,

John Singer Sargent's 1919 painting *Gassed* depicts soldiers poisoned by mustard gas during World War I, as author Richard Aldington was before he returned to Britain and began writing *Death of a Hero*. © JOHN SINGER SARGENT / IMPERIAL WAR MUSEUM / THE ART ARCHIVE / THE PICTURE DESK, INC.

AN IMAGIST IN THE TRENCHES: RICHARD ALDINGTON'S WAR POETRY

Although Aldington is now best known for *Death of a Hero* and for his prewar involvement with the avant-garde Imagist movement, he also published several influential volumes of poetry dealing with his war experiences. The companion volumes *Images of War* (1919) and *Images of Desire* (1919), written while Aldington was a soldier and in the months just after, describe his experiences in the trenches, his struggle to reintegrate himself into civilian life, and his attempts to work through the breakup of his marriage with H.D.

His poems describe the horrors of trench warfare as well as registering the effects of the war on the intellectual classes. In "In the Library," for example, Aldington reflects on

the shift in his interest in languages and literature, describing "a strange void in my brain." He continues "What is it / I am reading? Greek? What does / Greek matter?"

In the preface to *An Imagist at War: The Complete War Poems of Richard Aldington*, editor Michael Copp explains that Aldington explicitly distinguished his war poems from those of such early war poets as Rupert Brooke, whose work he considered jingoistic. Aldington described his own poems as "bitter, anguish-stricken, realistic ... stern truth," saying that because of their raw nature he hesitated before publishing them but finally decided that to do so would be a cathartic experience, a way of exorcising some of the ghosts of the war.

the women in Winterbourne's life are based on H.D. and Dorothy Yorke, and, on the London arts scene, the characters Upjohn, Shobbe, Bobbe, and Tubbe are loosely disguised portraits of Ezra Pound, Ford Maddox Ford, D. H. Lawrence, and T. S. Eliot. When Aldington transforms his cohorts into objects of satire, however, his personal resentments are absorbed into a larger cultural critique. Translated into fiction, Aldington's life becomes an allegory for the culture that he despises.

The novel also expresses the hopelessness of atonement on the part of soldiers who survived the war. The narrator, a thinly disguised Aldington, describes his writing as an attempt to escape from "the curse—the blood guiltiness" that "poisons us," "mak[ing] us heartless and hopeless and lifeless—us the war generation, and the new generation too." However, the guilt persists in the narrator as it did for Aldington.

Aldington wanted to portray the atmosphere of the trenches accurately, which for him meant using the profane language of the soldiers. The 1929 edition of the novel was harshly censored, with the objectionable words replaced with asterisks. According to Willis, Aldington saw the expurgation as detracting from the realism of the novel. The author argued that, while his language was "at present taboo in England[,] I have recorded nothing which I have not observed in human life, said nothing I do not believe to be true." For Aldington, censorship was another example of postwar society's inability to understand the reality of the war. He believed that describing that world accurately was necessary to integrating the war into the national culture and memory. Although an unexpurgated version of *Death of a Hero* was published in 1930, it was not widely available until 1965.

Aldington extends his critique of Edwardian society in *Death of a Hero* by deconstructing the traditional form of the novel. In the letter prefacing the novel, he remarks that he "hates standardized art as well as standardized life," thus implicitly criticizing

both the conventional form of the Victorian novel and the social forms that it expresses. He differentiates his own novel from this tradition, declaring that "conventions of form and method in the novel [that] have been erected into immutable laws ... are entirely disregarded here. To me the excuse of the novel is that one can do any damn thing one pleases."

In *Death of a Hero*, Aldington's rebellion leads him to provide a minimal plotline and to devote much of the novel to the narrator's often angry opinions of Winterbourne's family and friends, who serve as examples of the straitlaced mores of society. Aldington's prose style resembles journal entries, and these often veer away from the actions of the characters into tirade and satiric commentary. The war scenes offer the most straightforward narrative, relaying events as they happen in a naturalistic style, though the confusion on the battlefields and in the trenches means that this part of the novel is no easier to follow.

CRITICAL DISCUSSION

Aldington's novel enjoyed immediate success, was reprinted several times, and received generally positive reviews. Despite its popularity, it did not achieve the continued success of Hemingway's and Remarque's novels. Aldington's 1955 vitriolic biography of T. E. Lawrence (*Lawrence of Arabia: A Biographical Inquiry*) later earned him the animosity of the British literary and military establishment, which damaged the reputations of both Aldington and Lawrence and caused sales of *Death of a Hero* to decline. Aldington's novel is often mentioned in discussions of works that address the psychological effects of war on soldiers, including shell shock and the difficulty soldiers face on reentering society. Writing in the journal *SubStance*, Evelyn Cobley cites Aldington's novel as an example of the shift in the chivalric mythos of war from "encoding the soldier as an honorable savior of society ... to encoding him as its noble sacrificial victim."

Death of a Hero is also frequently mentioned in examinations of homoeroticism and male intimacy in the literature of World War I. While the subject was long taboo, there have been a number of recent studies that address the emotional and physical interactions of soldiers in the trenches and attempt to define the sexual and psychological bonds between them. Santanu Das places the novel in the context of a larger culture of male intimacy in World War I literature, suggesting that Aldington's claim that there was nothing "sodomical" about the relationships he describes foregrounds the intense anxiety about masculinity that characterizes trench literature.

SOURCES

Aldington, Richard. *Death of a Hero*. London: Hogarth, 1984. Print.

Cobley, Evelyn. "Violence and Sacrifice in Modern War Narratives." *SubStance* 23.3 (1994): 75–99. Print.

Das, Santanu. "'Kiss me, Hardy': Intimacy, Gender, and Gesture in World War I Trench Literature." *Modernism/Modernity* 9.1 (2002). Web. 19 May 2011.

Ekstein, Modris. *Rites of Spring: The Great War and the Birth of the Modern Age*. New York: Houghton, 1989. Print.

Willis, J. H., Jr. "The Censored Language of War: Richard Aldington's *Death of a Hero* and Three Other War Novels of 1929." *Twentieth Century Literature* 45.4 (1999). Web. 23 May 2011.

Zilboorg, Caroline. "Richard Aldington in Transition: His Pieces for *The Sphere* in 1919." *Twentieth Century Literature* 34.4 (1988). Web. 23 May 2011.

FURTHER READING

Aldington, Richard. *An Imagist at War: The Complete War Poems of Richard Aldington*.

Ed. Michael Copp. Madison: Fairleigh Dickinson UP, 2002. Print.

Blunden, Edmund. *Undertones of War*. London: Cobden-Sanderson, 1928. Print.

Doyle, Charles. *Richard Aldington: A Biography*. Carbondale: Southern Illinois UP, 1989. Print.

Fussell, Paul. *The Great War and Modern Memory*. Oxford: Oxford UP, 1975. Print.

Gates, Norman. *Richard Aldington: An Autobiography in Letters*. University Park: Pennsylvania State UP, 1992. Print.

Graves, Robert, *Goodbye to All That: An Autobiography*. London: J. Cape, 1929. Print.

Hemingway, Ernest. *A Farewell to Arms*. New York: Scribner, 1929. Print.

Remarque, Erich Maria. *All Quiet on the Western Front*. Trans. A. W. Wheen. New York: Little, Brown, 1929. Print.

Jennifer Ludwig

THE GOOD SOLDIER ŠVEJK

And His Fortunes in the World War

Jaroslav Hašek

❖ **Key Facts**

Conflict:
World War I

Time Period:
Early 20th Century

Genre:
Novel

OVERVIEW

The Good Soldier Švejk: And His Fortunes in the World War (originally published in Czech as *Osudy dobrého vojáka Švejka za světové války*, 1921–23), by Jaroslav Hašek, is among the most influential Czech novels to emerge from World War I. The work revolves around the figure of its iconic title character, a hapless World War I Czech foot soldier whose seeming simplemindedness and naïveté produce a series of comic misunderstandings that successfully keep him from ever having to see combat. The good-natured Švejk confounds his superiors with his well-intentioned blunders, incessant chatter, and storehouse of parable-like tales, all of which appear to confirm his fervent desire to reach the front.

As the novel opens, Švejk learns of the assassination in Sarajevo of Austria's archduke Franz Ferdinand, the event that sparked the start of World War I. Švejk's military career is stalled by a variety of farcical incidents: he is diagnosed as an idiot and consigned to a mental institution, sent to an infirmary for suspected malingerers, and arrested as a suspected spy. Švejk's last escapade involves his misreading of a map, which leads to a case of mistaken identity when he is captured by his own unit and assigned to a gang of Russian prisoners of war. The unfinished novel concludes at this point in the narrative. Hašek died of heart failure and pneumonia at the age of thirty-nine on January 3, 1923, and was unable to complete all of the several projected volumes of *The Good Soldier Švejk*.

The Good Soldier Švejk developed out of the circumstances of Hašek's life. He was born in 1883 in Prague, at the time a city located in what was then known as Bohemia, one of several central European territories constituting the sprawling Austro-Hungarian Empire. A Czech nationalist and longtime critic of the monarchy, Hašek was drafted into military service for the empire in 1915, just after the start of World War I. His experiences in the 91st Regiment form the basis for the comic episodes that make up the loosely structured plot of the novel.

The Good Soldier Švejk appeared in booklet form in installments from 1921 to 1923. The first volume was privately printed and distributed by Hašek and his friend Franta Sauer in 1921. The publisher A. Synek brought out volumes two and three in 1922 and the incomplete fourth volume shortly after Hašek's death. Another friend, Karel Vaněk, composed an ending for the story, but it is now rarely included in published versions of the novel. A year after the author's death, the newspaper *České slovo* serialized an abridged version of the work, accompanied by 540 cartoon illustrations by Hašek's friend, the artist Josef Lada. The novel was translated into German in 1926 by Grete Reiner and adapted into a play by Max Brod and Hans Reimann two years later. Directed by Erwin Piscator in Berlin, this early stage production of the novel featured hundreds of cartoon drawings by German expressionist artist Georg Grosz. These drawings were converted into a filmstrip and projected as a backdrop to the performance. Grosz's grotesque, antireligious, and often violent imagery contrasted sharply with Lada's more whimsical drawings for the work. An abridged English translation appeared in 1930 as *The Good Soldier Schweik* (trans. Paul Selver). It was not until 1973 that the novel appeared in English in its entirety, Cecil Parrott's translation titled *The Good Soldier Švejk: And His Fortunes in the World War*.

For most modern critics, *The Good Soldier Švejk* is first and foremost an antiwar novel, one that lampoons the imperial pretensions of the Austro-Hungarian Empire. Švejk is the quintessential wise fool; his doubletalk and bumbling actions serve to expose the utter futility of World War I and the hypocrisies of the Austrian Hapsburg monarchy in entering and managing the conflict. At the same time, Hašek's novel belongs to a distinctly Czech tradition of literary satire, one that frequently targeted the subservient attitudes of Czech politicians to their Hapsburg rulers. Czech critics have also lauded the virtuosity of Hašek's storytelling in *The Good Soldier Švejk*, tracing the novel's various links to regional folklore and oral narrative traditions. The author's liberal use of slang and everyday speech also resonated with contemporary Czech readers, who found in the titular character echoes of the "common man" that were at once farcical and deeply familiar. Indeed these unique linguistic qualities have often eluded non-Czech commentators on the work.

Heinz Ruhmann as Švejk and Fritz Muliar as the Russian soldier in the 1960 film adaptation of *The Good Soldier Švejk*.
© EVERETT COLLECTION

HISTORICAL AND LITERARY CONTEXT

After the death of his father from alcoholism when Hašek was just thirteen, the teenager began to roam the streets of Prague, where he took part in antigovernment riots and got into other trouble with the vagabonds he befriended. As early as the age of seventeen, when he began publishing newspaper articles critical of the monarchy, Hašek became part of an increasingly vocal group of Czech nationalists in Prague who desired the overthrow of the Hapsburg dynasty seated in Vienna, Austria. He joined the anarchist movement, was arrested several times for his radical journalism, and frantically composed short stories to earn money to pay for the many nights he spent drinking and writing in Prague pubs. During these years, Hašek produced roughly fifteen hundred short stories, which were characterized both by their biting satire and their comic tone. These qualities later formed the basis of *The Good Soldier Švejk*.

The novel's irreverent irony, inspired by Hašek's intense political convictions and antiestablishment ethos, situates *The Good Soldier Švejk* within a tradition of comic satire that stretches back to the works of François Rabelais, Miguel de Cervantes, and Jonathan Swift. At the same time, *The Good Soldier Švejk* is judged innovative in its attack on the huge government and military bureaucracies of the Austro-Hungarian Empire that claimed control of the common people. In ridiculing the inefficiency and absurdity of

bureaucratic structures, *The Good Soldier Švejk* was a prototype for Joseph Heller's classic antiwar novel, *Catch-22*, the title of which refers to the circular logic of military commands.

The Good Soldier Švejk emerged out of the long-simmering discontent felt by the various national minorities living under Austro-Hungarian rule in the nineteenth and early twentieth centuries. This political instability finally reached a boiling point on June 28, 1914, when a Serbian nationalist assassinated Archduke Franz Ferdinand (heir to the Austro-Hungarian throne) and his wife in Sarajevo, the event that sparked the onset of World War I. Hašek's involvement in the war took him to the front in 1915 in the Austro-Hungarian province of Galicia. But he was quickly captured as a prisoner of war in a Russian counteroffensive. In the spring of 1916, Hašek enlisted in the Czech Foreign Legion, which had been formed in Russia to fight against Austria. After the Bolshevik Revolution, however, he defected from the legion and became a member of the Bolshevik party. He rose in the ranks of the party organization and did not return to Prague until 1920, when he began composing *The Good Soldier Švejk*.

THEMES A ND STYLE

Reflecting Hašek's rejection of authority in his own life, *The Good Soldier Švejk* was written in political protest over the domination of the Hapsburg monarchy and

ŠVEJK: HAŠEK'S ALTER EGO?

Hašek's biographers portray the author as an exhibitionist and consummate hoaxster. It is reported that in 1909 he lost his job as editor of the journal *Animal World* for writing articles about invented species.

Other Hašek pranks were not so innocuous. In 1911 he faked a suicide attempt in Prague by throwing himself off the Charles Bridge into the waters of the Vltava River at nearly the same location where St. John of Nepomuk had been drowned in the late 1300s. Later that year Hašek stood as a candidate for the Austro-Hungarian parliament under the banner of "The Party of Moderate and Peaceful Progress within the Limits of the Law," a bogus political party he concocted with some of his bohemian friends. In connection with the spoof, Hašek campaigned in cabaret performances mocking the monarchy at various pubs in Prague.

In an even bolder affront to the Austrian authorities, Hašek registered under a Russian-sounding name at a notorious Prague brothel and hotel at the inception of World War I. When questioned by the hotel staff about the reason for his visit to the city, Hašek reported that he was investigating Austrian generals. Law enforcement was immediately called in. When the police arrived at the hotel, they were embarrassed to discover that their familiar nemesis, Hašek, had perpetrated the charade. Even more humiliating to police was the fact that the name Hašek had used in the hotel registry spelled "Kiss my arse" when read backward.

its conscription of Czech soldiers into their war effort. Švejk is the instrument of Hašek's ridicule. Though Švejk is quick to declare himself a "certified idiot," he shows an uncanny ability to take the militaristic machinery of the empire to its absurd conclusions with his zealous execution of his orders. His ineptitude often sabotages his own regiment while at the same time allowing him to avoid active duty. The character of Švejk has been the subject of much debate. He has been alternately portrayed as a naïve and blundering patriot; a shrewd manipulator of circumstance, capable of ingenious subterfuge and artifice at just the right moments; and, in the words of René Wellek, "a coward and shirk who assumes the innocence and stupidity of an idiot to disarm railing officers, a happy-go-lucky skeptic as to war and military glory" (qtd. in Vlach). Regardless of the interpretive stance, the end result is the same: Švejk's peculiar brand of ironic double-talk underscores the pointlessness of the war and undermines the supposed rationality of Austrian military discipline.

Švejk's chief survival mechanism is his amazing gift of gab. With his aimless banter and inexhaustible arsenal of stories, he is able to proffer any number of innocent explanations to ward off danger or explain away the disasters he has wrought upon his unit. Hašek's satire emerges primarily through Švejk's speech, which features bawdy anecdotes, coarse language,

foreign quotations, rhyming jingles, and patriotic songs juxtaposed in such a way as to reveal the hypocrisy and corruption of the ruling powers and the military apparatus. Leslie Fiedler observed, "On [Švejk's] lips the noblest slogans become mockeries. Let him merely cry, 'God save the Emperor' and all who listen are betrayed to laughter." In addition to its more obvious political import, Švejk's barrage of talk has been seen to signal the alienation of the modern human condition. A reviewer for the *Times Literary Supplement* judged Švejk's blather a defense mechanism against the dehumanizing effects of the bureaucratic machine: "He gains an immense inner freedom through this trick but the price he has to pay is almost total loneliness." Hašek biographer Emanuel Frynta concluded that the collagelike assemblage of stories in Švejk's chatter was symbolic of the fragmentation of modern life in times of peace as well as war: "The chaos of war and the alienation of the soldier in the army, fighting for a cause that was unacceptable to him, probably seemed to Hašek to be, above all, a most suitable graphic form for depicting and expressing the utter discordance of social reality itself."

CRITICAL DISCUSSION

Most of Hašek's earliest Czech critics determined that Švejk truly was a "patent idiot," albeit a lucky one, and that his creator was an equally simpleminded writer given to coarse language, vulgar jokes, and carelessness. Hašek's infamous reputation as a Bolshevik and public drunkard did little to endear him to critics at home, many of whom complained that the novel made Czechs appear lazy and politically uninformed. Max Brod was an early champion of the work, placing Hašek's protagonist within a European comic tradition dating back to the novels of Cervantes and Rabelais. Indeed, the enthusiastic reception of *The Good Soldier Švejk* in Germany caused the novel to be reassessed in Czechoslovakia. Eventually, the character of Švejk became so embedded in Czech popular culture that the word *Schweikism* was introduced into the language to denote a type of passive resistance. Following World War II political dissidents of various casts embraced *The Good Soldier Švejk*, lending increased international stature to the novel, and Švejk was institutionalized in Czechoslovakia as a proletarian folk hero after the Communist takeover in 1948.

In the 1960s Czech philosopher Karel Kosík outlined the modernist elements in Hašek's novel, while comparing the author to his contemporary Franz Kafka. Hašek's more recent critics have tended to judge Švejk's imbecility as a clever mask he assumes to disguise his resistance to the war. Some have suggested that Švejk's dual nature is the result of Hašek having become accustomed to camouflaging his true sentiments due to repressive censorship laws in existence before the fall of the Hapsburgs. Though Hašek has received an outpouring of praise for his mastery of irony and parody and the sheer inventiveness of

Švejk's speech, he is still sometimes charged with sloppy writing, certain critics having pointed out that much of the book was dictated in a bar and sent to the publisher without benefit of proofreading. Švejk's iconic stature remains unchallenged in Czechoslovakia; reproductions of his likeness (based on the now-famous original drawings of Josef Lada) appear on everything there from postage stamps and bar paintings to freestanding statues. Revivals of Robert Kurka's 1957 operatic version of *The Good Soldier Švejk* in Chicago (2001) and Long Beach, California (2010), suggest that Švejk continues to resonate with modern American audiences as well.

SOURCES

"The Art of Survival." *Times Literary Supplement* 21 Sept. 1973: 1083–84. *Twentieth-Century Literary Criticism.* Ed. Sharon K. Hall. Vol. 4. Detroit: Gale, 1981. *Literature Resource Center.* Web. 6 July 2011.

Fiedler, Leslie A. "The Antiwar Novel and the Good Soldier Schweik." *Unfinished Business.* New York: Stein, 1972. 32–42. *Twentieth-Century Literary Criticism.* Ed. Sharon K. Hall. Vol. 4. Detroit: Gale, 1981. *Literature Resource Center.* Web. 6 July 2011.

Frynta, Emanuel. *Hašek: The Creator of Schweik.* Trans. Jean Layton and George Theiner. New York: Artia, 1965. *Twentieth-Century Literary Criticism.* Ed. Sharon K. Hall. Vol. 4. Detroit: Gale, 1981. *Literature Resource Center.* Web. 6 July 2011.

Hašek, Jaroslav. *The Good Soldier Švejk.* Trans. Cecil Parrott. London: Penguin, 1973. Print.

Parrott, Cecil. Introduction. *The Good Soldier Švejk.* By Jaroslav Hašek. Trans. Parrott. London: Penguin, 1973. vii-xxii. Print.

Vlach, Robert. "Gogol and Hašek—Two Masters of Poshlost." *Slavic and East-European Studies* 7 (1962): 239–42. *Twentieth-Century Literary Criticism.* Ed. Sharon K. Hall. Vol. 4. Detroit: Gale, 1981. *Literature Resource Center.* Web. 6 July 2011.

FURTHER READING

Ambros, Veronika. "The Great War as a Monstrous Carnival: Jaroslav Hašek's Švejk." In: *History of the Literary Cultures of East-Central Europe.* Philadelphia: Benjamins, 2004. 228–36. Print.

Heller, Joseph. *Catch-22.* New York: Simon, 1996. Print.

Kosík, Karel. "Hašek and Kafka 1883–1922/23." Trans. A. Hopkins. *Cross Currents* 2 (1983): 127. Print.

Parrott, Cecil. *The Bad Bohemian: A Life of Jaroslav Hašek.* New York: Cambridge UP, 1978. Print.

———. *Jaroslav Hašek: A Study of Švejk and the Short Stories.* New York: Cambridge UP, 1982. Print.

Quinn, Michael. "Svejk's Stage Figure: Illustration, Design, and the Representation of Character." *Modern Drama* 31.3 (1988): 330–39. *Literature Resources from Gale.* Web. 8 July 2011.

Thirlwell, Adam. "Czech Mates: Caught for Centuries between Warring Empires." *New Statesman (1996)* (17 May 2010): 42. *Literature Resources from Gale.* Web. 7 July 2011.

Janet Mullane

MADMEN AND SPECIALISTS

A Play

Wole Soyinka

❖ *Key Facts*

Conflict:
Nigerian Civil War

Time Period:
Mid-20th Century

Genre:
Play

OVERVIEW

Nigerian dramatist and poet Wole Soyinka composed his internationally renowned political play *Madmen and Specialists* (1970) after serving an extended prison sentence during the Nigerian Civil War (1967–70). Though the conflict is not explicitly referenced, it serves as the background for the drama, which describes the tragic end of a young, power-hungry doctor.

The action begins outside Dr. Bero's office after he has come home from war. Four beggars crouch before the house shooting dice. Wounded in the conflict, these crazed mendicants have returned to work for Bero to guard the Old Man (Bero's father) whom Bero has imprisoned in the cellar. Calling themselves the "Creatures of As," these "madmen" profess faith in a mysterious force that is revealed when Bero's sister and the village priest arrive to welcome the young man home. Facing his sister (Sí Bero) and the cleric, Bero confesses that the Old Man tricked him and his fellow officers into eating human flesh during the war. This was an attempt to demonstrate the ironic danger of worshiping "As," the Old Man's name for the oppressive forces of the corrupt governmental system, but the horrific ruse backfired: Bero and the men relished the meat and have become cannibals. "It was no brain-child of mine," Bero tells his sister. "We thought it was a joke. 'I'll bless the meat,' he said. And then—'*As* Was the Beginning, *As* is, Now, *As* Ever shall be … world without …'' We said amen with a straight face and sat down to eat." Sí Bero and the priest are sickened, but Bero only laughs. Before the war, he was a medical specialist, but in the army he became an intelligence officer, a specialist in torture who used his gifts to gain authority. "Afterwards I said why not?" he boasts. "What is one flesh from another? … It was the first step to power you understand. Power in its purest sense."

Bero informs his sister that the army has released the Old Man into his care and that he must either execute him for his crimes or keep him prisoner. Sí Bero is horrified but later confesses her own secret plan. She has engaged the services of two earth mothers, Iya Agba and Iya Mate, to help discover medical secrets that will balance the cosmic forces, pitting the healing power of herbs against the destructive power of war. Her quest for power is likewise thwarted. Disgusted

by Bero's behavior, the old women feel that their spiritual energies have been misappropriated and that the family is beyond redemption. When Bero shoots his father, the earth mothers burn the herb garden and depart, destroying any hope for future harmony in a single nihilistic act.

Soyinka finished *Madmen and Specialists* in June 1970, shortly after his release from prison. Seeking refuge from the Nigerian government's censorship, he commissioned a group of actors from Nigeria's Ibadan University Theatre Art Company, and together they premiered the piece at the National Playwrights Conference, an annual gathering for theater artists at the Eugene O'Neill Theatre Center in Waterford, Connecticut. An incisive critique of the corrupt dictators running rampant throughout Africa, the production attracted much attention and led to a series of free performances in New York City. Though seldom performed outside university settings today, *Madmen and Specialists* is often studied as a documentation of Nigeria's bloody quest for democracy. Frequently anthologized, the play is part of the canon of postcolonial Nigerian literature that opposes dictatorial rule.

HISTORICAL AND LITERARY CONTEXT

Madmen and Specialists alludes to the political uprisings that plagued postcolonial Africa throughout the mid- to late twentieth century. Though the playwright's homeland, Nigeria, celebrated its independence from the United Kingdom in 1960, civil unrest immediately beset the newly formed republic. Britain had designated the national borders with little regard for the more than three hundred ethnic and cultural groups occupying the region. Religious, linguistic, and political differences led to infighting and a struggle for power between the Islamic and theocratic Hausa-Fulani who dominated the northern part of the country, the monarchical Yoruba in the southwest, and the largely democratic Igbo in the southeast. In January 1966 economic tensions mounted, and an Igbo contingent staged a military coup, killing more than thirty major political leaders, including the prime minister, Abubakar Tafawa Balewa. On May 30, 1967, the southeastern region declared itself the Republic of Biafra, officially beginning the Nigerian Civil War. Though the democratic aims of the Biafran cause

WAR OF SOLIDITY FOR SOLIDITY

Though most of Nigeria's intellectual elite, such as the writers Chinua Achebe, Pius Ike, Christopher Okigbo, and John Munonye, had claimed solidarity with the Biafran secessionists during the war, Soyinka adopted a distinctly nationalistic and humanistic position. Rejecting both factional complaints, he called instead for a complete overhaul of Nigeria's political and economic system. In his prison diaries, later published in the book *The Man Died* (1972), Soyinka writes, "What is clear, miserably and humiliatingly clear is that a war is being fought without a simultaneous programme of reform." Arguing that Nigerians were not waging a war of unity, but a "war of solidity

for solidity," he laments that the outcome would only consolidate the cult of "As" portrayed in *Madmen and Specialists*. In other words, "victory" for either side would only serve to cement "the very values that gave rise to the war in the first place." *Madmen and Specialists* and *The Man Died* (1972) are just two parts of a tetralogy that frames the author's reflections on Nigeria's civil war. The collection also includes a book of poetry written in prison called *A Shuttle in the Crypt* (1972) and the antiwar novel, *Season of Anomy* (1973). Together, the four works represent a period of change in Soyinka's writing that was a direct result of his imprisonment.

helped the movement to gain sympathizers throughout Europe and Africa, Nigeria's economy depended on the region's oil resources, and the central government resolved to reunite the country. With the help of British troops, they instituted a reign of terror, cutting off the rebels' food supply and staging extermination raids in southeastern cities. An estimated three million Nigerians (more than ninety percent of them from the southeastern region) died before the northern government reabsorbed the failed republic.

Soyinka, a Yoruba, questioned the moral and ideological claims of both sides in the conflict, claiming that the war only served to emphasize the factional differences between the conservative north and the more westernized south. He argued for a nationalist agenda that would improve the living conditions of all Nigerian peoples. His outspokenness earned him many enemies, and when General Yakubu Gowon took charge of the Nigerian military government after a coup in 1966, he had Soyinka imprisoned for treason. The writer spent the majority of his twenty-two-month sentence in solitary confinement. This traumatic experience, combined with what literary scholar Chidi Amuta calls in "The Ideological Content of Soyinka's War Writings" the "mental and moral indignation" induced by the national conflict, forced Soyinka to reexamine his portrayal of history and society. The author's previous works, such as *The Trials of Brother Jero* (1960), *A Dance of the Forests* (1960), and *The Strong Breed* (1966), employed a mythic, atemporal approach that cast historical events as recurrent tropes divorced from context. According to Amuta, Soyinka's postwar prose took on an "overt political edge." Beginning with *Madmen and Specialists*, his works sought to critique present-day injustices rather than simply compare them with past atrocities. "One of Soyinka's cardinal preoccupations in his war writings," Amuta observes, "is the question of leadership and its overall import as a determinant of social

morality and political ideology. ... He came to see the wartime military administration of Nigeria as the epitome of elite misrule, a fact which seemed to have been confirmed by his personal experience." Soyinka persisted with these themes throughout his later work, with such plays as *Jero's Metamorphosis* (1974) and *A Play of Giants* (1984) deepening his critique of corrupt dictatorial power.

THEMES AND STYLE

Although most Nigerian writers explore political topics, Eldred Jones cites Soyinka's work as unique in emphasizing universal themes while discussing African concerns. "Although his characters and their mannerisms are African," he notes in *The Writing of Wole Soyinka*, "the essential ideas which emerge from a reading of Soyinka's work are not specially African ideas." Soyinka, Jones asserts, is a humanist, concerned with a "man on earth" that "represents the whole race." Regarding *Madmen and Specialists*, he contends that the playwright exploits dramatic structure and themes reminiscent of Classical Greek tragedy. Bero's defiance of the gods, or in this case natural law, transforms him from a promising youth to a tragic antihero whose hamartia (fatal mistake) and hubris (pride) lead to his inevitable corruption. Unlike the catharsis that follows a Greek hero's recognition of his misfortune, however, Soyinka affords neither his audience nor his characters such redemption. "Once you begin there is no stopping," the Old Man warns Bero. "For those who want to step beyond, there is always one further step."

In this debate between the young man and his father, Soyinka complicates the relationship between good and evil. While Bero's cannibalism is reprehensible, it was the Old Man who led him down the path of destruction by feeding him the cursed meat. The Old Man declares that he has "stolen the salvation" of the warring men: though the soldiers claim just cause in their attack on the enemy, the universal sinfulness

Madmen and Specialists author Wole Soyinka at his home in Ibadan, Nigeria, on October 21, 1969, shortly after his release from prison. He had been imprisoned for two years for questioning the Nigerian government's suppression of the Biafran independence movement. © KEYSTONE / HULTON ARCHIVE / GETTY IMAGES

of eating human flesh robs them of any claim to righteousness. Thus, the Old Man's trickery exposes the inherently cannibalistic nature of civil warfare. "Oh yes, you rushed out and vomited. You and the others," he taunts Bero. "But afterwards you said I had done you a favour. Remember? I'm glad you remember. Never admit you are a recidivist once you've tasted the favourite food of As." According to African theatre scholar Frances Harding's article "Soyinka and Power: Language and Imagery in *Madmen and Specialists*," the playwright's ambiguities "enable us to see that there is no single question as to whether this or that person is good or bad and no simple answer—there is 'no separable moral judgment' ... only people, families, struggling to survive in a war-torn society."

To this end, the characters of *Madmen and Specialists* represent symbols or philosophical ideas rather than individuals. The two supernatural characters of the play, Iya Agba and Iya Mate, provide an alternative to the destructive tendencies of the men and stand in for a traditional, animist cultural influence. Likewise, Sí Bero is an aspiring earth mother, herself aligned with the fruitfulness of nature. Bero embodies nihilism, and the Old Man is his Socratic antagonist who exposes falsehood without regard for questions of moral justice. The priest's conventional Western morality plays a foil to the earth mothers—his dualist mind cannot fathom the depths of cosmic forces—and the mendicants, finally, are the pawns and "inadequate protégés" of the will of "As."

Iya Agba and Iya Mate's herbs, which the mothers grow in hopes of purging the world's hostilities, are the symbol of nature's secrets. Because only the honorable have access to this power, neither Bero nor the Old Man can acquire it. Nature, the old women remind us, is not a hierarchical system but rather operates according to reciprocity. "We put back what

we take, in one form or another. Or more than we take," the old woman tells him. "It's the only law." When the old women set fire to the herbs, Soyinka underlines the play's inherent pessimism. In this universe, corruption forces nature to withdraw its gifts. In addition, these women defy Bero's quest to find a "natural" cure for war, maintaining that there is no secret truth of power.

CRITICAL DISCUSSION

Soyinka is arguably Africa's most celebrated playwright, and most critics consider the American and European productions of his plays to have been catalysts for the renewed interest in Nigerian literature in the West. Outside Africa, the playwright is praised for blending mythic stories from his native Yoruban folk-drama with European dramatic forms to great effect. According to Charles Larson's *New York Times* review, *Madmen and Specialists*, in particular, demonstrated Soyinka's talent. Without mentioning the conflict directly, Larson notes, Soyinka's use of allegory and irony "leveled a wholesale criticism of life in Nigeria since the Civil War: a police state in which only madmen and spies can survive, in which the losers are mad and the winners are paranoid about the possibility of another rebellion." In the *Times Literary Supplement*, D. A. N. Jones calls the play both grotesque and horrible but concedes that these qualities contributed to the work's overall effect. "The rhetoric is quite powerful," he writes, though he adds that the play is one of Soyinka's most difficult. "It is clearly not expected that many in the audience will be able to follow the verbal argument. Meaninglessness is the theme of this play: it demonstrates failure in communication, dramatizing the solitude and despair of a playwright who was once a source of optimism."

Some of Soyinka's African contemporaries, however, consider the writer's global inspirations cryptic, irresponsible, and ideologically suspect. In his article "Soyinka and His Radical Critics," scholar Brian Crow observes that the playwright's "Nigerian critics have persistently accused Soyinka of obscurantism and of being too much immersed in private myth-making ... at the expense of communicating with a popular audience about issues which directly concern it." Crow quotes one detractor, Nigerian theater artist Yemi Ogunbiyi, who calls Soyinka's work morally ambiguous, saying that "a committed work of art ... must lay bare unambiguously the causal historical and socio-economic network of society in such a way as to enable us to master reality and, in fact, transform it."

Soyinka, however, rails against this perspective. In his article "Neo-Tarzanism: The Poetics of Pseudo-Tradition," he questions the "more-committed-than-thou breast-thumping" of his radical critics. "Social commitment is a citizen's commitment and embraces equally the carpenter, the mason, the banker, the farmer, the customs officer etc., etc., not forgetting the critic," he writes. "Yet none of these thousand and one categories of contributors to social progress spends twenty-four hours a day being 'socially committed.' That non-stop mandate is miraculously reserved for the artist alone." In an interview with *New York Times* writer Jason Berry, Soyinka confirms that as an artist in the African cultural tradition, he "has always functioned as the record of the mores and experience of [my] society," but he is reticent to speak for an entire continent. "I'm not sure I'm trying to communicate a message. I'm just trying to be part of the movement away from the unacceptable present."

SOURCES

Amuta, Chidi. "The Ideological Content of Soyinka's War Writings." *African Studies Review* 29.3 (1986): 43–54. *JSTOR*. Web. 16 Oct. 2011.

Berry, Jason. "A Voice out of Africa." *New York Times* 18 Sept. 1983. SM92. *ProQuest Historical Newspapers*. Web. 16 Oct. 2011.

Crow, Brian. "Soyinka and His Radical Critics: A Review." *Theatre Research International* 12.1 (1987): 61–70. *Cambridge Journals Online*. Web. 16 Oct. 2011.

Harding, Frances. "Soyinka and Power: Language and Imagery in *Madmen and Specialists*." *African Languages and Cultures* 4.1 (1991): 87–98. *JSTOR*. Web. 16 Oct. 2011.

Jones, D. A. N. "The Devotees of As." *Times Literary Supplement* 31 Dec. 1971: 1632. *TLS Historical Archive*. Web. 20 Nov 2011.

Jones, Eldred D. *The Writing of Wole Soyinka*. 3rd ed. London: Currey, 1988. Print.

Larson, Charles R. "Wole Soyinka: Nigeria's Leading Social Critic." *New York Times Book Review* 24 Dec. 1972: 6. *ProQuest Historical Newspapers*. Web. 16 Oct. 2011.

Soyinka, Wole. *Madmen and Specialists; A Play*. New York: Hill, 1971. Print.

Soyinka, Wole. *The Man Died: Prison Notes of Wole Soyinka*. New York: Harper, 1972. Print.

———. "Neo-Tarzanism: The Poetics of Pseudo-Tradition." *Transition* 48 (1975): 38–44. *JSTOR*. Web. 18 Nov 2011.

FURTHER READING

Graf, William D. *The Nigerian State: Political Economy, State Class and Political System in the Post-Colonial Era*. London: Currey, 1988. Print.

—*Perspectives on Wole Soyinka: Freedom and Complexity*. Ed. Biodun Jeyifo. Jackson: UP of Mississippi, 2001. Print.

Jeyifo, Biodun. *Wole Soyinka: Politics, Poetics, and Postcolonialism*. Cambridge: Cambridge UP, 2004. Print.

McLuckie, Craig W. *Nigerian Civil War Literature: Seeking an "Imagined Community."* Lewiston: E. Mellen, 1990. Print.

Msiska, Mpalive-Hangson. *Postcolonial Identity in Wole Soyinka*. Amsterdam: Rodopi, 2007. Print.

Soyinka, Wole. *A Shuttle in the Crypt*. New York: Hill, 1972. Print.

———. *Season of Anomy*. New York: Third, 1974. Print.

Sara Taylor

M*A*S*H
The Story of Three Army Doctors
Richard Hooker

✤ **Key Facts**

Conflict:
Korean War

Time Period:
Mid-20th Century

Genre:
Novel

OVERVIEW

*M*A*S*H: The Story of Three Army Doctors* (1968) is a novel based on the experiences of author Richard Hooker in a mobile army surgical hospital (MASH) during the Korean War (1950–53). Hooker, whose real name was H. Richard Hornberger, served as a thoracic surgeon in the U.S. Army Medical Corps. In the novel, he portrays life in the fictional 4077th MASH, which is located in South Korea near the thiry-eighth parallel. Like Hooker's army colleagues, protagonists Benjamin Franklin "Hawkeye" Pierce, Augustus Bedford "Duke" Forrest, and John "Trapper" McIntyre—all new to the 4077th—are "exposed to extremes of hard work, leisure, tension, boredom, heat, cold, satisfaction and frustration that most of them had never faced before."

The novel opens with the arrival of Hawkeye and Duke to the 4077th. Trapper John soon joins them in their tent, which is known as "The Swamp." Together, the quirky, irreverent Swampmen cope with life in the MASH by adopting a detached, ironic view of army rules and regulations, religion, and other forms of orthodoxy. They wind up long shifts with a few martinis or several hands in the ongoing card game run by Captain Waldowski, the unit's dentist, at the Painless Polish Poker and Dental Clinic.

To avenge themselves on their by-the-book colleagues Major Margaret "Hot Lips" Houlihan and Major Frank Burns, they contrive a host of ruthless practical jokes. They also make several excursions away from the 4077th. On one trip, Hawkeye and Trapper John perform surgery on a U.S. congressman's son and then don traditional Korean costume before entering a golf tournament. Along the way, they party at a brothel operating out of a hospital, save an infant's life, and take compromising photographs of a general.

Their outside adventures are balanced, however, with graphic scenes in the operating tent, where Hooker depicts the harrowing nature of life in a MASH. The novel ends with the repatriation of Hawkeye and Duke, who, drunk and disbelieving, return to the arms of their wives and children.

Hooker's novel is the basis for the award-winning film *M*A*S*H* (1970), directed by Robert Altman. The book was also adapted into a television series, which aired from 1972 to 1983 and has become one of the most popular in the history of television.

HISTORICAL AND LITERARY CONTEXT

The Korean War was the first armed conflict of the Cold War era. It is known as a proxy war because forces from third-party countries did much of the fighting. The United States entered the war not because of any direct threat but because it wished to protect Japan from communist encroachment. Later, China joined the conflict in order to bolster its communist neighbor and to repel a potential threat to its border by Western powers.

When Japan's surrender brought World War II to an end in 1945, the Korean peninsula was divided along the thirty-eighth parallel, with troops from the Soviet Union occupying territory north of the dividing line and American troops occupying territory to the south. In 1948 the two Korean divisions established separate governments—communist in the north and anticommunist in the south. U.S. and Soviet troops had withdrawn by 1949.

On June 25, 1950, after several years of armed attacks along the border, the North Korean People's Army (KPA) invaded South Korea. The UN Security Council condemned the invasion and recommended that its members offer military aid to South Korea. American forces began fighting in the war in early July 1950, and other UN allies soon joined the conflict. China entered the war in October 1950. By the summer of 1951, the conflict had settled into a stalemate. Fighting continued, but the line separating the combatants barely changed. Negotiations for an armistice began in July 1951, but an agreement was not signed until July 1953. The armistice established a demilitarized zone between the two Koreas that roughly follows the thirty-eighth parallel.

The MASH, first used in World War II, was a portable medical unit designed to provide lifesaving treatment near the front lines of battle. During the Korean War, MASH units became more sophisticated and more effective in treating battlefield trauma and reducing the death rate among injured soldiers. Patients in need of specialized care (for example,

SERIOUS COMEDY

The television series *M*A*S*H*, based on Robert Altman's film adaptation of Richard Hooker's novel, became a staple of American prime-time programming in the 1970s. In 1983, eleven years after the show was almost canceled because of poor ratings, more than 105 million viewers watched the final episode, a record that remained unbroken until the 2010 Super Bowl attracted an audience of 106,500,000.

*M*A*S*H* pushed the boundaries of network television; its creators incorporated taboo language and topics and unprecedented amounts of blood into its scenes while making the effort to remain true to the show's historical roots. The series writers gathered story ideas for some episodes from interviews with Korean War surgeons. Later medical shows, including the hit series *ER* (1994–2009) and *House* (2004-), made use of techniques pioneered on *M*A*S*H*.

In a *USA Today* report on a reunion of some of the *M*A*S*H* cast in 2009, producer Larry Gelbart says that, despite popular perceptions, the series was intended to be "'pro-peace' rather than 'anti-war.'" Actor Alan Alda, who played doctor Hawkeye Pierce and wrote and directed numerous episodes, denies that the show served as a political soapbox. Instead, he says, "We were, for the first time on TV in a comedy show, taking [war] seriously."

neurosurgery) were evacuated to specialty centers. The Korean War saw the first use of helicopters to transport wounded soldiers. Many innovations in surgical and medical treatment implemented in MASH units were later adopted in hospitals around the world.

Hooker's novel reflects that many doctors who served in MASH units in Korea were young and still in the medical residency stage of their training. Often, they had little or no military background. The relative inexperience of these military doctors could explain the irreverent attitudes of the *M*A*S*H* protagonists with regard to military protocol.

As a work of war fiction, *M*A*S*H* is a gentle satire that lacks the sharp political edge of Joseph Heller's *Catch-22* (1961) and Kurt Vonnegut's *Slaughterhouse-Five* (1969). Hooker's novel has little in common with other fictional works about the Korean War, such as James Salter's *The Hunters* (1956) or James A. Michener's *The Bridges at Toko-Ri* (1953), both of which focus more on combat.

Hooker was not a professional writer. He worked on *M*A*S*H* for twelve years and endured numerous rejections from publishers before consulting journalist W. C. Heinz for help. After publishing *M*A*S*H*, Hooker wrote two sequels: *M*A*S*H Goes to Maine* (1972) and *M*A*S*H Mania* (1977). Although Hooker's name appears on other sequels, he did not contribute to their writing.

THEMES AND STYLE

While the film and television adaptations of *M*A*S*H* emphasize antiwar themes, Hooker's novel does not. In the book, Hooker is sometimes critical of army procedures and of typical military officer behaviors, and his characters invariably wish they were somewhere other than the battlefield. Yet, the war and the army are not the targets of his satire. Instead, he takes aim at those who do not care as deeply about the hospital's mission as Hawkeye, Trapper John, and Duke. Sticklers for codes and procedures are persecuted mercilessly—especially when they interfere with saving lives. However, the unit commander, Colonel Henry Blake, and the chaplain, John Patrick Mulcahy, whose soberness could have made them targets of the surgeons' pranks, escape the abuse because they value the doctors' dedication to the work of healing.

The Swampmen's practical jokes are a means of coping with an unpredictable environment. As Hooker notes in his foreword, among many army doctors, "the various stresses … produced behavior … that, superficially at least, seemed inconsistent with their earlier, civilian behavior patterns. A few flipped their lids, but most of them just raised hell, in a variety of ways and degrees."

Although the novel is considered a humorous work, it contains long passages that describe intense, bloody episodes in the operating tent. These harrowing experiences give rise to an equally intense release in what the film critic Roger Ebert describes as the doctors' "inspired and utterly heartless" revenge on those who get in the way of their work. "If the surgeons didn't have to face the daily list of maimed and mutilated bodies," Ebert writes, "none of the rest of their lives would make any sense."

Although Hooker may not have written the novel as an antiwar book, he nonetheless captures the absurdity of life in the midst of war. The surgeons are supremely dedicated in their efforts to heal the wounded; yet many of the soldiers they treat will return to the frontlines only to be wounded again or killed. During the Battle of Old Baldy in the summer of 1952, Hawkeye's devil-may-care attempts to cope with a seemingly endless stream of wounded men fall short, and anger, frustration, and depression set in. He relieves his melancholy by pranking an army psychiatrist. Nevertheless, a sense of futility continues to hover throughout the novel.

In this scene from the 1970 film adaptation of *M*A*S*H*, Army medical personnel play cards after a long shift. © 20TH CENTURY FOX FILM CORP. / EVERETT COLLECTION

CRITICAL DISCUSSION

*M*A*S*H* was not widely reviewed upon publication. In a *New York Times* review of Altman's film version of the novel, Roger Greenspun describes the book as "barely passable." When the sequel *M*A*S*H* Goes to Maine* was published, another *New York Times* reviewer wrote, "I couldn't find much humor in [the doctors'] activities. Nor much harm, either, come to think of it." When Ring Lardner Jr. adapted Hooker's original story into a screenplay for Altman's film, Ebert read it and "found it uninteresting."

What critics found flat on the page, however, became dynamic on film. Hooker's laconic one-liners gain new resonance when delivered by Donald Sutherland's thoroughly eccentric Hawkeye. In his review, Ebert touches on a number of the appealing features that the film and novel share. Noting that the three main characters are "almost metaphysically cruel," Ebert finds the film funny "because it is so true to the unadmitted sadist in all of us."

The surgeons are cruel to Major Houlihan because she is unmoved by the soldiers' broken, bleeding bodies, and the doctors want her to experience empathy through her suffering. The surgeons' tricks occasionally seem overzealous and fall flat in the novel, but the immediacy of film intensifies both the disapproval of Major Houlihan's unfeeling reverence for rules and the thrill of revenge. As Ebert observes, "Most comedies want us to laugh at things that aren't really funny; in this one we laugh precisely because they're not funny. We laugh, that we may not cry."

Whereas Ebert declares that "the flat-out, poker-faced hatred in *M*A*S*H* ... makes it work," Greenspun finds the film and its story less satisfying. Greenspun notes that the film, like the novel, "makes no profoundly radical criticism either of war or of the Army." Although he acknowledges that the film "is impudent, bold, and often very funny," he criticizes its lack of "the sense of order (even in the midst of disorder) that seems the special province of successful comedy." Ultimately, he concludes that the story "fails to build toward either significant confrontation or recognition."

SOURCES

Ebert, Roger. Rev. of *M*A*S*H*, by Robert Altman. *rogerebert.com*. Chicago Sun-Times, 1 Jan. 1970. Web. 27 June 2011.

Gehring, Wes. "*M*A*S*H* Turns 30: The TV Series' Dark Comedy Was a Paean to the Ludicrousness of War." *USA Today*. USA Today, 1 Sep. 2002. Web. 27 June 2011.

Greenspun, Roger. Rev. of *M*A*S*H*, by Robert Altman. *New York Times*. New York Times, 26 Jan. 1970. Web. 27 June 2011.

Hooker, Richard. *M*A*S*H: The Story of Three Army Doctors*. New York: Morrow, 1968. Print.

King, Booker, and Ismail Jatoi. "The Mobile Army Surgical Hospital (MASH): A Military and Surgical Legacy." *Journal of the National Medical Association* 97.5 (2005): 648–56. Web. 27 June 2011.

Rev. of *M*A*S*H* Goes to Maine*, by Richard Hooker. *New York Times*. New York Times, 5 Mar. 1972. Web. 27 June 2011.

Mifflin, Lawrie. "H. Richard Hornberger, 73, Surgeon behind *M*A*S*H*." *New York Times*. New York Times, 7 Nov. 1997. Web. 27 June 2011.

FURTHER READING

Apel, Otto F. *MASH: An Army Surgeon in Korea*. Lexington: UP of Kentucky, 1998. Print.

Ehrhart, W. D., and Philip K. Jason. *Retrieving Bones: Stories and Poems of the Korean War*. New Brunswick: Rutgers UP, 1999. Print.

Halberstam, David. *The Coldest Winter: America and the Korean War*. New York: Hyperion, 2007. Print.

Hastings, Max. *The Korean War*. New York: Simon, 1987. Print.

Jin, Ha. *War Trash: A Novel*. New York: Pantheon, 2004. Print.

Lardner, Ring, Jr. *M*A*S*H: The Screenplay*. Monterey Park: OSP, 1994. Print.

McWilliams, Bill. *On Hallowed Ground: The Last Battle for Pork Chop Hill*. Annapolis: Naval Institute, 2003. Print.

Wittebols, James H. *Watching M*A*S*H, Watching America: A Social History of the 1972–1983 Television Series*. Jefferson: McFarland, 1998. Print.

MEDIA ADAPTATIONS

*M*A*S*H*. Screenplay by Ring Lardner Jr. Dir. Robert Altman. Perf. Donald Sutherland, Elliott Gould, Tom Skerritt, Sally Kellerman, and Roger Bowen. Twentieth Century-Fox, 1970. Film.

*M*A*S*H*. Dir. Charles S. Dubin and others. Twentieth Century-Fox Television, 1972–83. Television.

Janet Moredock

OH WHAT A LOVELY WAR!

Joan Littlewood

OVERVIEW

A unique mixture of popular World War I songs, dance numbers, sketches, gags, and newsreel-like documentation, *Oh What a Lovely War!* was designed as musical entertainment charged with a stinging political indictment of war. It was written and performed beginning in 1963 by the members of the East London-based Theatre Workshop under the direction of Joan Littlewood, one of the troop's founders. *Oh What a Lovely War* expressed Littlewood's left-wing political sentiments to dazzling effect by manipulating the conceit of the pierrot show popular during the World War I era. She took the idea of pierrot—entertainers dressed as classic French clowns who sang, danced, and mimed at seaside resorts—and transferred it to a stage meant to recall the dance halls of the early twentieth century. Littlewood and her stage manager, Gerry Raffles, conceived the idea for the show in response to a 1961 BBC radio broadcast written and produced by Charles Chilton that contrasted the songs sung by World War I soldiers on the Western Front with the songs sung by civilians at home. Littlewood transformed what she considered Chilton's sentimental approach to the war into a satire on the strategies of the British government and its commanding officers in managing perceptions of the conflict.

Oh What a Lovely War exploited the political climate of the times, warning in its program notes that "a third, nuclear world war could kill as many in four hours as were killed in the whole of World War One." The play resonated with audiences fearful of escalating tensions in Vietnam and fresh in the memory of the Soviet buildup of missiles in Cuba. *Oh What a Lovely War* debuted to both popular and critical acclaim at the Theatre Royal, Stratford East, in the London borough of Newham on March 19, 1963. It won the Grand Prix on its tour to the Théâtre des Nations festival in Paris in 1963 and was nominated for four Tony awards for its 1964 to 1965 Broadway run at New York's Broadhurst Theater. Afterward the musical remained a part of local repertory theater, but because of restrictions placed on its performance by Littlewood, it was not revived for a national tour until 1998.

Oh What a Lovely War is performed in two acts, its dramatic scenes developed against the structuring device of the songs. The show features close to three dozen songs from the World War I era, each carefully chosen and placed within the text to develop an ironic contrast between their patriotic jingoism and the gruesome realities of trench warfare. Act One opens with an emcee introducing the audience to "the ever-popular War Game." A circus parade of actors dressed as pierrots, each representing a different country involved in World War I, appears onstage as the early events of the conflict are sketched. Initial optimism and rousing renditions of war anthems slowly give way to a more somber mood as slides depicting life in the trenches flash on a background screen and a panel board that traverses the width of the stage announces the numbers of war dead. As Act Two begins, the emcee apologizes for the bombing and artillery shelling that have interrupted the festivities. There follow scenes depicting munitions manufacturers reaping millions in profits from the war and elegant dinner parties attended by British commanding officers and their wives. These are joined with images of clouds of poison gas, suicide attacks on German lines, soldiers digging mass burial pits, and the always-present tally of the death toll. The soldiers begin to supply their own more cynical words to the program of patriotic anthems as self-satisfied officers continue to gamble with their lives.

HISTORICAL AND LITERARY CONTEXT

The Theatre Workshop was established in 1945 on a working-class ethos, and its productions had much in common with the agitprop theater of the 1930s in which Littlewood learned her trade. *Agitprop*, a word derived from the combination of two other words, *agitation* and *propaganda*, is a type of left-wing political theater, didactic in intent and often documentary in character. The term originated in Soviet Russia to describe the dissemination of communist ideas. As it was adapted by playwrights in Europe and the United States beginning in the 1920s, it came to denote any type of leftist political theater aimed at inculcating in the public a sense of class consciousness. Like most other creations of the Theatre Workshop, *Oh What a Lovely War* had a socialist agenda, in this case meant to educate the working classes about the incompetence of the army command and the callous disregard of politicians and profiteers for the men who sacrificed their lives in World War I combat. The performance played a central role in cementing popular perceptions of the "futility myth" of World War I, which gained

Key Facts

Conflict:
World War I

Time Period:
Early 20th century

Genre:
Play

Awards:
Grand Prix, Theatre des Nations Festival, Paris, 1963;
Antoinette Perry Award nomination, Best Book of a Musical, 1965

JOAN LITTLEWOOD'S FEUD WITH THE NATIONAL THEATRE OF LONDON

The Theatre Workshop of Joan Littlewood, author of *Oh What a Lovely War!*, operated out of the dilapidated Theatre Royal, Stratford East, beginning in 1953 and survived without paying its actors. The British Arts Council distrusted Littlewood's communist sympathies, and it gave scarce funding to the workshop in its start-up years.

Littlewood harbored a legendary animosity toward the National Theatre of London, an institution of the old guard that always received generous endowments from the Arts Council. In 1994, when Richard Eyre, the artistic director of the National, approached Littlewood with the idea for a new production of *Oh What a Lovely War*, she was characteristically caustic. Eyre recorded their exchange in a diary entry for April 20 of that year:

Joan Littlewood has refused us the rights of OWALW [*Oh What a Lovely War*]. I sent her a card on her eightieth birthday. I got a pc [postcard] back: 'Thanks for your card, Richard. I really don't know what you're up to. Whatever it is you'd do better to bomb that building. *I* had to put up with an *old* slum in London, yours need never have been." (*National Service: Diary of a Decade at the National Theatre*, 2003)

Littlewood eventually reached a compromise with Eyre. In keeping with her egalitarian idea of theater, she granted the National rights to *Oh What a Lovely War* under the condition that the show tour the country in a big top tent. The National's mobile production stopped in eleven cities in the spring of 1998.

renewed significance in the 1960s as it was adapted by the radical left in their critiques of such contemporary political issues as the arms race and the Vietnam War. As part of a 2008 education pack designed to aid students, history professor Dan Todman explained,

Certainly the 'musical entertainment' has been blamed by modern military historians for falsifying popular perceptions of the First World War. They would argue that, if Britons now think of the war in terms of mud, blood, futility and asinine generals, it is not because that accurately represents what happened, but because in the intervening years a false version of the war has become culturally dominant … Here, it is claimed, *Oh What a Lovely War* was a crucial text: creating powerful images of the betrayal of soldiers by their stupid, uncaring generals which have become embedded in British popular culture.

The pierrots, the vaudeville humor, and the music-hall renditions of patriotic war songs were meant to portray the innocence of life in England before the war. These comic aspects of the show were integrated with an objective chronicling of some of the shocking truths of World War I. Littlewood and the company were concerned to show that the war had been protracted unnecessarily for economic reasons without regard to the tragedy of human suffering and loss of life. The numbers recorded on the newsboard—sixty thousand men killed on the first day of the Battle of the Somme, for example—combine with the soldiers' parodies of the war anthems to present a version of war at the front that contrasts sharply with the propaganda being disseminated at home. It is estimated that eight

million soldiers and twelve million civilians were killed in World War I. The introduction of tank technology, chemical weaponry such as poison gas, and high explosive shells greatly escalated the death toll and made the manner of death exceptionally gruesome. As the conflict dragged on, many people came to question the morality of mass warfare; when it was over, ideals of heroism and freedom, such as those proclaimed in many of the songs featured in *Oh What a Lovely War*, seemed but hollow abstractions.

The title of the play is taken from a famous World War I music-hall song, "Oh! It's a Lovely War." Composed in 1917—three years into the fighting—the song contains some cynical verses, made all the more ironic in this production when sung by pierrots and employed against a backdrop recording the 59,275 soldier casualties at the Battle of Ypres: "As soon as reveille has gone / We feel just as heavy as lead, / But we never get up till the sergeant / Brings our breakfast up to bed." (The title of this song and that of the play and the film version, *Oh! What a Lovely War*, are frequently confused and used interchangeably.)

In the years after the initial runs of *Oh What a Lovely War*, Littlewood was vocal in her denunciation of subsequent productions that sentimentalized the material. In 2000 she republished the Theatre Workshop text in an effort to restore the play to its original spirit.

THEMES AND STYLE

The themes of *Oh What a Lovely War* are overtly political, and the play is obvious in its use of varying theatrical techniques to develop a startling contrast between the propaganda of war and its reality. The "War Game" that is announced at the play's beginning is stylized through the singing and clowning of the pierrots; other techniques are also used in Act One to develop the idea of the war as play, such as the scene in which French cavalry officers ride wooden poles meant to resemble hobbyhorses. Once the image of the war as its own form of entertainment is firmly established, reality begins to intrude on the stage in the form of documentary effects, including the newsboard that reports the rising death count and the background screen flashing actual images of trench combat. Narrated scenes and dialogue based on historical sources are also important to the irony. At one point in the play, for example, an actor reads a letter from a real-life combat nurse describing the terrible suffering of the wounded: "It is beyond belief, the butchery." The actor then offers a version of a 1914 song, "Keep the Home Fires Burning," the lyrics of which are rendered meaningless because it is clear that very few of the soldiers will make it home alive.

The primary targets of the play's political satire are the politicians and commanding officers who engineered the war and the industrial magnates who profited from it. Thus, the invective against war is intimately connected with a scheme to represent the polarization of the class structure. The motives and conduct of the upper-class men who managed the war are thoroughly discredited, while the working-class men who fought the battles are portrayed as their pawns. As Steve Lewis notes in his introduction to a 2006 edition of the revised text, the play emphasizes that "the commanders of the British operation were more concerned about their own standing in society and their personal reputations than the safety and security of the men under their command." The historical figure chiefly exposed is Field Marshall Sir Douglas Haig. In one scene his confused orders result in Irish soldiers progressing behind enemy lines and being shot down by their own side. In another, as soldiers sing "I Want to Go Home" and the newsboard records 2,500,000 men dead on the Western Front, Haig thanks God for his successes in battle. In yet another scene, his strategy at the Battle of the Somme is likened to a game of leapfrog. The last line of the last song in the show, "They Wouldn't Believe Me," is a final reminder to the audience that they have witnessed the war as told from the perspective of the powerless: "There was a front, but damned if we knew where."

CRITICAL DISCUSSION

Reviews of the London Theatre Workshop production of *Oh What a Lovely War* were generally positive, with critics praising its seamless meshing of comedy, satire, song, and historical documentation. Still, many commentators cited the play's vilification of General Haig as evidence of what Bernard Levin referred to in the *Daily Mail* as its "lopsided" presentation of the facts clearly favoring common soldiers over officer personnel (quoted in Lewis, Theatre Workshop). Much like Levin, a reviewer for the *Times* noted that *Oh What*

a Lovely War portrayed the conflict as "a criminally wasteful adventure in which the stoic courage of the common soldiers was equaled only by the sanctimonious incompetence of their commanders and the blind jingoism of the civilians" (quoted in Lewis, Theatre Workshop).

Although the text of the play frequently appears on high school and college reading lists in Britain, some recent critics have been less accepting than their 1960s counterparts of the play's politically biased view of the war. *Oh What a Lovely War* is now sometimes viewed as contributing to a leftist mythology of World War I. Like any literary text with an ideological agenda, the play is not necessarily completely based on fact and represents one view amongst many on World War I. Recent scholarship in literary and cultural studies shows that the journey from war enthusiasm to disillusionment sketched in the play was by no means a universal experience. Todman explained the powerful antiwar message of *Oh What a Lovely War* as a politically inspired oversimplification of the facts, noting that Littlewood's "intention was to make this representation of the war dramatic and didactic from an extremely left-wing perspective. For this reason she rejected scripts which offered a purely realistic depiction of life in the trenches … The result of these efforts was an original production which offered a black and white picture. Officers at all levels are stupid, callous cowards, while their men are sardonic heroes." *Oh What a Lovely War* has become symbolic of the antiestablishment mythology of the 1960s. In a 2007 *Spectator* review of a new British production, Robert Gore Langton remarked, "A chipper Edwardian music-hall knees-up with a comedy Kaiser is sabotaged by newsclips and savage stuff about politicians, profiteers, brass hats and capitalists. It was all very Sixties, according to almost everyone who saw the original—totally unforgettable." Todman added that the play became sentimentalized, but for reasons other than those Littlewood worried about. He reflected on the irony of the 1998 national revival having "sparked a new wave of nostalgia, not for the comradeship of the trenches but for a mythical, hedonistic, radical 1960s. … So famous had [the play] become as an emblem of the 1960s that it was itself viewed in nostalgic terms." With some relaxation on restraints to the play's production since Littlewood's death, theater companies have sought to update the material for contemporary circumstances while adhering to the original version of the text as provided by Littlewood in 2000. Ian Barge wrote of the play's continuing relevance in a *Stage* review of a 2008 tour of the show by the United Kingdom's Blackeyed Theatre:

> The counterpoint between slide-projected war images, stark statistics and the delusional hypocrisy of official attitudes assumes a lacerating contemporary relevance with the inclusion of images drawn from Iraq, the Falklands and Northern Ireland, as well as the familiar

iconic First World War trench photographs. Any assumption that *Oh! What a Lovely War* is a period piece is shot to shrapnel. Forty years on we need Littlewood's vision more than ever.

SOURCES

Barge, Ian. Rev. of *Oh What a Lovely War*. *Stage* 15 Sept. 2008. Web. 11 July 2011.

Langton, Robert Gore. "Packing a Punch: Robert Gore Langton on Why a Sixties Satire on the First World War Still Has Enduring Power." *Spectator* 20 Oct. 2007: 73. *Literature Resources from Gale*. Web. 11 July 2011.

Lewis, Steve. Commentary. *Oh What a Lovely War*, by Theatre Workshop. London: Methuen, 2006. xxi-lxxi. Print.

Theatre Workshop. *Oh What a Lovely War!*. Rev. ed. London: Methuen, 2000. Print.

Todman, Dan. "*Oh What a Lovely War*: Retelling the First World War in Post-War Britain." *Education Pack*, by the Educ. and Outreach Dept. Partnership of Blackeyed Theatre, Courtyard Centre for the Arts, and South Hill Park. 2008. Web. 13 July 2011.

FURTHER READING

Ebert, Roger. "Oh, What a Lovely War." Rev. of *Oh! What a Lovely War*, dir. Richard Attenborough. *Chicago Sun-Times* 30 Oct. 1969. Web. 9 July 2011.

Hickling, Alfred. Rev. of *Oh What a Lovely War*. *Guardian* [London] 29 Oct. 2007. Web. 11 July 2011.

———. Rev. of *Oh What a Lovely War*. *Guardian* [London] 11 Mar. 2010. Web. 11 July 2011.

Paget, Derek. "*Oh What a Lovely War*: The Texts and Their Context." *New Theatre Quarterly* 6 (1990): 244–60. Print.

"Commentary: Effects of the Musical Work *Oh What a Lovely War*." Narr. Robert Siegel. *All Things Considered*. Natl. Public Radio. 24 Sept. 2002. *Literature Resources from Gale*. Web. 11 July 2011. Transcript.

MEDIA ADAPTATION

Oh! What a Lovely War. Dir. Richard Attenborough. Perf. Wendy Allnutt, Colin Farrell, and Malcolm McFee. Paramount Pictures, 1969. Film.

Janet Mullane

PARENTHESES OF BLOOD

Sony Labou Tansi

OVERVIEW

Best known for his biting critiques of the postcolonial dictatorships that followed African independence, Congolese novelist and theater artist Sony Labou Tansi was one of the most prolific and internationally celebrated Francophone African writers of the twentieth century. His play *Parentheses of Blood* (1977), a farce notable for its ferocious satire and nightmarish atmosphere, is set in an imaginary war-ravaged country where the foot soldiers of a brutal authoritarian regime search tirelessly for the freedom fighter "Anamata Lansa, alias Libertashio," despite the fact that he is already dead. "We're looking for *a* Libertashio," the Sergeant explains. "We need one. Real or supposed, it doesn't matter. In the end we'll find one we suppose to be real."

The action begins as soldiers approach Libertashio's family home and demand the freedom fighter's surrender. His daughter Ramana, however, insists that the regime sent his head and bloodied clothes home for burial six months prior. When the Sergeant finally agrees to take the freedom fighter's head back to the capital, he is shot dead by his second-in-command. With a brief ceremony, the man promotes himself to Sergeant, explaining that "deserters are shot, that's military justice. … A deserter is a uniformed soldier who says Libertashio is dead. … The law forbids belief in Libertashio's death, whether he's dead or not. Thus, he is not dead." The charade continues as the new Sergeant declares the freedom fighter's nephew, Martial, the "new Libertashio" and places the entire family under arrest.

By morning, three more Sergeants have been deposed in the same manner as the first; the junior officer Cavacha takes command and insists that each prisoner be given a dying request. To buy time, Libertashio's youngest daughter, Aleyo, asks if she may marry the Sergeant, and her request to be the "future late Madame Sergeant Cavacha" is granted. The symbolic marriage of the child of the freedom fighter to the new totalitarian regime is, ironically, presided over by the white colonial powers. Trouble begins immediately when a French diplomat, Dr. Portès, falls in love with Aleyo and refuses to leave her side. He is promptly arrested, and Cavacha orders the remaining soldiers to lock up the prisoners and cut off their ears. Together in the dark, each uncertain about being

alive or dead, they scream "Long Live Libertashio!" in frustration between moans of pain and regret. This situation changes with the arrival of a new soldier from the capital. The country has been united, democracy has been proclaimed, and Libertashio is a national hero. There are sounds of celebration in the streets, and it becomes clear that the captives *are* still alive. The Sergeant is suddenly a prisoner himself, but screaming "Down with Libertashio!" he starts a new revolution, calling for supporters as he picks up his gun and showers the stage with bullets.

Sony Labou Tansi became an international sensation after *Parentheses of Blood* won high honors at the Inter-African Theatrical Contest sponsored by Radio France International. Following productions in Paris and Dakar, the Ubu Repertory Theater, an American production company dedicated to bringing Francophone works to the United States, commissioned a translation that premiered on their New York stage in 1986. Though *Parentheses of Blood* was Sony Labou Tansi's third published play, it was the first to appear in English, and it prompted a new interest in Francophone African writing in the Anglophone world. Despite its initial success, the play is rarely performed outside of university settings today. A vital critique of the history of African independence, *Parentheses of Blood* nevertheless remains important to the fields of Francophone and postcolonial literatures.

HISTORICAL AND LITERARY CONTEXT

Sony Labou Tansi was born Marcel Ntsoni in the former Belgian Congo (known in his lifetime as Zaire and today as the Democratic Republic of the Congo), but he was educated and lived in Brazzaville in the bordering French colony of Middle Congo. The French colony gained independence in 1960 and is today the Republic of Congo, but the country was known as the People's Republic of the Congo (1970–91) during most of Sony Labou Tansi's adult life. Though no single leader there achieved the international notoriety of Zaire's infamous despot Mobutu Sese Seko, repressive dictatorial rule was ever-present. Party censors quashed all but the most veiled criticisms of the government; thus, Sony Labou Tansi's works are most often set in imaginary African countries that more closely approximate the "other Congo." Scholar Dominic Thomas, in his book *Nation-Building, Propaganda, and Literature*

Key Facts

Conflict:
Congo Crisis;
Decolonization of Africa

Time Period:
Mid-20th Century

Genre:
Play

Award:
Concours Théâtral
Interafricain de
Radio-France
Internationale

"AFTER INDEPENDENCE ≠ BEFORE INDEPENDENCE"

Despite gaining political independence, the newly formed Republic of the Congo had few native military officers; in fact, no Congolese in the entire military had earned a rank higher than sergeant when the country gained its independence from Belgium in 1960. As a result, the Congolese Force Publique was obliged to keep paying Belgian officers to lead the corps while training its own military leadership. On his first day in office, however, Prime Minister Lumumba made the fatal mistake of raising the pay for all government employees except those in the armed services. On July 5, 1960, the military's commander, Lieutenant General Émile Janssens, called a meeting of the entire garrison, where he provoked the Congolese soldiers by writing on a blackboard, "After independence = before independence."

The outraged Congolese mutinied against its white officers and began attacking numerous European targets. In a single act, Lumumba had forever lost the allegiance of his native military forces and inadvertently created the ragtag group of citizen soldiers led by a rotating cast of sergeants that was ridiculed by Sony Labou Tansi in *Parentheses of Blood*.

in Francophone Africa, calls this practice an "effective device" that enables the author to wage a war of words on the government while avoiding both censorship and potential charges of treason. "By transposing his narrative in Zaire, Sony Labou Tansi can attack authoritarianism without actually naming the People's Republic of the Congo," Thomas writes. "The reality he describes and the interconnectedness of the respective colonial and postcolonial histories of the two Congos are close enough for the criticism to apply to both spheres."

The "atmosphere of war" that pervades *Parentheses of Blood* evokes the Congo Crisis (1960–66), a period of turmoil that began with the country's independence from Belgium. As much as an anticolonial struggle as it was an internal secessionist conflict and a Cold War proxy battle between the United States and the Soviet Union, the Congo Crisis led to the deaths of more than one hundred thousand people, including the assassination of the country's first Prime Minister, Patrice Lumumba. Much like Sony Labou Tansi's fabled Libertashio, Lumumba was viewed as the Congo's savior and his assassination as its original sin. French philosopher Jean-Paul Sartre observed in his book *Colonialism and Neocolonialism* that "The dead Lumumba ceased to be a person and became Africa in its entirety, with its unitary will, the multiplicity of its social and political systems, its divisions, its disagreements, its power, and its impotence: he was not, nor could he be, the hero of pan-Africanism. He was its martyr." Sony Labou Tansi credits this deification

of Lumumba with making the Congo vulnerable to corruption. By murdering Libertashio's "children," the playwright demonstrates that those who refuse to take an active role in the political matters at hand choose oppression by default. "When you go to the ballot box, why don't you say, 'We don't want this man,'" the soldiers ask. "Once you make someone your leader, he makes the laws. You're the real devils. We have a democracy in our country; the army doesn't vote. So tell me, where does the fault lie … the blame?"

Although Sony Labou Tansi's opposition to oppressive regimes allies him with contemporary African writers such as Tchicaya U Tam'si, Wole Soyinka, and Henri Lopes, literary critic Jonathan Ngate notes in his book *Francophone African Fiction* that the playwright's avant-garde approach to writing "signalled a clean break" with the tradition of *littérature engagée*. Committed largely to decolonization, these "engaged" writings use techniques of witnessing and reporting to prod readers into a critical consciousness that might bring about social change. Their authors, however, focus on the encroachment of the colonial Other as the sight of persecution, whereas Sony Labou Tansi looks to Africa's postindependence dictatorships for an imbalance of power. Proffering a *littérature engageante*, or "engaging literature," that emphasizes experimentation and collective creation, he views authorship "as a mode of invention, a way of writing oneself into being with words" that relies on breaking the traditions of Western literary models. By abandoning realism's safety and manipulating linguistic conventions, texts like *Parentheses of Blood* ask readers and spectators to reach beyond the moralizing conundrums of postcolonial politics and interact with the text as its cocreator, making meaning through actively "engaging" with the author's words.

THEMES AND STYLE

From the very title of the play Sony Labou Tansi alerts his audience that the events onstage in *Parentheses of Blood* are extraordinary, bracketed, and set apart from the normal flow of existence. This is perhaps more clearly delineated in the original French title, *La parenthèse de sang*. This singular form, "parenthesis of blood," suggests a digression as much as a punctuation mark. "It's begun in this sad century," the prologue states. "Whether open or closed—this parenthesis of blood, this parenthesis of the intestines, it's begun, but won't end." Describing the bloody interlude between colonial rule and an imagined future democracy, Sony Labou Tansi's title connects power to grammar. Sociologists Ronjon Paul Datta and Laura MacDonald, in their article "Time for Zombies," describe parentheses as playing "with(in)" existence and linguistics. "They provide further explanation, a reference, the meta moment, another level or layer, back story, a revealing secret or joke, a self-conscious aside, a rem(a)inder, a side note or marginalia," they write.

Sony Labou Tansi's *Parentheses of Blood* does all these things. Simultaneously history and satire, the play does not relate the details of the Congo Crisis; instead, it reflects on their incongruity within the larger narrative of independence. The play is itself a parenthesis describing a parenthesis. According to Datta and MacDonald, these parentheses are not supposed to interpret reality but instead "impart something related or supplementary and outside the main throughline." In this view, Sony Labou Tansi disrupts the idea that corrupt leaders are a natural byproduct of colonial repression. He challenges his audience to reflect on the agency of the individuals within the parentheses. "My only sin is to believe in freedom," Libertashio's daughter Yavilla asserts as if reflecting on this point. "I've spent my life shouting 'Long Live Libertashio.' I am only a force that says down with dictatorship—dictatorship by men, by things, and by God if He exists."

Questions of being likewise plague the characters in Sony Labou Tansi's play. Because their existence is parenthetical to reality, they are forever unsure whether they are experiencing "death within life" or "life within death." While they suffer in the dark after the wedding, Aleyo and her family convince themselves that they are dead, working hard to resist Dr. Portès's deflating, scientific stance. "I'm in pain. I'm in pain, and so I'm alive," he insists, to which Aleyo replies, "What a joke. Who ever told you the dead don't suffer too?" Thomas attributes this discord to Sony Labou Tansi's rejection of the "framework of Cartesian logic." Because the ambiguous results of the atrocities depicted in *Parentheses of Blood* defy logic, Thomas argues that they become a call to action. "Rebellion functions as proof of life in an environment where death is a part of everyday existence," he writes. Martial's assertion that "the time to die is over" as he is led to his executioners underscores this point. By killing the family of freedom fighters, Sony Labou Tansi extends their rebellion beyond life for the good of future generations and therefore beyond the parenthesis. Dr. Portès, however, with all his trappings of conservative Western humanism, remains a prisoner of physical reality because he cannot understand existence after the death of his body. "No, death. You can't. You have no right," he wails as Libertashio's family lies dead around him. "You can't close me off in these parentheses."

CRITICAL DISCUSSION

Though he died at the age of forty-seven, Sony Labou Tansi's impressive body of work remains one of the most frequently studied among Francophone African authors. "Like many of his fictional characters," Thomas remarks, "Sony Labou Tansi thus continues to 'live' in death. ... His physical death has not silenced his resistance to tyranny in the African postcolonial state." This success outside of Africa, however, posed certain difficulties for a playwright intent on securing

A photograph of black African soldiers evicting a white man from the former Belgian Congo, which became independent from Belgium's colonial rule on June 30, 1960, on the cover of *Paris Match* magazine on July 23, 1960. © ARCHIVES CHARMET / THE BRIDGEMAN ART LIBRARY INTERNATIONAL

the public's mandate, forcing Sony Labou Tansi to walk a thin line between critical recognition and political efficacy.

In order to gain the support of the academic elite who possessed the power to affect social change in the Congo, Sony Labou Tansi wrote in French. This bias in his work toward the upper classes coupled with the playwright's celebrated status in fashionable circles in France led many to accuse him of pandering to the colonizers. "Recognizing the futility of censoring Sony Labou Tansi's work in what essentially constituted a non-book-consuming society," Thomas remarks, "the authorities [in the People's Republic of the Congo] proceeded instead to discredit him by underlining and questioning the appropriateness of his links with the former colonial powers." In light of his numerous awards and invitations to speak at international events, the argument was easily made. This line of questioning, however, which framed the playwright as a colonial supporter, was tantamount to accusing Sony Labou Tansi of being an agent of imperialism himself.

In his book *Thresholds of Change in African Literature*, Kenneth Harrow observes that Sony Labou Tansi "has repeatedly affirmed his intention to write a literature of combat while at the same time choosing a literary style that is not easily accessible. ... We can say that his protest is anchored in a reality whose images he refuses to recast in realist terms." Rather than limiting his reach, however, Harrow argues that this obfuscation "gives Sony Labou Tansi access to a discourse whose multifaceted features lend his protest far greater force than would be the case had his work remained circumscribed by the narrow bounds of realism." His unwillingness to be direct, therefore, is its own site of rebellion against another oppressive force.

SOURCES

Datta, Ronjon Paul, and Laura MacDonald. "Time for Zombies: Sacrifice and the Structural Phenomenology of Capitalist Futures." *Race, Oppression and the Zombie*. Ed. Christopher Moreman and Cory Rushton. Jefferson: McFarland, 2011. 77–104. Print.

Harrow, Kenneth. *Thresholds of Change in African Literature: The Emergence of a Tradition*. Portsmouth: Heinemann, 1994. Print.

Labou Tansi, Sony. *Parentheses of Blood*. Trans. Lorraine Alexander Veach. New York: Ubu Repertory Theater, 1986. Print.

Ngate, Jonathan. *Francophone African Fiction: Reading a Literary Tradition*. Trenton: Africa World, 1988. Print.

Sartre, Jean-Paul. *Colonialism and Neocolonialism*. Trans. Azzedine Haddour, Steve Brewer, and Terry McWilliams. London: Routledge, 2006. Print.

Thomas, Dominic. *Nation-Building, Propaganda, and Literature in Francophone Africa*. Bloomington: Indiana UP, 2002. *eBrary*. Web. 12 Oct. 2011.

FURTHER READING

Devésa, Jean-Michel. *Sony Labou Tansi: écrivain de la honte et des rives magiques du Kongo*. Paris: L'Harmattan, 1996. Print.

Gyasi, Kwaku Addae. *The Francophone African Text: Translation and the Postcolonial Experience*. Francophone Cultures and Literatures. New York: P. Lang, 2006. Print.

Kadima-Nzuji, Mukala, Abel Kouvouama, and Paul Kibangou. *Sony Labou Tansi, ou, la quête permanente du sens*. Paris: L'Harmattan, 1997. Print.

Mbanga., Anatole. *Les procédés de création dans l'oeuvre de Sony Labou Tansi.: systèmes d'interactions dans l'écriture*. Paris: L'Harmattan, 1996. Print.

Mbembé, J. A. *On the Postcolony*. Trans. A. M. Berrett, Murray Last, Janet Roitman, and Steven Rendall. Berkeley: U of California P, 2001. Print.

Yewah, Emmanuel. "Congolese Playwrights as Cultural Revisionists." *The Performance Arts in Africa*. Ed. Frances Harding. London: Routledge, 2002. 208–21. Print.

Sara Taylor

SCATTERED CRUMBS

Muhsin Al-Ramli

OVERVIEW

In *Scattered Crumbs* (2000) Muhsin Al-Ramli satirizes the rise of Saddam Hussein and Iraqi militarism during the Iran-Iraq War (1980–88) by documenting the sad, and at times absurd, history of an impoverished Iraqi family split apart by the war and by its various reactions to the dictator. Referred to only as "the Leader" and kept at the fringes of the novel, the figure of Hussein nevertheless casts a shadow over all aspects of family life and determines the fate of each of the eight children. At the heart of the novel is the clash between Ijayel, the patriarch and a foolish patriot who judges his children solely by the degree of their loyalty to the despot, and Qasim, his eldest son, an artist who is executed for desertion. On one hand, Al-Ramli leaves the father-son tragedy by chronicling the unlikely rise of Saadi, the village idiot and the other deserter in the family, to national fame by shamelessly offering sexual favors to the members of the Leader's inner circle. On the other hand, Al-Ramli shows the level of resentment a figure like Hussein breeds through the story of Warda, the beautiful but daft sister who marries a man only because he has dedicated his life to assassinating the Leader.

The novel opens when the unnamed narrator, an ex-patriot living in Spain, returns to Iraq to search for Mahmoud, a cousin who, like the narrator years before, "slunk away to the North one night" without telling anyone where he was going. Overcome by the beauty of the Iraqi landscape, the narrator soon forgets the object of his quest and focuses instead on the people who stayed home—at first the entire community but eventually just Mahmoud's seven siblings and their parents. The narrator also modifies his weary, nostalgic tone and reminds himself that sad stories like the one he originally seeks to tell "become monotonous in Iraq because of their abundance."

Disregarding Mahmoud, the narrator begins to reminisce about how local villagers discuss local events and gossip throughout the day until he recalls a tale about his uncle Ijayel's mishap with a hedgehog. According to the legend a hedgehog shot one of its needles into young Ijayel's neck after he attempted to pet it. When she saw the thin stream of blood flowing from the wound, Ijayel's frantic mother begged him for an explanation, but, so the story goes, the boy could only bah like a sheep. By way of this tragicomic anecdote Al-Ramli signals the beginning of a story about living in a volatile, unpredictable country among people tied to the land, a tale the narrator finds more compelling than the story of a fellow exile nobody at home even remembers.

HISTORICAL AND LITERARY CONTEXT

Like other works by Iraqi writers who experienced Hussein's rule, *Scattered Crumbs* objects to Hussein's ruthless governance and laments the fear he inspired in average Iraqi citizens. However, Al-Ramli is more circumspect in his criticism of the former president than many of his contemporaries, and his work is more given to humor. Mahmoud Saeed's *Saddam City*, for example, chronicles the trials of Mustafa Ali Noman, a teacher in Baghdad who is arrested without explanation and brutally tortured in each of the prisons where he is incarcerated. Likewise, in *I'jaam* Sinan Antoon's protagonist languishes in jail for the better part of the novel. Al-Ramli, on the other hand, treats jail comically, lampooning Hussein's henchman to show their vapidity and hypocrisy rather than exposing their brutality. When the authorities imprison Ijayel's son Saadi, the lecherous young man happily offers himself to all of the guards and inmates interested in having sex with him. Word of Saadi's exploits soon reaches the warden, who transfers Saadi to a cell closer to his office, buys him a wardrobe of beautiful dresses, and visits him nightly through a secret tunnel he has constructed.

Rather than continuously recreating Hussein's violence, Al-Ramli makes only one reference to his heavy-handed tactics. As he meditates on the bank of the Tigris River, Qasim recalls a story he has heard about how the Leader casually declared war on Iran before his hand-picked representatives in parliament. According to the story, when he asked if anyone objected, the Leader was surprised to see one of the representatives raise his hand. Shortly after he left the room ostensibly to discuss the matter privately with the official, the rest of the assembly heard a gunshot. The Leader then returned and asked if anyone else objected. Aside from this moment, the reader senses the reach of the Leader's power solely by the way he influences the choices that Ijayel and his children make in response to the war with Iran.

Initiating the Iran-Iraq War on September 22, 1980, Hussein claimed that he was acting in response

✛ *Key Facts*

Conflict:
Iran-Iraq War

Time Period:
Late 20th Century

Genre:
Novel

to alleged Iranian attacks on Iraq's eastern border. Many historians, however, maintain that Hussein invaded Iran because he saw the internal turmoil there as an opportunity for Iraq to displace Iran as the preeminent power in the Persian Gulf. Iran's Islamic Revolution had lasted from October 1977, when protestors began demonstrating against reigning monarch Shah Mohammad Reza Palavi, until April 1, 1979, when Ayotallah Ruhollah Khomeini formally assumed control after the Shah's departure the previous January. Iraqi forces made limited advances into Iran during the opening months of the war, but Iran quickly halted their progress and by 1982 had regained control of all lost territory. Hussein asked for a cease-fire in June 1982, but Khomeini refused. The fighting continued for six more years until the two sides agreed to a cease-fire on August 20, 1988, when all original borders were restored. It is estimated that during the eight years of the war a total of 1.3 million soldiers and civilians were killed or wounded and that each

side lost up to the equivalent of $500 billion. In *Scattered Crumbs* Al-Ramli mentions only two casualties: the narrator's father, who died in the second year of the war, and Ijayel's most patriotic son, Abdul-Wahid, who is killed within days after he arrives at the front.

THEMES AND STYLE

Al-Ramli uses the conflict between Ijayel and his eldest son, Qasim, to mock the uncritical loyalty of Iraqis who continued to trust Hussein blindly even as the Iran-Iraq War dragged on. Throughout the text Qasim is the voice of well-considered dissent, while Ijayel represents obtuse patriotism. Al-Ramli underscores the silliness of Ijayel's views with the language the old man uses to compliment everyone and everything. Those people and objects that are agreeable to him Ijayel calls "nationon," a mispronunciation of the English word "national" that Ijayel has stubbornly carried with him from his youth, despite having been corrected many times. For example, Ijayel calls his kerosene space heater "nationon." However, when he discovers that Qasim and Saadi have left their military posts, he says, "They are not nationon at all because they deserted the army just when the war heated up!"

In contrast, throughout the dispute with his father Qasim's words and actions are more measured and likely represent something closer to Al-Ramli's assessment of Hussein and the war. Ijayel's quarrel with Qasim comes to a head when Qasim refuses to paint a picture of the Leader for Ijayel's living room wall. By way of explanation, Qasim tells one of his siblings, "Father thinks that the land is more important than the people, and I think the reverse, and the Leader takes advantage of this difference by pitting us against each other without giving a damn about the land or the people." Eventually, Qasim compromises and instead of drawing a picture of the leader offers his father a stylized painting of Iraq in which Qasim has drawn a green heart around the shape of Iraq, which he has colored red. The Tigris and Euphrates rivers are white.

According to Harold Braswell, in a review of the novel that appeared in *New Republic Online,* "The painting showcases Qasim's love for his country, not its head of state. It also reveals an appreciation for the tragic dimension of Iraqi life: The red of the country represents the country's blood, and the white Tigris and Euphrates are filled with the country's tears. Around them, the green heart rises as a symbol of transcendental love." After he dies, Qasim's sister Warda draws a black arrow through the heart, filling the last of the four colors of the Iraqi flag (red, green, white, and black) into the picture. Thus Qasim's sincere love of country stands against the folly of Ijayel's patriotism. However, as Braswell notes, this haunting image also indicates that the Leader's destruction of the family "is relentless and complete; the 'scattered crumbs' of the title are, in the end, those citizens who have been pulverized by the Leader's regime."

The heart with the arrow passing through it also recalls an image from the opening portion of the novel when Al-Ramli documents Warda's first romantic encounter in a tragicomic tale rife with sexual overtones. The story begins with a young Kurd who sprays the village homes with a milky white poison to kill rodents. Whenever he sees an attractive girl the boy sprays a heart with an arrow on her home. He's so taken with Warda that he inadvertently fills her milk bucket with the substance, which she feeds to the cow, accidentally killing the animal and causing her mother immeasurable grief. Just as the hedgehog from Ijayel's mishap can be interpreted as the politically volatile Iraq, the slain cow could be seen to represent a country deprived of the chance to nourish its people.

CRITICAL DISCUSSION

Reviewers agree that *Scattered Crumbs* addresses a need among Western readers for more stories about Iraq that ignore American political concerns and instead shed light on daily life there. Writing for the *Chronicle of Higher Education*, Scott McLemee calls *Scattered Crumbs* a "lyrical, comic, and bitterly satirical" novel that wisely keeps Hussein on its periphery and focuses instead on "members of a rural clan" who are "absorbed in the local politics of clashing temperaments." Braswell claims that *Scattered Crumbs* "provides at least a first step towards a greater understanding of daily life in Iraq" and predicts that the novel "will certainly add some much needed complexity to our politically suffocated image of the Iraqi people." Likewise, in a review posted in *Al Jadid*, a U.S.-based magazine that focuses on Arab arts and culture, Lynn Rogers argues that *Scattered Crumbs* documents "a hilarious family history" and that the novel "confirms the vibrancy of contemporary Arabic culture and testifies to the comprehensive need for more Arabic translations."

In "Under Western Eyes," an article from 2006 that appeared in the *New York Times Book Review*, Rachel Donadio highlights the need for more English translations of Arabic literature by noting the challenges that Western writers face when they attempt to write about terrorism from the Arab perspective. Donadio considers the limitations of John Updike's *Terrorist*, a novel about an American-born Arab teenager who is seduced by radical Islam ideology, and Martin Amis's "The Last Days of Muhammad Atta," a fictional account of how the man who crashed American Airlines Flight 11 into the North Tower of the World Trade Center spent the days leading up to the attack. Of Amis and Updike, Donadio observes that "a vast cultural and linguistic divide separates them from their chosen subjects." Both writers, she contends, focus on terrorist cells and the end result of their plans but offer little insight into the circumstances that directed their protagonists toward violence. In the article Donadio quotes Algerian novelist Yasmina Khadra, who says, "It's hard for a Westerner to get to the bottom of things. He's forced to dwell on the networks, the operations and motivations of terrorist organizations and to ignore the essential: the mentality, the fundamentalist philosophy."

On the other hand, Donadio claims that novels such as Al-Ramli's *Scattered Crumbs* and Hoda Barakat's *Disciples of Passion* (1993) examine, firsthand, the sexual repression and economic hardship that make people vulnerable to fundamentalist doctrine. Donadio quotes Arabic translator Marilyn Booth, who says that Arabic writers such as Al-Ramli and Barakat "are dealing with the conditions and situations that lead young people to consider violent reactions." Because such writers focus on the process, their work, unlike that of Western writers, is not likely "to resemble a front-page news story in an American newspaper." Donadio closes by quoting Updike, who admits that Western writers are "all a little slow maybe to wrap our minds around this fundamental new factor in American life, in Western life really. These are deep waters that have us all kind of puzzling."

SOURCES

Al-Ramli, Muhsin. *Scattered Crumbs*. Trans. Yasmeen S. Hanoosh. Fayettville: U of Arkansas P, 2003. Print.

Braswell, Harold. "Family Matters." Rev. of *Scattered Crumbs*, by Muhsin Al-Ramli. *New Republic Online* 23 Sept. 2004. Web. 31 Oct. 2011.

Donadio, Rachel. "Under Western Eyes." *New York Times Book Review* 11 June 2006: 35(L). *Literature Resource Center*. Web. 31 Oct. 2011.

McLemee, Scott. "An Undistorted View of Iraqi Misery; Recalling the Golden Age of Arabic Intellectual Life." *The Chronicle of Higher Education* 49.48 (2003). *Gale Biography in Context*. Web. 31 Oct. 2011.

Rogers, Lynne. "A Small Feast: Iraqi Satire Explores Lost Homeland." *Al Jadid* 11.52 (2004). Web. 31 Oct. 2011.

FURTHER READING

Blasim, Hassan. *The Madman of Freedom Square*. Trans. Jonathan Wright. Print.

Brands, Hal. "Why Did Saddam Invade Iran? New Evidence on Motives, Complexity, and the Israel Factor." *Journal of Military History* 75.3 (2011): 861+. *EBSCO*. Web. 31 Oct. 2011.

Donovan, Jerome. *The Iran-Iraq War: Antecedents and Conflict Escalation*. Abington: Routledge, 2011. Print.

Hiro, Dilip. *The Longest War: The Iran-Iraq Military Conflict*. New York: Routledge, 1991. Print.

Karsh, Efraim. *The Iran-Iraq War 1980–1988*. Colchester: Osprey, 2002. Print.

Mustafa, Skakir, ed. *Contemporary Iraqi Fiction: An Anthology*. Trans. Mustafa. Syracuse: Syracuse UP, 2008. Print.

Rajaee, Farhang, ed. *The Iran-Iraq War: The Politics of Aggression*. Darby: Diane, 1993. Print.

Takeyh, Ray. "The Iran-Iraq War: A Reassessment." *Middle East Journal* 64.3 (2010): 365+. *EBSCO*. Web. 31 Oct. 2011.

Joseph Campana

SIEGE OF KRISHNAPUR

James Gordon Farrell

✣ *Key Facts*

Conflict:
Indian Mutiny

Time Period:
Mid-19th Century

Genre:
Novel

Award:
Booker Prize, 1973

OVERVIEW

The Siege of Krishnapur is the second novel in J. G. Farrell's satirical Empire Trilogy. Based on the Siege of Lucknow in the Indian Mutiny of 1857, *The Siege of Krishnapur* subverts the standard themes and structure of the genre known as the mutiny novel, thus creating a serious critique of empire within a satirical framework.

In the months before the (fictional) Indian Mutiny, Krishnapur's highest ranking British official, Mr. Hopkins, foresees the possibility of violence and makes preparation for a possible siege, despite the laughter of the British community. When the mutiny occurs, the British community is besieged in the official Residency, an elegant home designed for entertaining rather than for defense. They defend themselves against attack, using household items as weapons when they run out of ammunition. (A metal bust of Shakespeare proves to be a particularly effective, and symbolic, missile.) They cope with inadequate supplies, lack of sanitation, a cholera epidemic, and the gradual disintegration of both the existing social order and their personal beliefs. After three months of confinement, the besieged garrison is so focused on survival that the people do not realize they have been rescued when the British army relieves the siege.

The British of Krishnapur survive, but their relationship with India does not. As Hopkins observes, "India itself was now a different place; the fiction of happy natives being led forward along the road to civilization could no longer be sustained."

Published in 1973, Farrell's novel looked at the empire with a satirical eye at a time when the British public had begun to look back at its Indian empire with nostalgia. This sentimental reconsideration of Britain's imperial past produced a market for novels, picture books, and films about the days of the Raj, beginning with Mark Bence-Jones's *Palaces of the Raj* (1973) and reaching its height in 1984 with the wildly popular television miniseries based on Paul Scott's *Raj Quartet*.

At the time of his death, Farrell was writing a second novel dealing with British India, *The Hill Station*, set in the British hill station of Simla in the 1880s. Because the novel's protagonist plays a role in *The Siege of Krishnapur*, *The Hill Station* is often discussed as a sequel to the earlier novel. The later work was published in a fragmentary form in conjunction with Farrell's diaries as *The Hill Station: An Unfinished Novel, and an Indian Diary* in 1981.

HISTORICAL AND LITERARY CONTEXT

The Siege of Lucknow is one of the best-known incidents of the Indian Mutiny of 1857. In 1856 the British government had seized the principality of Oudh on the grounds that the government was corrupt and the king lazy and capricious. The people of Oudh deeply resented the annexation of the territory. Their resentment had implications for the East India Company's army, which employed forty thousand high-caste sepoys (Indian soldiers) from Oudh. When the sepoys at the garrison at Meerut mutinied on May 10, 1857, the three regiments stationed in Oudh soon followed.

At the end of June, Sir Henry Lawrence, the newly appointed chief commissioner of Oudh, received word that the mutineers were gathering north of Lucknow, the region's capital. He ordered the entire European and Christian population of Lucknow into the British Residency, which he had fortified and provisioned with food and ammunition. Lawrence was killed early in the siege, and Colonel John Inglis took command. Roughly 1,700 men, including civilian volunteers and 500 or 600 Indian sepoys, defended the Residency, where more than 1,200 noncombatants had taken refuge, against an Indian army estimated at eight thousand.

On September 25 a small British force headed by Major Generals Sir James Outram and Sir Henry Havelock stormed their way through Lucknow's attackers to the Residency, only to be besieged in turn. Lucknow remained under siege until mid-November, when a column under the command of General Colin Campbell relieved the siege and evacuated the Residency. The British were not able to reoccupy Lucknow until March 1858.

The Indian Mutiny was a popular subject of British fiction from 1859 through the first quarter of the twentieth century. The subject quickly developed into a subgenre, with clearly defined conventions of adventure and romance set against the background of the familiar events of the mutiny. Known as mutiny novels, they often dealt with besieged garrisons in which British soldiers defended civilians, including women

and children, against numerically superior Indian forces. The best known of these novels today is Flora Annie Steel's *On the Face of the Waters*, which remained constantly in print from 1896 to Steel's death in 1929.

Typically these narratives closely follow the narrative arc of the historical events of the mutiny. They begin shortly before the revolt at Meerut, establishing a picture of "normal life" for the protagonists. They often use May 9 as the occasion for a festive event that is set in contrast to the violence on May 10. After a series of adventures, tribulations, and romances for the main characters, the novels end with the relief of the besieged by British troops, the reestablishment of British political and military control, and the engagement or marriage of the central couple.

The cast of characters typically includes a young imperial hero who is either an army officer or a civil servant, a beautiful young girl, and a visitor from England who is trapped by the violence. With the exception of loyal servants and an occasional villain based on Indian leaders of the mutiny, Indian characters are limited to an undifferentiated mass of rebels.

With a few exceptions, mutiny novels written after independence retain the basic formula. Their main characters, however, often oppose British policy in the years before the mutiny and anticipate Indian resentment and even violence.

THEMES AND STYLE

Looked at in terms of its plot, *The Siege of Krishnapur* is just another mutiny novel based on the siege of Lucknow. In fact, Farrell creates something quite different from this familiar material. As David Rubin describes the work in his book *After the Raj*, Farrell "breaks the stranglehold of the tradition by adopting it and, with cool intelligence, pushing it to extremes," creating a novel "that gathers together all the stereotypes and employs them brilliantly for a completely contrary purpose."

One way in which Farrell pushes the stereotypes is to expose the characters to the physical realities of what Ronald Binns, in *J. G. Farrell*, summarizes as "the condition of an isolated community caught up in the dramatic experience of being besieged." In addition to

Thomas Henry Kavanagh (1821–82) is disguised as a Sepoy so he can sneak through the city, retrieve the British relief forces, and lead them back to the beleaguered Garrison in the Residency during the Siege of Lucknow, which is also the setting of J. G. Farrell's satirical novel *The Siege of Krishnapur*. © THOMAS HENRY KAVANAGH VC BEING DISGUISED AS A NATIVE DURING THE INDIAN MUTINY AT THE SIEGE OF LUCKNOW, 9TH NOVEMBER 1857, C.1860 (OIL ON CANVAS), DESANGES, CHEVALIER LOUIS-WILLIAM (FL.1846–87) / NATIONAL ARMY MUSEUM, LONDON / THE BRIDGEMAN AR

THE EMPIRE TRILOGY

In an interview with George Brock in 1978 titled "Epitaph for Empire" Farrell says, "It seemed to me that the really interesting thing that's happened during my lifetime has been the decline of the British Empire." Together, the three satirical novels that make up his Empire Trilogy—*Troubles* (1970), *The Siege of Krishnapur* (1973), and *The Singapore Grip* (1978)—present a picture of that decline.

Like *The Siege of Krishnapur*, the other novels in the trilogy focus on times and places in which the British Empire is in crisis. *Troubles* is set in 1919, at the beginning of the civil war that led to the partition of Ireland. *The Singapore Grip* takes place during the fall of Singapore to the Japanese in 1942. The characters in *Troubles* are mostly elderly residents of the once-grand Majestic Hotel in Kilnalough who are aware of but insulated from the violence around them. The main character in *The Singapore Grip* is appalled to learn that his family fortune is based on the exploitation of the rubber industry.

Each novel is based on extensive historical research. Their combined effect, however, is a relationship to history that Keith M. Booker, in *Colonial Power, Colonial Texts*, describes as "complex, fragmentary and multiple."

heroism, his characters display greed, selfishness, and fear. The progress of romance, in particular, is accompanied by the progressive dirt and smells of life in cramped and insalubrious quarters.

Farrell uses Western knowledge as a way to describe the changing relationship between his British characters and India. Hopkins, the British collector, is inspired by his visit to the Crystal Palace exhibition of 1851, where he saw the latest achievements of Victorian science and culture. He believes that part of his mission in India is to expose Indians to Western civilization. Once besieged in the British compound in Krishnapur, he turns to his library for assistance, certain that his books will provide the knowledge he needs to withstand the siege. Eventually, however, Hopkins loses his faith in Britain's scientific and industrial progress as being applicable to India.

Farrell's romantic hero, George Fleury, represents a different aspect of Western civilization and a different approach to India. He is a hazy Pre-Raphaelite aesthete who is touring India with his sister. In addition to visiting his mother's grave, he has been "commissioned by the Court of Directors to compose a small volume describing the advances that civilization had made in India under the Company rule." Like Hopkins, Fleury is transformed by his experiences in the Mutiny; he abandons his Pre-Raphaelite ideals in favor of a new-found ability to deal with practical affairs. When the two characters meet by chance in England "one day in the seventies," Fleury believes in the Victorian notions of material progress that Hopkins has since disavowed.

Following the standard conventions of the mutiny novel, Fleury's ignorance of India is initially set in contrast to the collector's knowledge. As the novel progresses, however, both men come to the conclusion that they know little about India. Hopkins realizes that "there was a whole way of life of the people of India which he would never get to know and which was totally indifferent to him." Similarly, Fleury is confronted with "what a lot of Indian life was unavailable to the Englishman who came equipped with his own religion and habits."

Building on a solid base of journals, memoirs, and other documentary evidence related to the Indian Mutiny, Farrell plays with the style of the Victorian novel. He combines an omniscient narrator and referential asides to the works of Thackeray, Tennyson, and Matthew Arnold with what Rubin describes as "ironic distancing of the style tinged with affection, impartial in its view of everybody concerned, but tending to compassion rather than distaste." The result is summed up by Binns as a "pastiche Victorian novel, written from an ironic twentieth-century perspective."

CRITICAL DISCUSSION

The novels of Farrell's Empire Trilogy, including *The Siege of Krishnapur*, received favorable responses from both critics and readers when they were first published. His use of irony has been compared to that of E. M. Forster and John Fowles, while his sense of historical process has been compared to Sir Walter Scott. In "History and the Art of Fiction," A. V. Krishna Rao mourns Farrell's early death as the loss of what might have been "one of the greatest historical novelists that England has ever produced."

In the decade after his death, scholars found themselves troubled by both Farrell's subject matter and his style. Some treated the novel as a clever variation on the traditional mutiny adventure story, without reference to its ironic use of the genre's themes. Others were concerned by the absence of meaningful Indian characters. Since the 1990s, critical work on Farrell has focused on the uncomfortable relationship of his work to postcolonial fiction and postcolonial theory, a position John McLeod describes in "J. G. Farrell and Post-Imperial Fiction" as "too experimental to be realist, not innovative enough to be truly postmodern." *The Siege of Krishnapur* won the Booker Prize in 1973. It was one of the six finalists in the international Best of the Booker vote that marked the prize's fortieth anniversary in 2008.

SOURCES

Binns, Ronald. *J. G. Farrell*. London: Metheun, 1986. Print.

Booker, Keith M. *Colonial Power, Colonial Texts: India in the Modern British Novel*. Ann Arbor: U of Michigan P, 1997. Print.

Farrell, J. G. "Epitaph for Empire." Interview by George Brock. *Observer Magazine* 24 September 1978. 73+. Print.

————. *The Siege of Krishnapur*. New York: Carroll, 1997. Print.

McLeod, John. "J. G. Farrell and Post-Imperial Fiction." *J. G. Farrell: The Critical Grip*. Ed. Ralph J. Crane. Portland: Four Courts, 1999. Print.

Rao, A. V. Krishna. "History and the Art of Fiction: J. G. Farrell's Example: *The Siege of Krishnapur*." *Literary Criterion* 23:3 (1988) 38–48. Print.

Rubin, David. *After the Raj: British Novels of India since 1947*. Hanover: UP of New England, 1986. Print.

FURTHER READING

Chakravarty, Gautam. *The Indian Mutiny and the British Imagination*. New York: Cambridge UP, 2005. Print.

Crane, Ralph J., ed. *J. G. Farrell: The Critical Grip*. Portland: Four Courts, 1999. Print.

Crane, Ralph J., and Jennifer Livett. *Troubled Pleasures: The Fiction of J. G. Farrell*. Portland: Four Courts, 1997. Print.

Edwardes, Michael. *Battles of the Indian Mutiny*. London: Pan, 1970. Print.

Farrell, J. G. *The Hill Station: An Unfinished Novel, and an Indian Diary*. Ed. John Spurling. London: Weidenfeld, 1981. Print.

————. *J. G. Farrell in His Own Words: Selected Letters and Diaries*. Ed. Lavinia Greacen. Cork: Cork UP, 2009. Print.

————. *The Singapore Grip*. London: Weidenfeld, 1978. Print.

————. *Troubles*. London: Cape, 1970. Print.

Greacen, Lavinia. *J. G. Farrell: The Making of a Writer*. London: Bloomsbury, 1999. Print.

Hibbert, Christopher. *The Great Indian Mutiny: India 1857*. New York: Penguin, 1980. Print.

Morley, Peter. *Fictions of India: Narrative and Power*. Edinburgh: Edinburgh UP, 2000. Print.

Pamela Toler

SIMPLICIUS SIMPLICISSIMUS

Jakob Christoffel von Grimmelshausen

❖ *Key Facts*

Conflict:
Thirty Years' War

Time Period:
17th Century

Genre:
Novel

OVERVIEW

Simplicius Simplicissimus (1669) is the title most often used in English for *Der Abentheuerliche Simplicissimus Teutsch* (*The Adventurous German Simplicissimus*), a picaresque novel by Hans Jakob Christoffel von Grimmelshausen (c. 1621–76). Widely considered to be among the most important works of seventeenth-century German literature, *Simplicissimus* presents a vivid picture of life during the extensive and destructive European conflict known as the Thirty Years' War (1618–48).

The original subtitle provides an excellent summary of *Simplicissimus*: "The Description of the Life of a Peculiar Wanderer Named Melchior Sternfels von Fuchshaim, Including Where and in What Manner He Came into This World, What He Saw, Learned, Experienced and Put Up With Therein; Also Why He Voluntarily Left It." Although the narrative is related in the first person, each chapter begins with a description of what happens to the protagonist, who is referred to as "Simplicissimus" (a Latin word meaning "most simple, plain, or frank"). In the course of the novel's five books, he is orphaned and kidnapped; becomes a court jester, a soldier, a singer, a servant, and a con artist; participates in several battles; and romances a variety of women. At several pivotal points he encounters Olivier, a wicked character, and Herzbruder, the model of a good man. Simplicissimus eventually learns that he is not a lowborn peasant but the son of a noble hermit, and by the end of the novel he has decided to leave worldly things behind and retreat into a secluded life of spiritual reflection.

The combination of lively writing, clever storytelling, and relevance to recent events made *Simplicissimus* an immediate success. Grimmelshausen quickly wrote the *Continuatio*, an addition to the original story in which Simplicissimus leaves his hermitage, has several adventures, and is cast away on an island paradise, where he chooses to remain. Over the next decade Grimmelshausen produced a succession of so-called Simplician works, each of which take up characters and themes from the original novel. Though he was a prolific and popular writer in his own time, Grimmelshausen was little known by the early eighteenth century, and it was not until the later nineteenth century that literary scholars began to recognize *Simplicissimus* as both a masterpiece of world literature

and an invaluable account of conditions during the Thirty Years' War.

It was assumed at one time that the character Simplicissimus is a fictionalized version of Grimmelshausen, and there are some commonalities. Grimmelshausen was descended from the lower nobility, grew up in a small town, lost his parents at an early age, and was kidnapped as a teenager. He served in various armies and fought in several battles. However, Grimmelshausen's life also differed considerably from that of his famous character. He received a basic education in the local school and, after being abducted into the army, rose through a series of increasingly responsible positions, ending as a regimental secretary. He went on to become a mayor, an innkeeper, and the father of ten children.

Though largely self-educated, the author was well read, and *Simplicissimus* is by no means a naive account of Grimmelshausen's personal experiences. The novel draws on many literary influences, from Mateo Alemán's *Guzmán de Alfarache* (1599), an important example of the Spanish picaresque, to the pastoral novel *Arcadia* (1590) by the Elizabethan poet Sir Philip Sidney. Grimmelshausen's work has far outlasted his era, influencing modern German writers such as Thomas Mann, Bertolt Brecht, and Günter Grass.

HISTORICAL AND LITERARY CONTEXT

Although less familiar today than other world conflicts, the Thirty Years' War was a major turning point in European history. Most of the military action took place in what would later become Germany, and by the time hostilities concluded in 1648, the population of that country had been reduced by as much as one-quarter. Because the war was fought largely by undisciplined armies that depended for compensation or even survival on what they could plunder, many civilians were killed by marauding soldiers. In addition, a large number of deaths occurred owing to famine and disease.

Although the fighting began over religious disputes among Catholics and Protestants, it expanded to include a variety of economic, political, and dynastic issues, and almost every European country became involved at some point. Outcomes of the war, as determined through a series of treaties known collectively as

Claude Callot (1620–86) painted *The Hanging* in 1635 after an etching by Jacques Callot, who had created it as part of a series depicting the destruction of the Thirty Years' War. Oil on canvas. © THE ART GALLERY COLLECTION / ALAMY

the Peace of Westphalia, included the establishment of limited religious tolerance, increased independence for German territories, and a significant rearrangement of European power structures. In addition, the prolonged conflict brought about cultural changes that contributed to the Enlightenment and eventually to the rise of modernity.

Dreadful conditions created by the war were described at the time in a wide variety of written materials, and according to John Theibault's essay "The Rhetoric of Death and Destruction in the Thirty Years War," this informal documentation produced an "image of death and destruction [that] has defined the social history of the Thirty Years War to a greater extent than almost any other event in early modern European history." Modern scholars have debated the degree to which contemporaneous accounts may have been exaggerated in the service of personal or political aims, and there is some disagreement about the amount of destruction and suffering that actually occurred during the conflict.

There is ample evidence, however, that civil society was severely disrupted in many areas and that some soldiers engaged in the kinds of amoral behavior depicted in *Simplicissimus* and described in other documents. R. G. Asch contends in "'Wo der soldat hinkömbt, da ist alles sein': Military Violence and Atrocities in the Thirty Years' War Re-examined" that the brutality exhibited by some soldiers during the fighting resulted not only from practical issues, such as the lack of rules and the competition for resources, but also from a tendency for soldiers—many of whom

were effectively mercenaries—to establish status by harsh treatment of civilians. One consequence of the war seems to have been a shift away from the use of mercenaries and toward the development of regular armies.

THEMES AND STYLE

Despite its sometimes unsparing depiction of wartime mayhem, *Simplicissimus* is for the most part a spirited, imaginative, and often ribald adventure. This marriage of social realism and colorful mischief is characteristic of the picaresque novel. The form is described by Ulrich Wicks in *Dictionary of Literary Themes and Motifs* as an "episodic narrative in which an economic and social outsider relates, from birth to a point of moral/spiritual conversion (either overt or implied), the trick-or-be-tricked techniques necessary for physical, emotional, social, and moral survival in a [hostile] world." In fact, *Simplicissimus* is considered to be a definitive example of the picaresque, fitting the model in almost every respect.

Like most picaresque works, the novel is told in the first person, incorporates a variety of familiar materials (ranging from folk tales to moral discourses), contrasts the upper and lower classes, includes a good deal of bawdiness, and satirizes the age in which it was written. The protagonist, often referred to as a *picaro*, must live by his wits in a world that is for some reason disordered, and as his fortunes rise and fall he ends up in improbable places and situations.

At the same time, *Simplicissimus* differs from the typical picaresque in several ways. First, it depicts

SIMPLICISSIMUS LIVES ON

Although German baroque literature is not considered a major source of creative ideas in the modern world, *Simplicius Simplicissimus* has been the inspiration for a surprising variety of artistic works. Over the last 150 years Grimmelshausen's masterpiece has been reincarnated—or at least referenced—as follows:

- 1881—*Simplicius* the etchings, a suite of four works by the German symbolist artist Max Klinger that depict Grimmelshausen's famed character in different scenes.

- 1887—*Simplicius* the operetta, by composer Johann Strauss II and librettist Victor Léon.

- 1896—*Simplicius Simplicissimus* the satirical magazine, published weekly or biweekly in Germany until 1967.

- 1935—*Simplicius Simplicissimus* the antiwar, anti-Nazi chamber opera by Karl Amadeus Hartmann.

- 1961—*Simplicius Simplicissimus* the movie, directed by Hans Harleb.

- 1975—*Abenteuerlicher Simplizissimus* the next movie, directed by Fritz Umgelter.

- 1999—*Simplicius* the Swiss movie, directed by Thomas Grimm.

- 2010—*Simplicius Simplicissimus* the WordPress Website template created by themeforest, appropriately offering "unlimited combinations of basic elements designed for universal application."

Hartmann's opera is especially noteworthy. Not long after Hitler came to power, the young German expressionist began work on a kind of musical warning to his countrymen, even though he knew it would not be heard. The opera was finally performed for the first time in 1949 and has gradually claimed a place in the modernist repertoire. In 2007 a production by the Stuttgart State Opera was made available on DVD. Though based on Grimmelshausen's novel, Hartmann's work retains none of the picaresque elements, focusing relentlessly on the terrible consequences of war.

extreme conditions—created by a prolonged and violent war—that go well beyond the usual level of disorder confronted by the picaro. The world around Simplicissimus is marked not merely by social dysfunction but by wanton cruelty, catastrophic devastation, and rampant moral decay. Second, unlike most picaros, Simplicissimus focuses not just on personal safety, material acquisition, or romantic conquest but also on his own spiritual nature. Third, the novel not only exposes conditions of poverty and inequity using satire, but also adds a level of reflection on historical events and social conditions. Writing two decades after the end of the Thirty Years' War, Grimmelshausen was in a position to understand both the true extent of the suffering endured by Germany's peasants and the continuing consequences of the conflict.

Simplicissimus is recognized by literary scholars as a complex and inventive work that defies simple genre classifications and incorporates a wide variety of themes and styles. As Lynne Tatlock observes in *Seventeenth Century German Prose*, the narrative "is now farcical, now allegorical, now picaresque, now encyclopedic, now satirical, now chiliastic." Although the accumulation of these effects may seem on the surface to be a matter of entertainment, there is also evidence that Grimmelshausen meant these varied layers to carry a deeper message as well.

One key to understanding the book's unifying theme is found in the so-called phoenix copper, an engraving that served as its original frontispiece. The image depicts a chimeric creature (part human, part bird, part goat, part fish) holding an open book and surrounded by symbols (a crown, a fool's cap, dice, a sword, a cannon, a ship, and so on) that relate to episodes in the novel. Scholars have speculated that the illustration was intended as a substitute for the type of introduction common to books of the time, which guided the reader's interpretation of the work. Beneath the image on the frontispiece of *Simplicissimus* is a poem that begins "I was born out of fire like the Phoenix," speaks of many journeys, and ends by explaining that the tale has been set down in a book "so that the reader may, like myself, avoid folly and live in peace." While this inscription undoubtedly suggests a moral and spiritual dimension of the novel, it may also refer to the desire for peace that was often expressed during the Thirty Years' War.

CRITICAL DISCUSSION

In a 1948 survey titled "*Simplicissimus* and the Literary Historians," Carl Hammer summarizes several centuries of critical attention this way:

> After brief popularity, *Simplicissimus* was lost to view in the early stages of the Enlightenment and not rediscovered until the latter half of the eighteenth century, at which time it met with limited favor. The positivistic literary historians of the nineteenth century, while esteeming it rather highly, nevertheless treated it as a unique phenomenon standing apart from all contemporaneous writings. To twentieth century criticism, which considers Grimmelshausen's novel in the light of the whole *Geistesgeschichte* [spirit of the age] of that day, it has been revealed as the crowning achievement of Baroque literature in Germany.

In the early twentieth century, interest in *Simplicissimus* was stimulated and shaped by the two world wars, both of which brought new attention to Germany's war literature. Since that time scholars have undertaken fresh approaches to the novel, often adopting literary rather than historical perspectives. For example, there have been explorations of its relationship to the bildungsroman, or novel of self-discovery, and Arnold L. Weinstein has discussed *Simplicissimus* in terms of the emerging self in fictive autobiography. Commentaries concentrating on Grimmelshausen's use of literary motifs include Ewa M. Thompson's comparison of the character Simplicissimus with the archetype of the fool in Russian literature and Anne Leblans's analysis of carnivalesque elements, such as role reversal and the suspension of rules. Jeffrey Ashcroft has provided a detailed consideration of the emblems and imagery that function to expand the novel's field of meaning.

Although newer studies have not focused on *Simplicissimus* in terms of the literature of war, textual analysis is contributing insight into Grimmelshausen's use of war in the novel. As Monique Rinere points out in *Transformations of the German Novel: Simplicissimus in Eighteenth-Century Adaptations*, "Only thirteen of the 139 chapters [in *Simplicissimus*] refer to people, places, objects or events relating to war," and of the thirteen, only two mention particulars. By contrast, an anonymous 1756 adaptation of *Simplicissimus* mentions soldiers, armies, weapons, and other aspects of war in nearly half of its chapter headings. Such shifts in emphasis reveal the extent to which war can be seen in the book as an allegorical element, rather than as a dramatic device. For Grimmelshausen, Rinere suggests, the Thirty Years' War was a symbol of the *Verkehrtheit der Welt* (craziness of the world), but for his later adapters, "the battles and war-torn landscapes of the last century's war" were little more than "a credible and vivid historical setting."

SOURCES

Asch, R. G. "'Wo der soldat hinkömbt, da ist alles sein': Military Violence and Atrocities in the Thirty Years' War Re-examined." *German History* 18 (2000): 291–309. Print.

Ashcroft, Jeffrey. "Ad Astra Volandum: Emblems and Imagery in Grimmelshausen's *Simplicissimus*." *Modern Language Review* 68.4 (1973): 843–62. Print.

Hammer, Carl. "*Simplicissimus* and the Literary Historians." *Monatshefte* 40.8 (1948): 457–64. Print.

Leblans, Anne. "Grimmelshausen and the Carnivalesque: The Polarization of Courtly and Popular Carnival in *Der Abenteuerliche Simplicissimus*." *MLN* 105.3 (1990): 494–511. Print.

Rinere, Monique. *Transformations of the German Novel: Simplicissimus in Eighteenth-Century Adaptations*. Oxford: Lang, 2009. Print.

Tatlock, Lynne. *Seventeenth Century German Prose*. New York: Continuum, 1993. Print.

Theibault, John. "The Rhetoric of Death and Destruction in the Thirty Years War." *Journal of Social History* 27.2 (1993): 271–90. Print.

Thompson, Ewa M. "The Archetype of the Fool in Russian Literature." *Canadian Slavonic Papers/Revue Canadienne des Slavistes* 15.3 (1973): 245–73. Print.

Weinstein, Arnold L. *Fictions of the Self, 1550–1800*. Princeton: Princeton UP, 1981. Print.

Wicks, Ulrich. "Picaresque." *Dictionary of Literary Themes and Motifs*. Ed. Jean-Charles Seigneuret. New York: Greenwood, 1988. Print.

FURTHER READING

Bjornson, Richard. *The Picaresque Hero in European Fiction*. Madison: U of Wisconsin P, 1977. Print.

Black, Jeremy. *European Warfare, 1494–1660*. London: Routledge, 2002. Print.

Gillespie, Gerald. "From Duplicitous Delinquent to Superlative Simpleton: *Simplicissimus* and the German Baroque." *The Picaresque: A Symposium on the Rogue's Tale*. Ed. Carmen Benito-Vessels and Michael Zappala. Newark: U of Delaware P, 1994. 107–22. Print.

Helfferich, Tryntje. *The Thirty Years War: A Documentary History*. Indianapolis: Hackett, 2009. Print.

Menhennet, Alan. *Grimmelshausen the Storyteller: A Study of the "Simplician" Novels*. Columbia: Camden, 1997. Print.

Metzger, Michael, and Erika Metzger. "The Thirty Years War and its Impact on Literature." *German Baroque Literature: The European Perspective*. Ed. Gerhard Hoffmeiser. New York: Ungar, 1983. 38–51. Print.

Mortimer, Geoff. *Eyewitness Accounts of the Thirty Years War, 1618–48*. Houndmills: Palgrave, 2002. Print.

Otto, Karl F. *A Companion to the Works of Grimmelshausen*. Rochester: Camden, 2003. Print.

Wagener, Hans. *The German Baroque Novel*. New York: Twayne, 1973. Print.

Wilson, Peter H. *The Thirty Years War: Europe's Tragedy*. Cambridge: Belknap, 2009. Print.

MEDIA ADAPTATION

Simplicius Simplicissimus. Dir. Hans Hartleb. Perf. Ingeborg Bremert. Norddeutscher Rundfunk, 1961. Television.

Cynthia Giles

SLAUGHTERHOUSE-FIVE
or, The Children's Crusade: A Duty-Dance with Death
Kurt Vonnegut Jr.

❖ *Key Facts*

Conflict:
World War II;
Vietnam War

Time Period:
Mid-20th Century

Genre:
Novel

Awards:
Nebula Award
nomination, 1969;
Hugo Award nomination,
1970

OVERVIEW

Slaughterhouse-Five; or, The Children's Crusade: A Duty-Dance with Death is experimental writer Kurt Vonnegut's sixth and perhaps best-known novel. Published in 1969, the book describes events that took place during World War II and at the same time alludes to the Vietnam War, which was generating increasing protest in the United States. Vonnegut draws parallels between these two major twentieth-century military conflicts to critique war and human brutality more generally. Based on his own experiences as an infantryman during World War II, the novel took Vonnegut twenty years to write; he attributed this to the difficulty of finding language to communicate the enormous violence he had witnessed and the trauma he had suffered.

Slaughterhouse-Five is the story of Billy Pilgrim, an optometrist from Indiana who is drafted into military service and taken prisoner by the German army. Imprisoned in a former slaughterhouse in Dresden, he is one of very few people sheltered from the Allied bombs that destroy the city. As a survivor, Billy struggles to find a refuge from the guilt that constantly plagues him. He claims to have been abducted by a flying saucer from the planet Tralfamadore and displayed in a zoo alongside a movie star named Montana Wildhack. Billy henceforth experiences the sensation of being "unstuck in time," living his life out of sequence and flashing from one moment to another in his past, present, and future. The novel's nontraditional structure mirrors this experience, moving back and forth through time and shifting abruptly between settings.

The novel is noted for the complexity of its thematic concerns; its mix of social satire, black humor, autobiography, and moral philosophy; and its powerful antiwar message. It draws on techniques of science fiction to address ethical and formal questions regarding the psychological effects of war on soldiers and violence in modern culture. It also employs tactics of metafiction, self-consciously displaying its own fictionality.

Set in the past and looking toward the future, *Slaughterhouse-Five* holds a unique place in the canon of war literature. It is most closely allied with Joseph Heller's novel *Catch-22* (1961), a satirical critique of World War II. Vonnegut's novel encourages readers to reconsider the branding of World War II as the "last just war" and espouses the growing pacifist movement of the 1960s, a movement that Vonnegut himself openly supported.

HISTORICAL AND LITERARY CONTEXT

World War II, a global military conflict between the Axis powers (Germany, Italy, and Japan) and the Allies (Britain, France, the Soviet Union, the United States, and China), lasted from 1939 to 1945. As the war in Europe moved toward its conclusion in the early months of 1945, Allied forces sought to launch an air offensive that would be substantial enough to interrupt the movement of German troops and to lower German morale. The Allies eventually settled on the city of Dresden as their target. Dresden was an important cultural center, and the Allies later cited intelligence suggesting that it was a major site of military manufacturing. Between February 13 and 15, 1945, the U.S. Army Air Force and the British Royal Air Force conducted a series of coordinated bombing raids, dropping more than three thousand tons of high explosive and incendiary bombs on the city, which was filled with German refugees fleeing from the advancing Soviet army. The bombing ignited a firestorm that wiped out a fifteen-square-mile swath of Dresden. *Slaughterhouse-Five* draws on Vonnegut's experiences as a prisoner of war in Dresden, where, like Billy, he witnessed the city's destruction during the raids. The book describes the bombing of Dresden as the "greatest massacre in human history"; it reduced the city to a jagged ruin that Vonnegut likens to the surface of the moon. It is unclear how many people died, but estimates range from 18,000 to more than 135,000.

The destruction of Dresden is one of the most controversial military actions of World War II, second only to the dropping of atomic bombs on Hiroshima and Nagasaki, Japan. The Allies' disregard for civilian lives in Dresden reflects the nature of World War II combat more generally. The conflict is often referred to as a "total war" because both sides marshaled all available resources to overwhelm strategic targets in the enemies' homelands. Germany had employed a similar strategy in the 1942 bombings of London, known collectively as the Blitz. The justification for the Dresden bombing has been the focus of greater ethical scrutiny, however, because it was carried out when most experts felt that German surrender was already imminent. The details of the raid, including classified documents assessing its objectives and military effectiveness, were not officially released until 1978. Vonnegut's novel narrates his frustrated attempts to get information from the government about the bombing and openly questions the decision to keep the papers secret. Some historians and critics believe that the publication of *Slaughterhouse-Five* and the release of the film in 1972 were instrumental in the eventual release of the information.

Published at the height of the Vietnam War, *Slaughterhouse-Five* was one of the first major literary texts of the antiwar movements of the 1960s. In 1965 President Lyndon Johnson had authorized air strikes on North Vietnam and committed ground troops to help the South Vietnamese army defeat the Vietcong, communist troops attempting to overthrow the government of South Vietnam. The 1968 Tet offensive incited many Americans to massive protests against the war. Vonnegut's novel implicitly compares the incendiary bombs deployed in Dresden to napalm, the burning chemical used by the United States during the Vietnam War.

In *Slaughterhouse-Five*, Vonnegut builds on the satiric vision of Heller's *Catch-22*. Heller, a World War II veteran, was also deeply concerned with the social and psychological effects of witnessing atrocities, as well as with the struggle to convey his experiences and vision to a general public. Both novels deploy an absurdist style to critique the idea of necessary violence.

THEMES AND STYLE

In the semiautobiographical introduction to *Slaughterhouse-Five*, Vonnegut remarks that "there is nothing intelligent to say about a massacre." The novel's main theme is in its critique of war and the unnecessary deaths it causes, epitomized by the sheer number of innocent civilians who died in the Dresden bombings.

Slaughterhouse-Five is an example of metafiction—literature that takes the writing of fiction as a topic, revealing and examining its own processes. From the first line of the novel, "All of this happened, more or less," Vonnegut addresses questions of narrative truth. In a strategy typical of metafiction, the narrator draws attention to himself as the book's creator. At one point, referring to an American prisoner who shares a latrine with Billy, the narrator says, "That was I. That was me. That was the author of this book." Vonnegut also suggests that science fiction, with its abilities to convey both objective and subjective truth, to generate new ideas and visions, and to produce alternative narrative schemes, is the form best suited to describing modern life. One character in *Slaughterhouse-Five* remarks that, while Fyodor Dostoyevsky's *The Brothers*

In this still from the film adaptation of *Slaughterhouse-Five*, German guards force the captured Billy Pilgrim to pose for a photograph. © UNIVERSAL / THE KOBAL COLLECTION

Karamazov holds everything there is "to know about life," the nineteenth-century Russian realistic novel "isn't *enough* anymore." Because it does not attempt to mimic reality, science fiction provides an expanded imaginative space that, according to the narrator, can be "a big help" to traumatized veterans "trying to re-invent themselves and their universe."

Although Vonnegut did not consider himself a writer of science fiction, his novel reproduces some of the major characteristics of the genre. Space and time travel allow him to create the Tralfamadorians, who are two feet high and green and who live in four dimensions. They are able to experience all moments in time simultaneously. In addressing Billy's grief and guilt, they tell him that death is ephemeral, that "the dead person is in bad condition at that particular moment but that same person is just fine in plenty of other moments." Billy absorbs this lesson, but the novel ultimately satirizes it. The Tralfamadorian saying about death—"So it goes"—conveys death's irrelevance to existence. Throughout the course of the narrative, Vonnegut repeats the phrase after every death—whether of an individual person, a group of people, an animal, or an object—often reiterating it more than once on a single page. The effect of this repetition is to accentuate the omnipresence of death, especially in the war; it reminds the reader that, from the three-dimensional perspective of earthlings, death is central, signifying an ending.

One element of the Tralfamadorian point of view is that everything is known and nothing can

THE BOMBING OF DRESDEN

In *Slaughterhouse-Five*, Kurt Vonnegut brings to light one of the most devastating attacks by the Allied forces during World War II. In 1941 and 1942, the U.S. and British air forces began to use the strategy of area bombing—spreading bombs over large portions of German cities and towns with the intent of lowering morale among German citizens and thereby weakening the German armed forces. In February 1945, when the war in Europe was nearly over—Italy and Germany's other European allies had been defeated, and the Soviet armies were rapidly occupying the eastern portions of Germany—air marshal Arthur Harris engineered the bombing of the city of Dresden, which had been flourishing since the Middle Ages. Essentially untouched during the war, Dresden was home to thousands of refugees who had fled the Soviet troops. It was basically undefended by antiaircraft guns. On February 13, 14, and 15, 1945, under Harris's direction, hundreds of British and American planes dropped incendiary bombs containing highly combustible chemicals, including magnesium, phosphorus, and petroleum jelly (napalm), over large swaths of the city. The attack devastated Dresden and killed tens of thousands of its residents. As Vonnegut describes the event in his novel, the city and its inhabitants were essentially melted into the ground, leaving it nearly impossible to determine the exact number of fatalities. In the decades since the end of World War II, the military necessity of bombing Dresden has been much debated, and it is generally considered one of the more controversial decisions made by Allied commanders.

be changed; all beings are "bugs in amber." Billy remarks to a Tralfamadorian, "You sound to me as though you don't believe in free will." According to the Tralfamadorians, free will is an imagined construct particular to Earth. The novel appears to critique this distanced, cold conviction, promoting instead the human belief that free will is necessary to any kind of ethical action and that individuals can effect change. In this way Vonnegut implicitly supports the growing numbers of young men who in the 1960s were choosing to dodge the draft. Many debated whether the true patriot was the man who sacrificed for his country unconditionally or the one who stood up against an errant government in accordance with a higher moral code.

Aside from Vonnegut's introduction and conclusion, the narrative follows Billy's life as he experiences it, switching rapidly from one moment in time to another, from Earth to Tralfamadore and, most markedly, from World War II to scenes of his earlier and later civilian existence: "He has seen his birth and death many times, he says, and pays random visits to all the events in between." While Billy himself is convinced that his travels in time are real, the novel's structure uses the classic approach of flashbacks and flash-forwards. In one instant he is in the present, a "senile widower," and in the next he returns to his

time as a soldier in the war. The novel leaves open the possibility that he may in fact have suffered a nervous breakdown, as his daughter believes. The narrative, formal, and thematic use of time travel may therefore be seen as a way of explaining the incidence of flashbacks caused by wartime trauma. It can function as a metaphor for post-traumatic stress disorder, or PTSD, which first gained widespread attention during the Vietnam War and which encouraged a reevaluation of the treatment of veterans from previous wars as well.

CRITICAL DISCUSSION

The earlier success of Vonnegut's novels *Cat's Cradle* (1963) and *God Bless You, Mr. Rosewater* (1965) brought him renown and an association with the 1960s counterculture. One of the first reviews of *Slaughterhouse-Five*, published in the *New York Times*, refers to Vonnegut as "an indescribable writer whose seven previous books are like nothing else on earth." The reviewer calls the book "very tough and very funny; it is sad and delightful; and it works." Of particular importance, the reviewer suggests, is the introduction, which "should be read aloud to children, cadets and basic trainees."

Because of its readability, clear language, and concern with the ethics of war in contemporary culture, *Slaughterhouse-Five* is frequently studied by high school and undergraduate college students as an example of the modern novel. Its use of profanity and its confrontation with difficult issues, however, have made it the target of several instances of censorship in schools. In 1975 *Slaughterhouse-Five*, along with eight other works of fiction, was banned from school libraries in a Long Island school district for being "anti-American, anti-Christian, anti-Semitic and just plain filthy." In 1982 the case went before the U.S. Supreme Court in *Board of Education v. Pico*. English teacher Donald B. Veix remarks in "Teaching a Censored Novel: *Slaughterhouse-Five*" that the satiric novel "holds a mirror up to our society and the image is repulsive." He maintains that the novel does not attack the American way of life but rather lays bare such myths as the romance of war, the innate nobility of the American soldier, the innate corruption of the enemy soldier, and above all the idea of morally righteous war.

Some studies of modern and postmodern fiction, such as Gerald Graff's *Literature Against Itself* (1977) and John Gardner's *On Moral Fiction* (1978), criticize Vonnegut's novel for ignoring formal novelistic concerns and concentrating instead on ethical questions. Later critics such as Leonard Mustazza, however, laud Vonnegut for his psychological acuity and for the use of experimental forms to explore the psychology of soldiers and veterans and the aftereffects of traumatic experience. In "War Stories: Myths of World War II," Samuel Hynes points out that Vonnegut's vision of the war, like that of such authors as Primo Levi and Kenzaburo Oe, is concerned with "scenes of civilian suffering" rather than views of the battlefields, which would depict "the active, potentially heroic side of war." According to Hynes, *Slaughterhouse-Five* "should be at the center of our myth of the Second World War."

Twenty-first-century academics have continued the discussion along these same lines. In *War, Literature and the Arts*, Christina Jarvis refers to the novel as an example of the "Vietnamization" of World War II, in which postmodern novels reenvision the moral certainty of the earlier war through questions raised by the Vietnam War. Criticism has also focused on the novel's concept of free will, often comparing it to Heller's *Catch-22* and Thomas Pynchon's *Gravity's Rainbow*. Writing in the journal *Critique*, Alberto Cacicedo observes that, while Heller's novel is generally seen as an unambiguous call to "ethical social action," critics are divided about whether *Slaughterhouse-Five* espouses fatalism and therefore encourages moral lassitude or satirizes the nihilistic viewpoint attributed to the Tralfamadorians.

SOURCES

"At Last, Kurt Vonnegut's Famous Dresden Book." Rev of *Slaughterhouse-Five*, by Kurt Vonnegut. *New York Times*. New York Times, 31 Mar. 1969. Web. 5 May 2011.

Cacicedo, Alberto. "'You Must Remember This': Trauma and Memory in *Catch-22* and *Slaughterhouse-Five*." *Critique* 46.4 (2005): 357–69. Web. 5 May 2011.

Hynes, Samuel. "War Stories: Myths of World War II." *Sewanee Review* 100.1 (1992): 98–105. Web. 5 May 2011.

Jarvis, Christina. "The Vietnamization of World War II in *Slaughterhouse-Five* and *Gravity's Rainbow*." *War, Literature and the Arts* 15.1–2 (2003): 95–117. Web. 5 May 2011.

Veix, Donald B. "Teaching a Censored Novel: *Slaughterhouse-Five*." *English Journal* 64.7 (1975): 24–33. Web. 5 May 2011.

Vonnegut, Kurt, Jr. *Slaughterhouse-Five; or, The Children's Crusade: A Duty-Dance with Death*. New York: Delacorte, 1969. Print.

FURTHER READING

Abele, Elizabeth. "The Journey Home in Kurt Vonnegut's World War II Novels." *New Critical Essays on Kurt Vonnegut*. Ed. David Simmons. New York: Macmillan, 2009. 67–90. Print.

Addison, Paul, and Jeremy A. Crang, eds. *Firestorm: The Bombing of Dresden, 1945*. Chicago: Dee, 2006. Print.

Bloom, Harold. *Kurt Vonnegut's "Slaughterhouse-Five": Modern Critical Interpretations*. Philadelphia: Chelsea, 2001. Print.

Grayling, A. C. *Among the Dead Cities: The History and Moral Legacy of the WWII Bombing of Civilians in Germany and Japan*. New York: Walker, 2006. Print.

Heller, Joseph. *Catch-22*. New York: Simon, 1961. Print.

Klinkowitz, Jerome. *"Slaughterhouse-Five": Reforming the Novel and the World*. Boston: Twayne, 1990. Print.

Lundquist, James. *Kurt Vonnegut*. New York: Ungar, 1977. Print.

McCoppin, Rachel. "'God Damn It, You've Got to Be Kind': War and Altruism in the Works of Kurt Vonnegut." *New Critical Essays on Kurt Vonnegut*. Ed. David Simmons. New York: Macmillan, 2009. 47–65. Print.

Simmons, David. "'The War Parts, Anyway, Are Pretty Much True': Negotiating the Reality of World War II in *Slaughterhouse-Five* and *Catch-22*." *Critical Insights: "Slaughterhouse-Five."* Ed. Leonard Mustazza. Pasadena: Salem, 2011. 64–79. Print.

MEDIA ADAPTATION

Slaughterhouse-Five. Screenplay by Stephen Geller. Dir. George Roy Hill. Perf. Michael Sacks, Ron Leibman, and Eugene Roche. Universal Pictures, 1972. Film.

Jennifer Ludwig

THE SWORD OF HONOUR TRILOGY
The Final Version of the Novels
Evelyn Waugh

OVERVIEW

Sword of Honour, by Evelyn Waugh, is a fictional trilogy set during World War II that describes an English soldier's earnest attempt to restore his character through military service, only to be confounded by the absurdities of regimental life and the bleak futility of war. The trilogy comprises *Men at Arms* (1952), *Officers and Gentlemen* (1955), and *Unconditional Surrender* (1961, released in the United States under the title *The End of the Battle*). It tells the story of Guy Crouchback, the dispirited son of a declining aristocratic Roman Catholic family, who enlists in the army in 1939 with the intention of defending Christian values from the Nazi and communist onslaught. Through a host of comic characters and an epic sweep of wartime deployments, Waugh's heroic trilogy explores the difficulty of maintaining one's faith amid tragic circumstances, and the challenges of reconciling a personal mission with a public cause.

Many aspects of Waugh's trilogy are semiautobiographical. He had served in the Royal Marines during World War II, and his own service in North Africa, Crete, and Yugoslavia roughly parallels that of his protagonist. Waugh converted to Catholicism at age 26, following his divorce (Guy Crouchback, too, was divorced), and his conservative Catholic views gain greater voice in the war trilogy than in his other novels, most of which are more farcical. As a result, some critics hold that the trilogy suffers from tedious moralizing despite the presence of Waugh's familiar acerbic humor and keen social satire. Although its commercial success never matched that of his most popular novel, *Brideshead Revisited*. Nonetheless, the influential English writer and critic Cyril Connolly, who was skeptical of the series at its outset, came to regard the satiric trilogy as "the finest novels to have come out of the war" (quoted in Katharyn Crabbe, *Evelyn Waugh*).

HISTORICAL AND LITERARY CONTEXT

At the outbreak of war in September 1939, Waugh was already an accomplished author, but he was determined to join the war effort. At 36, he was too old to be called up immediately to service, but he applied for a commission with the Royal Marines, which he received in November.

Waugh was, like his protagonist, Guy Crouchback, motivated to service by fear of the potential triumph of atheistic communism and the 1939 signing of the Nazi-Soviet nonaggression pact. Conquest by the Russians, he wrote in his diary, would be "a more terrible fate for the allies we are pledged to defend than conquest by Germany." Waugh (again, like Crouchback) was enthusiastic to receive his commission as an officer, but after feeling frustrated by his unit's lack of action, he transferred to the British Commandos. His Commando unit was sent to Egypt and then to Libya, to harass German and Italian forces. In a nighttime reconnaissance raid on the coastal town of Bardia, the first troops ashore mistakenly killed their own commander and alerted enemy troops to their presence. Waugh was dismayed by the bungled operation.

In May 1941 his unit was sent to the island of Crete, a pivotal air and naval stronghold in the eastern Mediterranean. Axis forces had already taken Greece and Yugoslavia and saw Crete as key to the conquest of Egypt. German paratroopers invaded the island, catching the British forces by surprise. By the time Waugh's Commando unit arrived, it was clear that all was lost and the British forces were in full retreat. Waugh was again disgusted by the cowardice and lack of will he perceived in the Allied effort.

After returning to England, he was sanctioned for writing (without proper clearance) a propagandistic article on the Bardia raid for *Life* magazine, and he was refused promotions and chances to serve in combat. His illusions of winning valor in battle hopelessly broken, he spent the last year of the war on a military mission to Yugoslavia, where he reported on conditions of Christians in Croatia under the communist dictator Josip Tito.

The *Sword of Honour* trilogy, like *Brideshead Revisited*, is considered one of Waugh's explicitly Catholic works. Waugh had rejected Anglicanism while at Lancing College and Christianity altogether until 1930. He ultimately converted to Roman Catholicism, which he held to be the "genuine form of Christianity." In later writings Waugh expressed his conviction that the Protestant Reformation had derailed the United Kingdom from its intended course and unjustly severed it from the true seat of Christian faith in Rome. Many scholars have seen this spiritual and ideological backdrop as the decay from which Waugh's protagonist in *Sword of Honour* attempts to free himself by contributing to the war effort.

By the time Waugh began to publish the trilogy, his position as both a satirist and commentator on the subject of war was well established. In addition, the widely celebrated humor of his early novels *Decline and Fall* (1928), *Vile Bodies* (1930), and *A Handful of Dust* (1934) was compared favorably to the wit of P. G. Wodehouse, of whom Waugh was an admirer. His novels *Put Out More Flags* (1942) and *Brideshead Revisited* (1945) respectively express Waugh's optimism that World War II might provide Britons with an ennobling cause and his dismay over the enduring cost of the conflict. By the 1950s and the writing of *Sword of Honour*, Waugh's attitude toward the war had grown even more jaundiced, and with his epic satirical trilogy he expounded more than ever on his own military experience and his staunch Catholic beliefs.

THEMES AND STYLE

At the beginning of the trilogy, when Crouchback learns of the newly formed Soviet-German alliance, the prospect of confronting a worthy enemy seems to offer new meaning in his otherwise lonely, idle life. Before the tomb of a failed crusader, Sir Roger of Waybroke, Crouchback runs a hand along the reposing warrior's sword and asks, "Sir Roger, pray for me, and for our endangered kingdom." Thus begins Crouchback's quixotic quest for justice and personal salvation.

The sword from which the series derives its title quickly takes on ironic significance, as Crouchback's adolescent illusions of honor and martial chivalry bear little similarity to the realities of military life. Crouchback imagines himself "sprinting at the head of a platoon," yet for much of *Men at Arms* he is engaged in haphazard training, far from combat, with men who see the war as an opportunity for a comfortable career. Crouchback's first deployment to Dakar reflects an Allied effort that is comically disorganized and inglorious. Even his comrade Apthorpe, supposedly a veteran of African service, becomes a caricature of Crouchback's noble delusions. Apthorpe's vaunted experiences turn out to be fictions and he meets an ignominious end fueled by whiskey and tropical illness.

The second book of the series, *Officers and Gentlemen*, delves further into the themes of moral, social, and political disillusion. Friends turn out to be traitors. Crouchback endures the humiliation of serving under the man for whom his ex-wife, Virginia, left him. The ineptitude of his brothers-in-arms is painstakingly detailed in the withdrawal from Crete, where Crouchback witnesses the appalling crisis of Allied leadership. Then Crouchback's crusade is undercut by the unholy alliance between the United Kingdom and the Soviet Union. Like Sir Roger the crusader, whose memory remains vital to Crouchback throughout the trilogy, his mission has failed. His precious "endangered kingdom" is as threatened from within as it is from any fascist or communist regime.

In the final installment, *Unconditional Surrender*, his apathy and disillusionment with the war complete,

Anthony Gross's painting *The Garrett Landing* depicts the Royal Marines, led by Major Garrett, retreating from Crete and landing at Sidi Barrani, Egypt, on June 9, 1941. Author Evelyn Waugh fought with the Royal Marines in the same disappointing Crete campaign. © ANTHONY GROSS / IMPERIAL WAR MUSEUM / THE ART ARCHIVE / THE PICTURE DESK, INC.

THE WAR BEFORE THE WAR IN WAUGH'S *PUT OUT MORE FLAGS*

A decade before publishing his acclaimed *Sword of Honour* trilogy, Evelyn Waugh authored *Put Out More Flags* (1942), his first book dedicated to the subject of World War II. The novel chronicles the early stages of that conflict, when England and its allies were engaged in what became known as the "Phony War"—the period between September 1939, when Germany embarked on its devastating military campaign against Poland, and May 1940, when the Germans expanded the theater of war through their sweeping invasions of France, Belgium, and Holland.

Although the Allies formally declared war on Germany shortly after the Polish invasion, the ensuing months were characterized by a conspicuous lack of military engagement with the enemy. In *Put Out More Flags*, Waugh satirizes this period of dormancy by chronicling the ostensibly pointless activities of British soldiers, who have been called into duty without clear directives or goals. In particular, Waugh's portrayal of Alistair Trumpington, a well-meaning British combatant who finds himself engaged in one meaningless military exercise after another, captures the mood of uncertainty and confusion that came to define this period.

Put Out More Flags is also noteworthy for resuscitating several characters from some of Waugh's earlier fiction, including his celebrated debut novel, *Decline and Fall* (1928).

Crouchback begins to find redemption in the wisdom of his father. When Crouchback complains, "it doesn't seem to matter now who wins," his father replies, "that sort of question isn't for soldiers." He criticizes Crouchback for being too concerned with the appearance of victory, and thinking too little of charity. "Quantitative judgments don't apply," he counsels, "if only one soul was saved that is full compensation for any amount of loss of 'face.'" Crouchback thereafter abandons his immature notions of a grand triumph, finding consolation instead in personal agency and relationships. He remarries and raises Virginia's orphaned son. Crouchback moves from a public to a personal mission, from seeking glory in battle to cultivating his relationship with God.

In contrast to Crouchback's earlier affinity with Sir Roger's sword, he refuses to pay homage to the Sword of Stalingrad—a ceremonial gift from the British to their new Soviet allies—which completes in his eyes the war's failure as holy crusade. It also confirms the notion that public crusades distort noble intentions into farce and shame. Having matured in the face of these distortions, Crouchback feels that the great challenge of life lies in fitting one's faith to the world as it is, rather than superimposing a religious order upon it.

Among his contemporaries, Waugh's satires were never regarded as bearing the intellectual ambition of Aldous Huxley or the spleen of Wyndham Lewis. His reputation for comic artfulness and literary craftsmanship, however, exceeded that of his peers, and his reputation as a serious writer—often in spite of his acerbic wit and absurdist social satire—was substantially elevated by the allegorical characters and serious themes he addressed with *Sword of Honour*. In his later career his biting humor and trademark sense of irony were still present, but his tone became mollified by a more practical type of conservatism, what critic Bernard Bergonzi described as a kind of "Tory Romanticism."

CRITICAL DISCUSSION

Critical responses to Waugh's trilogy varied widely as the individual volumes were published. Many felt skeptical that Waugh could incorporate his arch humor with such seemingly weighty themes as spiritual salvation and disillusionment about collective human endeavor.

Among the most outspoken of these critics was Kingsley Amis, who felt that the moral seriousness of the work signaled the end of Waugh's career as a satirist. However, Waugh's later biographer (and friend) Christopher Sykes observed in a favorable review of the second book that Waugh succeeded by extending the boundaries of his technique: "a primary rule of style is broken: farce is mixed with comedy, with tragi-comedy, and even with tragedy … The result is abundantly successful."

Amis also accused Waugh of suffering from a common flaw among satirists: falling in love with his protagonist—assigning positive attributes only to him and to a handful of aged peripheral characters such as Crouchback's father, who signifies Waugh's traditionalist Catholic ideals. In a 1994 introduction to the combined volumes, critic Frank Kermode, too, observes this separation:

> There has always been much made about Waugh's snobbery, and what sometimes seems to be his identification of human value with the English Catholic aristocracy. Mr. Crouchback simply believes there are only two kinds of people, his kind and everybody else. He will treat the outsiders with courtesy and charity, but it does not occur to him to question the distinction.

Penelope Lively has commented on the social distinctions in the novel as well. She observes in a 2001 issue of the *Atlantic Monthly*, "Fifty years ago, British society was polarized in a way that is hard to conceive of now: there were two nations in terms of how people lived and how they perceived one another. Waugh evoked that vanishing world and nailed its assumptions, its prejudices, its mysterious fault lines."

Lively adds that contemporary readers might experience in the trilogy a sharp contrast to the celebratory view of World War II presented to the public through such works as Tom Brokaw's bestselling *The Greatest Generation*. Lively notes that Waugh's bias heightens the contemporary perception of the trilogy and its idiosyncratic approach to war and morality as a sort of "maverick aspect of historical writing." In his study *The Satiric Art of Evelyn Waugh*, James Carens comments on the different representations of the era, describing the breadth of "impulses being released in World War II" that are communicated through historical writings and noting particularly the counterpoint of absurdly drawn characters. He sees Waugh's contrasting of the surreal, ignoble elements of battle with the novel's central ideal, the chivalrous, fallen crusader, as "ironic realism."

SOURCES

Carens, James. *The Satiric Art of Evelyn Waugh*. Seattle: U of Washington P, 1966. Print.

Crabbe, Katharyn. *Evelyn Waugh*. New York: Continuum, 1988. Print.

Davis, Robert Murray. *Evelyn Waugh, Writer*. Norman: Pilgrim, 1981. Print.

Heath, Jeffrey. *The Picturesque Prison: Evelyn Waugh and His Writing*. Montreal: McGill-Queen's UP, 1982. Print.

Lively, Penelope. "A Maverick Historian." *Atlantic Monthly* 287.2 (2001): 128–29. Web. 3 July 2011.

Patey, Douglas Lane. *The Life of Evelyn Waugh*. Oxford: Blackwell, 1998. Print.

Waugh, Evelyn. *The Sword of Honour Trilogy*. Introd. Frank Kermode. New York: Everyman, 1994. Print.

FURTHER READING

Adam, Karl. *The Spirit of Catholicism*. Garden City: Image, 1954. Print.

Davie, Michael, ed. *The Diaries of Evelyn Waugh*. London: Weidenfeld, 1976. Print.

Greenblatt, Stephen Jay. *Three Modern Satirists: Waugh, Orwell, and Huxley*. New Haven: Yale UP, 1965. Print.

Heinimann, David. "An Ethical Critique of Waugh's Guy Crouchback." *Renascence* 46.3 (1994): 175–85. Academic Search Premier. Web. 3 July 2011.

MacLeod, Lewis. "'They Just Won't Do, You Know': Postcolonial Discourse and Evelyn Waugh's *Sword of Honour*." *Literature Interpretation Theory* 21.2 (2010): 61–80. Web.

Stannard, Martin. *Evelyn Waugh: The Later Years, 1939–1966*. New York: Norton, 1992. Print.

Sykes, Christopher. *Evelyn Waugh: A Biography*. Boston: Little, 1975. Print.

Voorhees, R. J. "Evelyn Waugh's War Novels," *Queens Quarterly* 65 (1958): 53–63. Print.

Thomas Colligan

WORLD WAR I POEMS

"Counter-attack," "The General," "The Glory of Women," and "The Hero"

Siegfried Sassoon

✤ **Key Facts**

Conflict:
World War I

Time Period:
Early 20th Century

Genre:
Poetry

OVERVIEW

Siegfried Sassoon's World War I poems are furious satires of the British government and the administrators responsible for what he saw as an unnecessary war. The poems expose the flawed decisions of the generals, the poor leadership of officers, the miserable conditions of the trenches, and the unbearable violence of the battlefield. Sassoon, who fought as a member of the Royal Welch Fusiliers, was one of the few trench poets—as the numerous soldier-poets of the war were known—to survive the conflict, though he was wounded at the Battle of the Somme in 1916, injured again in 1918, and suffered from extreme shellshock.

The poet Edmund Blunden referred to Sassoon's work in the latter years of the war and afterwards as a "war on the war." Sassoon was outspokenly critical of the British military leadership and of the response of those on the home front, whom he believed to be unaware of what the soldiers were going through and insensitive to the deaths and wounds of those who were fighting in the trenches.

In 1917 he produced his famous antiwar salvo, "A Soldier's Declaration," a self-described "act of willful defiance of military authority," produced "because I believe that the war is being deliberately prolonged by those who have the power to end it." Sassoon argued that what had been a "war of defense and liberation" had become a "war of aggression and conquest." He hoped his statement might "help to destroy the callous complacence with which the majority of those at home regard the continuance of agonies which they do not share, and which they have not sufficient imagination to realize." Sassoon's statement, which nearly led to his being court-martialed (fellow poet Robert Graves managed to have him sent to a sanitarium instead) describes the satiric aim of his most accomplished war poems.

The four poems that are the focus of this essay illustrate the main aspects of Sassoon's work. "Counter-attack" and "The General" are scathing depictions of officers who seem unaware of the difficulties faced by their men. In "The Glory of Women," Sassoon accuses women of being too invested in heroic myths to see the true brutality of war. "The Hero" exposes the government's role in keeping factual accounts of the battlefield from the public.

"The Hero" was first published in *The Old Huntsman and Other Poems* (1917). "The Glory of Women," "Counter-attack," and "The General" first appeared in *Counter-attack and Other Poems* (1918).

HISTORICAL AND LITERARY CONTEXT

The First World War (1914–19), known at the time as the Great War, began as a conflict between the Allied powers (Britain, France, and Russia) and the Central powers (Germany, Austro-Hungary, the Ottoman Empire, and Bulgaria). While Britain was not directly threatened by the German invasion of Belgium at the beginning of the war, British politicians felt that they were morally obligated to defend Belgium because of treaties between the two nations.

The war was heavily propagandized in Britain as an ethical struggle to protect civilized nations from the barbaric Germans, and thousands of young men signed up to fight. Britain was certain enough of its military prowess that it was said the war would be "over by Christmas," the fighting would be brief, and few lives would be lost. But the Allied and Central powers were evenly matched in terms of military technology, and a long war of attrition ensued.

A defining feature of the conflict was trench warfare, in which soldiers dug themselves into trenches on either sides of a stretch of unoccupied land known as "no-man's-land." The use of long-range missiles, guns, and poisoned gas to attack the enemy in their trenches was both brutal and ineffective in terms of gaining a decisive advantage and led to millions of casualties on both sides. The shocking casualty rate and the concomitant realization that the war that was supposed to save civilization was distinctly uncivilized caused great disillusionment among soldiers and civilians alike. These feelings are most strongly expressed in the works of the poets who wrote verse from the trenches and from behind the lines in an attempt to convey the terror, pain, and death of the war to those at home.

Sassoon, at first fully in support of the war, rapidly became one of the most disillusioned of the trench poets, having come to believe that the continuation of the war was no longer an ethical decision but one based on the pride of the government and officers, who were willingly sacrificing their men. Among

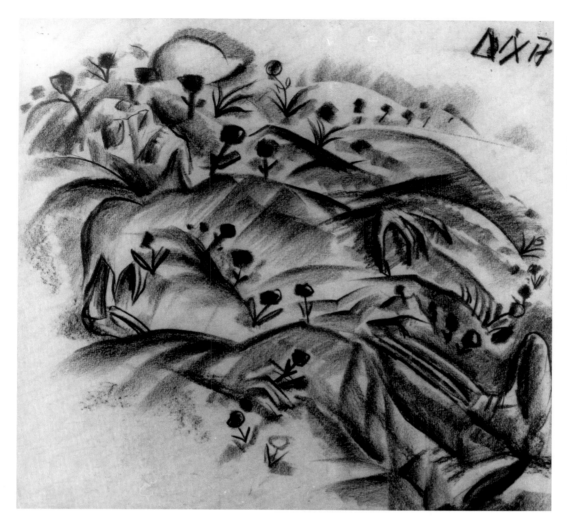

the major trench poets, whose ranks included Wilfred Owen (1893–1918), Edmund Blunden (1896–1974), Isaac Rosenberg (1890–1918), Ivor Gurney (1890–1937), and Herbert Read (1893–1968), Sassoon is noted for his frank expression of anger at the leaders of the nation and the war and for his scathingly satiric voice.

THEMES AND STYLE

Sassoon's poems thematize the difference between the life of a soldier and the life of a civilian or officer. His most famous poem, "Counter-attack," is a first-person account of a morning in the trenches, beginning with a description of the soldiers' preparation for an attack and ending when their counterattack fails. The first part of the poem alternates between the slang of the trenches, the technical vocabulary of war, and more figurative poetic language that ironically reveals the destroyed landscape around the soldiers, where "green clumsy legs / High booted, sprawled and groveled along the saps / And trunks." The second half of the poem, which describes the attack itself, uses staccato

rhythms to evoke the fear of the soldiers and to convey the rapid-fire unfolding of events during the German attack and the British attempt to fight back.

Sassoon's narrative focuses on an officer who "came blundering down the trench," "gasping and bawling" orders. The officer, rather than the soldiers, is the one who panics, screaming, "O Christ, they're coming at us," before nearly forgetting his gun and then dying in the confusion. Although the officer is shown as a combatant like the rest, and his death is another tragedy amidst many, his incapacity to lead redounds to the detriment of his men. The irony echoes that of Sassoon's poems in general, which accuse higher officers of leaving their men unprepared and of standing back while young soldiers are slaughtered in the trenches.

Sassoon's short poem "The General" offers another ironic depiction of the relationship between a commanding officer and his men, revealing the hypocrisy of the general who merrily greets his soldiers— "Good morning; good morning!"—then sends them off to fight. "Now the soldiers he smiled at are most

REGENERATION: THE PSYCHOLOGICAL EFFECTS OF TRENCH WARFARE

Pat Barker's 1991 novel *Regeneration* is a fictional account of soldiers during World War I being treated for shell shock at Craiglockhart War Hospital. At the start of the novel, the main character, a semifictionalized Siegfried Sassoon, has been diagnosed with "shell-shock" after the publication of his declaration against the continuation of the war. The head psychiatrist at Craiglockhart, Dr. W. H. R. Rivers, doubts this diagnosis, and, indeed, it seems likely that the authorities had Sassoon declared mentally ill to discredit his public condemnation of the war. In addition, while Sassoon published his manifesto hoping to be court-martialed, which would allow his views on the war to be aired, writer and soldier Robert Graves arranged for him to stand before a medical board so that he would be institutionalized instead.

Although Sassoon's diagnosis is in question, a number of the other soldiers at Craiglockhart in Barker's novel are indeed exhibiting intensely debilitating psychological symptoms as a result of their experiences in the trenches. Anderson, a surgeon, is made ill by the sight of blood and suffers intense recurring nightmares. Burns, a former soldier, has hallucinations in which he relives the more horrific moments of his wartime experiences. While these men have been diagnosed as "mad," Rivers eventually questions whether these psychological responses to the war should be qualified as madness, or simply a reasonable human response to the horrors of war.

Regeneration, the first of Barker's World War I trilogy, was followed by *The Eye in the Door* (1993) and *The Ghost Road* (1995), which won the 1995 Booker Prize.

of 'em dead, / And we're cursing his staff for incompetent swine." The cheerful general represents the poor military leadership that led to the loss of thousands of soldiers' lives in brutal battles like Arras, the setting for "The General."

The poem's language points out the class differences between the soldiers and the officers who command them. The soldiers' diction ("he's a cheery old card"), the fact that they regularly drop the "th" in "them," and their names—"Harry and Jack"—identify them as regular "Tommies," ordinary lower-class foot soldiers. Harry and Jack are portrayed as good-hearted; despite the fact that they are "slogging up to Arras," Harry "grunts" his unresentful comments about the general's good cheer. The narrator of the poem, however, writes with the benefit of hindsight, aware that such ordinary men die, while the generals who sent them to the front live on. The poem's galloping meter and perfect rhyme scheme accentuate this difference by echoing the rhythm of the jovial greeting of the general, which contrasts with the grim story told by the poem.

The poems "The Hero" and "The Glory of Women" address the reactions of those on the home front to the war. In a famous line from his *Memoir of an Infantry Officer*, Sassoon remarks that "the man who really endured the War at its worst was everlastingly differentiated from everyone except his fellow soldiers." Both poems narrate the response of women to the war dead, capturing the distance that Sassoon believed the war had erected between soldiers and noncombatants.

"The Hero" contrasts the story told to a mother by an officer who knocks at her door to tell her that her son is dead, with the actual circumstances of his death. Both the "Brother Officer" and the colonel's letter he bears tell her "some gallant lies / That she would nourish all her days"; they allow her to believe that her son had "been so brave, her glorious boy," though the officer thinks of him as a "cold-footed, useless swine" who "had panicked … [and] tried / To get sent home." The poem itself does not blame the dead soldier, but exposes the gap between the actuality of the war in which so many men "died / Blown to small bits" and the necessity of placating those who remained behind. The tales told to the mother are a kindness, especially since "No one seemed to care [about the soldier's death] / Except that lonely old woman with white hair." While gently mocking the woman, the poem reveals the hypocrisy of the war.

The sonnet "The Glory of Women" provides a less sympathetic depiction of those on the home front, this time of young, middle-class women. The image of the soldier as courageous and noble allows them to "love us when we're heroes, home on leave, / Or wounded in a mentionable place" but reduces the soldiers to "decorations" to be "worshipped." Not only is this a falsely ironic vision of the war—a vision in which all British soldiers are unfailingly loyal and brave, earning accolades and winning battles through their unselfish and valiant actions—but it also implies that such heroic behavior is the only reason for soldiers to be loved, or mourned. The poem implies that women would no longer respect or worship the men if they were aware that British troops "retire / When hell's last horror breaks them, and they run, / Trampling the terrible corpses—blind with blood." The final three lines of the poem expand this view to include all women, describing a "German mother" who is equally unaware of her own son's predicament, who knits socks while "his face is trodden deeper in the mud."

CRITICAL DISCUSSION

Sassoon, a well-known poet before the war, was immediately recognized as one of the most important figures of trench poetry and as the genre's central satiric voice. In a 1917 article titled "Some Soldier Poets," Edmund Gosse includes him in the category of soldier-writers of verse who, "in my judgment, expressed themselves with most originality during the war," remarking that

Sassoon differs from other soldier-poets in the intensity of his anger towards the war and his sense of disillusionment.

Early critical accounts of Sassoon generally agree with Gosse's assessment, emphasizing the poet's anger and resentment about the war and its violence, the unfairness of the innumerable deaths, and the poet's frustration that what could have been an age of beauty was subsumed in a useless war. Paul Fussell's account of Sassoon in *The Great War and Modern Memory* remarks on the way that Sassoon's initial passionate engagement in the war waned as he became "appalled by what he saw there."

Critics usually read Sassoon's war poems, his ironic use of figurative language to describe war's horrors, and his use of army slang in a poetic context as a central example of trench poetry's reconfiguration of the poetic tradition. This reconfiguration enabled the trench poets to describe experiences that were essentially indescribable. In his study of World War I literature, Bernard Bergonzi sums up this account of trench poetry with the comment that "the literary records of the Great War can be seen as a series of attempts to evolve a response that would have some degree of adequacy to the unparalleled situation in which the writers were involved."

In recent years a number of critics have argued that the identification of World War I poetry with trench poetry, an association motivated by the idea that combat experience is necessary to write authentic war literature, has led to a restricted definition of war poetry. Writing in *New Literary History*, James Campbell contests the concept he calls "combat Gnosticism," the idea that combat is a nearly mystical experience and that only it can produce the spiritual awakening that inspires war poetry. Campbell argues instead that the experience of war is larger than the experience of the battlefield and that the definition of war poetry needs to be expanded to include the work of noncombatants. Sassoon's work, because of his scathing critiques of women on the home front and his belief that combat experience erected an impenetrable barrier between soldiers and noncombatants, is particularly vulnerable to this critique.

SOURCES

Barker, Pat. *Regeneration*. New York: Dutton, 1992. Print.

Bergonzi, Bernard. *Heroes' Twilight: A Study of the Literature of the Great War*. New York: Palgrave Macmillan, 1980. Print.

Campbell, James. "Combat Gnosticism: The Ideology of First World War Criticism." *New Literary History* 30.1 (1999): 203–215. *JSTOR*. Web. 24 June 2011.

Fussell, Paul. *The Great War and Modern Memory*. Oxford: Oxford UP, 1975. Print.

Gosse, Edmund. "Some Soldier Poets." *Some Diversions of a Man of Letters*. London: Heinemann, 1920. *Project Gutenberg*. Web. 24 June 2011.

Sassoon, Siegfried. *Counter-attack and Other Poems*. New York: Dutton, 1918. *Bartleby.com*. Web. 6 June 2011.

———. "Declaration against the War." *The First World War Poetry Digital Archive*. University of Oxford/JISC, n.d. Web. 7 June 2011.

———. *Memoirs of an Infantry Officer*. New York: Faber, 1980. Print.

———. *The Old Huntsman and Other Poems*. New York: Dutton, 1918. *Bartleby.com*. Web. 7 June 2011.

FURTHER READING

Blunden, Edmund. *Undertones of War*. Chicago: U of Chicago Press, 2007. Print.

Campbell, Patrick. *Siegfried Sassoon: A Study of the War Poetry*. Jefferson: McFarland, 1999. Print.

Egremont, Max. *Siegfried Sassoon: A Life*. New York: FSG, 2005. Print.

Hemmings, Robert. *Modern Nostalgia: Siegfried Sassoon, Trauma, and the Second World War*. Edinburgh: Edinburgh UP, 2008. Print.

Sassoon, Siegfried. *The War Poems*. Ed. Rupert Hart-Davis. London: Faber, 1983. Print.

———. *The Collected Poems, 1908–1956*. London: Faber, 1986. Print.

Reilly, Catherine, ed. *Scars Upon My Heart: Women's Poetry and Verse of the First World War*. London: Virago, 2006. Print.

Ward, Candace, ed. *World War I British Poets: Brooke, Owen, Sassoon, Rosenberg and Others*. London: Dover, 1997. Print.

Jennifer Ludwig

℮ Experiments

L'ALLEGRIA

Giuseppe Ungaretti

OVERVIEW

L'Allegria (best translated into English as "The Joy," or simply "Joy") is a collection of lyric poems written by Italian author Giuseppe Ungaretti (1888–1970) between 1915 and 1919. These concise and evocative compositions depict the author's painful experience of the First World War, giving voice to the grief felt over the loss of fellow soldiers. Despite this grief, the story also highlights the joy that comes from a hopeful, if saddening, vision of the human condition. In the definitive edition of the collection, published in 1931 (although the poet continued revising the poems for many years after this date), Ungaretti unifies and organizes into an organic whole a series of his prior publications. The first of these earlier publications was a 1916 collection titled *Il porto sepolto* ("The Buried Port"), which then formed the nucleus of the expanded collection, *Allegria di naufragi* ("Joy of Shipwrecks"), in 1919. This collection, in turn, was subsumed into *L'Allegria* in 1931. The powerfully brief lyrics of *L'Allegria* juxtapose the concrete with the philosophical, avant-gardism with personal poetic vision, and experience in battle with abstract reflection on the overarching meaning of warfare for humankind.

HISTORICAL AND LITERARY CONTEXT

Literary experts often consider Ungaretti a leading exponent of the Italian poetic movement known as Hermeticism. Influenced somewhat by French symbolism and flourishing in the experiential literary climate of early twentieth-century Italy, Hermeticism espoused an intense, purified form of lyric characterized by cryptic brevity and metaphysical contemplation. *L'Allegria* engenders some key aspects of the Hermetic style, which allows for the poetry's historically specific content (many of the poems are accompanied by the date and place, showing when and where during the war they were written) to resonate with a timeless, existential perplexity that transcends geographic and historical specificity.

Born in Alexandria, Egypt, where his Italian parents had settled, Ungaretti received a European education, studying at the Sorbonne in Paris in 1912. While there he was introduced to avant-garde literature, having direct contact with major authors of the time, including the French poet Guillaume Apollinaire as well as a number of prominent Italian Futurists.

Moving to Milan in 1914, Ungaretti became an interventionist, or a member of the popular movement favoring Italy's entry into World War I. The poet volunteered for military service when Italy joined the war in 1915 and served as a private in the country's infantry. His deployment to the northeastern Italian front, in the rugged and rocky Carso region, led to both traumatic and illuminating experiences that he distilled into poetry. During lulls between battles, whether in the trenches or in his tent at night, Ungaretti wrote in a poetic diary, which became the foundation of his first cluster of poems published as *Il porto sepolto*. This wartime poetry immediately distinguished Ungaretti as a new visionary voice in Italian letters.

In a literary context, one of the best illustrations of Ungaretti's synthesis of the concrete with the contemplative is the poem "Veglia" ("Vigil"). "Vigil" is the earliest of *L'Allegria*'s dated war poems and one of the most startling in its imagistic vividness. The physical setting for this poem is "Cima Quattro," or "Peak Four," on the alpine front; the location is given using a military designation, increasing the sense of historical specificity intersecting with personal experience. The date of the poem is December 23, two days before Christmas, which allows the reader to understand the reference to the "letters full of love" (Christmas greetings to loved ones back home). Set in this frigid and craggy atmosphere on a day that, in the civilian world, would be one of happy anticipation of the holiday, the poet spends the night awake, in an enforced and acrid sort of "vigil" in the trenches next to a dead comrade.

The emphasis in "Vigil" (as in other poems in *L'Allegria*) is predominantly on the horrors of battle: the "congestion" of the "hands" of the dead soldier can be seen as an objective correlative (a single image encapsulating the emotion of a poem) for the chaos and trauma permeating the war front. The concluding stanza complicates the emotion of the poem by affirming an unprecedented "attachment to life" in the face of the personal and collective horror expressed earlier. Indeed, the last lines of the lyric exemplify a key theme of *L'Allegria* overall—namely, the belief in the life-generating potentiality of the poetic word. Writing becomes a site of purification and salvation in a world in decline, and, on this note, it is significant that in "Vigil" the writing process is emphasized by the reference to "letters full of love" and by the coda

Key Facts

Conflict:
World War I

Time Period:
Early 20th Century

Genre:
Lyric Poetry

RADICAL LITERATURE AND WORLD WAR I

Giuseppe Ungaretti's radical poetic experimentation in *L'Allegria* finds echoes in other European verse of the period. Among the most innovative—and idiosyncratic—literary figures of the First World War was the poet Guillaume Apollinaire, whom Ungaretti met while studying in Paris. Apollinaire was closely associated with the numerous avant-garde writers and artists who were living in Paris in the years leading up to the war, including Pablo Picasso, Gertrude Stein, and Pierre Reverdy. Influenced by the radical developments in painting and literature that emerged during these years, Apollinaire set out to invent a new language to describe the increasingly unfamiliar and unsettling aspects of modern existence. In 1913 he published his most influential verse collection, *Alcools*. The volume includes such poems as "Zone" and "Le Pont Mirabeau," and

is characterized both by its radical stylistic experimentation and its unprecedented treatment of such subjects as technology and the alienation of the individual. In this sense, *Alcools* seemed to anticipate some of the concerns that would shape literary modernism in the years following World War I. A year after the book's publication, Apollinaire enlisted in the French army and was later gravely wounded in the head by shrapnel. During his recovery, he revised his early play *The Breasts of Tiresias* (1917), in which the word *surreal* first appeared. On November 9, 1918, Apollinaire died of influenza in the great pandemic. *Calligrammes: Poems of War and Peace, 1913–1916* (1918), a volume of experimental poems inspired by Apollinaire's experiences in the war, was published just weeks after his death.

that points to the author's activity as a diarist of war. As critic Margaret Brose notes in her article in *Italica*, "the poetic word, for Ungaretti our only *vestigium Dei*, could cleanse language of its temporal taint. Dead to history but reborn to eternal life, the poetic word points the way back to Eden."

Like a number of other poets writing during and immediately after the First World War (for instance, T. S. Eliot, William Butler Yeats, and Rainer Maria Rilke), Ungaretti seeks a mode of transcendence in the gritty reality of lived experience in the here and now. Physical reality is by no means glossed over or prettied up in a poem such as "Vigil," but this brutal reality is nonetheless accompanied by a call to celebration of life in this world. In *L'Allegria*, the poet is not a privileged intellectual or an armchair interpreter of history (as was often the case in more traditional Italian poetry) but is rather part of the mass of soldiers struggling to survive on the battlefield, clinging to life among thousands of other, largely anonymous, human beings.

THEMES AND STYLE

The style of *L'Allegria* is arguably its greatest innovation. Its themes of war, purification, and transcendence—as well as, in some sections of the collection, the treatment of nonwar themes such as memories of Egypt and of the contrast between urban life and nature—are intimately bound up with Ungaretti's quest for a new kind of poetic language. His style in *L'Allegria* avoids the classical eloquence and complex syntax characterizing much poetry in the Italian tradition, highlighting instead the power of the single word. In this respect, Ungaretti is influenced by Italian Futurists such as Filippo Marinetti, who advocated the style of *parole in libertà*, or "words in freedom," unhinged from syntax and punctuation. Unlike Marinetti and

most of the Futurists, however, Ungaretti presents a coherent vision of the complexities of warfare and of the yearning for peace. The emphasis on the single word in *L'Allegria* creates a sense of musicality, clarity, and truth stripped of ornament. What is sought is an Edenic poetic language that might transform this troubled, discordant world into one of harmony and innocence.

These aspirations of a return to innocence are reflected in the form of the poems, which have short lines (often only one or two words in length) and simplified syntax. The absence of most punctuation can make it seem as if the short phrases are simply floating in the air, liberated from their conventional contexts and the layers of acquired meaning that can otherwise hinder (from the Hermeticist perspective) the pure impact of language. Despite the simplicity of their form, the poems in *L'Allegria* are rigorously contemplative and morally complex. This intersection of unadorned language and nuanced introspection is the hallmark of Ungaretti's poetic innovation in *L'Allegria*.

An example of the interweaving of formal experiment in the direction of "pure" poetry, on the one hand, and the theme of a desired return to innocence, on the other, is the poem "Fratelli" ("Brothers"), written in 1916 and gradually revised, by 1931. In this poem, the word "brothers" (*fratelli*) is rediscovered in its primal and absolute meaning, salvaged from the commonplaces of conventional usage. Pronouncing this familiar word in the alien environs of the war, in the dark of night, makes it resonate anew and sets in motion a seemingly spontaneous chain of analogies: the word "brothers" is a "leaf just born" and a "revolt" against human "fragility." In the original Italian, strong alliteration connects the poem's key words: *fratelli* (brothers), *foglia* (leaf), and *fragilità* (fragility).

The brevity of the poem's lines emphasizes each of these words in its own right and highlights its sonic and thematic connection to the others. The "brothers" on the battlefield are powerfully, if tenuously, united by their shared fragility, their condition analogous, in its impermanence, to a leaf just born and destined soon to fall. The fragmentation of the poetic line and the lyrical sublimation of physical reality make for a poem that is immediate yet abstract, concrete yet profoundly idealistic.

In the poetry of *L'Allegria*, language aims to become a site of purification and salvation in a world in decline. At times the poetic word contains a life-generating potentiality, as in the poem "Commiato" ("Farewell," or "Envoy," the final poem in *Il porto sepolto*, the first edition of what became *L'Allegria*). In this poem, Ungaretti makes his vision of poetry explicit: "poesia / è il mondo l'umanità / la propria vita / fioriti dalla parola …" ("poetry / is the world humanity / one's own life / flowering from word …"). In Ungaretti's compressed and paratactic style, this passage succinctly expresses the stylistic and thematic concerns of the collection.

CRITICAL DISCUSSION

One of the first prominent critical appraisals of *L'Allegria* appeared in *La poesia ermetica* ("Hermetic Poetry"), published in 1936 by Italian critic Francesco Flora. In this work, Flora popularized the term *Hermetic*, using it disparagingly to identify what he saw as a lack of clarity and overall coherence in *L'Allegria*. Flora disapproved of the poems' suggestiveness and brevity—what he called their "atomic impressionism." He also grouped Ungaretti with the Futurists, whom he disliked, accusing both strains of poetry as being a sensationalistic and chaotic presentation of ideas and emotions. The critic's main point was that the meaning of Ungaretti's poems, with their subjective and vague analogies, would remain hermetically sealed.

The term *Hermeticism* is still used in reference to Ungaretti's poetry today, although without the derogatory connotations Flora intended. In her book *Mirage and Camouflage*, contemporary critic Vivienne Suvini-Hand sums up more recent appraisals:

> Apart from the fact that, with the passing of time and the development of ever more 'sophisticated' writing techniques, Ungaretti's poetry is no longer considered as difficult or obscure as it seemed when it first appeared, *L'Allegria* now tends to be *appreciated* precisely for those features which Flora condemned. Critics now praise its fresh immediacy, its apparent spontaneity ('apparent,' because all of Ungaretti's poems underwent meticulous revisions, as demonstrated by the numerous 'versions'), and, above all, its 'atomic impressionism.' … [T]he beauty of Ungaretti's poetry lies in its ability to

Bayonet assault in the Alps, published in the newspaper *La Domenica del Corriere*, 1917. © ALFREDO DAGLI ORTI / THE ART ARCHIVE AT ART RESOURCE, NY

exploit the manifold potentials of language; to use words not only in their literal meanings or for their traditional associations, but also, and above all, for their symbolic and musical values, and for their suggestive overtones.

Writing in *The Cambridge Companion to Modern Italian Culture*, Shirley W. Vinall and Tom O'Neill give another characteristic positive appraisal of *L'Allegria*. They state:

> Perhaps the most lasting synthesis of modern experimentation with the essential elements of tradition appears in Ungaretti's First World War Poems …. Ungaretti succeeds in exploring his complex experience with war: both the destruction, suffering, isolation and loss, and the intoxicating moments of harmony with nature and the revitalizing sense of comradeship … At the same time he celebrates the power of art to give permanence to fleeting human experience.

In summary, like many experimental works of literature, *L'Allegria* was condemned at the time of its publication by established critics. It has, however, passed into posterity as what many consider to be the most remarkable poetic chronicling of World War I written in the Italian language.

SOURCES

Brose, Margaret. "Ungaretti's Promised Land: The Mythification of *L'Allegria*." *Italica* 54.3 (1977): 341–66. Print.

Flora, Francesco. *La poesia ermetica*. Bari: Laterza, 1942. Print.

Ó Ceallacháin, Éanna. *Twentieth-Century Italian Poetry: A Critical Anthology (1900 to the Neo-Avantgarde)*. Leicester: Troubador, 2007. Print.

————— *Mariano, July 15, 1915* (Barca trans.)

Pazzaglia, Mario. *Letteratura italiana: Testi e critica con lineamenti di storia letteraria*. Bologna: Zanichelli, 1992. Print.

————— *Peak Four, December 23, 1915* (Rebay trans. with alterations by Lisa Barca)

Rebay, Luciano. *Italian Poetry: A Selection*. New York: Dover, 1969. Print.

Suvini-Hand, Vivienne. *Mirage and Camouflage: Hiding behind Hermeticism in Ungaretti's L'Allegria*. Market Harborough: Troubador, 2000. Print.

Ungaretti, Giuseppe, and Allen Mandelbaum. *Selected Poems of Giuseppe Ungaretti*. Ithaca: Cornell UP, 1975. Print.

Vinall, Shirley W., and Tom O'Neill. "Searching for New Languages: Modern Italian Poetry." *The Cambridge Companion to Modern Italian Culture*. Ed. Zygmunt G. Barański and Rebecca J. West. Cambridge: Cambridge UP, 2001. Print.

FURTHER READING

Barański, Zygmunt G., and Rebecca J. West. *The Cambridge Companion to Modern Italian Culture*. Cambridge: Cambridge UP, 2001. Print.

Cambon, Glauco. *Giuseppe Ungaretti*. New York: Columbia UP, 1967. Print.

Cary, Joseph. *Three Modern Italian Poets: Saba, Ungaretti, Montale*. Chicago: U of Chicago P, 1993. Print.

Condini, Ned. *An Anthology of Modern Italian Poetry in English Translation, with Italian Text*. New York: MLA, 2009. Print.

Jones, Frederic J. *Giuseppe Ungaretti: Poet and Critic*. Edinburgh: Edinburgh UP, 1977. Print.

Lang, Ariella. "The Sounds of Silence: Words of Exile and Liberation in Ungaretti's Desert." *Rivista di letterature moderne e comparate* (2000): 323–36. Print.

Ungaretti, Giuseppe, and Patrick Creagh. *Selected Poems*. Harmondsworth: Penguin, 1971. Print.

Lisa Barca

ANTIGONE

Jean Marie Lucien Pierre Anouilh

OVERVIEW

One of the twentieth century's most prolific playwrights, French dramatist Jean Anouilh rose to international fame with his 1942 play *Antigone*—an adaptation of the Greek poet Sophocles' tragedy—which premiered in Paris in the midst of the Nazi occupation of France during World War II (1939–45). Anouilh's basic story line closely follows Sophocles' classical version of the myth.

After King Oedipus of Thebes learns that he has unknowingly killed his father and slept with his mother, he departs the city in shame, leaving four children from the incestuous union in the care of their uncle, Créon. Upon coming of age, Oedipus's twin sons, Eteocles and Polyneices, quarrel over the throne, and when Eteocles refuses joint rule, Polyneices launches an armed attack on Thebes. In the ensuing battle the brothers kill each other, and Créon takes up the role of sovereign. Attempting to restore order to the ravaged city, he makes an example of Polyneices' revolt, declaring that, while Eteocles will be given a hero's funeral, Polyneices' body will be left to rot in the open air. Anyone who attempts to perform burial rites for the traitor's corpse will also be found guilty of treason and condemned to death.

The action of Anouilh's play begins on the morning after this decree. Oedipus's youngest daughter, Antigone, has disobeyed Créon's edict and scattered soil over her brother's body in a symbolic act of burial. Though both her sister Ismène and the king attempt to deter her, Antigone is determined to die for her cause, and she thwarts any attempt to conceal her crime. After Antigone announces that she intends to continue covering the body as long as she lives, the king regretfully sentences her to death. She is sealed inside a cave, where she hangs herself in defiance. Haemon, Créon's son and Antigone's fiancé, discovers her body and joins her in death, stabbing himself in the heart. When a messenger relates the details of the grisly scene, Créon's wife, Eurydice, slits her own throat, leaving Créon alone to contemplate the circle of tragedy that has left him the ultimate victim.

The play is known for the extended philosophical debate between Créon and Antigone that makes up more than a third of the text. Philosopher Jean-Paul Sartre points to this dialogue when asserting that Anouilh's *Antigone* is one of the great early examples of existentialist theater, noting that the argument dramatizes the notion that men are not created but instead create themselves through choice. Antigone chooses to die rather than face the bourgeois mediocrity that Créon lays out for her, and in this act critics see evidence of the character's relationship to the young French radicals who opposed German occupation.

Anouilh's play, which was eventually embraced by liberation forces worldwide, had two major revivals in France before 1946, in addition to performances in the United States, England, India, Egypt, Greece, and several Southeast Asian countries over the next five years. The play remains a favorite among radicals and is frequently revived in small professional theaters, particularly in times of extreme political conservatism.

HISTORICAL AND LITERARY CONTEXT

Though the playwright vehemently denied interest in the political struggle between the collaborationist French government and its detractors, literary scholar Donald Heiney confirms that the original audience of *Antigone* interpreted the play "as a thinly-veiled allegory of France under the Vichy regime." In the midst of a territorial war, Anouilh's idealistic young protagonist rails against the clinical pragmatism of an unjust ruler lacking a political mandate. This paralleled the real-life outrage of the Resistance, the half million freedom fighters working clandestinely to undermine the legitimacy of what came to be called Vichy France.

Nazi forces invaded France in 1940, capturing Paris and forcing the national government into exile. Cabinet leaders quickly surrendered, ceding more than 60 percent of French land to German military administration and granting nominal control of the country to the newly appointed head of state, Marshal Henri-Philippe Pétain. The aging general was beloved among the French for his military heroism during World War I, and the retreating rulers of France's Third Republic thus granted him unprecedented legislative power.

Pétain, however, blamed the egalitarian political system for France's loss of sovereignty and promptly eliminated the republic, replacing it with an authoritarian government that he called the French State. He described this new France as a "social hierarchy" that would embrace the German philosophy of ethnic purification. Historian Mark Mazower quotes Pétain

Key Facts

Conflict:
World War II

Time Period:
Mid-20th century

Genre:
Play

ANOUILH'S SILENCE

Anouilh's stubborn silence on political matters during World War II frequently led critics to speculate that the dramatist was a Nazi sympathizer. These rumors escalated as a result of Anouilh's public clashes with General Charles de Gaulle, the leader of the Free French Forces and later president of the Fifth Republic. The playwright confessed that, even in the midst of controversy surrounding fascist support of *Antigone*, he had been astonished by the reaction to his play in its early days of production. W. D. Howarth quotes a letter from the early 1980s in which Anouilh wrote, "In my naïvety I was a little bewildered. As a man who had always felt free, I had not had felt that I was risking something."

Howarth acknowledges, however, that Anouilh's "naïve idealism" ended abruptly in 1945 when Allied forces liberated Paris. The French provisional government immediately called for a purge of all collaborationist leaders still living in the country. Poet and journalist Robert Brasillach, who edited the fascist journal *Je Suis Partout*, was one of the first tried and condemned to death. Though Anouilh hardly knew Brasillach, he was deeply offended by the notion of a writer being convicted for intellectual crimes and, at last, took a stand.

Circulating a petition for a pardon at great personal risk, the playwright appealed directly to de Gaulle to commute Brassillach's sentence. The petition was ultimately unsuccessful, and Brasillach was executed eight days later. His death marked a turning point for Anouilh, who later admitted that what was left of his youth and optimism died along with Brasillach that day.

as saying that his regime would reject "the false idea of the natural equality among men." Just as Créon replaces the corrupt sibling rulers in Anouilh's play, Pétain's stern paternalistic administration supplanted the traditional French notion of "brotherhood." He even replaced the republican motto *Liberté, égalité, fraternité* (liberty, equality, brotherhood) with the new credo *Travail, famille, patrie* (work, family, fatherland).

Critics of every ilk recognized Pétain's totalitarian practicality and proclivity for ethical compromise in the speeches made by Anouilh's fictional Créon. Despite the play's obvious allusions to events of the day, however, critics were unsure of the playwright's message. There is no obvious victor in the battle between Créon and Antigone; according to theater historian Kenneth Krauss, "In the same houses in which some audience members saw Antigone as the Resistance and Creon as Vichy, there were fascist sympathizers who saw Creon as a necessary force against the Anarchist Antigone, and many more who recognized them as being equal forces that were both, in a fundamental sense, right."

This ambiguity enabled the play to pass by Nazi censors with ease while still appealing to a public hungry for insurrection. In fact, *Antigone* was one of many classical myths adapted by modern playwrights during the occupation, including *The Flies*, Sartre's retelling of Aeschylus's *Oresteia* trilogy, and *Caligula* by Albert Camus, a drama in which the troubled Roman emperor orchestrates his own assassination upon realizing the futility of existence.

Krauss refers to the period as a renaissance of French theater, noting that the new government happily funded existentialist dramas because it saw in the authors' rejection of the bourgeois world a "celebration of revolutionary fascist values." By pointing out the folly of protagonists who destroyed themselves through their individual ambitions, German ideologues and their French sympathizers could advocate the moral superiority of a totalitarian state, regarding the pieces as inadvertent propaganda. While nationalists claimed that the title character's stubborn quest for personal liberty at any cost embodied the spirit of a free France, the German government praised the work as a glorification of strong leadership that denounced free will as a path to imminent destruction.

THEMES AND STYLE

Unlike the prewar modernists, Anouilh and his fellow existentialists used myth not to highlight universal themes of human existence but to demonstrate the eternal plight of the individual condemned to choice. Their characters are not ruled by fate or religious duty like their Greek counterparts; rather, they actively choose to perform their roles in the tragedy.

Anouilh highlights this idea of choice through his use of what English scholar Redmond O'Hanlon calls the "metatheatrical frame." Bodies onstage represent both actors in the play and characters in the story. This is most clearly indicated through the figure of the Chorus. Anouilh compressed the traditional Greek chorus into a one-man commentator who can enter and exit the action of the play at will. From the curtain's rise he is present onstage along with the full cast. "Well, here we are," he begins, directing his speech toward the house. "These people are about to act out the story of Antigone." He introduces each character in turn, pausing only when he arrives at Antigone, sitting alone in the corner:

> What's she thinking? That any minute she'll have to become "Antigone." To somehow break the bounds of what she was, the rather pale, withdrawn young girl who no one in the family really takes seriously and become *Antigone* … She's thinking that she's going to die, that she's young, and that she'd rather not. But when your name is Antigone, there is only one part you can play; she will have to play hers through to the end.

In this passage Anouilh makes an important distinction between fate and destiny. Although the presence of an a priori myth or theatrical playscript might seem to dictate the actions of the characters within a story, Anouilh argues that, though the outcome is

anticipated, individuals within a set of given circumstances must choose to act before any destiny can
become reality. Unlike pawns controlled by an exterior
hand of fate, Anouilh's characters are responsible for
their own actions.

In the world of occupied France, this philosophy
implies that all citizens are to be held accountable for
the country's situation; those who do not resist choose
to collaborate by default. According to O'Hanlon,
the use of this frame places the drama in the context of its philosophical moment, transforming what
he dismisses as the "quasi-naturalist ethico-political
drama" of Sophocles into the "highly theatricalized
and self-conscious" social commentary that emerges in
Anouilh's adaptation.

Anouilh's theatrical metaphors continue through
Antigone's famous debate with Créon after her arrest.
The king cannot understand her seemingly arbitrary
motivations. "You have cast me for the villain in this
little play of yours," he says. "And positioned yourself
for the heroine." Créon offers to cover up the crime
and spare her life, but Antigone bristles, determined
to expose the injustice of Créon's ruling by compelling him to follow through with his cruel decree. In
forcing his hand, Antigone has exposed the king's role
in her destiny. She must die only because her will as
an individual clashes with his. Though he would prefer to save her life, the desire must be suppressed if
he is to maintain authority. It appears that Créon is
trapped. Antigone refuses, however, to let him off so
easily. "You could have said no," she presses, forcing
him to examine his motives; eventually Créon resigns.
"I could. But … it wouldn't have been honest," he
replies. "So I said yes."

In this scene Anouilh dramatizes the political gulf
between the French citizens who said no to German
occupation and those, like Marshal Pétain, who said
yes, even when it meant succumbing to moral compromise. Though he makes no overt claim as to which
side is more firmly in the right, the playwright takes
great pains to argue that both parties have clear agency
in the outcome.

This is underscored by Anouilh's decision to
eliminate the character of Tiresias, the blind prophet
in Sophocles' tragedy who warns Créon that his persecution of Antigone will result in his own undoing. In
the Greek myth Tiresias is a symbol of Créon's blindness, but literary scholar Murray Sachs points out that
the presence of the prophet would weaken the existentialist argument. "Blindness is not the essence of
Anouilh's Creon," he writes, noting that the king is,
"on the contrary, completely lucid."

CRITICAL DISCUSSION

Anouilh earned approval from German censors soon
after *Antigone*'s completion in 1942, and despite financial delays the production opened in 1944 to huge
commercial success. Theatergoers from both ends of the
political spectrum embraced the work, each annexing a

La France avait perdu une bataille.
Mais la France va gagner la guerre !
C. de Gaulle

In this 1943 *Allegory of the French Resistance*, the Allies, flags waving, are led by lady Liberty to crush the Nazis. Some critics think that Jean Anouilh's *Antigone* was intended as an allegory for the French Resistance, yet was veiled enough to avoid censors. Signature of Charles de Gaulle (1890–1970). Color litho. © FRENCH SCHOOL, (20TH CENTURY) / PRIVATE COLLECTION / ARCHIVES CHARMET / THE BRIDGEMAN ART LIBRARY INTERNATIONAL

portion of the play to support their respective causes.
The production earned critical acclaim from major
journals, although the high volume of favorable reviews
eventually led to a backlash.

Anouilh biographer W. D. Howarth observes that,
in the "highly-charged political atmosphere" of occupied Paris, accolades from critics with known collaborationist tendencies could ultimately be "far more harmful
than any adverse criticism." Some of the most damning
press came from the extraordinary praise of Alain Laubreaux, who wrote at least four laudatory pieces in the
collaborationist journal *Je Suis Partout*. Laubreaux was
not alone among pro-German writers in his exaltation
of the work, and within the year the French left had
boycotted the piece, calling it a "Nazi play."

When the play was commended by *Au Pilori*, a
notoriously anti-Semitic publication, Anouilh suffered
even greater damage to his reputation, but it was not
until the play's revival after the Paris liberation that
the playwright faced real danger. Howarth quotes Pol

Gaillard's call for Anouilh's indictment, in a November 1945 edition of the Communist journal *L'Humanité*, on the grounds that *Antigone*'s continued production endangered the new provisional government. "Let us be clear because it seems there are still doubts," he wrote. "Jean Anouilh's Antigone is no masterpiece, and it can only hurt the French … No work better served the purposes of the Nazis during the occupation, and no thing can more easily stop the rise of the French today." Though Anouilh was never formally blacklisted, he faced years of scrutiny following the occupation.

Outside France, however, *Antigone* was almost universally received as a positive political parable, earning praise from revivals in New York and London and in North Africa and Asia. It remains a touchstone in the canon of antiwar drama and is generally considered to oppose Nazi sentiments. Krauss defends Anouilh's long silence, maintaining that the author, with his mastery of literary structure and deft dramatic technique, would not have endowed *Antigone* with the potential to serve as an anthem for the Resistance if he had not wished the public to at least consider this possibility.

SOURCES

Anouilh, Jean. *Antigone*. Trans. Jeremy Sams. New York: Samuel French, 2002. Print.

Heiney, Donald. "Jean Anouilh: The Revival of Tragedy." *College English* 16.6 (1955): 331–35. Web. 13 Aug. 2011.

Howarth, W. D. *Anouilh, Antigone*. Studies in French Literature. London: E. Arnold, 1983. Print.

Krauss, Kenneth. *The Drama of Fallen France: Reading La Comédie Sans Tickets*. Albany: SUNY P, 2003. Print.

Mazower, Mark. *Dark Continent: Europe's Twentieth Century*. New York: A. A. Knopf, 1999. Print.

O'Hanlon, Redmond. "Metatragedy in Anouilh's *Antigone*." *Modern Language Review* 75.3 (1980): 534–46. *JSTOR*. Web. 12 Aug. 2011.

Sachs, Murray. "Notes on the Theatricality of Jean Anouilh's *Antigone*." *The French Review* 36.1 (1962): 3–11. *JSTOR*. Web. 13 Aug. 2011.

FURTHER READING

Albert, Walter. "Structures of Revolt in Giraudoux's *Electre* and Anouilh's *Antigone*." *Texas Studies in Literature and Language* 12.1 (1970): 137–50. Print.

Freeman, Ted. *Theatres of War: French Committed Theatre from the Second World War to the Cold War*. Exeter: U of Exeter P, 1998. Print.

Kaplan, Alice Yaeger. *The Collaborator: The Trial & Execution of Robert Brasillach*. Chicago: U of Chicago P, 2000. Print.

Sartre, Jean Paul. "Forgers of Myths." *Theatre Arts* 30.6 (1946): 324–35. Print.

MEDIA ADAPTATIONS

Antigone. By Jean Anouilh. Trans. Lewis Galantiere. Dir. Gerald Freedman. Perf. Geneviève Bujold, Stacy Keach, and Leah Chandler. PBS Theatre in America. Public Broadcasting Service. 13 Feb 1974. Television.

Antigone. By Jean Anouilh. Dir. Stellio Lorenzi. Perf. Jean Topart, Alain Cuny, and Marie-Hélène Breillat. Institut National de l'Audiovisuel. 21 Dec 1974. Television.

Antigone. By Jean Anouilh. Trans. Christopher Nixon. Dir. Brendan Fox. Perf. Elizabeth Marvel, Francis Guinan, and Alan Mandell. L.A. Theatre Works: Venice, CA, 2005. CD.

Sara Taylor

Aria da Capo

A Play in One Act

Edna St. Vincent Millay

OVERVIEW

American author Edna St. Vincent Millay, best remembered for her lyric verse, was the first woman to receive the Pulitzer Prize for Poetry (1923). A few years earlier her short play *Aria da Capo* (1919), presented in New York by the Provincetown Players, launched the young poet to international fame.

The play begins with a harlequinade, an eighteenth-century take on Italian commedia dell'arte, with its stock characters and comic scenarios. In *Aria da Capo* the curtain rises on Pierrot, the melancholy clown, and his love interest, the coquettish servant Columbine. Seated at a banquet table in a "merry black and white interior," they converse in a hollow fashion that Millay declares, in her author's note, should seem both "indolent and indifferent."

Their small talk is quickly interrupted by Cothurnus, who demands that Pierrot and Columbine clear out so that he may direct his own play. The two grumble, but Cothurnus, an imposing figure embodying the Greek tragic chorus, prevails. He calls two shepherds to the stage to act out a pastoral scene. The friends, Thyrsis and Corydon, frolic in the countryside, but the idyllic scene quickly sours. Abandoning lighter games, they decide to build a crepe-paper wall and, according to Thyrsis, "say that over there belongs to me, / And over here to you!" What had been lighthearted play devolves into jealous plotting. The scene ends when each succeeds in murdering the other in a covetous rage.

After arranging the bodies under the table, Cothurnus claps his hands, and Pierrot and Columbine return to play the harlequinade. When they discover the dead bodies, they balk, wondering how they can continue the scene. "Pull down the tablecloth," Cothurnus replies. "And play the farce. The audience will forget." They nod in agreement and restart the play from the beginning. The curtain falls on a comic scene identical to the first, as if the tragedy had never happened.

The play premiered just six months after the Paris Peace Conference marked the official end to World War I, and though Millay does not mention the conflict, public perception overwhelmingly classified *Aria da Capo* as an antiwar drama. Dealing with the universal themes of jealousy, greed, vanity, and loss, Millay's story resists being fixed to a specific time period. It is perhaps this quality that has made the play a political satire for the ages.

Edd Winfield Parks of the *Sewanee Review* notes that Millay is able, in her "brief allegory," to embody "all the futility and the tragic absurdity of war" that is communicated in epic dramas of three times the length. *Aria da Capo* remains in production at regional and university theaters worldwide. In addition to its notoriety as a piece of dramatic literature, the play has also inspired operatic adaptations.

HISTORICAL AND LITERARY CONTEXT

There were approximately 37,500,000 military and civilian casualties during World War I, making the so-called Great War the sixth-deadliest conflict in human history. Particularly startling was that most World War I casualties, unlike those of previous wars, resulted from combat rather than disease. According to theater historian Ronald Wainscott, "The aftershock of World War I reverberated in the American theater, not only in plays about warfare … but in the growth of seriousness in subject matter now deemed appropriate for the stage." The incredulity of the populace, he notes, afforded theater artists the opportunity to abandon the more patriotic themes of the war era and to experiment with both content and form.

The Provincetown Players were among the most influential of these experimental theater groups, which later became known collectively as the "Little Theatre Movement." Comprising small, subscription-based playhouses modeled on the independent theaters of Europe, the movement was instrumental in preparing Americans for the growing trend of politically charged symbolist and expressionistic theater productions catching on worldwide.

After moving to Greenwich Village in 1917, Millay was unable to support herself with her poetry and joined the Provincetown Players in hopes of supplementing her income. Though in her personal correspondence she mentions working on "a Pierrot play" as early as 1916, it was not until reaching New York City that the young writer from rural Maine could grasp the disparity between the positions of soldiers fighting for a "noble cause" and the attitudes of self-interested bourgeoisie awaiting the soldiers' return stateside. News of

··· Key Facts

Conflict:
World War I

Time Period:
Early 20th century

Genre:
Play

WAR AS SLAPSTICK: WILLIAM BOYD'S *AN ICE-CREAM WAR*

In her World War I play *Aria da Capo*, Edna St. Vincent Millay employs stylistic experimentation as a means of exposing the grotesque irrationality of war. Writing more than six decades later, British novelist William Boyd offers his own absurd take on the Great War in his award-winning novel *An Ice Cream War* (1982). At once a satirical glimpse at the British war effort and a shocking depiction of the devastating effects of combat, *An Ice-Cream War* continually juxtaposes the mundane, often comic concerns of the people who have stayed behind in Britain and the hapless maneuvers of the forces fighting their way through East Africa.

Throughout the novel, Boyd's narrative moves seamlessly, and at times jarringly, between moments of ridiculous humor and incidents of grim violence. In one instance, a British officer's inopportune sneeze causes one of his troops to discharge his weapon, accidentally killing one of his comrades. In another scene, the British army finds itself repelled by a swarm of bees as it tries to lay siege to a German stronghold. Believing the bees to be a sophisticated new form of weapon, the soldiers cannot help but ponder the ruthless cunning of their enemy. Constant throughout this absurdist drama is Boyd's abiding sympathy for his main characters, all of whom struggle to find meaning amidst the chaos of world conflict.

the conflict abroad infiltrated much of Millay's early work, according to literary critic Harriet Monroe, who noted that Millay "was powerfully moved by the contrast between [the war's] tragic futilities and the gay little pleasantries of Greenwich Village life."

In addition to exposing the foolishness of territorial warfare, Millay criticized what she viewed as the irresponsible isolationist policies of the American government. Though the United States initially remained uninvolved in World War I, German submarine attacks on American ships forced participation in the international conflict, marking the first breach of U.S. neutrality policies since the 1800s.

Despite Woodrow Wilson's efforts to engage America in more responsible foreign policy measures after the war, the Senate repudiated the Treaty of Versailles, refusing to join the League of Nations. In the 1940s Millay appealed to Americans directly, giving speeches and publishing verse about the necessity of American involvement in World War II. In her poem "There Are No Islands Anymore," she wrote, "No man, no nation is made free, / By stating it intends to be."

This mocking tone, though couched in allegory, is evident from the play's first and last lines, as Columbine exclaims, "Pierrot, a macaroon! I cannot *live* without a macaroon!" To classify want of a cookie as a life and death matter is a clear affront to those who lost family members in the war, and Millay emphasizes the persistence of American indifference to the foreign cause by bookending her war tragedy with the buffoonery of the Harlequin elite.

New York Times theater critic Alexander Woollcott agreed that, though this subtle jab at American apathy might be lost on most audiences,

> surely no mother from a gold-starred home, who
> saw the war come and go like a grotesque comet
> and who now hears the rattlepated merriment

of her neighbors all the more distinctly because of the blank silence in her own impoverished home—surely no such mother will quite miss the point of *Aria da Capo*.

THEMES AND STYLE

The term *da capo aria* refers to a type of musical composition, popular in the baroque era, made up of two distinct sections and a coda. *Aria da Capo* takes its name from this unique three-part repeating structure. The first section is the aria, a self-contained musical entity that could, in principle, be sung alone. The second section, dependent on the first, usually supplies a contrast in key, texture, and mood. The coda is typically specified only by the direction *da capo*, an Italian phrase meaning "from the head," which signifies that the melody should repeat the beginning verse in its entirety.

By inverting the phrase, Millay implies that the "aria," or farce, of the Harlequinade has already taken place and will continue "da capo," or from the beginning, in perpetuity. In this way the short play is strangely prophetic, as a return to isolationism left the United States unprepared for the attack on the American military base in Pearl Harbor that forced U.S. engagement in World War II.

The contrast evidenced between the worlds of the Harlequinade and Millay's rendering of the traditional medieval shepherds' play advance the conceit of a da capo aria. While both forms utilize character archetypes as stand-ins for larger metaphorical ideas, the juxtaposition of the clowns' comic burlesque to the shepherds' morality play allows Millay to showcase the disparity between the decadence of isolationism and sacrifice of engagement without ever overtly making a political comment.

Even though the shepherds are enacting their play on the setting originally fixed for the Harlequinade, their actions speak more clearly to the idea of justice being "black and white" than do those of Pierrot and Columbine. In her own production, Millay further emphasized this idea with stylized costume choices. She specifies that Pierrot and Columbine should wear lilac and pink, respectively, ghostly shades next to the high contrast of the stage setting. On the other hand, according to her author's note, the two shepherds should have cloaks of bright red and blue that "must be so strong and vivid in every way that when Columbine comes in and says, 'Is this my scene or not?' it will seem to the audience that it is she, not the shepherds, who is hopelessly out of the scene."

This sense of discord is carried into the stage properties as well. Thyrsis and Corydon, thrust upon the Harlequinade to perform their tragedy before they have had time to prepare, complain to their director, Cothurnus, "We cannot act / A tragedy with comic properties!" Cothurnus replies ominously, "Try it and see. I think you'll find you can." The shepherds then proceed to enact their violent deeds with the bits of ribbon and tissue paper flowers left over from the comic scene. They build the wall with streamers and pretend that the brightly colored pieces of confetti from the table are variously jewels and poison, acknowledging all along that they must stretch their imagination to construct these "truths."

This practice of metatheatricality, in which characters tend to recognize that they are performing in a play, heightens the tension felt when their pretended weapons result in their "actual" deaths. By demonstrating that the shepherds can indeed murder each other with trifles, Millay seems to assert that even when participants in military conflict acknowledge that they are simply "playing a dangerous game," the results are the same: war ends in death.

The highly stylized nature of *Aria da Capo* builds on the symbolist tradition that had been gaining ground in literature and drama since the mid-nineteenth century. Unlike the verisimilitude of stage setting and naturalistic themes that had dominated theater productions for nearly a hundred years, works like Millay's *Aria da Capo* sought to embody heroic ideals rather than humble reality. Millay uses allegorical characters to evoke the values attached to such genres as commedia dell'arte, Greek tragedy, medieval verse drama, and classical opera. Her political message is thus interpolated through these comparisons.

CRITICAL DISCUSSION

Woollcott's *New York Times* review of *Aria da Capo* was the only noteworthy commentary to follow the play's premiere in 1919. Nonetheless, his unabashed praise—calling Millay's one-act drama "the most beautiful and most interesting play in the English language now to be seen in New York"—earned the piece considerable attention.

Millay's biographer Nancy Milford remarks that the volume of the poet's correspondence doubled in the months following the Provincetown Players'

production. She received so many requests for performance licenses and information about her interpretation of the script that she felt the need to add an appendix describing her staging in the drama's formal release by Harper & Brothers in 1920. The Provincetown Players revived the work at least three times before 1921, which added to the fervor surrounding the play. Even thirty years later, licensing statements show that *Aria da Capo* was performed in 471 different theaters in the United States during the 1950–51 season alone.

Millay considered the play to be among her best works: "On the stage, all its intricacies move into place in a clear and terrible pattern. I am very proud of *Aria da Capo*. I wish I had a dozen more, not like it, but as good." The success of the drama turned the poet from a cult favorite in Greenwich Village to an international sensation. Her newfound name recognition resulted in the subsequent publication of some of her most treasured lyric poetry.

Her newfound standing as the "It-girl of the hour," however, subjected Millay and her unconventional lifestyle to considerable criticism. A self-proclaimed bohemian in the habit of entertaining both male and female lovers, Millay seemed to share many of the characteristics of the decadent and irresponsible youth who were the objects of her critique.

After rival playwright William Carlos Williams's play *The Old Apple Tree* was passed over for *Aria da Capo* at a prominent New York theater, Williams wrote a scathing parody of Millay's play where he lampooned her reputation for promiscuity and sentimental writing style. Transforming *Aria da Capo*'s shepherds into pseudointellectual jazz babies, *Paterson* attacked both Millay's literary work and her personal life. According to literary critic Sandra Gilbert, "The most unpleasant representative of female art [in Williams's play] is the foolish lesbian 'poetess' Corydon, whose flirtation with a nymphet named Phyllis Williams dramatizes in terms of bad metaphors and banal literary history."

Millay's quiet victory, though, was her enduring success. Monroe defies critics who dismiss Millay's writing on the grounds of its femininity, calling this its lasting virtue: "In this brief, swiftly moving, symbolic Pierrot play, she was able to strike the hardest blow at the War-god which has ever been dealt him by a poet of our language—and this, paradoxically, with the lightest possible touch."

SOURCES

Gilbert, Sandra, and Susan Gubar. "Female Female Impersonators." *No Man's Land: The Place of the Woman Writer in the Twentieth Century.* New Haven: Yale UP, 1988. 57–120. Print.

Milford, Nancy. *Savage Beauty: The Life of Edna St. Vincent Millay.* New York: Random, 2001. Print.

Millay, Edna St. Vincent. *Aria Da Capo: A Play in One Act.* New York: Harper, 1920. Print.

Monroe, Harriet. "Advance or Retreat?" *Poetry* 38.4 (1931): 216–21. *JSTOR.* Web. 6 Aug. 2011.

Parks, Edd Winfield. "Edna St. Vincent Millay." *Sewanee Review* 38.1 (1930): 42–49. *JSTOR.* Web. 8 Aug. 2011.

Schweik, Susan M. *A Gulf So Deeply Cut: American Women Poets and the Second World War.* Madison: U of Wisconsin P, 1991. Print.

Wainscott, Ronald Harold. *The Emergence of the Modern American Theater, 1914–1929.* New Haven: Yale UP, 1997. Print.

Woollcott, Alexander. "Second Thoughts on First Nights: There Are War Plays and War Plays." Rev. of *Aria da Capo*, by Edna St. Vincent Millay. *New York Times.* 14 Dec. 1919: XX2-XX2. *ProQuest Historical Newspapers.* Web. 8 Aug. 2011.

FURTHER READING

Baudelaire, Charles. *Flowers of Evil: From the French of Charles Baudelaire.* Trans. Edna St. Vincent Millay. Ed. George Dillon. New York: Harper, 1936. Print.

Gurko, Miriam. *Restless Spirit: The Life of Edna St. Vincent Millay.* New York: Crowell, 1962. Print.

Millay, Edna St. Vincent. *Collected Poems.* 1956. Alexandria: Chadwyck, 1999. Print.

Women Writers of the Provincetown Players: A Collection of Short Works. Ed. Judith E. Barlow. Albany: Excelsior, 2009. Print.

Sara Taylor

ATONEMENT

Ian McEwan

OVERVIEW

Atonement (2001) is a highly acclaimed novel by British author Ian McEwan. Set in Europe during the buildup to World War II and the eventual German occupation of France, the story follows the life Briony Tallis, an upper-middle-class British adolescent with an active imagination and a talent for writing. As the title suggests, *Atonement* explores questions of guilt and redemption, but it is also a story about storytelling itself, a metanarrative that explores the role of the author in shaping our understanding of tragedies, both personal and shared.

As a thirteen-year-old, the inquisitive and precocious Briony glimpses a raw, furtive love scene between her older sister Cecilia and Robbie Turner, the housekeeper's son. She subsequently witnesses the apparent sexual assault of her cousin Lola. Briony accuses Robbie of the rape, and her allegations lead to devastating consequences: he is torn from Cecilia, imprisoned, and subsequently sent to fight against the Germans in France. During the following years Briony attempts to make amends for Robbie's unwarranted punishment, first by serving as a nurse during the war and later by apologizing to her estranged sister and promising Robbie complete exoneration through the courts.

In a sudden switch, however, Briony takes over the previously third-person narrative and reveals that her reconciliations with Cecilia and Robbie never actually occurred. Now seventy-seven, she admits that she has written the entire preceding account over and over during the years since her adolescence, treating herself as a character in it, and that she invented the resolution in an attempt to finally come to terms with the misdeeds of her youth. In her final, still possibly deceptive version, Robbie has died on the beaches of Dunkirk in France and Cecilia has been killed in the 1940 bombing of London's Balham Tube station by the *Luftwaffe* (the German air force). If it is not possible to atone for her transgressions, Briony concludes, it is her duty as an author (as it is McEwan's) to create something of value, however fictional, from the tragic events.

Widely considered McEwan's masterpiece, *Atonement* has been praised for its psychological complexity and thoroughly researched depictions of life during wartime, both on the front lines during the German invasion of France and in the London hospitals where thousands of British soldiers were treated for their wounds. The correlation between Briony's falsified conclusion to her narrative and the tendency of the British to reimagine the evacuation at Dunkirk as a victory despite their heavy losses highlights the difficulty of writing a "true" account of the war—one that portrays the human toll of its senseless and irredeemable violence rather than the soldiers' heroism and victory.

Atonement received the 2002 National Book Critics Circle Award and was named the best novel of 2001 by *Time* magazine. It was subsequently made into a BAFTA- and Academy Award-nominated film.

HISTORICAL AND LITERARY CONTEXT

Atonement begins in the summer of 1935, as all of England is immersed in a heat wave and the British government nervously keeps watch on an increasingly and more openly militarized and racist Germany. Briony's father, Jack, is a civil servant who is absent from the family's Surrey estate during much of the opening section of the novel; he is presumably in London engaging in British policy decisions, which wavered between appeasement and preparation for conflict. At one point Jack's wife, Emily, sneaks a look at some of his documents, where she finds calculations of projected war casualties. Although Lola's rape and Briony's erroneous accusation dominate this part of the novel, McEwan makes it clear that even four years before Britain officially entered World War II, its imminence weighed heavily on British minds.

The second section of the novel is set in 1940. Cecilia has become a nurse, moved to London, and cut off all contact with her family because of their part in Robbie's imprisonment. The narrative follows Robbie to northern France. Recently released from prison on the condition that he join the British Expeditionary Force (BEF), he is among the first troops sent to fight in Europe.

The BEF was deployed along France's border with Belgium in September 1939 but did not engage in combat until May 10, 1940, when the Germans invaded France. By the end of the month, German troops had pushed the BEF and their French and Belgian counterparts to the northwestern coast near the city of Dunkirk. The British soldiers had only a dim prospect of survival. In a surprising move, however, the Germans halted their advance on

⁙ Key Facts

Conflict:
World War II

Time Period:
Mid-20th Century

Genre:
Novel

Awards:
Shortlisted for Man Booker Prize, 2001; Time Magazine Best Novel of the Year, 2001; National Book Critics Circle Award, 2002

THE WAR EFFORT AT SEA: THE EVACUATION OF DUNKIRK

Throughout World War II, civilians across Western Europe played a critical role in the Allied defense efforts, whether by providing food and provisions to soldiers, participating in organized resistance movements, or harboring Jewish fugitives from the Nazi extermination program. In addition to their activities on land, noncombatants also proved critical to the war effort at sea.

Nowhere was the role of civilians more vital than during the evacuation of Dunkirk. Between May 27 and June 4, 1940, after German forces inexplicably halted their advance on British and French forces trapped along France's northeastern coast, the British navy orchestrated the escape of more than 338,000 troops. In what became known as Operation Dynamo, the navy requisitioned approximately seven hundred civilian ships, including fishing vessels, commercial ferries, and private yachts, to assist with the evacuation.

Launching from the English coastal town of Ramsgate, these small vessels helped transport thousands of stranded British and French troops to England. The mission was particularly perilous because most of the ships had never before crossed the English Channel. Notable among these civilian boats was the *Royal Daffodil*, a ferryboat that serviced the River Mersey, which transported nearly 7,500 soldiers over the course of five channel crossings.

Dunkirk for three days, leaving just enough time for the British Royal Navy, with the vital help of seven hundred "little ships" (most of which were commandeered private pleasure boats and yachts) to evacuate more than 300,000 soldiers from the area. The event was hailed as a victory snatched from the jaws of defeat; government propagandists touted a national unity that made the mismatched battle more palatable. This led to the term "Dunkirk spirit," which the British still use to describe their ability to endure in the direst circumstances. McEwan's fictional portrayal of these events is based largely on stories he heard from his father, who had experienced them firsthand as a member of the BEF.

Atonement turns next to Briony's service as a nurse in London's St. Thomas' Hospital, where many of the wounded British and French soldiers evacuated from Dunkirk were treated. It served as an important medical center for British forces until a portion of it was destroyed during the German bombing of London. Much of this part of the book is based on *No Time for Romance*, the 1977 autobiography of Lucilla Andrews, a novelist and World War II nurse stationed at St. Thomas' Hospital. When marked similarities were discovered, London's *Mail on Sunday* criticized McEwan for possible plagiarism.

In the novel's final section, titled "London 1999," Briony admits that she fabricated her account of a reunion between Robbie (on military leave) and Cecilia and that she even made up the circumstances of their deaths during the war. This section is purposely fragmented and unreliable. In the vein of Kurt Vonnegut's *Slaughterhouse-Five* (1969) and Tim O'Brien's short story "How to Tell a True War Story" (1990), *Atonement* employs techniques of metafiction: it is not about the war itself but is rather about the process of writing about war.

Each of these three postmodern works presents a variety of perspectives, refuting the notion that a unified narrative can approach the truth of events. Unlike Vonnegut, O'Brien (who wrote about the Vietnam War), and most authors of canonical World War II texts, McEwan did not experience the war firsthand. In "The Anxiety of Authenticity," Maria Margonis explores the difficulties this causes in the text: "Why did McEwan … frame his carefully researched fictionalization of the experience of Dunkirk in an elaborate set of narrative games that call into question not only what novelists do with their research and experience but their motives for doing it?"

McEwan actively participates in delving into these dilemmas and pointedly leaves them unresolved. Rather than searching for truth or accuracy, Briony offers romance and myth to satisfy the reader's desire for closure before she admits to having lied. The novel's ending is in some senses unfulfilling, mimicking our equally distorted cultural memory of the period. This is the value of the postmodern and metafictional aspects of McEwan's book: they juxtapose the grand narrative construct of popular memory about World War II England with a messier reality that he insists cannot be represented.

THEMES AND STYLE

Atonement is a complex novel with a diverse set of concerns, among them cause and effect, guilt, reconciliation, authorial responsibility, and the elusiveness of the past. McEwan uses an array of writing styles and perspectives to explore these often interdependent themes.

The initial scenes are written in a languid prose reminiscent of early-nineteenth-century English novels of manners, which often take place in country homes and reflect what are now considered naive, antiquated concerns with etiquette and social class. The young Briony attempts to be a writer by ventriloquizing earlier literary styles and their aesthetics. When she is older and refines the narrative, she adds another level, using her character to elucidate British attitudes in the years leading up to the Second World War.

The tone of the middle sections shifts drastically, portraying in stark, unflinching language the gruesome realities of Robbie and Briony's wartime experiences. Briony's quest for redemption correlates her painful journey into adulthood with the country's transition into the postwar era. Until this point in the novel, the third-person omniscient point of view has created a seemingly objective narrative.

In the final section, there is a sudden shift to Briony's first-person perspective, which allows for the reflective, measured tones of her long-deliberated confession. The intrusive moral judgments and one-sided interpretations of her teenage years vanish, and her assessment of the possibility of expiation takes shape.

McEwan underscores the futility of Briony's attempts at atonement: "Everyone was guilty, and no one was. No one would be redeemed by a change of evidence, for there weren't enough people, enough paper and pens, enough patience and peace, to take down the statements of all the witnesses and gather in the facts." At the novel's conclusion, however, Briony explains the necessity of her undertaking: that true reconciliation with the past "was always an impossible task, and that was precisely the point. The attempt was all."

Atonement suggests that although narratives of the horrors and atrocities of World War II can only offer a fraction of the truth, the search for meaning is in itself a noble pursuit, because it is a reflection of our basic human need to wring order out of chaos. Paradoxically, both McEwan and Briony must lie to their readers to give an honest account of the war. An outsider to the love story between Cecilia and Robbie, Briony invents the romantic reunion between the two to give her narrative a sense of balance and closure. McEwan manipulates fragments of the past—gleaned from his research at the Imperial War Museum, Andrews's autobiography, and his father's stories about the Dunkirk evacuation—to reconcile a brutal episode that has played a major role in defining our present-day lives.

In an interview in Margaret Reynolds and Jonathan Noakes's *Ian McEwan*, the author himself calls *Atonement* "a novel full of other writers." The work's epigraph is from Jane Austen's *Northanger Abbey* (1818), which also concerns the spiraling consequences of an overactive imagination. Critics have identified a number of twentieth-century influences on the novel, including the works of Henry James, E. M. Forster, Virginia Woolf, and Elizabeth Bowen, whose *Heat of the Day* (1948) deals with events at Dunkirk and their impact.

McEwan has said that in his book's first section, he consciously challenged early modernism, with its tendency to value stream-of-consciousness observations and literary acrobatics over plot and characters. Geoff Dyer notes in a *Guardian* review that *Atonement* "is less about a novelist harking nostalgically back to the consoling certainties of the past than it is about creatively extending and hauling a defining part of the British literary tradition up to and into the twenty-first century."

CRITICAL DISCUSSION

Early in his career McEwan found critical favor with such novels as *The Comfort of Strangers* (1981), *Enduring Love* (1997), and *Amsterdam* (1998), but it was *Atonement* that established him as a major figure in contemporary English literature. Reviewers have been nearly unanimous in praising the novel.

Esteemed literary critic Frank Kermode writes in the *London Review of Books* that "no contemporary of [McEwan's] has shown such passionate dedication to the art of the novel," and in the *International Fiction Review*, Nora Foster Stovel calls the work "a great novel in the grand tradition." Reviewers who dislike the book most often object to its ending, finding it contrived or too self-consciously postmodern in its attempt to undermine our understanding of the plot. Nevertheless, *Atonement* spent more than three months on the *New York Times* best-seller list, and popular interest in the novel was rekindled in 2007 after the release of its film adaptation.

Criticism of *Atonement* has particularly focused on McEwan's experimentation with narrative techniques, emphasizing the way in which he adroitly shifts from the writing style of the late nineteenth and early twentieth centuries—making free use of interior monologue and indirect discourse—to the gritty realism of modern war literature and finally to the frank, meditative reflections on authorial responsibility that constitute the final section. Criticism of the text as war literature is relatively scarce; more commonly the war is seen as a backdrop against which McEwan plays out his theoretical concern with the morality of historical fiction.

Still, some reviewers see McEwan's manipulation of language, time, and perspective as an exploration of the continuing influence that World War II exerts on contemporary life. In "Briony's Stand against Oblivion: The Making of Fiction in Ian McEwan's *Atonement*," Brian Finney writes, "World War Two, which introduced the world to mass ethnic cleansing, the subsequent Cold War, and the permanent threat of nuclear war, appears to have elicited aesthetic structures that reflect the complexity and horror of life in the second half of that century."

SOURCES

Dyer, Geoff. "Who's Afraid of Influence?" Rev. of *Atonement*, by Ian McEwan. *Guardian* [London]. Guardian News and Media, 22 September 2001: 8. Web. 24 May 2011.

Finney, Brian. "Briony's Stand against Oblivion: The Making of Fiction in Ian McEwan's *Atonement*." *Journal of Modern Literature* 27.3 (2004): 68–82. Print.

Kermode, Frank. "Point of View." Rev. of *Atonement*, by Ian McEwan. *London Review of Books* 4 Oct. 2001: 8–9. Print.

Margonis, Maria. "The Anxiety of Authenticity: Writing Historical Fiction at the End of the Twentieth Century." *History Workshop Journal* 65 (2008): 138–60. Print.

McEwan, Ian. *Atonement*. London: Cape, 2001. Print.

———. Interview by John Noakes. *Ian McEwan: The Essential Guide*. Ed. Margaret Reynolds and Jonathan Noakes. London: Vintage: 2002. 10–26. Print.

Stovel, Nora Foster. Rev. of *Atonement*, by Ian McEwan. *International Fiction Review* 31.1–2 (2004): 114. Print.

FURTHER READING

Albers, Stephanie, and Torsten Caeners. "The Poetics and Aesthetics of Ian McEwan's *Atonement.*" *English Studies* 90.6 (2009): 707–20. Print.

Cormack, Alistair. "Postmodernism and the Ethics of Fiction in *Atonement.*" *Ian McEwan: Contemporary Critical Perspectives.* Ed. Sebastian Groes. London: Continuum, 2009. 57–69. Print.

Crosthwaite, Paul. "Speed, War, and Traumatic Affect: Reading Ian McEwan's *Atonement.*" *Cultural Politics* 3.1 (2007): 51–70. Print.

Hidalgo, Pilar. "Memory and Storytelling in Ian McEwan's *Atonement.*" *Critique* 46.2 (2005): 82–91. Print.

Mathews, Peter. "The Impression of a Deeper Darkness: Ian McEwan's *Atonement.*" *English Studies in Canada* 32.1 (2006): 147–60. Print.

McLoughlin, Kate. "Duration." *Authoring War: The Literary Representation of War from the Iliad to Iraq.* Cambridge: Cambridge UP, 2011. 107–34. Print.

MEDIA ADAPTATION

Atonement. Dir. Joe Wright. Perf. Saoirse Ronan, Brenda Blethyn, Julia West, and James McAvoy. Universal Pictures, 2007. Film.

Jacob Schmitt

Austerlitz

W. G. Sebald

OVERVIEW

Austerlitz (2001) is the last completed work of German prose writer W. G. Sebald. The novel tells the story of Jacques Austerlitz, who escaped Czechoslovakia as part of the *Kindertransport*, an effort to evacuate Jewish children from Nazi-occupied territories and place them with British families in the months leading up to World War II. Austerlitz comes of age believing he is Dafydd Elias, the son of a Welsh minister. While in boarding school, he discovers his real name due to legal technicalities related to his supposed father's death, and he becomes vaguely aware that he had been a war refugee as a small child. Over the next several decades, he largely suppresses direct knowledge of his origins, going so far as to avoid information about World War II and the events that made him an orphan.

Upon taking early retirement from his job as an architectural historian in 1991, Austerlitz sets out to write a large-scale synthesis of his architectural theories, but the weight of what he refers to as his "self-censorship" catches up with him, and he suffers a nervous breakdown. After his collapse Austerlitz begins to excavate his past, forcing himself to confront his fragmentary memories. He consults the state archives in Prague, the city of his birth, where he finds evidence that leads him to a family friend who can provide him with further details about his origins. He uncovers important facets of his identity in conversation with the woman, who was his nanny and next-door neighbor during his infancy, and he continues his search for his identity in the archives of Theresienstadt, the concentration camp where his mother was interned, and in archives in Paris.

Told in the first person, *Austerlitz* unfolds between the late 1960s and late 1990s. The work measures the psychological toll suffered by its protagonist, a result not only of the original distress of losing his parents but also of the decades-long suppression of his early years. At the same time, the book gauges the degree to which emotional devastation and repression is enabled by modern systems of power and knowledge, as embodied most prominently in architecture and in public archives that purport to document the past. As such, *Austerlitz* is as much a meditation on memory and historical trauma as it is a novelistic portrait of a unique character.

HISTORICAL AND LITERARY CONTEXT

For many late twentieth-century artists and intellectuals, including Sebald, the horrors committed by the Nazi regime challenged basic assumptions upon which Western civilization rested. While high cultural achievement had been historically linked with social progress, and the superiority of reason-based systems of power had seemed self-evident to many, the Nazis manipulated both reason and culture to promote their nihilistic political agenda.

In his nonfiction work and various interviews, Sebald indicates that he did not believe traditional literary forms, themselves a product of historical assumptions predating the Nazi period, were capable of telling the truth about the Holocaust. As a non-Jewish German and the son of a Wehrmacht soldier, Sebald was in a particularly precarious position. He had no authority to speak from the points of view of Holocaust victims or their descendants. In this respect his liberal interweaving of multiple literary genres can be seen as a response to the ethical stakes imposed by the Holocaust on artists and intellectuals. Sebald's prose writings are framed as documentary narratives rather than works of traditional fiction and largely comprise observations, conversations, and historical anecdotes. The book's accompanying photographs enhance this documentary quality, while also reframing the written text so as to call into question its legitimacy. By confining his text to material that the narrator discovers on his own, while eschewing the conventional novelistic technique of imagining characters' internal lives, Sebald presents a narrative that has clear limits. In this way he attempts to honor those who died or were traumatized by his country's history without presuming to speak for them.

This approach is particularly striking in *Austerlitz*. On the surface the work seems to conform to novelistic conventions, in contrast to Sebald's other books. It takes as its subject a single character with a remarkable life history and attempts to acquaint the reader with the person and his life. While Austerlitz is the book's subject, however, the narrative is revealed through a series of documented conversations between him and the narrator. Photographs and other images in the text, many of which purport to have been taken or collected by Austerlitz, further the illusion of the text's documentary status. As artifacts of past moments, ranging

+ *Key Facts*

Conflict:
World War II

Time Period:
Mid-20th Century

Genre:
Novel

Awards:
Independent Foreign
Fiction Prize, 2002;
Koret Jewish Book Award,
special award, 2002;
National Book Critics Circle
Award for Fiction, 2002

THE TWO MODELS FOR JACQUES AUSTERLITZ

Each of W. G. Sebald's works intentionally straddles the border between fact and fiction, exhibiting the trappings of nonfiction while consistently pointing to the inherently fictional nature of all storytelling and personal reflection. Readers might be tempted to believe that Jacques Austerlitz is an actual acquaintance of the author-narrator of the book that bears his name, but in fact Sebald modeled him on two different people, one of whom was an actual acquaintance, the other of whom he learned about by watching television.

Sebald was acquainted in real life with a London-based architectural historian whom he had met repeatedly by chance in out-of-the-way locations in Belgium. When they would meet, Sebald, like the narrator of *Austerlitz*, would listen with great admiration to his acquaintance's intellectually stimulating disquisitions on architecture. Onto the shape of this acquaintance's life, meanwhile, Sebald grafted the childhood experience of a woman whose story he had learned about via a television broadcast. The woman had been evacuated from Germany as a toddler, and she was brought up by fundamentalist Christians in Wales who kept her in ignorance of her identity.

from the seemingly inconsequential (a contemporary street scene) to the profound (a photograph of Austerlitz's mother, who was killed in a Nazi death camp), the images in Sebald's text ceaselessly point to a past that can never be truly recaptured. Taken together, these techniques provide a semblance of "proof" that what is being stated actually happened, while also hinting at numerous details that remain missing—thus pointing to the limits of language and narrative.

THEMES AND STYLE

The conversations between the narrator and Austerlitz unfold in long sections unbroken by paragraph breaks. In this way Austerlitz's voice becomes nested within the narration itself rather than being set off by punctuation or any pronounced shift in tone. The story's major events occur during two distinct time periods. The first spans the years 1967 to 1975, when Austerlitz and the narrator become acquainted during a series of coincidental encounters in Belgium. Each time they meet, as the narrator says, "we simply went on with our conversation, wasting no time in commenting on the improbability of our meeting again." These early discussions revolve almost exclusively around architectural history; indeed, the narrator learns almost nothing about Austerlitz's personal life during this first period of their acquaintance. Beginning in 1975 the narrator and Austerlitz lose touch for two decades, only to be reunited in 1996—again purely by chance. In the interim Austerlitz discovers the truth about his life, and it is during their second period of friendship that he tells the narrator about his attempt to reconstruct his past.

On one level this reconstruction amounts to an elegy for the Austerlitz family and for European Jewry as a whole. Like many elegies dating from the modernist period onward, it appears to offer little in the way of consolation. Austerlitz's encounter with his past and his recognition of what he has lost represent a rediscovery of self. The value of such a rediscovery, however, particularly in the face of the Holocaust, remains uncertain. The process of reconstruction itself incapacitates Austerlitz and can never be completed or satisfyingly concluded. What is recovered is not an intact self but scraps of information and sets of fragmentary memories without any center. In this way the book suggests that the losses suffered by European Jews in the 1930s and 1940s is ongoing and immeasurable, extending beyond the actual lost lives to include an erasure of historical consciousness that has devastated entire cultures.

At the same time, *Austerlitz* points to numerous facets of modern life that conspire to enable both its atrocity and its erasure from the historical record. As the narrator relates, Austerlitz studies "the architectural style of the capitalist era," particularly "the compulsive sense of order and the tendency towards monumentalism evident in law courts and penal institutions, railway stations and stock exchanges, opera houses and lunatic asylums, and the dwellings built to rectangular grid patterns for the labor force." As he uncovers the story of how the Nazi regime destroyed his family, Austerlitz realizes that these various architectural structures actually echo the design of concentration camps. Sebald thus suggests that Nazism, far from being antithetical to other modern societies, arose from the same mix of intellectual currents, economic forces, and cultural traditions found in those nations that opposed Germany during World War II. Acquiescence to the norms of modern society, then, not only fails to honor the full nature of the atrocities committed by the Nazis but also risks enabling other forms of cruelty in the future.

To reconstruct history as Sebald (via Austerlitz) does is to counter such tendencies. Throughout his writings, Sebald demonstrates a preoccupation with systems of historical preservation, from local museums to national archives. Such archival institutions serve different functions from text to text, but they all embody the author's abiding concern for the preservation of history and, perhaps more significantly, knowledge. As *Austerlitz* makes clear, however, archival preservation is also an expression of political power. Victims of history, such as Austerlitz's parents, leave scant traces on the historical record. As beings whose lives were devalued by those very powers responsible for documenting history, in other words, they are not substantially part of official history.

Still, for Sebald's protagonist the archive represents an unavoidable and necessary starting point for historical reconstruction. Austerlitz, as J. J. Long points out in *W. G. Sebald: Image, Archive, Modernity*, depends for his sense of identity on the archives of Prague, Theresienstadt, and Paris, because these places bear clues into his parents' lives. The scraps of archival information that Austerlitz finds, however, repeatedly open up the need for further forms of investigation. "The epistemological promise of the archive is never fulfilled," Long writes, "which is why it leaves the end of this particular text open and the subjectivity of Austerlitz in a permanent state of incompletion."

In the same way, architecture plays a central role in both the preservation and erasure of knowledge. The novel closes with a passage about the Bibliotéque Nationale in Paris, a gigantic building that seems, in Sebald's view, to be constructed in such a way as to prevent the preservation and dissemination of knowledge. In other words, the building's very architecture stands in direct opposition to its avowed reason for existing. The metaphorical significance of this dysfunctional institution becomes unmistakable when the author reveals that the site on which the building stands was previously the location of a warehouse where the confiscated possessions of Parisian Jews were stored during World War II. The institution's very foundation, Sebald suggests, obscures the atrocity in which those who built it were complicit.

CRITICAL DISCUSSION

At the time of its publication, *Austerlitz* was already being hailed as a classic, with many reviewers suggesting that it represented an artistic advance over Sebald's previous work. Although Sebald died in a car crash shortly after the book's publication, in the ensuing years he has become the subject of an extraordinary amount of attention among both German- and English-language scholars. No consensus exists as to which of Sebald's four prose texts represents his highest artistic achievement. Furthermore, the consistency of Sebald's style and thematic concerns across all four works is such that the study of any one of the texts necessarily requires familiarity with the others. *The Emergence of Memory: Conversations with W. G. Sebald* (2007), edited by Lynne Sharon Schwartz, includes reviews, essays, and interviews drawn from the mainstream press. Together they offer a lucid and concise overview of Sebald's thematic preoccupations, including his concern with the ethics of Holocaust representation and the importance of cultural memory. Mark R. McCulloh's *Understanding W. G. Sebald* (2003) proceeds systematically through the four major prose texts and usefully delineates the ways in which Sebald's approaches to form and style relate to his sense of history. *W. G. Sebald: A Critical Companion*, edited by J. J. Long and Anne Whitehead (2004), is composed of scholarly essays on what the editors see as Sebald's signature concerns, including "the effects of political history on nature and on the lives of individuals, as well as the nature of memory, be it collective, familial,

A still from the documentary, *Into the Arms of Strangers: Stories of the Kindertransport*, which illuminates the experiences of children who were transported out of danger, without their parents, during World War II. © SABINE FILMS / THE KOBAL COLLECTION

or individual." Long's *W. G. Sebald: Image, Archive, Modernity* (2007), meanwhile, considers Sebald's four prose texts in relation to Michel Foucault's theory of modern archival systems.

More specialized considerations of *Austerlitz* and of Sebald's relationship to the Holocaust abound as well. A 2006 article in *MLN* by John Zilcosky situates the novel relative to postmodern conceptions of history and literature, while addressing the ethical implications of Sebald's representation of the Holocaust. Brad Prager's 2005 piece in *New German Critique* likewise assesses the ethics of Sebald's approach to his subject matter, but it does so via a consideration of the entirety of his creative and scholarly writings on the Holocaust and the World War II period. James L. Cowan's two-part essay in *Monatshefte*, meanwhile, considers the balance of documentary versus fictional material in *Austerlitz* as a means of pursuing a more complex view of Sebald's ethics of historical representation.

SOURCES

Cowan, James L. "W. G. Sebald's *Austerlitz* and the Great Library: History, Fiction, Memory. Part I." *Monatshefte* 102.1 (2010): 51–81. *Project MUSE*. 20 June 2011. Web.

———. "W. G. Sebald's *Austerlitz* and the Great Library: History, Fiction, Memory. Part II." *Monatshefte* 102.2 (2010): 192–207. *Project MUSE*. 20 June 2011. Web.

Long, J. J. *W. G. Sebald: Image, Archive, Modernity.* New York: Columbia UP, 2007. Print.

Long, J. J., and Anne Whitehead. *W. G. Sebald: A Critical Companion.* Seattle: U of Washington P, 2004. Print.

McCulloh, Mark R. *Understanding W. G. Sebald.* Columbia: U of South Carolina P, 2003. Print.

Prager, Brad. "The Good German as Narrator: On W. G. Sebald and the Risks of Holocaust Writing." *New German Critique* 96 (2005): 75–102. JSTOR. 20 June 2011. Web.

Schwartz, Lynne Sharon, ed. *The Emergence of Memory: Conversations with W. G. Sebald*. New York: Seven Stories, 2007. Print.

Sebald, W. G. *Austerlitz*. Trans. Anthea Bell. New York: Random, 2001. Print.

Zilcosky, John. "Lost and Found: Disorientation, Nostalgia, and Holocaust Melodrama in Sebald's *Austerlitz*." *MLN* 121.3 (2006): 679–98. *Project MUSE*. 20 June 2011. Web.

FURTHER READING

Denham, Scott, and Mark McCulloh, eds. *W. G. Sebald: History-Memory-Trauma*. Berlin: De Gruyter, 2006. Print.

Fischer, Gerhard, ed. *W. G. Sebald: Schreiben ex patria/ Expatriate Writing*. Amsterdam: Rodopi, 2009. Print.

Fuchs, Anne, and J. J. Long, eds. *W. G. Sebald and the Writing of History*. Würzburg: Königshausen, 2007. Print.

Patt, Lise, and Christel Dillbohner. *Searching for Sebald: Photography after W. G. Sebald*. Los Angeles: Institute of Cultural Inquiry, 2007. Print.

Sebald, W. G. *Campo Santo*. New York: Random House, 2005. Print.

———. *On the Natural History of Destruction*. New York: Random House, 2003. Print.

Zisselsberger, Markus, ed. *The Undiscover'd Country: W. G. Sebald and the Poetics of Travel*. Rochester: Camden, 2010. Print.

Mark Lane

LA CASA GRANDE

Álvaro Cepeda Samudio

OVERVIEW

La casa grande (1962; English edition 1991), the only novel by Colombian author and journalist Álvaro Cepeda Samudio, is considered, along with Gabriel García Márquez's *One Hundred Years of Solitude*, a seminal work of twentieth-century Colombian literature. It focuses on the banana massacre, the 1928 assault by the Colombian military on striking *bananeros* (banana workers) employed by the United Fruit Company in the northern town of Ciénaga, an event also treated by García Márquez in his novel. Excerpts of *La casa grande* were published in literary journals throughout the 1950s during a period of extreme political unrest in Colombia known as La Violencia (the violence), widely seen as a consequence of the same intense conflict between workers and a conservative, capitalist regime that had led to the banana massacre. For this and other reasons, *La casa grande* is often regarded as a political statement on matters beyond its immediate historical concerns.

The novel is broken into ten chapters and features a nonlinear plot that jumps between the first-, second-, and third-person perspectives of a number of unnamed characters and narrators, including an anonymous omniscient narrator, soldiers, townspeople, and, most prominently, several generations of a wealthy family that live in the "big house," a gaudy mansion overlooking the town that provides a physical and metaphoric representation of the accumulation of power in the hands of the few. The first chapter, "Soldiers," presents a debate between two soldiers over the morality of their orders to quell the bananeros's demonstrations, with one arguing that "it's a strike, and we should respect it and not get involved." The second chapter, "Sister," set after the massacre has occurred, introduces in the form of an interior monologue one of the family members, a young woman, who describes her father returning from the carnage and saying "those were the last ones, we've wiped them out." The third chapter, "Father," further introduces the head of the household through a brief third-person narrative, followed by several passages of dialogue in which the townspeople describe killing him. The fourth chapter provides a brief description of Ciénaga and the townspeople, and the next chapter features "Decreto No. 4," an exact transcription of a historical document, a decree (*decreto*), that expresses the government's official reaction to the strike, declaring the strikers "rebels" and "a gang of criminals." The sixth and seventh chapters take place on the day of and the day after the massacre, respectively, and present the perspectives of the townspeople in the hours leading up to and following the killings without ever directly engaging with the incident itself. The eighth chapter returns to the morning of the massacre, and provides a third-person narration detailing the events that took place from 5:10 a.m. to 10:00 a.m., just before the soldiers opened fire on the workers. The final two chapters, "Brother" and "Children," return to the perspectives of the family members, with the older brother describing his reactions to the events of the novel and reminiscing about his past while a younger brother makes preparations to depart for boarding school, respectively. The novel never once describes the massacre as it occurred but simply alludes to it, creating a work that, as Jonathan Tittler writes in *Hispania*, "spins kaleidoscopically about the central scene, showing its motivations (both collective and individual), its antecedents, its by-products, and its principal consequences, but never acquiesces to dramatizing the actual slaughter."

HISTORICAL AND LITERARY CONTEXT

The United Fruit Company, an American corporation, gained a near monopoly of the U.S. banana market in the late nineteenth and early twentieth centuries by employing laborers throughout Latin America at incredibly low wages and striking tax deals with local governments. The company amassed a great deal of capital through its shrewd business practices, creating small pockets of wealth in otherwise poor countries. In most cases the majority of profits were sent to the United States, with the remaining money distributed among a group of elite landowners (like the father in *La casa grande*) who oversaw the laborers and doled out their meager payments, exacerbating an already large gap between the wealthy and the poor in these microeconomies.

The United Fruit Company and its overseers also acquired a considerable amount of political power as governments became increasingly dependent on the money generated by the fruit trade. The prevalence of such political and economic exploitation and inequality throughout Latin American and

✦ *Key Facts*

Conflict:
Banana Massacre;
La Violencia

Time Period:
Mid-20th Century

Genre:
Novel

THE BANANA MASSACRE:
A LITERARY LEGACY

Like Cepeda Samudio, Gabriel García Márquez makes the Banana Massacre of 1928 a central event of his acclaimed novel *Cien años de soledad* (1967: *One Hundred Years of Solitude*, 1967). The novel traces the decline of the fictional town of Macondo, Colombia, from its founding by José Arcadio Buendía through seven generations of his descendents. While Macondo begins as a magical, utopian "city of mirrors," political unity and economic prosperity begin to decline after Mr. Herbert and Mr. Brown, two American businessmen, decide to open a banana plantation in the area. They build fences around the plantation and provide insufficient wages to the exploited workers. One of Arcadio Buendía's descendents, José Arcadio Segundo, helps to organize a strike among the laborers, and the government responds by opening fire upon their demonstrations from nearby rooftops. The massacre results in more than three thousand dead, with Segundo and a small child whom he places on his shoulders during the chaos being the only survivors.

Many critics suggest that the small child on Segundo's shoulders represents Cepeda Samudio, who often claimed to have been present in Ciénaga, the site of the actual Banana Massacre. While there is little evidence to support the claim, García Márquez's insistence in *One Hundred Years of Solitude* that "many years later that child would still tell, in spite of people thinking that he was a crazy old man, how José Arcadio Segundo had lifted him over his head and hauled him, almost in the air, as if floating on the terror of the crowd, toward a nearby street," is taken as a subtle acknowledgment of the importance of his friend Cepeda Samudio's treatment of the Banana Massacre in *La casa grande*.

Caribbean nations led to the coinage of the term *banana republic* in the early 1900s.

Labor organizers in Colombia, appalled by the poor working conditions on the banana plantations and the wealth disparity in their country, sought to counter these conditions in the 1920s by facilitating the rise of communism. They encouraged workers on the banana plantations to organize into unions. In November 1928 workers in Ciénaga began a strike, demanding that their workdays be reduced to eight-hour periods and that the workweek be reduced to six instead of seven days. Thousands of laborers and sympathetic liberals demonstrated in the town square throughout November. As December neared, the conservative government of President Miguel Abadía Méndez—at the behest of the United Fruit Company—called on the Colombian army, led by General Carlos Cortés Vargas, to disperse the crowds and put an end to the strike. On December 6 a military unit set up machine guns on rooftops around the plaza, and after a brief warning period, opened fire on the crowd. Reports of casualties numbered anywhere from the forty to several thousand, though no official

investigation into the massacre was ever completed. In the ensuing years tensions between liberal and conservative groups increased. In 1948 the assassination of liberal politician Jorge Eliécer Gaitán, an outspoken critic of the banana massacre, led to *El Bogotazo*, a riot in the capital city of Bogotá that left thousands dead and numerous buildings destroyed. An extended period of political chaos followed that lasted throughout the twentieth century. Guerrilla groups and militias formed on both sides of the political spectrum, and disappearances, tortures, and murders were commonplace. To this day several left-wing organizations, including the National Liberation Army and the Revolutionary Armed Forces of Colombia, seek to topple the capitalist government of Colombia and institute Marxist economic policies.

Cepeda Samudio is rumored to have been a witness, as a child, to the banana massacre, but there is little evidence to support this claim besides his own (false) assertion that he was born in Ciénaga. During La Violencia, he was a journalist with the Colombian newspapers *El Nacional* and *El Heraldo*, to which he also contributed a number of short stories. He and a group of other journalists and authors, including Germán Vargas, Alfonso Fuenmayor, and García Márquez, formed a literary circle known as the Barranquilla Group, named for the city in which they congregated. The group read and discussed works of early twentieth-century literature, including the experimental narratives of Ernest Hemingway and William Faulkner. Their own writing began to reflect the disjointed, multiperspective style of their modernist influences, leading Michael Palencia-Roth to remark in *World Literature Today* that *La casa grande* is "drawn with typical Faulknerian circularity" and "the sentence structure and the author's sense of dialogue owe much to Hemingway." Although most literary critics make similar claims, they also note that Cepeda Samudio's work incorporates other distinctly Latin American features, most prominently an emphasis on oral storytelling, as seen in the novel's dependence on dialogue rather than straightforward narration.

Many other authors have explored the consequences of the banana companies' presence in Latin America. For example, Ramón Amaya Amador's *Prisión verde* (1945; Green prison) describes the exploitation of Honduran laborers that he witnessed while working on a banana plantation there, while Carlos Luis Fallas's *Mamita Yunai: El Infierno de las Bananeras* (1940; Mama united: The hell of the banana plantations) presents a similar reaction to the United Fruit Company's operations in Costa Rica. Most notably, Nobel Prize-winning Guatemalan author Miguel Ángel Asturias produced a trio of celebrated works commonly known as the Banana Trilogy: *Viento fuerte* (1950; *Strong Wind*, 1968), *El Papa Verde* (1954; *The Green Pope*, 1971), and *Los ojos de los enterrados* (1960; *The Eyes of the Interred*, 1960).

THEMES AND STYLE

The dominant theme of *La casa grande* is the widespread social and economic injustice in Colombia. Tittler notes, "What emerges from beneath the turbulent textural surface is a constant abuse of power that results in hatred and reprisals, fatal tendencies that are passed through a family's and a nation's bloodlines from generation to generation." The relative lack of detail in the novel—in which the characters are identified only by their role within the family or the town, and the massacre itself is only alluded to through the people's reactions to it—give the narrative a mythological dimension that allows the incident and the novel itself to serve as a larger commentary on the underlying causes of La Violencia. The ambiguity of the ending, in which the young son of the murdered father prepares to leave for boarding school, a symbol of his privileged position in society, suggests that the cycle of social domination by a minority of elites will continue well into the future, an assertion that was solidified by the social circumstances in Colombia at the time of the novel's publication.

Cepeda Samudio's fragmentary technique in *La casa grande*, which depicts the chaos of the massacre by providing glimpses of the action as reflected in the conversations and inner thoughts of those who experienced it rather than through a traditional authoritative third-person narrative, also reflects the fact that no government report was ever released on the tragedy in Ciénaga, leading to the facts of the event being heatedly debated among the people. As Raymond Leslie Williams writes in his discussion of the novel in *The Twentieth-Century Spanish American Novel*, "In a world in which written history is an act of exercising political power, what is (subversively) said rather than what is (officially) written becomes essential to an understanding of reality." Thus the deliberately political language of the decree reprinted in chapter five becomes an eerie, inhuman counterpoint to the impassioned language of the people who experience the incident firsthand. In his foreword to the 1991 English translation of *La casa grande*, García Márquez asserts:

> The super dialogues, the straight-forward and virile richness of the language, the genuine compassion aroused by the characters' fate, the fragmentary and somewhat loose structure which so closely resembles the pattern of memories— everything in this book is a magnificent example of how a writer can honestly filter out the immense quantity of rhetorical and demagogic garbage that stands in the way of indignation and nostalgia.

By choosing not to depict soldiers opening fire on the laborers (or of the father's subsequent murder, for that matter), Cepeda Samudio does not in fact downplay the horrible violence of the massacre. Instead, he draws attention to the "rhetorical and demagogic garbage" that obfuscates the reality of the massacre and of La Violencia in the Colombian national consciousness, thereby encouraging an open and honest discourse that takes into account what has been left unacknowledged in the official record for decades.

CRITICAL DISCUSSION

La casa grande was recognized throughout Latin America as an important and foundational work of literature. Palencia-Roth notes that the novel's "surrealistic qualities anticipate such significant Latin American experiments in fragmentation as *The Death of Artemio Cruz* by [Carlos] Fuentes and *The Green House* by [Mario] Vargas Llosa." The Colombian playwright Carlos José Reyes adapted the first chapter of *La casa grande* into a celebrated play, *Soldados*, in 1966, and Cepeda Samudio's friend and colleague Daniel Samper Pizano compiled an anthology of his work in 1977. Although Cepeda Samudio died in 1972, just ten years after the publication of *La casa grande*, García Márquez and others continued to champion his work. *La casa grande* has since been translated into a number of languages, with an English translation by Seymour Menton appearing in 1991 to generally positive reviews.

Scholarly work on *La casa grande* is more abundant in Spanish than in English, but scholars of both languages tend to focus on the novel's stylistic elements: its sources, impact on the text, and influence on later writers. Others discuss the historical background of the text and its relationship to the ongoing cultural upheaval in Colombia. Studies of other writers in the Barranquilla Group, especially García Márquez, often devote lengthy passages to Cepeda Samudio's influence on these authors' works and on twentieth-century Colombian literature in general. Although a number of Colombian writers are far more familiar to readers throughout the world, Cepeda Samudio is widely acknowledged as being a major factor in the development of a distinct Colombian literary style, in large part the result of his innovative and powerful *La casa grande*.

The Santa Marta region of Colombia, where the Banana Massacre took place on December 6, 1928. This photograph was taken the following day. © BETTMANN / CORBIS

SOURCES

Cepeda Samudio, Álvaro. *La casa grande*. Trans. Seymour Menton. Austin: U of Texas P, 1991. Print.

García Márquez, Gabriel. Foreword. *La casa grande*. By Álvaro Cepeda Samudio. Trans. Seymour Menton. Austin: U of Texas P, 1991. ix-x. Print.

———. *One Hundred Years of Solitude*. Trans. Gregory Rabassa. New York: Harper, 1967. Print.

Palencia-Roth, Michael. Rev. of *La casa grande*, by Álvaro Cepeda Samudio. *World Literature Today* 66.2 (1992): 317–18. Print.

Tittler, Jonathan. Rev. of *La casa grande*, by Álvaro Cepeda Samudio, and *A Saint Is Born in Chimá*, by Manuel Zapata Olivella. *Hispania* 75.5 (1992): 1203–04. Print.

Williams, Raymond Leslie. "Rereading the Spanish American Novel beyond the Boom." *The Twentieth-Century Spanish American Novel*. Austin: U of Texas P, 2003. 149–62. Print.

FURTHER READING

Ángel Asturias, Miguel. *The Eyes of the Interred*. Trans. Gregory Rabassa. New York: Delacorte, 1973. Print.

———. *The Green Pope*. Trans. Gregory Rabassa. New York: Delacorte, 1971. Print.

———. *Strong Wind*. Trans. Gregory Rabassa. New York: Delacorte, 1968. Print.

Bost, David H. "The Poetics of History in Alvaro Cepeda Samudio's *La casa grande*." *SECOLAS Annals: Journal of the Southeastern Council of Latin American Studies* 21 (1990): 24–32. Print.

Bucheli, Marcelo. *Bananas and Business: The United Fruit Company in Colombia, 1899–2000*. New York: New York UP, 2005. Print.

Edwards, Jennifer Gabrielle. *The Flight of the Condor: Stories of Violence and War from Colombia*. Madison: U of Wisconsin P, 2007. Print.

Roldán, Mary. *Blood and Fire: La Violencia in Antioquia, Colombia, 1946–1953*. Durham: Duke UP, 2002. Print.

Striffler, Steve, and Mark Moberg, eds. *Banana Wars: Power, Production, and History in the Americas*. Durham: Duke UP, 2003. Print.

Tittler, Jonathan. "Álvaro Cepeda Samudio: Neo-Colombian Literature's Source?" *Readerly/Writerly Texts* 3.1 (1995): 151–60. Print.

Jacob Schmitt

GRAVITY'S RAINBOW

Thomas Pynchon

OVERVIEW

Thomas Pynchon's *Gravity's Rainbow* is generally considered one of the most influential novels of twentieth-century fiction. Set primarily during World War II, the book chronicles many key historical events, including Germany's intensive bombing campaign against England during the late stages of the war, the development of the V-2 rocket by Nazi scientists, and the emergence of the German industrial complex as an integral aspect of that nation's war effort. At the same time the work repeatedly leaps beyond the confines of the war to explore a wide range of seemingly incongruous subjects and themes: the eradication of the dodo bird on the island of Mauritius in the seventeenth century, the racially tinged Los Angeles "Zoot Suit" riots of June 1943, and the American antiwar movement of the 1960s and 1970s. Most significantly, *Gravity's Rainbow* captures the phenomenon of American global economic and military dominance that characterized the postwar period, suggesting powerful parallels between German fascism and U.S. imperialism. *Gravity's Rainbow* is composed of many subtly interconnected and often fragmentary stories. Although there is no conventional plot or protagonist, the novel primarily concerns a U.S. intelligence officer named Tyrone Slothrop, whose erections are improbably correlated with the pattern of German rocket attacks on and around London. Slothrop's unique sexual condition soon attracts the attention of a clandestine military organization, the Agents of the Firm, who seek to uncover the mystery of his uncanny prophetic powers. Pursuing his own explanation of his unusual condition, he ventures into the Zone, a surreal wasteland spanning the ruins of Europe. He learns that as a child he may have been subjected to behavioral conditioning experiments carried out by a Harvard researcher. With the onset of World War II, the same researcher has become a scientist working for the Nazi government, charged with developing a new rocket codenamed 00000. The novel ends with 00000 poised to strike a movie theater. Throughout the work Slothrop's narrative is disrupted and interpenetrated by extensive anecdotes, vignettes, and subplots wherein precise historical references and incisive cultural critique are mixed with elements of farce, eroticism, and wordplay. Either overtly or implicitly, it touches on almost every aspect of twentieth-century culture, from social and political problems to post-Newtonian

science and emerging technology. At the heart of the novel is Pynchon's grim vision of what Dale Carter calls the modern "Rocket State," in which technology serves the purposes of violence and allows multinational corporations to achieve world domination. In this sense *Gravity's Rainbow* is at once an epic novel of World War II and a sweeping philosophical meditation on what it means to be human in the technological age. The work owes much of its enormous scope to its ambitious structure and style. More than seven hundred pages long and populated with roughly four hundred characters, *Gravity's Rainbow* unfolds in the complex, allusive, and extravagant prose typical of postmodern literature. Encyclopedic and sprawling, the work defies straightforward categorization, freely interweaving history and fantasy, high art and pop culture, somber reflections on human mortality and slapstick comedy. For the most part, Pynchon's view of human nature is brutal and dark; he explores the depths of depravity and paranoia that lurk beneath the surface of official recorded history. At the same time, the novel's satirical tone and subversive approach to its subject are representative of American black humor, a style marked by its morbid sensibility and its willingness to tackle outrageous, at times controversial, subject matter.

HISTORICAL AND LITERARY CONTEXT

In his essay "War, Optics, Fiction," Paul Saint-Amour observes that *Gravity's Rainbow* is "set at the hinge moment between conventional and nuclear warfare." Indeed, Pynchon situates his narrative at the point in history when scientists began to recognize the vast destructive potential of modern technology. During World War II, Germany and the United States raced to develop weapons that could kill larger numbers of people at greater distances. Although the United States succeeded in developing the atomic bomb, Germany took the lead in conventional weaponry with the V-2 rocket, the first human-made object ever to attain suborbital space flight. Before the V-2, bombs were delivered to distant targets by piloted aircraft, which could be shot down by ground-based defenses or by other planes. The V-2 evaded conventional antiaircraft defensive strategies by launching in an arc-shaped trajectory beyond earth's atmosphere before hurtling back toward its target at supersonic speed. Since the V-2 traveled faster than the speed of sound, people on

❖ Key Facts

Conflict:
World War II

Time Period:
Mid-20th Century

Genre:
Novel

Awards:
National Book Award, 1974 (declined); William Dean Howells Medal, best novel of the decade, American Academy of Arts and Letters

WAR IN THEIR OWN WORDS

We Shall Cut off All the Evil Enemies' Communications 1942, Russian poster. © THE ART ARCHIVE / EILEEN TWEEDY

Epic in scope, Thomas Pynchon's *Gravity's Rainbow* delves into virtually all facets of World War II. In tackling the historical underpinnings of the conflict, Pynchon makes continual reference to the diverse military and political leaders who oversaw the conduct of the war, frequently mocking their authority and prestige with mordant satire. In *Warlords: An Extraordinary Recreation of World War II through the Eyes and Minds of Hitler, Churchill, Roosevelt, and Stalin* (2006), Simon Berthon and Joanna Potts provide a more measured, serious exploration into the roles played by some of the conflict's principal actors. Written from the alternating perspectives of each of the four leaders, *Warlords* reimagines the complex strategizing that unfolded during moments of intense crisis, pitting one man's thoughts against another in an elaborate global chess game. Through these interior monologues, the authors depict the various psychological factors behind each leader's decision making, while simultaneously reenacting the intricate intellectual drama that occurred in the shadows of actual combat. In addition to elucidating the stark ideological contrasts between the Allies and Hitler, the book also explores the various rifts that existed between Roosevelt, Churchill, and Stalin, examining their efforts both to collaborate in the fight against Nazism and outmaneuver each other in pursuit of postwar spoils. Although crafted in the manner of a thriller, *Warlords* is solidly rooted in scholarship, providing surprising insights into the intricate political machinations that sometimes go unreported in more conventional histories.

the ground could not hear it approach, so the explosive impact seemed to come out of nowhere.

The Nazi's V-2 rocket program was led by Wernher von Braun, who later played a critical role in the expansion of the U.S. space program in the 1950s and 1960s. During this period of the Cold War, other exiled German scientists working in the United States and the Soviet Union developed intercontinental

ballistic missiles (ICBMs) capable of carrying nuclear warheads across long distances. Both countries amassed thousands of nuclear missiles and bombs in order to guarantee that any offensive ("first-strike") use of nuclear weapons would trigger a devastating cycle of retaliation. The theory behind this strategy was known as Mutually Assured Destruction (MAD). By 1969 the arms race had become so threatening that the United States and the Soviet Union began a series of negotiations known as the Strategic Arms Limitation Talks (SALT). Throughout *Gravity's Rainbow*, Pynchon continually links advances in modern warfare to the emergence of the global economy during both World War II and the ensuing Cold War. This militarized world, in which corporate interests and politics become inextricably intertwined, is at once haunting and farcical. The novel's conclusion offers one of the strangest evocations of the new world order: Pynchon depicts U.S. president Richard Nixon as a paranoid theater owner attempting to quell politically subversive behavior—which he describes as "irresponsible use of the harmonica"—in the moments before his theater is destroyed by a rocket.

Composed between 1966 and 1973, *Gravity's Rainbow* emerged at a time when the American war novel was undergoing a radical transformation. During the 1960s a new generation of authors, notably Joseph Heller and Kurt Vonnegut, had begun to explore the fundamental absurdity of modern warfare. These writers mingled historical revisionism with pointed satire to expose the hypocrisy and deceit at the heart of American political and military agendas. By undermining the conventional belief that World War II was an unequivocally "just" conflict, Pynchon, Heller, and Vonnegut raise difficult questions concerning the obscure motives behind contemporary wars. Like Heller's *Catch-22* and Vonnegut's *Slaughterhouse Five*, *Gravity's Rainbow* reimagines modern war as an ambiguous process motivated by a tangle of economic, cultural, and political forces.

THEMES AND STYLE

Although *Gravity's Rainbow* focuses primarily on World War II, the novel is more broadly concerned with the long-term ramifications of the conflict on American society and culture. At the time Pynchon was writing *Gravity's Rainbow*, the United States was struggling with both the enormous monetary costs of the arms race and the increasing human cost of the war in Vietnam. By the late 1960s many Americans openly opposed the conduct of the war, which included the use of technologically advanced weaponized chemicals such as Agent Orange and napalm. At the same time, many young people were growing disillusioned with the prevailing American value system, which seemed increasingly based on consumerism and materialism. An ideological rift soon developed, dividing supporters of "the establishment," or existing sociopolitical structures, from members of a loosely organized countercultural movement that opposed traditional mores and experimented with unconventional lifestyles. *Gravity's Rainbow* expresses this fundamental conflict between differing American values through a wildly unorthodox literary style. With its cryptic allusiveness and slang-driven prose, the novel intentionally alienates readers unwilling to break free of cultural and societal norms. It is dense with arcane symbolism, layer upon layer of cultural and historical references, obscure literary puns, mathematical equations, and in-depth descriptions of complicated scientific processes, effectively transforming the act of reading into a process of extensive decoding. Pynchon also skewers traditional sexual mores, using grotesque depictions of licentiousness. In one particularly striking orgy scene, a woman sodomizes a transvestite with a glass dildo filled with baby piranhas; in another, a German spy brings sexual pleasure to a British brigadier by forcing him to eat her feces. Pynchon further subverts traditional narrative forms with his sudden and unexpected leaps from somber depictions of death to episodes of madcap comedy, and his elegant, often poetic, descriptive sentences are punctuated throughout the work by juvenile songs, scatological jokes, and fatuous utterances by his characters.

This spectroscopic, even manic, virtuosity lends *Gravity's Rainbow* a unique air of literary authority. At the same time, Pynchon's style raises a number of unsettling questions. As the narrative continues its exhaustive exploration into its subject matter, the book's mystery only deepens: the idea of meaning becomes increasingly elusive in the face of mounting complexity. The author enhances the overall sense of distrust and fear with repeated allusions to secret societies and plots. In the end, he seems to suggest that individual consciousness is ultimately incapable of grasping the intricate and dark historical forces that shape human existence. The novel's central symbol, the rainbow, refers not only to the arc of the V-2 rocket but also to the cyclical quality of the narrative itself; in fact, a rainbow is actually a circle, interrupted only by the horizon. In the final scene, theatergoers await the start of a film that never begins, as the text abruptly ends with the line "Now everybody—." Left with an unsatisfactory conclusion, the reader is drawn directly back to a haunting phrase from novel's opening lines: "it's all theatre."

CRITICAL DISCUSSION

In 1974 *Gravity's Rainbow* was unanimously nominated for a Pulitzer Prize by the fiction jury. The advisory board overruled their recommendation, however, describing the book as "unreadable," "turgid," "overwritten," and, in parts, "obscene." This dispute over the merits of Pynchon's novel resulted in a stalemate, and no Pulitzer Prize for fiction was awarded in 1974. The board's assessment reflected not only a conservative view of what constitutes good literature but also a discomfort with Pynchon's radical

re-presentation of World War II. In "The Vietnamization of World War II in *Slaughterhouse-Five* and *Gravity's Rainbow*," Christina Jarvis points out that *Gravity's Rainbow* "deconstructed the binary framing of America's 'good war,' offering a 'Vietnamized' version, full of discontinuities, fragmented bodies, and multiple shades of gray." Similarly, in "War as a Background in *Gravity's Rainbow*," Khachig Tölölyan calls the work a "new kind of war novel [that] redefines not only the genre but our idea of war itself." Tölölyan describes the book as "a fictional alternative to available historical versions of the real world" and notes the contrast between it and traditional war novels such as those by Ernest Hemingway, Norman Mailer, and James Jones, which strive to capture the "real" war experience. Incorporating accurate historical and scientific information, *Gravity's Rainbow* provides a different kind of realism. Pynchon, who studied engineering before he turned to writing, writes with authority on the weaponization of new technology. Saint-Amour notes that "no other novel knows as much as [*Gravity's Rainbow*] about the history of twentieth-century reconnaissance and bombing, treating obscure techniques as if they were common knowledge."

A 49-foot, 3-ton German V-2 rocket that was captured by the Allies is exhibited in London's Trafalgar Square during celebrations at the end of World War II. © MARY EVANS PICTURE LIBRARY / EVERETT COLLECTION

The novel has generated a large number of critical books and articles, as well as several guides to the novel's copious references. At the broadest level, opinions have diverged on whether the work is a purely nihilistic satire, an indictment of mainstream culture that also contains themes of love and hope, or a mischievous labyrinth meant to confound (and ultimately defeat) both readers and scholars. Steven Weisenburger and others have addressed this facet of the work by producing comprehensive manuals aimed at helping readers organize and decode the novel's complex plot and symbolic structure.

Since the early days of scholarly fascination with *Gravity's Rainbow*, approaches to the novel have generally followed prevailing trends in literary criticism. In the early 1980s, in keeping with the current of deconstructionist and poststructuralist orientations, the study of meaning in *Gravity's Rainbow* shifted to a greater attention to the book's unique literary style. The later 1980s and 1990s introduced new avenues of interpretation, including studies that focused on mythic and spiritual dimensions, psychoanalytic influences, the use of allegory, and other topics that reflect a postmodernist view of *Gravity's Rainbow*. As literary criticism moved into the twenty-first century, commentaries such as Margaret Lynd's "Science, Narrative, and Agency in *Gravity's Rainbow*" showed the effect of postcolonial and feminist trends. According to Lynd, although Pynchon's "critique of science posits white male desire as the central motivating factor in virtually every act of violence since the Renaissance, from schoolyard bullying to genocide," his analysis is undercut in *Gravity's Rainbow* "by [the] near exclusion of female and nonwhite voices."

Other critical perspectives have focused on Pynchon's critique of the corporate underpinnings of modern warfare. That theme is picked up by another of the novel's primary symbols: the German chemical conglomerate IG Farben, a real company that produced both rocket fuel (used in the V-2) and Zyklon B gas (used in Nazi extermination facilities). In "IG Farben's Synthetic War Crimes and Thomas Pynchon's *Gravity's Rainbow*," Robert McLaughlin explains that for Pynchon, "IG Farben (and, more importantly, the mindset it represents) is, even more than Hitler, the villain of World War II." According to McLaughlin, Pynchon effectively incorporates the actual history of the firm and "uses IG Farben as an important structuring and thematic device to represent Western civilization's tendency to control and corrupt the natural and transform it from the purposes of life to the purposes of death." In the twenty-first century, some scholars have devoted attention to the theme of universal extinction at the core of Pynchon's attitude toward technology. In *Ethical Diversions: The Post-Holocaust Narratives of Pynchon, Abish, Delillo, and Spiegelman*, Katalin Orbán observes,

"The arc-shaped trajectory of the Rocket—the [V-2] that is the white whale of Pynchon's encyclopedic fiction—is invariably linked to disease, distraction, dreams of expansion and domination." The rocket exemplifies what Pynchon calls the "purest form of European adventuring"—a state, Orbán explains, in which "dreams of transcendence and extermination go hand in hand."

SOURCES

Jarvis, Christina."The Vietnamization of World War II in *Slaughterhouse-Five* and *Gravity's Rainbow*." *War, Literature, and the Arts* 15.1–2 (2003): 95–117. Print.

Lynd, Margaret. "Science, Narrative, and Agency in *Gravity's Rainbow*." *Critique: Studies in Contemporary Fiction* 46.1 (2004): 63+. Print.

McLaughlin, Robert. "IG Farben's Synthetic War Crimes and Thomas Pynchon's *Gravity's Rainbow*." *Visions of War: World War II in Popular Literature and Culture*. Ed. M. Paul Holsinger and Mary Anne Schofield. Bowling Green: Popular, 1992. 85–95. Print.

Orbán, Katalin. *Ethical Diversions: The Post-Holocaust Narratives of Pynchon, Abish, Delillo, and Spiegelman*. New York: Routledge, 2005. Print.

Saint-Amour, Paul K. "War, Optics, Fiction." *Novel: A Forum on Fiction* 43.1 (2010): 93–101. Print.

Tölölyan, Khachig. "War as a Background in *Gravity's Rainbow*." *Approaches to Gravity's Rainbow*. Ed. Charles Clerc. Columbus: Ohio State UP, 1983. 31–69. Print.

Weisenburger, Steven. *A "Gravity's Rainbow" Companion: Sources and Contexts for Pynchon's Novel*. Athens: U of Georgia P, 2006. Print.

FURTHER READING

Adair, W. G. *The American Epic Novel in the Late Twentieth Century: The Super-Genre of the Imperial State*. Lewiston: E. Mellen, 2008. Print.

Ashe, Frederick. "Anachronism Intended: *Gravity's Rainbow* in the Sociopolitical Sixties." *Pynchon Notes* 28–29 (1991): 59–75. Print.

Baker, Jeffrey S. "Amerikkka uber Alles: German Nationalism, American Imperialism, and the 1960s Antiwar Movement in *Gravity's Rainbow*." *Critique* 40.4 (1999): 323–41. Print.

Best, Steven, and Douglas Kellner. *The Postmodern Adventure: Science, Technology, and Cultural Studies at the Third Millennium*. New York: Guilford, 2001. Print.

Carter, Dale. *The Final Frontier: The Rise and Fall of the American Rocket State*. London: Verso, 1988. Print.

Hume, Kathryn. *Pynchon's Mythography: An Approach to "Gravity's Rainbow."* Carbondale: Southern Illinois UP, 1987. Print.

Nadeau, Robert L. *Readings from the New Book of Nature: Physics and Metaphysics in the Modern Novel*. Amherst: U of Massachusetts P, 1981. Print.

Steve Meyer

IN PARENTHESIS

David Jones

OVERVIEW

In Parenthesis is a book-length literary work by Welsh-English poet David Jones (1895–1974), who utilized memories of his first year as a soldier in World War I to create an epic view of modern warfare as seen through the lens of history, literature, and religious symbolism. The work has been widely praised both for its accurate, detailed evocation of life in the trenches and for its brilliant use of poetic expression and literary allusion. Jones, who was also a noted artist and engraver, worked for almost a decade on the seven-part poetic work before it was published in 1937.

In Parenthesis takes place during a few months in 1915 as protagonist John Ball and his fellow soldiers undergo training and fight in their first battle. Using language and imagery drawn from everyday speech and from a variety of literary sources, Jones depicts both the banality and the terror of war. The text is a mixture of poetry and prose, description and suggestion, designed to amplify the individual experience of war through the addition of mythic dimensions.

In his introduction to the 1961 edition, T. S. Eliot calls *In Parenthesis* "a work of genius" and ranks Jones among eminent modernists Ezra Pound, W. B. Yeats, and Eliot himself. Other literary luminaries, including W. H. Auden and Yeats, agreed. Yet *In Parenthesis* never gained a large audience, in part because of its difficulty and in part because it appeared at a time when interest in World War I had waned. For the balance of his life, Jones continued to develop a distinctive approach to both literary and visual art, writing influential essays on the relationship of art and sacrament, as well as an ambitious sequence of poems about Western civilization, published in 1952 as *The Anathemata*. In 1955 he was awarded the title Commander of the Order of the British Empire (CBE), and in 1959 he received the Bollingen Prize for poetry.

Although never as well known as some of his contemporaries, Jones has continued to attract scholarly interest and is regarded among those who know his work as one of the most important writers of the twentieth century. John Johnston, in his seminal 1962 essay "David Jones: The Heroic Vision," observes that "if the poetry directly inspired by World War I is viewed as a continuity with a rather rapid expansion or development toward a more comprehensive artistic statement, *In Parenthesis* stands as a remarkable, and almost completely unrecognized, culmination of that development."

HISTORICAL AND LITERARY CONTEXT

In the summer of 1914, when the assassination of Archduke Franz Ferdinand of Austria touched off long-simmering tensions among the European nations, almost everyone on both sides expected the conflict to be resolved in a few months. Many of Britain's best-educated and most talented young men, including David Jones, immediately volunteered for service. For the most part, these volunteers expected a chivalric combat in which they might prove their mettle, experience the existential intensity of battle, and defend the highest values of British culture. None were prepared for the realities of a war that dragged on for years and killed millions on both sides.

Nor could these young men have imagined such a poorly planned and executed conflict. Living in deep trenches on either side of a deadly no-man's-land, common soldiers like Jones were constantly vulnerable to artillery assaults and sniper fire. Battles, when they occurred, might last for days and result in extensive casualties yet gain no ground for either side. Opposing sides were stalemated during most of the war, and soldiers died not only of battlefield wounds but also of diseases that developed in the trenches and horrific poison gas attacks launched at times by both sides.

Jones was one of the writers who survived World War I and turned their experiences into poetry, memoirs, and autobiographical fiction. Among the best known of these authors were Robert Graves and Siegfried Sassoon, both of whom, like Jones, joined the Royal Welch Fusiliers. The three never met (Graves and Sassoon were officers, while Jones served as an infantryman throughout the war), but all suffered for many years after the war from post-traumatic stress.

The first volume of Sassoon's fictionalized memoir was published in 1928, and Graves's iconoclastic autobiography *Good-bye to All That* appeared the following year. Jones took much longer to produce his own document, however. Following the war, he had become a devout Roman Catholic, and throughout the 1920s, his time was divided between spiritual inquiry and his artistic career. His health was frail as well, and in 1932 he suffered the first in a series of severe mental breakdowns. *In Parenthesis* was not published until

Conflict:
World War I

Time Period:
Early 20th Century

Genre:
Poetry, Prose

AMONG THE CONVERTS

David Jones was one of several British artists and intellectuals who converted to Roman Catholicism in the early twentieth century. It was a dramatic decision at the time, when the modern world was becoming increasingly secular—but strong opposition to secular modernism was a characteristic shared by most of these converts. Among the best known of the group were writer G. K. Chesterton (who converted in 1922 at the age of forty-five) and historian Christopher Dawson (converting in 1914, aged twenty-five), as well as novelists Graham Greene (1926, aged twenty-two) and Evelyn Waugh (1930, aged twenty-seven). Influential authors T. S. Eliot and C. S. Lewis are often considered part of this group, although they became Anglicans (rather than Roman) Catholics.

According to Joseph Pearce's *Literary Converts: Spiritual Inspiration in an Age of Unbelief*, "David Jones became a Catholic on 7 September 1921 but the embryonic roots of his faith went back to the trenches of 1917." Jones was very moved when he chanced on soldiers gathered for a battlefield mass, and he began to discuss religion with the chaplain attached to his battalion at Ypres. The mass—and especially the doctrine of transubstantiation, which holds that sacramental bread and wine literally become Christ's body and blood—remained central to Jones's spirituality and to his understanding of art as a form of spiritual signification.

Some of the converts, like Jones, were sustained and inspired by their faith, some became extreme in their views, and others—like Graham Greene—struggled to reconcile behavior with belief. Collectively, however, they represented what Pearce characterizes as "an evocative artistic intellectual response to the prevailing agnosticism of the age."

two years before World War II broke out—the same year that Neville Chamberlain became prime minister of England and Picasso commemorated the German bombing of Spain in his vitally important painting *Guernica*.

THEMES AND STYLE

Poet W. S. Merwin writes in his foreword to the 2003 edition that "as a 'war book' *In Parenthesis* is incomparable." He goes on to note that "in his account of those months of stupefying discomfort, fatigue, and constant fear in the half-flooded winter trenches, and then of the mounting terror and chaos of the July assault on the Mametz Wood, David Jones made intimate and inimitable use of sensual details of every kind." Jones's narrative strategy interweaves the ordinary with the exceptional, layering the colloquial normality of his Cockney trench-mates and the dialect of his own Welsh heritage with poetic excursions that range from the arcane to the sublime. The many allusions he employs are not only literary but also historical and scriptural, with references as diverse as Shakespeare's *Henry V*, Coleridge's *Rime of the Ancient Mariner*,

Lewis Carroll's *Alice in Wonderland*, Sir Thomas Malory's *Le Morte D'Arthur*, the medieval Welsh story cycle *Mabinogion*, and the Book of Revelation.

The complexity and density of *In Parenthesis* is not merely an exercise in literary style. As John Johnston observes, Jones "employs both character and action as textures upon which the essence of modern warfare is projected and interpreted." Ball and his fellows emerge as real people, their experiences as real events, which in turn makes the depiction of war in *In Parenthesis* seem almost journalistically accurate. In a plainly autobiographical parallel, *In Parenthesis* ends after a character is wounded, possibly fatally, at Mametz Wood; Jones had been critically injured there, too. Overlaying all is what Gerald Russello calls, in his 2006 essay "David Jones and the Sacrament of Art," a "tone of Celtic wildness" that gives the work a "distinctive, bardic tincture." In Russello's words, "Merlin and Guinevere seem to hover just beyond the trenches." This mythic resonance reflects the fact that "Jones was not, as we now use the terms, 'pro-' or 'anti-' war; combat for him was a basic fact of human existence, and for him a searing experience, to be understood and explained in the context of tradition."

Jones characterizes his work this way in a preface to the original edition of *In Parenthesis*: "I did not intend this as a 'War Book'—it happens to be concerned with war. I should prefer it to be about a good kind of peace … [but] we find ourselves privates in foot regiments. We search how we may see formal goodness in a life singularly inimical, hateful, to us." Jones believed that the only way to make sense of the war was to find its commonalities with the great sweep of human experience, and as a consequence he situates his account of World War I in the early months, when the conflict could still be imagined within the context of traditional warfare. The "wholesale slaughter of the later years," according to Jones, became a "relentless, mechanical affair" that bore little resemblance to the common experience that had for so many centuries united Roman legionnaires, Welsh warriors, and knights of the Round Table.

CRITICAL DISCUSSION

Although critics have almost universally admired Jones and his work, two less positive views have raised points of discussion. The first comes from influential historian Paul Fussell, whose 1975 study *The Great War and Modern Memory* is among the most important studies of World War I and its cultural impact. Although Fussell considers Jones an "unclassifiable genius," he describes *In Parenthesis* as an "honorable miscarriage" that ultimately romanticized the war. "The effect of the poem, for all its horrors," Fussell contends, "is to rationalize and even to validate the war by implying that it somehow recovers many of the motifs and values of medieval chivalric romance." He concludes that Jones's "deeply conservative work" uses the past "not as it often pretends to do, to shame the present, but really to ennoble it." From Fussell's perspective, World War I was a radically new kind of conflict, and the past evoked by Jones offered "no precedent for an understanding of war as a shambles and its participants as victims." Even so, Fussell concludes that *In Parenthesis* "remains in many ways a masterpiece impervious to criticism."

To the extent that Fussell's critique rings true, part of the reason may be that Jones's interests lay in illumination of historical dimensionality rather than in characterization of particular events. His approach was intended to reveal—rather than recount—what Charles Andrews calls in his 2007 essay "War Trauma and Religious Cityscape in David Jones's *In Parenthesis*" the "traumatic fragmentation" of war. Andrews suggests that the "the rupture of linear history experienced by war survivors, combatants, and non-combatants alike, gave particular weight to artistic experimentation," and that the "overall form of *In Parenthesis* displays an excess that functions as the traumatic kernel rupturing the narrative from the inside."

The difference between these two critical viewpoints is visible in their different responses to the thirty pages of explanatory endnotes Jones included with *In Parenthesis*. For Fussell, these "rather pedantic notes at the end bespeak the literary insecurity of the autodidact; they sometimes prop up the text where the author suspects the poetry has miscarried." Andrews, on the other hand, characterizes the notes as "a self-reflexive gesture that accentuates the sense of fragmentation" that Jones has created through the allusions.

A more negative view of Jones and his work is put forth by Elizabeth Ward in her 1983 book *David Jones, Myth-Maker*. Although Ward acknowledges the exceptional achievement of *In Parenthesis*, she contends that "this brilliant first work has been eclipsed by the shadow of David Jones's subsequently earned reputation as a Catholic ideologue and a primitivist." Ward offers an extensive and often unflattering analysis of Jones's writing, including his essays, letters, and poems. From this process she concludes that his political beliefs were highly conservative.

Kathleen Staudt responds, in her survey "Recent Criticism on David Jones," with an acknowledgment that Ward had made an important contribution to Jones scholarship by "raising the issue of his relation to the conservative, even reactionary political climate of Britain in the thirties, and particularly to the ideological commitments of a circle of British Catholics who were Jones's close friends and associates." At the same time, however, Staudt expresses concerns about Ward's selective use of material to support her own interpretive agenda, as well as her unsupported assumption that Jones's political views followed those of his acquaintances. Providing a more detailed refutation of Ward in his 1986 essay in *Journal of Modern Literature*, Jones scholar Thomas Dilworth argues that though the poet had a short-lived flirtation with Nazism, it was merely a naïve intellectual interest; his

work "during and after the Second World War is thoroughly and explicitly anti-totalitarian."

SOURCES

Andrews, Charles. "War Trauma and Religious Cityscape in David Jones's *In Parenthesis*." *Journal of the Midwest Modern Language Association* 40.1 (2007): 87–96. Print.

Dilworth, Thomas. "David Jones and Fascism." *Journal of Modern Literature* 13.1 (1986): 149–62. Print.

Fussell, Paul. *The Great War and Modern Memory*. New York: Oxford UP, 1975. Print.

Johnston, John H. "David Jones: The Heroic Vision." *Review of Politics* 24.1 (1962): 62–87. Print.

Jones, David, William S. Merwin (foreword), and Thomas S. Eliot (introduction). *In Parenthesis*. New York: NY Review, 2003. Print.

Russello, Gerald J. "David Jones and the Sacrament of Art." *New Criterion* 25.3 (2006): 33. Print.

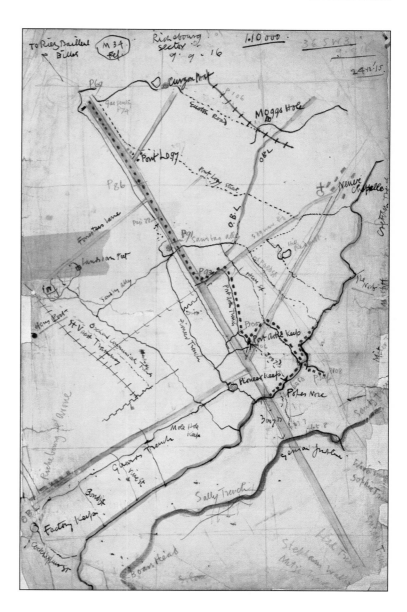

David Jones (1895–1974) created this sketch map to accompany his epic poem about World War I, "In Parenthesis". © TATE GALLERY ARCHIVE TGA 8222221 / ART RESOURCE, NY / REPRODUCED BY PERMISSION OF THE ESTATE OF DAVID JONES.

Staudt, Kathleen Henderson. "Recent Criticism on David Jones." *Contemporary Literature* 27.3 (1986): 409–22. Print.

Ward, Elizabeth. *David Jones, Myth-Maker*. Manchester: Manchester UP, 1983. Print.

FURTHER READING

Blissett, William. *The Long Conversation: A Memoir of David Jones by William Blissett*. New York: Oxford UP, 1981. Print.

Dilworth, Thomas. *Reading David Jones*. Cardiff: U of Wales P, 2008. Print.

Edwards, Paul. "British War Memoirs. "*The Cambridge Companion to the Literature of the First World War*. Ed. Vincent B. Sherry. Cambridge: Cambridge UP, 2006. Print.

Halsey, Alan, and David Annwn. *Stalking Within Yer Chamber: Some Notes for a Reading of David Jones"In Parenthesis.'* Hay-on-Wye: West House, 1996. Print.

Jones, David. *Epoch and Artist*. London: Faber, 2009. Print.

Miles, Jonathan, and Derek Shiel. *David Jones: The Maker Unmade*. Bridgend: Seren, 1995. Print.

Robichaud, Paul. *Making the Past Present: David Jones, the Middle Ages, and Modernism*. Washington, D.C.: Catholic U of America P, 2006. Print.

Sherry, Vincent B. *The Cambridge Companion to the Literature of the First World War*. Cambridge: Cambridge UP, 2005. Print.

Staudt, Kathleen H. *At the Turn of a Civilization: David Jones and Modern Poetics*. Ann Arbor: U of Michigan P, 1994. Print.

Welch, Robert A. "David Jones: A Re-Assessment of the Major Works." *Studies: An Irish Quarterly Review* 62.246 (1973): 165–72. Print.

Cynthia Giles

THE KINGDOM OF THIS WORLD

Alejo Carpentier

OVERVIEW

Alejo Carpentier's *El reino de este mundo* (1949; *The Kingdom of this World*, 1957) remains one of the most influential novels in the history of Hispano-American letters. The novel tells the story of a 1751 slave rebellion in Haiti and explores its implications for the country's move toward independence from France in the nineteenth century, as well as its abolition of slavery. The work is seen as a prominent antecedent of magical realism, a literary genre that infuses and emphasizes everyday objects and events with a sense of the fantastic or miraculous. Carpentier's fundamentally political version particularly highlights the incongruities of uneven cultural and historical advances in developing Latin American countries. *The Kingdom of this World* is thought to have inspired the magical realism of the so-called "boom" generation of Latin American authors of the 1950s, '60s, and '70s, which included Gabriel García Márquez, Julio Cortázar, Carlos Fuentes, and Mario Vargas Llosa.

The Kingdom of this World portrays the historical events of the Haitian Revolution from the perspective of a fictional slave named Ti-Noël. Set in the mid-1700s, Part 1 of the novel introduces Ti-Noël, who works on a sugar plantation owned by a French colonist named Lenormand de Mézy. Another slave on the plantation, Mackandal, is a legendary and charismatic Angolan who loses his left arm in an accident and flees to the mountains, where he gains knowledge of various herbs and natural medicines and becomes a powerful practitioner of voodoo, a religion that incorporates traditional African beliefs with elements of Catholicism. Mackandal facilitates a revolt among the slaves by distributing poisonous mushrooms that they use to kill livestock and slave owners, including Lenormand de Mézy's wife. Several years later, after he acquires the ability to assume the shape of various animals and insects, Mackandal returns to the plantation, where he is captured and burned at the stake by the French. The slaves, however, are sure that he was saved by the African gods and simply laugh at the spectacle.

In Part 2, Boukman, a slave of Jamaican descent, organizes a second revolt in 1791 in which the slaves openly attack the plantation owners, killing many of them. Ti-Noël participates in the revolt, raping the mistress of Lenormand de Mézy. When Boukman is killed, the uprising comes to a temporary halt. Lenormand de Mézy, who survived in hiding, gathers up his slaves and flees to Cuba, where he gambles away all of them, including Ti-Noël. Eventually, Ti-Noël saves enough money to buy his freedom and returns to Haiti.

Part 3 describes the conditions Ti-Noël finds in Haiti upon his return. Though the slaves had continued to rebel against the French and had won their independence, the new king of the island, a former cook named Henri Cristophe, retains many of the policies that the rebellion was supposed to end. Despite being of African descent himself, Cristophe uses slave labor to build the new nation, and Ti-Noël is soon captured and forced back into slavery. He eventually escapes and takes refuge on the former Lenormand de Mézy plantation. After some time, King Christophe commits suicide in torment over the pain he has inflicted on his fellow Haitians.

In the fourth and final section of the novel, Ti-Noël attempts to organize a peaceful society at the former Lenormand de Mézy plantation, but his efforts are thwarted when the mulattoes—mixed-race Haitians whom the French deemed superior to the black slaves but inferior to the white landowners—come to power and begin to enslave the black Haitians again. Disheartened by the seemingly endless cycle of violence and exploitation, Ti-Noël decides, like Mackandal, to assume the form of an animal and escape. After he succeeds in becoming a goose, however, he realizes that even the society of geese is stratified and unequal. Ti-Noël returns to human form, and his armchair ascends into the air. The novel's ending is ambiguous, leaving uncertain whether Ti-Noël is still seated in the chair and suggesting that it may instead have been a vulture flying across the sky.

HISTORICAL AND LITERARY CONTEXT

In the eighteenth century the French colony of Saint Domingue (now Haiti) produced most of the world's sugar supply through a network of plantations; thus, the colony required the most manual labor. This need was fulfilled by transporting hundreds of thousands of Africans to the island. The slaves worked for a small group of landowners whose members included both whites and blacks. Although the French king Louis XIV established legal guidelines in 1685 to ensure the well-being of slaves in the colonies, the laws did little

⁜ *Key Facts*

Conflict:
Haitian Revolution

Time Period:
Late 18th–early 19th Centuries

Genre:
Novel

FREEDOM FIGHTERS: THE ROLE OF THE MAROONS IN HAITIAN INDEPENDENCE

Escaped slaves, commonly known as *maroons*, played an important role in the independence struggles of many Latin American nations, including Haiti. Also known by the Haitian Creole word *mawon*, Haitian maroons in the 1600s and 1700s fled to the dense forests and mountainous regions, where they formed close-knit societies with other escaped slaves and such indigenous peoples as the Taino Indians. These societies acted as sources of inspiration and support for those still in captivity, often engaging in armed raids against the plantation owners.

Two of the most famous maroons appear in *The Kingdom of this World*: François Mackandal and Dutty Boukman. Mackandal was a renowned practitioner of voodoo. During the uprisings he distributed poisonous herbs and mushrooms to the slaves, who used them to kill plantation owners and their livestock. Furthermore, Mackandal led attacks against the French and is said to have been responsible for the deaths of more than six thousand colonists. In 1791 Boukman, also a voodoo priest, prophesied the overthrow of French rule and encouraged the slaves to revolt. The resulting rebellion is considered the catalyst for the Haitian Revolution and the eventual establishment of Haitian independence. To commemorate the maroons' contributions, President François Duvalier erected a statue titled Nèg Mawon ("Black Maroon") near the National Palace in 1959.

to protect the slaves from the abuses of landowners and the harsh working conditions on sugar and coffee plantations. The slave rebellions depicted in *The Kingdom of this World* were a reaction against these intolerable conditions. The 1751 rebellion was led by François Mackandal, who, as described in the novel, became legendary for his practice of voodoo and his reputed ability to change his shape at will. Following the suppression of this first rebellion and the execution of Mackandal, a period of relatively peaceful instability began that lasted until one of Mackandal's successors, Dutty Boukman, vowed to renew the fight against France in 1791.

After more than ten years of armed conflict in which both Spain and Britain participated, Haiti obtained its independence in 1804. At that point slavery was also abolished on the island, and it became the first monarchy ever instituted in the Americas, with Henri Christophe, a former member of the free black population of Saint Domingue, the first king. His reign (1804–20) is depicted in Carpentier's novel as holding the seeds of later dictatorships and tyrannies in Latin America. While at first Christophe adopted French revolutionary ideals, he was soon behaving as an absolute monarch, implementing a system of *corvée* labor in which lower-class citizens, usually of African descent, were forced to work for little or no pay on plantations or on one of the king's massive building projects. In August 1820 Christophe suffered a stroke and, afraid of being assassinated, he committed suicide. Jean-Pierre Boyer, a mulatto who was president of a rival government in southern Haiti toward the end of Christophe's autocratic rule, then gained undisputed control of the island.

In 1825, under renewed threat of invasion by France, Boyer agreed to pay 150 million francs to ensure the recognition of Haiti as a free and independent nation. Although the debt was later reduced to sixty million francs, the payments proved an impossible burden on the Haitian economy, and Boyer instituted a system of government-enforced agriculture in the hope of generating more revenue. The scheme worsened an already severe economic gap between the privileged urban mulatto class and the rural black population, and in 1843 a rebellion led by the black military officer Charles Rivière-Hérard overthrew the Boyer regime. A series of bloody revolts marked the latter half of the 1800s and early 1900s, leading the United States to occupy and effectively govern Haiti from 1915 to 1934. Many historians regard the U.S. intervention as an attempt to assert sovereignty over the region and to quell further uprisings in independent, black-ruled countries. In 1949, the year in which *The Kingdom of this World* was published, the black general Paul Magloire took control of the country by military force. He was later ousted in a popular uprising that led to the thirty-year dictatorship of François Duvalier and his son, Jean-Claude ("Baby Doc"), which ended in another popular uprising in 1986. To this day poverty, racial tensions, oppressive debt, foreign interventions, and political strife remain major obstacles to Haitian progress and national unity.

Alejo Carpentier's fascination with Haiti, and with Latin America in general, began early in his life. Born in 1904 in Lausanne, Switzerland, to French and Russian parents, he moved with his family to Havana, Cuba, in 1905 and always considered himself thoroughly Cuban. During his childhood, Carpentier lived on a farm in the countryside, an experience that informs the imagery and references of the first part of the novel. A 1943 vacation to Haiti with the French theatrical director Louis Jouvet inspired him to depict the Haitian Revolution from a distinctly

Latin American perspective. Although he consciously incorporates elements of the European literary tradition into the novel (for example, the elevated, florid prose reminiscent of the Spanish baroque period; his frequent use of counterpoint, a technique common to baroque music in which two contrasting perspectives are presented; and his incorporation of passages from the works of such Spanish authors as Miguel de Cervantes and Miguel Félix Arturo Lope de Vega y Carpio as epigraphs), Carpentier strives to expand upon a distinctly New World aesthetic in *The Kingdom of this World*, one that captures what he terms in the novel's prologue *lo real maravilloso* ("the marvelous reality") of Latin American culture.

THEMES AND STYLE

Carpentier's prologue to *The Kingdom of this World* has been the focus of much commentary. In it, he attempts to introduce readers to Latin American sensibilities and experiences and to promote the possibilities of a unique literature based on several key traits of the underlying culture, particularly the vitality of its daily life and the heterogeneity of its ritualistic and artistic expression. According to Carpentier, these aspects of Latin American reality need to be rediscovered and given the literary attention they deserve. Specifically, he discusses them as fundamental to the *real maravilloso*, which has Latin American literary antecedents in the modernist tales of Uruguayan author Horacio Quiroga (1878–1937) and the indigenist (or native nationalist) novels of Miguel Angel Asturias (1899–1974).

In the prologue Carpentier explains that an epiphany provoked by his trip to Haiti in 1943 determined the subject of *The Kingdom of this World*. The magical atmosphere that Carpentier felt in Haiti gave rise to the author's particular aesthetic vision, in which Latin America could be a source of new, very different mythologies than the already exhausted ones produced in Europe centuries earlier. In terms of the novel, the literary space of Haiti differs from that of Europe in the strong faith of the slave community in the power of miracles. For example, when Mackandal is killed, the slaves' belief that he has been saved by the African gods ensures that their vision of liberation does not die with him. The miracle sets the stage for the rise of Boukman (who is considered to be the embodiment of Mackandal's spirit) and the rebellion that will lead to Haitian independence.

The Kingdom of this World uses the struggle for Haitian independence to illustrate a fundamental difference between Latin American and European understandings of reality and history. It can be read as an attempt to explain the political and intellectual logic of the Haitian Revolution and the way in which that logic is distorted when viewed through the framework of an outdated and spiritually bankrupt European mindset. The empty, formal language that the pseudo-aristocratic French landholders use to describe the Haitian belief system and the contrasting spiritual energy of the slaves' culture together create the disjunction at the heart of the novel's magical realism. Only through a firm understanding of the "marvelous reality" of the Afro-Caribbean experience can one view the recurrence of violence and social upheaval that has gripped Haiti for so many years as part of a necessary process toward the establishment of a culturally and politically liberated Caribbean region. By acknowledging the centrality of such fantastical elements as the slaves' belief in the power of miracle, Carpentier underscores that the Haitian people were motivated by much more than bloodthirsty revenge or political greed, an assertion that ran counter to the historical representation of the Haitian Revolution in his day.

CRITICAL DISCUSSION

Because the prologue of *The Kingdom of this World* explores the essential dissimilarity of Latin American cultures and those of their European colonizers, as well as the possibilities of a distinctively Latin American artistic sensibility, the "boom"-generation authors came to regard it as their foundational text. In consequence, literary critics virtually ignored the fictional narrative of the novel for several decades, preferring to focus their discussion on the prologue.

During the 1970s and '80s, however, such critics as Roberto González Echevarría and Emir Rodríguez Monegal began to praise the novel itself as a foundational text in Latin American literature. In particular, they argue that Alejo Carpentier not only revised the official, Eurocentric historical account of Haitian independence but that, in so doing, he also gave voice to a distinctly Haitian version of the story, one that emphasizes the role of seemingly powerless slaves in their own liberation. Carpentier does not mention the traditional heroes of the independence movement, including the Haitian military leader Jean-Jacques Dessalines, preferring to filter the revolution through the experiences of characters like Ti-Noël. This unique approach to history set a further precedent for the novels of the "boom" era. Gabriel García Márquez's *The General in his Labyrinth* (1990) and Mario Vargas Llosa's *The Feast of the Goat* (2000), for example, both focus on the consequences of political power struggles for ordinary people.

Recent scholarship on *The Kingdom of this World* has in some ways run counter to the initial assessments of the novel. Lizabeth Paravisini-Gebert, for example, writes in *Research in African Literatures* that the ambiguous ending of the novel and Carpentier's blurring of historical fact reveal his "hopelessness concerning the Haitian land and its people." In *Colonialism and Race in Luso-Hispanic Literature*, Jerome Branche suggests the presence of an "antiblack" sentiment in the novel that "undercuts the superficial rhetoric of cultural vindication that has led some critics to see the novel as a celebration of negritude." Nevertheless, Carpentier remains one of the most highly regarded figures in Latin American letters, and his birthday is celebrated annually as a national holiday in Cuba.

SOURCES

Branche, Jerome. "Menegildo, Macandal, and Marvelous Realism." *Colonialism and Race in Luso-Hispanic Literature*. Columbia: U of Missouri P, 2006. 212–48. Print.

Carpentier, Alejo. *The Kingdom of this World*. Trans. Harriet de Onis. New York: Knopf, 1957. Print.

González Echevarría, Roberto. "The Dictatorship of Rhetoric/the Rhetoric of Dictatorship: Carpentier, García Márquez, and Roa Bastos." *Latin American Research Review* 15.3 (1980): 205–28. Print.

Paravisini-Gebert, Lizabeth. "The Haitian Revolution in Interstices and Shadows: A Re-Reading of Alejo Carpentier's *The Kingdom of This World*." *Research in African Literatures* 35.2 (2004): 114–27. Print.

Rodríguez Monegal, Emir. "Lo real maravilloso y *El reino de este mundo*." *Asedios a Carpentier*. Ed. Klaus Müller-Bergh. Santiago: Editorial Universitaria, 1972. 101–32. Print.

FURTHER READING

Anderson, J. Bradford. "The Clash of Civilizations and All That Jazz: The Humanism of Alejo Carpentier's *El reino de este mundo*." *Latin American Literary Review* 35.69 (2007): 5–28. Print.

Bell, Steven M. "Carpentier's *El reino de este mundo* in a New Light: Toward a Theory of the Fantastic." *Journal of Spanish Studies: Twentieth Century* 8.1 (1980): 29–43. Print.

Brennan, Timothy. Introduction. *Music in Cuba*. Trans. Alan West-Durán. Minneapolis: U of Minnesota P, 2001. 1–58. Print.

De Armas, Frederick A. "Metamorphosis as Revolt: Cervantes' *Persiles y Segismunda* and Carpentier's *El reino de este mundo*." *Hispanic Review* 49.3 (1981): 297–316. Print.

García Márquez, Gabriel. *The General in his Labyrinth*. Trans. Edith Grossman. New York: Knopf, 1990. Print.

Goldberg, Florinda F. "Patterns of Repetition in *The Kingdom of this World*." *Latin American Literary Review* 19.38 (1991): 23–34. Print.

González Echevarría, Roberto. *Alejo Carpentier: The Pilgrim at Home*. Austin: U of Texas P, 1990. Print.

James, Cyriel Lionel Robert. *The Black Jacobins*. London: Secker, 1938. Print.

———. *The Future in the Present: Selected Writings*. Westport: Hill. 1977. Print.

Shaw, Donald. *Alejo Carpentier*. Boston: Twayne, 1985. Print.

Vargas Llosa, Mario. *The Feast of the Goat*. Trans. Edith Grossman. New York: Farrar, 2001. Print.

Elizabeth Gansen

LEAVES OF HYPNOS
A War Journal (1943–1944)
René Char

OVERVIEW

Leaves of Hypnos (*Feuillets d'Hypnos*) is a wartime journal that the poet René Char kept in 1943–44 while serving as a leader of the French Resistance in the Vaucluse department. The book, whose title refers to one of the code names, Hypnos, that Char used in communicating with other Resistance fighters, consists of a preface, 237 numbered sections, and a conclusion. The sections range in scope from sentence fragments to several paragraphs, with only a few occupying more than half of a printed page. Formally they tend toward aphorism, anecdote, and diaristic reflection, but in their highly suggestive language and oblique relationship to the context of their composition, they also read like prose poems. *Leaves of Hypnos* addresses a range of topics, including camaraderie, freedom, death, bravery, nature, social turmoil, and possibilities for the renewal of the self and community. As Char writes in the preface, the poems "were written under stress, in anger, fear, emulation, disgust, stealth, in furtive meditation, in illusory hope for the future, in friendship and in love." While he claims to have neither revised nor read the text thoroughly beyond the initial period of composition, recent scholarship suggests that he may have altered it to some degree. In a letter he sent his friend the writer Gilbert Lély immediately after the war, Char described having buried the original version of *Leaves of Hypnos* in a wall somewhere near the village of Céreste before he left France in July 1944 to participate in resistance efforts in Algiers. Sources indicate that he subsequently retrieved the writings and transcribed (and possibly edited) them for publication before burning the original manuscript.

Char had published numerous volumes of poetry and had been an instrumental figure in the surrealist movement in 1930s Paris, but he did not achieve widespread acclaim prior to the war years. With the publication in 1945 of his first postwar collection of poems, *Seules demeurent*, his reputation spread, and he became friends with Albert Camus, among other prominent French intellectuals and artists. *Leaves of Hypnos* appeared in 1946, as public enthusiasm for heroes of the French Resistance was at a high point, and it increased Char's fame as well as his moral stature. Like his friend Camus, to whom *Leaves of Hypnos* is dedicated, Char considered his literary work part of a larger emancipatory effort, and he was widely seen in the postwar years as a model for combining moral engagement with literary achievement. *Leaves of Hypnos* itself, which demonstrates a commitment to poetry, personal sacrifice, and action for the sake of the greater good, supports such a view of the author.

Once it became widely available in translation in the 1950s, *Leaves of Hypnos* was a central text in the English-language reception of Char's work, and it remains a valuable document of the Resistance movement. His 1948 volume, *Fureur et mystère* (*Furor and Mystery*), which Camus proclaimed among the most important works of French poetry since Arthur Rimbaud's *Illuminations*, established him as one of the most important poets of his time.

HISTORICAL AND LITERARY CONTEXT

From 1929 Char was a vital figure in the surrealist movement in Paris, coauthoring a book with André Bréton and Paul Éluard and helping to found a journal for the group. Although he did not make a definitive break with the movement, by the mid-1930s he was living primarily in his native L'Isle-sur-la-Sorgue in the Vaucluse department of southeastern France. There he developed a style of poetry in which surrealist techniques and imagery were placed in the service of a more personal vision. During this time he was particularly influenced by the poetry of Rimbaud, with whom he has often been compared.

In 1939 Char served in the French artillery on the Alsatian border with Germany. After Germany invaded and occupied France in 1940, he was demobilized, and he returned to L'Isle-sur-la-Sorgue. Soon after his return Char was denounced by the occupation Vichy government because of his affiliations with leftists and his marriage to a Jew, and he had to flee for his safety. He made contact with the Resistance networks fighting for the country's liberation from the Vichy regime, and by 1942 he was actively fighting as a leader of the Maquis, as the Resistance fighters in the French countryside were called. Since the Resistance operated in secret within occupied France, Char assumed code names to protect his identity. One of

Conflict:
World War II

Time Period:
Mid-20th Century

Genre:
Journal

THE RESOLUTION OF OPPOSITES

As many of his commentators have pointed out, René Char's embrace of the aphorism as a poetic form is at least partly attributable to his admiration for Heraclitus, the pre-Socratic Greek philosopher. Heraclitus, whose own aphorisms exist today only as quotations in the work of other philosophers and writers, believed that all things arise out of the tension between opposites and that a hidden harmony unifies apparently contradictory elements. Char's work, including his embrace of the aphorism, demonstrates substantial adherence to these concepts. As the leading Char translator and scholar Mary Ann Caws writes in "René Char—Resistance in Every Way," "Aphoristic condensation is such that thought is resolved only in tension … while in a poem or essay the tension can drag itself out at greater length."

There are many aphorisms in *Leaves of Hypnos* that illustrate this principle: "Be married and not married to your house;" "An act is virgin, even when repeated;" "Acquiescence lights up the face. Refusal gives it beauty;" "Keep with others what you have promised yourself alone. That is your contract." Furthermore, Char's overall project in *Leaves of Hypnos*, which might be summarized as the seeking of poetic individuality through communal activity, has a similarly paradoxical flavor.

these was le Capitaine Alexandre; the other was Hypnos, after the Greek god of sleep.

In 1943–44, during breaks from military responsibilities, when Char was writing the short fragments of text that were collected as *Leaves of Hypnos*, he was the head of a parachute reception unit. Some passages in *Leaves of Hypnos* accordingly have substantial documentary value, reflecting, for example, the reality of waiting for secret nighttime parachute drops, the precariousness of relying on ordinary villagers to keep the identity of Resistance fighters secret, and the feelings of solidarity that develop with fellow fighters when the possibility of death is always imminent. Char was wounded in a 1944 skirmish against German forces but continued to fight, participating in Resistance efforts in Algeria and Provence as the war drew to a close.

THEMES AND STYLE

Although *Leaves of Hypnos* was written while Char was a Maquis leader in the French Resistance and while it was intended at least partly as a record of his wartime experiences, it is by no means a straightforward diary. The first numbered section of the text establishes the tone and the mode of delivery that characterize the whole: "As far as possible, teach them to be efficient, for the purpose at hand but not beyond. Beyond is smoke. Where there is smoke there is change."

While this set of statements obliquely reflects Char's situation as the leader of a Resistance unit,

responsible for teaching "them" (the men over whom he has command) how to act in relation to "the purpose at hand," the statements' lack of documentary detail announces a desire to capture truths that transcend the particular historical moment. As the critic Northrop Frye, writing in the *Hudson Review*, notes in a review of *Hypnos Waking*, the early English translation of selected works that includes the full text of *Leaves of Hypnos*, "These sentences are oracular, like the aphorisms of Heraclitus, a philosopher who has deeply impressed Char. Linear reading, of the kind we apply both to ordinary prose and to meter, will not do for them. The aphorism works on the principle of the Bloody Mary: it has to be swallowed at a gulp and allowed to explode from inside."

Nevertheless, *Leaves of Hypnos* is directly tied to its historical circumstances. In addition to the overarching oracular mode of the aphorisms, the text includes sections that are more anecdotal, closer to what might be found in a diary. Entry 9, for example, consists of a character sketch of one of Char's comrades:

> After a few cautious moves at the start, Crazy Arthur has now thrown the whole of his strong, determined nature into our gamble. His lust for action has to be satisfied with the exact job I assign him. He is obedient and holds himself in, fearing a reprimand! Otherwise, God knows what final hornet's nest this daredevil would get into! Good, loyal Arthur, like a trooper of the old days!

There are also memorable anecdotal sections recounting close escapes from German troops, the wrenching deaths of comrades, and Char's own brushes with death and injury. Together these documentary fragments root the text in the particularities of the clandestine life of the Maquis, and they accumulate into a portrait of a noble and unified community of fighters.

Char's goals go further than a desire for documentation and portraiture, however; he looks to his experience as part of this community for insights into how to behave as an individual and a poet. As the scholar Virginia A. La Charité writes in *The Poetics and the Poetry of René Char*,

> The poet recognizes that while each being has a distinct personality, each is also a member of the community of men who share a common destiny of suffering and death. Furthermore, he becomes aware that this community refuses to acquiesce to the overwhelming forces which try to overcome it; in order to live, it accepts the risk of destruction. In this common will to act, the poet discovers the inherent dignity of man.

Moreover, Char is sensitive to the temptations of sentimentalizing this dignity and the solidarity on which it is based. As he writes in section 65,

"Too bad that the quality of partisans [of the Resistance cause] is not everywhere the same! … [H]ow many slippery charlatans there are, more anxious to profit than to produce! It is to be expected that these cocks of the Void will crow in our ears, once the Liberation has come …" Thus, the dignity and vision that the poet achieves as a result of fighting in solidarity for a worthy cause do not represent a destination that society as a whole will reach upon vanquishing the Nazis: "Resistance is nothing but hope," he writes in section 168. "Like the moon of Hypnos, full tonight in every quarter, tomorrow a vision of poems passing."

"All through *Leaves of Hypnos,*" Frye writes, "we read of a new world dawning." He adds, "Yet this feeling is not the usual donkey's carrot of people at war who hypnotize themselves into believing that the war is worthwhile because of all the wonderful things that will happen after it … The 'real' world that produced the war is always here, and only poetry can do anything effective about it."

CRITICAL DISCUSSION

Char, associated with the existentialists in the immediate postwar period, was widely regarded as one of the major poets of his time. Among the contributions to French poetry for which he was recognized was his instrumental role in establishing the prose poem as a form to be taken as seriously as verse.

He was also lionized as an archetype of the morally engaged artist. For Char poetry was coterminous with a commitment to extending freedom and dignity to all humans, and his service in the Resistance, as documented in *Leaves of Hypnos,* lent legitimacy to this stance.

Char's influence on American poetry in the postwar period was pronounced. The poet William Carlos Williams not only translated Char's work but also included a reference to him in the 1954 poem "To a Dog Injured in the Street":

> René Char
> you are a poet who believes
> in the power of beauty
> to right all wrongs.
> I believe it also.

Leaves of Hypnos was the centerpiece of *Hypnos Waking* (1956), the first selection of Char's work to appear in translation in the United States, and the book was reviewed enthusiastically in American periodicals, including the *New York Times Book Review* and *Time* magazine, both of which focused on his identity as a Resistance fighter and as a poet of moral engagement. Then, as L. C. Breunig observes in "René Char in English," recounting the history of the poet's early reception in the United States, "As we moved along into the sixties, however, the interest seemed to taper off, and Char was obliged to cross a bit of a wasteland before reaching—like many a good poet, native or foreign, in the United States—the 'p'oasis' of the university campus." Accordingly, a number of biographical and critical studies have appeared on Char and his work.

SOURCES

Breunig, L. C. "René Char in English." *World Literature Today* 51.3 (1977): 396–400. *JSTOR*. Web. 27 Sept. 2011.

Caws, Mary Ann. "René Char—Resistance in Every Way." *Brooklyn Rail*. The Brooklyn Rail, Dec. 2007-Jan. 2008. Web. 27 Sept. 2011.

Char, René. *Hypnos Waking: Poems and Prose by René Char*. New York: Random, 1956. Print.

Frye, Northrop. "Poetry of the Tout Ensemble." *Hudson Review* 10.1 (1957): 122–25. *JSTOR*. Web. 27 Sept. 2011.

La Charité, Virginia A. *The Poetics and the Poetry of René Char*. Chapel Hill, U of North Carolina P, 1968. Print.

FURTHER READING

Caws, Mary Ann. *René Char*. Boston: Twayne, 1977. Print.

———. *The Presence of René Char*. Princeton: Princeton UP, 1976. Print.

Eichbauer, Mary E. *Poetry's Self-Portrait: The Visual Arts as Mirror and Muse in René Char and John Ashbery*. New York: P. Lang, 1992. Print.

Lawler, James R. *René Char: The Myth and the Poem*. Princeton: Princeton UP, 1978. Print.

Minahen, Charles D., ed. *Figuring Things: Char, Ponge, and Poetry in the Twentieth Century*. Lexington, KY: French Forum, 1994. Print.

Noland, Carrie Jaurès. "The Performance of Solitude: Baudelaire, Rimbaud, and the Resistance Poetry of René Char." *French Review* 70.4 (1997): 562–74. *JSTOR*. Web. 27 Sept. 2011.

Piore, Nancy Kline. *Lightning: The Poetry of René Char*. Boston: Northeastern UP, 1981. Print.

Mark Lane

LITTLE MOUNTAIN

Elias Khoury

OVERVIEW

One of the most significant of the many works of fiction inspired by the Lebanese civil war (1975–90), *Al-jabal al-saghir* is a loosely autobiographical novel based on Elias Khoury's own experience of the conflict in his native Beirut.

First published in 1977 in Arabic, *Al-jabal al-saghir* was widely praised as boldly innovative in its use of a complex narrative viewpoint and floating temporal and spatial sequences to portray the fractured reality of a country torn apart by bitter factional hatreds. The first English translation of the novel, *Little Mountain*, appeared in 1989 with a foreword by the famous Palestinian-born American literary theorist Edward Said. Said emphasizes the groundbreaking nature of *Little Mountain*, noting that it marked a break with the realist tradition of the Arab novel as represented by its best-known practitioner, the Egyptian Nobel Prize winner Naguib Mahfouz. Said remarks,

> The startling originality of *Little Mountain* is its avoidance of the melodramatic and the conventional; Khoury plots episodes without illusion or foreseeable pattern, much as a suddenly released extraterrestrial prisoner might wander from place to place, backward and forward, taking things in through a surprisingly well-articulated earth-language … Khoury's work embodies the very actuality of Lebanon's predicament, so unlike Egypt's majestic stability as delivered in Mahfouz's fiction.

As Said's commentary suggests, *Little Mountain* depicts a world surreal in its disorder. The novel focuses on the first years of the civil war as fighting broke out between Palestinian and Christian militias and spread throughout the streets of Beirut and the surrounding mountains. Although Khoury fought with the Palestinian resistance, he does not openly favor a religious or political position in the novel. His purpose is rather to illustrate the mass of confused and overlapping ideologies that fueled the fighting. Khoury employs a variety of experimental stylistic and narrative devices to replicate the chaos.

The novel consists of five chapters ostensibly told from separate points of view: a Christian adolescent in chapter one, Palestinian fighters in chapters two and three, a middle-class Beirut civil servant in

chapter four, an intellectual exiled to Paris in chapter five. The prose style of the novel is alternately matter-of-fact and lyrical, mixing telescopic accounts of the fighting with poetic ruminations on Beirut before the war and vague philosophical asides on the meaning of war and revolution. As the narrative compresses and expands, the point of view shifts constantly, sometimes from sentence to sentence. The integrity of the separate speaking voices at times collapses; the child in chapter one is very possibly one of the Palestinian guerrillas as well as the displaced intellectual. Khoury's blurring of the boundaries between space and time results in a story that never coalesces into a coherent whole.

HISTORICAL AND LITERARY CONTEXT

The facts of Khoury's life are a record of the religious and political strife in Lebanon that finally erupted into civil war in 1975. Khoury was born in 1948 into an Orthodox Christian family in Ashrafiyyeh, the hilltop neighborhood of East Beirut known as "Little Mountain" that is nostalgically recalled by the child narrator of the novel. Although the civil war was increasingly characterized by a complicated mix of shifting religious and political rivalries and foreign interventions, it erupted along fairly clear-cut lines between right-wing Christian militiamen, who were pro-Israel in their sympathies, and a combined fighting force of Lebanese Muslims and Palestinians.

Tensions between Christians and Muslims had steadily escalated due to the growing presence of Palestinians in Lebanon. The first great influx of Palestinian refugees into Lebanon occurred in 1948 after the creation of Israel. A second wave of displaced Palestinians entered the country after the Arab-Israeli War of 1967. As a nineteen-year-old undergraduate at Lebanese University in Beirut, Khoury traveled to Amman, Jordan, to enlist in the Fatah, the largest resistance group in the Palestinian Liberation Organization (PLO). When the PLO was expelled from Jordan in 1970 it established headquarters in Lebanon.

Amidst the growing polarization in Beirut, Khoury decided to finish his studies in Paris. He returned home in 1972 and joined the ranks of the Palestinian sympathizers when war broke out. Khoury was severely wounded in the fighting, losing his eyesight for a time. He withdrew from active fighting in

Key Facts

Conflict:
Lebanese Civil War

Time Period:
Late 20th Century

Genre:
Novel

THE TRUTH OF THE CIVIL WAR

Lebanese novelist Elias Khoury, who has suffered censorship in his homeland for writing honestly, reads at a PEN Freedom to Write event called Face-to-Face: Confronting the Torturers on April 29, 2010, in New York City. © CHARLES ESHELMAN / WIREIMAGE / GETTY IMAGES

Khoury has stated in interviews that he considers Lebanese intellectuals fortunate in having the freedom to express their opinions in writing without fear of censorship. However, he has also noted that his fourth novel, *Al-wujuh al-baidha'* (1981; *White Masks*), caused a considerable stir because it openly criticized his own political camp, the Palestinian resistance. *White Masks* exposes atrocities committed in January 1976 at Damour, a town south of Beirut, where hundreds of Christian civilians were murdered by PLO fighters in response to a Christian assault on a Palestinian refugee camp. The following exchange between a pro-Palestinian filmmaker and one of the PLO fighters provides an example:

> "Listen, you don't listen we have to make our just cause
> known and reveal the fascist practices, killing, rape,
> theft, expulsion and destruction of houses. This is the
> role of the engaged cinema …"
>
> "But we, too … I told her that we, too, had committed
> crimes, had killed and …"
>
> "That's not true, it isn't true."
>
> "I swear it's true, Damour …"
>
> "No, that's not the truth. The truth has to serve the revolution.
> This kind of truth makes our camp get mixed up."
>
> "The truth has to serve the truth."

When *White Masks* was first published, the PLO effectively banned the book by threatening distributors. It was not until a few years later, after Khoury had published several articles denouncing the Israeli invasion of Beirut, that the novel was made available for sale.

1976 and afterward became increasingly skeptical of applying a military solution to Lebanon's troubles. He turned to critiquing the war in a variety of writings,

including newspaper articles, essays, and novels. The second in a series of novels that currently has more than ten entries, *Little Mountain* brought Khoury to international attention.

Khoury has traced his innovative writing approach to a variety of factors, including the childhood influence of his maternal grandmother, who introduced him to classical Arabic poetry, oriental Christian myths, and popularized versions of the Middle Eastern stories and folktales of *One Thousand and One Nights*. In an interview with Sonja Mejcher published in *Banipal* magazine, he recalls, "I think that these three elements: poetry, stories, and religious stories later played an important role in my novels, especially in my efforts to cross the frontiers between reality and the imaginary and to read life as a journey in unknown places. … Ashrafiyya lives inside me at this crossing point between reality and imagination."

Khoury also professes to being profoundly affected by the conventional view of Arab history as a progression from a medieval Golden Age to an epoch of decline (*inhitat*), followed by a stage of renaissance (*nahdah*) commencing at the turn of the twentieth century. In his conversation with Mejcher he expresses the opinion that this periodization had resulted in an incomplete view of Lebanon's past.

> The hypothesis of the *nahdah* was that we had
> to go back to the sources of our culture. … But
> there was also another neglected heritage: the
> heritage of the *inhitat* (often referred to as the
> Ottoman decadence), the heritage of the spoken and the lived. … In the 1970s many Arab
> writers tried to give voice to this other heritage
> in one way or another. It was as if we found a
> new kind of narrative that was neither a repetition of the glorious Arab past nor an imitation
> of the modern Western novel—like the novels
> of the famous Egyptian writer and Nobel prize
> winner Naguib Mahfouz. For the first time our
> writing corresponded to our very hybrid way
> of living.

THEMES AND STYLE

Little Mountain is, as Said observes, "the story of an unraveling society." The novel registers Khoury's disillusionment with the war in the absurdity of the situations it documents. Through its random structure, splintering of time, and shifting perspectives, the novel depicts a society so deranged that a bomb blast on the street is perceived as more of a threat to parked cars than to innocent passersby, and the life of a soldier is reduced to a marketing strategy: "We die for the sake of a poster. A color photograph, with colored writing underneath," one Palestinian fighter concludes.

Contradictory and ill-formed notions of freedom and justice devolve into chaotic fighting that takes on its own momentum detached from any ideological aims. In an essay included in *Sexuality and*

War: Literary Masks of the Middle East, Evelyn Accad observes, "Like the war itself, the narrative is often disconnected and absurd, expressing a hopelessness and meaninglessness spreading to the rest of the world through phrases, sentences, and descriptions that recur with the monotony of despair."

Accad is among a number of critics who have commented upon Khoury's use of the stylistic device of repetition, which causes the narrative to constantly circle back on itself, suggesting an endless cycle of confusion and violence. Said notes that the repetition, as well as Khoury's reliance on gallows humor, helped to convey the idea of war's insanity:

> Style in *Little Mountain* is, first of all, repetition, as if the narrator needed reiteration to prove to himself that improbable things actually *did* take place … Style for Khoury is also comedy and irreverence. For how else is one to apprehend those religious verities for which one fights—the truth of Christianity, for instance—if churches are also soldiers' camps, and if priests like the French Father Marcel in Chapter Two of *Little Mountain*, are garrulous and inebriated racists?

In the interview with Mejcher, Khoury explains how the nightmarish reality of war had destroyed his initial enthusiasm for the Palestinian resistance:

> *Al-jabal al-saghir* was written two years before it was published—in 1975/76 during the civil war. Everybody who read it thought that I was not a real revolutionary because I was fighting and at the same time criticizing the civil war in my writing. There was a contradiction between the euphoric optimistic ideology we were living and what I was writing … Ideology cannot work in literature and it cannot really work in life either because it covers reality and it covers atrocities and I cannot be part of that.

CRITICAL DISCUSSION

Criticism of *Little Mountain* has focused on Khoury's break with the tradition of the Arab novel through his use of experimental strategies most often associated with Western postmodernist fiction. In a review of the novel for the London *Sunday Times*, Austin MacCurtain observes, "Elias Khoury eschews plot. Instead he offers a series of isolated scenes of shooting, prisons and disrupted family life. The closest comparison that the Western tradition could offer is the postmodernist novel."

In an essay titled "The Patchwork Novel: Elias Khoury," Stephen J. Meyer argues that Khoury made a deliberate attempt to undermine the classic form of the novel in *Little Mountain* by structuring the work as a series of interweaving short stories. Meyer characterizes *Little Mountain* as a "virtual grab bag" of postmodernist devices meant to "unsettle, dislocate, and fragment the narrative to the optimum degree." In a 2007 interview with Maya Jaggi for the *Guardian*, Khoury recalls, "I didn't know what postmodern was. I was

This photograph of Beirut in June, 1982, during the Lebanese Civil War, captures the landscape Elias Khoury depicts in *Little Mountain*—the surreal chaos of the war-torn city. © PATRICK CHAUVEL / SYGMA / CORBIS

trying to express the fragmentation of society. Beirut's past is not of stability, but of violent change. Everything is open, uncertain. In my fiction, you're not sure if things really happened, only that they're narrated."

Scholars have praised Khoury's remarkable insight into the character of the war as a whole. Reviewing the 1990 English translation for *World Literature Today*, Roger Allen avers,

> The fracturing of time and the switching between differing modes of narration serve as apt reflections of the complex, disordered environment being portrayed, as Lebanon is tossed and turned in the political upheavals of the region during the lifespan of this generation. Indeed, the portrayal given here may be seen as a prescient foretaste of what has actually happened since its publication more than a decade ago.

Said also judges *Little Mountain* a perceptive appraisal of the turmoil in Lebanon:

> The work's five chapters … exfoliate outward from the family house in Ashrafiyyeh, to which neither Khoury nor the narrator can return given the irreversible dynamics of the Lebanese Civil Wars, and when the chapters conclude, they come to no rest, no final cadence, no respite. For indeed Khoury's prescience in this work of 1977 was to have forecast a worsening of the situation, in which Lebanon's modern(ist) history was terminated, and from which a string of almost unimaginable disasters (the massacres, the Syrian and Israeli interventions, the current political impasse with partition already in place) have followed.

SOURCES

Accad, Evelyn. "Elias Khoury: Ambivalence, Fear of Women, and Fascination with Death and Destruction." *Sexuality and War: Literary Masks of the Middle East*. Trans. Elizabeth Loverde-Bagwell. New York: NYU, 1990. 135–59. Print.

Allen, Roger. Rev. of *Little Mountain*, by Elias Khoury. *World Literature Today* 64.2 (1990): 358–59. JSTOR. Web. 10 Oct. 2011.

Asfour, Nana. "On the Trail of Elias Khoury." *New Yorker*. Condé Nast, 13 May 2010: n. pag. Web. 18 Oct. 2011.

Jaggi, Maya. "A Circle of Madness." *Guardian* [London] 27 July 2007. *Guardian News* and *Media Limited*. Web. 3 Oct. 2011.

MacCurtain, Austin. Rev. of *Little Mountain*, by Elias Khoury. *Sunday Times* [London] 13 Jan. 1991. *LexisNexis*. Web. 18 Oct. 2011.

Mejcher, Sonja, with Elias Khoury. "The Necessity to Forget—and Remember." *Banipal Magazine of Modern Arab Literature* [UK], 12 (2001): 8–14. *banipal.co.uk*. Web. 18 Oct. 2011.

Meyer, Stephen J. "The Patchwork Novel: Elias Khoury." *The Experimental Arabic Novel: Postcolonial Literary Modernism in the Levant*. New York: SUNY, 2001. Print.

Said, Edward. Foreword. *Little Mountain*. By Elias Khoury. Trans. Maia Tabet. New York: Picador, 2007. ix-xxi. Print.

FURTHER READING

Adnan, Etel. *Sitt Marie-Rose: A Novel*. Trans. Georgina Kleege. Sausalito: Post, 1982. Print.

Hirst, David. *Beware of Small States: Lebanon, Battleground of the Middle East*. New York: Nation, 2010. Print.

Khoury, Elias. *Gate of the Sun*. Trans. Humphrey Davies. New York: Archipelago, 2005. Print.

———. *The Journey of Little Gandhi*. Trans. Paula Haydar. New York: Picador, 2009. Print.

———. *White Masks*. Trans. Maia Tabet. New York: Archipelago, 2010. Print.

———. *Yalo*. Trans. Peter Theroux. New York: Picador, 2009. Print.

Lalami, Laila. "Bound by Tragedy." *Los Angeles Times* 13 Jan. 2008. Los Angeles Times. Web. 3 Oct. 2011.

Mejcher-Atassi, Sonja. "On the Necessity of Writing the Present: Elias Khoury and the 'Birth of the Novel' in Lebanon." *Arabic Literature: Postmodern Perspectives*. Ed. Angelika Neuwirth, Andreas Pflitsch, and Barbara Winckler. London: Saqi, 2010. 87–96. Print.

Werner, Louis. "Arab Novellas Reflect Changing Mideast Social Milieu." *Christian Science Monitor* 21 Nov. 1989. *LexisNexis*. Web. 18 Oct. 2011.

Janet Mullane

MARAT/SADE

Peter Ulrich Weiss

OVERVIEW

Widely regarded as one of the most innovative political dramas of the twentieth century, *The Persecution and Assassination of Jean-Paul Marat as Performed by the Inmates of the Asylum of Charenton Under the Direction of the Marquis de Sade* (1964) is the best-known work by German painter, writer, and filmmaker Peter Weiss. A complex and multilayered theatrical piece, it engages in a critique of political philosophy; by blurring the lines between the characters, the actors, and the real-life spectators, the play complicates the moral relationships between performance and reality. As the title suggests, *Marat/Sade* is a play within a play set in the bathhouse of the Charenton lunatic asylum, where patients perform in a musical spectacle written and directed by their fellow inmate, the Marquis de Sade. Under the auspices of the asylum's director, the Abbé de Coulmier, the piece functions as both a means of therapy for the inmates and an evening of entertainment for the curious Paris elite in attendance (represented by the real-life spectators of Weiss's play), who have come to witness the lunatics' "exercises" and are forced to participate in the events unfolding onstage. Sade's play dramatizes the 1793 assassination of the French Revolution's charismatic leader Jean-Paul Marat by the twenty-three-year-old minor aristocrat Charlotte Corday. Sade—a sexual libertine and an opponent of Marat's extreme revolutionary tactics—plays himself in the absurdist tragedy, while the part of Marat is enacted by a paranoiac who, true to his namesake, has a skin disease that confines him to a warm bath. A young woman suffering from sleeping sickness portrays Corday, and an ensemble cast of spastics, schizophrenics, depressives, and erotomaniacs round out the ranks of the French citizenry united in their perpetual refrain, "We want our rights and we don't care how / We want our Revolution now."

The action begins with an "Homage to Marat," sung by four balladeers who elevate the leader to the status of demigod, regarding him as the one true revolutionary. This veneration is contrasted, however, in the balladeers' subsequent introduction of Corday. According to the singers, she and her fellow royalist Girondists view Marat as a despot who will lead France on a death march to the guillotine. As if to illustrate this point, Marat interrupts Corday's initial assassination attempt to narrate the history of the

Reign of Terror. While he lists the victims, the other patients pantomime the executions with delight, going so far as to play football with the severed heads before nurses restrain them. Coulmier admonishes Sade for overexciting the inmates, and the play continues, progressing in this chaotic fashion, not as a causally connected sequence of events leading up to the assassination but rather as a succession of disjointed episodes. Tirades from such historical figures as the philosopher Voltaire, the chemist Antoine-Laurent Lavoisier, and the priest Jacques Roux punctuate the extended philosophical discussion between Marat and Sade that emerges between the revolutionary ballads. When Corday finally stands with her dagger poised to kill Marat for the third time, Sade again interrupts the action, this time ostensibly so that "Marat can hear and gasp with his last breath / at how the world will go after his death." The full cast breaks into song, relating the history of the "fifteen glorious years" following Napoleon Bonaparte's rise to power with an ironic gusto before Corday finally plunges her knife into Marat's chest. In the epilogue Coulmier's enthusiasm for the new emperor, however, incites the inmates to rage. They begin to riot, attacking Coulmier, the nurses, and finally the audience as Roux screams over the din. "When will you learn to see?" he pleads. "When will you finally understand?"

Marat/Sade premiered in West Berlin on April 29, 1964, to critical acclaim but achieved international notoriety only after British director Peter Brook's groundbreaking production with London's Royal Shakespeare Company that fall. The show moved to Broadway the next year and was made into a feature film by Brook in 1967. The popularity of Brook's production established *Marat/Sade* as a modern classic, and the play is frequently studied and performed by university theaters. The Royal Shakespeare Company mounted the play's first major professional revival for their 2011 fiftieth anniversary season.

HISTORICAL AND LITERARY CONTEXT

Weiss acknowledges that certain parts of *Marat/Sade* are based on actual events. The Marquis de Sade was in fact imprisoned at the Charenton asylum from 1801 until his death in 1814. He did write and produce several dramas with the other inmates there, but he never wrote a play featuring Marat, the physician

Key Facts

Conflict:
French Revolution

Time Period:
Early 19th Century

Genre:
Play

Awards:
Named production of the year Theater Heute, 1964; Lessing Prize, 1965; Antoinette Perry Award, best play, 1966; New York Drama Critics' Circle Award, 1966

SOCIAL JUSTICE AND THE FRENCH REVOLUTION

Peter Weiss's avant-garde play *Marat/Sade* represents an unorthodox and provocative interpretation of the French Revolution and its aftermath as seen through the eyes of the residents of an asylum. A more traditional account of the revolution appears in the classic novel *A Tale of Two Cities* (1859) by Charles Dickens. In that work, Dickens portrays the hardships suffered by the French peasantry in the years leading up to the revolution, as well as the bloodshed, chaos, and terror that followed the violent overthrow of King Louis XVI. Dickens alternates chapters set in Paris with chapters that give glimpses into the social and economic life of London during the same period, revealing a culture equally rife with inequality and injustice. While Dickens clearly sympathizes with the underprivileged classes in the novel, he stops short of endorsing revolutionary violence, and his depictions of the barbaric actions of some of the participants are unflinching in their candor. At the novel's core lies Dickens's concern for issues of social justice, as well as his continual plea for compassion and restraint. Populated with the author's trademark idiosyncratic characters and driven by a complex plot, *A Tale of Two Cities* remains not only the most famous work to emerge from the French Revolution but also one of the most popular novels in the history of English literature.

and political theorist considered to be one of the more extreme voices of the French Revolution (1789–99). As a member of the radical Jacobin faction, Marat made impassioned public speeches and produced a radical newspaper, drumming up public support for what has come to be known as the Reign of Terror, a period of violence early in France's civil war during which Marat, Maxmilien de Robespierre, and the Jacobin rebels sought to exterminate all "enemies of the revolution." Between sixteen and forty thousand such "enemies" were guillotined during the eleven months of the Terror, most of them members of the Girondist faction with whom Corday sympathized. Weiss's portrayal of Corday's views are accurate. A disenfranchised member of the aristocracy, she felt that Marat had become an evil dictator symbolizing the violence that had reigned since the beginning of the war.

In his book *Performing History*, Freddie Rokem highlights the tensions that are created by staging historical incidents. The process, he notes, "draws attention not only to the theatrical medium itself, but also to the deeper thematic concerns of such performances." Sade witnessed the atrocities of the Terror in 1793 and was jailed for his vocal opposition to the radical tactics. Although he had given up his aristocratic title and much of his personal property in support of revolutionary ideals, he vehemently condemned the use of capital punishment for political gain. Rokem points out that while Weiss does not dramatize the

events of the Terror, he stages Sade's resistance. During an infamous whipping scene in the play, Sade forces Corday to beat him with a cat-o'-nine-tails while he is driven about the stage in an executioner's cart sharing his views on the revolution:

> At first I saw in the revolution a chance
> for a tremendous outburst of revenge
> an orgy greater than all my dreams
> But then I saw
> when I sat in the courtroom myself …
> I couldn't bring myself
> to deliver the prisoners to the hangman …
> as the tumbrels ran regularly to the scaffolds
> and the blade dropped and was winched up
> and dropped again
> all the meaning had drained out of this
> revenge.

According to Rokem, this penitential beating is a stand-in for Sade's personal epiphany and psychological self-flagellation. "Corday and the chorus accompanying her have all become integrated in this mechanized expression of violence on the Charenton stage," he notes, adding that Sade, as a former participant in the revolution and current inmate of the asylum, "has created the scene to illustrate what happened when the Revolution turned against itself and became the tool for its own destruction." Because the acknowledgement that events are historical naturally leads to some assumption of authenticity onstage, Rokem argues, the actors also function as historians. "Whatever else they are doing," he writes, "they are also telling us something about the French Revolution as a historical event through the energies of their bodies."

The battle cry of Weiss's inmates—"Revolution Revolution, Copulation Copulation"—articulates the opposing tacks of the play's protagonists. While Marat might sacrifice the masses for social gain, Sade advocates a radical humanism that stresses the supremacy of the individual. Neither Marat nor Sade, however, is able to employ his ideas in advance of a successful revolution. In his idealism Weiss's Marat advocates action that is unreasonable for starving citizens whose most basic needs remained unfulfilled. Sade's pessimistic view, however, which proclaims humans by nature incapable of acting beyond themselves, ultimately leads to his personal destruction.

Brook's interpretation of *Marat/Sade* highlighted the inherent dichotomy between Marat's revolutionary mandate and Sade's endorsement of individual liberation by approaching the play through two seemingly opposite twentieth-century theater theories. Weiss's play clearly took inspiration from German director Bertolt Brecht's dialectical theater tradition, which favored an aloof spectator capable of analyzing the author's political argument. In accordance with Brecht's "alienation effect," *Marat/Sade*'s episodic plot structure is interrupted by musical interludes and theatrical devices that break continuity and jar the audience into approaching the work intellectually rather than emotionally. Brook chose to combine this Brechtian approach with tactics made famous by the French theater artist Antonin Artaud, who sought to appeal to the spectators' precognitive response: by immersing them in spectacle-rich "total theater," he attempted to eliminate the psychological boundaries between performance space and audience space. Both Brecht and Artaud strove to create a politically engaged and impassioned audience primed for social revolution. Their combined techniques empowered Brook to craft a production that relied both on the political message presented in the text and the reality of an onstage revolution.

Although Brook's staging of the play has come to be seen as a landmark interpretation of both *Marat/Sade* and the writings of Brecht and Artaud, Weiss preferred a 1965 East German production directed by Konrad Swinarski. He felt that the exuberant theatricality of Brook's interpretation gave undue weight to the Artaudian "cruelty" of Sade, whereas Swinarski's more balanced approach foregrounded Marat's social consciousness. Roger Gross's article " *Marat/Sade's* Missing Epilogue" examines an epilogue included in the original German text (and cut from Brook's production), revealing that "[Weiss] personally took the Marxist/Marat side." Gross notes, however, that the playwright's "intended effect" depends on presenting a clear, balanced argument from moment to moment in order to delve into the specific function of each new outbreak of violence." Nevertheless, the memory of Brook's production endures, and when *Marat/Sade* was revived by the Royal Shakespeare Company in 2011, it was the Weiss/Brook version that made it back onto the stage.

THEMES AND STYLE

In spite of any factual accuracies, the scope of *Marat/Sade's* philosophical debate extends beyond a historical account of the French Revolution. Though the inmates' performance is set fifteen years after Marat's murder, numerous theatrical devices—including flashbacks, repetitions, rapid scene changes, and the inmates' periodic lapses into madness—confuse the chronology of events, turning the narrative into a general critique of revolutionary ideas that may lead to dictatorships—a point relevant to Weiss's difficult coming of age during the Nazi and Soviet regimes. "Weiss deliberately rebuts the presumption of historical authenticity," Marshall Cohen writes in the *Partisan Review*. "The debate is openly proleptic, its subject less the French than the Russian and the Nazi revolutions." The playwright, he argues, stages a "conversation" between Marat and Sade, two polarizing figures of the nineteenth century, in order to explore the philosophical conundrum plaguing those divided between socialist and capitalist systems in the modern world. The two characters' arguments are well matched, Cohen notes, emphasizing Weiss's own personal ambivalence about man's "correct" role in social action. In his article "*Marat/Sade*: A Portrait of the Artist in Bourgeois Society," Ladislaus Löb shares Cohen's sentiment. "While the play ostensibly deals with the French Revolution and its aftermath, the deliberate anachronisms emphasize the problem of revolution today," he observes. "Although he antedates Marx, Marat is presented as a Marxist revolutionary … [who] explains the revolutionary terror as counter-violence provoked by the violence of the rulers," Löb writes. In order to accomplish this feat, "Weiss works on three different levels of time and with a multitude of intricately linked locations and events."

The three levels of time that Löb references are the 1793 narrative of the French Revolution, the 1808 performance of Sade's play within the play in the Charenton asylum, and the present-day audience that is re-created anew each time the play is staged. "In Weiss's play, the performance is witnessed by Coulmier, the timeserving, 'progressive' director of the asylum," Cohen notes, as well as the audience, which stands in for the "fashionable, thrill-seeking Parisian audience" that came to gawk at the historical inmates of the eighteenth-century Charenton Asylum. As a result of shifting temporality, spectators viewing *Marat/Sade* are asked to interpret several layers of consciousness, simultaneously maintaining awareness of the historical figures being portrayed within Sade's drama, the Charenton lunatics who have been cast in those roles, and the living reality of the present-day actors onstage. Together audience and actors share the performance space as coparticipants, and they all become metacharacters in the play as a result of this mutually acknowledged self-awareness. It is this complex temporality that allows *Marat/Sade* to achieve both Brecht's ideal of distance and Artaud's concept of immersion. The patients are alternately "alienated" Brechtian actors, merely "showing" the characters they portray in Sade's play, and practitioners of psychological realism, fully immersed in what Cohen calls a "lunatic consummation" of authentic experience. It is in the instant when Weiss's stage directions call for the actors to engage the audience that "these panting, rioting madmen, exhibiting freshly spilt blood, celebrating the festival of the guillotine, performing mimes of copulation and whipping the Marquis de Sade, create a shocking and beautiful mise-en-scène inspired by Artaud's conception of an anti-literary theater of the senses." In addition, at the conclusion of the performance, the assembled patients applaud the audience, refusing to leave the theater space until the viewers begin to retreat in discomfort. This reversal of the relationship between actors and audience calls into question the sanity of the viewers, as their role in the theatrical event becomes even more uncertain.

CRITICAL DISCUSSION

In both London and New York, the press's reaction to *Marat/Sade* was almost unanimously positive, though the theatricality of Brook's production often received the most attention. In his retrospective on *Marat/Sade* printed in the performance journal *Maske und Kothurn*, theater scholar Ward B. Lewis cites three levels of response to *Marat/Sade*. "The first confined itself to appreciation of Brook's effects and some of the lines without any recognition of the political or philosophical issues posed by Weiss," he notes. At the secondary level, the reviewer tended to appreciate the presence of a political message but was "unable to perceive that Marat and Sade defined two philosophical poles about which the work turned." The tertiary level of appreciation, though, "consisted of full recognition" of the two leaders' political positions. Lewis concludes, however, that "critics whose response relegated them to this category were already familiar with the arguments and their implications, knew that the positions were irreconcilable or at least not resolved by Weiss before their eyes, and became dissatisfied with the drama," adding that this frustration reverted a sophisticated critic's response back to the spectacle of level one.

Many of the issues of intelligibility likely stemmed from the fact that the dense verse spoken by the principal characters was often obscured by the wild antics of the other actors onstage. In his book *Great Directors at Work*, theater scholar David Richard Jones maintains that "most audiences experienced [the performance] as powerful" regardless of their level of appreciation of the text. "Viewers showed that they were strongly affected by its magnitude, whether they walked out in anger or stayed seated, shaking, at the end." Jones reports that some audience members stormed out of performances, some became ill from the intensity of the experience, and "at least one spectator, the German actress Ruth Arrack, died in the auditorium during a performance." These stories only added to *Marat/Sade*'s overall mystique, but viewer response to the play's frank violence and brutality combined with Weiss's ambiguous assertions about the proper method of social change led many of the play's detractors to label it as nothing more than "shock theater."

In New York's *Herald Tribune*, theater critic Walter Kerr questions the merit of Weiss's text without Brook's embellishments, calling the Broadway premiere "the substitution of theatrical production for dramatic structure," and observing that "[*Marat/Sade*] is stimulating only in its externals, literally in its stage management." In his review in London's *Times Literary Supplement*, George Steiner shares Kerr's feeling, writing, "The debate between Marat and Sade on the nature of justice and revolution, which is pivotal to the work, falls flat. What we know of both men, and what they wrote, is more disturbing, more exciting, than what emerges in the text. ... It may be that the future of *Marat/Sade*,

like that of a number of the major nineteenth-century operas, lies wholly with the impresario."

SOURCES

Cohen, Marshall. "Review of *Marat/Sade*." *Partisan Review* 33.2 (1966): 270–73. *Literature Resource Center*. Web. 16 Oct. 2011.

Gross, Roger. "Marat/Sade's Missing Epilogue." *Journal of Dramatic Theory and Criticism* 2.2 (1988): 61–67. *Freely Accessible Arts & Humanities Journals*. Web. 6 Dec. 2011.

Jones, David Richard. *Great Directors at Work: Stanislavsky, Brecht, Kazan, Brook*. Berkeley: U of California P, 1986. Print.

Kerr, Walter. "Kerr reviews *Marat/Sade*." *Herald Tribune*. 28 Dec. 1965. Rpt. in *New York Theatre Critics' Reviews* 26.19 (1965): 215. Print.

Lewis, Ward B. "The American Reception of Peter Weiss' *Marat/Sade*." *Maske und Kothurn* 31 (1985): 65–72. *Literature Resource Center*. Web. 16 Oct. 2011.

Löb, Ladislaus. "Peter Weiss's *Marat/Sade*: A Portrait of the Artist in Bourgeois Society." *The Modern Language Review* 76.2 (1981): 383–95. Print.

Rokem, Freddie. *Performing History: Theatrical Representations of the Past in Contemporary Theatre*. Iowa City: U of Iowa P, 2000. *ebrary*. Web. 16 Oct. 2011.

Steiner, George. "*Marat/Sade* and the Theatre of Unrealism." *Times Literary Supplement* 17 Sept. 1964: 855. *TLS Archive*. Web. 16 Oct. 2011.

Weiss, Peter. *The Persecution and Assassination of Marat as Performed by the Inmates of the Asylum of Charenton under the Direction of the Marquis of Sade; a Play*. Trans. Geoffrey Skelton. Verse adapt. Adrian Mitchell. London: Calder, 1965. Print.

FURTHER READING

Beauvoir, Simone de. *Must We Burn De Sade?* Trans. Annette Michelson. London: Nevill, 1953. Print.

Brook, Peter, et al. "Marat/Sade Forum." *Tulane Drama Review* 10.4 (1966): 214–37. *JSTOR*. Web. 16 Oct. 2011.

Cohen, Robert. *Understanding Peter Weiss*. Trans. Martha Humphreys. Columbia: U of South Carolina P, 1993. Print.

Holderness, Graham. "Weiss/Brook: Marat/Sade." *Twentieth-Century European Drama*. Ed. Brian Docherty. New York: St. Martin's, 1994. 162–71. Print.

Mckenzie, J. R. P. "Peter Weiss and the Politics of 'Marat-Sade.'" *New Theatre Quarterly* 1.3 (1985): 301. *JSTOR*. Web. 15 Oct. 2011.

Roberts, David. "Marat/Sade, or the Birth of Postmodernism from the Spirit of the Avantgarde." *New German Critique* 38 (1986): 112–30. *JSTOR*. Web. 15 Oct. 2011.

Sontag, Susan. "Marat/Sade/Artaud." *Partisan Review* 32.2 (1965): 210–19. Print.

Sara Taylor

TEN DAYS THAT SHOOK THE WORLD
John Reed

OVERVIEW

John Reed's *Ten Days That Shook the World* (1919) is considered invaluable as a firsthand account of the 1917 Bolshevik (or October) Revolution in Russia. Reed was rare among international journalists in Russia in that he had an insider's perspective on the momentous events that brought about the overthrow of the provisional government and the ascendance of the Bolsheviks.

A Harvard-educated poet-turned-radical journalist, Reed was sympathetic to the socialist cause and fervently believed in the idealistic aims of the Bolsheviks: the transfer of political power to the proletariat, an end to Russian involvement in World War I, and international socialist revolution. Reed was a personal friend of Vladimir Lenin and Leon Trotsky, the two principal architects of the revolution. Although they did not confide in him the secret plans of the Bolsheviks, Reed nonetheless witnessed some of their most important political maneuverings. In addition to taking part in street protests, Reed participated in the proceedings at the Smolny Institute, the headquarters of the Bolshevik party in Petrograd, and attended many of the meetings of the soviets, or councils of workers, peasants, and soldiers.

Reed based *Ten Days That Shook the World* on documentary evidence, much of which is reprinted in his book. Accounts of his personal experience are integrated with excerpts from speeches, interviews, street conversations, newspaper articles, handbills, broadsides, proclamations, and decrees. The last of these were posted on various walls in Petrograd, where the revolution was fomented.

The bulk of *Ten Days That Shook the World* is a chronological narrative of the crucial first days of the Bolshevik coup. On November 7, 1917, the Bolshevik army took over the government buildings in Petrograd and invaded the czar's former Winter Palace, where the provisional government was still sitting. Ten days later the Bolsheviks' seized the Kremlin in Moscow. Reed's text is made accessible to general readers through its inclusion of extensive explanatory notes and introductory chapters that outline the circumstances leading to the revolution.

Reed was in Russia as the representative of the *Masses*, the leading socialist journal of the United States. The *Masses* had come under attack from the U.S.

government for violating the *Espionage Act of 1917*, which made it a crime to publish material that criticized American involvement in World War I. When Reed returned to New York City on April 28, 1918, he was immediately arrested. He was released on bail, but the substantial archive of papers he carried with him—the raw materials for the book he intended to write—was seized by customs officials and not returned for seven months. Once he was finally in possession of these documents, Reed secluded himself in a Greenwich Village apartment and began writing. In his book *Heroes I Have Known*, Max Eastman (Reed's editor at the *Masses*) recalls a brief meeting with him during this time:

> "Max, don't tell anybody where I am. I'm writing the Russian revolution in a book. I've got all the placards and papers up there in a little room and a Russian dictionary, and I'm working all day and all night. I haven't shut my eyes for thirty-six hours. I'll finish the whole thing in two weeks. And I've got a name for it too—*Ten Days That Shook the World*."

Reed's book was first published in 1919 by the New York-based Boni & Liveright, known for their sponsorship of avant-garde and nontraditional writers. Using a forged passport and hiding on a Scandinavian frigate, Reed made his way back to Moscow in 1920 to seek official recognition of the American Communist Labor party. While there, he gave a copy of his book to Lenin, who wrote an admiring preface that appeared in the 1922 Boni & Liveright edition. Reed died of typhoid in Moscow on October 17, 1920. With him at his death was his wife and fellow journalist, Louise Bryant, whose own eyewitness account of the revolution, *Six Red Months in Russia*, had appeared in 1918.

HISTORICAL AND LITERARY CONTEXT

The Bolsheviks were the radical left wing of the Russian Social Democratic Labour Party, renamed the Communist Party in 1918. As Reed explains in his preface to *Ten Days That Shook the World*, "In considering the rise of the Bolsheviki, it is necessary to understand that Russian economic life and the Russian army were the logical result of a process which began as far back as 1915."

Reed goes on in the book to describe how the feeble Russian state was completely unequipped to engage

+ *Key Facts*

Conflict:
Bolshevik Revolution

Time Period:
Early 20th Century

Genre:
History

JOHN REED REPEATEDLY ARRESTED

While Reed was in Russia covering the revolution, the socialist journal that had sent him there, the *Masses*, was prosecuted for violating the *Espionage Act of 1917*, which had made it a crime to publish any material that might undermine America's efforts in World War I. The *Masses* trial ended in a hung jury the day before Reed returned home. When Reed arrived in New York Harbor on April 28, 1918, he was immediately arrested and ordered to stand trial with the original defendants in a second criminal proceeding against the *Masses*. This trial also resulted in a hung jury.

Reed's troubles with the authorities did not end there. On May 31, 1918, he was charged with inciting a riot in Philadelphia by disseminating communist propaganda. On September 15, 1918, he was again arrested, this time for violating the *Sedition Act*, a May 1918 amendment to the *Espionage Act* that outlawed any language deemed injurious or disloyal to the U.S. government. This arrest stemmed from Reed's appearance the day before at a large rally in the Bronx in support of the Bolsheviks. Reed was acquitted in the May incident. He never stood trial on the sedition charge. He escaped the United States in early October 1919, bound for a second visit to Russia.

in a conflict on the scale of World War I. Fighting on the side of the Allied powers, which included France, Britain, Japan, and eventually the United States, the poorly fed and outfitted Russian troops suffered humiliating military defeats by the Central powers of Germany and Austria-Hungary on the Eastern Front in 1915.

Inflation soared, the railroads were strained, and food shortages were widespread. Discontent with the autocracy of Czar Nicholas II escalated as millions of people went hungry. In February 1917 food riots and other large demonstrations and strikes broke out in Petrograd. On the advice of the Duma, the Russian legislature, the czar abdicated. The Duma politicians set up a temporary, or provisional, government led by the moderate Socialist Alexander Kerensky. After another disastrous military offensive, directed by Kerensky, soldiers fled the front in increasing numbers, workers deserted the factories, and bread lines swelled.

In the chaos, the Bolsheviks had by September 1917 gained control of the Red Guards (the local regiments of soldiers, workers, and sailors) and they held a majority in several key soviets as well, including those in Petrograd and Moscow. With Trotsky and Lenin now out of exile, the Bolsheviks began to plan the October coup that would bring down Kerensky's provisional government.

Reed's detailed account of the coup begins on November 7 (October 25) with the convening of the Second All-Russian Congress of Soviets and the arrests of the members of the provisional government. During the course of the next several days, the Bolsheviks struggled to consolidate their power amidst threats of insurrection from opposing political factions. More pressing difficulties followed in the coming months, including Allied and other foreign retaliation for the coup and Russia's withdrawal from World War I. In addition, a lengthy civil war (1918–22) ensued from which the communists emerged victorious to establish the Union of Soviet Socialist Republics (USSR).

The Bolshevik Revolution turned out to be one of the most consequential historical events of the twentieth century. The Communists remained the only official political party until the dissolution of the Soviet Union in 1991. But the actual progress of the Bolshevik Revolution was remarkably peaceful. Just four people—one sailor and four Red Guards—were killed on November 7, 1917. Many retrospective accounts of the revolution, however, have tended to portray it as a bloodbath.

Although *Ten Days That Shook the World* is not the work of a detached historian, it is generally regarded as a mostly factual accounting of the coup. Still, A. J. P. Taylor noted in his introduction to a modern reprint of *Ten Days That Shook the World*, "7 November is the central point of Reed's narrative. Himself tense and excited, he did not perhaps stress enough the small scale of the dramatic events he recounted. This was not a rising of the masses … It was a conflict between two small groups, neither of which had much taste for fighting."

THEMES AND STYLE

The themes of *Ten Days That Shook the World* are those subjects that most occupied the Bolsheviks. The Bolsheviks demanded an end to the classism of imperial rule and appealed to the masses to seize the machinery of the state. Committed to improving the lives of the poor, the Bolsheviks aimed to redistribute the lands of the estates to the peasants and to confer upon them localized power. In the immediate aftermath of the coup, they raised wages, shortened the workday, and confiscated all private bank accounts. They resolved to bring all Russian troops home from the front in a war they were convinced was being fought on behalf of capitalist interests.

Reed reprinted a resolution of the Second All-Russian Congress of Soviets addressed to all workers, soldiers, and peasants:

> The Soviet authority will at once propose an immediate democratic peace to all nations, and an immediate truce on all fronts. It will assure the free transfer of landlord, crown, and monastery lands to the Land Committee, defend the soldiers' rights, enforcing a complete democratization of the Army, establish workers' control over production … take means to supply bread to the cities and articles of first necessity to the villages.

Lenin and other Bolsheviks, along with Reed, were convinced that downtrodden workers throughout

Europe would be inspired to revolt by the example of the Russian coup, which they considered a mere preliminary to international socialism.

Critics often discuss the style of *Ten Days That Shook the World* in relation to Reed's earlier journalistic writings, especially *Insurgent Mexico* (1914) and *The War in Eastern Europe* (1916), which have both been described as florid in their lionization of peasants and workers. By contrast, Reed is judged to have been more conscious of his role as a professional reporter in *Ten Days That Shook the World* and to have used language more appropriate to the context. Robert A. Rosenstone wrote in his 1975 biography of Reed, "With descriptions toned down, with far fewer consciously poetic flights than in earlier books, Reed keeps the eye centered on concrete places and events."

Although historians now confirm that Reed either invented or incorrectly recalled some of the events described in *Ten Days That Shook the World*, it is generally agreed that he aimed at a factual reconstruction of the revolution that would allow the Russian people to speak for themselves.

CRITICAL DISCUSSION

Reed is reported to have become frustrated with the Russian Communist Party on his second trip to the country, fearful that centralization of leadership and intolerance toward divergent views within the party would dismantle the revolution. His disenchantment did little to alter his hero status. After his death in 1920, Reed was honored with a state funeral and became the first American buried at the Kremlin Wall. *Ten Days That Shook the World*, which had been translated into Russian in 1923, was embraced as a communist rallying cry.

In honor of the tenth anniversary of the Bolshevik revolution, the Soviet government commissioned a movie adaptation, silent film director Sergei Eisenstein's 1927 *October: Ten Days That Shook the World*. Reed's book was soon banned in Russia, however, with the rise of communist leader Josef Stalin, who is said to have been angered that Reed discounted his part in the revolution.

In the United States, *Ten Days That Shook the World* was immediately recognized as an important eyewitness account of a defining moment in history that signaled the complete transformation of Russian society. Some reviewers opposed to Reed's politics complained that he was biased in his reporting, but most noted that Reed was concerned to present Bolshevik as well as anti-Bolshevik viewpoints.

In the years since its first appearance in the United States, *Ten Days That Shook the World* has continued to be praised for its dramatic immediacy. Much emphasis has been placed on Reed's preface, where he explains, "This book is a slice of intensified history—history as I saw it ... [My] sympathies were not neutral. But in telling the story of those great days I have tried to see

Vladimir Lenin addresses Second Soviet Congress on November 8, 1917. The meeting was a key event in the Bolshevik Revolution, which John Reed documents in *Ten Days That Shook the World*. © HERITAGE IMAGES / CORBIS

events with the eye of a conscientious reporter, interested in setting down the truth."

Critics have insisted that it is precisely because of Reed's emotional connection with his subject that he was able to create such a powerful book, many of them arguing that he achieved a deeper form of poetry because the facts were filtered through his penetrating political sensibilities. John Stuart remarked in a 1955 introduction to a selection of Reed's writings, "[His] identification with the revolution was complete and lasting ... His writing thus gained an emotional charge and an intellectual dimension beyond a skilled use of words in a rhythmically constructed sentence." Bertram Wolfe observed of Reed in his 1965 *Strange Communists I Have Known*, "[With] the artist's gift of selection, heightening and unifying, he assimilated all the chaotic impressions into a picture more impressive and more beautiful than life itself."

Though largely reportage, *Ten Days That Shook the World* has continued to be analyzed as literature into the twenty-first century. Daniel Lehman's 2002 *John Reed and the Writing of Revolution* presents a sustained consideration of *Ten Days That Shook the World* as literary nonfiction.

SOURCES

Eastman, Max. "An Apotheosis: John Reed and the Russian Revolution." *Heroes I Have Known: Twelve Who Lived Great Lives.* New York: Simon, 1942. 201–24. Print.

Reed, John. *Ten Days That Shook the World.* New York: Penguin, 1977. Print.

Rosenstone, Robert A. *Romantic Revolutionary: A Biography of John Reed.* New York: Knopf, 1975. *Twentieth-Century Literary Criticism.* Ed. Dennis Poupard. Vol. 9. Detroit: Gale, 1983. *Literature Resource Center.* Web. 30 July 2011.

Stuart, John. Introduction. *The Education of John Reed: Selected Writings*. By John Reed. New York: International, 1955. 7–38. *Twentieth-Century Literary Criticism*. Ed. Dennis Poupard. Vol. 9. Detroit: Gale, 1983. *Literature Resource Center*. Web. 30 July 2011.

Taylor, A. J. P. Introduction. *Ten Days That Shook the World*. By John Reed. New York: Penguin, 1977. vii-xix. Print.

Wolfe, Bertram. "The Harvard Man in the Kremlin Wall." *Strange Communists I Have Known*. New York: Stein, 1965. 23–51. *Twentieth-Century Literary Criticism*. Ed. Dennis Poupard. Vol. 9. Detroit: Gale, 1983. *Literature Resource Center*. Web. 30 July 2011.

FURTHER READING

Bryant, Louise. *Six Red Months in Russia: An Observer's Account of Russia before and during the Proletarian Dictatorship*. New York: Doran, 1918. Print.

Duke, David C. *John Reed*. Boston: Twayne, 1987. Print.

Gelb, Barbara. *So Short a Time: A Biography of John Reed and Louise Bryant*. New York: Norton, 1973. Print.

Hicks, Granville. *John Reed: The Making of a Revolutionary*. 2nd ed. New York: B. Blom, 1968. Print.

Lehman, Daniel. *John Reed and the Writing of Revolution*. Athens: Ohio UP, 2002. Print.

MEDIA ADAPTATIONS

October (orig. title *Oktyabr*). Dir. Sergei Eisenstein and Grigori Aleksandrov. Perf. Vladimir Popov and Vasili Nikandrov. Sovkino, 1927. Film.

Ten Days That Shook the World. Perf. Orson Welles, Robert Stephens, Barbara Jefford, and Hugh Burden. Granada, 1967. Television.

Reds. Dir. Warren Beatty. Perf. Warren Beatty, Diane Keaton, Jack Nicholson, Paul Sorvino, and Maureen Stapleton. Paramount Pictures, 1981. Film.

Janet Mullane

THE THINGS THEY CARRIED
A Work of Fiction

Tim O'Brien

OVERVIEW

The Things They Carried (1990) is widely regarded as one of the most important fictional accounts of the lives of U.S. soldiers during the Vietnam War. The collection of twenty-two short stories began as a single piece of short fiction that was published in *Esquire* in 1986. Its author, Tim O'Brien, is a Vietnam veteran who had previously won praise for his Vietnam War novel *Going after Cacciato*, a chapter from which he later adapted as one of the stories in *The Things They Carried*. The stories are sometimes considered to be a composite novel, because the characters and events described are related.

The collection tells the story of a platoon of American soldiers under the command of Lt. Jimmy Cross. The narrator is a fictional forty-three-year-old man named Tim O'Brien, whose life parallels that of the author in many ways. The narrator O'Brien, a writer, is reflecting on his experiences and on those of his comrades during the war, several decades earlier. Many of the stories respond to the death of Ted Lavender, who is shot in the head on the way back from relieving himself during a mission. Lavender's death profoundly affects the men in the platoon, especially Cross, who feels responsible for it. As the stories unfold, "the things they carried" comes to refer not only to the lists of equipment and mementos O'Brien uses in the title story but also to the immense emotional burdens of the war. The collection repeatedly emphasizes the importance of storytelling as a means of coping with these burdens and as a way of rearranging events to get at the "real" truth. O'Brien has been praised for his ability to seamlessly blend fact and fiction.

The publication of *The Things They Carried* helped to confirm O'Brien's reputation as one of the leading voices of contemporary fiction. In 1991 the book was nominated for both the Pulitzer Prize and the National Book Critics Circle Award.

HISTORICAL AND LITERARY CONTEXT

Much of the action of *The Things They Carried* takes place in Quang Ngai Province during the Vietnam War, a conflict that ultimately claimed the lives of more than 58,000 American soldiers. Combat in the Vietnam War was particularly dangerous because of the tactics used by the Vietcong, a branch of the Vietnamese National Liberation Front that relied on guerrilla warfare. The Vietcong were best known for their booby traps, pit traps, and mines, many of which were homemade. Aware that they were at a disadvantage when facing American troops in open combat, they relied primarily on ambushes, which were made possible by an extensive system of underground tunnels. In the short stories in O'Brien's collection, the platoon is assigned to search and destroy the Vietcong tunnels near the village of Than Khe. The job of entering a tunnel without knowing whether traps or Vietcong forces might be inside is especially perilous. In the title story the soldiers draw numbers to see who will assume the risk. The unlucky scout survives the tunnel, but Ted Lavender's haphazard death occurs immediately afterward. In later stories in the collection, a member of the platoon named Curt Lemon is killed by a Vietcong booby trap, and another, the Native American soldier Kiowa, is killed during an ambush.

Before he wrote the stories that make up *The Things They Carried*, O'Brien had earned status as a war writer with the memoir *If I Die in a Combat Zone, Box Me Up and Send Me Home* (1973) and the novel *Going after Cacciato* (1978), which chronicles the adventures of a deserter in Vietnam and which won the National Book Award. O'Brien's own war experience makes his writing particularly visceral. He was stationed from 1969 to 1970 in Quang Ngai Province, one of the deadliest areas in the war zone. His unit regularly passed through My Lai, a village where hundreds of unarmed peasants had been brutally massacred by U.S. troops only a few months earlier. Although that fact was concealed from the soldiers, O'Brien felt tension and evil in the area. After his return from the war, he suffered from nightmares, depression, and suicidal thoughts. His repeated return to the conflict in his fiction reflects his commitment to telling the stories of the war and its victims and to conveying the senselessness of war in general.

Commentators have noted parallels between O'Brien's short stories and works of war literature by

❖ Key Facts

Conflict:
Vietnam War

Time Period:
Mid-20th Century

Genre:
Novel

Awards:
Chicago Tribune Heartland Prize, 1990; Prix du Meilleur Livre Étranger, 1990; National Book Critics Circle Award nomination, 1991; Pulitzer Prize nomination, 1991

THE PRESSURES ON THE HUMAN HEART

In addition to being one of the most critically acclaimed American books about the Vietnam War, Tim O'Brien's *The Things They Carried* is also one of the most popular books of contemporary fiction about any war. Since its publication it has sold over two million copies, and it continues to find enthusiastic readers among groups as diverse as aspiring writers, veterans of war, and high school students. In fact, the book is often taught in high schools, not simply for its value as a historical document but also for its applicability to everyday life. It has been effective in reaching troubled adolescents, who are encouraged to think of their own problems as the "things they carry."

Given that O'Brien does not think of himself in a strict sense as a war writer, the book's wider relevance should perhaps not be surprising. In an interview published in the literary journal *Artful Dodge* in 1992, O'Brien says:

> I've used [war] in the way Conrad writes about the sea, life on the water, stories set on boats … But Conrad is no more writing about the sea than I am writing about war. That is, he's not writing about marine biology and dolphins and porpoises and waves. He's writing about human beings under pressure, under the certain kinds of pressure that the sea exerts … My content is not bombs and bullets and airplanes and strategy and tactics. It is not the politics of Vietnam. It too is about the human heart and the pressures put on it.

a diverse group of writers, including the Greek poet Homer (ca. eighth century BCE), the British novelist Joseph Conrad (1857–1924), the American fiction writer Ambrose Bierce (1842–1913), and the German novelist Erich Maria Remarque (1898–1970).

THEMES AND STYLE

As its title suggests, *The Things They Carried* emphasizes the theme of the burdens carried by the soldiers it depicts. The title story catalogues the many objects carried by the soldiers in Cross's platoon, among them such necessities as "P-38 can openers, pocket knives, heat tabs, wristwatches, dog tags, mosquito repellent, chewing gum, candy, cigarettes, salt tablets, packets of Kool-Aid, lighters, matches, sewing kits, Military Payment Certificates, C rations, and two or three canteens of water." These innocuous lists of equipment, which often include detailed information about the size and weight of each object, are interspersed throughout the story with depictions of the emotional weight the soldiers also bear. While this and other stories describe the soldiers' struggles to "hump" their heavy equipment in the heat and humidity, it quickly becomes clear that they are weighed down by more than material objects. The narrator explains that Cross, obsessed with a college girl back home,

"humped his love for Martha up the hills and through the swamps." He is fantasizing about her when Lavender is shot, and he blames his preoccupation for his comrade's death. This death and those of several other members of the platoon in later stories are among the greatest burdens the men carry. O'Brien makes this clear in the book's opening pages, when he connects Lavender's death to the soldiers' gear with the simple observation "In April, for instance, when Ted Lavender was shot, they used his poncho to wrap him up."

The role and purposes of storytelling are also thematically central to *The Things They Carried*, which continually blurs the distinction between invention and reality. In addition to giving his fictional character his own name, O'Brien dedicates the book to "the men of Alpha Company, and in particular Jimmy Cross, Norman Bowker, Rat Kiley, Mitchell Sanders, Henry Dobbins, and Kiowa," despite the fact that they are fictional characters. O'Brien the narrator mentions "his" authorship of *If I Die in a Combat Zone* and *Going After Cacciato*, yet the author gives the narrator an invented young daughter who, in a pivotal moment, asks him if he killed anyone in the war.

The importance of storytelling and healing power arises in many of the narratives, as the fictional O'Brien ruminates on his postwar life and his career as a writer. One of the tales, "How to Tell a True War Story," reflects extensively on the nature of war narratives. O'Brien describes storytelling at one point as "a natural, inevitable process, like clearing the throat." It is also a way to honor or repay important figures in his life, such as his comrades in Vietnam, a classmate who died when she was only nine, and the old man with whom he stayed while contemplating fleeing to Canada to avoid going to war. At other times he uses storytelling as therapy, something he does because he is haunted by memories of the young man he killed with a grenade. Later, however, he confesses that he was not the one who killed the man but that "story-truth is truer sometimes than happening-truth," a statement that can be applied to the work as a whole. Such reflections on the craft of writing qualify *The Things They Carried* as a work of metafiction—fiction that treats its own devices as a central topic.

CRITICAL DISCUSSION

Prior to the release of *The Things They Carried*, five of its stories had been published in such periodicals as *Esquire* and the *Massachusetts Review*, where they were met with critical acclaim, garnering O'Brien a National Magazine Award in 1987. When the collection was published in 1990, it was immediately embraced by readers and critics alike. Reviewers noted the ways in which the stories, old and new, combined to create a cohesive whole. It won the Chicago Tribune Heartland Prize in 1990, and its French translation was awarded the prestigious Prix du Meilleur Livre Étranger.

Commentators frequently note O'Brien's skill at recreating the experiences and emotions of the war.

Writing in the *Christian Science Monitor*, Jeff Danziger says that the stories "never forget the utter hopelessness and loneliness of the fighting" and suggests, "If [O'Brien] deserves credit for anything, it is keeping an unvarnished version of the war alive in spite of the vast wash of nonsense that has spewed out of Hollywood and the networks." Although the book depicts experiences specific to Vietnam, many commentators also note its near-universal appeal and applicability. In the *Los Angeles Times Book Review*, Richard Eder asserts that "the best of these stories … are memory as prophecy. They tell us not where we were but where we are; and perhaps where we will be." Similarly, Robert B. Harris's review in the *New York Times* states that O'Brien "not only crystallizes the Vietnam experience for us, he exposes the nature of all war stories."

In the decades since its publication, *The Things They Carried* has attracted a sizable body of scholarship. The relationship between fact and fiction in the stories is of continued interest to scholars of O'Brien's work, and many have looked to his life in an attempt to understand his blending of the two in the pursuit of truth. In an essay in *College Literature*, Marilyn Wesley reads O'Brien's memoir, *If I Die in a Combat Zone*, alongside *The Things They Carried* and argues that, while the former is a more factual reflection of O'Brien's war experiences, the latter is truer. She says that "whereas the first book relies on the standard of the representation of truth, the second, by abandoning literary realism, comes closer to presenting a polemic vision that insists on the problematic nature of the Vietnam experience." Wesley's essay is also representative of a body of scholarship devoted to considering the role of storytelling in both O'Brien's story collection and his life and examining the ways in which storytelling affects the relationship between the remembered past and the present.

In part because *The Things They Carried* centers on a group of men and the masculine experience of war, some literary critics have been drawn to studying the role of women in the stories and the effect of the text on female readers. Exploring these issues in the *Massachusetts Review*, Pamela Smiley concludes that the work engages the sympathy of women by depicting men who glorify women and long for "a love of epic proportions in which soul mates merge and their union contains everything."

SOURCES

Danziger, Jeff. "True to Life Combat." Rev. of *The Things They Carried*, by Tim O'Brien. *Christian Science Monitor* 13 July 1990: 13. Print.

Eder, Richard. "Has He Forgotten Anything?" Rev. of *The Things They Carried*, by Tim O'Brien. *Los Angeles Times Book Review* 1 Apr. 1990: 3. Print.

Harris, Robert B. "Too Embarrassed Not to Kill." Rev. of *The Things They Carried*, by Tim O'Brien. *New York Times* 11 Mar. 1990: 8. Print.

O'Brien, Tim. *The Things They Carried*. Boston: Houghton, 1990. Print.

Smiley, Pamela. "The Role of the Ideal (Female) Reader in Tim O'Brien's *The Things They Carried*: Why Should Real Women Play?" *Massachusetts Review* 43.4 (2002–03): 602–13. Print.

Wesley, Marilyn. "Truth and Fiction in Tim O'Brien's *If I Die in a Combat Zone* and *The Things They Carried*." *College Literature* 29.2 (2002): 1–18. Print.

FURTHER READING

Bruckner, D. J. R. "Storyteller for a War That Won't End." *New York Times* 3 Apr. 1990: C15. Print.

Caputo, Philip. *A Rumor of War*. New York: Holt, 1977. Print.

Chen, Tina. "'Unraveling the Deeper Meaning': Exile and the Embodied Poetics of Displacement in Tim O'Brien's *The Things They Carried*." *Contemporary Literature* 39.1 (1998): 77–98. Print.

O'Brien, Tim. Interview by Martin Naparsteck. *Contemporary Literature* 32.1 (1991): 1–11. Print.

O'Brien, Tim. *Going after Cacciato: A Novel*. New York: Delacorte, 1978. Print.

———. *If I Die in a Combat Zone, Box Me Up and Ship Me Home*. New York: Delacorte, 1973. Print.

———. *In The Lake of the Woods*. Boston: Houghton, 1994. Print.

———. *July, July*. Boston: Houghton, 2002. Print.

———. "The Vietnam in Me." *New York Times*. New York Times, 2 Oct. 1994. Web. 13 June 2011.

Pasternak, Donna. "Keeping the Dead Alive: Revising the Past in Tim O'Brien's War Stories." *Irish Journal of American Studies* 7 (1998): 41–54. Print.

MEDIA ADAPTATION

A Soldier's Sweetheart. Adapted from the excerpt "Sweetheart of the Song Tra Bong." Dir. Thomas Michael Donnelly. Perf. Tony Billy and Christopher Birt. Paramount Pictures, 1998. Film.

Greta Gard

U.S. soldiers near Bong Son, Vietnam, in February 1966, carry the body of a fallen comrade across a rice paddy to a helicopter for evacuation. In *The Things They Carried*, author Tim O'Brien writes about the physical and emotional burdens soldiers bore. © AP IMAGES / RICK MERRON

UNDER FIRE
The Story of a Squad
Henri Barbusse

✦ *Key Facts*

Conflict:
World War I

Time Period:
Early 20th Century

Genre:
Novel

OVERVIEW

Henri Barbusse's *Le feu: Journal d'une escouade* (1916; translated as *Under Fire: The Story of a Squad*, 1917), the major French contribution to World War I literature, was published while the horrific devastation of the conflict was still unfolding. Barbusse, who had volunteered for service, wrote the novel while recovering from injuries sustained in the war, and it reflects his attempts to come to terms with the unthinkable destruction and loss of life he witnessed. *Under Fire* was the first major work of world literature to offer realistic commentary on the conflict and to critique its disproportionate burden on the lower classes, who are depicted as slaves dying for the cause of wealth and power they will never enjoy.

Upon publication, *Under Fire* was immediately recognized as an important piece of literature. It was awarded France's prestigious Prix Goncourt in 1916. Its brutal realism, coarse language, and use of slavery imagery were, however, controversial. While the book's message resonated with those who, like the author, were struggling to come to terms with the realities and horrors of the ongoing conflict, some complained that Barbusse had taken his critique too far, or that he had taken too many liberties with the truth. Despite the controversy the novel generated in France, a popular English translation soon followed, and the appearance in 2003 of a new translation by Robin Buss attests to its enduring appeal.

HISTORICAL AND LITERARY CONTEXT

Published in 1916, *Under Fire* reflects the experience of soldiers during the early years of World War I. Soon after the war began in 1914, German forces launched an offensive against France through Belgium. After having a difficult time capturing Belgium, especially Liege, the German offensive slowed further when it reached France in August 1914. Despite initial victories that brought them within fifty miles of Paris, the Germans were repelled in early September at the First Battle of the Marne. By 1915 the war on the Western Front was largely a stalemate, with both sides hunkered down in fortified trenches made necessary by the devastating power of weaponry such as the machine gun and high-powered artillery shells.

Barbusse's novel, which chronicles events through December 1915, depicts life on the Western Front. The story focuses on an unnamed narrator and the members of his battalion, a group of predominantly working-class men drawn from different regions of the country who bond over the course of their service. In a chapter titled "Fire," the narrator describes the fear and chaos of trench warfare, from the sounds of shells and machine-gun fire filling the air to the "chunks of shrapnel whizzing past one's head with the sound of red-hot iron hitting the water." After the battle ends, he describes an unreal scene in which "there is no human wave preceding ours; no one alive in front of us, though the ground is peopled with the dead, recent bodies still in poses of suffering or sleep."

As one of the first major literary responses to the utter desolation wrought by the conflict, *Under Fire* helped to usher in a new mode of literature, one that sought not to glorify war or acts of military heroism but to bear witness to the experience of war and its effects on the millions who served. Barbusse emphasizes his desire to speak for those who died in battle by dedicating his book "to the memory of the comrades who fell beside me at Crouy and on Hill 119." Because of his personal involvement in the war and the realism of his novel, Barbusse is subsequently considered among the first of a group of writers or "moral witnesses" whom Jay Winter describes as storytellers "with a terrible tale to tell, whose very lives are defined by these stories." Later works in this tradition of realistic testimony include texts specific to the First World War, such as Siegfried Sassoon's fictionalized autobiography *Memoirs of an Infantry Officer* (1930) and Robert Graves's memoir *Goodbye to All That* (1929), as well as works about later conflicts, including Tim O'Brien's Vietnam War novel *Going After Cacciato* (1978) and John Crawford's Iraqi War memoir *The Last True Story I'll Ever Tell* (2005).

THEMES AND STYLE

Under Fire is written in an informal, first-person style that has the feel of a diary. The narrator reflects on the events that he and his comrades experience as their service unfolds. The episodic nature of the "entries" and the frequent use of the historic present (in which the present tense is used to describe events that happened in the past) combine to cultivate the impression that the novel describes actual happenings and to give them a sense of immediacy. Describing an offensive, for example, the narrator explains, "Bursts of gunfire clatter out with such monstrous resonance that one feels annihilated by the very noise of these thunderclaps, these great stars of debris forming in the air." The use of the historic present contributes as well to what Kate McLoughlin describes in her book *Authoring War* as an attempt to recreate the unique sense of time (and timelessness) experienced by soldiers, who are forced to live in what she terms the "perpetual present." The novel, McLoughlin suggests, depicts the soldiers' experience of the war as never-ending, both in the sense that the sounds of artillery fire are frighteningly and constantly present ("the rifles and the big guns have gone on from morning to night and from night to morning") and in the sense that there is no end in sight to the war itself, leaving the soldiers unable even to imagine it.

Barbusse's desire to bear accurate witness to the war experience is also reflected in his choice of words. Throughout the work, he attempts to replicate as closely as possible the language used by the *poilus*, or French soldiers, in the trenches. The novel's dialogue is frequently marked by slang and coarse language. In his introduction to his English translation of the novel,

Robin Buss reflects on the unique stylistic properties of Barbusse's work and their implications for translation, noting that "slang is the language of a specific social group at a particular time, and trying to translate it into the specific language of another group raises more problems than it solves." He explains that the best solution available to him as Barbusse's translator was to "adopt a language that conveys the feel of the slang Barbusse uses without making it too specific or too obscure."

Experimenting with language also helped Barbusse emphasize that war is not a glorious event but a dirty and grueling experience, the burden of which falls most heavily on average men drawn from the working classes. The narrator, who professes his desire to write about his war experiences, promises his comrades in the battalion that he will "put the swearwords in, because it's the truth." The work also insists on portraying the physical and psychological truths of war as experienced by average soldiers, whom the author likens to slaves fighting a battle that does not represent their own interests. In the first chapter, "A Vision," Barbusse critiques the ignorance and greed that contributed to the war, depicting upper-class characters who are blind to its consequences for the lower orders of society—"the thirty million slaves who have been thrown on top of one another by crime and error into this war." Living in miserable conditions and bearing

The horror of having to charge into enemy fire, described by Henri Barbusse in his novel *Under Fire*, is illuminated in this drawing. Henri de Groux, (1867–1930), *The Assault, Verdun.* Pencil & w/c on paper. © MUSEE DES DEUX GUERRES MONDIALES, PARIS, FRANCE / THE BRIDGEMAN ART LIBRARY INTERNATIONAL

the overwhelming anxiety of unpredictable trench warfare, the men are unable to control even the most basic decisions of daily life, from when and what they will eat to when they can rest or with whom they can spend their free time. Barbusse emphasizes the way in which the war steals the soldiers' humanity in a passage in which a member of the battalion, realizing that they are near his hometown, "wants to see the village where he used to live happily, in former times, when he was a man." The novel ends by reiterating the pointlessness of the war and once again undercutting the conventional depiction of its glory: "a soldier's glory is a lie like everything in war that seems beautiful. In reality the sacrifice of soldiers is a dark repression."

CRITICAL DISCUSSION

When it was originally published in French, Barbusse's novel was received with a mixture of critical acclaim and disapprobation. While many readers and critics appreciated its attempts to depict the experiences of soldiers in a new and realistic way, others felt that Barbusse had taken too many liberties with the truth or were turned off by the work's critique of the soldiers as pawns in a capitalist war machine. The controversy over the book's message continued with its English release. In an article in the *New York Times*, H. A. Watt outlines the controversy,

noting that "it was the author's evident aim to strip off war's trappings and reveal the skull and bones beneath, and he has done this powerfully." He objects, however, to what he sees to be the subtext of the novel: "The most dangerous of the lies concealed beneath Barbusse's wonderful descriptions is the insidious perpetuation of the false idea that in a democracy the army is but a mass of slaves dying horribly that the name of some nobleman may be greater or the coffers of some rich man fuller." Despite such criticism, however, *Under Fire* was recognized as a unique and important work. Writing in the *Dial* in 1918, Robert Herrick describes it as "the most searching, the most revealing statement of what modern warfare means both morally and physically."

Although the controversy surrounding it has dissipated, Barbusse's novel continues to exert an undeniable influence on war literature. Contemporary scholars credit it with paving the way for later works of antiwar literature, and one enduring thread of scholarly discussion traces its influence on specific texts. Most notably, scholars including Jon Stallworthy and Simon Wormleighton have drawn parallels between the novel and the World War I poetry of Wilfred Owen (1893–1918), who was known to have read Barbusse's work in English translation.

HENRI BARBUSSE AND THE ARAC

The World War I experiences that inspired *Under Fire* also changed Barbusse's outlook on war and politics. In 1917 he became a founding member (along with three other veterans) of *L'association républicaine des anciens combattants* (the Republic Association of Veterans and War Victims, ARAC), and served as the organization's first president. ARAC's expressed goals included protecting the rights of veterans and victims of war, promoting peace and solidarity, advancing republican ideals such as freedom and equality, and opposing fascism and colonialism. The organization grew quickly, becoming one of the largest of its kind during the interwar years.

In the years following World War I, Barbusse, like many intellectuals of his generation, became increasingly committed to communism. He joined the French Communist Party in 1923. Barbusse's communism in turn influenced the direction of the already left-leaning ARAC, which became officially affiliated with the communist party. In fact the organization is often credited with helping to promote the cause of communism in France.

Nearly a century since its inception, ARAC remains active in France and around the world, and Barbusse's political accomplishments are nearly as well known as his literary ones. In 1953 France honored Barbusse's legacy with a postage stamp commemorating his eightieth birthday.

Today, commentators tend to view *Under Fire* as an important transitional work that helped to push war writing in a new direction. Because Barbusse's anticapitalist stance has been unpopular with many readers, and because it was later eclipsed by better-known texts, the novel has yet to attract as large a body of English-language criticism as other works treating the First World War. While Barbusse's novel has often been neglected by scholars, however, few would deny its impact on better-known works of war literature.

SOURCES

Barbusse, Henri. *Under Fire: The Story of a Squad*. Trans. Robin Buss. London: Penguin, 2003. Print.

Buss, Robin. Translator's Note. *Under Fire: The Story of a Squad*. By Henri Barbusse. Trans. Robin Buss. London: Penguin, 2003. xxi-xxii. Print.

Herrick, Robert. "Unromantic War." Rev. of *Under Fire*, by Henri Barbusse. *Dial* 14 Feb. 1918: 133–34. Print.

McLoughlin, Kate. *Authoring War: The Literary Representation of War from the* Iliad *to Iraq*. Cambridge: Cambridge UP, 2011. Print.

Stallworthy, Jon. *Wilfred Owen: A Biography*. London: Oxford UP, 1974. Print.

Watt, H. A. "Barbusse Under Fire." Rev. of *Under Fire*, by Henri Barbusse. *New York Times* 30 Dec. 1917: E2. Print.

Winter, Jay. "Henri Barbusse and the Birth of the Moral Witness." Introduction. *Under Fire: The Story of a Squad*. By Henri Barbusse. Trans. Robin Buss. London: Penguin, 2003. viii-xix. Print.

Wormleighton, Simon. "Some Echoes of Barbusse's *Under Fire* in Wilfred Owen's Poems." *Notes and Queries* 33.2 (1986): 190–91. Print.

FURTHER READING

Barbusse, Henri. *I Saw It Myself*. Trans. Brian Rhys. New York: Dutton, 1928. Print.

Crawford, John. *The Last True Story I'll Ever Tell: An Accidental Soldier's Account of the War in Iraq*. New York: Riverhead, 2005. Print.

Eksteins, Modris. *Rites of Spring: The Great War and the Birth of the Modern Age*. Boston: Houghton, 1989. Print.

Ferguson, Niall. *The Pity of War*. New York: Basic, 1999. Print.

Marwick, Arthur. "The Great War in Print and Paint: Henri Barbusse and Fernand Léger." *Journal of Contemporary History* 37.4 (2002): 509–21. Print.

O'Brien, Tim. *Going After Cacciato: A Novel*. New York: Delacorte, 1978. Print.

AWARDS

Prix Goncourt (1916)

Greta Gard

"THE WALLS DO NOT FALL"

H. D.

✧ *Key Facts*

Conflict:
World War II

Time Period:
Mid-20th Century

Genre:
Poetry

OVERVIEW

The Walls Do Not Fall (1944), *Tribute to the Angels* (1945), and *The Flowering of the Rod* (1946) make up an epic poetic sequence written by H. D. (Hilda Doolittle) in response to her experiences while living in London during World War II. The three poems were published together in a volume titled *Trilogy* in 1973. The forty-three sections of *The Walls Do Not Fall* connect the destruction of London with fallen civilizations of the past, drawing parallels between the cultural and physical remains of the ancient world and the ruins of the British capital, and placing the city in a chronology of human continuity. Drawing on religious and mythological imagery, H. D. examines the relationships between poetic inspiration, the production of the self, the place of the feminine in the modern world, and the role of the poet in wartime.

HISTORICAL AND LITERARY CONTEXT

The Walls Do Not Fall, written between 1942 and 1944, is nominally set during the last years of World War II. Unlike World War I, which was largely a land war, World War II was fought on land, in the air, and at sea. Both Axis and Allied powers deployed their air forces on bombing raids that targeted many major European cities. The war affected civilians in these cities much as it did soldiers on the battlefield. The United Kingdom declared war on Germany in September 1939, whereupon the British immediately began preparing for the possibility of German bombing raids. The London Blitz, an eight-month campaign of nearly nightly air raids, began on September 7, 1940, when German bombers and fighter planes attacked the city throughout the night. Similar raids occurred almost every night, killing tens of thousands of civilians and destroying buildings, roads, railways, and gas and sewer lines. Londoners responded by taking refuge in the London Underground and other shelters at night, emerging at the all clear, quickly repairing damage to infrastructure, and going about their daily lives. German dictator Adolf Hitler hoped that the campaign of terror against the citizens of London and other major cities would force Britain to surrender.

An American citizen, H. D. moved to London in 1911 to further her association with Ezra Pound (1885–1972) and his literary circle. Her poetry from the period of World War I does not address the conflict. She came to associate it with a series of personal losses, including a late miscarriage and the deaths of her brother and father. In contrast, World War II marked a highly productive period for H. D. as she mined ancient myth and history for the prefigurements of the war's destructiveness that appear in *The Walls Do Not Fall* and the other poems of *Trilogy*.

As a poet, H. D. is most closely associated with the Imagists, the early modernist poetic group that was inaugurated in 1912 when Ezra Pound declared H. D. to be the first "Imagiste." While her poems of the period conform to the Imagist aesthetic, H. D. was an individualist and uncomfortable with labels and movements. After World War I, when her marriage to the Imagist poet and novelist Richard Aldington (1892–1962) dissolved, she withdrew from literary society almost entirely to live in seclusion with her lover, Bryher (Annie Winifred Ellerman [1894–1983]). *The Walls Do Not Fall* is generally seen as an example of H. D.'s departure from Imagist aesthetics in her later work. Though its fragmentary form makes it a classic example of the modernist long poem, the poem eschews the Imagist ideal of compression and brevity for complex explorations of history, mythology, religion, and ideas about the self.

In a 1944 article in the *Sewanee Review*, Horace Gregory includes H. D. in his short list of the "elder generation of poets in both Britain and America," among such luminaries as E. E. Cummings, William Carlos Williams, Wallace Stevens, and T. S. Eliot. Gregory comments of this group generally that they "assert the merits of individual distinction, and not of group influences," and that they value "self-respect," or "a healthy relationship between the poet and what he writes." While these poets "have written poems that contain reference to the war," he continues, "the war has by no means engulfed the poetry, nor do we feel that it has been fortuitously introduced" so that the poems will be unimportant after the war ends. Gregory implies that such older writers stand in positive contrast to the generation of W. H. Auden and Stephen Spender, whose poetry was much more overtly political and whose topicality might render their verse less universal and therefore less lasting. Harold H. Watts, also writing in the *Sewanee Review*, describes *The Walls Do Not Fall* as exemplary of a tendency towards mythology in the poetry of the age.

"A good many poets agree," he surmises, "that it is the poet's task at present to trace a way out" of the "blind, bombed alley" of the current age. It is a "fact of our era," he continues, that "having in the last century or so gotten rid of myths … we seem constrained to set to work and discover" them again.

THEMES AND STYLE

The Walls Do Not Fall is a poem of witness. In it, H. D. observes civilian life in London during war, describing the broken-down city around her and capturing the direct effects of the violence on ordinary lives. H. D. and Bryher lived near the antiaircraft batteries in Hyde Park, an area in constant danger of air attacks. Susan Stanford Freeman points out in *Psyche Reborn* that the poet pointedly placed herself in the "harsh reality of the contemporary world," where "the gaping walls and constant death … surround[ed] her." However, Friedman notes, H. D. did not "limit her understanding of the destruction to the material rubble in front of her" but drew on historical knowledge, mythology, and religion to present a transhistorical and transcultural vision of poet and psyche attempting to make sense of a world in fragments. Sarah Graham, though she argues that the poem should be read as a war poem, finds the idea that it represents "the poet as war correspondent, reporting back from the civilian front line, and offering readers nothing less than the zeitgeist" far too simplistic. She suggests, rather, that the poem demonstrates H. D.'s complicated relationship with language as a vehicle for reality, "show[ing] evidence of a struggle between the urge to communicate and the will to obscure, the simultaneous desire for and fear of free will."

While *The Walls Do Not Fall* describes London's "ruin everywhere," is not set in a time of violence but in the quiet aftermath. The poem begins quietly—"An incident here and there, and rails gone (for guns) / from your (and my) old town square"—and slides almost immediately into memory and myth, drawing parallels between London and the ancient cities of Pompeii and Luxor, as well as the Greek temples H. D. had recently visited. The layers of historical, mythological, and religious references make *The Walls Do Not Fall* a challenging poem to read.

The Walls Do Not Fall self-consciously addresses its own status as a poem and as a war poem, thematizing the responsibilities of the poet during a time of political turmoil. Echoing the disparagements of those who would say that "poets are useless, / … are not only 'non-utilitarian', / we are pathetic," H. D. articulates an anxiety about the seeming unimportance of culture in wartime: "but we fight for life, / we fight, they say, for breath, // so what good are your scribblings?" The poem responds in the affirmative, making a strong argument for the importance of cultural artifacts and, in particular, of words as the cultural artifacts that preserve meaning and enable civilizations to rebuild after war: "I know, I feel, / the meaning that words hide; //

SEEKING REFUGE UNDERGROUND

In her long poem *The Walls Do Not Fall*, H. D. employs historical allusion and imagery to depict the devastation that swept across London in the early years of World War II. During much of 1940 and 1941, when England was subjected to a series of massive bombing attacks known as the Blitz, many London residents began to seek shelter in the city's extensive Underground, a subway system also known as the Tube. For the price of a halfpenny, Londoners could gain admittance to the Tube's train platforms, where they camped for the night in relative warmth and safety. At first the British government attempted to curtail this practice, believing that it posed a potential obstacle to critical troop maneuvers. The people resisted the government's efforts, however, and the practice continued throughout the Blitz. Although the Tube stations provided many Londoners with protection, and peace of mind, during the German bombings, they were actually far from bombproof. Because the bombs dropped by German planes had the power to penetrate up to fifty feet into the ground, they often inflicted heavy damage on these encampments. One of the most destructive attacks on the London Tube came in October 1940, when six hundred Londoners were killed or wounded in the bombing of Balham Station.

they are anagrams, cryptograms, / little boxes, conditioned // to hatch butterflies."

Of the poem's 43 sections, the first contains unrhymed tercets, while all of the remaining sections are made up of unrhymed couplets. Although its enigmatic, largely symbolic style resembles that of H. D.'s short Imagist poems, *The Walls Do Not Fall* is not composed of discrete lyrics. Rather, the interconnected stanzas form a layered historical and mythological matrix which points towards a way of rebuilding the present by drawing attention to the shared experience of contemporary London with great civilizations of the past. H. D. writes that "gods always face two-ways, / so let us search the old highways // for the true-rune, the right-spell, recover old values." Likening London to past archaeological ruins, H. D. draws connections between the gods of the past and the Judeo-Christian deity to reveal a common divine source. Invoking Isis, Osiris, Jehovah, Amen-Ra, and Hermes in turn, she concludes with the "secret of Isis, / which is: there was One // in the beginning, Creator, / Fosterer, Begetter, the Same-forever // in the papyrus-swamp / in the Judean meadow."

CRITICAL DISCUSSION

When it was published in 1944, *The Walls Do Not Fall* was widely and positively reviewed. Most notably, Osbert Sitwell of the *Observer* wrote, "We want—we need—more." While critics noted that *The Walls Do Not Fall* is set during the London Blitz, they generally agreed with Gregory that it is not strictly a war poem.

Elizabeth Atkins, for example, writes in *Poetry* that while it is "the best poem that I have seen arising out of the present war," it does not relate "horrors or heroism," nor does it "echo the war poems of 1914"; rather, "it is a proud answer to the philistines who reproach the introspective poets for daring to exist in a time of raining bombs and falling roofs."

Most of H. D.'s work was out of print by the time of her death in 1961. There was renewed interest in her work among poets in the 1960s, resulting most famously in Robert Duncan's unfinished homage, *The H. D. Book*. But there were few serious critical studies of her poetry before the feminist revival of the 1970s, when she became the focus of a challenge to the masculine canon of modernist poetry. As Susan Stanford Friedman observes in a 1975 article for *College English*, H. D. was overshadowed by her male contemporaries because "she was a woman, she wrote about women, and all the ever-questioning, artistic, intellectual heroes of her epic poetry and novels were women. … H. D. explored the untold half of the human story, and by that act set herself outside of the established tradition." On the other hand, Lawrence Rainey, writing in *College Literature*, warns against characterizing H. D.'s removal from the mainstream as a necessarily progressive act. Her isolation and relative obscurity, he argues, resulted from her lack of interest "in addressing anyone who stood outside of the coterie that surrounded her and Bryher," not just those who were not of her gender or sexuality.

There is little critical work addressing H. D. specifically as a war poet. Graham remarks in *Texas Studies in Literature and Language* that the critical response to *Trilogy* has "shied away from addressing it as war poetry, as if that were too obvious a response and therefore undeserving of sustained attention." She contests such readings of the poem, saying that "'from London 1942' is the context that all readers should take with them into the poem itself; through this epigraph H. D. neatly conveys that her poetry has both personal and global concerns." In an earlier article in *English*, Graham deploys trauma theory to elaborate this relationship, showing that, "in *Trilogy*, fallen walls represent, not only the traumatized city, but the traumatized self." She disputes the idea that "the poem [is] a celebration of the power of creativity over destruction," yet argues that H. D.'s likening of the city to the individual psyche, and of the "experiences of wartime (fear, betrayal, bereavement and dispossession)" to "the crises of self that her female protagonists endure"; allows her to show that the traumatized city, like the traumatized subject, "suffers damage yet survives." Rachel Blau DuPlessis makes a similar argument in *Contemporary Literature*, arguing that, for H. D., the First World War represented "aspects of that destructive force which shattered the possibility of a cultural life" and the "profound psychic damage from sexual and spiritual thralldom [which] continued to torment her." These issues, concludes DuPlessis, "recurred to be resolved during World War II."

German bombs fall around St. Paul's Cathedral, London, December 29, 1940. Photo taken by Herbert Mason from the roof of Northcliffe House. © THE ART ARCHIVE / CULVER PICTURES

As is true of H. D.'s work in general, *The Walls Do Not Fall* is seen by many critics to mirror a process of the psychic construction of the self that is specifically feminine. In *Contemporary Literature* Susan Gubar finds a "paradigm of a uniquely female quest for maturation" in H. D.'s "most ambitious poetic narratives." Gubar identifies that quest with the need to rejuvenate culture "in a world that worships coercion, [where] the sword takes precedence over the word," arguing that the search is successfully resolved when the poet manages to "recover the secret of Isis," a specifically feminine language of power. Other critics emphasize the poem as the product of the Freudian analysis that H. D. underwent, pointing to its ideas of layered consciousness and a hidden spiritual past as examples of Freudian tropes applied to history and myth.

SOURCES

Atkins, Elizabeth. "A Brilliant New Defense of Poetry." Rev. of *The Walls Do Not Fall*, by H. D. *Poetry* 65.6 (1945): 327–30. Print.

DuPlessis, Rachel Blau. "Romantic Thralldom in H. D." *Contemporary Literature* 20.2 (1979): 178–203. Print.

Friedman, Susan Stanford. *Psyche Reborn: The Emergence of H. D.* Bloomington: Indiana UP, 1981. Print.

———. "Who Buried H. D.?: A Poet, Her Critics and Her Place in 'The Literary Tradition.'" *College English* 36.7 (1975): 801–14. Print.

Graham, Sarah. "Falling Walls: Trauma and Testimony in H. D.'s *Trilogy.*" *English* 56 (2007): 299–319. Print.

Graham, Sarah H. S. "'We Have a Secret. We are Alive': H. D.'s *Trilogy* as a Response to War." *Texas Studies in Literature and Language* 44.2 (2002): 161. Web. 18 June 2011. Print.

Gregory, Horace. "Of Vitality, Regionalism and Satire in Recent American Poetry." *Sewanee Review* 52.4 (1944): 572–93. Print.

Gubar, Susan. "The Echoing Spell of H. D.'s *Trilogy.*" *Contemporary Literature* 19.2 (1978): 196–218. Print.

H. D. *Trilogy.* Rev. ed. New York: New Directions, 1998. Print.

Rainey, Lawrence. "Canon, Gender, and Text: The Case of H. D." *College Literature* 18.3 (1991): 106–25. Print.

Watts, Harold H. "H. D. and the Age of Myth." *Sewanee Review* 56.2 (1948): 287–303. Print.

FURTHER READING

Gelpi, Albert. "Re-membering the Mother: A Reading of H. D.'s *Trilogy.*" *H. D.: Woman and Poet.* Ed. Michael King. Orono: National Poetry Foundation, 1986. Print.

H. D. *Helen in Egypt.* New York: Grove, 1961. Print.

———. *Palimpsest.* Boston: Houghton, 1926. Print.

———. *Sea Garden.* Boston: Houghton, 1916. Print.

Hacker, Marilyn. "Brooks, H. D., and Rukeyser: Three Women Poets in the First Century of World Wars." *American Poet* 35 (2008): 8–12. Print.

Hughes, Gertrude Reif. "Making It *Really* New: Hilda Doolittle, Gwendolyn Brooks, and the Feminist Potential of Modern Poetry." *American Quarterly* 42.3 (1990): 375–401. Print.

Morris, Adalaide. "Signaling: Feminism, Politics and Mysticism in H. D.'s War Trilogy." *Sagetrieb* 9.2 (1990): 121–33. Print.

Ostriker, Alicia. "What Do Women (Poets) Want?: H. D. and Marianne Moore as Poetic Ancestresses." *Contemporary Literature* 27.4 (1986): 475–92. Print.

Jenny Ludwig

WAR MUSIC

Christopher Logue

† Key Facts

Conflict:
Trojan War

Time Period:
11th Century BCE

Genre:
Epic poem

OVERVIEW

War Music comprises a series of works by British poet Christopher Logue based on *The Iliad*, the Greek poet Homer's epic poem about the Trojan War. Logue started adapting portions of the ancient poem in 1959 when Donald Carne-Ross of the BBC invited him to contribute to a new version of *The Iliad* he planned to commission. Logue did not know ancient Greek, so Carne-Ross supplied word-for-word translations to guide him, in addition to standard translations by George Chapman (1611), Alexander Pope (1720), A. T. Murray (1924), and E. V. Rieu (1950). Rather than produce another translation in the strict sense, as Logue explains in his Author's Note, he "hoped [the work] would turn out to be a poem in English dependent on whatever … [he] could guess about a small part of *The Iliad*." The result is a poem that is distinctly modern, with cinematic shifts in pacing and focus, and with language and images drawn from all quarters of contemporary life.

Logue began work on his "Homer poem" with Book 16, also called the *Patrocleia*, which describes events surrounding the death of the Greek warrior Patroclus. With the completion of *Pax* (1967), based on Book 19, Logue's status as his generation's preeminent interpreter of *The Iliad* was acknowledged by many critics. In *After Babel*, George Steiner describes Logue's work as "the most magnificent act of translation going on in the English language at the moment."

Patrocleia and *Pax* were revised and published together with a bridging section, *GBH* (Grievous Bodily Harm), a conflation of Books 17 and 18), as *War Music* (1981). In the 1990s Logue published two prequels, *Kings: An Account of Books 1 and 2 of the* Iliad (1991) and *The Husbands: An Account of Books 3 and 4 of the* Iliad (1994). *All Day Permanent Red* (2003) recounts the battle scenes in Book 5. The penultimate installment of *War Music*, *Cold Calls* (2005), which draws on Books 5 through 9, won the 2005 Whitbread Poetry Award.

HISTORICAL AND LITERARY CONTEXT

The composition of *The Iliad* is conventionally dated to the late eighth or early seventh century BCE. More than fifteen thousand lines long, the epic is traditionally attributed to Homer, although debate continues about whether the poem is the work of a single author or a number of authors, who may have revised and added to it over time. The work recounts events of the Trojan War. The historical reality of this conflict between the Greeks and Trojans is hotly contested today; some seek to locate its origins in the twelfth century BCE.

The Iliad focuses on the final year of the decade-long conflict. As the Greek hero Achilles sulks on the sidelines, the Trojans have gained the upper hand in the war. Patroclus, Achilles' closest friend, finally leads Achilles' warriors into battle himself. Patroclus is killed in the fighting by Hector, Priam's son. Deranged with grief and rage, Achilles returns to the war, giving the advantage back to the Greeks. Achilles kills Hector but is himself ultimately killed by Paris. In the end the Greeks prevail, and Troy is razed to the ground.

Over the centuries *The Iliad* has continued to appeal powerfully to both scholars and lay readers. John Gross, in his review of *War Music* for the *New York Times*, cites Steiner's calculation that there have been "more than 200 complete or selected English versions" of *The Iliad* and *The Odyssey* in the past four centuries. These translations are based on an ancient written work that was itself a rendering of an oral performance piece. Working at such a remove from the source, translators of the ancient epics can never hope for the accuracy achieved in translations of contemporary writings. The uncertainties that challenge modern rendering have contributed to the decision of some translators to aim to capture the energy or essence of an ancient work rather than a mirror image in English language and meter. Logue's work provides a dramatic example of this trend.

THEMES AND STYLE

The violence of war is the overriding theme of *War Music*. Logue's poetry delivers high-definition images and sounds, allowing the reader no distance from the chaos and terror of combat. In contrast to Homer's *Iliad* (and traditional translations of it), *War Music* contains no time or space for the war's participants (or readers) to reflect on a past peace or to imagine a future free of the war. There is only blood lust and killing, to which gods and mortals alike dedicate themselves with an ecstatic zeal:

> Head-lock, body-slam,
> Hector attacking;
> His anger, his armour, his:
> *"Now, now, or never, O Infinite, Endless Apollo,"*

WAR MUSIC AS PERFORMANCE

As the title of Christopher Logue's *War Music* implies, sound plays a crucial role in the poem's emotional and thematic impact. The concept of creating an oral (and aural) foundation for the poem dates to the origins of Homer's *Iliad* itself.

Believed to have been composed sometime between the eighth and sixth centuries BCE, *The Iliad* was originally intended to be performed or sung and was used for both educational and ritual purposes among the ancient Greeks. In reviving this long-neglected aspect of the work, Logue aimed to adapt the epic poem's oral qualities to the modern era, altering the work at numerous points in order to render it more meaningful for twentieth-century audiences.

The first audio performance of the work was staged in 1959, when Logue adapted Book 21 of *The Iliad* for the BBC. More recently, in September 2001 the Verse Theatre Manhattan (VTM) in New York City produced a stage performance of *War Music*, with three women performers taking turns reciting the work. In the aftermath of the September 11, 2001, terrorist attacks, however, the production was suspended until the following March, when it reopened at New York's Wings Theatre. The production was particularly striking for its lack of props or scenery, leaving the audience to focus only on the three women's recitation of Logue's haunting verse.

> But silent,
> *"In my omnipotence I beg to cast*
> *All thought of peace on earth for me away*
> *Until I own that corpse."*

As Lorna Hardwick notes in the *Cambridge Companion to Homer*, Logue's poem "exposes the unpalatable aspects of the culture represented in Homer." It offers no relief from that culture's glorification of the battlefield; however, the sheer ubiquity of the carnage gives the lie to the glory. In *War Music*, violence does not honor but, rather, mocks greatness: "Hard to say who is who: the fighters, the heroes, / Their guts look alike."

The entwined themes of loss and grief also come into play in *War Music*, especially in the passages that focus on Achilles after Patroclus's death. But in this crucial instance loss and grief are quickly subsumed in Achilles's rage against Hector. As Achilles grieves at the beginning of *Pax*, his love for Patroclus is not even mentioned; rather, the telling image of Achilles is "his eyes like furnace doors ajar." Soon, Achilles is back in his armor, and "though it is noon, the helmet screams against the light; / Scratches the eye, so violent it can be seen / Across three thousand years."

As the foregoing suggests, Logue's style, built on a foundation of rapid-fire lines and high-impact verbs, is particularly suited to the depiction of action and emotions at high pitch and to the linguistic embodiment of violence. Compressed syntax—which involves many lines consisting of only one word— and rapid shifts in perspective and scene produce a "general effect (though there are more lilting passages, too) [that] is jagged and abrupt, which is only as it should be—for the most obvious feature of the action in *War Music* is its extreme violence," Gross observes. Michael O'Leary comments in the *Chicago*

Review that Logue's poem "looks like a screenplay on the page," a format that "allows the poem quickly to shift proportion and perspective," as in the opening passage of *Pax*:

> Rat.
> Pearl.
> Onion.
> Honey.
> These colours came before the sun
> Lifted above the ocean,
> Bringing light
> Alike to mortals and Immortals.

War Music, like *The Iliad*, was intended to be read aloud. The poem has been choreographed and set to music in onstage performances, and readings of Logue's renderings of Homer were released in 2001 as part of a seven-CD set titled *Audiologue*.

CRITICAL DISCUSSION

War Music has been hailed as one of the greatest works of British poetry since World War II. Although reviews of the first installments in Logue's native England were mixed, American commentators were more enthusiastic. As the work progressed, the consensus grew among critics that Logue was, in the words of Garry Wills in the introduction to *War Music*, one of the "few poets to bring Homer crashing into their time, like a giant trampling forests."

Logue's emphasis on violence and his stylistic decisions have divided critical opinion of the work. In "A Single-Minded Homer," André Naffis-Sahely decries the marginalization of Andromache and other female characters, whose words in opposition to war give Homer's poem "much nobility and therefore humanity." The "jettisoning" of such features, combined with Logue's "fetishism" of the battle scenes,

In this illustration by Marc Charmet of a scene from the Iliad, Achilles triumphantly drags Hector's body behind his chariot. circa 1900. © MARC CHARMET / THE ART ARCHIVE / THE PICTURE DESK, INC.

claims Naffis-Sahely, "has the effect of reducing [*War Music*] to a virtual spreadsheet of battles, victories, and defeats. Violence in Logue is no longer a medium for speech, but a military strategist's guide to Asia Minor; in short, banal."

These same qualities, however, have moved other critics to praise the poem for its energy and contemporaneity. In his *Guardian* review, for example, Charles Bainbridge draws attention to the poem's "exhilarating narrative drive and … remarkable sensitivity to the energies of contemporary language." Asserting that "Logue's is a modernist Homer," Mark Rudman writes in *American Poetry Review* that "[Logue] does to Homer what Pound did to Eliot's early version of *The Waste Land*: he retains only those verbal clusters whose energy is most intense."

In a study of the acoustic qualities of Logue's work, Emily Greenwood notes that Logue's adaptations of Homer retain their freshness "because contemporary referentiality and language are blended effortlessly with the diction and sound patterns of English literature across several centuries: Chaucer is present, as are Chapman, Shakespeare, Milton, Pope, Keats, and Pound."

The striking differences in the appearance and sound of Logue's Homer from traditional translations have been the focus of a great deal of criticism. Rudman argues that Logue's cinematic approach sacrifices the narrative continuity of the original epic to lyric intensity. Thus, the length of the narrative is significantly reduced, but "the effect … is enlarged, given added torque," notes Rudman. Gross describes the way in which, using "primarily a flexible form of blank verse," Logue captures in his jagged lines a world thrown out of balance by hatred and bloodshed.

Not all commentators believe that the work offers readers a substantial advantage over more straightforward renderings. Writing for the *London Review of Books*, Claude Rawson argues that Logue's stylistic pyrotechnics "[divert] attention from the poem, old or new, to the jumpy performing tricks of the poet."

Logue's decision to update or otherwise revise the extended similes that appear throughout Homer's work has also drawn critics' attention. Gross particularly praises Logue's handling of the extended simile in which the Greek soldiers are compared to a pack of wolves that has just killed and devoured a stag, contending that Logue's version is "at least as powerful as [George] Chapman's or Alexander Pope's, and a good deal more graphic than the equivalent passage in Robert Fitzgerald's *Iliad*." Similarly, *World Literature Today*'s Michael Leddy praises Logue's "startling" similes as the poet's "most remarkable invention."

SOURCES

Bainbridge, Charles. Rev. of *Cold Calls: War Music Continued*, by Christopher Logue. *Guardian* [London]. Guardian News and Media, 8 Oct. 2005. Web. 23 May 2011.

Greenwood, Emily. "Sounding Out Homer: Christopher Logue's Acoustic Homer." *Oral Tradition* 24.2 (2009): 503–18, Web. 28 Aug. 2011.

Gross, John. Rev. of *War Music: An Account of Books 16–19 of Homer's "Iliad,"* by Christopher Logue. *New York Times.* New York Times, 8 May 1987. Web. 23 May 2011.

Hardwick, Lorna. "'Shards and Suckers': Contemporary Receptions of Homer. *The Cambridge Companion to Homer.* Ed. Robert Louis Fowler. Cambridge: Cambridge UP, 2004. Print.

Leddy, Michael. Rev. of *All Day Permanent Red*, by Christopher Logue. *World Literature Today* 78.3–4 (2004). Web. *Literature Resource Center.* 23 May 2011.

Logue, Christopher. *War Music: An Account of Books 1–4 and 16–19 of Homer's "Iliad."* Chicago: U of Chicago P, 1997. Print.

Naffis-Sahely, André. "A Single-Minded Homer: On Christopher Logue's *War Music.*" *PN Review.* PN Review, May-June 2011. Web. 23 May 2011.

O'Leary, Michael. Rev. of *War Music*, by Christopher Logue. *Chicago Review* 43.4 (1997). Web. *Literature Resource Center.* 23 May 2011.

Rawson, Claude. "War and Pax." *London Review of Books.* LRB, 2 July 1981. Web. 23 May 2011.

Rudman, Mark. Rev. of *War Music*, by Christopher Logue. *American Poetry Review* 22.2 (1993). Web. *Literature Resource Center.* 23 May 2011.

Steiner, George. *After Babel.* London: Oxford UP, 1975. Print.

FURTHER READING

Carson, Anne. *An Oresteia.* New York: Faber, 2009. Print.

Fowler, R. L. *Cambridge Companion to Homer.* Cambridge: Cambridge UP, 2004. Print.

Homer. *The Iliad.* Trans. Robert Fagles. New York: Viking, 1990. Print.

Logue, Christopher. Interview. "Christopher Logue, the Art of Poetry No. 66." By Shusha Guppy. *Paris Review.* Paris Review, Summer 1993. Web. 23 May 2011.

Tipton, John. Rev. of *All Day Permanent Red*, by Christopher Logue. *Chicago Review* 49.3–4 (2004). Web. *Literature Resource Center.* 23 May 2011.

Walcott, Derek. *Omeros.* New York: Farrar, 1990. Print.

Wills, Garry. "Homer Alive." Rev. of *Kings: An Account of Books 1 and 2 of Homer's* Iliad, by Christopher Logue. *New York Review of Books* 23 Apr. 1992. Print.

Janet Moredock

THE WAR OF THE WORLDS

H. G. Wells

❖ *Key Facts*

Conflict:
Fictional

Genre:
Novel

OVERVIEW

The War of the Worlds, by H. G. (Herbert George) Wells (1866–1946), is regarded as one of the most influential and prophetic works of early science fiction. Published in 1898, the novel both reflects and exploits the pervasive fin de siècle anxieties that afflicted Victorian society, offering an imaginative scenario in which human civilization is almost—but not quite—annihilated by bloodthirsty extraterrestrials. In addition, *The War of the Worlds* presents a thinly veiled indictment of nineteenth-century imperialism and a philosophical commentary on controversial concepts such as "social Darwinism" (in which the fittest leave the weak behind) and "total war" (in which civilians are targeted along with military forces).

The novel is set in and around London, near the end of the nineteenth century. Its unnamed narrator recounts the arrival on Earth of hostile creatures from Mars. They attack the human population from enormous tripod-shaped mobile towers, using heat rays and poison gas. Human defenses ultimately prove useless against the Martian technology, and it turns out that the invaders intend to utilize human blood as a food source.

The narrator, who goes through a series of ordeals while trying to reunite with his wife, observes varied responses to the invasion and has lengthy conversations with a clergyman whose faith is shaken by the events and an artilleryman who articulates a grim plan for survival. Both the idealistic clergyman and the utilitarian artilleryman become demented, and the general populace runs mad. But the narrator—who is a student of science and moral philosophy—keeps his wits and eventually gets home. In the end, humanity is unexpectedly saved when the Martians succumb to infectious microorganisms. Following these events, which are told in flashback, scientists speculate that the Martians were an ancient race whose brains had become overevolved while their physical strength and resilience had atrophied.

The War of the Worlds was an immediate popular success, as were Wells's other early works of science fiction, which included *The Time Machine* (1895), *The Island of Doctor Moreau* (1896), and *The Invisible Man* (1897). Wells, who referred to the novels as "scientific romances," always claimed they were unimportant by comparison to his later work, which included not only dozens of novels and short stories but also a wide array of nonfiction books and articles. Yet *The War of the Worlds* has become the best known of all his works, in part because a radio dramatization of the novel caused public panic in some areas of the northeastern United States when it aired in 1938. Wells's story has retained a place in the popular imagination, influencing many later works of science fiction through its depiction of human vulnerability in the face of superior technology.

HISTORICAL AND LITERARY CONTEXT

At the beginning of the nineteenth century, the British Empire was the predominant colonial and military power on earth. As the century came to a close, however, it was becoming apparent that the empire was stagnating or beginning to decline. In addition, the certainties of religious belief and social theory were disturbed by publication of Charles Darwin's *On the Origin of Species* in 1859, and throughout the nineteenth century industrialization not only displaced workers from the countryside into the cities but also disrupted traditional class structures.

Germany's unexpected victory in the Franco-Prussian war of 1870 raised fears that a military invasion of the United Kingdom was possible. George Chesney capitalized on these national insecurities in his 1871 novel *The Battle of Dorking*, which depicted Germans invading an English market town. Chesney's novel was so popular that it spawned a thriving genre of "invasion literature" that persisted into the twentieth century. The United Kingdom was also struck by millennial anxiety and growing social unrest as the turn of the century approached.

Taken altogether, these factors created a perfect environment for *The War of the Worlds*, which combined two popular fascinations: invasion literature and stories about Mars. Interest in interplanetary adventures had begun in 1880 with Percy Greg's *Across the Zodiac* and was intensified in 1894 by reports that a French astronomer had observed "strange lights" on Mars. The following year, American astronomer Percival Lowell's book *Mars* suggested that features on the planet's surface could be irrigation channels, possibly constructed to support life on an arid world.

Those bits of news served as inspirations for *The War of the Worlds*, in which the flashes of light became

WELLS AND WELLES: THE GREAT SCARE

Orson Welles broadcasting a radio adaptation of H. G. Wells's The War of the Worlds in 1938. © FORTEAN / TOPFOTO / THE IMAGE WORKS. REPRODUCED BY PERMISSION.

H. G. Wells hit upon a powerful idea in 1898 when he depicted the helplessness of human beings faced with an otherworldly invasion. In the century after *The War of the*

Worlds was published, its premise inspired many works of science fiction and disaster drama. The first film based on the novel attracted enthusiastic audiences in 1953 and is widely considered a classic of science fiction cinema.

Yet it was radio that made *The War of the Worlds* a landmark of popular culture. An ambitious young writer named Orson Welles adapted the novel for performance on the radio drama series Mercury Theatre on the Air. Welles broadcast the story on the night before Halloween in 1938 in a simulated-reality format, beginning with "news flashes" that interrupted a music show to report strange lights in the sky. Soon the news story took over the broadcast, presenting mock interviews with experts and gradually escalating into an account of Martian machines overrunning humans.

At several points before and during the presentation, announcements explained that it was a dramatization, not a real news event. A number of people did not hear the disclaimers, however, and there was some amount of panic behavior, though no one is really sure how much. It is certain, however, that the highly publicized event propelled Orson Welles into a legendary career that included not only acting but also writing and directing such classic films as *Citizen Kane* and *The Magnificent Ambersons*.

It is also certain that six deaths occurred in Ecuador after Radio Quito aired a Spanish-language version of Welles's radio drama in 1949. A panic sparked by the broadcast turned into a deadly riot after the hoax was revealed, demonstrating once again how much the idea of alien invasion plays on humanity's deepest fears.

departing spacecraft and the Martians were imagined as canal-builders forced to leave their depleted planet in search of a new home. Along with these seemingly scientific ideas, Wells incorporated the horrifying notion that Martians might imbibe human blood, not unlike the vampire featured in Bram Stoker's popular 1897 novel *Dracula*.

Wells's audience was troubled not only by threats that could be imagined from past and present experience, but also by fears of what they could not yet foresee. As the pace of social and scientific change accelerated, there was an increasing awareness that new forms of technology would soon alter human life—perhaps beyond recognition. Wells tapped into that concern by depicting the Martians as humanoids who had become (after eons of evolution) so intellectually overdeveloped that they were dependent on machine technology to supplement or even replace their physical capabilities.

The technology they created for survival also gave them an insurmountable advantage over the conventional weaponry of Earth. Wells, who had been educated in the sciences, used *The War of the Worlds* to depict a new military might that would be characterized by motor-driven killing machines, deadly heat rays, inescapable poison gas, and unpreventable assaults from the air. Just two decades later, this "Martian" style of warfare became a human reality when tanks, chemical weapons, and even airplanes appeared in World War I.

THEMES AND STYLE

For most of its early readers, *The War of the Worlds* was merely a satisfying mixture of gory sensationalism and lightly philosophical commentary, offered up in a journalistic style that was both efficient and entertaining. (An anonymous reviewer for *The Critic* aptly described the novel as "an Associated Press dispatch, describing a universal nightmare.")

Wells points to the irony of colonizers becoming colonized in an early passage, as the narrator muses on the morality of the Martian invasion:

And before we judge of them too harshly we must remember what ruthless and utter destruction our species has wrought, not only upon animals, such as the vanished bison and the dodo, but upon its own inferior races. The Tasmanians, in spite of their human likeness, were entirely swept out of existence in a war of extermination by European immigrants, in the space of fifty years. Are we such apostles of mercy as to complain if the Martians warred in the same spirit?

Here, the Tasmanians represent the most extreme consequences of European colonialism, in which the indigenous population is effectively wiped out by deprivation, disease, and military force. Those who survived the European colonization of Africa, Asia, the Americas, and the South Pacific saw their lands and natural resources seized by a foreign army, their labor exploited by foreign companies, and their traditional cultures destroyed.

The War of the Worlds is ironically titled, because the war is so one-sided, the forces so unequal, that there is never any meaningful combat, just the rapid collapse of human civilization. There is little or no time or opportunity for romantic patriotism, heroism, or brotherhood in arms. In fact, once it becomes plain that Earth can put up no defense against the Martians, Wells's demoralized humans revert to selfish, savage behavior. In the end they survive only by an intervention of luck, or perhaps divine providence.

Although Wells was not an absolute pacifist, his opposition to imperialism and nondefensive war is subtly evident in *The War of the Worlds*. At the same time, there is a complementary subtext in which the Martian colonizers are wiped out by disease, just as native populations were decimated by European diseases for which they had no immunity. Similarly, the Martians are not motivated by the imperial desire for "more" (land, goods, political power) but rather by an instinct for survival. These Darwinian aspects—which are also reflected in the evolutionary exhaustion that has befallen the Martians—complicate the theme of anti-imperialism and create ambiguities which make the novel an intriguing work of fiction rather than an ideological tract.

CRITICAL DISCUSSION

In the twentieth century, as Wells shifted his attention from dark fantasies to progressive social commentary, he came to regard his early works as inconsequential. That view was generally shared by the critical community until 1961, when Bernard Bergonzi's *The Early H. G. Wells: A Study of the Scientific Romances* argued persuasively that Wells's popular speculative fictions deserved to be taken seriously. For example, Bergonzi points out that the fantastic surface of *The War of the Worlds* conceals important insights into "the secret fears and lack of confidence of late Victorian bourgeois society."

The subsequent renewal of interest in Wells's early novels proved fortunate for his posthumous reputation, since—as Frank McConnell explains in his 1980 essay "H. G. Wells: Utopia and Doomsday"—his works of speculative fiction are now regarded as classics, while "the rest of Wells seems to have vanished without a trace." Few people today, McConnell observes, are "aware that Wells's imprint on [the early

The Martians launch an attack from their three-legged fighting machines in Steven Spielberg's 2005 film version of *The War of the Worlds*. © DREAMWORKS / PARAMOUNT / THE KOBAL COLLECTION / THE PICTURE DESK, INC.

twentieth century] was equal to or greater than that of D. H. Lawrence, Virginia Woolf, C. S. Lewis, or W. H. Auden." By that time the doomsday visions that had suited the mood of fin de siècle England had been replaced in Wells's work by utopian ideals of progress and social reform.

While Wellsian socialism found an enthusiastic audience at first, by mid-century Wells and his ideas had faded from view. As Allan Chavkin points out in "Mr. Sammler's War of the Planets," when the protagonist of Saul Bellow's acclaimed 1970 novel *Mr. Sammler's Planet* muses on his affinities with Wells, he does not identify with the Wells who became an apostle of optimism. Instead he resonates with "the Wells of *The War of the Worlds*, the dark Wells who, like Sammler, is anxious about the survival of the species and ponders whether evolution will lead toward progress or extinction."

Since the late twentieth century, *The War of the Worlds* has attracted the attention of scholars whose interests range from the history of ideas to postcolonialist criticism. In his 1992 study *Voices Prophesying War: Future Wars, 1763–3749*, for example, I. F. Clarke finds *The War of the Worlds* to be "the perfect nineteenth-century myth of the imaginary war." It offers a symbolic representation of ideas already abroad in the culture and therefore immediately understood. Ingo Cornils takes a comparative approach in his 2003 essay "The Martians Are Coming! War, Peace, Love, and Scientific Progress in H. G. Wells's *The War of the Worlds* and Kurd Laßwitz's *Auf zwei Planeten*," which considers Wells's novel in relation to a German work (*Two Planets*) also written in 1897. (Laßwitz's novel—until the 1930s one of the most popular German science fiction works—transcends the war plot the two books have in common and ends in a mutually beneficial cooperation between Earthlings and Martians).

Patricia Kerslake, in her 2007 survey *Science Fiction and Empire*, examines *The War of the Worlds* as a narrative that "speaks of colonialism and the imperial drive from the most violent and dystopian of viewpoints." Bed Paudyal, in his 2009 essay "Trauma, Sublime, and the Ambivalence of Imperialist Imagination in H. G. Wells's *The War of the Worlds*," considers the novel in relation to philosopher Edmund Burke's aesthetic theories, particularly his theory of the sublime.

SOURCES

Bergonzi, Bernard, and H. G. Wells. *The Early H. G. Wells: A Study of the Scientific Romances*. Manchester: Manchester UP, 1961. Print.

Chavkin, Allan. "Mr. Sammler's War of the Planets." *The Critical Response to H. G. Wells*. Ed. William J. Scheick. Westport: Greenwood, 1995: 33–48. Print.

Clarke, I. F. *Voices Prophesying War: Future Wars, 1763–3749*. Oxford: Oxford UP, 1992. Print.

Cornils, Ingo. "The Martians Are Coming! War, Peace, Love, and Scientific Progress in H. G. Wells's *The War of the Worlds* and Kurd Laßwitz's *Auf zwei Planeten*." *Comparative Literature*. Winter 2003: 24–41. Print.

Kerslake, Patricia. *Science Fiction and Empire*. Liverpool: Liverpool UP, 2007. Print.

McConnell, Frank D. "H. G. Wells: Utopia and Doomsday." *Wilson Quarterly*. Summer 1980: 176–186. Print.

Paudyal, Bed. "Trauma, Sublime, and the Ambivalence of Imperialist Imagination in H. G. Wells's *The War of the Worlds*." *Extrapolation* 50.1 (2009): 102+. Print.

Wells, Herbert G., David Y. Hughes, and Harry M. Geduld. *A Critical Edition of the War of the Worlds: H. G. Wells's Scientific Romance*. Bloomington: Indiana UP, 1993. Print.

FURTHER READING

Flynn, John L. *"War of the Worlds": From Wells to Spielberg*. Owings Mills: Galactic, 2005. Print.

Hillegas, Mark R. *The Future as Nightmare: H. G. Wells and the Anti-Utopians*. New York: Oxford UP, 1967.

Huntington, John. *The Logic of Fantasy: H. G. Wells and Science Fiction*. New York: Columbia UP, 1982. Print.

Ketterer, David. *Flashes of the Fantastic: Selected Essays from "The War of the Worlds" Centennial, 19th International Conference on the Fantastic in the Arts*. Westport: Greenwood, 2004. Print.

Parrinder, Patrick, and H. G. Wells. *H. G. Wells: The Critical Heritage*. London: Routledge, 1997. Print.

Rieder, John. "Science Fiction, Colonialism, and the Plot of Invasion." *Extrapolation* 46 (2005): 373–94. Print.

Scheick, William J. *The Critical Response to H. G. Wells*. Westport: Greenwood, 1995. Print.

Trushell, John. "Mirages in the Desert: *The War of the Worlds* and *Fin du Globe*." *Extrapolation* 43.4 (2002): 439–455. Print.

Wells, H. G., and Martin A. Danahay. *The War of the Worlds*. Peterborough: Broadview, 2003. Print

Wells, Herbert G., and Glenn Yeffeth. *War of the Worlds: Fresh Perspectives on the H. G. Wells Classic*. Dallas: BenBella, 2005. Print.

MEDIA ADAPTATIONS

The War of the Worlds. Adapt. and perf. Orson Wells. CBS-Radio, 30 Oct. 1938. Radio.

The War of the Worlds. Dir. Byron Haskin. Perf. Gene Barry, Ann Robinson, and Les Tremayne. Paramount Pictures, 1953. Film.

The War of the Worlds. Dir. Steven Spielberg. Perf. Tom Cruise, Dakota Fanning, and Tim Robbins. Paramount Pictures, 2005. Film.

Cynthia Giles

ZANG TUMB TUUUM

Filippo Marinetti

❖ *Key Facts*

Conflict:
First Balkan War

Time Period:
Early 20th Century

Genre:
Poetry

OVERVIEW

One of the major works of early twentieth-century avant-gardism, *Zang Tumb Tuuum* (also referred to as *Zang Tumb Tumb*) is a long experimental poem written between 1912 and 1914 by Italian poet, editor, and performance artist Filippo Tommaso Marinetti (1876–1944). *Zang Tumb Tuuum* is based on Marinetti's impressions of the Battle of Adrianople (1913), in which the Ottoman Empire fought against the Bulgarian Second Army during the First Balkan War. Marinetti witnessed this battle as a reporter for the French political newspaper *L'Intransigeant.*

The poem *Zang Tumb Tuuum* is written in an experimental genre that Marinetti invented, called *parole in libertà* ("words in freedom"). This genre, which Marinetti claimed was better suited than traditional literary forms to express the vigorous, technological dynamism of modern life, uses the new versatility of industrial typography to make its visual, often visceral impact. The *parole in libertà* style in general, and *Zang Tumb Tuuum* in particular, juxtaposes different typesets, font sizes, and geometric arrangements of letters and graphic elements on the page. It is an early example of what came to be known as concrete poetry, or poetry that uses visual and typographic elements to convey its message. In addition to these visual features, the book also makes prolific use of onomatopoeia, or words that mimic sounds (such as the "zang tumb tuuum" of the book's title, which seeks to imitate the nonlinguistic sounds of armed combat).

Marinetti was the founder of the Italian artistic and social movement known as Futurism, the first major European avant-garde trend of the twentieth century. He and his followers created art, literature, and public performances celebrating themes that they saw as modern and forward-looking, such as technology, speed, youth, and violence. *Zang Tumb Tuuum,* a prime example of Futurists' fascination with these themes. It first appeared as a series of journal publications and was then collected into a single, 228-page, soft-cover artist's book and published in Milan in 1914, almost simultaneously with the outbreak of World War I.

HISTORICAL AND LITERARY CONTEXT

Like his Futurist colleagues, Marinetti strongly favored Italy's entry into the war; in fact, he saw war in general as a good thing, often claiming in his writings that "war is the only hygiene of the world." Marinetti's point of view was common during that time, with militant nationalism prevalent in many European countries in the early twentieth century. The climate of nationalist unrest was especially pronounced in Italy, which had only become a politically unified entity in 1871 (five years before Marinetti was born). This tenuous unification was the result of a decades-long period of political struggle called the Risorgimento (c. 1815–71), or "Uprising." Even after national unification and well into the first decades of the twentieth century, Italy was still, for all intents and purposes, culturally and linguistically fragmented. It remained a collection of disparate regions unified only in name. Many of its citizens, including Marinetti and other eventual adherents of fascism, believed that Italy had no clear national identity and that it could only achieve one through extreme, militant measures and in contest with other nations. *Zang Tumb Tuuum*'s predominantly celebratory representations of war were brought forth during these unsettled times. Although expressed in an especially vigorous tone of provocation, Marinetti's pro-war views were generally consonant with those of many European intellectuals at the time.

Futurist philosophy rejected the rhetorically florid aspects of the work of Gabriele D'Annunzio (at that time arguably the most influential poet in Italian letters), but it embraced and amplified D'Annunzio's vision of the *superuomo,* or superman. This concept was derived from certain aspects of the thought of German philosopher Friedrich Nietzsche (1844–1900). This vision of the *superuomo* shows up in the work of Marinetti as a vitalistic and heroic attitude that exalts unbridled energy and the immediate impulses of the irrational side of the psyche. Breaking with tradition and condemning the literary and cultural past in all its forms, Futurists considered direct psychological experience the only true source of art and poetry.

Marinetti published "The Futurist Manifesto" ("Il Manifesto del Futurismo") in February 1909 in the French journal *Le Figaro.* An announcement of the founding of the Futurist movement and an outline of its agenda, the "Manifesto" contains a list of eleven imperatives to which Futurists must aspire and adhere. These imperatives include the following:

2. Courage, audacity, and rebellion will be essential elements of our poetry.
3. Until today, literature has exalted pensive immobility, inner ecstasy, and dreaminess. We plan to exalt aggressive movement, feverish insomnia, running on the double, daredevil leaps, the slap and the punch.
9. We want to glorify war—the only hygiene of the world—militarism, patriotism, the destructive act of liberators, the worthy ideas for which one dies, and the denunciation of women.

Intentionally provocative, the rhetoric of Marinetti's "Manifesto," exemplified by the excerpts above, sheds light on the content of *Zang Tumb Tuuum*. To a great extent *Zang Tumb Tuuum* performs a direct, visceral communication of the ideas outlined in the "Manifesto": violence, speed, "masculine" dynamism and restlessness, and militant ideals.

THEMES AND STYLE

Informative for an understanding of *Zang Tumb Tuuum*'s style is Marinetti's 1912 treatise titled "The Technical Manifesto of Futurist Literature." As its title suggests, this later document outlines the linguistic features that ensure the most effective delivery of the ideology conveyed in the "Futurist Manifesto." Overall, the "Technical Manifesto" advises the abolition of grammatical and typographical features that constrict poetry in formalities and, in Marinetti's view, render it static and introspective. For instance, Marinetti wants Futurist poets to "destroy syntax, arranging nouns randomly as they spring forth." He also insists that they use verbs only in the infinitive, so that the verbs "adapt themselves elastically to nouns rather than subjecting them to the 'I' of the writer." He condemns the use of any adjectives, adverbs, or standard punctuation, and he advocates what might be called free association, or analogy between nouns that arises spontaneously and without conscious reflection.

All these attributes are clearly present in *Zang Tumb Tuuum*. Evoking the sights, sounds, and sensations of the bombardment of Adrianople by the Bulgarian artillery, the poem is full of onomatopoeia and a frenetic juxtaposing of words and phrases that want to burst off the page in the style of the bombardment itself. The Battle of Adrianople marked one of the first known uses of airplanes for bombing, and Marinetti's poem can be viewed as evoking the mechanical whirring of planes and the vertical descent of bombs as well as their explosions on the ground. Since the text loses much in translation because of its reliance on wordplay and formal distortions of language, below is an example of the

Le Petit Journal

ADMINISTRATION
61, RUE LAFAYETTE, 61
5 CENT. SUPPLÉMENT ILLUSTRÉ 5 CENT.
24ᵐᵉ Année — Numéro 1 167
DIMANCHE 2 MARS 1913

SORTIE DES ÉTRANGERS D'ANDRINOPLE

text presented first in the original Italian and then in an approximated translation:

Ogni 5 secondi cannoni da assedio sventrrrare spazio con un accordo ZZZANG TUMB TUMB ammutinamento di cento echi per azzannarlo sminuzzarlo sparpagliarlo all'infiiiiiiinito del centro di quel zzzang tumb tumb spiacciato (ampiezza 50 kmq.) balzare scoppi tagli pugni batterie tiro rapido Violenza ferocia re-go-la-ri-tà questo basso grave scandere strani folli agiatissimi acuti della battaglia.

Every 5 seconds assault cannons rrrrrrip open space with a unison ZZZANG TUMB TUMB mutiny of a hundred echoes to maul it demolish it scatter it to the infiiiiiiiinite of the center of that zzzang tumb tumb crushed (50 sq. kilometers) leaping blasts punches rapid-fire attacks Violence ferociousness re-gu-la-ri-ty this low heavy rising strange mad agitated sharp of the battle.

As depicted in *Le Petit Journal* on March 2, 1913, foreigners are allowed to leave the Turkish city of Edirne (formerly Adrianople), which is being bombarded by the Bulgarians. © MARY EVANS PICTURE LIBRARY / EVERETT COLLECTION

MARINETTI AND THE PARTITO POLITICO FUTURISTA

Filippo Marinetti not only published manifestos about the Futurist agenda, but he also took this agenda literally to the streets by organizing frequent *serate*, or "nights out." During these *serate*, Futurists put on provocative theatrical performances that directly involved the audience in action and often culminated in violence. In 1914 and 1915, Marinetti organized a number of events in Milan to support Italy's entry into World War I. In such a demonstration in May 1915, both Marinetti and eventual leader of the National Fascist Party, Benito Mussolini, were arrested. Taking his pro-war views beyond the realm of literary expression and street demonstrations, Marinetti formed the Partito Politico Futurista ("Futurist Political Party") in 1918.

Although the exact nature and extent of the relationship between Futurism and Fascism is debated by scholars, it seems clear that Marinetti was influential in the founding of the National Fascist Party. Marinetti knew Mussolini well, and although he broke with the fascist leader in 1920, Marinetti continued to support the regime and remained loyal to it until his death in 1944. After the 1922 March on Rome, during which Mussolini came to power, Marinetti claimed that fascism had actualized at least some of the demands outlined by Futurists. Marinetti became secretary of the Fascist Writers' Union in 1929, even though he had earlier condemned such institutions as restrictive and bureaucratic. In general, with its appeals to ancient Roman history and its drive toward conformity, fascism was less radical than was Marinetti's Futurist agenda; nonetheless, the two movements shared a mutually beneficial alliance for many years.

This passage reflects the prescriptions set out by Marinetti in the "Technical Manifesto." The absence of punctuation, the random arrangement of nouns, the infinitive verbs and corresponding lack of any specific grammatical subject, and the use of sound and typographical irregularities characterize the iconoclastic style of Marinetti's poem. The style also enacts the violent character of the poem's subject matter, so that form and content work in conjunction to create a virtual bombardment of words on the page.

CRITICAL DISCUSSION

Futurism had value primarily as a transitional movement, supplanting a classical, oratory literary style that had run its course and providing inspiration for a great many European avant-garde movements, including surrealism and Dada. It also interested proletarian activists in the years surrounding the publication of *Zang Tumb Tuuum*: the factory workers of Turin, whom political philosopher Antonio Gramsci was helping to organize and educate during these years, responded positively to Futurism and to Marinetti's seditious form of artistic expression. Even in revolutionary Russia his work had resonance. (In hindsight these positive identifications

by left-wing factions are ironic given Marinetti's avidly right-wing orientation, especially during the fascist years.) What the proletarian groups likely identified with was less a specific political agenda than a more general antiestablishment attitude and aesthetic. At least on the surface, Marinetti's futurist work pitted itself against the cultural markers of the wealth and prestige enjoyed by the old aristocracy and constituted a conscious, radical break with the past.

Another distinctive feature of Futurism that appealed to a wide audience of politically and artistically revolutionary individuals and groups was its intentional involvement of the public. Marinetti rejected the idealized identification with the artist demanded by older romantic and postromantic poetry. Instead, he invited the public, including critics, to disagree with him, to challenge his work, and even to dispute directly with him and the other Futurist participants in the public *serate*, or "nights out," which featured theatrical performances. Because of this, Marinetti earned both friends and enemies during the arc of his greatest prominence. More traditional critics dismissed and disparaged him while the more radical-minded embraced and emulated him.

Because of its official alliance with fascism, Futurism fell into general disfavor in Italy after World War II, and this attitude has persisted somewhat. Contemporary critics are divided on the question of literary Futurism's artistic merit and lasting significance. Prominent Italian literary critic Mario Pazzaglia sees Marinetti's poetry as an important transitional phenomenon and little else, remarking that Marinetti never quite went past mere pretense and that his work often bordered on parody. A number of critics identified with the new avant-gardes of the 1960s and 1970s, such as Caroline Tisdall, have given a more sympathetic appraisal of Marinetti's poetry and especially of *Zang Tumb Tuuum*. In collaboration with Angelo Bozzola, Tisdall writes:

> [The] masterpiece of Words-in-freedom and of Marinetti's literary career was ... 'Zang Tumb Tuuum' ... The dynamic rhythms and onomatopoetic possibilities that the new form offered were made even more effective through the revolutionary use of different typefaces, forms and graphic arrangements .... In 'Zang Tumb Tuuum,' they are used to express an extraordinary range of ... moods and speeds .... Audiences in London, Berlin and Rome alike were bowled over by the tongue-twisting vitality with which Marinetti declaimed 'Zang Tumb Tuuum.'

Although critics' and general audiences' opinions of *Zang Tumb Tuuum*'s literary depth and excellence may vary, it is certain that this work had an important influence on many twentieth-century avant-garde movements. Such movements were able to embrace the spirit of the work's audacious experimental style, either in conjunction with or independently of its pro-war content.

SOURCES

Barański, Zygmunt G., and Rebecca J. West. *The Cambridge Companion to Modern Italian Culture.* Cambridge: Cambridge UP, 2001. Print.

Berghaus, Günter. *Futurism and Politics: Between Anarchist Rebellion and Fascist Reaction, 1909–1944.* Providence: Berghahn Books, 1996. Print.

Gentile, Emilio. *The Struggle for Modernity: Nationalism, Futurism, and Fascism.* Westport: Praeger, 2003. Print.

Jensen, Richard. "Futurism and Fascism." *History Today* 45.11 (1995): n. pag. Web. 21 Sept. 2011.

Marinetti, Filippo Tommaso. *Les Mots en Liberté Futuristes.* Milan: Edizioni futuriste di "Poesia," 1919. *Reed Digital Collections: Artists' Books.* Web. 15 Sept. 2011.

———. *Zang Tumb Tuuum.* Milano: Edizioni futuriste di "Poesia," 1914. Print.

Nänny, Max, and Olga C. M. Fischer. *Form Miming Meaning: Iconicity in Language and Literature.* Amsterdam: J. Benjamins, 1999. Print.

Orban, Clara E. *The Culture of Fragments: Words and Images in Futurism and Surrealism.* Amsterdam: Rodopi, 1997. Print.

Pazzaglia, Mario. *Letteratura italiana: Testi e critica con lineamenti di storia letteraria.* Bologna: Zanichelli, 1992. Print.

Tisdall, Caroline, and Angelo Bozzolla. *Futurism.* London: Thames and Hudson, 1977. Print.

FURTHER READING

Bru, Sascha. *Democracy, Law and the Modernist Avant-Gardes: Writing in the State of Exception.* Edinburgh: Edinburgh UP, 2009. Print.

Drucker, Johanna. *The Visible Word: Experimental Typography and Modern Art, 1909–1923.* Chicago: U of Chicago P, 1994. Print.

Freeman, Ellis. *Conquering the Man in the Street: A Psychological Analysis of Propaganda in War, Fascism, and Politics.* New York: Vanguard, 1940. Print.

Hewitt, Andrew. *Fascist Modernism: Aesthetics, Politics, and the Avant-Garde.* Stanford: Stanford UP, 1993. Print.

Humphreys, Richard. *Futurism.* Cambridge: Cambridge UP, 1999. Print.

Marinetti, Filippo T., and R. W. Flint. *Marinetti: Selected Writings.* New York: Farrar, 1972. Print.

Perloff, Marjorie. *The Futurist Moment: Avant-Garde, Avant Guerre, and the Language of Rupture.* Chicago: U of Chicago P, 2003. Print.

Rainey, Lawrence S., Christine Poggi, and Laura Wittman. *Futurism: An Anthology.* New Haven: Yale UP, 2009. Print.

Taylor, Christiana J. *Futurism: Politics, Painting, and Performance.* Ann Arbor: UMI Research, 1979. Print.

Webster, Michael. *Reading Visual Poetry After Futurism: Marinetti, Apollinaire, Schwitters, Cummings.* New York: Lang, 1995. Print.

Lisa Barca

Thematic Outline

The thematic outline includes all volumes and chapters, in order, for the entire set of *The Literature of War*.

Volume 1

Approaches

Theories

The Art of War by Niccolò Machiavelli

The Art of War by Sun Tzu

"Civil Disobedience" by Henry David Thoreau

Guerrilla Warfare by Ernesto "Che" Guevara

On Guerrilla Warfare by Mao Zedong

On War by Carl von Clausewitz

Strategy by B. H. Liddell Hart

Histories

An Account, Much Abbreviated, of the Destruction of the Indies by Fray Bartolomé de las Casas

Backlands by Euclides da Cunha

Bloods by Wallace Houston Terry II

The Broken Spears by Miguel León-Portilla

The Civil War by Shelby Foote

The Crusades through Arab Eyes by Amin Maalouf

Eighteen Fifty-Seven by Surendra Nath Sen

Facundo by Domingo Faustino Sarmiento

Forty Miles a Day on Beans and Hay by Don Rickey Jr.

The Gallic War by Gaius Julius Caesar

Hiroshima by John Richard Hersey

The Histories by Herodotus

Histories by Tacitus

The History of the Peloponnesian War by Thucydides

The History of the Rebellion and Civil Wars in England, Begun in the Year 1641 by Edward Hyde

The Last of the Mohicans by James Fenimore Cooper

Mao's Generals Remember Korea by Xiaobing Li

Royal Commentaries of the Inca and General History of Peru by El Inca Garcilaso de laVega

Three Kingdoms by Luo Guanzhong

Eye-Witnessing

The Araucanaid by Alonso de Ercilla y Zúñiga

The Battle of Tomochic by Heriberto Frías

The Boer War Diary of Sol T. Plaatje by Solomon Tshekisho Plaatje

Cartucho and My Mother's Hands by Nellie Campobello

Decent Interval by Frank Snepp

Dispatches by Michael Herr

The Eagle and the Serpent by Martín Luis Guzmán

Echoes of Violence by Carolin Emcke

The Face of War by Martha Gellhorn

"Fireman Flower" by William Sansom

Homage to Catalonia by George Orwell

Man's Hope by André Malraux

Memory for Forgetfulness by Mahmoud Darwish

Nella Last's War by Nella Last

Requiem for Battleship Yamato by Yoshida Mitsuru

A Rumor of War by Philip Caputo

Russell's Despatches from the Crimea, 1854–1856 by William Howard Russell

A Small Corner of Hell by Anna Politkovskaya

Tales of Soldiers and Civilians by Ambrose Bierce

True History of the Conquest of New Spain by Bernal Díaz del Castillo

We Wish to Inform You That Tomorrow We Will Be Killed with Our Families by Philip Gourevitch

Zlata's Diary by Zlata Filipovic

Propaganda

The American Crisis by Thomas Paine

"Astraea Victrix," "The Transvaal," and "A Word for the Navy" by Algernon Charles Swinburne

What Price Glory? by Maxwell Anderson
World War I Poems by Wilfred Owen
Zinky Boys by Svetlana Alexievich

WOMEN AT WAR

And the Rain My Drink by Han Suyin
Destination Biafra by Buchi Emecheta
Don't Mean Nothing by Susan O'Neill
The Forbidden Zone by Mary Borden
Hospital Sketches by Louisa May Alcott
Iola Leroy by Frances Ellen Watkins Harper
Last Night I Dreamed of Peace by Đặng Thùy Trâm
Mary Chesnut's Civil War by Mary Boykin Chesnut
Mother Courage and Her Children by Bertolt Brecht
Mothers of the Revolution by Irene Staunton
Poems on Various Subjects Religious and Moral by Phillis Wheatley
Sitt Marie-Rose by Etel Adnan
Testament of Youth by Vera Brittain
Under Two Flags by Marie Louise de la Ramée
When Heaven and Earth Changed Places by Le Ly Hayslip
Wonderful Adventures of Mrs. Seacole in Many Lands by Mary Seacole

PRISONERS, REFUGEES, AND EXILES

Auschwitz and After by Charlotte Delbo
The Autobiography of a Runaway Slave by Miguel Barnet
The Complete Maus by Art Spiegelman
Days of Dust by Halim Barakat
Diary of a Young Girl by Anne Frank
The Enormous Room by e. e. cummings
Fatelessness by Imre Kertész
First They Killed My Father by Loung Ung
The Great Escape by Paul Brickhill
If This Is a Man by Primo Levi
Journey into the Whirlwind by Eugenia Ginzburg
Night by Elie Wiesel
No-No Boy by John Okada
Nowhere Man by Aleksandar Hemon
The Prison Poems by Miguel Hernández
Returning to Haifa by Ghassan Kanafani
Scatter the Ashes and Go by Mongane Wally Serote
Schindler's List by Thomas Michael Keneally
The Sovereignty and Goodness of God by Mary White Rowlandson
Tamas by Bhisham Sahni
This Way for the Gas, Ladies and Gentlemen; and Other Stories by Tadeusz Borowski
War Trash by Ha Jin

THE HOME FRONT

All Our Yesterdays by Natalia Ginzburg
Barefoot Gen by Keiji Nakazawa
Comedy in a Minor Key by Hans Keilson
The Girls of Slender Means by Muriel Spark
The Linwoods by Catharine Maria Sedgwick
"Meditations in Time of Civil War" by William Butler Yeats
A Night in May by A. B. Yehoshua
"The Rainy Spell" by Yoon Heung-gil
The Sea and Poison by Endō Shūsaku

CHANGE

Blue Dragon, White Tiger by Dinh Van Tran
The Campaign by Carlos Fuentes
Co. Aytch by Samuel Rush Watkins
Explosion in a Cathedral by Alejo Carpentier
The Forever War by Dexter Filkins
The General in His Labyrinth by Gabriel García Márquez
Girls at War and Other Stories by Chinua Achebe
A Grain of Wheat by Ngugi Thiong'o
Harry Gold by Millicent Dillon
The Insurrection by Antonio Skármeta
The Killer Angels by Michael Shaara
"Lessons of the War" by Henry Reed
The Long Song by Andrea Levy
The March by E. L. Doctorow
Persepolis by Marjane Satrapi
The Quiet American by Henry Graham Greene
The Sun Shines over the Sanggan River by Ling Ding
Tamburlaine the Great by Christopher Marlowe
Under the Yoke by Ivan Minchov Vazov
The Underdogs by Mariano Azuela
Wolf Dreams by Yasmina Khadra

VOLUME 3

IMPACTS

THE BODY

Black Rain by Masuji Ibuse
Born on the Fourth of July by Ron Kovic
Drum-Taps by Walt Whitman
Johnny Got His Gun by Dalton Trumbo
The Stone Virgins by Yvonne Vera

THE MIND

Afterwards by Rachel Seiffert
Battle-Pieces and Aspects of the War by Herman Melville
Ceremony by Leslie Marmon Silko

Clive of India by Mark Bence-Jones
Epic of Sunjata
Epitaphs of the War by Rudyard Kipling
"For the Fallen" by Laurence Binyon
Granada by Radwa Ashour
Mahābhārata

Malvinas Requiem by Rodolfo Enrique Fogwill
"Monody on Major André" by Anna Seward
My Grandmother by Fethiye Çetin
Son of Man by Augusto Roa Bastos
Spain in Our Hearts by Pablo Neruda
"Today I Invoke Waris Shah" by Amrita Pritam

CHRONOLOGY

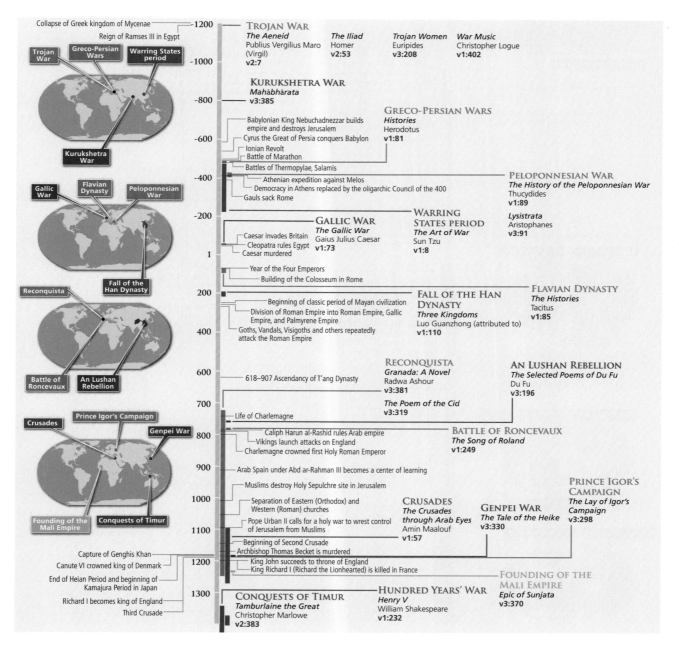

Collapse of Greek kingdom of Mycenae
Reign of Ramses III in Egypt

Trojan War
Greco-Persian Wars
Warring States period

Kurukshetra War

Gallic War
Flavian Dynasty
Peloponnesian War

Reconquista
Fall of the Han Dynasty

Battle of Roncevaux
An Lushan Rebellion

Crusades
Prince Igor's Campaign
Genpei War

Founding of the Mali Empire
Conquests of Timur

-1200

TROJAN WAR
The Aeneid
Publius Vergilius Maro
(Virgil)
v2:7

The Iliad
Homer
v2:53

Trojan Women
Euripides
v3:208

War Music
Christopher Logue
v1:402

-1000

KURUKSHETRA WAR
Mahābhārata
v3:385

-800

GRECO-PERSIAN WARS
Histories
Herodotus
v1:81

Babylonian King Nebuchadnezzar builds empire and destroys Jerusalem
Cyrus the Great of Persia conquers Babylon
Ionian Revolt
Battle of Marathon
Battles of Thermopylae, Salamis

-600

PELOPONNESIAN WAR
The History of the Peloponnesian War
Thucydides
v1:89

Athenian expedition against Melos
Democracy in Athens replaced by the oligarchic Council of the 400
Gauls sack Rome

-400

GALLIC WAR
The Gallic War
Gaius Julius Caesar
v1:73

WARRING STATES PERIOD
The Art of War
Sun Tzu
v1:8

Lysistrata
Aristophanes
v3:91

-200

Caesar invades Britain
Cleopatra rules Egypt
Caesar murdered

1

Year of the Four Emperors
Building of the Colosseum in Rome

200

FALL OF THE HAN DYNASTY
Three Kingdoms
Luo Guanzhong (attributed to)
v1:110

FLAVIAN DYNASTY
The Histories
Tacitus
v1:85

Beginning of classic period of Mayan civilization
Division of Roman Empire into Roman Empire, Gallic Empire, and Palmyrene Empire
Goths, Vandals, Visigoths and others repeatedly attack the Roman Empire

400

RECONQUISTA
Granada: A Novel
Radwa Ashour
v3:381

AN LUSHAN REBELLION
The Selected Poems of Du Fu
Du Fu
v3:196

600

618–907 Ascendancy of T'ang Dynasty

The Poem of the Cid
v3:319

700

Life of Charlemagne

BATTLE OF RONCEVAUX
The Song of Roland
v1:249

800

Caliph Harun al-Rashid rules Arab empire
Vikings launch attacks on England
Charlemagne crowned first Holy Roman Emperor

900

Arab Spain under Abd ar-Rahman III becomes a center of learning

PRINCE IGOR'S CAMPAIGN
The Lay of Igor's Campaign
v3:298

Muslims destroy Holy Sepulchre site in Jerusalem

1000

CRUSADES
The Crusades through Arab Eyes
Amin Maalouf
v1:57

GENPEI WAR
The Tale of the Heike
v3:330

Separation of Eastern (Orthodox) and Western (Roman) churches
Pope Urban II calls for a holy war to wrest control of Jerusalem from Muslims

1100

Beginning of Second Crusade
Archbishop Thomas Becket is murdered

Capture of Genghis Khan
Canute VI crowned king of Denmark

1200

King John succeeds to throne of England
King Richard I (Richard the Lionhearted) is killed in France

FOUNDING OF THE MALI EMPIRE
Epic of Sunjata
v3:370

End of Heian Period and beginning of Kamajura Period in Japan
Richard I becomes king of England
Third Crusade

1300

HUNDRED YEARS' WAR
Henry V
William Shakespeare
v1:232

CONQUESTS OF TIMUR
Tamburlaine the Great
Christopher Marlowe
v2:383

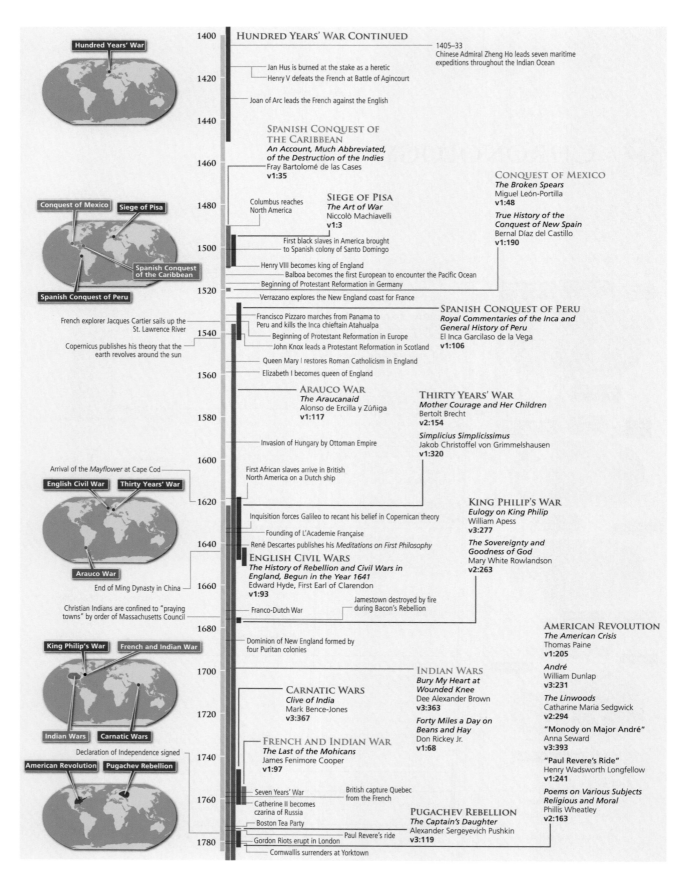

Hundred Years' War

Conquest of Mexico | Siege of Pisa

Spanish Conquest of the Caribbean

Spanish Conquest of Peru

French explorer Jacques Cartier sails up the St. Lawrence River

Copernicus publishes his theory that the earth revolves around the sun

Arrival of the *Mayflower* at Cape Cod

English Civil War | Thirty Years' War

Arauco War

King Philip's War | French and Indian War

Indian Wars | Carnatic Wars

American Revolution | Pugachev Rebellion

1400 — HUNDRED YEARS' WAR CONTINUED

1405–33
Chinese Admiral Zheng Ho leads seven maritime expeditions throughout the Indian Ocean

1420
— Jan Hus is burned at the stake as a heretic
— Henry V defeats the French at Battle of Agincourt

— Joan of Arc leads the French against the English

1440

SPANISH CONQUEST OF THE CARIBBEAN
An Account, Much Abbreviated, of the Destruction of the Indies
Fray Bartolomé de las Cases
v1:35

1460

CONQUEST OF MEXICO
The Broken Spears
Miguel León-Portilla
v1:48

SIEGE OF PISA
The Art of War
Niccolò Machiavelli
v1:3

1480
Columbus reaches North America

True History of the Conquest of New Spain
Bernal Díaz del Castillo
v1:190

— First black slaves in America brought to Spanish colony of Santo Domingo

1500
— Henry VIII becomes king of England
— Balboa becomes the first European to encounter the Pacific Ocean
— Beginning of Protestant Reformation in Germany

1520
— Verrazano explores the New England coast for France

SPANISH CONQUEST OF PERU
Royal Commentaries of the Inca and General History of Peru
El Inca Garcilaso de la Vega
v1:106

— Francisco Pizarro marches from Panama to Peru and kills the Inca chieftain Atahualpa

1540
— Beginning of Protestant Reformation in Europe
— John Knox leads a Protestant Reformation in Scotland

— Queen Mary I restores Roman Catholicism in England
— Elizabeth I becomes queen of England

1560

ARAUCO WAR
The Araucanaid
Alonso de Ercilla y Zúñiga
v1:117

THIRTY YEARS' WAR
Mother Courage and Her Children
Bertolt Brecht
v2:154

1580

— Invasion of Hungary by Ottoman Empire

Simplicius Simplicissimus
Jakob Christoffel von Grimmelshausen
v1:320

1600
First African slaves arrive in British North America on a Dutch ship

1620

KING PHILIP'S WAR
Eulogy on King Philip
William Apess
v3:277

— Inquisition forces Galileo to recant his belief in Copernican theory

— Founding of L'Academie Française
— René Descartes publishes his *Meditations on First Philosophy*

The Sovereignty and Goodness of God
Mary White Rowlandson
v2:263

ENGLISH CIVIL WARS
The History of Rebellion and Civil Wars in England, Begun in the Year 1641
Edward Hyde, First Earl of Clarendon
v1:93

— End of Ming Dynasty in China
1660

— Franco-Dutch War

— Jamestown destroyed by fire during Bacon's Rebellion

Christian Indians are confined to "praying towns" by order of Massachusetts Council

1680

AMERICAN REVOLUTION
The American Crisis
Thomas Paine
v1:205

— Dominion of New England formed by four Puritan colonies

1700

INDIAN WARS
Bury My Heart at Wounded Knee
Dee Alexander Brown
v3:363

André
William Dunlap
v3:231

CARNATIC WARS
Clive of India
Mark Bence-Jones
v3:367

The Linwoods
Catharine Maria Sedgwick
v2:294

1720

Forty Miles a Day on Beans and Hay
Don Rickey Jr.
v1:68

"Monody on Major André"
Anna Seward
v3:393

FRENCH AND INDIAN WAR
The Last of the Mohicans
James Fenimore Cooper
v1:97

"Paul Revere's Ride"
Henry Wadsworth Longfellow
v1:241

1740

Poems on Various Subjects Religious and Moral
Phillis Wheatley
v2:163

— Seven Years' War
— British capture Quebec from the French
1760
— Catherine II becomes czarina of Russia
— Boston Tea Party

PUGACHEV REBELLION
The Captain's Daughter
Alexander Sergeyevich Pushkin
v3:119

— Paul Revere's ride
— Gordon Riots erupt in London
1780
— Cornwallis surrenders at Yorktown

Declaration of Independence signed

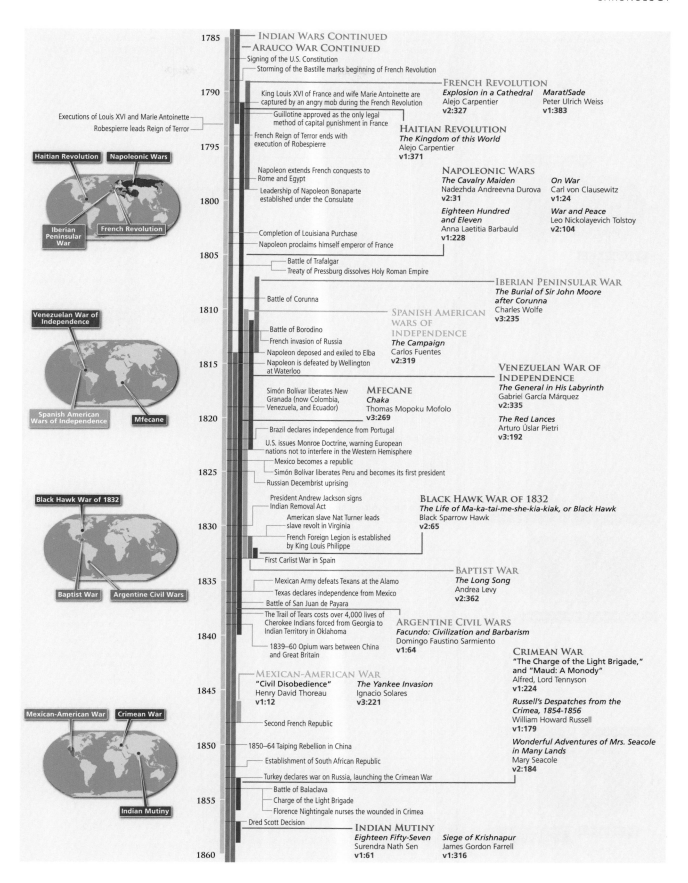

1785
INDIAN WARS CONTINUED
ARAUCO WAR CONTINUED
Signing of the U.S. Constitution
Storming of the Bastille marks beginning of French Revolution

FRENCH REVOLUTION
Explosion in a Cathedral   *Marat/Sade*
Alejo Carpentier   Peter Ulrich Weiss
v2:327   **v1:383**

1790
King Louis XVI of France and wife Marie Antoinette are
captured by an angry mob during the French Revolution
Guillotine approved as the only legal
method of capital punishment in France

HAITIAN REVOLUTION
The Kingdom of this World
Alejo Carpentier
v1:371

Executions of Louis XVI and Marie Antoinette
Robespierre leads Reign of Terror

1795
French Reign of Terror ends with
execution of Robespierre

Haitian Revolution   Napoleonic Wars

NAPOLEONIC WARS
The Cavalry Maiden   *On War*
Nadezhda Andreevna Durova   Carl von Clausewitz
v2:31   **v1:24**

Napoleon extends French conquests to
Rome and Egypt
Leadership of Napoleon Bonaparte
established under the Consulate

1800
Eighteen Hundred   *War and Peace*
and Eleven   Leo Nickolayevich Tolstoy
Anna Laetitia Barbauld   **v2:104**
v1:228

Iberian
Peninsular   French Revolution
War

Completion of Louisiana Purchase
Napoleon proclaims himself emperor of France

1805
Battle of Trafalgar
Treaty of Pressburg dissolves Holy Roman Empire

IBERIAN PENINSULAR WAR
The Burial of Sir John Moore
after Corunna
Charles Wolfe
v3:235

Battle of Corunna

1810
Venezuelan War of
Independence

SPANISH AMERICAN
WARS OF
INDEPENDENCE
The Campaign
Carlos Fuentes
v2:319

Battle of Borodino
French invasion of Russia
Napoleon deposed and exiled to Elba
Napoleon is defeated by Wellington
at Waterloo

1815
VENEZUELAN WAR OF
INDEPENDENCE
The General in His Labyrinth
Gabriel García Márquez
v2:335

Simón Bolívar liberates New
Granada (now Colombia,
Venezuela, and Ecuador)

MFECANE
Chaka
Thomas Mopoku Mofolo
v3:269

The Red Lances
Arturo Úslar Pietri
v3:192

Spanish American
Wars of Independence   Mfecane

1820
Brazil declares independence from Portugal
U.S. issues Monroe Doctrine, warning European
nations not to interfere in the Western Hemisphere
Mexico becomes a republic

1825
Simón Bolívar liberates Peru and becomes its first president
Russian Decembrist uprising

President Andrew Jackson signs
Indian Removal Act

Black Hawk War of 1832

BLACK HAWK WAR OF 1832
The Life of Ma-ka-tai-me-she-kia-kiak, or Black Hawk
Black Sparrow Hawk
v2:65

American slave Nat Turner leads
slave revolt in Virginia

1830
French Foreign Legion is established
by King Louis Philippe
First Carlist War in Spain

BAPTIST WAR
The Long Song
Andrea Levy
v2:362

1835
Mexican Army defeats Texans at the Alamo
Texas declares independence from Mexico
Battle of San Juan de Payara

Baptist War   Argentine Civil Wars

The Trail of Tears costs over 4,000 lives of
Cherokee Indians forced from Georgia to
Indian Territory in Oklahoma

ARGENTINE CIVIL WARS
Facundo: Civilization and Barbarism
Domingo Faustino Sarmiento
v1:64

1840
1839–60 Opium wars between China
and Great Britain

CRIMEAN WAR
"The Charge of the Light Brigade,"
and "Maud: A Monody"
Alfred, Lord Tennyson
v1:224

MEXICAN-AMERICAN WAR
"Civil Disobedience"   *The Yankee Invasion*
Henry David Thoreau   Ignacio Solares
v1:12   **v3:221**

Russell's Despatches from the
Crimea, 1854-1856
William Howard Russell
v1:179

1845
Mexican-American War   Crimean War

Second French Republic

Wonderful Adventures of Mrs. Seacole
in Many Lands
Mary Seacole
v2:184

1850
1850–64 Taiping Rebellion in China
Establishment of South African Republic
Turkey declares war on Russia, launching the Crimean War

1855
Battle of Balaclava
Charge of the Light Brigade
Florence Nightingale nurses the wounded in Crimea
Dred Scott Decision

Indian Mutiny

INDIAN MUTINY
Eighteen Fifty-Seven   *Siege of Krishnapur*
Surendra Nath Sen   James Gordon Farrell
v1:61   **v1:316**

1860

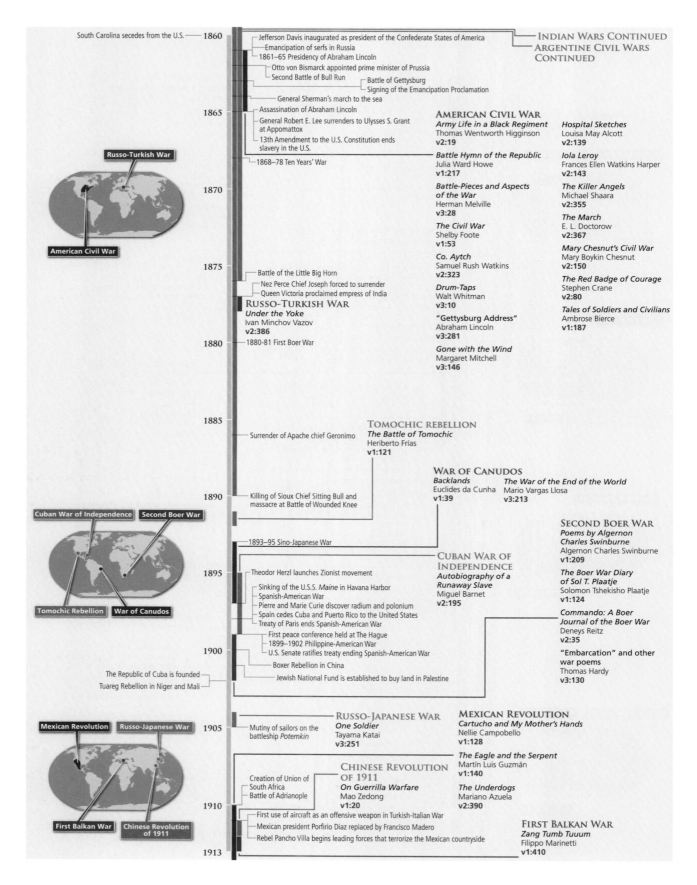

South Carolina secedes from the U.S. — **1860**

Jefferson Davis inaugurated as president of the Confederate States of America
Emancipation of serfs in Russia
1861–65 Presidency of Abraham Lincoln
Otto von Bismarck appointed prime minister of Prussia
Second Battle of Bull Run
Battle of Gettysburg
Signing of the Emancipation Proclamation

General Sherman's march to the sea

1865
Assassination of Abraham Lincoln
General Robert E. Lee surrenders to Ulysses S. Grant at Appomattox
13th Amendment to the U.S. Constitution ends slavery in the U.S.

1868–78 Ten Years' War

1870

1875
Battle of the Little Big Horn
Nez Perce Chief Joseph forced to surrender
Queen Victoria proclaimed empress of India

1880
1880-81 First Boer War

1885
Surrender of Apache chief Geronimo

1890
Killing of Sioux Chief Sitting Bull and massacre at Battle of Wounded Knee

1893–95 Sino-Japanese War

1895
Theodor Herzl launches Zionist movement
Sinking of the U.S.S. *Maine* in Havana Harbor
Spanish-American War
Pierre and Marie Curie discover radium and polonium
Spain cedes Cuba and Puerto Rico to the United States
Treaty of Paris ends Spanish-American War
First peace conference held at The Hague
1899–1902 Philippine-American War
U.S. Senate ratifies treaty ending Spanish-American War
Boxer Rebellion in China

1900
The Republic of Cuba is founded
Tuareg Rebellion in Niger and Mali
Jewish National Fund is established to buy land in Palestine

1905
Mutiny of sailors on the battleship *Potemkin*

Creation of Union of South Africa
Battle of Adrianople

1910
First use of aircraft as an offensive weapon in Turkish-Italian War
Mexican president Porfirio Diaz replaced by Francisco Madero
Rebel Pancho Villa begins leading forces that terrorize the Mexican countryside

1913

INDIAN WARS CONTINUED
ARGENTINE CIVIL WARS CONTINUED

AMERICAN CIVIL WAR

Army Life in a Black Regiment
Thomas Wentworth Higginson
v2:19

Battle Hymn of the Republic
Julia Ward Howe
v1:217

Battle-Pieces and Aspects of the War
Herman Melville
v3:28

The Civil War
Shelby Foote
v1:53

Co. Aytch
Samuel Rush Watkins
v2:323

Drum-Taps
Walt Whitman
v3:10

"Gettysburg Address"
Abraham Lincoln
v3:281

Gone with the Wind
Margaret Mitchell
v3:146

Hospital Sketches
Louisa May Alcott
v2:139

Iola Leroy
Frances Ellen Watkins Harper
v2:143

The Killer Angels
Michael Shaara
v2:355

The March
E. L. Doctorow
v2:367

Mary Chesnut's Civil War
Mary Boykin Chesnut
v2:150

The Red Badge of Courage
Stephen Crane
v2:80

Tales of Soldiers and Civilians
Ambrose Bierce
v1:187

RUSSO-TURKISH WAR

Under the Yoke
Ivan Minchov Vazov
v2:386

TOMOCHIC REBELLION

The Battle of Tomochic
Heriberto Frías
v1:121

WAR OF CANUDOS

Backlands
Euclides da Cunha
v1:39

The War of the End of the World
Mario Vargas Llosa
v3:213

SECOND BOER WAR

Poems by Algernon Charles Swinburne
Algernon Charles Swinburne
v1:209

The Boer War Diary of Sol T. Plaatje
Solomon Tshekisho Plaatje
v1:124

Commando: A Boer Journal of the Boer War
Deneys Reitz
v2:35

"Embarcation" and other war poems
Thomas Hardy
v3:130

RUSSO-JAPANESE WAR

One Soldier
Tayama Katai
v3:251

MEXICAN REVOLUTION

Cartucho and My Mother's Hands
Nellie Campobello
v1:128

The Eagle and the Serpent
Martín Luis Guzmán
v1:140

The Underdogs
Mariano Azuela
v2:390

CHINESE REVOLUTION OF 1911

On Guerrilla Warfare
Mao Zedong
v1:20

CUBAN WAR OF INDEPENDENCE

Autobiography of a Runaway Slave
Miguel Barnet
v2:195

FIRST BALKAN WAR

Zang Tumb Tuuum
Filippo Marinetti
v1:410

Russo-Turkish War
American Civil War

Cuban War of Independence
Second Boer War
Tomochic Rebellion
War of Canudos

Mexican Revolution
Russo-Japanese War
First Balkan War
Chinese Revolution of 1911

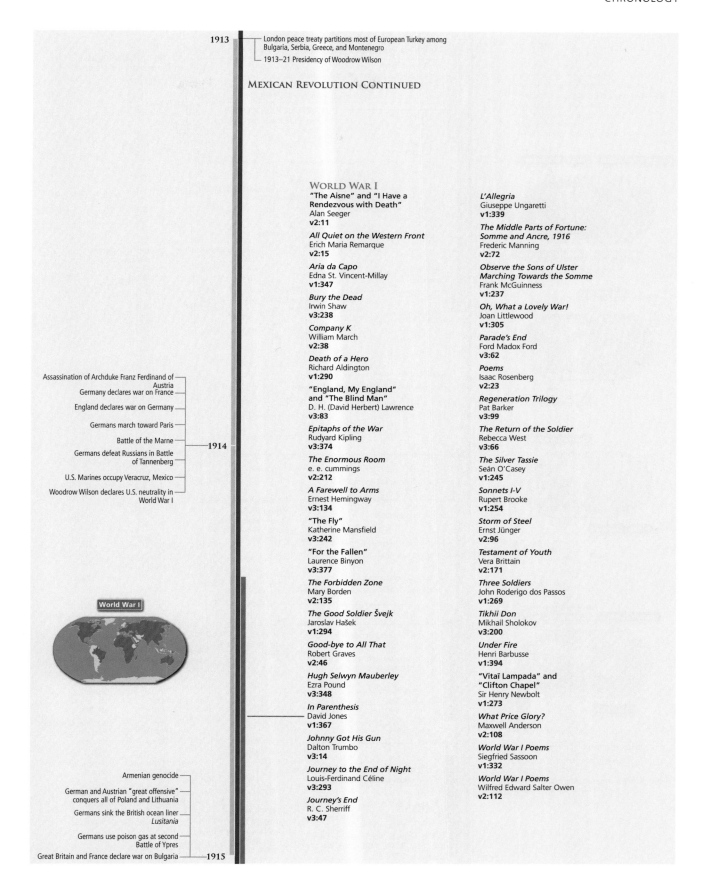

1913 — London peace treaty partitions most of European Turkey among Bulgaria, Serbia, Greece, and Montenegro
— 1913–21 Presidency of Woodrow Wilson

MEXICAN REVOLUTION CONTINUED

Assassination of Archduke Franz Ferdinand of Austria
Germany declares war on France
England declares war on Germany
Germans march toward Paris
Battle of the Marne
Germans defeat Russians in Battle of Tannenberg
U.S. Marines occupy Veracruz, Mexico
Woodrow Wilson declares U.S. neutrality in World War I

1914

World War I

Armenian genocide
German and Austrian "great offensive" conquers all of Poland and Lithuania
Germans sink the British ocean liner *Lusitania*
Germans use poison gas at second Battle of Ypres
Great Britain and France declare war on Bulgaria

1915

WORLD WAR I

"The Aisne" and "I Have a Rendezvous with Death"
Alan Seeger
v2:11

All Quiet on the Western Front
Erich Maria Remarque
v2:15

Aria da Capo
Edna St. Vincent-Millay
v1:347

Bury the Dead
Irwin Shaw
v3:238

Company K
William March
v2:38

Death of a Hero
Richard Aldington
v1:290

"England, My England" and "The Blind Man"
D. H. (David Herbert) Lawrence
v3:83

Epitaphs of the War
Rudyard Kipling
v3:374

The Enormous Room
e. e. cummings
v2:212

A Farewell to Arms
Ernest Hemingway
v3:134

"The Fly"
Katherine Mansfield
v3:242

"For the Fallen"
Laurence Binyon
v3:377

The Forbidden Zone
Mary Borden
v2:135

The Good Soldier Švejk
Jaroslav Hašek
v1:294

Good-bye to All That
Robert Graves
v2:46

Hugh Selwyn Mauberley
Ezra Pound
v3:348

In Parenthesis
David Jones
v1:367

Johnny Got His Gun
Dalton Trumbo
v3:14

Journey to the End of Night
Louis-Ferdinand Céline
v3:293

Journey's End
R. C. Sherriff
v3:47

L'Allegria
Giuseppe Ungaretti
v1:339

The Middle Parts of Fortune: Somme and Ancre, 1916
Frederic Manning
v2:72

Observe the Sons of Ulster Marching Towards the Somme
Frank McGuinness
v1:237

Oh, What a Lovely War!
Joan Littlewood
v1:305

Parade's End
Ford Madox Ford
v3:62

Poems
Isaac Rosenberg
v2:23

Regeneration Trilogy
Pat Barker
v3:99

The Return of the Soldier
Rebecca West
v3:66

The Silver Tassie
Seán O'Casey
v1:245

Sonnets I–V
Rupert Brooke
v1:254

Storm of Steel
Ernst Jünger
v2:96

Testament of Youth
Vera Brittain
v2:171

Three Soldiers
John Roderigo dos Passos
v1:269

Tikhii Don
Mikhail Sholokov
v3:200

Under Fire
Henri Barbusse
v1:394

"Vitaï Lampada" and "Clifton Chapel"
Sir Henry Newbolt
v1:273

What Price Glory?
Maxwell Anderson
v2:108

World War I Poems
Siegfried Sassoon
v1:332

World War I Poems
Wilfred Edward Salter Owen
v2:112

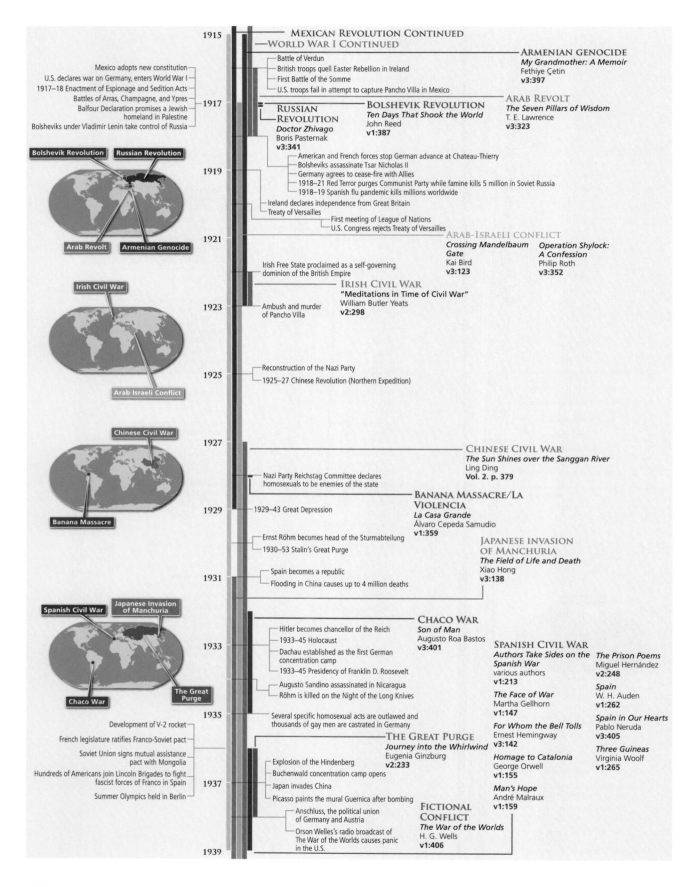

1915

MEXICAN REVOLUTION CONTINUED
WORLD WAR I CONTINUED

Mexico adopts new constitution
U.S. declares war on Germany, enters World War I
1917–18 Enactment of Espionage and Sedition Acts
Battles of Arras, Champagne, and Ypres
Balfour Declaration promises a Jewish
homeland in Palestine
Bolsheviks under Vladimir Lenin take control of Russia

Battle of Verdun
British troops quell Easter Rebellion in Ireland
First Battle of the Somme
U.S. troops fail in attempt to capture Pancho Villa in Mexico

1917

ARMENIAN GENOCIDE
My Grandmother: A Memoir
Fethiye Çetin
v3:397

ARAB REVOLT
The Seven Pillars of Wisdom
T. E. Lawrence
v3:323

RUSSIAN
REVOLUTION
Doctor Zhivago
Boris Pasternak
v3:341

BOLSHEVIK REVOLUTION
Ten Days That Shook the World
John Reed
v1:387

Bolshevik Revolution   Russian Revolution

1919

American and French forces stop German advance at Chateau-Thierry
Bolsheviks assassinate Tsar Nicholas II
Germany agrees to cease-fire with Allies
1918–21 Red Terror purges Communist Party while famine kills 5 million in Soviet Russia
1918–19 Spanish flu pandemic kills millions worldwide
Ireland declares independence from Great Britain
Treaty of Versailles
First meeting of League of Nations
U.S. Congress rejects Treaty of Versailles

Arab Revolt   Armenian Genocide

1921

ARAB-ISRAELI CONFLICT
Crossing Mandelbaum Gate
Kai Bird
v3:123

Operation Shylock: A Confession
Philip Roth
v3:352

Irish Free State proclaimed as a self-governing
dominion of the British Empire

Irish Civil War

IRISH CIVIL WAR
"Meditations in Time of Civil War"
William Butler Yeats
v2:298

1923

Ambush and murder
of Pancho Villa

Arab Israeli Conflict

1925

Reconstruction of the Nazi Party
1925–27 Chinese Revolution (Northern Expedition)

Chinese Civil War

1927

CHINESE CIVIL WAR
The Sun Shines over the Sanggan River
Ling Ding
Vol. 2. p. 379

Nazi Party Reichstag Committee declares
homosexuals to be enemies of the state

BANANA MASSACRE/LA
VIOLENCIA
La Casa Grande
Álvaro Cepeda Samudio
v1:359

1929

1929–43 Great Depression

Banana Massacre

Ernst Röhm becomes head of the Sturmabteilung
1930–53 Stalin's Great Purge

JAPANESE INVASION
OF MANCHURIA
The Field of Life and Death
Xiao Hong
v3:138

1931

Spain becomes a republic
Flooding in China causes up to 4 million deaths

Spanish Civil War   Japanese Invasion
of Manchuria

CHACO WAR
Son of Man
Augusto Roa Bastos
v3:401

Hitler becomes chancellor of the Reich
1933–45 Holocaust
Dachau established as the first German
concentration camp
1933–45 Presidency of Franklin D. Roosevelt
Augusto Sandino assassinated in Nicaragua
Röhm is killed on the Night of the Long Knives

1933

SPANISH CIVIL WAR
Authors Take Sides on the Spanish War
various authors
v1:213

The Face of War
Martha Gellhorn
v1:147

For Whom the Bell Tolls
Ernest Hemingway
v3:142

Homage to Catalonia
George Orwell
v1:155

Man's Hope
André Malraux
v1:159

The Prison Poems
Miguel Hernández
v2:248

Spain
W. H. Auden
v1:262

Spain in Our Hearts
Pablo Neruda
v3:405

Three Guineas
Virginia Woolf
v1:265

Chaco War   The Great
Purge

1935

Development of V-2 rocket
French legislature ratifies Franco-Soviet pact
Soviet Union signs mutual assistance
pact with Mongolia
Hundreds of Americans join Lincoln Brigades to fight
fascist forces of Franco in Spain
Summer Olympics held in Berlin

Several specific homosexual acts are outlawed and
thousands of gay men are castrated in Germany

THE GREAT PURGE
Journey into the Whirlwind
Eugenia Ginzburg
v2:233

Explosion of the Hindenberg
Buchenwald concentration camp opens
Japan invades China
Picasso paints the mural Guernica after bombing

1937

Anschluss, the political union
of Germany and Austria
Orson Welles's radio broadcast of
The War of the Worlds causes panic
in the U.S.

FICTIONAL
CONFLICT
The War of the Worlds
H. G. Wells
v1:406

1939

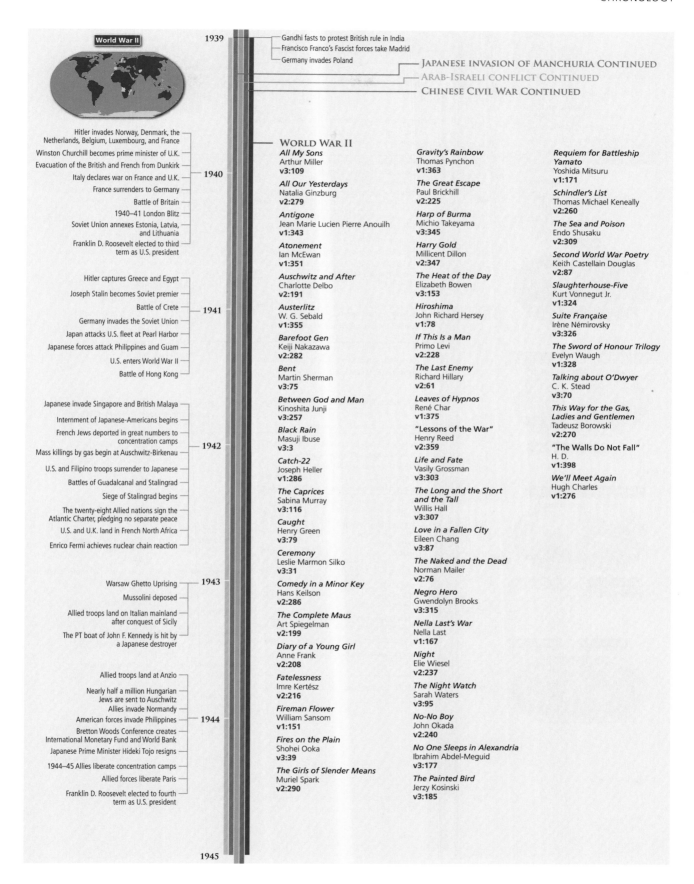

World War II

1939
- Gandhi fasts to protest British rule in India
- Francisco Franco's Fascist forces take Madrid
- Germany invades Poland

JAPANESE INVASION OF MANCHURIA CONTINUED
ARAB-ISRAELI CONFLICT CONTINUED
CHINESE CIVIL WAR CONTINUED

Hitler invades Norway, Denmark, the Netherlands, Belgium, Luxembourg, and France
Winston Churchill becomes prime minister of U.K.
Evacuation of the British and French from Dunkirk
Italy declares war on France and U.K.
France surrenders to Germany
Battle of Britain
1940–41 London Blitz
Soviet Union annexes Estonia, Latvia, and Lithuania
Franklin D. Roosevelt elected to third term as U.S. president

1940

Hitler captures Greece and Egypt
Joseph Stalin becomes Soviet premier
Battle of Crete
Germany invades the Soviet Union
Japan attacks U.S. fleet at Pearl Harbor
Japanese forces attack Philippines and Guam
U.S. enters World War II
Battle of Hong Kong

1941

Japanese invade Singapore and British Malaya
Internment of Japanese-Americans begins
French Jews deported in great numbers to concentration camps
Mass killings by gas begin at Auschwitz-Birkenau
U.S. and Filipino troops surrender to Japanese
Battles of Guadalcanal and Stalingrad
Siege of Stalingrad begins
The twenty-eight Allied nations sign the Atlantic Charter, pledging no separate peace
U.S. and U.K. land in French North Africa
Enrico Fermi achieves nuclear chain reaction

1942

Warsaw Ghetto Uprising
Mussolini deposed
Allied troops land on Italian mainland after conquest of Sicily
The PT boat of John F. Kennedy is hit by a Japanese destroyer

1943

Allied troops land at Anzio
Nearly half a million Hungarian Jews are sent to Auschwitz
Allies invade Normandy
American forces invade Philippines
Bretton Woods Conference creates International Monetary Fund and World Bank
Japanese Prime Minister Hideki Tojo resigns
1944–45 Allies liberate concentration camps
Allied forces liberate Paris
Franklin D. Roosevelt elected to fourth term as U.S. president

1944

1945

WORLD WAR II

All My Sons
Arthur Miller
v3:109

All Our Yesterdays
Natalia Ginzburg
v2:279

Antigone
Jean Marie Lucien Pierre Anouilh
v1:343

Atonement
Ian McEwan
v1:351

Auschwitz and After
Charlotte Delbo
v2:191

Austerlitz
W. G. Sebald
v1:355

Barefoot Gen
Keiji Nakazawa
v2:282

Bent
Martin Sherman
v3:75

Between God and Man
Kinoshita Junji
v3:257

Black Rain
Masuji Ibuse
v3:3

Catch-22
Joseph Heller
v1:286

The Caprices
Sabina Murray
v3:116

Caught
Henry Green
v3:79

Ceremony
Leslie Marmon Silko
v3:31

Comedy in a Minor Key
Hans Keilson
v2:286

The Complete Maus
Art Spiegelman
v2:199

Diary of a Young Girl
Anne Frank
v2:208

Fatelessness
Imre Kertész
v2:216

Fireman Flower
William Sansom
v1:151

Fires on the Plain
Shohei Ooka
v3:39

The Girls of Slender Means
Muriel Spark
v2:290

Gravity's Rainbow
Thomas Pynchon
v1:363

The Great Escape
Paul Brickhill
v2:225

Harp of Burma
Michio Takeyama
v3:345

Harry Gold
Millicent Dillon
v2:347

The Heat of the Day
Elizabeth Bowen
v3:153

Hiroshima
John Richard Hersey
v1:78

If This Is a Man
Primo Levi
v2:228

The Last Enemy
Richard Hillary
v2:61

Leaves of Hypnos
René Char
v1:375

"Lessons of the War"
Henry Reed
v2:359

Life and Fate
Vasily Grossman
v3:303

The Long and the Short and the Tall
Willis Hall
v3:307

Love in a Fallen City
Eileen Chang
v3:87

The Naked and the Dead
Norman Mailer
v2:76

Negro Hero
Gwendolyn Brooks
v3:315

Nella Last's War
Nella Last
v1:167

Night
Elie Wiesel
v2:237

The Night Watch
Sarah Waters
v3:95

No-No Boy
John Okada
v2:240

No One Sleeps in Alexandria
Ibrahim Abdel-Meguid
v3:177

The Painted Bird
Jerzy Kosinski
v3:185

Requiem for Battleship Yamato
Yoshida Mitsuru
v1:171

Schindler's List
Thomas Michael Keneally
v2:260

The Sea and Poison
Endo Shusaku
v2:309

Second World War Poetry
Keith Castellain Douglas
v2:87

Slaughterhouse-Five
Kurt Vonnegut Jr.
v1:324

Suite Française
Irène Némirovsky
v3:326

The Sword of Honour Trilogy
Evelyn Waugh
v1:328

Talking about O'Dwyer
C. K. Stead
v3:70

This Way for the Gas, Ladies and Gentlemen
Tadeusz Borowski
v2:270

"The Walls Do Not Fall"
H. D.
v1:398

We'll Meet Again
Hugh Charles
v1:276

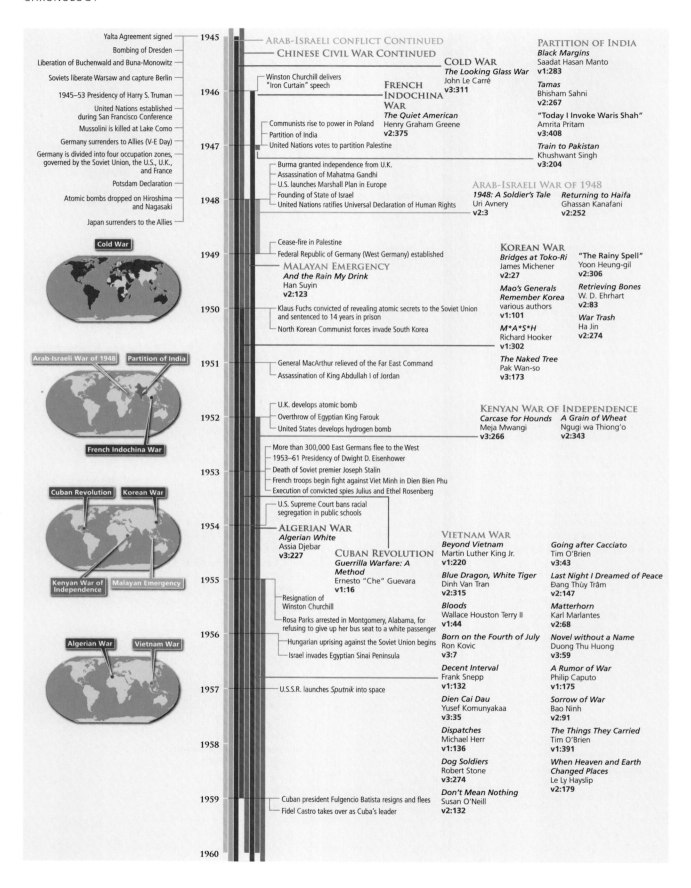

1945
- Yalta Agreement signed
- Bombing of Dresden
- Liberation of Buchenwald and Buna-Monowitz
- Soviets liberate Warsaw and capture Berlin

1946
- 1945–53 Presidency of Harry S. Truman
- United Nations established during San Francisco Conference
- Mussolini is killed at Lake Como
- Germany surrenders to Allies (V-E Day)

1947
- Germany is divided into four occupation zones, governed by the Soviet Union, the U.S., U.K., and France
- Potsdam Declaration

1948
- Atomic bombs dropped on Hiroshima and Nagasaki
- Japan surrenders to the Allies

Cold War

Arab-Israeli War of 1948 | **Partition of India**

French Indochina War

Cuban Revolution | **Korean War**

Kenyan War of Independence | **Malayan Emergency**

Algerian War | **Vietnam War**

ARAB-ISRAELI CONFLICT CONTINUED
CHINESE CIVIL WAR CONTINUED

- Winston Churchill delivers "Iron Curtain" speech
- Communists rise to power in Poland
- Partition of India
- United Nations votes to partition Palestine
- Burma granted independence from U.K.
- Assassination of Mahatma Gandhi
- U.S. launches Marshall Plan in Europe
- Founding of State of Israel
- United Nations ratifies Universal Declaration of Human Rights
- Cease-fire in Palestine
- Federal Republic of Germany (West Germany) established

MALAYAN EMERGENCY
- Klaus Fuchs convicted of revealing atomic secrets to the Soviet Union and sentenced to 14 years in prison
- North Korean Communist forces invade South Korea
- General MacArthur relieved of the Far East Command
- Assassination of King Abdullah I of Jordan
- U.K. develops atomic bomb
- Overthrow of Egyptian King Farouk
- United States develops hydrogen bomb
- More than 300,000 East Germans flee to the West
- 1953–61 Presidency of Dwight D. Eisenhower
- Death of Soviet premier Joseph Stalin
- French troops begin fight against Viet Minh in Dien Bien Phu
- Execution of convicted spies Julius and Ethel Rosenberg
- U.S. Supreme Court bans racial segregation in public schools

ALGERIAN WAR

CUBAN REVOLUTION
- Resignation of Winston Churchill
- Rosa Parks arrested in Montgomery, Alabama, for refusing to give up her bus seat to a white passenger
- Hungarian uprising against the Soviet Union begins
- Israel invades Egyptian Sinai Peninsula
- U.S.S.R. launches *Sputnik* into space
- Cuban president Fulgencio Batista resigns and flees
- Fidel Castro takes over as Cuba's leader

COLD WAR
The Looking Glass War
John Le Carré
v3:311

FRENCH INDOCHINA WAR
The Quiet American
Henry Graham Greene
v2:375

ARAB-ISRAELI WAR OF 1948
1948: A Soldier's Tale
Uri Avnery
v2:3

Returning to Haifa
Ghassan Kanafani
v2:252

KOREAN WAR
Bridges at Toko-Ri
James Michener
v2:27

Mao's Generals Remember Korea
various authors
v1:101

*M*A*S*H*
Richard Hooker
v1:302

The Naked Tree
Pak Wan-so
v3:173

"The Rainy Spell"
Yoon Heung-gil
v2:306

Retrieving Bones
W. D. Ehrhart
v2:83

War Trash
Ha Jin
v2:274

KENYAN WAR OF INDEPENDENCE
Carcase for Hounds
Meja Mwangi
v3:266

A Grain of Wheat
Ngugi wa Thiong'o
v2:343

PARTITION OF INDIA
Black Margins
Saadat Hasan Manto
v1:283

Tamas
Bhisham Sahni
v2:267

"Today I Invoke Waris Shah"
Amrita Pritam
v3:408

Train to Pakistan
Khushwant Singh
v3:204

And the Rain My Drink
Han Suyin
v2:123

VIETNAM WAR
Beyond Vietnam
Martin Luther King Jr.
v1:220

Blue Dragon, White Tiger
Dinh Van Tran
v2:315

Bloods
Wallace Houston Terry II
v1:44

Born on the Fourth of July
Ron Kovic
v3:7

Decent Interval
Frank Snepp
v1:132

Dien Cai Dau
Yusef Komunyakaa
v3:35

Dispatches
Michael Herr
v1:136

Dog Soldiers
Robert Stone
v3:274

Don't Mean Nothing
Susan O'Neill
v2:132

Going after Cacciato
Tim O'Brien
v3:43

Last Night I Dreamed of Peace
Đang Thùy Trâm
v2:147

Matterhorn
Karl Marlantes
v2:68

Novel without a Name
Duong Thu Huong
v3:59

A Rumor of War
Philip Caputo
v1:175

Sorrow of War
Bao Ninh
v2:91

The Things They Carried
Tim O'Brien
v1:391

When Heaven and Earth Changed Places
Le Ly Hayslip
v2:179

ALGERIAN WAR
Algerian White
Assia Djebar
v3:227

CUBAN REVOLUTION
Guerrilla Warfare: A Method
Ernesto "Che" Guevara
v1:16

1945 1946 1947 1948 1949 1950 1951 1952 1953 1954 1955 1956 1957 1958 1959 1960

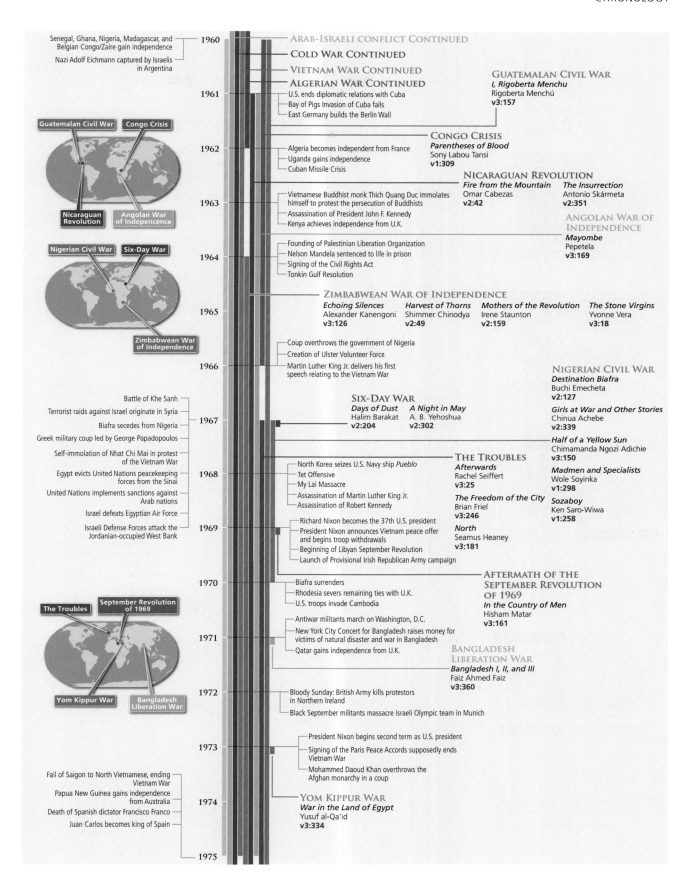

1960

Senegal, Ghana, Nigeria, Madagascar, and Belgian Congo/Zaire gain independence

Nazi Adolf Eichmann captured by Israelis in Argentina

ARAB-ISRAELI CONFLICT CONTINUED

COLD WAR CONTINUED

VIETNAM WAR CONTINUED

GUATEMALAN CIVIL WAR
I, Rigoberta Menchu
Rigoberta Menchú
v3:157

1961

ALGERIAN WAR CONTINUED

U.S. ends diplomatic relations with Cuba

Bay of Pigs Invasion of Cuba fails

East Germany builds the Berlin Wall

Guatemalan Civil War   Congo Crisis

1962

Algeria becomes independent from France

Uganda gains independence

Cuban Missile Crisis

CONGO CRISIS
Parentheses of Blood
Sony Labou Tansi
v1:309

NICARAGUAN REVOLUTION
Fire from the Mountain   *The Insurrection*
Omar Cabezas   Antonio Skármeta
v2:42   **v2:351**

1963

Vietnamese Buddhist monk Thich Quang Duc immolates himself to protest the persecution of Buddhists

Assassination of President John F. Kennedy

Kenya achieves independence from U.K.

ANGOLAN WAR OF INDEPENDENCE
Mayombe
Pepetela
v3:169

Nicaraguan Revolution   Angolan War of Indepencence

1964

Founding of Palestinian Liberation Organization

Nelson Mandela sentenced to life in prison

Signing of the Civil Rights Act

Tonkin Gulf Resolution

1965

ZIMBABWEAN WAR OF INDEPENDENCE
Echoing Silences   *Harvest of Thorns*   *Mothers of the Revolution*   *The Stone Virgins*
Alexander Kanengoni   Shimmer Chinodya   Irene Staunton   Yvonne Vera
v3:126   **v2:49**   **v2:159**   **v3:18**

Nigerian Civil War   Six-Day War

Zimbabwean War of Independence

1966

Coup overthrows the government of Nigeria

Creation of Ulster Volunteer Force

Martin Luther King Jr. delivers his first speech relating to the Vietnam War

NIGERIAN CIVIL WAR
Destination Biafra
Buchi Emecheta
v2:127

Girls at War and Other Stories
Chinua Achebe
v2:339

1967

Battle of Khe Sanh

Terrorist raids against Israel originate in Syria

Biafra secedes from Nigeria

Greek military coup led by George Papadopoulos

Self-immolation of Nhat Chi Mai in protest of the Vietnam War

Egypt evicts United Nations peacekeeping forces from the Sinai

United Nations implements sanctions against Arab nations

Israel defeats Egyptian Air Force

Israeli Defense Forces attack the Jordanian-occupied West Bank

SIX-DAY WAR
Days of Dust   *A Night in May*
Halim Barakat   A. B. Yehoshua
v2:204   **v2:302**

Half of a Yellow Sun
Chimamanda Ngozi Adichie
v3:150

1968

North Korea seizes U.S. Navy ship *Pueblo*

Tet Offensive

My Lai Massacre

Assassination of Martin Luther King Jr.

Assassination of Robert Kennedy

THE TROUBLES
Afterwards
Rachel Seiffert
v3:25

The Freedom of the City
Brian Friel
v3:246

Madmen and Specialists
Wole Soyinka
v1:298

Sozaboy
Ken Saro-Wiwa
v1:258

1969

Richard Nixon becomes the 37th U.S. president

President Nixon announces Vietnam peace offer and begins troop withdrawals

Beginning of Libyan September Revolution

Launch of Provisional Irish Republican Army campaign

North
Seamus Heaney
v3:181

1970

Biafra surrenders

Rhodesia severs remaining ties with U.K.

U.S. troops invade Cambodia

AFTERMATH OF THE SEPTEMBER REVOLUTION OF 1969
In the Country of Men
Hisham Matar
v3:161

1971

Antiwar militants march on Washington, D.C.

New York City Concert for Bangladesh raises money for victims of natural disaster and war in Bangladesh

Qatar gains independence from U.K.

BANGLADESH LIBERATION WAR
Bangladesh I, II, and III
Faiz Ahmed Faiz
v3:360

The Troubles   September Revolution of 1969

1972

Bloody Sunday: British Army kills protestors in Northern Ireland

Black September militants massacre Israeli Olympic team in Munich

Yom Kippur War   Bangladesh Liberation War

1973

President Nixon begins second term as U.S. president

Signing of the Paris Peace Accords supposedly ends Vietnam War

Mohammed Daoud Khan overthrows the Afghan monarchy in a coup

1974

Fall of Saigon to North Vietnamese, ending Vietnam War

Papua New Guinea gains independence from Australia

Death of Spanish dictator Francisco Franco

Juan Carlos becomes king of Spain

YOM KIPPUR WAR
War in the Land of Egypt
Yusuf al-Qa'id
v3:334

1975

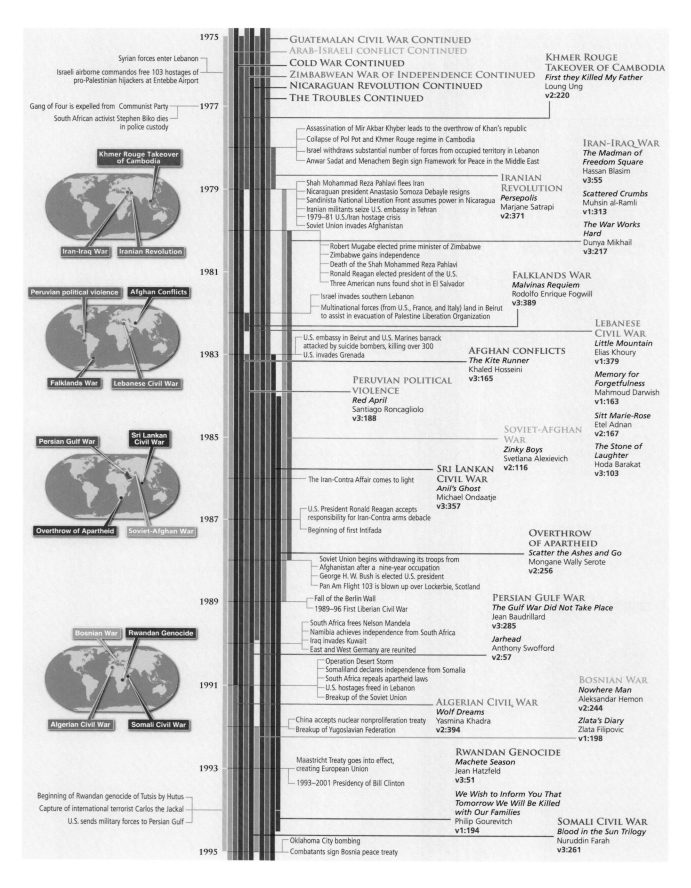

1975

GUATEMALAN CIVIL WAR CONTINUED
ARAB-ISRAELI CONFLICT CONTINUED

Syrian forces enter Lebanon

Israeli airborne commandos free 103 hostages of
pro-Palestinian hijackers at Entebbe Airport

COLD WAR CONTINUED
ZIMBABWEAN WAR OF INDEPENDENCE CONTINUED
NICARAGUAN REVOLUTION CONTINUED
THE TROUBLES CONTINUED

KHMER ROUGE
TAKEOVER OF CAMBODIA
First they Killed My Father
Loung Ung
v2:220

Gang of Four is expelled from Communist Party — **1977**
South African activist Stephen Biko dies
in police custody

Assassination of Mir Akbar Khyber leads to the overthrow of Khan's republic
Collapse of Pol Pot and Khmer Rouge regime in Cambodia
Israel withdraws substantial number of forces from occupied territory in Lebanon
Anwar Sadat and Menachem Begin sign Framework for Peace in the Middle East

IRAN-IRAQ WAR
*The Madman of
Freedom Square*
Hassan Blasim
v3:55

Khmer Rouge Takeover
of Cambodia

1979
Shah Mohammad Reza Pahlavi flees Iran
Nicaraguan president Anastasio Somoza Debayle resigns
Sandinista National Liberation Front assumes power in Nicaragua
Iranian militants seize U.S. embassy in Tehran
1979–81 U.S./Iran hostage crisis
Soviet Union invades Afghanistan

IRANIAN
REVOLUTION
Persepolis
Marjane Satrapi
v2:371

Scattered Crumbs
Muhsin al-Ramli
v1:313

*The War Works
Hard*
Dunya Mikhail
v3:217

Iran-Iraq War | Iranian Revolution

Robert Mugabe elected prime minister of Zimbabwe
Zimbabwe gains independence
Death of the Shah Mohammed Reza Pahlavi
Ronald Reagan elected president of the U.S.
Three American nuns found shot in El Salvador

1981

Peruvian political violence | Afghan Conflicts

Israel invades southern Lebanon
Multinational forces (from U.S., France, and Italy) land in Beirut
to assist in evacuation of Palestine Liberation Organization

FALKLANDS WAR
Malvinas Requiem
Rodolfo Enrique Fogwill
v3:389

LEBANESE
CIVIL WAR
Little Mountain
Elias Khoury
v1:379

U.S. embassy in Beirut and U.S. Marines barrack
attacked by suicide bombers, killing over 300
U.S. invades Grenada

1983

AFGHAN CONFLICTS
The Kite Runner
Khaled Hosseini
v3:165

*Memory for
Forgetfulness*
Mahmoud Darwish
v1:163

Falklands War | Lebanese Civil War

PERUVIAN POLITICAL
VIOLENCE
Red April
Santiago Roncagliolo
v3:188

Sitt Marie-Rose
Etel Adnan
v2:167

*The Stone of
Laughter*
Hoda Barakat
v3:103

1985

Persian Gulf War | Sri Lankan
Civil War

SOVIET-AFGHAN
WAR
Zinky Boys
Svetlana Alexievich
v2:116

The Iran-Contra Affair comes to light

SRI LANKAN
CIVIL WAR
Anil's Ghost
Michael Ondaatje
v3:357

U.S. President Ronald Reagan accepts
responsibility for Iran-Contra arms debacle

1987
Beginning of first Intifada

Overthrow of Apartheid | Soviet-Afghan War

OVERTHROW
OF APARTHEID
Scatter the Ashes and Go
Mongane Wally Serote
v2:256

Soviet Union begins withdrawing its troops from
Afghanistan after a nine-year occupation
George H. W. Bush is elected U.S. president
Pan Am Flight 103 is blown up over Lockerbie, Scotland

1989
Fall of the Berlin Wall
1989–96 First Liberian Civil War

PERSIAN GULF WAR
The Gulf War Did Not Take Place
Jean Baudrillard
v3:285

South Africa frees Nelson Mandela
Namibia achieves independence from South Africa
Iraq invades Kuwait
East and West Germany are reunited

Jarhead
Anthony Swofford
v2:57

Bosnian War | Rwandan Genocide

Operation Desert Storm
Somaliland declares independence from Somalia
South Africa repeals apartheid laws
U.S. hostages freed in Lebanon
Breakup of the Soviet Union

1991

BOSNIAN WAR
Nowhere Man
Aleksandar Hemon
v2:244

ALGERIAN CIVIL WAR
Wolf Dreams
Yasmina Khadra
v2:394

China accepts nuclear nonproliferation treaty
Breakup of Yugoslavian Federation

Zlata's Diary
Zlata Filipovic
v1:198

Maastricht Treaty goes into effect,
creating European Union

1993
1993–2001 Presidency of Bill Clinton

RWANDAN GENOCIDE
Machete Season
Jean Hatzfeld
v3:51

Algerian Civil War | Somali Civil War

Beginning of Rwandan genocide of Tutsis by Hutus
Capture of international terrorist Carlos the Jackal
U.S. sends military forces to Persian Gulf

*We Wish to Inform You That
Tomorrow We Will Be Killed
with Our Families*
Philip Gourevitch
v1:194

SOMALI CIVIL WAR
Blood in the Sun Trilogy
Nuruddin Farah
v3:261

Oklahoma City bombing
Combatants sign Bosnia peace treaty

1995

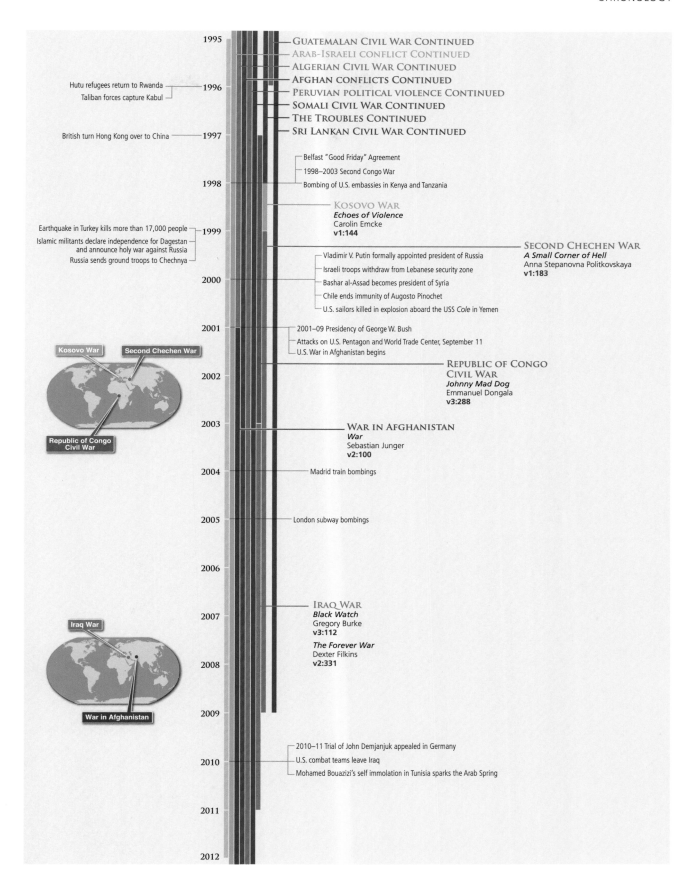

1995

ARAB-ISRAELI CONFLICT CONTINUED

GUATEMALAN CIVIL WAR CONTINUED

Hutu refugees return to Rwanda

Taliban forces capture Kabul

1996

ALGERIAN CIVIL WAR CONTINUED

AFGHAN CONFLICTS CONTINUED

PERUVIAN POLITICAL VIOLENCE CONTINUED

SOMALI CIVIL WAR CONTINUED

THE TROUBLES CONTINUED

British turn Hong Kong over to China

1997

SRI LANKAN CIVIL WAR CONTINUED

Belfast "Good Friday" Agreement

1998–2003 Second Congo War

1998

Bombing of U.S. embassies in Kenya and Tanzania

KOSOVO WAR

Echoes of Violence
Carolin Emcke
v1:144

Earthquake in Turkey kills more than 17,000 people

1999

SECOND CHECHEN WAR

A Small Corner of Hell
Anna Stepanovna Politkovskaya
v1:183

Islamic militants declare independence for Dagestan and announce holy war against Russia

Russia sends ground troops to Chechnya

Vladimir V. Putin formally appointed president of Russia

Israeli troops withdraw from Lebanese security zone

2000

Bashar al-Assad becomes president of Syria

Chile ends immunity of Augosto Pinochet

U.S. sailors killed in explosion aboard the USS *Cole* in Yemen

2001

2001–09 Presidency of George W. Bush

Attacks on U.S. Pentagon and World Trade Center, September 11

U.S. War in Afghanistan begins

REPUBLIC OF CONGO CIVIL WAR

Johnny Mad Dog
Emmanuel Dongala
v3:288

2002

Kosovo War   Second Chechen War

2003

Republic of Congo Civil War

WAR IN AFGHANISTAN

War
Sebastian Junger
v2:100

2004

Madrid train bombings

2005

London subway bombings

2006

2007

IRAQ WAR

Black Watch
Gregory Burke
v3:112

The Forever War
Dexter Filkins
v2:331

Iraq War

2008

2009

War in Afghanistan

2010–11 Trial of John Demjanjuk appealed in Germany

2010

U.S. combat teams leave Iraq

Mohamed Bouazizi's self immolation in Tunisia sparks the Arab Spring

2011

2012

CONFLICTS

This list includes the conflicts and corresponding entries represented in *The Literature of War,* with volume and page numbers.

GENRES

This list includes genres and corresponding entries represented in *The Literature of War,* with volume and page numbers.

NATIONALITIES

Following are the nationalities of authors represented in *The Literature of War*.

ALGERIAN

Assia Djebar (1936–)
Yasmina Khadra (1955–)

AMERICAN

Louisa May Alcott (1832–88)
Maxwell Anderson (1888–1959)
William Apess (1798–1839)
Ambrose Bierce (1842–c. 1914)
Kai Bird (1951–)
Mary Borden (1886–1968)
Gwendolyn Brooks (1917–2000)
Dee Alexander Brown (1908–2002)
Philip Caputo (1941–)
Mary Boykin Chesnut (1823–86)
James Fenimore Cooper (1789–1851)
Stephen Crane (1871–1900)
E. E. Cummings (1894–1962)
Millicent Dillon (1925–)
E. L. Doctorow (1931–)
John Roderigo Dos Passos (1896–1970)
William Dunlap (1766–1839)
W. D. Ehrhart (1948–)
Dexter Filkins (1961–)
Shelby Foote (1916–2005)
Martha Gellhorn (1908–98)
Philip Gourevitch (1961–)
H. D. (1886–1961)
Frances Ellen Watkins Harper (1825–1911)
Le Ly Hayslip (1949–)
Joseph Heller (1923–99)
Ernest Hemingway (1899–1961)
Aleksandar Hemon (1964–)
Michael Herr (1940–)
John Richard Hersey (1914–93)
Thomas Wentworth Higginson (1823–1911)
Richard Hooker (1924–97)
Khaled Hosseini (1965–)

Julia Ward Howe (1819–1910)
Ha Jin (1956–)
Sebastian Junger (1962–)
Martin Luther King Jr. (1929–68)
Yusef Komunyakaa (1947–)
Jerzy Kosinski (1933–91)
Ron Kovic (1946–)
Abraham Lincoln (1809–65)
Henry Wadsworth Longfellow (1807–82)
Norman Mailer (1923–2007)
William March (1893–1954)
Karl Marlantes (1945–)
Hisham Matar (1970–)
Herman Melville (1819–91)
James A. Michener (1907–97)
Arthur Miller (1915–2005)
Margaret Mitchell (1900–49)
Sabina Murray (1968–)
Tim O'Brien (1946–)
Susan O'Neill (1947–)
John Okada (1923–71)
Ezra Pound (1885–1972)
Thomas Pynchon (1937–)
John Reed (1887–1920)
Don Rickey Jr. (1925–2000)
Philip Roth (1933–)
Catharine Maria Sedgwick (1789–1867)
Alan Seeger (1888–1916)
Michael Shaara (1929–88)
Irwin Shaw (1913–84)
Martin Sherman (1938–)
Leslie Marmon Silko (1948–)
Frank Snepp (1943–)
Art Spiegelman (1948–)
Edna St. Vincent-Millay (1892–1950)
Robert Stone (1937–)

Anthony Swofford (1970–)
Wallace Houston Terry II (1938–2003)
Henry David Thoreau (1817–62)
Dalton Trumbo (1905–76)
Dinh Van Tran (1927–2011)
Kurt Vonnegut Jr. (1922–2007)
Samuel Rush Watkins (1839–1901)
Walt Whitman (1819–92)
Elie Wiesel (1928–)

Angolan

Pepetela (1941–)

Argentine

Rodolfo Enrique Fogwill (1941–2010)
Ernesto "Che" Guevara (1928–67)
Domingo Faustino Sarmiento (1811–88)

Australian

Paul Brickhill (1916–91)
Richard Hillary (1919–43)
Thomas Michael Keneally (1935–)
Frederic Manning (1882–1935)

Bosnian

Zlata Filipovic (1980–)

Brazilian

Euclides da Cunha (1866–1909)

British

Richard Aldington (1892–1962)
W. H. Auden (1907–73)
Anna Laetitia Barbauld (1743–1825)
Pat Barker (1943–)
Mark Bence-Jones (1930–2010)
Laurence Binyon (1896–1943)
Vera Brittain (1893–1970)
Rupert Brooke (1887–1915)
Gregory Burke (1968–)
Hugh Charles (1907–95)
Marie Louise de la Ramée (1839–1908)
Keith Castellain Douglas (1920–44)
James Gordon Farrell (1935–79)
Ford Madox Ford (1873–1939)
Robert Graves (1895–1985)
Henry Green (1905–73)
Henry Graham Greene (1904–91)
Willis Hall (1929–2005)
Thomas Hardy (1840–1928)
B. H. Liddell Hart (1895–1970)
Edward Hyde, First Earl of Clarendon (1609–74)

David Jones (1895–1974)
Rudyard Kipling (1865–1936)
Nella Last (1889–1968)
D. H. Lawrence (1885–1930)
T. E. Lawrence (1888–1935)
John Le Carré (1931–)
Andrea Levy (1956–)
Joan Littlewood (1914–2002)
Christopher Logue (1926–)
Christopher Marlowe (c. 1564–93)
Ian McEwan (1948–)
Sir Henry Newbolt (1862–1938)
George Orwell (1902–50)
Wilfred Edward Salter Owen (1893–1918)
Henry Reed (1914–1996)
Isaac Rosenberg (1890–1918)
William Sansom (1912–76)
Siegfried Sassoon (1886–1967)
Rachel Seiffert (1971–)
Anna Seward (1747–1809)
William Shakespeare (c. 1564–1616)
R. C. Sherriff (1896–1975)
Muriel Spark (1918–2006)
Algernon Charles Swinburne (1837–1909)
Alfred, Lord Tennyson (1809–92)
Sarah Waters (1966–)
Evelyn Waugh (1903–66)
H. G. Wells (1866–1946)
Rebecca West (1892–1983)
Virginia Woolf (1882–1941)

British-American

Thomas Paine (1737–1809)
Mary White Rowlandson (c. 1631–1711)

Bulgarian

Ivan Minchov Vazov (1850–1921)

Cambodian

Loung Ung (1970–)

Chilean

Pablo Neruda (1904–73)
Antonio Skármeta (1940–)

Chinese

Ling Ding (1904–86)
Du Fu (712–70)
Luo Guanzhong (fl. c. 1330–1400)
Xiao Hong (1911–42)
Han Suyin (1917–2011)

Sun Tzu (c. 544–c. 496 BCE)
Mao Zedong (1893–1976)

CHINESE AMERICAN
Eileen Chang (1920–95)

COLOMBIAN
Gabriel García Márquez (1927–)
Álvaro Cepeda Samudio (1926–72)

CONGOLESE
Emmanuel Dongala (1941–)
Sony Lab'Ou Tansi (1947–95)

CUBAN
Miguel Barnet (1940–)
Alejo Carpentier (1904–80)
Esteban Montejo (1860–1973)

CZECH
Jaroslav Hašek (1883–1923)

EGYPTIAN
Ibrahim Abdel-Meguid (1946–)
Yusuf al-Qa'id (1944–)
Radwa Ashour (1946–)

FRENCH
Jean Marie Lucien Pierre Anouilh (1910–87)
Henri Barbusse (1873–1935)
Jean Baudrillard (1929–2007)
Louis-Ferdinand Céline (1894–1961)
René Char (1907–88)
Charlotte Delbo (1913–85)
Jean Hatzfeld (1949–)
André Malraux (1901–76)
Irène Némirovsky (1903–42)

GERMAN
Bertolt Brecht (1898–1956)
Carolin Emcke (1967–)
Anne Frank (1929–45)
Ernst Jünger (1895–1998)
Hans Keilson (1909–2011)
Erich Maria Remarque (1898–1970)
W. G. Sebald (1944–2001)
Jakob Christoffel von Grimmelshausen
   (c. 1621–76)

GREEK
Aristophanes (c. 448–380 BCE)
Euripides (c. 480–c. 406 BCE)
Herodotus (484–c. 425 BCE)
Thucydides (c. 455/460–c. 395 BCE)

GUATEMALAN
Rigoberta Menchú (1959–)

HUNGARIAN
Imre Kertész (1929–)

INDIAN
Amrita Pritam (1919–2005)
Bhisham Sahni (1915–2005)
Surendra Nath Sen (1890–1962)
Khushwant Singh (1915–)

IRANIAN
Marjane Satrapi (1969–)

IRAQI
Muhsin al-Ramli (1967–)
Hassan Blasim (1973–)
Dunya Mikhail (1965–)

IRISH
Elizabeth Bowen (1899–1973)
Brian Friel (1929–)
Frank McGuinness (1953–)
Seán O'Casey (1880–1964)
William Howard Russell (1820–1907)
Charles Wolfe (1791–1823)
William Butler Yeats (1865–1939)

ISRAELI
Uri Avnery (1923–)
A. B. Yehoshua (1936–)

ISRAELI/PALESTINIAN
Mahmoud Darwish (1941–2008)

ITALIAN
Natalia Ginzburg (1916–91)
Primo Levi (1919–87)
Niccolò Machiavelli (1469–1527)
Filippo Marinetti (1876–1944)
Giuseppe Ungaretti (1888–1970)

JAMAICAN
Mary Seacole (1805–81)

JAPANESE
Masuji Ibuse (1898–1993)
Kinoshita Junji (1914–2006)
Tayama Katai (1872–1930)
Yoshida Mitsuru (1923–79)
Keiji Nakazawa (1939–)
Shōhei Ōoka (1909–88)
Endō Shūsaku (1923–96)
Michio Takeyama (1903–84)

KENYAN
  Meja Mwangi (1948–)
  Ngugi wa Thiong'o (1938–)

LEBANESE
  Hoda Barakat (1952–)
  Elias Khoury (1948–)
  Amin Maalouf (1949–)

LEBANESE/AMERICAN
  Etel Adnan (1925–)

LESOTHOAN
  Thomas Mopoku Mofolo (1876–1948)

MEXICAN
  Mariano Azuela (1873–52)
  Nellie Campobello (1900–86)
  Heriberto Frías (1870–1925)
  Carlos Fuentes (1928–)
  Martín Luis Guzmán (1887–1976)
  Miguel León-Portilla (1926–)
  Ignacio Solares (1945–)

NEW ZEALANDER
  Katherine Mansfield (1888–1923)
  C. K. Stead (1932–)

NICARAGUAN
  Omar Cabezas Lacayo (1950–)

NIGERIAN
  Albert Chinualumogu "Chinua" Achebe (1930–)
  Chimamanda Ngozi Adichie (1977–)
  Buchi Emecheta (1944–)
  Ken Saro-Wiwa (1941–95)
  Wole Soyinka (1934–)

NORTHERN IRISH
  Seamus Heaney (1939–)

PAKISTANI
  Faiz Ahmed Faiz (1911–84)
  Saadat Hasan Manto (1912–55)

PALESTINIAN
  Ghassan Kanafani (1936–72)

PARAGUAYAN
  Augusto Roa Bastos (1917–2005)

PERUVIAN
  El Inca Garcilaso de la Vega (1539–1616)
  Mario Vargas Llosa (1936–)
  Santiago Roncagliolo (1975–)

PRUSSIAN
  Carl von Clausewitz (1780–1831)

ROMAN
  Gaius Julius Caesar (100–44 BCE)
  Tacitus (c.56–c.117 CE)
  Virgil (70 BCE–19 BCE)

RUSSIAN
  Tadeusz Borowski (1922–51)
  Nadezhda Andreevna Durova (1783–1866)
  Vasily Grossman (1905–64)
  Boris Pasternak (1890–1960)
  Anna Stepanovna Politkovskaya
    (1958–2006)
  Alexander Sergeyevich Pushkin (1799–1837)
  Mikhail Sholokov (1905–84)
  Leo Nickolayevich Tolstoy (1828–1910)

SAUK NATION (AMERICAN)
  Black Sparrow Hawk (1767–1838)

SCOTTISH
  Gregory Burke (1968–)

SENEGALESE/AMERICAN
  Phillis Wheatley (c. 1753–84)

SOMALI
  Nuruddin Farah (1945–)

SOUTH AFRICAN
  Deneys Reitz (1882–1944)
  Mongane Wally Serote (1944–)

SOUTH KOREAN
  Yoon Heung-gil (1942–)
  Pak Wan-so (1931–2011)

SOVIET
  Eugenia Ginzburg (1904–77)

SPANISH
  Alonso de Ercilla y Zúñiga (1533–94)
  Fray Bartolomé de Las Cases
    (c.1484–1565)
  Bernal Díaz del Castillo (c.1496–c.1584)
  Miguel Hernández (1910–42)

SRI LANKAN
  Michael Ondaatje (1943–)

SWEDISH
  Peter Ulrich Weiss (1916–82)

SYRIAN
    Halim Barakat (1936–)

TURKISH
    Fethiye Çetin (1950–)

UKRAINIAN
    Svetlana Alexievich (1948–)

VENEZUELAN
    Arturo Úslar Pietri (1906–2001)

VIETNAMESE
    Đang Thùy Trâm (1942–70)
    Duong Thu Huong (1950–)
    Bao Ninh (1952–)

ZIMBABWEAN
    Shimmer Chinodya (1957–)
    Alexander Kanengoni (1951–)
    Irene Staunton (not found)
    Yvonne Vera (1964–2005)

AWARD WINNERS AND NOMINEES

AFTERWARDS BY RACHEL SEIFFERT
Long-listed for the Orange Prize for Fiction, 2007

ALL MY SONS BY ARTHUR MILLER
New York Drama Critics Circle Award, 1947
Antoinette Perry Award for Best Play, 1947
Antoinette Perry Award for Best Direction, 1947

ANIL'S GHOST BY MICHAEL ONDAATJE
Governor General's Award for English-language fiction, 2000
Prix Médicis étranger, 2001
Kiriyama Pacific Rim Book Prize, 2000
Giller Prize, 2000
Irish Times International Fiction Award, 2001

ATONEMENT BY IAN McEWAN
National Book Critics Circle Award, 2002
Time Magazine Best Novel of the Year, 2001
Short-listed for Man Booker Prize, 2001

AUSTERLITZ BY W. G. SEBALD
National Book Critics Circle Award for fiction, 2002
Independent Foreign Fiction Prize, 2002
Koret Jewish Book Awards, special award, 2002

BENT BY MARTIN SHERMAN
Pulitzer Prize nomination for drama, 1980
Antoinette Perry Award nomination, best new play, 1980

BRIDGES AT TOKO-RI BY JAMES A. MICHENER
Booker Prize, 1973

CARCASE FOR HOUNDS BY MEJA MWANGI
Jomo Kenyatta Prize, 1974

CEREMONY BY LESLIE MARMON SILKO
American Book Award, Before Columbus Foundation, 1980

CHAKA BY THOMAS MOPOKU MOFOLO
Named one of the top 12 best African books of the twentieth century, Zimbabwe International Book Fair

THE CIVIL WAR BY SHELBY FOOTE
Fletcher Pratt Award, Civil War Round Table of New York, 1964

COMEDY IN A MINOR KEY BY HANS KEILSON
National Book Critics Circle Award nomination

THE COMPLETE MAUS BY ART SPIEGELMAN
Pulitzer Prize for *The Complete Maus* and other writngs, 1992

CROSSING MANDELBAUM GATE BY KAI BIRD
National Book Critics Circle Award finalist

DOCTOR ZHIVAGO BY BORIS PASTERNAK
Nobel Prize for literature, 1958 (declined)
Bancarella Prize, 1958

DOG SOLDIERS BY ROBERT STONE
National Book Award (1975)

ECHOES OF VIOLENCE BY CAROLIN EMCKE
Political Book Award, Friedrich Ebert Foundation, 2005

FIRES ON THE PLAIN BY SHŌHEI ŌOKA
Yomiuri Prize, 1951

FIRST THEY KILLED MY FATHER BY LOUNG UNG
Excellence in Adult Nonfiction Literature Award, Asian/Pacific American Librarians' Association, 2001

FOR WHOM THE BELL TOLLS BY ERNEST HEMINGWAY
Pulitzer Prize nomination, 1941.

THE FOREVER WAR BY DEXTER FILKINS
Julia Ward Howe Award, Boston Authors Club, 2009
"Best Book" awards from several U.S. magazines and newspapers
National Book Critics Circle Award, 2009

GONE WITH THE WIND BY MARGARET MITCHELL
Pulitzer Prize, 1937

GRANADA BY RADWA ASHOUR
Book of the Year Award, Cairo International Book Fair, 1994
First Prize, Arab Women's Book Fair, Cairo, Egypt, 1995

GRAVITY'S RAINBOW BY THOMAS PYNCHON
National Book Award, 1974 (declined)
William Dean Howells Medal, best novel of the decade, American Academy of Arts and Letters

HALF OF A YELLOW SUN BY CHIMAMANDA NGOZI ADICHIE
David T. Wong International Short Story Prize, PEN Center, 2002, for "Half of a Yellow Sun"
Beyond Margins Award, International Pen, 2007
Orange Broadband Prize for fiction, 2007
Anisfield-Wolf Book Award, 2007

HARRY GOLD BY MILLICENT DILLON
PEN/Faulkner Award nomination, 2001

HARVEST OF THORNS BY SHIMMER CHINODYA
Commonwealth Writers Prize, Africa region, 1990

I, RIGOBERTA MENCHÚ BY RIGOBERTA MENCHÚ
Casas de las Américas Award, best testimonial, 1983

IN THE COUNTRY OF MEN BY HISHAM MATAR
Short-listed for Man Booker Prize, 2006

AN INDIAN HISTORY OF THE AMERICAN WEST BY DEE ALEXANDER BROWN
Christopher Award, 1971

JOHNNY GOT HIS GUN BY DALTON TRUMBO
National Book Award, 1939

JOHNNY MAD DOG BY EMMANUEL DONGALA
Cezam Prix Littéraire Inter CE, 2004

THE KILLER ANGELS BY MICHAEL SHAARA
Pulitzer Prize for fiction, 1975

THE KITE RUNNER BY KHALED HOSSEINI
Original Voices Award, Borders Group, 2004

THE LONG AND THE SHORT AND THE TALL BY WILLIS HALL
Evening Standard Play of the Year, 1959

THE LONG SONG BY ANDREA LEVY
Walter Scott Prize for historical fiction, 2011
Short-listed for Man Booker Prize
Long-listed for Orange Prize

MACHETE SEASON BY JEAN HATZFELD
Prix Femina, essay category, 2003
Prix Josseff Kessel, 2004

MARAT/SADE BY PETER ULRICH WEISS
Production of the year, *Theater Heute*, 1964
Antoinette Perry Award, best play, 1966
Lessing Prize, 1965
Drama Critics Circle Award, 1966.

THE MARCH BY E. L. DOCTOROW
National Book Critics Circle Award, 2005
Nominated for the National Book Award, 2005
PEN/Faulkner Award, 2006
Finalist for the Pulitzer Prize, 2006

MARY CHESNUT'S CIVIL WAR BY MARY BOYKIN CHESNUT
Pulitzer Prize (for the 1981 edition by C. Vann Woodward)

MATTERHORN BY KARL MARLANTES
William E. Colby Award, Pritzker Military Library, 2011

MAYOMBE BY PEPETELA
Angolan National Prize for Literature

MOTHER COURAGE AND HER CHILDREN BY BERTOLT BRECHT
Antoinette Perry Award nomination, best play, 1963

MOTHERS OF THE REVOLUTION BY IRENE STAUNTON
Outstanding Book of the Year Award, Zimbabwe Book Publishers' Association, 1990

A NIGHT IN MAY BY A. B. YEHOSHUA
Israel Drama Critics Award
Harp of David Award

THE NIGHT WATCH BY SARAH WATERS
Lambda Literary Award for Lesbian Fiction, 2007

NO ONE SLEEPS IN ALEXANDRIA BY IBRAHIM ABDEL-MEGUID
Special award for best novel of the year, Cairo International Book Fair, 1996

NORTH BY SEAMUS HEANEY
W. H. Smith Award
Duff Cooper Memorial Prize

NOWHERE MAN BY ALEKSANDAR HEMON
Los Angeles Times Book Award, 2002
National Book Critics Circle Award nomination, 2002

OBSERVE THE SONS OF ULSTER MARCHING TOWARDS THE SOMME BY FRANK MCGUINNESS
London Evening Standard Award for Most Promising Playwright

OH! WHAT A LOVELY WAR BY JOAN LITTLEWOOD
Grand Prix, Theatre des Nations Festival, Paris, 1963
Antoinette Perry Award nomination, Best Book of a Musical, 1965

OPERATION SHYLOCK BY PHILIP ROTH
PEN/Faulkner Award, 1993

THE PAINTED BIRD BY JERZY KOSINSKI
Prix du Meilleur Livre Etranger, 1966

PARENTHESES OF BLOOD BY SONY LAB'OU TANSI
Concours Théâtral Interafricain de Radio-France Internationale, 1978

PERSEPOLIS BY MARJANE SATRAPI
Angoulême Coup de Coeur Award, 2001
Alex Award, Young Adult Library Services Association

RED APRIL BY SANTIAGO RONCAGLIOLO
Alfaguara Prize, 2006
Independent Foreign Fiction Prize, 2011

REGENERATION TRILOGY BY PAT BARKER
Booker Prize, 1995, for "The Ghost Road"
London Guardian Fiction Prize, 1993, for "The Eye in the Door"

A RUMOR OF WAR BY PHILIP CAPUTO
Sidney Hillman Foundation Award, 1977

SCATTER THE ASHES AND GO BY MONGANE WALLY SEROTE
Nomination for South Africa *Sunday Times* fiction prize, 2003

SCHINDLER'S LIST BY THOMAS MICHAEL KENEALLY
Booker Prize for Fiction, 1982
Los Angeles Times Fiction Prize, 1982

SLAUGHTERHOUSE-FIVE BY KURT VONNEGUT JR.
Hugo Award nomination, 1970
Nebula Award nomination, 1969

SON OF MAN BY AUGUSTO ROA BASTOS
Concurso Internacional de Narrativa, Editorial Losada, 1959

SORROW OF WAR BY BAO NINH
Independent Foreign Fiction Prize, 1994

THE STONE OF LAUGHTER BY HODA BARAKAT
Al-Naqid Prize, 1990

THE STONE VIRGINS BY YVONNE VERA
Macmillan Writers Prize for Africa, 2002
San Francisco Chronicle Best Book of the Year, 2002

STORM OF STEEL BY ERNST JÜNGER
Oxford-Weidenfeld Translation Prize for Michael Hofmann's translation, 2004

SUITE FRANÇAISE BY IRÈNE NÉMIROVSKY
Renaudot Prize, 2004
Independent Booksellers Book of the Year, 2007

THE SUN SHINES OVER THE SANGGAN RIVER BY LING DING
Stalin Prize for literature, 1951

THE SWORD OF HONOUR TRILOGY BY EVELYN WAUGH
James Tait Black Memorial Prize for Best Novel, University of Edinburgh, for "Men at Arms" volume

TALKING ABOUT O'DWYER BY C. K. STEAD
Montana New Zealand Book Award finalist, 2000

TAMAS BY BHISHAM SAHNI
Sahitya Akademi Award, 1975
Uttar Pradesh Government Award, 1975

THE THINGS THEY CARRIED BY TIM O'BRIEN
Chicago Tribune Heartland Prize, 1990.
Prix du Meilleur Livre Étranger, 1990
Pulitzer Prize nomination, 1991.
National Book Critics Circle Award nomination, 1991.

TRAIN TO PAKISTAN BY KHUSHWANT SINGH
Grove Press India Fiction Prize, 1956

TROJAN WOMEN BY EURIPIDES
Second place award from City Dionysia Festival, Athens, 415 BCE

UNDER FIRE BY HENRI BARBUSSE
Prix Goncourt, 1916

WAR TRASH BY HA JIN
PEN/Faulkner Award, 2005
Pulitzer Prize nomination, 2005

***THE WAR WORKS HARD* BY DUNYA MIKHAIL**
PEN Translation Award
Short-listed for Griffin Poetry Prize

***WE WISH TO INFORM YOU THAT TOMORROW WE WILL BE KILLED WITH OUR FAMILIES* BY PHILIP GOUREVITCH**
Guardian First Book Award, 1999
Los Angeles Times Book Prize, 1998

George Polk Award for Foreign Reporting, 1998

Helen Bernstein Award, New York Public Library, 1999

PEN/Martha Albrand Award for First Nonfiction, 1999

***WHAT PRICE GLORY?* BY MAXWELL ANDERSON**
Pulitzer Prize nomination, 1924

MEDIA ADAPTATIONS

ALL MY SONS BY ARTHUR MILLER

All My Sons. Dir. Irvin Reis. Perf. Edward G. Robinson, Burt Lancaster, Mady Christians, and Louisa Horton. Universal-International Pictures, 1948. Film.

All My Sons. Dir. Jack O'Brien. Perf. James Whitmore, Aidan Quinn, Michael Learned, and Joan Allen. Brandman Productions, 1987. Film.

ALL QUIET ON THE WESTERN FRONT BY ERICH MARIA REMARQUE

All Quiet on the Western Front. Dir. Lewis Milestone. Perf. Lew Ayres, Louis Wolheim, and John Wray. Universal, 1930. Film.

ANTIGONE BY JEAN MARIE LUCIEN PIERRE ANOUILH

Antigone. By Jean Anouilh. Trans. Lewis Galantiere. Dir. Gerald Freedman. Perf. Geneviève Bujold, Stacy Keach, and Leah Chandler. PBS Theatre in America. Public Broadcasting Service. 13 Feb 1974. Television.

Antigone. By Jean Anouilh. Dir. Stellio Lorenzi. Perf. Jean Topart, Alain Cuny, and Marie-Hélène Breillat. Institut National de l'Audiovisuel. 21 Dec 1974. Television.

Antigone. By Jean Anouilh. Trans. Christopher Nixon. Dir. Brendan Fox. Perf. Elizabeth Marvel, Francis Guinan, and Alan Mandell. L.A. Theatre Works: Venice, CA, 2005. CD.

THE ART OF WAR BY SUN TZU

Art of War: Sun Tzu's Legendary Victory Manual Comes to Life. Dir. David Padrusch. Perf. James Wong. A&E Television, 2009. Television special.

Art of War Dir. Kuang Hui. 1981. Documentary film.

ATONEMENT BY IAN MCEWAN

Atonement. Dir. Joe Wright. Perf. Saoirse Ronan, Brenda Blethyn, Julia West, and James McAvoy. Universal Pictures, 2007. Film.

BAREFOOT GEN BY KEIJI NAKAZAWA

Barefoot Gen. Dir. Tenjo Yamada. Perf. Kenta Sato, Sachiko Hodari, Yotaro Komatsu, Chizuko Iwahara. Tengo Yamada, 1976. Film.

Barefoot Gen. Dir. Mori Masaki. Perf. Issei Miyazaki, Masaki Koda, Seiko Nakano. Gen Productions, 1983. Anime film.

Barefoot Gen. Dir. Masaki Nishiura, Shosuke Murakami. Perf. Ren Kobayashi, Kiichi Nakai, Yuriko Ishida, Akiyoshi Nakao. Fuji Television, 2007. Television broadcast.

BENT BY MARTIN SHERMAN

Bent. Dir. Sean Mathias. Adapted by Martin Sherman from his play. Perf. Lothaire Bluteau, Clive Owen, Mick Jagger. Metro-Goldwyn-Mayer, 1997. Film.

BLACK MARGINS BY SAADAT HASAN MANTO

Toba Tek Singh. Dir. Afia Nathaniel, 2005. Film.

BLACK RAIN BY MASUJI IBUSE

Kuroi Ame. Dir. Shoehi Imamura. Perf. Yoshiko Tanaka, Kazuo Kitamura, Etsuko Ichihara. Imamura Productions, 1988. Film.

BORN ON THE FOURTH OF JULY BY RON KOVIC

Born on the Fourth of July. Dir. Oliver Stone. Perf. Tom Cruise, Kyra Sedgwick, Raymond J. Berry, Carolina Keva. Universal Pictures, 1989. Film.

BRIDGES AT TOKO-RI BY JAMES A. MICHENER

The Bridges at Toko-Ri. Dir. Mark Robson. Perf. William Holden, Grace Kelly, Fredric March, Mickey Rooney. Paramount Pictures, 1954. Film.

THE CAPTAIN'S DAUGHTER BY ALEXANDER SERGEYEVICH PUSHKIN

La figlia del capitano. Dir. Mario Camerini. 1947. Film.

La Tempesta. Dir. Alberto Lattuada. 1958. Film.

The Captain's Daughter. Dir. Ekaterina Mikhailova. 2005. Animated film.

CARCASE FOR HOUNDS BY MEJA MWANGI

Cry Freedom. Dir. Ola Balogun. Perf. Candy Brown, Jorge Coutinho, Prunella Gee, and Albert Hall. 1981. Film.

CATCH-22 BY JOSEPH HELLER

Catch-22. Dir. Mike Nichols. Perf. Alan Arkin, Martin Balsam, Richard Benjamin, Art Garfunkel, Jack Gilford, Buck Henry, and Bob Newhart. Paramount Pictures, 1970. Film.

Catch-22. Dir. Richard Quine. Perf. Richard Dreyfuss, Dana Elcar, Stewart Moss, and Andy Jarrell. American Broadcasting Company (ABC), 1973. Television.

"THE CHARGE OF THE LIGHT BRIGADE" BY ALFRED, LORD TENNYSON

The Charge of the Light Brigade. Dir. J. Seatle Dawley. Perf. Ben F. Wilson, Richard Neill, James Gordon, and Charles Sutton. General Film Company, 1912. Film.

The Charge of the Light Brigade. Dir. Michael Burtiz. Perf. Errol Flynn and Olivia de Havilland. Warner Bros. Pictures, 1936. Film.

The Charge of the Light Brigade. Dir. Tony Richardson. Perf. Trevor Howard, Vanessa Redgrave, and John Gielgud. United Artists, 1968. Film.

DIARY OF A YOUNG GIRL BY ANNE FRANK

The Diary of Anne Frank. Dir. George Stevens. Perf. Millie Perkins, Shelley Winters, Richard Beymer, Diane Baker. Twentieth Century-Fox, 1959. Film.

The Diary of Anne Frank. Perf. Katharine Schlesinger, Steven Mackintosh, Nigel Anthony, Daniel Moynihan. British Broadcasting Corporation, 1987. Television miniseries.

The Diary of Anne Frank. Perf. Ellie Kendrick, Kate Ashfield, Iain Glen, Felicity Jones. British Broadcasting Corporation, 2009. Television miniseries.

DOCTOR ZHIVAGO BY BORIS PASTERNAK

Dr. Zhivago. Dir. David Lean. Perf. Omar Sharif, Julie Christie, Rod Steiger. Metro-Goldwyn-Mayer, 1965. Film.

Doctor Zhivago. Dir. Giacomo Campiotti. Perf. Sam MacLintock, Sam Neill, Keira Knightley, Hans Matheson. Independent Television. 2003. Television miniseries.

DOG SOLDIERS BY ROBERT STONE

Who'll Stop the Rain. Dir. Karel Reisz. Perf. Nick Nolte, Tuesday Weld, and Michael Moriarty. United Artist, 1978. Film.

A FAREWELL TO ARMS BY ERNEST HEMINGWAY

A Farewell to Arms. Dir. Frank Borzage. Perf. Helen Hayes, Gary Cooper, and Adolphe Menjou. Paramount Pictures, 1932. Film.

A Farewell to Arms. Adapt. Ernest Kinoy. Perf. Frederic March and Florence Eldridge. NBC Star Playhouse, 13 Dec. 1953. Radio. Mark 56 Records, 1976. Audio recording.

A Farewell to Arms. Dir. Charles Vidor. Perf. Rock Hudson, Jennifer Jones, and Vittorio De Sica. Twentieth Century-Fox, 1957. Film.

FATELESSNESS BY IMRE KERTÉSZ

Fateless. Dir. Lajos Koltai. Perf. Marcell Nagy. Released with English subtitles by THINKFilm in 2006. Film.

FIRE FROM THE MOUNTAIN BY OMAR CABEZAS LACAYO

Fire from the Mountain. Dir. Deborah Shaffer. 1987. Documentary film.

FIRES ON THE PLAIN BY SHŌHEI ŌOKA

Fires on the Plain. Dir. Kon Ichikasa. Perf. Eiji Funakoshi, Osamu Takizawa, and Mickey Curtis. Daiei, 1959. Film.

FOR WHOM THE BELL TOLLS BY ERNEST HEMINGWAY

For Whom the Bell Tolls. Dir. Sam Wood. Perf. Gary Cooper, Ingrid Bergman, and Katina Paxinou. Paramount Pictures, 1941. Film.

THE GIRLS OF SLENDER MEANS BY MURIEL SPARK

The Girls of Slender Means. Dir. Moira Armstrong. Perf. Jane Cussons, Marilyn Finlay, and Patricia Hodge. British Broadcasting Corporation, 1975. Television.

GONE WITH THE WIND BY MARGARET MITCHELL

Gone with the Wind. Dir. Victor Fleming. Perf. Clark Gable, Vivien Leigh, Leslie Howard, and Olivia de Havilland. Metro-Goldwyn-Mayer, 1939. Film.

THE GREAT ESCAPE BY PAUL BRICKHILL

The Great Escape. Dir. John Sturges. Perf. Steve McQueen, James Garner, Richard Attenborough, Charles Bronson, Donald Pleasence, James Coburn. United Artists, 1963. Film.

HARP OF BURMA BY MICHIO TAKEYAMA

The Burmese Harp (Biruma No Tategoto). Dir. Kon Ichikawa. Perf. Rentaro Mikuni, Shoji Yasui, Jun Hamamura, Taketoshi Naito, and Ko Nishimura. Nikkatsu, 1956. Film.

The Burmese Harp (Biruma No Tategoto). Dir. Kon Ichikawa. Perf. Kôji Ishizaka, Kiichi Nakai,

Takuzo Kawatani, and Atsushi Watanabe. Fuji Television Network, 1985. Film.

THE HEAT OF THE DAY BY ELIZABETH BOWEN

The Heat of the Day. Dir. Christopher Morahan. Perf. Michael Gambon, Patricia Hodge, Michael York. Broadcast on Masterpiece Theater. Public Broadcasting Service, 1989. Television special.

HENRY V BY WILLIAM SHAKESPEARE

Henry V. Dir. Laurence Olivier. Perf. Laurence Olivier, Robert Helpmann, Felix Aylmer. United Artists, 1946. Film.

Henry V. Dir. Peter Watts. Perf. John Clements, John Garside. British Broadcasting Corporation, 1953. Television movie.

Henry V. Dir. Kenneth Branagh. Perf. Kenneth Branagh, Simon Shepherd, James Larkin. Samuel Goldwyn Company, 1989. Film.

HIROSHIMA BY JOHN RICHARD HERSEY

Hiroshima. Adapt. John Valentine. Dir. Michael Haney. Perf. Tyne Daly, Ruby Dee, and Roscoe Lee Brown. Pacifica Radio Archives, 2004. Radio.

THE HISTORY OF THE PELOPONNESIAN WAR BY THUCYDIDES

The War That Never Ends. Dir. Jack Gold. Perf. Ben Kingsley, David Calder, Nathaniel Parker. British Broadcasting Corporation, 1991. Television movie.

IF THIS IS A MAN BY PRIMO LEVI

Primo. Adapt. Antony Sher. Dir. Richard Wilson. Perf. Sher. Royal National Theatre, 2004. Performance; British Broadcasting Corporation/ HBO, 2005. Film; British Broadcasting Corporation, 2007. Radio.

Primo Levi's Journey. Dir. Davide Ferrario. Narr. Chris Cooper. Cinema Guild, 2007. Documentary film.

THE ILIAD BY HOMER

Troy. Dir. Wolfgang Peterson. Perf. Brad Pitt, Eric Bana, Orlando Bloom, and Diane Kruger. Warner Brothers, 2004. Film.

AN INDIAN HISTORY OF THE AMERICAN WEST BY DEE ALEXANDER BROWN

Bury My Heart at Wounded Knee. Dir. Yves Simoneau. Perf. Aidan Quinn, Adam Beach, August Schellenberg, and Anna Paquin. HBO Films, 2007. Television movie.

THE INSURRECTION BY ANTONIO SKÁRMETA

Der Aufstand. Dir. Peter Lilienthal. Basis-Film-Verleih, 1980. Film.

JARHEAD BY ANTHONY SWOFFORD

Jarhead. Dir. Sam Mendes. Perf. Jake Gyllenhaal and Jamie Foxx. Universal Pictures, 2005. Film.

JOHNNY GOT HIS GUN BY DALTON TRUMBO

Johnny Got His Gun. Dir. Arch Oboler. Perf. James Cagney. Arch Oboler's Plays. NBC-Radio, 9 Mar. 1940. Radio.

Johnny Got His Gun. Dir. Dalton Trumbo. Perf. Timothy Bottoms and Donald Sutherland. Cinemation Industries, 1971. Film.

JOHNNY MAD DOG BY EMMANUEL DONGALA

Johnny Mad Dog. Dir. Jean-Stéphane Sauvaire. Perf. Carlos Badawi, Teddy Boy, Maxwell Carter. TFM Distribution, 2007. Film.

JOURNEY INTO THE WHIRLWIND BY EUGENIA GINZBURG

Within the Whirlwind. Dir. Marleen Gorris. Perf. Emily Watson, Pam Ferris, Ian Hart. Wild Bunch Benelux, 2010. Film.

JOURNEY'S END BY R. C. SHERRIFF

Journey's End. Dir. James Whale. Perf. Colin Clive, Ian Maclaren, and David Manners. Tiffany Pictures, 1930. Film.

Journey's End. Dir. Michael Simpson. Perf. George Baker, Gary Caby, and John Forgeham. British Broadcasting Corporation, 1988. Television.

THE KILLER ANGELS BY MICHAEL SHAARA

Gettysburg. Dir. Ronald F. Maxwell. Perf. Tom Berenger, Martin Sheen, Jeff Daniels. New Line Cinema, 1993. Film.

THE KITE RUNNER BY KHALED HOSSEINI

The Kite Runner. Dir. Marc Forster. Perf. Zekeria Ebrahimi, Khalid Abdalla, Atossa Leoni, and Shaun Toub. Paramount Pictures, 2007. Film.

THE LAST ENEMY BY RICHARD HILLARY

The Last Enemy. Dir. Peter Graham Scott. Perf. Tarn Bassett, John Breslin, Michael Bryant. Independent Television (ITV), 1956. Television.

THE LAST OF THE MOHICANS BY JAMES FENIMORE COOPER

Last of the Mohicans. Dir. Arthur Wellin. Perf. Emil Mamelok, Herta Heden, and Bela Lugosi. Luna Film, 1920. Film.

The Last of the Mohicans. Dir. George B. Seitz. Perf. Randolph Scott, Phillip Reed, and Robert Barrat. United Artists, 1936. Film.

The Last of the Mohicans. Dir. Michael Mann. Perf. Daniel Day-Lewis, Russell Means, and Eric Schweig. Twentieth Century-Fox, 1992. Film.

LAST NIGHT I DREAMED OF PEACE BY ĐANG THÙY TRÂM

Don't Burn. Dir. Nhật Minh Đặng. Perf. Minh Huong. BHD, 2009. Film.

LIFE AND FATE BY VASILY GROSSMAN

La dernière lettre. Dir. Frederick Wiseman. Comédie-Française, 2002, subtitled version, Zipporah Films, 2003. Film.

Life and Fate. Perf. Kenneth Branagh, David Tennant. British Broadcasting Corporation, Sep. 2011. Radio miniseries.

THE LONG AND THE SHORT AND THE TALL BY WILLIS HALL

The Long and the Short and the Tall [also known as *Jungle Fighters*]. Dir. Leslie Norman. Perf. Laurence Harvey, Richard Harris, Richard Todd, and David McCallum. Associated British Picture Corp., 1961. Film.

The Long and the Short and the Tall. Dir. Ronald Smedley. Perf. Michael Kitchen, Mark McManus, and Richard Morant. British Broadcasting Corporation School Broadcasting, 9 Apr. 1979. Television.

THE LOOKING GLASS WAR BY JOHN LE CARRÉ

The Looking Glass War. Dir. Frank Pierson. Perf. Anthony Hopkins, Ralph Richardson, Christopher Jones, Pia Degermark, Paul Rogers. Columbia Pictures, 1970. Film.

The Looking Glass War. Perf. Ian McDiarmid, Patrick Kennedy, Piotr Baumann, Simon Russell Beale. British Broadcasting Corporation, 2009. Radio play.

LOVE IN A FALLEN CITY BY EILEEN CHANG

Qing cheng zhi lian. Dir. Ann Hui. Perf. Yun-Fat Show, Cora Miao, Gerry Barnett. Golden Harvest Company, Shaw Brothers, 1984. Film.

LYSISTRATA BY ARISTOPHANES

Lysistrata, or Triumph of Love. Dir. Kaspar Loser. Perf. Judith Helzmeister, O. W. Fischer, and Marie Kramer. Distinguished Films, 1947. Film.

Lysistrata. Dir. Ludo Mich. Perf. Jacques Ambach, Annie Cré, and Armand De Heselle. Varia Films, 1976. Film.

Lysistrata: Female Power and Democracy. Dir. James Thomas. Perf. Jane Fonda and Katrina Vanden Heuvel. MacMillan Films for Public Broadcasting Service, 2009. DVD.

M*A*S*H BY RICHARD HOOKER

M*A*S*H. Screenplay by Ring Lardner Jr. Dir. Robert Altman. Perf. Donald Sutherland, Elliott Gould, Tom Skerritt, Sally Kellerman, and Roger Bowen. Twentieth Century-Fox, 1970. Film.

M*A*S*H. Dir. Charles S. Dubin and others. Twentieth Century-Fox Television, 1972-83. Television.

MAHĀBHĀRATA

The Mahabharata. Perf. Erika Alexander. MK2 Productions, 1990. Television miniseries.

Mahabharat. Dir. B. R. Chopra, Ravi Chopra. Perf. Arun Bakshi, Aloka Mukerjee, Virendra Razdan. B.R. Films, 1988-90. Television series.

Bhagvad Gita: Song of the Lord. Dir. G. V. Iyer. Perf. Neena Gupta, Gopi Manohar, G. V. Ragavendra, Govind Rao. 1993. Film.

MAN'S HOPE BY ANDRÉ MALRAUX

L'espoir. Dir. André Malraux and Boris Peskine. Perf. Andrés Mejuto, Nicolás Rodríguez, José Sempere. Lopert Pictures Corporation, 1945. Film.

MARAT/SADE BY PETER ULRICH WEISS

The Persecution and Assassination of Jean-Paul Marat as Performed by the Inmates of the Asylum of Charenton Under the Direction of the Marquis de Sade. Dir. Peter Brook. Trans. Geoffrey Skelton. Verse adaptation by Adrian Mitchell. Music by Richard Peaslee. Geoffrey Skelton. Perf. Ian Richardson, Patrick Magee, and Glenda Jackson. United Artists. 22 Feb 1967. Film.

MOTHER COURAGE AND HER CHILDREN BY BERTOLT BRECHT

Mother Courage and Her Children. Perf. Anna Fierling, Olive McFarland. British Broadcasting Corporation, 1959. Television movie.

Mother Courage and Her Children. Dir. Peter Palitzsch, Manfred Weckwerth. Perf. Helen Weigel, Angelika Hurwicz. Constantin Film, 1961. Film.

THE NAKED AND THE DEAD BY NORMAN MAILER

The Naked and the Dead. Dir Raoul Walsh. Perf. Aldo Ray, Cliff Robertson, Raymond Massey, and Lili St. Cyr. Warner Bros. Pictures, 1958. Film.

NELLA LAST'S WAR BY NELLA LAST

Housewife, 49. Dir. Gavin Miller. Perf. Victoria Wood, David Threlfall, Christopher Harper. ITV, 2006. Television movie.

THE NIGHT WATCH BY SARAH WATERS

The Night Watch. Dir. Richard Laxton. Perf. Jenna Augen, Neal Barry, Claudie Blakley, and Lucy Briers. British Broadcasting Corporation, London, 12 Aug. 2011. Television.

OH! WHAT A LOVELY WAR BY JOAN LITTLEWOOD

Oh! What a Lovely War. Dir. Richard Attenborough. Perf. Wendy Allnutt, Colin Farrell, and Malcolm McFee. Paramount Pictures, 1969. Film.

PERSEPOLIS BY MARJANE SATRAPI

Persepolis. Dir. Vincent Paronnaud and Marjane Satrapi. Perf. Chiara Mastroianni, Catherine Deneuve, Danielle Darrieux, Simon Abkarian, Gabrielle Lopes Benites. 2.4.7.Films, 2007. Film.

THE POEM OF THE CID

Il Cid. Dir. Mario Caserini. Perf. Maria Caserini, Amleto Novelli. Società Italiana Cines. 1910. Silent film.

El Cid. Dir. Anthony Mann. Perf. Charlton Heston, Sophia Loren. Allied Artists, 1961. Film.

THE QUIET AMERICAN BY HENRY GRAHAM GREENE

The Quiet American. Dir. Joseph L. Mankiewicz. Perf. Audie Murphy, Michael Redgrave, and Claude Dauphin. United Artists, 1958. Film.

The Quiet American. Dir. Phillip Noyce. Perf. Michael Caine, Brendah Fraser, Do Thi Hai Yen, and Rade Serbedzjia. Miramax Films, 2002. Film.

THE RED BADGE OF COURAGE BY STEPHEN CRANE

The Red Badge of Courage. Dir John Huston. Perf. Audie Murphy, Bill Mauldin, and Andy Devine. Metro-Goldwyn-Mayer, 1951. Film.

The Red Badge of Courage. Dir. Lee Philips. Perf. Richard Thomas, Michael Brandon, and Wendell Burton. National Broadcasting Companies (NBC), 1974. Television.

REQUIEM FOR BATTLESHIP YAMATO BY YOSHIDA MITSURU

Senkan Yamato. Dir. Yutaka Abe. Perf. Toru Abe, Minoru Arita, Hiroshi Ayukawa, Miyuki Chiaki, Susumu Fujita, and Gen Funabashi. Shintoho. 1953. Film.

THE RETURN OF THE SOLDIER BY REBECCA WEST

The Return of the Soldier. Dir. Alan Bridges. Perf. Julie Christie, Ian Holm, Glenda Jackson, and Ann-Margret. Twentieth Century Fox, 1985. Film.

A RUMOR OF WAR BY PHILIP CAPUTO

A Rumor of War. Dir Rob Holcomb. Perf. Brad Davis, Brian Dennehy, Keith Carradine, Michael O'Keefe, Stacy Keach, Lane Smith, and Christopher Mitchum. Charles Fries Productions, 1980. Film.

SCHINDLER'S LIST BY THOMAS MICHAEL KENEALLY

Schindler's List. Dir. Steven Spielberg. Perf. Liam Neeson, Ben Kingsley, Ralph Fiennes, and Caroline Goodall. Universal Pictures, 1993. Film.

THE SEA AND POISON BY ENDŌ SHŪSAKU

The Sea and Poison. Dir. Kei Kumai. Perf. Eiji Okuda, Ken Watanabe, and Takahiro Tamura. Sea and Poison Production Committee, 1986. Film.

SIMPLICIUS SIMPLICISSIMUS BY JAKOB CHRISTOFFEL VON GRIMMELSHAUSEN

Simplicius Simplicissimus. Dir. Hans Hartleb. Perf. Ingeborg Bremert. Norddeutscher Rundfunk, 1961. Television.

SLAUGHTERHOUSE-FIVE BY KURT VONNEGUT JR.

Slaughterhouse-Five. Screenplay by Stephen Geller. Dir. George Roy Hill. Perf. Michael Sacks, Ron Leibman, and Eugene Roche. Universal Pictures, 1972. Film.

SON OF MAN BY AUGUSTO ROA BASTOS

Hijo de hombre. Dir. Lucas Demare. Argentina Sono Film, 1961. Film.

THE SONG OF ROLAND

The Song of Roland. Dir. Frank Cassenti. Perf. Klaus Kinski. 1978. Film.

TALES OF SOLDIERS AND CIVILIANS BY AMBROSE BIERCE

Ambrose Bierce: Civil War Stories. Dir. Don Maxwell and Brian James Egen. Perf. Campbell Scott, Vivian Schilling, and Nathan Darrow. Hannover House, 2006. Television.

An Occurrence at Owl Creek Bridge. Dir. Brian James Egen. Perf. Bradley Egen and Jody Chansuolme. Hannover House, 2005. Film.

TAMAS BY BHISHAM SAHNI

Tamas (also known as *Darkness*). Dir. Govind Nihalani. 1986. Television miniseries.

TEN DAYS THAT SHOOK THE WORLD BY JOHN REED

October (orig. title *Oktyabr*). Dir. Sergei Eisenstein and Grigori Aleksandrov. Perf. Vladimir Popov and Vasili Nikandrov. Sovkino, 1927. Film.

Ten Days That Shook the World. Perf. Orson Welles, Robert Stephens, Barbara Jefford, and Hugh Burden. Granada, 1967. Television.

Reds. Dir. Warren Beatty. Perf. Warren Beatty, Diane Keaton, Jack Nicholson, Paul Sorvino, and Maureen Stapleton. Paramount Pictures, 1981. Film.

TESTAMENT OF YOUTH BY VERA BRITTAIN

Testament of Youth. Perf. Cheryl Campbell. British Broadcasting Corporation, 1980. Television miniseries.

THE THINGS THEY CARRIED BY TIM O'BRIEN

A Soldier's Sweetheart. Adapted from the excerpt "Sweetheart of the Song Tra Bong". Dir. Thomas Michael Donnelly. Perf. Tony Billy and Christopher Birt. Paramount Pictures, 1998. Film.

TIKHII DON BY MIKHAIL SHOLOKOV

And Quiet Flows the Don. Dir. Ivan Pravov, Olga Preobrazhenskaya. Perf. Nickolai Podgorny, Andrei Abrikosov, Emma Tsesarskaya. Amkino Corporation, 1932. Film.

And Quiet Flows the Don. Dir. Sergei Gerasimov. Perf. Pyotr Glebov, Elina Bystritskaya. United Artists, 1957. Film.

Quiet Flows the Don. Dir. Sergei Bondarchuk. Perf. Rupert Everett. Delphine Forest, F. Murray Abraham, Ben Gazzara. Entertainment 7, 2006. Film.

TRAIN TO PAKISTAN BY KHUSHWANT SINGH

Train to Pakistan. Dir. Pamela Rooks. American Vision International, 1998. Film.

TROJAN WOMEN BY EURIPIDES

The Trojan Women. Dir. Michael Cacoyannis. Perf. Katharine Hepburn and Vanessa Redgrave. Cinerama Releasing, 1971. Film.

The Trojan Women. Dir. Brad Mays. Perf. Willow Hale, Karen Kiegren, and Shelley Delayne. Ark, 2004. Film.

UNDER TWO FLAGS BY MARIE LOUISE DE LA RAMÉE

Under Two Flags. Dir. Lucius Henderson. Perf. William Russell, Katherine Horn, and William Garwood. Film Supply Company, 1912. Film.

Under Two Flags. Dir. J. Gordon Edwards. Perf. Theda Bara, Herbert Hayes, and Stuart Holmes. Fox Film Corporation, 1916. Film.

Under Two Flags. Dir. Frank Lloyd. Perf. Ronald Colman, Claudette Colbert, Victor McLaglen, and Rosalind Russell. Twentieth Century-Fox, 1936. Film.

UNDER THE YOKE BY IVAN MINCHOV VAZOV

Under the Yoke. Dir. Dako Dakovski, 1953. Film.

THE UNDERDOGS BY MARIANO AZUELA

Los de Abajo. Dir. Servando González. Corporación Nacional Cinematográfica, 1978. Film.

Los de Abajo. Dir. Chano Urueta. Nueva América, 1940. Film.

WAR AND PEACE BY LEO NICKOLAYEVICH TOLSTOY

War and Peace. Dir. King Vidor. Perf. Audrey Hepburn, Henry Fonda, Mel Ferrer, and Vittorio Gassman. Paramount Pictures, 1956. Film.

War & Peace. Perf. Anthony Hopkins, Morag Hood, Alan Dobie, and Rupert Davies. British Broadcasting Corporation, 1973. Television miniseries.

THE WAR OF THE WORLDS BY H. G. WELLS

The War of the Worlds. Adapt. and perf. Orson Wells. CBS-Radio, 30 Oct. 1938. Radio.

The War of the Worlds. Dir. Byron Haskin. Perf. Gene Barry, Ann Robinson, and Les Tremayne. Paramount Pictures, 1953. Film.

The War of the Worlds. Dir. Steven Spielberg. Perf. Tom Cruise, Dakota Fanning, and Tim Robbins. Paramount Pictures, 2005. Film.

"WE'LL MEET AGAIN" BY HUGH CHARLES

We'll Meet Again. Dir. Philip Brandon. Perf. Vera Lynn, Geraldo, and Patricia Roc. Columbia Pictures, 1943. Film.

WHAT PRICE GLORY? BY MAXWELL ANDERSON

What Price Glory. Dir. Raoul Walsh. Perf. Victor McLaglen, Edmund Lowe, and Dolores del Rio. Twentieth Century-Fox, 1926. Film

"War Babies". *Baby Burlesks.* Dir. Charles Lamont. Perf. Shirley Temple. Educational Films, 1932. Film.

What Price Glory. Screenplay by Phoebe Ephron and Henry Ephron. Dir. John Ford. Perf. James Cagney, Corinne Calvet, and Dan Daily. Twentieth Century-Fox Films, 1952. Film.

WHEN HEAVEN AND EARTH CHANGED PLACES BY LE LY HAYSLIP

Heaven and Earth. Dir. Oliver Stone. Perf. Tommy Lee Jones, Joan Chen, Haing S. Ngor, Hiep Thi Le, Debbie Reynolds. Warner Bros. Films, 1993. Film.

AUTHOR INDEX

The author index includes author names and name alternatives, as well as English and foreign language titles from *The Literature of War*. Main author names include birth and death dates. Numbers in **Bold** indicate volume, with page numbers following after colons.

TITLE INDEX

The title index includes works that are represented in *The Literature of War*, as well as original foreign language titles, if applicable, and publication dates. Bolded numbers refer to volumes, with page numbers following colons.